Which Way Forward?

People, Forests, and Policymaking in Indonesia

EDITED BY

Carol J. Pierce Colfer and
Ida Aju Pradnja Resosudarmo

RESOURCES FOR THE FUTURE
WASHINGTON, DC, USA

CENTER FOR INTERNATIONAL
FORESTRY RESEARCH
BOGOR, INDONESIA

INSTITUTE OF SOUTHEAST
ASIAN STUDIES
SINGAPORE

Printed in the United States of America

An RFF Press book
Published by Resources for the Future
1616 P Street, NW, Washington, DC 20036–1400

A copublication of Resources for the Future (www.rff.org), the Center for International Forestry Research (www.cifor.org), and the Institute of Southeast Asian Studies (www.iseas.edu.sg).

Library of Congress Cataloging-in-Publication Data
Which way forward?: people, forests, and policymaking in Indonesia / Carol J. Pierce Colfer and Ida Aju Pradnja Resosudarmo, editors.
    p.   cm.
    Includes bibliographical references and index.
    ISBN 1–891853–44–9 (lib. bdg.) — ISBN 1–891853–45–7 (pbk.)
    1. Forest policy—Indonesia. 2. Forest management—Indonesia. I. Colfer, Carol J. Pierce.
    II. Resosudarmo, Ida Aju Pradnja.

SD657.I5 W55 2001
333.75'09598—dc21   2001047675

f e d c b a

The paper in this book meets the guidelines for permanence and durability of the Committee on Production Guidelines for Book Longevity of the Council on Library Resources.

The geographical boundaries and titles depicted in this publication, whether in maps, other illustrations, or text, do not imply any judgement or opinion about the legal status of a territory on the part of Resources for the Future, the Center for International Forestry Research, the Institute for Southeast Asian Studies, or any other organization that has participated in the preparation of this publication.

The findings, interpretations, and conclusions offered herein are those of the contributing authors. They do not necessarily represent the views of Resources for the Future, its directors, or officers, and they do not represent the views of any other institution that has participated in the development of this publication.

ISBN 1–891853–44–9 (cloth)   ISBN 1–891853–45–7 (paper)

About Resources for the Future and RFF Press

Resources for the Future (RFF) improves environmental and natural resources policymaking worldwide through independent social science research of the highest caliber. Founded in 1952, RFF pioneered the application of economics as a tool to develop more effective policy about the use and conservation of natural resources. Its scholars continue to employ social science methods to analyze critical issues concerning pollution control, energy policy, land and water use, hazardous waste, climate change, biodiversity, and the environmental challenges of developing countries.

RFF Press supports the mission of RFF by publishing book-length works that present a broad range of approaches to the study of natural resources and the environment. Its authors and editors include RFF staff, researchers from the larger academic and policy communities, and journalists.

About the Institute of Southeast Asian Studies

The Institute of Southeast Asian Studies (ISEAS) was established in Singapore as an autonomous organization in 1968. It is a regional center for scholars and other specialists concerned with modern Southeast Asia, particularly the multifaceted problems of stability and security, economic development, and political and social change.

About the Center for International Forestry Research

The Center for International Forestry Research (CIFOR) was established in 1993 as part of the Consultative Group on International Agricultural Research (CGIAR) in response to global concerns about the social, environmental, and economic consequences of forest loss and degradation. CIFOR research produces knowledge and methods needed to improve the well-being of forest-dependent people and to help tropical countries manage their forests wisely for sustained benefits. This research is done in more than two dozen countries, in cooperation with numerous partners. Since it was founded, CIFOR has also played a central role in influencing global and national forestry policies.

Resources for the Future

iv

Contents

Contributors

Grahame Applegate is a forest scientist with the Sustainable Forest Management program at the Center for International Forestry Research (CIFOR). His research focuses on forest management as it relates to underlying causes of fire in Indonesia and improved practices in natural forests as part of sustainable forest management.

Graham Baines is a freelance consultant in tropical natural resources and environmental management. His academic training is in agricultural science, plant ecology, and environmental physics. He has participated in a number of short-term missions addressing biodiversity issues in Indonesia.

Christopher Barr is a policy scientist with CIFOR's Underlying Causes of Deforestation, Forest Degradation, and Changes in Human Welfare program. His current research focuses on the effect of the International Monetary Fund and World Bank structural adjustment policies on Indonesia's forest-based industries, corporate debt, and forest-sector finance. He also studies the likely effects of decentralization on forest administration in East Kalimantan and Riau.

Chris P. A. Bennett is an associate with the Food and Resource Economics Group, Faculty of Agricultural Sciences, University of British Columbia. He also teaches courses at the University of British Columbia. A plant pathologist who has moved into agroforestry and forest policy analysis, he has served as a consultant for the Harvard Institute for International Development, World Bank, United States Agency for International Development, U.K. Department for International Development (DFID), the Ford Foundation, and CIFOR.

David Brown was recently awarded a Ph.D. from the Department of Political Science of the University of Washington. His research examines the appropriation of timber rent by political elites in insular Southeast Asia. He has served as a consultant to DFID, studying the political-economic and supply-and-demand profiles of Indonesia's timber industry. He has worked as an equities analyst with the global investment bank Dresdner Kleinwort Benson.

Jeffrey Y. Campbell is a program officer in environment and development with the Ford Foundation. Currently posted in the foundation's New York Office, he spent six and one-half years with the foundation in India and three and one-half years in the Jakarta office. The primary focus of his work is facilitating the development of community-based natural resource management from the grass roots to the policy level.

Anne Casson is a research fellow in the Resource Management in Asia–Pacific Project, Australian National University. She has conducted research in Indonesia since 1991 and has recently completed her doctoral thesis on the political economy of the Indonesian oil palm subsector through the School of Resources, Environment, and Society of Australian National University. While performing research for her Ph.D., she was a consultant for CIFOR's Underlying Causes of Deforestation, Forest Degradation, and Changes in Human Welfare program. She continues to work on the oil palm subsector and the current process of decentralization in Indonesia's forest sector.

Carol J. Pierce Colfer is leader of the CIFOR program on Local People, Devolution, and Adaptive Collaborative Management. An anthropologist, she has conducted research in Indonesia since 1979, primarily in Kalimantan and Sumatra, where she has focused on rural people's interactions with forests. She has also conducted long-term fieldwork in Iran, Oman, and the United States, with shorter-term work on projects involving criteria and indicators for assessing human well-being in Cameroon, Côte d'Ivoire, Brazil, and Gabon. She is coeditor of *People Managing Forests: The Links between Human Well-Being and Sustainability*.

Ahmad Dermawan is research program assistant in the Underlying Causes of Deforestation, Forest Degradation, and Changes in Human Welfare program and the Sustainable Forest Management program at CIFOR. His work has focused on the effects of the economic crisis on forest cover, and the decentralization of policymaking and administration of policies affecting forests in Indonesia. He has researched the effects of the economic crisis on the foodcrop sector and has studied agroforestry and the role of extension to farmers in West Java.

Richard G. Dudley has more than 20 years experience working with developing-country scientists and administrators in the management of natural fish populations, conservation of aquatic and marine resources, and the assessment of environmental impacts on fisheries and other resources. He has a special interest in helping countries improve their own natural resource management capabilities. He has served as team leader on Asian Development Bank and U.S. Agency for International Development funded projects in Oman and Indonesia to develop new research programs in the management of fisheries and related resources. In Indonesia, he has worked both with local universities and the central government to review the qualifications of consultants and strengthen university teaching and research in marine science.

Chip Fay is a leading member of the research team at the International Centre for Research in Agroforestry (ICRAF) that works on land and tree tenure, assisting the governments in Indonesia and the Philippines in their efforts to develop and strengthen regulatory decrees and legislation, to implement programs that enable forest-dependent communities to maintain their livelihood, and to sustainably manage areas of state-defined forest zones. He has served as a project officer for Southeast Asia at Survival International, program officer for the Ford Foundation in Indonesia, and as director of the Southeast Asia Office of the Environmental Policy Institute.

James J. Fox is professor and director at the Research School of Pacific and Asian Studies. A social anthropologist, he has done research on a wide range of social, ecological, and resource policy issues in Indonesia, including rice intensification, integrated pest management, and marine and forest management and development. He is author of *Harvest of the Palm: Ecological Change in Eastern Indonesia.*

David Kaimowitz, an economist, is director general of CIFOR. He previously worked for the Inter-American Institute for Cooperation in Agriculture, the International Service for National Agricultural Research, and the Ministry of Agriculture of Nicaragua. He has published widely on issues in forest and agricultural policy.

Hariadi Kartodihardjo is a lecturer at the Faculty of Forestry, Bogor Agriculture Institute. He is in active collaboration with several local nongovernmental organizations and is one of the founders of the Indonesian Ecolabelling Institute. He also currently serves as an adviser to the Ministry of Forestry and Estate Crops as a member of the Forestry and Estate Crops Development Reform Committee.

Rita Lindayati is completing her Ph.D. in environmental studies at York University in Canada. Her research interests include community forestry, local-based resource management, policy studies, and political ecology in Southeast Asia. Her fieldwork has focused on Bali, Kalimantan, Sumatra, and Jakarta.

Andrew Mitchell is a graduate forester with more than 20 years of experience in both temperate and tropical forestry. He has consulted and worked on numerous projects and review missions throughout the world. He has undertaken work on the total economic valuation of ecosystems in Bangladesh and Belize and has worked on forest revenue systems in Suriname, Belize, and Bangladesh.

David Packham is a rural fire consultant based in Melbourne. A chemist by training, his major work has been in fire retardants, heat and mass transfer in wildfires, and fire detection systems for buildings. He has served as deputy director of the Australian Disaster College and as supervising meteorologist for rural fire warning services at the Australian Bureau of Meteorology.

Ida Aju Pradnja Resosudarmo is leader of the CIFOR Underlying Causes of Deforestation, Forest Degradation, and Changes in Human Welfare program. Her major areas of research are population and migration trends, forest and forestry-related policies, the decentralization process, and the effects of the economic crisis on forest cover and the well-being of forest villagers in Indonesia.

Emil Salim is professor of economics at the University of Indonesia. His positions in the Indonesian government include Minister for Population and the Environment. Internationally, he has served on advisory boards and committees at the United Nations and World Health Organization; he was president of the U.N. Environment Program Governing Council from 1985–1987. Currently, he is leading a review about the future role of the World Bank Group in the extractive industries to promote poverty reduction and sustainable development. He is co-chair of the World Commission on Forest and Sustainable Development and chair of the Board of Trustees of the Foundation for Sustainable Development (Jakarta). Pak Salim holds doctorates in economics from the University of Indonesia and the University of California at Berkeley. His books include *Masalah Pembangunan Indonesia* (*Development Problems in Indonesia*) and *Lingkungan Hidup dan Pembangunan* (*Environment and Development*).

Jeffrey A. Sayer was director general of CIFOR from its inception in 1992 until July 2001. An ecologist by training, he has long been involved in the field of conservation. He has worked with the Food and Agriculture Organization, the International Union for the Conservation of Nature/World Conservation Union, the World Bank, and now the World Wide Fund for Nature. He has conducted research in Africa, South America, and Asia.

Martua Sirait is a scientist at ICRAF. He is also working on community forestry policy in the Outer Islands of Indonesia to assist the Indonesian Forestry Department. His activities are part of the regional policy research project funded by the Asian Development Bank and the Ford Foundation. Previously he worked with the World Wide Fund for Nature's Indonesia Program on community mapping at Kayan Mentarang Nature Reserve, East Kalimantan.

Ross Smith is the assistant commissioner for the New South Wales Rural Fire Service. He worked with the New South Wales Forestry Commission from 1963 to 1994, specializing in forest fire management and environmental audit and compliance. Since joining the Rural Fire Service, he has provided forest fire and emergency management consultant services to agencies in Spain, Indonesia, Croatia, and China.

William D. Sunderlin is a sociologist working in CIFOR's Underlying Causes of Deforestation, Forest Degradation, and Changes in Human Welfare program. His main area of research has been the effect of economic crisis and structural adjustment policies on the well-being of forest villagers and on forest cover change in Cameroon and Indonesia. He has also conducted research on the relationship of livestock sector expansion and forest cover loss in Honduras and the relationship of mineral exports to tropical deforestation.

Nigel Tapper is head of the School of Geography and Environmental Science at Monash University, Melbourne, Australia. He is also joint coordinator of the Monash Atmospheric Science Program and deputy director of the Monash Environment Institute. His research interests include indigenous forecasting systems (i.e., local weather knowledge and its application) and environmental change and variability in Southeast Asia, with a focus on rainfall variability in the area of the El Niño–Southern Oscillation and the impact of the variability of crop production and fire in Indonesia.

Eva (Lini) Wollenberg is a researcher at CIFOR where she focuses on social learning among forest stakeholders and the means for empowering local communities, especially in the tropical regions of Asia. Before joining CIFOR in 1994, she worked for the Ford Foundation's Asia Rural Poverty and Resources Program. She has had extensive experience working in the Philippines and Borneo.

Rachel Wrangham is an associate professional officer with DFID and a Ph.D. candidate at the London School of Economics. Her social anthropology research in Indonesia has covered a wide range of issues, including local perceptions of development, changing resource management strategies, and poverty. Currently focusing on rural development in Mozambique, she has also worked in India and Thailand.

Acknowledgments

This book evolved in response to the availability of a number of relatively independent analyses of Indonesia's rapidly changing conditions in 1999. A diverse set of authors, writing from very different perspectives, were producing analyses that we felt shed significant light on the rapid evolution of Indonesian policy. This compilation includes contributions supported by a wide range of institutions, which we would like to highlight here.

Although some chapters include acknowledgments, we felt it important to recognize those who contributed in a more global way. The Center for International Forestry Research (CIFOR) demonstrated its institutional flexibility by allowing the editors the freedom to pursue this serendipitous opportunity under their auspices, with additional financial contributions as needed. Similarly, the closely affiliated International Centre for Agroforestry Research (ICRAF) responded flexibly by supporting some of their staff members to participate in this endeavor. We thank the many CIFOR and ICRAF colleagues who read and critiqued various drafts and served as sounding boards for our ideas. We also want to thank Rahayu Koesnadi, Linda Yuliani, and Atie Puntodewo at CIFOR, Rebecca Henderson and Don Reisman at Resources for the Future (RFF), and Chrysa Cullather for their assistance throughout the production process. We are grateful to Mark Poffenberger and David Kaimowitz who reviewed an early version of the entire book, as well as to the anonymous reviewers selected by RFF. The input of these reviewers improved the quality of our analyses and writing, and we very much appreciate their work.

Parts of this book have also been supported by the Asian Development Bank and the U.K. Department for International Development. We thank them most sincerely for their vital contributions. We also thank Institut Pertanian Bogor (Bogor Agricultural Institute) in Bogor, the Ford Foundation, Lembaga Ilmu Pengetahuan Indonesia (Indonesian National Science Foundation), the Australian National University and York University, with whom various of our authors are affiliated.

As book editors, we are particularly grateful to the authors who first wrote their chapters and then responded graciously without exception, to our repeated requests for revisions and additional information throughout this long process. The authors were also industrious in providing each other with constructive critiques, which also enriched the final product.

We are all particularly indebted to the many Indonesian government and industry personnel, researchers, and other Indonesia specialists who have contributed to our thinking and provided critical information. We are grateful to the Indonesian government, which has overseen a sea change in terms of Indonesia's acceptance of critical analysis since the Soeharto era. Had we written this book under Soeharto, it would have been a more perilous undertaking. Finally, we thank the rural people of Indonesia who have patiently survived our questions and curiosity with unfailing good humor. We hope that their help and cooperation is justified by the utility of this book, in the process of answering the question that the book's title poses: Which way forward?

Dedication

Carol dedicates this book to her husband, Richard G. Dudley. His deep concerns about the environment and Indonesian policies, combined with his continual, faithful, and strong support, have been important forces leading to this work. She also dedicates this book to her son, Andrew Balan Pierce (also known as "Alan"). Straddling the cultures of Indonesia and the United States even more than his mother, he cares about Indonesia, its people, and its future as much as she does. He is an eternal source of delight and pride.

Ida Aju Pradnja dedicates this book to her parents, Ida Pedanda Gede Nyoman Jelantik Oka and Jero Istri Nengah; to her husband, Budy; and to her children, Adhikara, Kalyana, and Wisesa.

Which Way Forward?

Foreword

One would like to think that governments exist to take care of the public good and that ensuring fairness in access to opportunities and resources for all their citizens, present and future, would be their fundamental role. But in so many of the forest-rich countries of the tropics, this has not been the case. Rather than holding forests in trust for the nation, many government officials have usurped rights to the forest for their personal enrichment. Forests have not been just victims of corruption, they have also fueled it. Economic growth, expansion of trade, and the availability of bigger machines for logging and clearing tropical forests have combined to provide irresistible opportunities for those in power. In many countries, the most visible symptom of bad governance has been abuse of forests and land, and the lightning rod for expression of public dissatisfaction with corrupt governments has been the struggle for equity in access to natural resources. It was, therefore, no surprise to find Indonesia's nascent environmental organizations at the forefront of the barricades during those tumultuous days in May 1998 that led to the overthrow of the Soeharto regime.

Since then, the country has been swept by a tidal wave of change. Reformist elements have struggled with the powerful forces of vested interest and conservatism in a game that is still far from being played out. Meanwhile, opportunists throughout the country, both the rich and powerful and the poor and marginalized, have seized the opportunities provided by huge vacuums in the power structures. With the uncertainty of the future and lucrative export opportunities created by the depreciation of the local currency, there has been an explosion of opportunistic forest exploitation and clearing. The very process of reform and democratization that should, in the long term, help to bring forests under better public control has, in the short term, exposed these forests to unprecedented threats.

This book documents the events of the past years in Indonesia and will help us to learn what went wrong. Indonesia may be unique in the magnitude of the forest problems created by corruption and the battles to eliminate it. But many of these problems occur to a greater or lesser extent in other forest-rich countries in the tropics; recently the same issues are emerging in the ex-Soviet Union. The question implicit in this book is, what might the forest conservation lobby have done differently to counter the pernicious evil of corruption and avert the more disastrous asset-stripping associated with the transition to democracy? After all, there were tens of millions of people in Indonesia who were bearing the cost of forest abuse. And a significant proportion of the billions of dollars generated by international efforts to save rain forests was invested in Indonesia. One irony is that rather than being the allies of the potential domestic constituency for forest conservation—the forest people—the international campaigners were marching to a different drum. They also wanted to expropriate the forests and set them aside for some lofty global environmental purpose—in the eyes of local people they were just as much a threat as the loggers.

Meanwhile, much of the official development assistance allocated to support better forest management was being used in feeble attempts to bring about marginal improvements in the technologies of forestry. Donor after donor set out to "demonstrate" its own particular model of how forests ought to be managed. In many cases the approaches advocated were little more than "technologists' dreams of what might, in theory, work." Much was totally alien to the social and political realities of the country.

So what might have been done differently? First, one must acknowledge that the students and nongovernmental organizations (NGOs) who brought about change were able to do so in part because of the empowerment that occurred through access to information and support from international networks of activists. Many, but not enough, development assistance agencies had been devoting their resources to education and professional development and to working with NGOs. They had a significant effect on the emergence of Indonesia's civil society. But much international assistance was, and to some extent still is, devoted to maintaining the institutional status quo. The burgeoning bureaucracies that fed on natural resources were being encouraged and promoted by international projects.

And what of the future? The worst abuses of the old regime are now, we hope, a thing of the past. But the country is destined to pass through a difficult period of transition. I personally doubt if the international community will achieve much by coming with "ready-made" solutions to Indonesia's problems. What it can do is help to build a generation of Indonesians with the knowledge and skills to find their own solutions. Exemplary centers of research and higher education, well connected to the outside world, will yield people with the knowledge and moral authority to steer the country in the right direction. And we must never forget that the main source of essential knowledge of Indonesian forests remains with the people who live in the forests. The empowerment of these people and the legitimization of their rights must be a major part of the solution.

The forests of Indonesia and the people who depend on them have suffered greatly from the events of recent years. But both the forests and the people are resilient, and the human and natural resources remain amongst the richest in the world. It is still possible to hope for a richer and more sustainable future for the country—but this outcome is by no means guaranteed. The abscess of bad governance has been lanced, but the patient is going to need a great deal of care and a considerable measure of luck if the potential of the forests is to be restored and sustained.

Jeffrey A. Sayer
World Wide Fund for Nature

Introduction

Indonesia is truly at a crossroads. Decades of Soeharto's autocratic rule under the New Order[1] regime have left the country crippled. Existing institutions are brittle with little capacity to deal with any fluidity of power—a prerequisite for a functioning democracy. Collusion, corruption, and nepotism (a phrase that became a rallying cry, also referred to as KKN—*kolusi, korupsi, dan nepotisme*) are deeply engrained practices that continue to hinder fair and transparent conduct of business and government. On the positive side, there is a vibrant, nascent civil society, led by students, nongovernmental organizations, and intellectuals, passionately committed to creating a fairer, better Indonesia. Their work is strengthened and supported by a newly free press. They in turn have helped to strengthen communities across the land who have begun to claim rights that were routinely usurped by central governments for centuries.

This crossroads at which Indonesia finds itself became obvious in 1998 after three dramatic crises had struck the nation.

- A devastating, El Niño–induced drought decimated food production in a number of provinces, and vast areas of Sumatra and Kalimantan were consumed by forest fires.[2]

1

- The Asian "tiger economies" were reduced to shambles, with Indonesia hit the hardest. The value of Indonesia's national currency dropped from Rp 2,500 to the U.S. dollar in July 1997 to Rp 17,000 in April 1998, and urban unemployment ran amok (ELSAM [Lembaga Studi dan Avokasi Masyarakat–The Institute for Policy Research and Advocacy]/CIEL [Center for International Environmental Law] 2001b estimates 8 million people lost their jobs).
- The 30-year regime of President Soeharto came under serious attack, with riots in Jakarta's streets and growing complaints by the citizenry about the special privileges of Soeharto's relatives and friends and the inequitable and corrupt distribution of the nation's resources.[3]

The growing discontent among the populace resulted in President Soeharto's handing the reins of power to his controversial and somewhat unpopular vice president, B.J. Habibie on May 21, 1998. The next few months brought dramatic changes in Indonesia:

- the first relatively democratic national election in decades,
- changed proportional representation by various groups—most notably, the military—within the parliament,
- a proliferation of opposition parties (48 parties total including Soeharto's party, Golkar),
- a significantly freer press,
- a referendum in East Timor that resulted in its independence from Indonesia,
- a rise in separatist movements in various parts of the country, and
- a rush to develop new policies to address the perceived shortcomings of Soeharto's New Order.

The most noticeable change has been the upsurge in free expression and action from all members of civil society—viewed with suspicion by some who see such freedom as bordering on anarchy. This near-anarchy, which is discussed in the next section, is particularly evident in Indonesia's forest areas.

Introduction to Indonesia

For readers unfamiliar with its history and human geography, it is important to provide a brief introduction to Indonesia as a nation. Indonesia, a nation of 13,677 islands covering 1,919,440 km^2 (Donner 1987; Factbook 2001), has the fourth largest population in the world (203,456,005), of which 38.4 million adults (older than 15 years of age) were employed in agriculture, forestry, hunting, and fishing in 1999 (BPS 2001). Situated directly on the equator between Australia to the south and Malaysia and the Philippines to the north, the country has always been a major pathway for maritime traffic between the Indian and Pacific Oceans. Its coastline spans 54,716 km (Factbook 2001).

On a macro level, Indonesia has seen many waves of cultural influence, from the arrival of Hinduism in the 4th Century, followed by Buddhism in the 5th Century, and then Islam via traders from the Northwest in the 13th Century (Miksic 1996). Eighty-eight percent of the country is Muslim at this stage (Factbook 2001). These various "great traditions" (Redfield 1956) have combined in a rich syncretic mix (Geertz 1960) with local animist beliefs, forming Indonesia's unique and complex cultural tradition. For more than 300 years, until August 17, 1945, the Dutch ruled most of Indonesia, leaving their footprint as well (Furnivall 1948).

On a micro level, the nation is characterized by one of the most ethnically diverse populations on earth, each segment having its own language and culture—though 45% of the population is Javanese with another 14% Sudanese (the two dominant ethnic groups on the island of Java). The national language, Bahasa Indonesia, is still not spoken by everyone, though great strides have been made since Independence through attempts at universal education (84% of the population is reported to be literate by Factbook 2001, although rates are lower in the Outer Islands, on which this book focuses). Multilingualism is the rule rather than the exception, and cultural diversity is taken in stride by Indonesians. Indeed, the national motto is "Unity in Diversity." Holding this insular nation together for the past 50 years has been a momentous accomplishment.

We focus on the Outer Islands in this book because of their comparative importance in recent decades as generators of foreign exchange; as sources of livelihood for a rich potpourri of ethnic groups, management styles, and cultural traditions; and because of the genetic diversity and ecological importance of the Outer Island forests. The Outer Islands are defined as those islands other than Java and Bali (Geertz 1963).[4] Java and Bali are densely populated ($946/km^2$ in Java); they are home to about 60% of Indonesia's population (BPS 2001) on 7% of its land mass (the most fertile regions of the nation).

From a forestry perspective, Indonesia technically has 120 million ha of forestland (Departemen Kehutanan 2001). It must be noted, however, that forestland is not identical to forests or forested land. In fact, in 1999 it was estimated that there were only about 90 million ha of forests (The World Bank 2001). This official "forest estate" covers more than 60% of the country and has been under state control for centuries. Peluso (1990) documents the European (primarily Dutch) influence and rule first under the East India Company (Verenigde Oost-Indische Compagnie) from the mid-17th Century to 1799 and by the Dutch colonial state from 1814 to 1940 (ELSAM/CIEL 2001; Harwell 2000; Wadley 2000).[5] For centuries, Dutch control of the forests was minimal, with their primary intent to keep the peace so that they could reap the benefits of trade. Indeed, the Indonesian government's presence was not seriously felt in remote forested areas until the last three decades, when the Outer Islands were opened to commercial timber extraction.

Barr (1999) describes how Soeharto's New Order played an active role in developing Indonesia as a world leader in timber: the *Hak Pengusahaan Hutan* concession system (discussed in later chapters) was introduced in 1967, and it allowed companies to log vast areas of Outer Island forests with almost no regulatory oversight. Then during the 1980s, a log ban was instituted and companies were pressured to develop downstream wood-processing plants. Plywood factories multiplied, resulting in an industry capable of producing 12.6 million m^3 per year by 1990. Meanwhile, senior government officials micromanaged the development of the plywood industry through approval and lending processes, ultimately concentrating capital ownership and control within the industry in the hands of large timber conglomerates, typically with strong ties to state elites. At the same time, the New Order leadership gave APKINDO (the Indonesian Wood Panel Association, under Mohamad "Bob" Hasan's leadership) far-reaching regulatory controls over the export of Indonesian plywood, resulting in an effective marketing cartel. During the 1990s, the country's panel producers were able to capture 70% of the world hardwood plywood exports (Barr 1999).

One clear result of this process was the highly centralized nature of forest management under the New Order, in pursuit of improved gross national product and the patronage of state elites and their business partners. Another result was the adverse effects of the Basic Forestry Law of 1967 and its associated *Hak Pengusahaan Hutan* system on the communities located within the forest estate (comprising 74% of the nation's area), who basically lost their traditional rights to local resources.

ELSAM/CIEL (2001) documents the legal history of local government from the Dutch arrival to the present and shows the state's increasing involvement in community affairs. One issue was the definition of a village as an administrative unit below the subdistrict. This hierarchical formulation was not an entirely appropriate concept outside Java and Madura. Following on this, one of the most significant legal changes for forest communities since Independence was the 1979 Village Governance law (*Undang-Undang* [UU] 5/1979). This law attempted to institute a uniform, bureaucratic structure across the nation, and it specified considerably more control over village governance than had been the case previously. The village headman was appointed by the subdistrict or district leader. The headman was to be literate, familiar with *Pancasila* philosophy,[6] and a member of the Golkar political party.

The law had three fundamental effects on local communities (ELSAM/CIEL 2001):

- loss of village rights to choose leaders, thus eroding traditional forms of authority and reformulating the characteristics required of a leader;

- centralization of authority in the village headman, not balanced by either the formal *Lembaga Musyawarah Desa* (the village consensus-reaching institution) or popular participation via indigenous institutions; and
- erosion of existing village institutions and replacement by an institution incapable of settling disputes and in some cases exacerbating them.

Besides their function as sources of timber, Indonesia's forests are the best remaining forests in Southeast Asia. They are, however, being cut at an ever-increasing rate (see Brookfield et al. 1995; Sunderlin and Resosudarmo 1996; and The World Bank 2001 for a thorough discussion of related losses in Borneo or the eastern Malay Peninsula). Sumatra, once rich in forest resources, has largely been converted to plantations (which in fact have a long history in Sumatra, cf. Pelzer 1982), with Kalimantan following a similar path. MacKinnon et al. (1996, 635) noted that 60% of Borneo was still under forest cover, but this figure has dropped significantly because of a series of trends that have already denuded vast areas of Sumatra.

The wealth of Indonesian forests in terms of biodiversity is also noteworthy. Borneo alone, covering 0.2% of the earth's land surface, has 1 in 25 of all known plants and 1 in 20 of all known birds and mammals (MacKinnon et al. 1996, 632). Its timber resources have been the draw to exploitation, particularly the valuable Dipterocarps.

Here we aim to examine the recent and ongoing political ferment against the backdrop of Indonesia's forest management during the Soeharto regime. Indonesia's forests, seen as "empty" from the perspective of overpopulated Java, were defined as part of a permanent forest estate whose management was ceded to Indonesia's powerful Ministry of Forestry (see Chapters 1 and 8). Logging and other concessions were handed out as favors to the politically or militarily well connected. Little attention was paid to the sustainability of management, and even less attention was paid to the communities that in fact had inhabited those forests—in most cases, sustainably—for generations.

There has been a predictable trajectory for Indonesian forests over the past three decades. A forest rich in timber was identified and given out by the government to a logging company to manage. That forest was typically home to one or more local communities whose traditional claims were not noted. The logging company logged the forest, with short-term negative effects on the environment and a somewhat ambivalent relationship with local people who appreciated the roads, improved transportation, and occasional work, and who did not suffer egregious losses by sharing their forest with others. The forest was then relabeled as "degraded." Degraded forest was eligible for use as an industrial timber or oil palm plantation or as a transmigration site.[7] All of these three options were considerably less compatible with continued customary use by local people (Barber et al. 1994; Colfer and Dudley 1993; Gonner 1999).

The cultural diversity that characterizes Indonesia may be unparalleled in the world. In the attempt to make one nation of these many ethnic and language groups, a potent taboo evolved on the use of the term *suku* (ethnic group). Indonesia's forests are home to hundreds of ethnic groups, each with its own ways of relating to the forest. The way in which these ethnic differences have been incorporated into public discourse has involved extensive use of the concept of *adat* (usually translated as tradition or custom). There is clear ambivalence in the nation about *adat*. In some cases, it can symbolize primitiveness and destruction; in other cases, it can symbolize cultural integrity and homegrown values. It served as a basis for agrarian law, but the stipulation that it applies only if it does not interfere with national interests has consistently resulted in interpretations that disadvantage forest dwellers, superseding the force of *adat* law in most forest contexts. *Adat* is recognized from the community level on up, and it has recently become something of a tool for environmentalists who have argued that traditional systems, reflected in *adat* law, serve conservation functions (Kemf 1993; Banuri and Marglin 1993; Zerner 1994 critiques this view). Local people typically value their own *adat* (though in varying degrees), and it remains a highly charged concept about which there has been and will continue to be considerable debate.

The low levels of population density, combined with an ongoing cultural onslaught against the "primitive" forest dwellers and supplemented by occasional repressive measures, effectively silenced, or at least muted, rebellion. Many forest dwellers were able to continue their own forest management practices by making minor compromises. But as the years and decades passed, and as more "favors" were allocated to outsiders, the required compromises became more serious. In recent years, forest dwellers' patience began to be tested, and the number of violent incidents surrounding logging, plantations, and transmigration sites increased dramatically. The condition and extent of Indonesia's beautiful and valuable forests—with their world-class levels of biodiversity and abundant supplies of timber and other forest products—deteriorated equally dramatically.

Recent History of Events

To return to the question of near-anarchy mentioned earlier, and to further orient the reader, we describe some of the political events of recent years. After Indonesia gained independence in the late 1940s, the charismatic and popular Soekarno came to power. He led Indonesia with a strong and vociferous international presence but with increasing chaos at home. In 1966 he was overthrown by Soeharto, in cooperation with the Indonesian military, ostensibly to rid the country of the godless Communists whom Soekarno was seen to favor (see Schwarz 1999 for a retrospective and skeptical view of this version of Indonesian history).

Soeharto instituted a much more low-key style of leadership, abandoning many democratic principles in favor of a strong center, which he felt was required to bring the nation back into some semblance of order and stability. Membership in his party, Golkar, was required of all civil servants, and elections bore little resemblance to a true democratic process. He was consistently backed by the military, and he developed a cadre of family and friends whose unswerving loyalty he required and rewarded generously with business concessions, tax exemptions, and bank loans. The Indonesian system evolved in such a way that corrupt practices became the norm. He called himself the "Father of Development," and indeed many parts of Indonesia prospered under his rule.

An informal philosophy characterized Indonesian bureaucracy during this period: *bapakism. Bapak* is the Indonesian term for father, but it is also used more widely, rather like "Mr." Bosses are called *bapak* (or *pak*, for short), and obedience to one's *bapak* is expected. Certain familial qualities, like caretaking, defending, and working together amicably, are expected in dealing with one's boss. Although there are important positive features to these kinds of relationships, they can also contribute to cronyism, corruption, and collusion. It is often difficult for someone lower in the bureaucracy, for instance, to give bad news to a superior (so problems may not be addressed), payments or shares of work-related benefits may be expected by a boss from a subordinate, and useful or profitable information may be kept "within the family" rather than shared for wider benefit. Soeharto was a quintessential *bapak*.

Education and income levels rose as Soeharto's immediate family grew in size and greed, as did the families of his cronies. People began to question the KKN that characterized his rule, and in May 1998 thousands of students took to the streets, demanding his resignation. When he resigned on May 21, 1998, his vice president, B.J. Habibie, was sworn in as president and ruled the country until the reasonably fair elections referred to earlier could take place in June 1999. The chapters in this book were almost all initially written during the time of Habibie's rule.

Habibie was an intellectual who was trained in Germany and lived there many years before returning home to lead Indonesia's aerospace program in 1974. As a longtime friend of Soeharto's and a recent political appointee (minister of research and technology), his credibility within the country was seriously compromised. He did, however, make apparent efforts to appoint more honest people to his cabinet. He successfully organized and carried off a comparatively fair national election, and he held things together through a touch-and-go period. From a forestry perspective, he appointed an agriculture specialist as the minister of forestry and changed the name to Ministry of Forestry and Estate Crops. The new Ministry of Forestry and Estate Crops minister, Muslimin Nasution, had long experience in the Ministry of Cooperatives and had been a deputy in the national planning agency. He was personally committed to the cooperatives concept (despite decades of comparatively unsuccessful efforts to organize *koperasi unit desa* (village unit cooperatives)—throughout the country).[8] Habibie's regime maintained freedom of the press, which has continued to date (June 2001). Legislation granting greater regional autonomy by January 1, 2001, was also promulgated at this time (UU 22/1999 on Regional Governance and UU 25/1999 on Fiscal Balance; Down to Earth 2001; ELSAM/CIEL 2001; Chapter 15 of this book).[9]

In the June 1999 election, the party of Megawati Soekarnoputri (daughter of the late Soekarno) won the largest number of votes, but she was not selected as president by the *Majelis Permusyawaratan Rakyat* (MPR). Instead, Abdurrahman Wahid (known informally as Gus Dur), a Muslim cleric who had headed Indonesia's largest Muslim organization (Nahdlatul Ulama) and was considered an honest moderate by most, was selected, with Megawati Soekarnoputri as his vice president.

Meanwhile Indonesia consistently made the nightly news based on events in East Timor, where an election resulted in East Timor's decision to separate from Indonesia, prompting weeks of bloodshed in which Indonesian troops as well as local militia were implicated. Indonesia came under a great deal of international criticism for human rights violations. In the same year, Wahid signed the National Human Rights Law 39, with specific recognition of governmental responsibilities to local people (including community land rights, in accordance with their development over time—Article 6, Sections 1, 2). This is in line with MPR's Act on Human Rights issued in the preceding year, Act of Parliament MPR XVII/MPR/1998, Article 41.

In response to events at a National Congress on Indigenous Peoples (the first of its kind), the minister of agrarian affairs (which includes the Bureau of Lands, charged with land titling) issued a ministerial decree on the Resolution of Traditional Rights Conflicts (Decree of State Minister of Agrarian Affairs 5), allowing for delineation and titling of *adat* lands and for communal and nontransferable private ownership (ELSAM/CIEL 2001).

There is no question that Abdurrahman Wahid took office during a difficult time. The financial crisis was not yet resolved, several other provinces (most dramatically, Aceh and Irian Jaya) were violently expressing interest in independence, and the role of the military remained in question. Indeed, the whole country was unsure about how to implement the situation it wanted: political freedom, an equitable economy, free expression, a functioning democracy, and an end to KKN.

Wahid's tenure has not been easy, nor were many of the problems resolved. Separatist movements continue to plague the central government, with continued accusations of unjust military actions in these areas. Attempts to prosecute cronies and family members have borne no fruit to date, despite continual discussion about the issue in the press. The infamous and well-connected timber baron, Bob Hasan, was under house arrest for 10 months, but he was sentenced in January 2001 to two years in jail for his role in the misuse of US$75 million of government funds in a mapping project (*The Jakarta Post* 2001a). The court decided to count his eight months under house arrest toward his sentence and let him serve the rest of his term under house arrest, without a jail term. Public outcry was sufficient to reverse this decision, and he is now in jail (as of mid-June 2001). Tommy Soeharto, son of the ex-president, was alleged to be involved in a scam with Bulog (the Logistical Bureau, which deals with such issues as ensuring the nation's rice supply, among other things) and Goro, one of Tommy's companies. He was on the verge of coming to trial when he went into hiding. The police have not succeeded in locating him.

Meanwhile, the planned decentralization of authority—long called for by many, because of the extreme centralization that characterized Indonesian politics and policies throughout the New Order regime—is proceeding, with mixed results. The number of provinces has risen from 27 to 32 (*The Jakarta Post* 2001b), and new regencies are proliferating. Some suspect that these new administrative units are designed to provide new opportunities for local bureaucrats to reap financial benefit. Although it is too early to be sure, some lower-level functionaries appear to be taking on the corrupt practices and habits previously reserved for those at the center.[10] Rates of illegal logging, though difficult to measure, are widely reported to have skyrocketed (cf. Curry and Ruwindrijarto 2000; McCarthy 2000; Obidzinski and Suramenggala 2000; Wadley 2001; Chapter 16 of this book).

There is a tug-of-war between the center and the regions, focusing on timber concessions and revenues. Although there appear to be many local interpretations, Down to Earth (2001, 4) summarizes a common view of recent events succinctly:

> Last year (2000), forestry minister Nur Mahmudi attempted to put all logging concessions in the hands of state forestry companies and suggested a division of resource revenue that differed from the ratios set out in the 1999 law (no. 25) on fiscal balance between centre and regions. This provoked anger among local authorities and pro-autonomy central government officials who saw the proposals as evidence of the forestry ministry's reluctance to relinquish control…Mahmudi later proposed a new state forestry agency to oversee the allocation of logging concessions and reforestation. In November, just two months before the start of regional autonomy, the forestry department dropped another bombshell: it announced it would issue 70 logging concessions. Most of these were extensions of expired concessions, but twenty-one were new. This was regarded as another slap in the face for the regions.
>
> A decree issued the same month then set out the new rules for timber concession management, still retaining a high level of central government control. The decree says provincial administrations may issue concessions of up to 100,000 hect-

ares, and district administrations up to 50,000 hectares[11].... It is not clear whether central government or local governments will be able to decide the location of concessions.... The payment of royalties will continue to be regulated by central government—a move that is bound to further displease local officials.

This practice has dwarfed the 1999 and early 2000 cooperatives fad among timber companies and entrepreneurs, some of whom helped communities establish a cooperative, in such a way as to ensure continuing outsider access to timber in the community territory (Colfer's observations in East Kalimantan in August 1999; Wadley 2001, on West Kalimantan practices in May 2000).

In June 2001, Abdurrahman Wahid was under serious pressure. The *Dewan Perwakilan Rakyat* has issued a statement implicating him in a series of recent corruption cases, which led to his impeachment in July. There were demonstrations in the streets of Jakarta and elsewhere, both in favor of Wahid and against him. Megawati Soekarnoputri was sworn in as Indonesia's fifth president on July 23, 2001. Although many specifics have changed since the chapters in this book were written, the essence remains the same: uncertainty about Indonesia's future.

Organization of the Book

In this collection we have three principal purposes: first, we document what is happening to the people and forests of Indonesia. The changes under way are making history with important parallels in other forest-rich countries. Issues of land reform and the formalization of the traditional rights of forest communities have been much discussed since Soeharto's fall, in marked distinction to previous times. Changes mandated by the World Bank as part of a structural adjustment program (resembling such programs in a number of other countries) have had a series of good and bad effects on Indonesia's people and natural resources. The effectiveness of governance in remote areas has diminished dramatically, from what most considered a rather low standard.

Second, we provide insights to policymakers, policy researchers, and concerned citizens who are interested in the development of policies that will benefit the nation. On the one hand, many people want to create a system marked by a more equitable distribution of the wealth from Indonesia's forests; on the other hand, many are calling for improved, more sustainable management of the nation's resources, which have in many cases been plundered without much thought for future use. One important hindrance to improving both distribution and management has been the pervasiveness of the KKN that marked the New Order. This issue must be understood and addressed in the Indonesian context, which is still marked by wealthy and powerful "special interests" and a formidable inertia characteristic of any vast and bloated bureaucracy. Transparency International (2000)[12] ranks Indonesia as the world's fourth most corrupt nation. Insights from Indonesia may well prove useful in the many other nations where corruption is a problem. There is some evidence that countries rich in natural resources may be more prone to corruption than are nations with other bases for their wealth (Gupta et al. 1998).

Finally, Indonesia's experience is of wider interest, particularly in the region.[13] Soeharto's regime was not alone in the pervasive granting of special privileges to family and friends in its autocratic exercise of centralized authority; in the lack of transparency in legal, military, political, and economic matters; and in its failure to provide mechanisms for citizen input into the policymaking process. Students of policy, policymakers, project managers, and researchers in other countries may be able to benefit from these analyses of Indonesia's rather dramatic and disastrous experience—both in helping to identify potential problems and in structuring new solutions to old ones.

The authors in this book represent a wide range of disciplines (anthropology, economics, fire, fisheries biology, forestry, geography, human ecology, natural resource management, policy analysis, sociology, and system dynamics). As such, the theoretical orientations and the perspectives differ markedly from chapter to chapter, as do the conventions of scholarship. We have tried to smooth over some of these differences, but we were torn because the differences in style sometimes reflect important and valuable differences in perspective. We realize that the chapters do not fit into a standard mold. The fact that people from many different disciplines share numerous conclusions, despite the different starting points of their respective studies, in our view, strengthens these conclusions.

We begin with a series of Chapters (1–6) that focuses on the links between the government's policies on forests and forest people. We present the chapters in a progression, beginning with analyses focused on abstract and conceptual matters (i.e., laws, bureaucratic norms of interaction, structures) and proceeding to more field-oriented implications of recent changes in the laws and policies for forest people and the forests. Our final section focuses on what has transpired between 1999, when most of these chapters were written, and June 2001.

In Chapter 1, Wrangham (an anthropologist) provides an overview of Indonesian laws and regulations that relate to communities and forests—drawing from bodies of law in various sectors. She focuses on competing discourses, one supporting the concentration of control over land in the hands of the state, further strengthened by a long-standing depiction of traditional communities as destroyers of the forest resource. The other discourse emphasizes the management capabilities and human rights of forest peoples in the practice of their *adat* institutions. In pursuing these themes, she provides a summary of the most important legislation and policy pertaining to these issues from the New Order and before.

In Chapter 2, Lindayati (an environmental and policy scientist) takes a more theoretical, political science perspective on policy, examining the history and process of forestry policy changes relating to communities in Indonesia's Outer Islands. She identifies three distinct stages in the evolution of policies on forest management in Indonesia, particularly as they relate to communities and their management: the late 1960s to the early 1980s, the mid-1980s to 1997, and 1998 to 1999. The bureaucratic decisionmaking process is put into context by examining the ideational and normative systems within which decisions have been made.

In Chapter 3, Bennett (an independent consultant who began as a plant pathologist and now calls himself a policy pathologist) examines the problems anticipated for Indonesia's decentralization process (which is now under way) and makes some concrete suggestions to address them. He specifically suggests involving communities directly in processes designed to ensure the accountability of local governments to their own areas. Bennett's suggestions are down-to-earth and practical and come at a time when Indonesian policymakers recognize the need for such mechanisms to prevent the simple devolution of KKN to lower levels of government.

Wollenberg (a social scientist) and Kartodihardjo (a forester) provide an analysis of the September 1999 forestry law and its implications for devolution of more authority to local communities in Chapter 4. This chapter focuses on the law's provisions relating to customary communities and cooperatives, concluding with some suggested actions to enhance the effect of this new legislation on devolution. Interestingly, although this law was published a year and a half ago, as of June 2001 we still know of no implementing regulations for it.

Chapter 5, by Campbell (a specialist in community-based natural resource management), presents two conflicting perspectives: one emphasizing local people's rights to their resources (based on traditional law) and one focusing on the people's economy. Campbell's discussion provides an analysis of some of the debate that has accompanied the law described in the previous chapter, as well as some other relevant legislation being considered in mid-1999. This discussion reflects ongoing philosophical disagreements within the country. Both the centrally determined emphasis on cooperatives and the push for decentralization have progressed along the trajectory described in this chapter.

Chapter 6, by Fay (a political scientist) and Sirait (a forester), covers some similar ground to Chapter 5 but deals with the process that has occurred in the development of legislation, again highlighting issues that relate to people living in forests. They report on the policy process, in which they were intimately involved, that resulted in *Kawasan dengan Tujuan Istimewa* (Zone with Special Purposes). These areas significantly represent the first formal recognition of customary rights to manage an area within the formal forestry estate of the nation. There remains hope that these areas can serve as precedents for more such areas in the future or can stimulate a more serious attempt to deal with the conflicting claims that currently characterize Indonesia's forest landscapes.

The next set of chapters (7–12) turns to in-depth, sector-level analyses of what happened in Indonesia immediately following Soeharto's fall. This series begins with Kartodihardjo's formal look at the structures and institutions involved in forestry-related policy development, in Chapter 7, from a forestry perspective. He talks first about the economic losses from "illegal logging" and from various corrupt practices as causes of the destruction in Indonesia's production forest areas. He then analyzes aspects of the institutional arrangements and bureaucratic roles that maintain and reinforce adverse practices. Finally he looks at the new policy reforms, with some discussion of the future implementation of the new forestry law.

Resosudarmo (a policy analyst) provides an account of the nature and development of the overall forestry sector in recent years in Chapter 8. She highlights the most important issues that have plagued those who would see Indonesia's forests managed sustainably, setting the stage for the related analyses of specific subsectors that follow.

Barr's analysis in Chapter 9 of Indonesia's concession system focuses on five assumptions underpinning what he calls the "sustainable logging paradigm." As a sociologist and policy analyst, he critiques each assumption based on changes that have occurred in Indonesia's forests and in related industries in recent years, concluding that profitable, sustainable logging is no longer possible in Indonesia's natural forests. If his conclusions were true in 1999, they are doubly so now, with the increasing pressures from illegal logging and the manner in which decentralization is being implemented.

Casson (another specialist in policy) has done a thorough analysis, part of which is reproduced in Chapter 10, of oil palm development and its implications for Indonesia's forests. Besides documenting the recent history of oil palm production and related problems, Casson argues that without significant changes in Indonesian policy, oil palm expansion continues to pose a serious threat to the nation's forests.

Chapter 11, by Sunderlin (a sociologist), provides an analysis of the effects of Indonesia's economic crisis on smallholders and the forest. The chapter provides details of changes, with possible effects on forests and people, as the crisis progressed. He presents the results of a five-province survey looking at the effects of the crisis on small farmers, and he documents changes in a number of extrasectoral factors affecting forests (e.g., export commodity policy and management, mining, roads). The chapter also provides some insights into specific forestry-related policies and how they changed during the crisis (e.g., area limits on forest concessions and resource rents, the auction system and cooperatives, the new forestry law).

Chapter 12, by Barr, Brown (a political scientist), Casson, and Kaimowitz (economist and director general of Center for International Forestry Research [CIFOR]), is a macroeconomic analysis of how Indonesia's corporate debt has affected the forestry sector, with some worrying prognoses for the future. They provide an estimate of the magnitude of the debt, discussion on how debt write-offs are being used as subsidies, and some discussion of who will have to pay for these write-offs and rescheduling.

The next section of this book focuses on Indonesia's experience of the fires in 1997–1998. In Chapter 13, Applegate (a forester) and his coauthors— Smith (a specialist in fire management and environmental audits), Fox (a social anthropologist), Mitchell (a forester), Packham (a rural fire consultant), Tapper (a geographer), and Baines (a consultant in tropical natural resources and environmental management)—provide a national view, documenting the extent of the damage and suggesting some ways to address future fires more constructively. This is particularly important now, as we are predicted to be facing another El Niño. Colfer (an anthropologist) provides a field-based view of the causes of the fires in Chapter 14, based on research in six communities in East Kalimantan. Both these analyses represent early efforts to systematize and prioritize fire causes so that better policies can be created to deal more effectively with future El Niños.

The final section updates the reader, focusing on the two most important trends at work in the Outer Islands of Indonesia at this time: decentralization and illegal logging. In Chapter 15, Resosudarmo and Dermawan (a socioeconomist specializing in policy) first explain the meaning and history of decentralization efforts in Indonesia, with special reference to forestry. They then elaborate on the two most pertinent recent laws on regional autonomy (on regional governance and fiscal balance). Building on evidence from recent field research, they demonstrate the tug-of-war on forestry issues under way between the levels of government. They conclude with some reflections on the implications of decentralization for communities and forests and on possible avenues for Indonesia to go forward.

In Chapter 16, Dudley (a modeler and a fisheries biologist) provides a preliminary version of a system dynamics model being developed to portray the factors encouraging illegal logging. By extensive use of causal loop diagrams, he first shows the logging situation under Soeharto's regime and since. He then provides views of illegal logging, as seen by local players and then as seen from the business perspective. Besides serving as a partial update on illegal logging, the analysis brings in many of the issues discussed throughout this book, reminding us of the systemic and interconnected nature of topics we typically address in bits and pieces.

Most of the issues we raise relating to Outer Island forests, forest communities, and policies with implications for forests remain at the forefront of

Indonesian debate. What rights should local communities have? How should previous abridgement of their rights be dealt with now? How should forest management and use be structured? What kinds of land use are appropriate for forested and previously forested areas? What effects do macropolicy shifts have on specific forests? How should Indonesia deal with fires in and around forests? The issues that came to the forefront right after Soeharto's fall are complex enough that they have not yet been resolved; nor do we expect them to be resolved in any final manner in the near future. The fact that they are now being openly discussed in government (and other) circles is a huge step forward.

The way that Indonesia has dealt with these problems reveals lessons for other areas. Natural resource management, the policy–environment interface, devolution and decentralization, and policymaking processes and indigenous land claims are recurrent themes throughout this book—themes that have applicability and appeal far beyond Indonesia's borders.

Most of the chapters in this book were written during the second half of 1999. Now (June 2001) Indonesia remains in an unusually fluid state, with major changes occurring regularly in an apparently spontaneous fashion. Continual revision of the manuscript is impossible (this book would never be published!), but we do try to give snapshot coverage of what has happened since 1999. Where possible we have revised specific chapters to incorporate relevant changes; other times, we have had to footnote the change. We have added chapters on Indonesia's implementation of decentralization and on illegal logging, as partial, more systematic updates of the situation. We provide a timeline of major legislation (Appendix), a list of Indonesian acronyms, and a glossary of Indonesian terms. It is our intention that this book capture the combination of worry and hope that the current situation comprises.

Endnotes

1. New Order is a term used to describe the Soeharto government of Indonesia from 1967 to 1998.

2. See Chapter 13 of this book, Colfer Forthcoming, Colfer et al. 2000, Dennis et al. 2000, Guhardja et al. 2000, Harwell 2000, Schweithelm 1999, Stolle and Tomich 1999, Suyanto 2000, Suyanto and Ruchiat 2000, and Vayda 1999 for discussions of the extent and effects of the fires.

3. See Ascher 1993, Barber 1997, and Schwarz 1999.

4. Forestry has also had an important role in Java, with an impressive (and strife-ridden) history of teak plantations (Peluso 1990, 1992). Indeed, conflicts over teak forests under government control continue in Java to this day. Our emphasis in this book, however, is on natural forests, of which few remain intact on the densely populated Java of today.

5. More specifically, the Verenigde Oost-Indische Compagnie came to Indonesia in 1596 and occupied Indonesia until the end of 1799. The Dutch colonial state started to occupy Indonesia on January 1, 1800, continuing until 1811, followed by the British for three years

(the Raffles' era). Control returned to the Dutch from 1814 until May 1942, followed by the Japanese occupation for three years, ending in August 1945.

6. *Pancasila* is the official state philosophy and includes five components: belief in one God, humanitarianism, national unity, people's sovereignty, and social justice.

7. Since Dutch times, Indonesia has had a transmigration program. In the earliest days, transmigration was designed to move poor people from Java to other islands to supply cheap labor to plantations, especially in Sumatra (Swasono 1986). Later it was designed to reduce the population on Java by resettling poor people to the Outer Islands; in more recent years, the program has focused on "developing the Outer Islands" by the same means. The program has now shifted its focus to dealing with the large numbers of refugees being produced by Indonesia's internal conflicts.

8. ELSAM/CIEL (2001) critiques the cooperative idea by pointing out its strictly commercial, as opposed to sustainable management, orientation; its overly bureaucratic nature; and its creation of opportunities for abuse because anyone (including timber companies) can form cooperatives without mechanisms for accountability to local communities.

9. Down to Earth also reports that under the 1999 UU 22/1999 and 25/1999, forestry is supposed to be managed at the district level, and 80% of the revenues they earn are to be retained in the regions.

10. Down to Earth (2001), for instance, says "One of the main risks of this approach [the current version of decentralization] is that the newly empowered *bupatis* (regency heads) will orchestrate the plunder of natural resources in their areas, repeating at local level the get-rich-quick approach of the central government during the Soeharto years."

11. A ministerial decree, quite difficult to interpret, was issued on November 6, 2000, specifying regulations on this issue; however, governors and regents had already begun allocating lands prior to that time. Stepi Hakim, a researcher from CIFOR, recently learned an official interpretation of the regulations from Paser, East Kalimantan. He was told by local officials that both the governor and the regent can give 100-ha plots of land to cooperatives (technically outside of the forest estate, although in reality much of this land is forested); both the governor and the regent can give out 50,000-ha concessions within the forest estate to cooperatives, small- and medium-scale enterprises, state companies (Badan Usaha Milik Negara), local government companies (Badan Usaha Milik Daerah), and private companies (Hakim 2001). Jean-Marie Bompard and Tim Nolan, also researchers, who recently returned from Berau in East Kalimantan, found the view that governors could issue 100,000-ha concessions and regents could issue 50,000-ha concessions. The officials they interviewed also reported having officially granted villages their territories within existing concessions and developing a joint venture involving a benefit sharing system (30% for the state forest company [Inhutani I], 30% for the province, 30% for the regency; and 10% for local communities [Bompard and Nolan 2001]). Decentralization will inevitably result in increasing variation in policies from place to place.

12. Transparency International describes itself as "a civil society organization dedicated to curbing both international and national corruption."

13. Though distant, Cameroon has suffered from similar economic crises (cf. Russell and Tchamou 2000, 2) and structural adjustment programs of the World Bank (Kaimowitz et al. 1998; Sunderlin et al. forthcoming, 2000).

References

Ascher, W. 1993. *Political Economy and Problematic Forestry Policies in Indonesia: Obstacles to Incorporating Sound Economics and Science.* Durham, NC: Center for Tropical Conservation, Duke University.

Banuri, T., and F.A. Marglin (eds.). 1993. *Who Will Save the Forest? Knowledge, Power and Environmental Destruction*. London: Zed Books.

Barber, C.V. 1997. *Environmental Scarcities, State Capacity, Civil Violence: The Case of Indonesia*. Washington, DC: American Academy of Sciences and University College, University of Toronto.

_____, N. Johnson, and E. Hafild. 1994. *Breaking the Logjam: Obstacles to Forest Policy Reform in Indonesia and the United States*. Washington, DC: World Resources Institute.

Barr, C. 1999. *Discipline and Accumulate: State Practice and Elite Consolidation in Indonesia's Timber Sector, 1967–1998*. MS thesis. Ithaca, NY: Cornell University.

BPS (Badan Pusat Statistik). 2001. *Hasil Sementara Sensus Penduduk 2000* (*Preliminary Results of the Population Census, 2000*). Berita Resmi Statistik no. 03/IV/3. January 2001. Jakarta, Indonesia: From the webpage of BPS at http://www.bps.go.id/releases/sp2000-sementara.pdf (accessed February 9, 2001).

Bompard, J.M., and T. Nolan. 2001. Personal communication with the authors, February 14.

Brookfield, H., L. Potter, and Y. Byron. 1995. *In Place of the Forest: Environmental and Socioeconomic Transformation in Borneo and the Eastern Malay Peninsula*. Tokyo: United Nations University Press.

Colfer, C.J.P. Forthcoming. Fire in East Kalimantan: A panoply of practices, views and (discouraging) effects. *Borneo Research Bulletin*.

Colfer, C. J. P., with R.G. Dudley. 1993. *Shifting cultivators of Indonesia: Marauders or managers of the forest? Rice production and forest use among the Uma' Jalan of East Kalimantan*. Community Forestry Case Study Series no. 6. Rome: Food and Agriculture Organization.

Colfer, C.J.P., R. Dennis, and G. Applegate. 2000. *The underlying causes and impacts of fires in Southeast Asia: site 8, Long Segar, East Kalimantan Province, Indonesia*. CIFOR Site Report. Bogor, Indonesia: CIFOR.

Curry, D., and A. Ruwindrijarto. 2000. *Illegal Logging in Tanjung Puting National Park, an Update to the Final Cut Report*. London: Environmental Investigation Agency and Bogor, Indonesia: Telapak Indonesia.

Dennis, R., J. Mayer, and F. Stolle. 2000. *Field Trip to West Kalimantan. February 17–23*. Bogor, Indonesia: CIFOR/International Centre for Research in Agroforestry.

Departemen Kehutanan. 2001. From the DepHut webpage at http://www. dephut.go.id/ informasi/umum/datainformasi/luas_hutan.htm (accessed February 12, 2001).

Donner, W. 1987. *Land Use and Environment in Indonesia*. Honolulu: University of Hawaii Press.

Down to Earth. 2001. *Down to Earth Newsletter* no. 48. From the webpage at www.gn.apc.org/dte (accessed in February).

ELSAM/CIEL (Lembaga Studi dan Avokasi Masyarakat–The Institute for Policy Research and Advocacy/Center for International Environmental Law). 2001. *Whose Nation? Whose Resources? Towards a New Paradigm of Environmental Justice and the Nationals Interest of Indonesia*. Jakarta, Indonesia, and Washington, DC: ELSAM/CIEL.

Factbook. 2001. From the webpage at http://www.cia.gov/cia/publications/factbook/geos/id.html (accessed February 9, 2001).

Furnivall, J.S. 1948. *Colonial Policy and Practice: A Comparative Study*. Cambridge: Cambridge University Press.

Geertz, C. 1960. *The Religion of Java*. London: The Free Press of Glencoe.

_____. 1963. *Agricultural Involution*. Berkeley: University of California Press.

Gonner, C. 1999. Causes and effects of forest fires: A case study from a sub-district in East Kalimantan, Indonesia. Paper presented at the International Centre for Research in Agroforestry Methodology Workshop: Environmental Services and Land Use Change: Bridging the Gap Between Policy and Research in Southeast Asia. May 31 to June 2, 1999, Chiang Mai, Thailand.

Guhardja, E., M. Fatawi, M. Sutisna, T. Mori, and S. Ohta (eds.). 2000. *Rainforest Ecosystems of East Kalimantan: El Niño, Drought, Fire and Human Impacts*. Tokyo: Springer.

Gupta, S., H. Davoodi, and R. Alonso-Terme. 1998. *Does corruption affect income inequality and poverty?* Working Paper of the International Monetary Fund (IMF). WP/98/76. Washington DC: IMF.

Hakim, S. 2001. Personal communication with the authors, February 15.

Harwell, E. 2000. Remote sensibilities: Discourses of technology and the making of Indonesia's natural disaster. *Development and Change* 31: 307–40.

The Jakarta Post. 2001a. Bob Hasan gets two years in jail, February 3, 1.

———. 2001b, Gorontalo inaugurated as the country's 32nd province, February 17, 2.

Kaimowitz, D., Erwidodo, O. Ndoye, P. Pacheco, and W. Sunderlin. 1998. Considering the impact of structural adjustment policies on forest in Bolivia, Cameroon and Indonesia. *Unasylva* 49(194):57–64.

Kemf, E. (ed.). 1993. *The Law of the Mother: Protecting Indigenous Peoples in Protected Areas*. San Francisco: Sierra Club Books.

MacKinnon, K., G. Hatta, H. Halim, and A. Mangalik. 1996. *The Ecology of Kalimantan*. Singapore: Periplus Editions.

McCarthy, J.F. 2000. *"Wild Logging": The Rise and Fall of Logging Networks and Biodiversity Conservation Projects on Sumatra's Rainforest Frontier*. CIFOR occasional paper no. 31. Bogor, Indonesia: CIFOR.

Miksic, J. (ed.). 1996. *Ancient history. In Indonesian Heritage* (Volume 1). Jakarta, Indonesia: Buku Antar Bangsa for Grolier International Inc.

Obidzinski, K., and I. Suramenggala. 2000. *Illegal Logging in Indonesia—A Contextual Approach to the Problem*. Draft paper. Bogor, Indonesia: CIFOR.

Peluso, N.L. 1990. A history of state forest management in Java. In *Keepers of the Forest: Land Management Alternatives in Southeast Asia*, edited by M. Poffenberger. West Hartford, CT: Kumarian Press, 27–55.

———. 1992. *Rich Forests, Poor People: Resource Control and Resistance in Java*. Berkeley: University of California Press.

Pelzer, K.J. 1982. Planters Against Peasants: The Agrarian Struggle in East Sumatra, 1947–1958. *Verhandelingen van het Koninklijk Instituut voor de Taal-Land-en Volkenkunde* 97. S'Gravenhage: Martinus Nijhoff.

Redfield, R. 1956. *Peasant Society and Culture: An Anthropological Approach to Civilization*. Chicago: University of Chicago Press.

Russell, D., and N. Tchamou. 2000. Soil fertility and the generation gap in southern Cameroon. In *People Managing Forests: The Links between Human Well Being and Sustainability*, edited by C. Colfer and Y. Byron. Washington, DC: Resources for the Future.

Schwarz, A. 1999. *A Nation in Waiting: Indonesia's Search for Stability*. St. Leonards, New South Wales, Australia: Allen and Unwin.

Schweithelm, J. 1999. *The Fire This Time: An Overview of Indonesia's Forest Fires in 1997–98*. Jakarta, Indonesia: World Wide Fund for Nature.

Stolle, F., and T. Tomich. 1999. The 1997–98 fire event in Indonesia. *Nature and Resources* 35(3):22–30.

Sunderlin, W.D., and I.A.P. Resosudarmo. 1996. *Rates and Causes of Deforestation in Indonesia: Towards a Resolution of the Ambiguities*. CIFOR occasional paper no. 9. Bogor, Indonesia: CIFOR.

Sunderlin, W.D., I.A.P. Resosudarmo, and O. Ndoye. Forthcoming. The effect of economic crises on small farmers and forest cover: A comparison of Cameroon and Indonesia. In *World Forests, Society, and Environment*, edited by M. Palo and J. Uusivuori. Dordrecht: Kluwer Academic Publishers.

Sunderlin, W.D., O. Ndoye, H. Bikié, N. Laporte, B. Mertens, and J. Pokam. 2000. Economic crisis, small-scale agriculture, and forest cover change in southern Cameroon. *Environmental Conservation* 27(3):284–90.

Suyanto, S. 2000. *Fire, Deforestation and Land Tenure in the Northeastern Fringes of Bukit Barisan Selatan National Park, Lampung.* Bogor, Indonesia: International Centre for Research in Agroforestry.

Suyanto, S., and Y. Ruchiat. 2000. *Impacts of Human Activities and Land Tenure Conflict on Fires and Land Use Change: Case of Menggala; Lampung; Sumatra.* Preliminary draft. Bogor, Indonesia: International Centre for Research in Agroforestry.

Swasono, S.E. 1986. Kependudukan, Kolonisasi dan Transmigrasi. In *Transmigrasi di Indonesia 1905–1985,* edited by S.E. Swasono and M. Singarimbun. Jakarta, Indonesia: Universitas Indonesia Press, 70–85.

Transparency International. 2000. *Transparency International's Corruption Index.* From the webpage at http://www.transparency.de/index.html 2000.

Vayda, A.P. 1999. *Finding Causes of the 1997–98 Indonesian Forest Fires: Problems/Possibilities.* Jakarta, Indonesia: World Wide Fund for Nature.

Wadley, R.L. 2000. *Histories of Natural Resource Use and Control in West Kalimantan, Indonesia: Danau Sentarum National Park and Its Vicinity (1800–2000).* A Report for the CIFOR Project "Local People, Devolution, and Adaptive Collaborative Management." Bogor, Indonesia: CIFOR.

_____. 2001. *Community Co-operatives, Illegal Logging, and Regional Autonomy: Empowerment and Impoverishment in the Borderlands of West Kalimantan, Indonesia.* Paper presented at "Resource Tenure, Forest Management, and Conflict Resolution: Perspectives from Borneo and New Guinea." April 2001. Australian National University, Canberra.

The World Bank. 2001. *Indonesia: Environment and Natural Resource Management in a Time of Transition.* Washington, DC: The World Bank.

Zerner, C. 1994. Through a green lens: The construction of customary environmental law and community in Indonesia's Maluku islands. *Law and Society Review* 28:1079–122.

C H A P T E R   O N E

Changing Policy Discourses and Traditional Communities, 1960–1999

Rachel Wrangham

Indonesia's forests are among the most diverse and spectacular in the world. Yet with an annual deforestation rate as high as 1.5 million ha, the state of the remaining forest is a matter of concern for the entire international community (see Chapter 5). So far Indonesia's record of managing its resources and responsibilities has been mixed. Before the Asian economic crisis, the country was lauded as a capitalist success story, with rising standards of living and rapid industrialization. Yet even before that bubble burst, Indonesia had a second face—the exploitation of not only resources but also people (specifically expropriation and corruption, the repression of indigenous peoples, and the unsustainable extraction of the country's natural wealth). In October 1999, Indonesia seemed to teeter between an extractive and centralist past and an uncertain future. This chapter provides a historical context in which to understand this ongoing transition.[1]

In this chapter, I consider the ways in which power over land and forest resources has been concentrated in the hands of the state, and I outline the discourses that I consider to have been associated with this process. The first of these is a discourse that identifies forest-dwelling communities as destroyers of national forest resources, outside modernity and the nation. The second is the discourse of national unity, modernity, national development, and nationhood that underlay the whole New Order system.[2] I also look at a third countervailing discourse that privileges the local and indigenous, considering that community management of forests is both the fairest and the most sustainable form of management (compare the discussion of policy narratives in the conclusion to this book). To situate this discussion and to indicate how the balance of influence has shifted between these discourses, I take a broadly chronological approach, looking at laws and policies to elucidate the ways in which these discourses have developed and changed.

This chapter is based largely on library research, interviews with individuals and organizations in Jakarta, and six months of fieldwork in the Tanimbar Islands, Southeast Maluku, in 1998. As a result of this research, my discussion focuses on the letter of the law and the ways laws have been used and interpreted by different groups during different periods.

Land Tenure: The Legislative Framework

Understanding the laws and decrees governing forest ownership, use, and conservation is extremely complicated. The confusion is worsened because these sometimes contradictory laws issue from several different ministries, which themselves have changed in composition over time.[3] In this section I give a brief and necessarily selective account of the changes in Indonesian law and policy on land tenure and how these changes have led to multiple layers of contested and often contradictory rights to land, to the use of land, or to its natural resources.

Land tenure law as developed by the Dutch can be seen as an early attempt to find a compromise between the recognition of preexisting rights systems and the desire of the colonial state to exploit and benefit from natural resources. At Independence, three systems of land law were recognized: (a) unwritten *adat* (traditional or customary) law, which varied from place to place and included both communal and individual rights; (b) land registered according to the Indonesian Civil Code; and (c) state land, which according to the agrarian law of 1870 included all land that could not be proved to be otherwise owned and could be leased for plantations. Conflicts over whether such lands were in fact unoccupied could and did arise, but in theory preexisting customary rights were recognized[4] (Thiesenhusen et al. 1997).

The Indonesian constitution of 1945 did nothing to clarify the situation. Article 18 specifically continued to recognize historical rights (*hak asal-usul*), while Article 33 (another frequently quoted passage) declared the right and responsibility of the state to control (*menguasai*) natural resources for the general good of the Indonesian people. Article 33 has been used to justify most New Order forest management practices and to explain why many of the fundamental reforms now being demanded are constitutionally impossible.

It was not until 1960 that the problem of these multiple systems of land tenure was addressed. The Basic Agrarian Law (*Undang-Undang* [UU] 5/1960) intended to end the confusion and create a uniform system. It allowed the registration of four different rights over land: (a) the right to own (*hak milik*); (b) the right to cultivate state land (*hak guna usaha*), which may be granted for up to 35 years and extended for an additional 35 years; (c) the right to build and own buildings on land owned by another (*hak guna bangunan*); and (d) the right to use or collect products from state or private land for a certain period (*hak pakai*). It also recognized but denied the registration of various other rights, including rights to clear land, gather forest products, use water, and raise and catch fish. Other forms of customary law were also recognized, so long as they did not interfere with state or national interests and were not superseded by rights granted under the Basic Agrarian Law. This law was very much a first step: its scope was extremely general, and so far it has required more than 3,000 implementing regulations (Thiesenhusen et al. 1997).

The next addition to the legislation governing land tenure, this time specifically relating to forests, came in 1967. This marked the end of the more socialist concerns of the Soekarno era and the beginning of the New Order's emphasis on economic development. The Basic Forestry Law ([BFL] UU 5/1967) gave the state legal authority to plan and regulate all forest tenure and to use arrangements in its jurisdiction. It stated that forests must be protected and used for the welfare of the Indonesian people. The government was left to determine the balance between these and a range of other objectives, including prevention of flooding, harvesting of forest products for national development, protection of the earnings of those in and around the forest, conservation, migration, agriculture, and plantations. The law centered authority on the minister, who was given the power to designate land as forest, determine the purpose and use of all forests, regulate forest management, stipulate and regulate judicial relations between citizens or corporations and forests, and regulate juridical deeds about forests. It granted minimal recognition to customary rights, although Article 17 stated that customary communities may have rights to obtain benefits from the forest, so long as these rights do not disturb the objectives of the BFL, as interpreted by the minister (Thiesenhusen et al. 1997).

At about the same time as the BFL, three other important laws were promulgated: the Basic Law on Mining (UU 11/1967), the Law on Foreign Investment (UU 1/1967), and the Law on Domestic Investment (UU 6/1968). In 1970 two government regulations were issued—*Peraturan Pemerintah* ([PP] government regulation) 21/1970 Forest Exploitation Rights and Forest Product Harvesting Rights and PP 33/1970 on Forest Planning. Together these laws and regulations created the framework for the systematic economic exploitation of Indonesia's natural resources by large companies. In the forestry sector this exploitation was made possible by a process of classifying and demarcating forestland and then prohibiting local access or resource use. This process started with the BFL in 1967 and has been governed by the Consensus Land Use Planning Decree from the Ministry of the Interior (*Surat Keputusan* [SK] or ministerial decree 26/1982) and the Spatial Planning Law (UU 24/1992). The text of these two laws was neither as anticommunity nor as nonparticipatory as their implementation has been, in a world dominated by forest concessions, ideas of forest exploitation (*pengusahaan*) rather than management (*pengelolaan*), and mistrust of communities. The result of these laws and the climate in which they have been implemented has been the gradual though incomplete extension of state control, via central and provincial forest departments, over about 70% of Indonesia's land.

My suggestion, which I explore in the remainder of this chapter, is that this climate displays a clash between the two contradictory sets of discourses that I sketched at the outset: on the one hand a modernist, centralist discourse of state-led management, backed by a justificatory discourse of local destruction, and on the other a rights-based discourse of indigenous forest use. Policies were developed and laws formulated and implemented in conversation between these discourses. Changes in the policy climate reflect the changing balance of power between the proponents of these discourses. In the next three sections I examine these discourses in more detail.

Who Controls, Who Destroys?

The majority of forest-related laws during the 1970s and 1980s were detrimental to the rights and livelihoods of traditional communities, based on customary law (or *masyarakat hukum adat*), as commercial timber extraction was privileged over local forest use.[5] For example PP 21/1970 (on Forest Exploitation Rights and Forest Product Harvesting Rights), PP 18/1975 (its revision), and PP 7/1990 (on Industrial Timber Plantations) did not give equal rights to traditional communities compared with private or nationalized companies. PP 28/1985 (on Forest Protection) minimized the role of traditional communities by centralizing forest protection functions, which reduced the scope for local involvement or responsibility. The Law on Forest Planning (PP 33/1970) did not allow for a participatory process of boundary setting, nor did it guarantee compensation for lost land. The conclusions drawn by Suharjito and his associates (1999, 62–63), on whose work the above analysis is based, is that the laws mentioned were not conducive to the development and growth of community-managed forestry. They also commented that the result of all sorts of policies that merely spoke of "community" was that the recognition of the traditional management of customary forests became hazy, and the character and existence of customary forests was sidelined.

Leaving aside the rights and wrongs of this situation, these policies and laws were based on an image of forest dwellers and local forest users as destroyers of the national forest resource and trespassers on state or concession land. The discourse of destruction had several roots and was extremely important in justifying state forest policy. Zerner (1992, 14) commented that the Indonesian government's assessment of shifting cultivation "continues to follow the trajectory of negative colonial assessments of these practices: that swidden and its practitioners are environmentally unsustainable, destructive and wasteful." Furthermore the government assumed that forest-dwelling communities traditionally lived in isolated integrity, their practices governed by unchanging customary laws. As this was self-evidently no longer the case, the argument then was that such communities were no longer traditional and were unfit to manage natural resources. The result was that for much of the New Order, the ministry's position on community involvement in any kind of forest management was negative; despite a limited rhetoric of participation, the different departments tended to regard forest communities as a threat, rather than as partners.[6] This discourse underlay approaches to forest management into the 1990s. For example SK 251/1993 identifies forest communities as a potential threat to timber companies; meanwhile it aims to protect their rights to nontimber forest products (NTFPs) and timber for consumptive use. In another instance the 1993 Joint Decree from the Ministries of Agriculture, Home Affairs, and Transmigration and Forest Dwellers 480/Kpts-II/1993 describes forest dwellers who practice shifting cultivation as destroyers of the forest resource.

The discourse of destruction is powerful and by no means confined to Indonesia. It tells a clear story about what has gone wrong, and it has equally clear recommendations of advisable improvements and changes. As Scott (1998) suggested, the management practices that follow from it can be seen as part of a broader attempt by the modern state to make the people, practices, and landscape under its aegis more legible in a bid to increase control. Yet it has remained a discourse, a story of how things ought to be, rather than an account of what has actually happened. It has proven impossible to bring the vast area of Indonesia's forest under state control. In some cases, branches of government have resorted to violence in their attempt to remove local people from state land, but in other cases traditional communities have stayed, generally with the connivance or cooperation of local government (Sirait et al. 1999). Thus while any community living on state land is in a vulnerable position, the legal tangle coupled with de facto decentralization of authority (despite ostensible centralization and uniformity—see the next section) means that policy implementation has depended to a great degree on personalities and place. The lack of certainty in the law, combined with the lack of a legal structure clearly linking the forest resource to its users, has created a free-for-all in which forest management has become the responsibility of no one (Seve 1999). The result is that the Ministry of Forestry (MoF)[7] has not succeeded in managing the forest, even according to its own limited definitions. It has been unable to regulate just access to land, nor does it have the enforcement capacity for sustainable forestry management.

The Centralizing State

A second discourse underlies much official policy toward Indonesia's forests: that of the unified and centralized state. Again this is not unique to Indonesia, but in Indonesia it reached an unusual level of elaboration and complication, and it was fundamental to the identity of the nation—hence the national motto, "Unity in Diversity."

In the field of forestry legislation, this concept was worked out in three ways. First, laws were drafted for the whole of Indonesia, taking no account of the diversity of the Indonesian environment. Laws and regulations were drafted in Jakarta, usually after negligible local consultation. Implementing regulations were also composed in Jakarta and tended to deal solely with the outputs, never the outcomes of laws. This meant that decisions were taken and actions were monitored far from the forest itself. Second, government bureaucratic systems were extended right down to the local level. As a result of two laws on local government (UU 5/1974 and UU 5/1979), village government and administration were drawn into the central and uniform bureaucratic net. These laws extended government control into villages and undermined *adat* leadership systems right at their roots. Villages were redefined to destabilize these traditional systems, and an Indonesia-wide pattern for village administration replaced the older arrangements. Third, there was almost complete government domination of the policy arena within a closed yet strikingly disunified bureaucratic system. The result was that policies tended to serve the interests of particular sections of government.

In the same way the discourse of destruction has been challenged, so has the trajectory of decentralization. The result has been that the government's domination of village-level government and the policy arena has not in fact been total. It is my suggestion that some of the contradictory rights-based discourse described next was in fact created by the very nature of the Indonesian state.

The Indonesian state, for all its centralization, can be pictured as being centered on a vacuum. By this I mean that there has been no legislative center at the heart of the governmental process. At the heart of Indonesia's pyramidal and centralized state has lain a range of executive agencies and ministries and the military rather than legislative bodies. This situation came about because of Soeharto's desire for a strong government; he believed that only this could guarantee economic development and political stability. It involved the concentration of power in the hands of the president and his ministers at the expense of the legislature and judiciary, and therefore most law and government policy has taken the form of ministerial decrees, rather than laws approved by parliament. Once again, Indonesia is not unique in privileging the executive, but the situation is more accentuated than in many other countries.

My suggestion is that one of the unintended consequences of concentrating power in the hands of competing ministries is that there has been a bit more space for alternative discourses to develop and for ministries to develop rather different policies.[8] The lack of policy harmony—for example, the contradictions between the BFL (1967) and the Basic Agrarian Law (1960)—has led to an ad hoc system of government with different laws being implemented in different places. Authority and the granting of exceptions have become highly personalized, so that demands and requests have been channeled through patron–client linkages rather than through representative institutions (Lindayati 1999). Thus, the overall role of civil society and its institutions has been very limited. Success has generally been confined to a few privileged individuals and groups, while consultation has been ad hoc and at governmental whim. Thus some donor projects have won highly preferential status, and they have managed to overcome the implementation and policy blockages that have stymied many unsupported customary communities.

It is in this complex situation—with powerful government rhetoric, sporadic but strong-armed implementation, and a vacuum at the center of the state—that nongovernment actors have been able to work. Both at the local and the central levels, some communities and nongovernmental organizations (NGOs) have negotiated exceptions or situated themselves in areas of interministerial conflict. The New Order government's vision was never truly all encompassing. Despite repression, many local and national actors continued to press for the recognition of alternative practices, viewpoints, and paradigms. The government has been challenged from all directions by the direct action of local people, NGO advocacy, research findings, and pressure from the international community to pay more attention to indigenous rights and environmental issues. Evidence that local people can manage their own land and resources, using local institutions, has been accumulating. The best-studied case is probably the damar agroforest of Krui (see Chapter 6), but other research has shown similar resilience and adaptability of management systems in other parts of Indonesia (e.g., Suyanto et al. 1998b). Consequently, there have been calls for a change in the government paradigm of economic exploitation of the forest and for the state to pay more attention to issues of community ownership, participation, sustainable forest management, human rights, and the rampant corruption that has characterized much of the forest concession system.

Indigenous Rights

At no point did the aforementioned discourses of control, modernity, or unity go unchallenged: running alongside them, in various forms, has been a less clearly elaborated discourse of indigenous rights and community management. The existence of this secondary discourse is indicated from the start: the earliest laws (e.g., the 1870 agrarian law, the 1945 Constitution) recognized the existence and validity of customary claims and rights to land and resources. Indeed there has been a long and dialectical relationship between these claims and the centralizing trajectory of the modern state. Yet proponents for the recognition of indigenous rights (either as a human rights issue or as a belief that this will ensure better forest management) have only started to influence the policy and implementation climate in the last decade.

This process really becomes noticeable from the early 1990s, with various legal and regulatory texts aiming to direct and facilitate the participation of local communities in the forestry sector dating from this time. Such texts include the Law on Spatial Planning (UU 24/1992), which involves communities in determining land use and recognizes appropriate compensation for losses; *Rencana Pembangunan Lima Tahun* VI (the sixth Five-Year National Development Plan), which calls for encouraging participation of forest-dwelling communities in the management of forest boundaries and maintenance of forest sustainability; and Article 6 of the Law on Population Development and Family Welfare (UU 10/1992), which guarantees the "right to the beneficial use of territory that constitutes a traditional customary inheritance" (Seve 1999). The new vocabulary in these laws is an indication of the slowly increasing influence of the rights-based discourse, but because they were drafted and implemented within the bounds of the centralist system, actual changes were minor.

After Djamaludin Suryohadikusumo became the minister of forestry in 1993, this process became more marked, and several important policy initiatives relating to community forestry began to be implemented. In 1995 the Village Development (*Bina Desa*) program established by SK 691/1991 was expanded into a new program called *Pembinaan Masyarakat Desa Hutan* ([PMDH] Forest Village Community Development) by SK 691. PMDH is a program that holders of *Hak Pengusahaan Hutan* (HPH) or *Hak Pengusahaan Hutan Tanaman Industri* (HPHTI) concessions[9] are obliged to run in villages within or near their concession area to mitigate some of the negative effects of their operations. Like Bina Desa, PMDH included social forestry (*hutan kemasyarakatan*) among a range of social projects ranging from scholarships to health centers to soft loans. Social forests here have often been little more than small-scale plantations, worked by villagers who are in effect contract laborers and who receive a salary for their work. Most studies have concluded that any positive effects of these projects are likely to be short term, as they are the result of a temporary increase in cash income (see Chapter 14 for potential links to increased fire susceptibility). The projects are permeated by the attitude that local people cannot take charge of their own development but must be guided by concessionaires (Suharjito et al. 1999). A similar program on social forestry was set up under SK 622/1995. It has been dogged by many of the same problems as the social forests set up under PMDH. The positive effects of the projects have not been sustained; people have abandoned or burned the trees they planted (often to get the incentives provided by the project at the outset and the food crops that they could plant between the trees) before they became productive (Aminuddin 1998).

During these years donor funding has been used to develop a number of different models of social or community forests (NRI 1998). One well-known example is the GTZ[10] Social Forestry Development Project, near Sanggau in West Kalimantan. It is an ambitious project that has developed from an early emphasis on afforestation and farm forestry to include the management of natural forest and timber exploitation. Though feted for several years as a rare success, this project suffered a series of setbacks, including arson in 1999. Communities have also been involved in the management of buffer zone forests at Gunung Palung National Park, West Kalimantan, with the support of Harvard University. This project aimed to develop a model of community forest management, integrating sustainable production forest management, community enterprise development, and protection of a national park. It is broadly similar to the GTZ project but with a greater emphasis on developing technologies appropriate for community-level management. It also suffered from violent conflicts in 2000. In both these cases technical assistance costs have been extremely high, and many exceptions have been gained (see the *Borneo Research Bulletin* 2000 for analyses from Danau Sentarum National Park, which used some similar approaches).

The mid-1990s also saw a new move toward decentralization, a process directed not by the MoF but by the Ministry of the Interior. In 1995 a law was passed (PP 8/1995) that required each province to choose one regency that would join a pilot decentralization scheme. Under this program, some 19 services and activities were transferred to regency level, with a corresponding transfer of funding, staff, and assets. Yet the scheme was beset by problems, including hasty enactment, limited local capacity, lack of adequate financial and human capital at the local level, and lack of coordination among ministries. More fundamentally, this was not a thoroughgoing attempt at devolution (especially not of forest responsibilities) but just a discharge of tasks, with the budgets (if not the actual money) for these tasks controlled by higher levels of administration.

What changes can be seen in the aforementioned initiatives? The main difference is that during these years positive action was taken to begin implementing the earlier laws in a rights-based atmosphere. This is a crucially important change in the entire policy landscape, although its importance is somewhat mitigated by the fact that these changes took the form of projects and thus did not feed directly into new initiatives in other areas. Many old attitudes in fact continued, and, as in the case of the social forests, the government used words that hid its true demeanor. The attitudes that the government knew best—that locals should comply, that swidden agriculture was destructive and unlawful, and that the projects existed to lure local people toward conversion to permanent cultivation—were still paramount. Lawmaking remained firmly top-down, so that in SK 622/1995 (on social forests) local people were treated as objects, not subjects, of the law, with a limited role and bargaining position.

A Changing Balance of Power? Conflicting Discourses since Soeharto's Fall

It is tempting to draw too sharp a line between Soeharto's New Order and the transitional government policies. After May 1998 the canvas of opportunities for NGOs and campaigners widened enormously; however, as the previous sections have shown, indicators of change date from the early 1990s. The speed of change has increased dramatically since May 1998 with many promises of reform and a stream of new decrees and new drafts of laws. In this section I discuss initiatives relating to the involvement of the traditional communities in forest management; the new laws on decentralization; and the new Forestry Law, which creates a new overall policy sphere.

The first decree that signaled a fundamental although still limited, change in attitudes toward traditional communities dates from before Soeharto's resignation. At the start of 1998 Minister Djamaludin signed decree SK 47/1998, which created a distinctive forest use classification: *Kawasan dengan Tujuan Istimewa* ([KdTI] Zone with Special Purpose). This designation granted the right to continue to manage 29,000 ha of damar agroforests on state forestland to local communities via traditional management structures (see Chapter 6). The classification is unprecedented because rights are provided without a time limit, and it is the first time that management responsibility for state forestlands has been devolved to a traditional community structure. Although this decree was a breakthrough, many Krui residents now believe that they could get more, and they are arguing for the recognition of their rights and the reclassification of their land as nonstate forest.

Passed a year after the decree on KdTI, the decree from the Ministry of Agrarian Affairs/National Land Agency, the Guidelines to Resolve *Adat* Communal Rights Conflicts (*peraturan menteri* or ministerial regulation 5/1999) is further step in the direction of recognizing customary management rights on forestland. This decree specifically recognizes customary rights over land (*hak ulayat*) within the forest zone, so long as the traditional communities still exist and there are rules about the use and management of *hak ulayat* land that are still respected by the traditional communities. The tenor of the law has been greeted with considerable enthusiasm, but there are grave concerns over the feasibility of implementation. These concerns involve dealing with overlapping rights and the fact that the law comes from the Ministry of Agrarian Affairs rather than the MoF (Ruwiastuti 1999).

SK 677/1998, passed by the MoF after Soeharto's resignation, is very different in scope from the two decrees just discussed. It updates SK 622/1995 (on social forests) and is another attempt by the government to increase the participation of communities living inside state forest in the management of forest resources. This law widens the opportunities for local communities to benefit from areas designated as social forests, which can be part of production or serve as protection or conservation areas; it also allows communities to harvest timber as well as NTFPs. Yet to be eligible for exploitation rights (*Hak Pengusahaan Hutan Kemasyarakatan*), communities have to form a cooperative and comply with a battery of bureaucratic reporting regulations. This emphasis on cooperatives and community shareholding can be seen in several other new initiatives, and it partly reflects the fact that the transition minister of forestry and estate crops, Muslimin Nasution, was for many years a senior administrator in the Ministry of Cooperatives. For example, it is now mandatory for commercial HPHs to give shares to community-level cooperatives, with a stake of 10% rising to 20% more than five years. Other new laws aim to make it easier for communities (via cooperatives) or community-level small businesses to win small HPH concessions (see Chapter 4).

A further important sphere of reform has been decentralization (see Chapter 15). Initiatives have been ongoing for many years, but since Soeharto's fall the process has accelerated remarkably. The new and important dimension of recent changes has been the synchronized passage of both a fiscal decentralization law and a regional autonomy law (UU 22/1999 and UU 25/1999, see Chapter 15). These laws create new models for revenue sharing, decentralize many functions currently held by central government to the regency level, and fundamentally reform the system of village-level government. Given the lack of clarity in the law about decentralization in the forestry sector, it is this reform of village-level governance that may have the greatest potential to affect traditional communities.

The most recent, and most important, law is the new Law on Forestry (UU 41/1999). Even the drafting process for the law signaled important changes. The original drafting process was highly consultative, although what actually went to Parliament was an internal ministry draft. There was intense lobbying, both during the abortive drafting process and while parliament was considering the law. The process gave campaigners the scope to develop, elaborate, and argue for radical changes, and even though their aspirations did not find a place in the legislation, a vision for the future now exists. Although the law disappointed many observers, it already signals a significant shift in the ministry's position. It shows increased state support for the devolution of forest management and forest benefits to local communities. It is regressive, however, in that it maintains state control over what is now called customary forest (unlike in earlier drafts where the customary forest was a distinct class from state and private forest). The state is also given the power to recognize or revoke the status of traditional community and, therefore, customary forest. In addition, and in a continuation of what has always been an important legal loophole, the rights of traditional communities are given only insofar as they do not conflict with national priorities. In fact, the status of land as customary forest so far confers little advantage—only the right to use the forest to meet daily needs and to undertake forest management according to customary rules, as long as these do not conflict with national priorities or other state laws (see Chapter 4).

These new initiatives and laws are evidence of a real and sustained change over the previous 18 months. Campbell (Chapter 5) identifies two competing strains within the reform process: (a) a rights-based call for the recognition of the rights of the indigenous communities, as suggested by customary leaders, some academics, and some NGOs, and (b) an approach focusing on the redistribution of access to forest resources and income away from the elite and toward small- and medium-sized enterprises organized by cooperatives. This is a line followed by many reformers within the transition government, led by former Minister Muslimin himself. An awareness of these two different reformist discourses helps to clarify some of what might otherwise be considered halfhearted reform on the part of the government.

First, it shows that the characterization of reform as a mere public relations exercise aiming to garner fresh and much-needed political support is too harsh. Some NGOs argued that the consultation preceding SK 677/1998 (on social forests) and the new forestry law (UU 41/1999) was phony and that so far reform was merely a new name for old practices. Instead, reform is indeed under way, but along an agenda different from that espoused by many organized groups of traditional communities and the NGOs that support them, with a focus on the people's economy rather than the rights of the traditional communities. Second, although there has been a rush of new legislation, there is still no evidence that the government is close to accepting the calls of traditional communities and many NGOs to recognize customary rights. It may now be accepted that local communities have a part to play in forest management, but this is more of a pragmatic, interest-based acceptance than a conversion to a rights-based approach. The new laws still show considerable mistrust of communities and customary institutions (as shown by the emphasis on cooperatives as the main management institution, for example).

Therefore, despite considerable pessimism and gloom among many of those I spoke to in August and September 1999, I would argue that the changes under the transition government have been fundamental. In particular the situation on the ground and the mental framework within which forest-dwellers and local government officials are working has changed out of all recognition.[11] What the central government (the ministry) says bears little resemblance to what is happening on the ground. This change in local rhetoric and in the attitude of the street-level bureaucracy (Lipsky 1980) is the key difference, because it is local officials who are ultimately responsible for implementation of any laws. Legislation is indeed important, because it is part of the enabling or disabling environment. But it is important to remember that the drafting of a law is only one small part of the general policy process. The law is not a policy on its own; it becomes policy through implementation. Therefore it is important not to spend too much time arguing about whether the law is drafted perfectly but to work on changing the mental frameworks of those who will be responsible for implementation (see Chapter 2). I argue that this change has already begun and is so far the most significant change that the reform process has seen, of far greater importance than shifting legal wording.

In addition, the NGO movement has developed rapidly over the last two years. Organizations like *Koalisi Untuk Demokratisasi Pengelolaan Sumberdaya Alam* (Coalition for the Democratization of Natural Resources), Forum *Komunikasi Kehutanan Masyarakat* (Communication Forum on Community Forestry), and *Aliansi Masyarakat Adat Nusantara* (Alliance of Indigenous Peoples of the Archipelago) have been established and have expanded rapidly. Along with other more established NGOs (e.g., Indonesian Center for Environmental Law and *Wahana Lingkungan Hidup Indonesia*) they have put forward policies, made press statements, demonstrated, and organized televised debates. The fact that there has been so much ongoing central-level discussion of the new forestry law owes as much to their tenacity as it does to a changing attitude toward consultation within the ministry; it may well have led to the recognition of the supportive role of NGOs and the creation of the Forest Watch Forum in the new Law on Forestry.

Furthermore, there is now evidence that an acceptance of the importance of community involvement in forest management is becoming increasingly mainstream. Policies toward communities have gradually been moving away from the public relations add-ons of earlier years, when forest policy was firmly directed toward national development and increasing the economic productivity of the forests to a situation in which customary management systems are seen more as a resource than as an obstacle. The increased involvement of local communities is only one strand of the current reform process, but it is the one that has drawn its impetus particularly from the internal Indonesian reform process (NRI 1998).

Conclusion

This chapter has aimed to do two things: first to give a brief and schematic account of some of the main laws and policies that have dealt with forest dwelling communities in Indonesia since 1960, and second to consider how the discourses relating to forest control, management, and ownership that I identified at the beginning have played out within these policies and their implementation.

The process of change that I have attempted to describe is complicated and not amenable to easy analysis, because of the number of cross-cutting themes and contradictory trends. The power and influence of the different discourses have waxed and waned, as evidenced by the changing laws and policies described. The political situation has changed too, and experience in forest management has been built up. The change to a more community-friendly set of policies has not happened overnight, and indeed has not happened completely: at no point has any discourse within Indonesian forest management approached hegemony, and policies have always been developed amidst conflicting voices.

So what does this continuing clash between these two discourses mean for the traditional communities and customary institutions of Indonesia? All parties in the debate caricature themselves and their opponents and make claims that they cannot or have not delivered. *Adat* rights are reified and overdefined both by those arguing for state control and those who want control to rest with customary institutions themselves. The result is that expectations of customary institutions are high. It remains unclear whether customary control will lead to sustainable forest management, as it is personally costly to farmers to leave forests in the state in which they can continue to perform a public function (e.g., Suyanto et al. 1998a). There is also the risk of losing sight of *adat*—that complex of tradition, law, custom, and belief that characterizes so many forest communities—as an evolving and dynamic process of community decisionmaking. Some of the other important things that NGOs argue for, like equity or democracy, may be lost in an oversimplifying emphasis on *adat* alone. Furthermore, oversimplifying and overaggregating may perhaps unintentionally create communalist discourses, based on the unproblematized idea of a unified community. This loses sight of the fact that there are different groups within a community who will use different resources within the forest at different times and in different ways and will attribute different social meanings to the forest (Leach 1999). As the government and NGOs work through the complex and difficult issues associated with the more equitable sharing of benefits from the forest and the recognition of alternative rights systems, it is important that the urge to simplify does not involve reducing the arguments to caricatures.

Endnotes

1. The date on which the research for this article was finished was the date on which the text of the new Law on Forestry, UU 41/1999, became public (September 16, 1999). Therefore, my analysis does not fully take into account of its potential effect (see Chapter 4 also).

2. New Order is a term used to describe the Soeharto government of Indonesia from 1967 to 1998.

3. Much Indonesian forest policy is not in the form of laws (UU—*undang-undang*—passed by parliament) but rather government regulations (PP—*peraturan pemerintah*) and ministerial decrees (SK—*surat keputusan*). When I refer to these collectively, however, I call them "laws," even though SKs and PPs are in fact the product of the executive. See Appendix for more information.

4. Dutch attempts to understand and codify *adat* laws and land claims have created the somewhat anomalous situation whereby many *adat* communities now refer back to these Dutch legal texts to validate their claims to land.

5. Throughout this chapter I refer to *masyarakat hukum adat* as traditional communities. Increasingly self-defined communities use the phrase *masyarakat hukum adat* to describe themselves, and they are central to much of the discussion that follows.

6. Although it is important to remember this, it is equally important to recall that the reality on the ground has never been squared with the rules and that throughout the history of the Indonesian Republic communities have continued to live on state-claimed land and to depend on forests for their livelihoods.

7. This agency was called the Ministry of Forestry and Estate Crops during much of 2000, and now (June 2001) is again called MoF.

8. This lack of "joined-up government" is a worldwide problem, one that is much easier to identify than to solve, as the Blairite British government has discovered.

9. HPH refers to commercial logging concessions, and HPHTI refers to commercial timber plantations.

10. GTZ refers to the German aid agency Deutsche Gesellschaft fuer Technische Zusammenarbeit.

11. This is a point contradicted by some field-level observations, which suggest that these changes have so far affected only Jakarta, while the same corrupt officials remain in positions of authority at the middle and lower levels. Indeed, in many areas the forest management situation has worsened considerably as illegal logging has spiraled out of control (Colfer 2000; Chapters 7, 9, 16 of this book).

References

Aminuddin.1998. Dampak sosial ekonomi dan sosial budaya dari pengembangan hutan kemasyarakatan di Propinsi Nusa Tenggara Barat. In *Kehutanan Masyarakat: Beragam Pola Partisipasi Masyarakat Dalam Pengelolaan Hutan*, edited by D. Suharjito and D. Darusman. Jakarta, Indonesia: Institut Pertanian Bogor & Ford Foundation, 71–85.

Borneo Research Bulletin. 2000. *Special Issue on Danau Sentarum National Park*. Volume 31.

Colfer, C.J.P. 2000. Personal communication with the author, July 10.

Leach, M. 1999. *Plural Perspectives and Institutional Dynamics: Challenges for Community Forestry*. Paper presented at International Agrarish Centrum executive seminar, Decision-Making in Natural Resources Management with a Focus on Adaptive Management. September 1999. Wageningen, The Netherlands.

Lindayati, R. 1999. *The New Order Public Policy Process: With Specific Reference to Social Forestry Policies*. Paper presented at International Conference on Good Governance: A Workable Solution for Indonesia? May 1999. McGill University, Montreal, Canada.

Lipsky, M. 1980. *Street-Level Bureaucracy: Dilemmas of the Individual in Public Services*. New York: Russell Sage Foundation.

NRI (Natural Resources Institute). 1998. *Overview of the Indonesian Forest Sector: A Report Prepared for the Department for International Development by NRI*. Chatham: NRI.

Ruwiastuti, M.R. 1999. *Pengakuan Hak Ulayat: Antara Harapan Dan Kenyataan. Catatan Kritis Terhadap Peraturan Menteri Negara Agraria/Kepala BPN 5/1999 Tentang Pedoman Penyelesaian Masalah Hak Ulayat Masyarakat Hukum Adat*. Paper presented at roundtable discussion between *Lembaga Studi dan Avokasi Masyarakat* (The Institute for Policy Research and Advocacy), Pusat Kajian Pembangunan Masyarukat (Center for Societal Development Studies) *Unika Atma Jaya*, and *Konsorsium Pembaruan Agraria*. July 1999. *Wisma Persatuan Kebum Binatang Indonesia*, Jakarta, Indonesia.

Scott, J.C. 1998. *Seeing Like a State: How Certain Schemes to Improve the Human Condition Have Failed*. New Haven, CT, and London: Yale University Press.

Seve, J. 1999. *A Review of Forestry Sector Policy Issues in Indonesia. Technical Report. Environmental Policy and Institutional Strengthening*. Jakarta, Indonesia: Natural Resources Management Programme.

Sirait, M., C. Fay, and A. Kusworo. 1999. *Bagaimana hak-hak masyarakat hukum adat dalam mengelola sumber daya alam diatur?* Part of a manuscript submitted to the Forestry Department in an attempt to accommodate rights of *adat* peoples within forest areas, and presented as a paper given at the meeting of the Consultative Group on Indonesian Forestry. September 1999, Jambi, Indonesia.

Suharjito, D., et al.1999. *Karakteristik pengelolaan hutan berbasiskan masyarak*at. Jogjakarta, Indonesia: Studi Kolaboratif Forum Komunikasi Kehutanan Masyarakat.

Suyanto, S., T. Tomich, and K. Otsuka 1998a. *Land Tenure and Farm Management Efficiency: The Case of Paddy and Cinnamon Production Areas of Sumatra*. Mimeo. Bogor, Indonesia: International Centre for Research on Agroforestry.

———. 1998b. *Land Tenure and Farm Management Efficiency: The Case of Smallholder Rubber Production in Customary Land Areas of Sumatra*. Mimeo. Bogor, Indonesia: International Centre for Research on Agroforestry.

Thiesenhusen, W., T. Hansted, R. Mitchell, and E. Rajagukguk. 1997. *Land Tenure Issues in Indonesia*. Report prepared for the U.S. Agency for International Development. Jakarta, Indonesia: GRIDEC Cultural Development Consultants.

Zerner, C. 1992. *Indigenous Forest Communities in Indonesia's Outer Islands: Livelihood, Rights and Environmental Management Institutions in the Era of Industrial Forest Exploitation*. Report commissioned by the World Bank in preparation for the Forestry Sector Review. Washington, DC: The World Bank.

CHAPTER TWO

Ideas and Institutions in Social Forestry Policy

Rita Lindayati

For the past decade, Indonesia's forestry community has witnessed growing opposition to the incumbent state-centered forest management system. The belief in the state as the sole legitimate resource developer and custodian has been condemned as the root cause of many contemporary forest-related problems (e.g., deforestation, forest-related social conflicts), particularly in the Outer Islands.[1] In response to the ailing centralized system, many have proposed the community forestry alternative.[2] This alternative is usually regarded as a better way to deal with the Outer Islands' social and ecological complexities as well as the perceived unjust distribution of forest-generated economic benefits. Nongovernmental organizations (NGOs), academics, international agencies, and other policy advocates have actively tried to influence such reform, albeit with varying degrees of success.[3] Incremental policy changes that have taken place for the last several years were primarily aimed at providing the legal means for greater local participation in forest management. Only recently have substantial reforms occurred, even with the basic tenet of a state-centralized management control remaining unaltered.

In this chapter, I will examine policymaking and policy change through an overview of the process of how community-based forest management ideas are translated into public decisions.[4] Social forestry policymaking and policy change processes are explored by looking at the interactions of state and societal actors within sectoral policy subsystems, within which ideas and institutions are central in shaping policy subsystem actors' decisions. Policymakers decide what policy choices are or are not made, yet their decisions are biased by prevailing policy ideology or ideologies within a given sociopolitical institution and historical context. I will elaborate this argument in more detail by discussing the following points:

- the conceptual framework to understanding sectoral policy processes, focusing on the role of ideas and institutions that condition policy actors' performances;
- the macro level institutions that shape institutionalized sectoral politics; and
- a historical overview of the social forestry policy subsystem, focusing on how the interaction of ideas and institutions enables and constrains the ability of policy actors to respond to changing socioeconomic conditions.

Sectoral Policy Process: The Role of Ideas and Institutions

Most Indonesia-based forestry policy studies emphasize elite and business-linked economic interests as the major forces underlying forestry policy creation (see Chapters 6, 8, 9, and 16). Although material stakes indisputably play an important role, they are only half of the story. Some policymakers do care about the country's forestry problems and are genuinely searching for solutions within an uncertain and continuously changing environment. Oftentimes the government is pressured to act under time, information, and resource constraints. Uncertainty with regard to the magnitude of the problem, the various interdependent social and ecological variables affecting the problem, and the competing interests surrounding it is a challenge routinely faced by policymakers. As Heclo (1974, 305) posited:

> Politics finds its sources not only in power but also in uncertainty—men [sic] collectively wondering what to do.... Policymaking is a form of collective puzzlement on society's behalf.... Much political interaction has constituted a process of social learning expressed through policy.

The dimensions of "social learning," pinpointed by Heclo, highlight the pivotal role that ideas play in influencing (and being influenced by) policy process politics and policy actors' collective decisions. Ideas, Stone (1988, 7) said, "are a medium of exchange and a mode of influence.... Shared meanings motivate people to action and meld individual striving into collective action." Every policy deliberation revolves around a set of ideas usually bounded by the way people see the world.[5] Policy actors' ideational conceptions of a particular public problem, therefore, are never impartial, for they carry assumptions of a given phenomenon's cause–effect relationship, which consequently shapes the choice of policy goals and instruments.

In light of this argument, Outer Islands' social forestry policy formation and change will be examined by mapping out different policy ideas that have encapsulated different modes of people–forest relations. To trace how a particular set of reform ideas can affect a policy outcome, it is useful to look at Howlett and Ramesh's (1998) concept of policy subsystem, which encompasses two interrelated dimensions: knowledge and interests. The former refers to the notion of a policy community, which suggests an arena where those with knowledge of certain policy issues engage in policy discourse; the latter refers to the concept of a policy network, which refers to the relationships among certain actors in the policy community who actively participate in policymaking to pursue their policy interests (Wilks and Wright 1987; Sabatier and Jenkins-Smith 1993; Howlett and Ramesh 1998). While a policy community may include various segments of society who demonstrate a common policy concern (government, the public, NGOs, academics, international agencies, media, associations), a policy network maintains fewer participants specifically involved in policy formulation (usually government and a few nongovernment representatives).

Policy subsystems perform within broader sociopolitical institutions that serve to constrain policy actors' preferences and actions. The institutional structures refer to the state and society's organizational and ideological properties, rules, and norms that guide the group of actors' relations (Ikenberry 1988). Once adopted, these institutions are usually very difficult to change and relatively unresponsive to individual preferences and idiosyncrasies (Ikenberry 1988); they may also recognize a particular set of policy ideas and interests as more legitimate than others. In the New Order era, for instance, the institutionalized belief of the supremacy of state control and centralized development pervaded all development sectors: school curricula were centrally designed, local administrative and governmental systems were made uniform and centrally supervised, people could only embrace religions permitted by the state, and so forth. This situation hindered any form of creative thinking that sought to promote development strategies based on diversity and unique local environments. The following section examines the institutional context of the New Order social forestry policy development process; it is followed by a discussion of the actual process itself.

The Influences of Macro Sociopolitical Institutions

The various dimensions of the social forestry policy subsystem (e.g., who has access to the policy process, who are the primary decisionmaking actors, what type of relationships do they develop, what kinds of policy ideas do they promote) cannot be understood in isolation from the broader political institutions in which the sectoral policy process takes place. Institutionalized policymaking mechanisms, which designate who has the legal decisionmaking authority, are shaped by the country's formal and informal rules. The 1945 National Constitution mandates the People's Consultative Assembly to amend the Constitution and formulate general state policy guidelines; the executive and House of Representatives to pass laws and regulations; and the Supreme Court to conduct judicial review, both on policy procedure and content. Yet analyzing the legal text is far from sufficient. Society's rules of conduct are also governed by a complex set of informal codes—stemming from social customs, cultural traditions, and historical experiences—which often provide the interpretive framework for how the legal precepts are exercised. A complex blend of these formal and informal codes shapes the political reality of state–society relations and power distribution, as well as reflecting "whose decisions count."

After a "traumatic" experience of parliamentary polity (1948–1959), Indonesia returned to the 1945 Constitution that is based on a very powerful presidential body. Following the bloody 1965 attempted Communist coup d'état, the ousted President Soekarno handed over power to his successor, Soeharto. In its early days of rule, the Soeharto government was confronted with a fractious nation with conflicting political lines, regional uprisings, and near economic bankruptcy. To keep the nation together, the New Order emphasized political stability and the boosting of badly needed economic development. This, it was argued, required a strong government, which was accomplished by consolidating power in the executive position (centered in the president's hands), gaining military support through various political–economic rewards and concessions, developing a strong and loyal bureaucracy to implement executive decisions, and systematically paralyzing potential state and societal adversaries. This strategy effectively calmed political strife and promoted several decades of economic growth. Yet it also resulted in a politically weak society and a highly centralistic and militaristic regime whose years of noncorrective power abuse eventually brought about its own recent demise.

So even though the constitution allocates policymaking authority to state agencies, other subordinate laws and informal political measures have systematically weakened the legislative and judicial bodies. The house's administrative and political rules were created in such a way that the executive (with bureaucratic and military backing) could dismiss house members who dared to criticize government policies, not to mention proposing legislation that the government disliked.[6] The Supreme Court, whose personnel and career development were controlled by the bureaucracy, also did not have the political power or the expertise to exercise its authority. The whole enterprise of legislative procedure and process lay entirely in the government's (especially the bureaucracy's) hands. Furthermore, through the "floating mass" doctrine,[7] a citizen's political participation was systematically crippled. People were disconnected from their political parties, which were more accountable to the government than to the people they were supposed to represent. The system created a hierarchical power configuration in which the president as the highest executive and military leader—was at the core, followed by the president's closest state and nonstate benefactors (e.g., families, friends), the bureaucracy and military, other political parties, and, lastly, ordinary citizens (Sanit 1998). While the line of command was from the core to the far end, the line of accountability was the reverse.

Political relationships were highly personalized, and legal mechanisms for making political demands (e.g., through political parties, the House of Representatives, pressure groups) were virtually nonexistent. Instead, the patron–client relationship based on personal reciprocities—cutting across lines of family connection, economic dependency, ethnic and religious bonds, alumni affiliations, and so forth—proliferated and became the primary institution through which to channel such demands. "Whose voice counts" was less dependent on the person's official rank than his or her proximity to the power center.

The "central power" is at the core of the state polity and symbolizes society's unity, so that power dispersion is conceived of as a threat to the state's existence (Anderson 1990). This prevailing ideology dictates the nature of state intervention, rendering legitimacy (or lack thereof) to proposed policy alternatives. Similarly, the legitimacy of social forestry policy alternatives depends on the degree to which they conform to the New Order's prevailing norms of the state's role. For most government policymakers, local forest management policies were conceivable as long as they came under state control and did not devolve significant power.

The primary point of the previous discussion is that the institutional and normative framework of a given political system sets the limits within which state and societal actors can pursue their policy initiatives. Following the 1998 New Order's collapse, demands to transform prevailing sociopolitical institutions, including the patron–client mode of political-economic relationships, mounted considerably. Many statutory laws (*Undang-Undang* [UU] and government regulations (*Peraturan Pemerintah* [PP]) were altered, mostly during the Habibie government, although the extent to which these reforms coherently advocate genuine democracy is still questionable. In the forestry sector, a new law has been ratified as well. UU 41/1999 (see Chapter 4) explicitly acknowledges community-based forest management systems, although the predominant ideology of state-centralized forestry control remains intact. The law, which indicates a major legal transformation of community-based forest management, is a milestone of lengthy reform deliberations.

Social Forestry Policymaking and Change: The Historical Dynamics of Policy Subsystems

With politically powerless citizens and a dysfunctional legislative and judicial system, New Order policymaking was often labeled as based on bureaucratic politics—where power and participation in national policy decisions were almost entirely controlled by state actors, particularly the bureaucracy (Jackson 1978). I take a slightly different approach by viewing the policy network, whose members are state actors, nonstate actors, or both, as the primary "driver" of policy formulation. The advantage of the policy network concept is that it captures the decisionmaking role of bureaucrats, either by themselves or in relation to other state and nonstate groups. Different from the bureaucratic policy approach that refers to strategies for action, a policy network is a form of an institutionalized social relation that is voluntarily formed on the basis of the network members' similar policy beliefs (as the primary glue for collective action).

The legal basis of New Order resource management policies is Article 33 of the 1945 Constitution, which is often interpreted as giving the state the absolute right to control all of Indonesia's national resources. At the forestry level, the primary legal framework was the Basic Forestry Law (BFL) UU 5/1967, which further elaborated state resource management sovereignty and which governed three decades of sectoral forestry policies. The law mandated the government to plan and regulate all forest tenure and use arrangements within its jurisdiction. It also gave the government the legal authority to seize "unowned" land, including traditional community forests, and to allocate exploitation rights to private companies or to use the land for other purposes. This situation led to overlapping customary and state-based forest access and use rights that brought about three decades of serious conflicts and resentment among various Outer Island forest users, particularly between local people and state-backed logging companies.

Despite the New Order government's claim otherwise, the 1967 BFL management philosophy did not differ significantly from its 1865 BFL colonial predecessor:

> state forestry serves the greatest good of the greatest number of people, scientific forestry is an efficient and rational form of resource use, and promoting economic growth through forest production for the state is the key component of the forester's role (Peluso 1992, 125).

Foresters are trained within this paradigm, and their belief in the supremacy of scientific management implicitly devalues other modes of resource institutional arrangements. As state agents, forestry bureaucrats are also implanted with the creed of centralized, power-based state unity. These dogmas are deeply ingrained in most policymakers' mindsets—rendering nonstate forest management policy ideas involving power devolution nearly inconceivable.

Before the New Order, most Outer Island forests were managed by customary (or *adat*) communities. Different regulations existed for different types of forest activities (e.g., hunting, timber felling, nontimber forest product gathering), but they were generally weak and inconsistent (Departemen Kehutanan RI 1986). State-centralized forest management that restricted local customary forest access was effective primarily in Java (Peluso 1992). The colonial Forest Service attempted to centrally control and exploit the Outer Islands' forests through uniform forestry laws, but it failed because of fierce internal opposition (Lindayati forthcoming). The 1967 BFL represented the culmination of extensive government deliberation on the application of uniform forest management policies for both Java and the Outer Islands. With this law, state-centralized forest control, which the Dutch had instituted in Java during the mid-19th and early 20th centuries, was applied to the Outer Islands. Not surprisingly, many government assumptions of Outer Island forest management problems were derived from Java's experiences, including social forestry. Java's social forestry policy was implemented to minimize ongoing conflicts between the State Forest Corporation (Perhutani) and local people (Barber 1989), and similar intentions held true for the Outer Islands.

Contemporary Outer Islands' social forestry policy development can be considered in three distinct periods, each distinguished according to the variety of policy instruments and approaches that the government used to deal with forest dwellers and local forestry systems. The first, or presocial, forestry phase (late 1960s to mid-1980s) occurred when the government reinforced its monopoly over forest control, strengthened negative attitudes toward local forest practices, and established a legal institutional framework that systematically excluded such systems from formal forestry discourse. The second phase (mid-1980s to 1997) occurred when social forestry schemes were adopted and gradually institutionalized into the state forest management system, although local indigenous forest use and tenurial rights were still illegal. The third phase (1998 to the present) is a point at which radical policy changes are occurring; local forest management is being incorporated into the overall legal forestry framework even though it remains subject to the government forestry system.

Late 1960s to Mid-1980s

This period was characterized by the adoption of policy instruments that reflected the government's complete rejection of local community forest access, including formal contempt toward forest dwellers' lifestyles and resource management practices. Forest communities were considered "backward" and thus in need of integration into mainstream society, and their shifting cultivation method was deemed economically unproductive and ecologically destructive.[8]

The practice was blamed for causing the degradation of approximately 500,000 ha of land annually, with the cumulative total of degraded land blamed on such practices reaching some 40 million ha in the mid-1980s (Departemen Kehutanan RI 1986, 29). Strict control of this agricultural system was one of the primary objectives of the first Five-Year National Development Plan (1969–1974) and remained so in the ensuing years.

The negative ideological inclination toward forest-dwelling communities resulted in a set of policies that attempted to keep them away from the forest (i.e., resettlement) or aimed at transforming their customary forest practices into lifestyles more in keeping with policymakers' preference (e.g., sedentary farming, urban-based livelihoods). Because it was believed that shifting cultivation was driven by desperate economic need, resettlement and permanent agriculture programs were seen as potential means of raising farmers' living standards (i.e., the farmers would, theoretically, be relocated in areas more accessible to government services and employment opportunities). Some 15,000 households were targeted for resettlement during 1973–1983, with a realization rate of approximately 75% (Departemen Kehutanan RI 1986, 148). In the new locations, every newly settled family was normally given a small house, 3 ha of land, a year's supply of basic foodstuffs (e.g., rice, sugar, dried-fish, vegetable oil), and government technical assistance for sedentary farming. After one or two years, they were left on their own.

In addition, restrictions on peasants' forest access were further reinforced by a gradual ban on small-scale timber felling and nontimber forest product gathering.[9] During the early years of the timber boom (late 1960s to early 1970s), forest exploitation was performed mechanically by a handful of logging companies as well as manually by individuals responding to lucrative international (especially Japanese) timber markets. At first, some 20–30% of total production forest was intended for small-scale logging, including those based on customary rights (Departemen Kehutanan RI 1986, 12). With PP 21/1970, the criteria and administrative mechanisms for both big and small concessionaires were defined; big concessionaire licenses (*Hak Pengusahaan Hutan* [HPH] or Forest Concession, Forest Exploitation Rights) were issued by the central government, while the smaller ones (*Hak Pemungutan Hasil Hutan* [HPHH] or Forest Product Harvesting Rights) were issued by the provincial government. The HPHH system allowed individuals and local businesses to collect forest products manually for either personal use or for local markets (not for export), although the same regulation also froze local customary resource access in HPH areas.[10]

Subsequent to the Japanese hand-cut log boycott, which caused the Government of Indonesia large economic losses, a harsher stance was taken toward small-scale and local-based timber cutting operations. The East Kalimantan government—concerned by the adverse social effects of thousands of suddenly jobless woodcutters (locals and migrants) partly caused by the rapid ecological deterioration that resulted from uncontrolled logging—was probably the first to withdraw from the provincial-based HPHH system. Several years later (mid-1980s), the HPHH was completely cancelled throughout Indonesia because it was neither economically and ecologically feasible nor easily controlled. The central government monopolized the issuance of concession rights from then on.

Resettlement and permanent agriculture programs, combined with coercive forest access policing, were the New Order's primary policy instruments for transforming and governing forest dweller–forest relationships in the Outer Islands. PP 21/1970 (Forest Exploitation Rights and Forest Product Harvesting Rights) and later PP 28/1985 (Environmental Protection) specifically banned local people's customary forest access in state-designated forest concession and protection zones. Criminalization of villagers' forest resource use was the primary cause of friction between the state and forest dwellers. Incidents between locals and government-backed business interests over forest use and ownership were reported throughout the country. When these conflicts turned violent, the government usually used its military power to resolve them.

The New Order's economist-dominated development planners emphasized growth-oriented modernization as the ultimate national development goal, with forestry policies formulated accordingly. Local-based and small-scale forestry practices were deemed irrelevant to the nation's modernization and industrialization process. Formal decisionmaking was kept in government hands, with the policy community and policy networks remaining small, exclusive, and monopolized by the bureaucracy and a handful of elites who uniformly believed in the supremacy of state-centralized and growth-oriented forest management. International donors, long important in government national and forest management planning, subscribed to this same modernization and industrial forestry paradigm.[11] Local (provincial) governments were also fully supportive of the resettlement policy and constantly requested that the central government pass regulations to ban shifting cultivation.[12] Academic communities, from which governments often requested technical policy advice, also held similar views.[13] The involvement of NGOs and nonforesters in forestry policymaking was quite rare, as the Ministry of Forestry (MoF) was confident in its in-house expertise. It was not until the 1990s, especially during the social forestry experimentation phase, that the government began to involve nonbureaucrats and nonforesters, as the department began to realize it was lacking both knowledge and experience in community development. The policy subsystem's homogenous membership, its hegemonic policy discourse, and the strong bureaucratic mandate of coercive forest control contributed to a high degree of state autonomy in forestry policymaking. This strong autonomy was further magnified (through the enactment of 1985 political laws) by a depoliticization of citizens and political parties, rendering popular participation in policy formation an alien concept.

National development and the forest management framework in this period provided ideological and institutional infrastructures through which the social forestry concept was later introduced. Meanwhile, various internal sectoral factors, as well as outside events, led to the second phase that was characterized by the MoF's increasing attention to social forestry programs and a slight attitudinal change toward community forestry. The 1978 Jakarta World Forestry Congress was obviously responsible for introducing the MoF to the social forestry concept and "forests for people" rhetoric. The conference marked the beginning of forest management that embraced distributional benefits to local people, arguing that the focus on industrial growth should be accompanied by strategies aimed at equity, popular participation, and the attainment of basic needs. Like other newly independent countries that relied on Western aid and technology, the New Order was quick to adopt international development ideas—promoting local participation, meeting people's basic needs, and addressing environmental concerns soon became rhetorical niches through which the New Order situated its goal to govern peasant–forest relationships. Yet the way these ideas were incorporated into national development and forestry policy was mediated through policymakers' well-established forestry ideology, the national sociopolitical institutions, and socioecological conditions and development priorities. The 1978 World Forestry Congress resolution was seen as consistent with current government ventures to improve the living conditions of forest villagers through resettlement and shifting cultivation control (Departemen Pertanian, Direktorat Jenderal Kehutanan 1979, 7).

Furthermore, changing state policy ideas were also influenced by sectoral factors, such as bureaucratic training and experience, information exchanges (e.g., workshops, seminars, research), and a flood of international aid for social forestry projects. The changing development orientation of many international donors during the 1970s—shifting from macro economic growth to meeting people's basic needs—allowed the government to access resources to put the social forestry idea into operational projects. In the early 1980s, the MoF and the Ford Foundation began to discuss social forestry programs, although it was not until 1985 that actual programs were launched, both in Java and the Outer Islands. The field experiences gained from these projects later became the foundation from which the MoF formulated its nationwide social forestry policy.

External events such as increasing and more widespread conflict between local people and logging companies, accelerating rates of deforestation, and an increasing number of environment- and human rights–oriented NGOs were also significant influences on policymakers. The presence of NGOs in the policy subsystem was unique: they stand at the interface between local communities and the government, and their close collaboration with the international community helped to spread the worldwide movement of indigenous rights and self-determination. Even though their policymaking roles were still insignificant—the government felt NGOs were just a nuisance—their strong international links meant that the government could not totally turn a deaf ear to these critics. *Wahana Lingkungan Hidup Indonesia* ([WALHI] or Indonesian Forum on the Environment) and *Sekretariat Kerjasama Pelestarian Hutan Indonesia* (NGO Network for Forest Conservation in Indonesia) were some of the pioneers that supported the local forestry system, and their advocacy work (as well as that of other NGOs) was probably one of the major forces that later brought the community-based forest management issue onto the formal policy agenda.

Mid-1980s to 1997

This period is notable for the adoption of social forestry programs. The core policy ideology, that the state is forest developer and steward and that local forest management systems are backward and destructive, remained intact. Yet some aspects (albeit secondary ones) started to change. Compared to the previous era, the policy goal remained the same (halt forest dwellers' destructive resource management practices), but the instruments used to achieve this goal were more diverse. In addition to repressive measures, a "prosperity" approach was given more emphasis and the social forestry concept was viewed as a potential policy option.

From the mid-1980s to early 1990, national attention increased toward local people's forest access and tenurial rights. This was marked by the growing realization (especially by nongovernmental actors) of the Outer Islands' diverse and complex local forestry systems. Various studies and field projects (including the MoF/Ford Foundation social forestry pilot projects in East Kalimantan, Irian Jaya, and Sulawesi) contributed to this understanding. Subsequent internationally funded social forestry projects followed this lead in an attempt to promote recognition of Outer Islands' local forestry diversity in formal policy. In the meantime, this period also witnessed increasing government concern over local forest encroachment.

Internal and external forces, as indicated earlier, played an important role in shaping these trends. Yet it was President Soeharto's official speech at the 1987 National Regreening Week indicating his serious concern about the widespread land degradation caused by shifting cultivation that was probably the primary reason for the MoF's decision to pay more serious attention to local forestry practices.[14] The president called for local governments, sectoral departments, and private companies to play an active role in controlling shifting cultivation. The MoF quickly responded by instructing governors in the Outer Islands to coordinate, vertically and horizontally, all relevant sectoral programs in their jurisdictions.[15] In addition to resettlement, programs such as Transmigration, People's Nucleus Estate Programs, Industrial Timber Plantations,

Development of Isolated Communities, Village Consolidation, and others, which were administered by different ministries, were expected to prioritize forest dwellers as the target groups.[16]

The changing national development orientation in favor of environment and peasant socioeconomic problems was reflected in *Rencana Pembangunan Lima Tahun VI* (the sixth Five-Year National Development Plan) (1994–1999). Environmental conservation, poverty alleviation, decentralization, and local participation were stated to be the primary policy guidelines, providing a favorable political climate for social forestry. The MoF slowly began to "loosen" its de jure forest control as it realized that the three decades–long complete ban on local forest access was ineffective—the government had neither the capacity nor the resources for enforcement. Conflicts between local people and state-sanctioned logging companies over forest access control frequently captured national headlines. Some prominent examples include Yamdena Island (Maluku Province), Sugapa (North Sumatra), Bentian (East Kalimantan), and Benakat (South Sumatra) (Barber 1998). Furthermore, as the international community became increasingly concerned with the adverse social and ecological consequences of current development practices, many donor agencies began to incorporate strong environmental and local participation criteria into their development project portfolios. The then forestry minister, Djamaludin Suryohadikusumo, also paid more attention to local forest access concerns.

Internal divisions existed within the ministry itself, as some foresters began promoting policy reforms whereas others wanted the status quo. In the late 1980s, attempts began to revise the 1967 BFL, with one of the major proposed changes being to clarify *adat* or customary forest rights. The reform proposal, however, was opposed by some senior officials who saw the 1967 BFL as an Indonesian foresters' masterpiece and worried that any reform would result in reduced MoF forest control and authority (Manurung 1997). After several years, the reform working group evolved to consist entirely of the reform proponents. Deliberations, however, were abruptly halted in 1997 when some MoF senior officials began to fear that the Agrarian Ministry (which believed forestlands should be under its jurisdiction) would challenge the MoF's jurisdictional authority during upcoming interdepartmental meetings (Manurung 1997). Nevertheless, MoF reform-minded individuals remain an important enabling factor in pushing MoF policy reforms.

Despite internal opposition to the 1967 BFL reform attempt, other subordinate regulations (e.g., ministerial decrees) were issued to gradually accommodate local forestry practices. In 1993, the MoF passed a regulation that obliged concessionaires to allow customary communities to collect forest products (for subsistence purposes) in concession areas.[17] Furthermore, it was assumed that by allowing villagers to participate in state forest management (i.e., through social forestry schemes), multiple social and environmental objectives would be met: locals would have access to productive capital (land, credits), allowing them to improve their socioeconomic well-being, and would therefore be willing to practice "ecologically sound" permanent agriculture (as promoted in social forestry programs). As a result, the government's limited resources would be saved because the community development goal could be achieved in addition to solving illegal squatter and deforestation problems.

The early 1990s to 1997 marked the beginning of the incorporation of local participation into formal forest management systems. Through the Ministerial Decree on Community Forestry (*Hutan kemasyarakatan*), first enacted in 1995, locals were granted limited user rights;[18] and through the Forest Village Community Development decree (*Pembinaan Masyarakat Desa Hutan*), first enacted in 1991, concessionaires were obliged to "help" in the economic development of forest villages. The Community Forestry decree's primary purpose was to rehabilitate degraded land while providing local economic opportunities. Therefore, it allowed local people to manage critical lands both in state-protected and production forests. Meanwhile, the Forest Village Community Development decree goal of improving villages' socioeconomic situation was often interpreted by the concessionaires as helping villagers with physical infrastructural development (e.g., building mosques, permanent agriculture demonstration plots, health clinics, schools). In contrast to the Community Forestry decree that did not seem to interest villagers (most villagers perceive the land as theirs, so joining a Community Forestry program would merely slash their de facto forest rights), the Forest Village Community Development program was implemented to a certain degree. One major reason was that funding for the latter was readily available from the private concessionaires,[19] whereas Community Forestry depended on a limited government budget.

Forest Village Community Development and Community Forestry program objectives were formulated in accordance with the New Order's political ideology. This meant that they did not address the Outer Islands' underlying forest management problems, which were rooted in state–society conflicts over resources. Nor did the two programs deal with the imbalance between state and societal power structures that underlay the paternalistic relationship between government and local people in any New Order policy intervention. Far from being a "partnership," the approach was more like "social welfare." Forest management and proprietary rights remained the exclusive domain of the MoF, with local people only entitled to limited user rights. Local forest access—even to a very limited extent—was deemed a privilege rather than a right.

Various changes in the bureaucracy and broader socioeconomic conditions also led to changes in the policy subsystem. New players—such as NGOs, academics, and international agencies—entered the policy community and facilitated the development of an alternative policy discourse that challenged mainstream state beliefs. Growing research on indigenous knowledge, combined with the spread of certain values (e.g., environmental conservation and sustainable development, grassroots democracy, human rights, cultural identity), helped to develop an alternative forest management ideology focused on community self-determination rights. In its most extreme form, this philosophy (often advocated by NGOs and a few academics) was the total opposite of state-centralized resource control. It recognized full community forest management and ownership authority and therefore demanded that the state relinquish forest functional and territorial control to local people. In the early 1990s, several NGOs established a nationwide network, called *Sistem Hutan Kerakyatan* (Community-based Forest System Management), focusing on research and advocacy to promote community-based forest management.

The formal policymaking network also saw the entrance of more innovative bureaucrats and nonstate players. Lacking the necessary information, unaccustomed to the new social forestry approach, and inexperienced in dealing with local complexities, the government invited nonstate actors to provide policy advice. The previous minister, Djamaludin Suryohadikusumo (1993–1998), also showed more concern for social forestry issues and was more accommodating of nonstate policy participation. The MoF did, however, still retain full authority to screen the participants and advice. Those who showed adversarial attitudes were quickly dropped from the invitation list, and policy recommendations that contested the state forest management philosophy were immediately discarded. Participants included provincial bureaucrats and other actors from different backgrounds (e.g., NGOs, international agencies, academics) and geographical settings (most were from Jakarta, and a few were from the provinces). Nongovernment participation was limited to the early stages of the policymaking process, which usually addressed technical issues. Final decisions involving more political considerations were the exclusive domain of the highest level bureaucrats.

Forest Village Community Development and Community Forestry policy formulation provides some illustrations of the process. Both regulations were at the level of ministerial decrees, which meant that the decisionmaking took place internally within the MoF. First drafts were prepared by middle-level officials, who then invited non-MoF stakeholders—usually those who had already developed some relationship with the bureaucracy—to comment on the drafts. Since first introduced, the Forest Village Community Development and Community Forestry decrees have changed several times, and numerous implementation guidelines were formulated (between 1991 and 1996, the MoF passed 28 Forest Village Community Development–related regulations). The middle-level officials who were interviewed indicated that they expected policy advice that was technically applicable, not harsh criticism with suggestions that were impossible to implement. Conceptual issues, like land tenure, were unpopular because they were perceived to directly challenge the MoF's position and authority. Resolving such issues would also require involvement of other land-use ministries (e.g., the Ministry of Mining, National Land Agency, Ministry of Agriculture)—the last thing the MoF middle-level officials wanted. The interdepartmental policy process was typically time- and resource-consuming; it produced frequent conflicts, particularly with regard to competing land-use controls.

From 1995 to early 1998, frequent meetings were held to discuss Forest Village Community Development and Community Forestry reforms. Meeting minutes show that policy recommendations dealt mainly with technical matters (e.g., methods to implement the programs). On a few occasions, some participants (mainly NGOs and expatriates) attempted to open up discussion to include the status of local peoples' forest management and ownership, but the MoF firmly responded that there should be no debate: state proprietary rights were absolute, and local people were only entitled to limited user rights. The NGOs and expatriates presented evidence of sustainable local forest management practices, although to no avail as the MoF's stance did not change. Even when the MoF did not categorically reject the suggestions, they were never ultimately adopted into final policy decisions. Typically, the draft (which was prepared beforehand by MoF mid-level bureaucrats) only underwent slight changes, such as settings/levels or the mechanisms for policy delivery.

The MoF's firm stance over local peoples' forest access and rights was also for practical reasons. The centralistic bureaucracy was not designed to serve local diversity. Allowing millions of local community groups to become primary forest players would require a fundamental bureaucratic (e.g., structure, standard operating procedures) transformation. The perceived risk and uncertainties of radical policy reform were probably too high for the MoF. Nonstate actors advocating *adat* and local forest rights often expressed frustration in dealing with the slow pace of change. Some claim, somewhat cynically, that the MoF's policy debate invitation was superficial, because none of their substantial recommendations were ever considered. Despite these criticisms, the MoF policy forums at least created a medium in which state and nonstate actors met, exchanged ideas, engaged and clarified each others' policy stance, and built networks with like-minded individuals. In the years to come, these networks would become increasingly significant in forestry policymaking.

Without significant changes in the wider sociopolitical institutions, the fundamental policy network power structure remained unaltered. The bureaucracy was still the ultimate decisionmaker, reflecting state policymaking autonomy. Changes in the network character, mainly caused by a lack of state policymaking and implementation capacity, were more nuances than profound systemic changes. With resource shortages (e.g., in-house experts, information, funds), the government searched for outside assistance, particularly from international donors. Various social forestry projects, both bilateral and multilateral in nature, mushroomed.[20] The objectives of these projects were primarily to generate policy-relevant information and to help the government with policy implementation.

1998 to Present

The conditions in the previous phases shaped social forestry development in the third period (1998 to present). This phase is marked by more meaningful changes in formal government social forestry policy. The utilitarian forestry philosophy is still well preserved, as is the belief that the state is the ultimate forest manager and steward. Yet the recognized means of achieving sustainable forest exploitation and conservation have been significantly amended. This includes a gradual acceptance of the government's limited policymaking and implementation capacity and of the ability of local people (especially indigenous communities) to manage forests. This change has not yet been implemented and institutionalized in the sense of being widely embraced or adopted as standard operating procedure. It is, however, imprinted in the recently enacted law and other government regulations. As will be described later, these substantial policy reforms are more a function of broader sociopolitical pressures and innovative policy individuals than of collective bureaucratic action.

The first landmark of the third phase was the 1998 Ministerial Decree of *Krui Kawasan dengan Tujuan Istimewa* ([KdTI] Zone with Special Purpose, see Chapter 6). This regulation marked the government's initial gesture to legally recognize local indigenous forest management.[21] The minister acknowledged that, by passing the KdTI, he took a political risk, because community forestry does not have a clear legal foundation under the 1967 BFL (Suryohadikusumo 1998). To avoid unconstitutional measures, the best he could do was to grant the people of Krui stewardship rights, with the forestlands still remaining under state tenurial control (Suryohadikusumo 1998). The minister's maneuver was indirectly facilitated by the political situation— Soeharto was preoccupied with International Monetary Fund threats and the worsening economic climate, and the minister had nearly completed his term in office. Futhermore, the lack of economic interests in Krui for Soeharto and his patrons was another major advantage.[22]

More substantial and nationwide social forestry policy reform took place during the recent political economic turbulence. Soon after Soeharto stepped down (May 1998), the Ministry of Forestry and Estate Crops's (MoFEC's)[23] new minister, Muslimin Nasution, established a reform committee whose members were drawn from both inside and outside government. The committee's primary task was to review and reformulate "oppressive" forestry regulations, including the 1967 BFL. Through several seminars, attended primarily by NGOs, academics, international agencies, provincial government, and forestry business associations, the committee welcomed public opinion and criticism of the proposed new Forestry Law and other regulations. Local people, however, still remained outside the process.

Most nonstate policy actors who had applauded this reform endeavor, because it was perceived to signal a more democratic and open MoFEC, were soon disappointed when they discovered that the MoFEC had established another internal (bureaucratic) commission with exactly the same mandate. Unhappy with the MoFEC's conduct, as well as the committees' draft Forestry Law reforms, the coalition of nonstate community forestry supporters, coordinated by the *Forum Komunikasi Kehutanan Masyarakat* ([FKKM] Communication Forum on Community Forestry), formulated its own Forestry Law proposal. There were, therefore, three Forestry Law drafts from three different groups, each representing different ideals of community–forest relations. The most radical policy changes were proposed by the FKKM; this version significantly reduced the state's forest management authority by, among other things, requiring that the state grant full forest management control and ownership rights to local, especially indigenous, people. For policymakers who believed in state unity and centralized power and who believed that foresters' raison d'être was to act as managers and guardians for the state, the idea of relinquishing total territorial control was far from persuasive.

The recently enacted Forestry Law UU 41/1999 was drawn primarily from the draft designed by the MoFEC internal committee (see Chapter 4). Compared with its predecessor, the new law contained substantial changes in relation to local people's forest access and rights. Like other forest user groups (e.g., big business, state enterprise), forest villagers are now granted equal access for forest use and management, especially if they form cooperatives. Indigenous people (or *adat* communities) are also given special status, and their unique resource management is legally recognized. Large concessionaires whose operations are located near villages are required to work with the local cooperatives. Unlike the FKKM proposal, the new law still defines the MoFEC as the highest institution that controls and oversees forest territorial functions, use, and tenurial arrangements. Many, however, are still unhappy with the new law, feeling that it is just another government tactic to control forests through government- or industry-controlled cooperatives.

Of the three decades of social forestry development that we have reviewed in this chapter, the last two years have demonstrated the most remarkable policy and subsystem changes. The collapse of the New Order and the ongoing political economic crises have damaged state legitimacy and significantly reduced state power vis-à-vis societal groups. The normative value of the state's absolute power and centralized control was strongly criticized, and a call for democracy and strengthened civil society quickly gained advocates across the nation. The transformation of political systems and norms pervaded the forestry sector, providing more legitimacy to alternative social forestry policy ideas that promote empowerment of local people. Debates over the "appropriate" state forest management role (for the new Forestry Law) no longer took place exclusively within the state domain but spilled over into the public sphere involving a much wider audience (including the media).

Social forestry policymaking is no longer monopolized by the state-centralized management philosophy. Policy networks were formed along two ideological lines—those who believe in state control and those who are convinced that this authority should be devolved to local communities. The former network was dominated primarily by state actors, although it also includes a few nonstate individuals. The latter was dominated by nonstate agents, especially NGOs. Each network, through various strategies, tries to pursue its policy idea, including affecting public opinion through means such as seminars, conferences, press releases, and public statements. Of the two networks, the government's network seems to be more receptive to amending its policy belief by assimilating elements of the other ideology into its own. This is demonstrated by the new Forestry Law UU 41/1999, which adopted many community forestry concepts into the philosophy of state management and control. At the same time, the need for collective action has seemed to enhance the non-state–dominated policy network's capacity. Through more organized and nationwide membership coalitions (or networking with groups such as the FKKM), societal interest associations seemed to enhance their position vis-à-vis the state.

Even though crisis-ridden change has not caused a social forestry policy paradigm shift, it has brought about substantial policy reform. This policy transformation has occurred not because of any bureaucratic learning process, as happened in the previous periods, but because of changing state–society power configurations and political norms. The bureaucracy is still the decisionmaking center, but it is less powerful than before. The House of Representatives and political parties are beginning to play their roles, and societal groups may also enhance their policy participation. If Indonesia continues on its path to democracy and a more pluralistic political system, social forestry policy development will be characterized by the participation of more diverse players. Understanding social forestry policy formation should, therefore, focus on these players' decisionmaking roles and their modes of interactions, political power, policy ideas, policy strategies, and institutional constraints.

Conclusion

Indonesia's experience demonstrates that policymaking is not simply driven by government interests; it also involves the policymakers' "learning" process in which policy ideas play a central role. The Outer Islands' social forestry development reveals a close relation between policy reform and policymakers' changing ideational conceptions. Every policy deliberation revolves around a particular set of ideas. Policy actors, both state and nonstate, pursue these ideas within the institutional boundaries that limit their actions and preferences. Policy ideas are not static—they change as policy actors interact with each other and with the broader sociopolitical world.

Yet the earlier social forestry historical analysis also demonstrates how an institutionalized dogma of state-centralized and scientific-based forestry hamstrung the adoption by policymakers of new ideas contrary to such dogma. It was not until the 1998 political economy crisis that substantial policy changes occurred. It is argued here that once a particular set of ideas—usually introduced to serve a particular mandate—is adopted and internalized as part of an institution's standard operating principles, it becomes very difficult to radically change. The extent of ensuing policy change is largely gradual because substantial reforms often involve very high short-term costs. More importantly, the institutionalized ideological principles within which policymakers operate are often perceived to be the raison d'être of a given institution; radical policy changes can be perceived to threaten the very existence of said institution.

The development of Outer Islands' social forestry policy can be divided into three stages, each of which is featured by modified state conceptions of local forestry systems and represented through different policy instruments. The first period (late 1960s to mid-1980s) was characterized by government's complete rejection of local communities' forest access and its contempt toward forest dwellers' resource management practices. Formal policy focused on policing local forest access, in addition to relocating forest dwellers outside of the forests and trying to change their mode of production. During the second phase (mid-1980s to 1997), government began to ease de jure restrictions on local forest access and adopted social forestry programs, such as Community Forestry and Forest Village Community Development, although the fundamental view of state and local people's roles and status remained the same. The third phase (1998 to present) is marked, at least theoretically, by a substantial improvement of local people's legal forest access and management rights, although this scheme is still under the state management framework.

The first three decades of social forestry history involved incremental policy changes that took place under "normal" political situations. These reforms were primarily a result of changing bureaucratic social forestry ideas and resulted in the alteration of policy instruments (such as the enactment of the Forest Village Community Development and Community Forestry programs) without substantial transformation in state and local forest management roles and authority. The only notable policy change under the "normal" state was in early 1998 (the third phase), when Djamaludin Suryohadikusumo passed the ministerial decree granting Krui the designation as a Zone with Special Purpose. This development suggests that meaningful policy reforms can happen in the presence of risk-taking policymakers. The minister's exceptional decision, however, was still made within the state-centralized forest management framework because his decision could not go beyond this institutional framework. The fact that Krui's experience did not have a direct nationwide effect—because it was restricted to the Krui region—and did not require bureaucratic organizational changes also minimized the minister's political risk.

During the first and second periods, the policy community was small and dominated by the bureaucracy. With the bureaucracy's permission, a handful of NGOs, international organizations, and academics was sometimes involved at the beginning of the policy process, although their involvement was restricted to helping the government deal with technical issues rather than political ones.[24] Bureaucratic control of the policy process and policy ideology resulted in high state policymaking autonomy. Alternative policy ideas promoting community forestry began to develop, but this was outside the mainstream public policy discourse because a closed and monolithic political system tends not to tolerate unconventional policy ideas.

After the fall of the New Order, social forestry policy entered a distinctive development phase marked by changing laws and regulations respecting local people's access to forest and forestry rights. The basic tenets of the state resource management role remain the same, but local community authority has been, at least on paper, significantly restored. Unlike the previous social forestry stages, the third phase policy reform occurred more because of the political situation than because of a bureaucratic internal learning process. State decisionmaking autonomy was reduced as state legitimacy was crippled. The experience of social forestry in the Outer Islands suggests that significant policy change entails several interrelated factors: (a) the presence of alternative policy ideas whose supporters have developed a fairly strong network; (b) the presence of risk-taking policymakers; and (c) changing sociopolitical institutions, which involves changing the power distribution and political norms. The first factor is the prerequisite for policy change, although it does not ensure that significant change will occur. The second and third factors accelerate the reform process, provided that the first factor exists.

The current, more open, political system resonates at the sectoral level. The policy community is a wider audience and includes more than a single policy ideology. The policy network includes more players and a changing decisionmaking mechanism. The bureaucracy is still the decisionmaking center but no longer the hegemonic player, as the House of Representatives has begun to play a significant role. Local governments, which have long been powerless, increasingly become significant players as well, particularly with the implementation of the current form of decentralization (see Chapter 15). In addition, NGO-based societal interest groups are more organized and have more capacity to bring their aspirations to the House of Representatives. Local people are still in the policymaking periphery, although their political participation is formally enhanced. This sectoral trend will likely continue, assuming the broader political system permits such changes.

With a more open policy subsystem that allows easier access to new players and ideas, struggles for policy change will likely be more dynamic. This does not necessarily mean that policy change will now be easier—more diverse players (with more dispersed power distribution) and policy ideas can lead to various policy change scenarios, depending on how different policy networks struggle to acquire policymaking power.

Endnotes

1. The Outer Islands refer to the areas outside Java and Bali (Inner Islands). The Outer Islands include approximately 90% of Indonesia's forests, and they have been the focus of the massive forest exploitation that has occurred during the last three decades. The Inner and Outer Islands' forest management histories have taken different paths, so it is important to distinguish between the two. For Java's forest management, see Barber (1989) and Peluso (1992).

2. A variety of terms such as social forestry, community forestry, local and community-based forest management, and joint forest management, are used to describe various modes of local people's involvement in forest management. I will use "social forestry" as an umbrella term to cover all government programs and policies that involve forest dwellers in forest management and that have the ultimate goal of improving their socioeconomic well-being. The terms community-based forest management and community forestry, unless indicated otherwise, will be used to refer to actual forest management practices of local communities. Social forestry may or may not promote community-based forest management.

3. The definition of success, of course, depends on one's standards and criteria for expected change. It may range from small policy adjustments to radical ideological transformations.

4. With the exception of Barber (1989) and Peluso (1992), most of Indonesia's social forestry policy studies focus on legal text analyses without paying attention to the incumbent policy process. For text-based analyses, see Moniaga (1993), Wangsadidjaja and Ismanto (1993), WALHI (1993), Lynch and Talbott (1995), Safitri (1995), and Chapter 1 of this book.

5. I use the term "policy idea" to encompass all other similar terminologies such as policy ideology, paradigm, and discourse. Idea is used here to acknowledge that it entails ascending levels of policy actors' belief systems, from the "core" (i.e., usually involving overall policy goals and causal theories) to "peripheral" aspects (i.e., usually involving policy instruments). Sabatier and Jenkins-Smith (1993) provide a detailed description of this matter.

6. Political parties had to request government approval for proposed legislative candidates, and through the "recall" mechanism, the government (through the political party) could dismiss a disliked house member without legal cause.

7. This phrase was used to imply, and sometimes state, that any dissent was Communist inspired.

8. This attitude was obviously passed down by the Dutch. During the 1930 summit of the East Indies Agriculture Extension Bureaus, for instance, one of the urgent recommendations dealt with the need to establish legal mechanisms (with or without conforming to the customary laws) to halt the "destructive" Outer Islands' shifting cultivation practices (Departemen Kehutanan RI 1986, 175).

9. The 1967 BFL itself neither explicitly outlawed nor promoted local forest use and access rights on state land.

10. In contrast to its primary objective, the HPHH did not seem to bring many economic advantages to forest farmers because they had neither the understanding of urban-based bureaucratic procedures nor the necessary start-up capital—the benefits were primarily reaped by a few urban rich.

11. Thanks to Hubert de Foresta for this contribution.

12. See Forest Department annual reports (i.e., Rapat Kerja Nasional Kehutanan 1975), especially between 1966 and 1979.

13. In 1975, for example, the Institut Pertanian Bogor (Bogor Agricultural Institute), which houses one of the country's biggest and most influential forestry faculties, in cooperation with the Department of Agriculture, discussed the problem of the Outer Islands' accelerating land degradation. Blame was again directed at shifting cultivators, and the recommendations made were to enforce existing resettlement and permanent agriculture policies (Tjondronegoro 1991, 26). Universities such as Gadjah Mada University and The University of Padjajaran, among others, played an active role in helping the government design its Resettlement Master Plan (Rapat Kerja Nasional Kehutanan 1975).

14. Land degradation became a serious issue, especially after the huge forest fire of 1983, which cleared some 3 million ha of forests. Smallholder farming practice was blamed as a major cause.

15. See MoF Instruction 088.

16. Transmigration (under the Ministry of Transmigration) formerly aimed at relieving the Inner Islands' population pressures by resettling Inner Island farmers in the Outer Islands. Since the mid-1980s, however, this program also included "local" transmigration, which relocated Outer Island smallholders to government-selected areas (the Ministry of Transmigration then became the Ministry of Transmigration and Resettlement of Forest Squatters). Forest farmers were also encouraged to join People's Nucleus Estate programs (under the Ministry of Agriculture) and Industrial Timber Plantations (MoF). The Development of Isolated Communities (Ministry of Social Affairs) focused on relocating "isolated" tribes into urban areas, while the Village Consolidation program (Ministry of Home Affairs) aimed at merging scattered, isolated, and sparsely populated villages into larger geographic and administrative units.

17. See MoF Decree 251.

18. For community forestry particulars, see MoF Decree 622.

19. The community development plan must become an integral part of the company's *Rencana Karya Pengusahaan Hutan* (Forest Exploitation Work Plan); without this document, the concessionaires' work plan could not be approved by the MoF bureaucracy.

20. Some examples include West Kalimantan's Social Forestry Development Project, community forestry in Gunung Palung National Park, the conservation project in Danau Sentarum Wildlife Reserve (now a national park), and East Kalimantan's Promotion of Sustainable Forest Management Systems.

21. In January 1998, for the first time in Indonesia's history under the New Order, the forestry minister (Djamaludin Suryohadikusumo), designated 29,000 ha of state-claimed forest in Krui (Lampung) as a special, formally recognized, grassroots-based forest management zone. Before such status was granted, Krui was yet another state forest area where local people's forest access was banned. In the early 1990s, government-licensed oil palm plantations began to aggressively raid and clear village damar (*Shorea javanica*) dominated agroforestry gardens. Krui villagers tried various methods to stop company operations, including seeking outside assistance. The International Centre for Research in Agroforestry and a few locally active NGOs acted as facilitators to help bring the Krui case to the attention of the MoF in Jakarta. After long and arduous negotiations, including the minister's visiting Krui, the minister agreed to grant Krui special status. Although the plantation threat has vanished, locals remain unhappy because this "special status" is reminiscent of user rights and hence does not eliminate the government's claim over the land.

22. The Bentian region of East Kalimantan had experienced developments similar to those in Krui, yet the designation as a Zone with Special Purpose status was never awarded to Bentian people. One of the reasons is that Bentian is directly linked to timber stakes held by key members of the elites, including those of Bob Hasan (Soeharto's closest economically).

23. At that time the MoF had been renamed the MoFEC (Ministry of Forestry and Estate Crops).

24. Business interests are not direct players in social forestry policymaking. Yet they have a powerful (albeit indirect) influence; the social forestry subsystem is politically and economically "subordinate" to the timber industry's. Accordingly, every policy instrument of the former is designed in such a way that it does not erode the latter's interests.

References

Anderson, B. 1990. *Language and Power: Exploring Political Cultures in Indonesia.* Ithaca, NY, and London: Cornell University Press.

Barber, C.V. 1989. *The State, the Environment, and Development: The Genesis and Transformation of Social Forestry Policy in New Order Indonesia.* Ph.D. dissertation. Berkeley: University of California.

———. 1998. Forest resource scarcity and social conflict in Indonesia. *Environment* 40(4):4–9.

Departemen Kehutanan RI. 1986. *Sejarah Kehutanan Indonesian I (Indonesian Forestry History I).* Jakarta, Indonesia: Departemen Kehutanan.

Departemen Pertanian, Direktorat Jenderal Kehutanan. 1979. *Rapat Kerja Instansi Kehutanan Se-Indonesia Tahun. Buku II: Ceramah dan Pidato Pengarahan.* Jakarta, Indonesia: Departemen Pertanian.

Heclo, H. 1974. *Modern Social Politics in Britain and Sweden.* New Haven, CT: Yale University Press.

Howlett, M., and M. Ramesh. 1998. Policy subsystem configurations and policy change: Operationalizing the postpositivist analysis of the politics of the policy process. *Policy Studies Journal* 26: 466–81.

Ikenberry, G.J. 1988. Conclusion: An institutional approach to American foreign economic policy. *International Organization* 42: 220–43.

Jackson, K.D. 1978. Bureaucratic polity: A theoretical framework for the analysis of power and communications in Indonesia. In *Political Power and Communications in Indonesia*, edited by K.D. Jackson and L. Pye. Berkeley: University of California Press, 3–22.

Lindayati, R. Forthcoming. Macro–Micro Linkages: Shaping Local Forest Tenure in National Politics. In *The Commons in the New Millennium: Challenges and Adaptation*, edited by N. Dolsak and E. Ostrom.

Lynch, O.J., and K. Talbott. 1995. *Balancing Acts: Community-Based Forest Management and National Law in Asia and the Pacific.* Washington, DC: World Resource Institute.

Manurung, T. 1997. *Political Economy in the Formulation of Forestry Law in Indonesia.* Bogor, Indonesia: Center for International Forestry Research.

Moniaga, S. 1993. Toward community-based forestry and recognition of *adat* property rights in the Outer Islands of Indonesia. In *Legal Frameworks for Forest Management in Asia*, edited by J. Fox. Honolulu, HI: East–West Center, 131–50.

Peluso, N.L. 1992. *Rich Forests, Poor People: Resource Control and Resistance in Java.* Berkeley: University of California Press.

Rapat Kerja Nasional Kehutanan. 1975. *Bahan Pembahasan Buku II: Naskah-naskah.* Bogor, Indonesia: Departemen Kehutanan.

Sabatier, P.A., and H. Jenkins-Smith (eds.). 1993. *Policy Change and Learning.* Boulder, CO: Westview.

Safitri, M. 1995. Hak dan Akses Masyarakat Lokal Pada Sumberdaya Hutan: Kajian Peraturan Perundang-undangan Indonesia (Local Community Access and Rights to Forest Resources: Analysis of Indonesia's Legal Framework). *Ekonosia* 3: 43–59.

Sanit, A. 1998. *Reformasi Politik (Political Reform).* Yogyakarta, Indonesia: Pustaka Pelajar.

Stone, D.A. 1988. *Policy Paradox and Political Reason.* Glenview, IL: Scott, Foresman.

Suryohadikusumo, D. 1998. Personal communication with the author, November1998.

Tjondronegoro, S.M.P. 1991. The utilization and management of land resources in Indonesia, 1970–1990. In *Indonesia: Resources, Ecology, and Environment,* edited by J. Hardjono. Singapore: Oxford University Press, 17–35.

WALHI (*Wahana Lingkungan Hidup Indonesia or Indonesian Forum on the Environment*). 1993. *Violated Trust: Disregard for the Forests and Forest Laws of Indonesia.* Jakarta, Indonesia: WALHI.

Wangsadidjaja, S., and A.D. Ismanto. 1993. The legal case for social forestry in the production forests of Indonesia. In *Legal Frameworks for Forest Management in Asia,* edited by J. Fox. Honolulu, HI: East–West Center, 115–29.

Wilks, S., and M. Wright. 1987. Comparing government–industry relations: States, sectors, and networks. In *Comparative Government–Industry Relations: Western Europe, United States, and Japan,* edited by S. Wilks. and M. Wright. Oxford, U.K.: Clarendon Press, 274–313.

CHAPTER THREE

Responsibility, Accountability, and National Unity in Village Governance

Chris P. A. Bennett

One institution has remained on the periphery of policy dialogue about decentralization to the regency level—the village. Proper integration of village governance into the wider system of decentralized governance may, however, offer the last hope for sustainable management of Indonesia's natural resources. More important still, it could be the most effective way to ensure responsible regency governance while strengthening the sense of national unity and tempering opportunistic calls for regional independence. Villages, however, are still typically perceived by national and regency governments as potential liabilities rather than unique social and political assets for an emerging democratic nation.

The mindset that led to the Village Governance Law (*Undang-Undang* [UU] 5) of 1979, which intended in part to subvert traditional forms of governance, still survives. Village government institutions have been essentially determined from above, not by village communities, and those communities have rarely been consulted about the allocation and use of natural resources within their village areas by the ubiquitous, government-approved private and parastatal companies. Lacking in the past, and critically lacking within the present decentralization program, higher levels of government (i.e., county, regency, provincial, national) have not been held formally accountable by the village communities affected by their decisions. With the full implementation of the decentralization law on January 1, 2001, Indonesia has the chance to fully recognize and integrate the crucial role of village governance in decentralization of natural resource management as well as the development of regency government within Indonesia.[1] There has been scant evidence that this opportunity will be seized (see Chapter 15).

Risks of Irresponsible Local Government

The literature and rhetoric of decentralization (in Indonesia and elsewhere) is replete with cautionary tales about the shortcomings of devolving authority to local government (Crook and Sverrisson 1999; Frerks and Otto 1996; Moore and Putzel 1999; Treisman 2000). More often than not, reality bears this out, although the underlying problems are often misunderstood. In Indonesia, national government agencies, particularly sectoral departments, and observers of decentralization rightly warn of the potent combination of local governments' lack of administrative capacity and eagerness to tax locally produced agricultural, forestry, and mineral commodities (Bennett 2000b). In recent months, the dubious efforts of a *bupati* (the executive in charge of a regency) in North Sulawesi to increase taxes paid by the Newmont mining company provided an early warning (see Annex 3–1). Since then other press reports have focused on similar problems. More recently, a *bupati* in South Sulawesi arbitrarily cancelled the outcome of an auction for lake fishing rights (Pedoman Rakyat 2000). The acute mismanagement of sandalwood resources by past governors of Nusatenggara Timur is finally coming to light (*Indonesian Observer* 2000).

Natural resources, it is feared, may be capitalized by local government for short-term gain rather than be well managed to sustain gains over the long term; they may, for instance, involve the conversion of natural forests to timber or oil plantations. Sustaining natural resources to reflect their true economic and social value is often, at best, a secondary consideration of local government. Furthermore, rights to natural resources may be captured by local elites consisting of senior bureaucrats and favored businessmen, typically excluding the poor, the majority of whom are heavily dependent on natural resources.[2] Incomes of the poor are directly reduced when their produce is taxed or their lands are assigned to large-scale development schemes. Given that poverty alleviation and improved environmental management are directly related (DFID 2000), concerns about decentralization of natural resource management are justified. Experience in other countries has shown that one of the more difficult challenges for decentralization is maintaining a sufficiently high policy priority at the local level for poverty alleviation efforts (Crook and Sverrisson 1999).

In many ways, regional government is now being criticized for wanting to follow the example set by the national government during President Soeharto's

New Order (during 1966–1998). True, there is a real danger of money politics deciding the outcome of local elections of the regional House of Representatives or the appointments of *bupatis* or village leaders, but the role of money in deciding such "elections" has a long history. Be that as it may, Indonesian government concerns over the prospect of (continued) irresponsible natural resource governance and inefficient service delivery as a result of decentralization remain legitimate. Part of the problem is the lack of local government capacity.

Crisis of Capacity

Undeniably, most regency governments lack sufficient capacity for responsible and efficient implementation of their new roles under decentralization (DCM 2000; U.S. Embassy in Jakarta 2000; *The Jakarta Post* 2000a); this applies both to the legislature and the *bupati*. Sound financial administration and effective service delivery by the time of full implementation of UU 22/1999 in 2001 appeared unlikely in 2000 (*The Jakarta Post* 2000a), and in fact this has not yet materialized in early 2001. Raising the capacity of regional government has both obvious and less apparent implications. First, and most obvious, is the question, how do you raise capacity? Second, how do you convince local government of the nature and extent of the capacity gap? Third, how do you encourage a continuous process of capacity improvement?

Training programs are necessary, but they are not a sufficient solution to the capacity problem. After all, if local government personnel and institutions were to be at the same level of capacity as central government, this alone would not guarantee good local governance, any more than it did at the center during the New Order. And will additional capacity at the regional level necessarily be put to good social use? If local government is captured by local elites, increased administrative ability could be turned to their advantage, thus helping them to conceal their activities from central government audits and oversight. As vital as developing capacity is, to be put to good use it must be linked to the development of what has for so long been lacking both in the regions and the center—accountability. Truly accountable local government must actively seek the capacity it needs or face the painful consequences of betraying the public's trust.

Local Government Responsibility and Accountability

Accountability, the cornerstone of good governance,[3] the light that can reach into the darkest recesses of a Byzantine bureaucracy and its business partners, is unfortunately not among the highest priorities of Indonesia's decentralization policymakers, decisionmakers, analysts, and observers.[4] In the new political establishment, not all who have just won the authority they have long struggled for find it easy to welcome the limits that increased accountability and decentralization set on what they can now do, whether in their own interests (*The Jakarta Post* 2000b) or in what they perceive to be the best interests of the nation.

Although Indonesia's new political order is more pluralistic, it is far from clear how committed it is to decentralization and the increased accountability upon which decentralization's success depends. Academics, nongovernmental organizations (NGOs), the press, the private sector, and donor agencies have added their voices to those in government who, often with good intentions, urge less decentralization and a slower pace for the process as a whole. Apart from warnings that local governments will excessively tax and capitalize natural resources, there is the added concern that there has been insufficient preparation for the necessary changes in financial administration and that therefore the provision of essential services will be neglected. Ideally, the process should be slower to be surer. But the history of past "decentralization" programs in Indonesia provides a warning that the argument of insufficient capacity can be used to delay the process interminably. Workable and meaningful mechanisms of accountability for both central and regional governments during the process of devolving authority are essential—and essentially lacking.

While regency governments are developing their democratic institutions and efforts are made by both central and provincial government agencies to provide appropriate oversight (a labor of decades), one institution can play an important role in fostering the kind of accountability that is consistent with national development goals—the village (as conceived in UU 22/1999). Village communities, properly represented, can and should be invited to hold regency governments accountable for the following consequences:

- poor service delivery,
- excessive taxation, and
- unsustainable management of natural resources.

During the New Order, either this was not the case or villages were "represented" by those approved by the *bupati*. Before exploring mechanisms by which villages might exert positive and participatory influence on regency government, it is important to take a brief look at the concept of government accountability as it has developed in Indonesia over the past three decades.

"Responsibility" and Responsibility

"Accountability" and other similar terms have been used in ways that, if not clarified, could undermine the development of mechanisms of real accountability. In Indonesian laws and regulations, the concepts of accountability and responsibility have tended to be interchangeable. Accountability, translated as *akuntabilitas*, is less familiar than the more commonly used *tanggung jawab*, meaning responsibility, literally being prepared to reply or answer. In practice, however, *tanggung jawab* has not meant being answerable. It has tended to be a statement of government-approved authority (i.e., responsibility for a certain task rather than its outcome). A term with more direct connotations of accountability has been conspicuous by its absence in the lexicon of civil servants (and politicians). *Tanggung gugat* is perhaps that missing term.[5]

Tanggung gugat is an expression heard rarely among those who proclaim government-sanctioned authority. It suggests being prepared to accept liability for the consequences of one's actions. *Tanggung gugat* invites establishment of the instruments of accountability such as transparency, information access, multistakeholder participation, opportunity for and responsiveness to public questions, and true responsibility. This is an invitation that only enlightened regency governments will want to send out. Acceptance that accountability is better understood as *tanggung gugat* than *tanggung jawab* would be a useful step forward, a significant symbolic gesture that decentralization does not simply mean doing locally what the center used to do from Jakarta. Perhaps the compromise would be to add *dan tanggung gugat* (*sosial*) wherever the term *tanggung jawab* appears in new policies. Mention of the new term would require formal definition, including the steps taken to ensure it, for the benefit of government agencies and village communities alike.

Immediate Accountability

At present, the political survival of the members of the regional House of Representatives and the *bupatis* they appoint does not depend sufficiently on formal accountability to the electorate. The five years between elections is time enough for a considerable degree of rent-seeking and misgovernment, such as issuing lucrative licenses to clear-cut natural forests, imposing multiple taxes on export commodities, and squandering road building and maintenance funds. One of the most serious disconnects between local government and the electorate is that regional House of Representatives members owe their primary allegiance to their parties rather than to a physically defined constituency within each regency.

Theoretically, the proximity of decisionmakers and policymakers under decentralization should discourage extreme abuses of power and encourage more suitable development strategies. After all, the *bupati's* house is within easier reach of village communities whose mangrove forests have been licensed without their consent for conversion to shrimp ponds than is the director general's house in Jakarta. Reliance on "mobocracy" to punish wayward local government, however, will not allow development of equitable and efficient local government that enjoys the public trust. Furthermore, it can too easily be manipulated by vested interests. What checks and balances, especially during the critical early stages of decentralization and democratization, can be applied to local government to instill adequate accountability? How can due process be invoked to achieve this?

Accountability to National Government

The problem of accountability of regency government is generally perceived as accountability to those institutions relinquishing some of their authority, that is, the national government and its central agencies. Financial, administrative, and environmental monitoring and evaluation by auditors from the center should prevent some problems of misuse of funds and resources. Such monitoring and evaluation mechanisms may prove less successful than the ability of national government to interrupt the process of policy development at the regional level. Thus, Articles 113 and 114 of UU 22/1999 (see Annex 3–2 and Appendix) allow for central government oversight of policy development by local government. Regency regulations and decisions can be overturned by central government. But such intervention will have to be used carefully if it is not to result in divisive accusations of excessive meddling by central government in regional affairs. A government regulation could establish such a mechanism for policy oversight acceptable to national and local governments (Bennett 2000a).

The ability of the center to rein in irresponsible policymakers in the regions should not be taken for granted. Notwithstanding the advent of a future national backlash against decentralization, the center is not negotiating with the regions from a position of unified strength. Distrustful of the center's commitment to decentralization, some regencies are warning that they will disregard unreasonable decisions made at the center (and there is anecdotal evidence that they have already begun to do so). The Kutai Regency, East Kalimantan, questioned the role of the Ministry of Forestry (MoF)[6] in forest conservation, suggesting that this could be handled locally. Central Kalimantan decided to continue with the community forestry program known as the *hutan kemasyarakatan* despite an MoF directorate general's instruction to halt the program until it was amended to be in line with UU 41/1999. Several regency governments have vehemently opposed ministry plans to nationalize production forest leases under so-called *perumisasi* (the process, quite popular among central ministry officials in 2000, of nationalizing forest companies). Regional challenges to the very legitimacy of government departments, as reasonable as some may be, nonetheless undermine the principle of accountability to the center.

Accountability to Village Communities

While central government worries about how to exert adequate control over provincial and regency governments to prevent taxation or rent-seeking excesses, let alone regional sentiments that might ultimately lead to calls for more autonomy, it has largely ignored potent allies for whom local government accountability is no less important—the 65,000 village communities. Once regarded as a threat to national unity because of their diverse and relatively independent forms of traditional governance, they hold the key to restraining, if not preventing, economic and political excesses of regency governments, particularly those related to natural resource management.

Rural communities stand to lose most from government policies that favor unsustainable and inequitable exploitation of natural resources. And the livelihoods of the poor, most of whom live and work in rural areas as smallholders or landless agricultural laborers, are at greatest risk. Most coastal seas, riparian and wetland waterways, forests, and agricultural lands in Indonesia are within or close to village areas. In the past, village communities had little formal or recognized say in resource allocation, management, and regulation or taxation of their agricultural and fisheries products. Since the reform era began, village communities have spoken out against a wide range of past injustices made possible by central government approval, such as confiscation of farmland, destruction of forest-based livelihoods, and degradation of waterways by high-impact logging. So far, however, villager grievances have been raised at the regency level in an ad hoc manner.

The obligation of regency government to provide adequate formal opportunities for villagers to present their questions or complaints and to publicly respond to such villager presentations, whether about natural resource management, taxation, or delivery of services, could exert a significant moderating force on local policymaking and decisionmaking. Public responses would mean written disclosure of the reasons for specific regency government policies and decisions, not, as in the past, dismissive oral answers that ended any further discussion. Alerted through the public process of receiving complaints, central government might then choose to intervene, perhaps by invoking Articles 113 and 114 of UU 22/1999, if serious problems between village and regency remained unresolved, strengthening the vital link between the people and national government (as discussed in the next section). Facing the prospect of formal and public complaints from those at the sharp end of inappropriate decisions and policies should encourage local government to invite community participation in planning and policy development.

Village Representation

In some ways, the democratic process has been at work longer in Indonesian villages than in the higher levels of regional and national government. Although in the past, village heads had to be approved by the *bupati* and were therefore not always the village community's first choice, their proximity to the members of their constituency and its natural resources made it difficult for them to be as detached and autocratic as the heads of higher levels of government, from county leaders to the president. Therefore they were more likely to be influenced by older and longer-established systems of governance, which were more familiar to the community—traditional systems that had themselves been adapting to a changing Indonesia. True, Village Governance Law (UU 5/1979) either disrupted or abolished traditional village governance by forcing villages to merge and creating counties that cut across larger traditional communities that had consisted of groups of villages (Marga of Jambi, the Nagari of West Sumatra, Binua of West Kalimantan, or Lembang of Toraja). But after 20 years, village communities have generally learned to live with these external administrative constraints and remain a potentially potent rural voice that should be permitted to hold regency (and higher levels of government) accountable for their policy and development actions.

New Order and New Village Government

While an increasing number of observers of decentralization warn of the risk of the "little king" syndrome (see Annex 3–1) and an array of other potentially negative outcomes, the development of village democracy, a vital force for local government accountability, has not been accorded sufficient attention by policymakers. UU 22/1999 offers the prospect of strengthening village democracy through elections of village councils and village heads without undue influence from higher levels of government. There is even a provision for the redrawing of village boundaries to better reflect the will of local communities. But will the spirit of UU 22/1999 survive its implementation?

Local government and old-style bureaucrats in Jakarta seem to be balking at the thought of more genuine village representation and the increased legitimacy and boldness it would bring to the process of holding regency governments liable for their misdeeds. Implementation is being left largely in the hands of local government. That seems reasonable enough until it is noted that some regency governments will not necessarily welcome the development of village institutions that will dare to hold them accountable.

Some fear that the village councils will be corrupted to become ineffectual institutional puppets of higher levels of government, something like the New Order versions (*Lembaga Ketahanan Masyarakat Desa* [LKMD] or Village Community Resilience Councils; *Lembaga Musyawarah Desa* [LMD] or Village Consensus-Reaching Organization). Current government insistence that village council members have a certain level of formal education would eliminate many village elders whom villagers would like to choose, people who have the standing, eloquence, and courage to challenge a county leader or a *bupati*. Village communities may feel, however, that the reform era has given them the right to choose their representatives. Without the heavy hand of the

New Order, the village councils may yet become democratic, despite the best efforts of the bureaucracy.

Concerns that implementation of greater village democracy and influence over higher levels of government might be abused (e.g., "captured" by the local elite) should be considered in the light of recent history. In the past, village leadership (e.g., the village head, LKMD, LMD) was sometimes controlled by corrupt or even criminal forces.[7] This was often made possible because legitimacy was derived from above. Anyone who questioned a government-approved village headman faced the prospect of being invited to present his or her complaints to unsympathetic government officials with the police or army in attendance. Over time, these practices have apparently become less common. Proper implementation of UU 22/1999 should consolidate this trend as representational legitimacy depends more on the sanction of the people than on the offices of higher levels of government.

Rural village areas cover most of Indonesia's natural land resources. Whether villager and government perceptions of village boundaries coincide, most forestland is accessed (traversed or used) by people from village settlements who have a clear stake in the fate of those lands. In short, villagers are major stakeholders in the outcome of natural resource management in Indonesia. At the very least, they should be more involved in decisionmaking about the allocation and management systems for the natural resources that affect their livelihood. They, especially their poor, are at the sharp end of natural resource policies.

Given that some of central government's worst fears about decentralization are about misallocation or excessive taxation of natural resources (e.g., forests, mines), village communities could play an important role in alerting the center of such policy misdeeds and in persuading regency government to think twice before issuing policies in a nonparticipatory manner. Village-driven accountability channeled through due public process could help to exert a moderating influence on decentralized government—but only if this role is formally recognized.

Mechanisms of Village-Driven Accountability

How can village-driven accountability work? How can we avoid mere lip service to accountability? Many *bupati* during the New Order received villagers, listened to their concerns, expressed thanks for their input, and then behaved as if such meetings had never taken place. Accountability obviously requires more than simple (passive) receptivity—responsiveness, responsibility for the outcome of decisions, transparency of decisionmaking processes, and social inclusivity (multistakeholder participation) are all essential. Village-driven accountability could work in two ways.

1. First, it could work through more participatory mechanisms of decisionmaking, including village contributions to spatial planning and allocation as well as

management of natural resources within village areas. This might involve such decisions as whether to grant a forest concession or timber estate license or whether to convert forestland to agricultural use. Participatory planning between local government and villages could be coordinated through formal (e.g., county) or traditional village groupings, as decided by the communities themselves (discussed later in this section).

2. A second and more crucial means for making it work is through a transparent and open-door process for receiving village community representatives with petitions or grievances, be they about poor services, inequitable land-use permits, or excessive commodity taxes. Even if the first approach is initially ignored, the second should ultimately persuade local government to be more participatory (i.e., by sharing responsibility for actions, thereby reducing the likelihood of village community protests). Doors must be opened in ways that allow meaningful participation of disadvantaged groups such as women, those who cannot read or write, and marginalized ethnic groups such as the Punan or Orang Rimba.[8]

Imagining the prospect of opening their doors in this way is likely to frighten regency governments. They would probably perceive the institutionalization of the second approach as more threatening than the first. Furthermore, local governments (and sectoral departments) might insist that they are already using principles of participation (*partisipasi* and *peran serta*) in their development planning and implementation. In reality, such "participatory" schemes generally fall far short of their declared intent and remain essentially top-down. Yet without meaningful community participation, development plans are unlikely to be appropriate or to generate trust between villagers and local government. One of the most common grievances of traditional village communities in Indonesia is that the government does not invite them to participate in the process of formal allocation of natural resources within their village areas (Tim Tujuh 1999). Lack of increased community participation in local government has been identified as one of the main failures of decentralization worldwide (Crook and Sverrisson 1999; Frerks and Otto 1996).

Village Grouping or Association

Opening the doors of regency government to village representatives is a necessary but not sufficient condition for village-driven accountability. After all, what could the representatives of a single village achieve in the alien environment of high bureaucracy? NGOs can help village communities articulate their concerns. Several villages could collaborate in conveying a message to local government. Decentralization has prompted the formation of an association of *bupatis*. Why not an association of villages to share information and experience about the development of village democracy according to UU 22/ 1999 (Federation of Community Forest Users in Nepal, a network of forest user groups in Nepal, has had some significant successes along these lines.) This could also provide a means of generating a voice loud enough to be heard by regency, provincial, or national government. An association would be able to help disseminate information to its members about relevant new national or regional policies. It could be the channel for alerting central government about unjust local government regulations. National government might then decide to investigate further or invoke Articles 113 and 114 of UU 22/1999 to halt the local regulation in question.

There should be the option of one or several villages coming together to convey their message. This would depend on the nature of the problem and would be a matter for individual village governments to decide. Following are some examples.

- One village primarily concerned about its water supply might object to a gold mining concession that was granted without due consultation with the local community.
- Several villages might join to oppose the nonparticipatory allocation of a clear-cut license in nearby natural forests, which harbor a range of forest products to which they have long had access.
- Tens of highland villages might combine in opposition to local taxes on smallholder coffee, which would in turn invite an array of informal levies by government agencies checking shipments of such a regulated commodity to ensure that paperwork (like tax forms) was in order.
- Most villages in a regency might make it clear that they are unhappy about the slow disbursement of development funds or services in general.

Empowered by Article 93 of UU 22/1999, villages might choose to present their case to the *bupati* or regional House of Representatives through old institutions that traditionally encompassed several villages, like Kasepuhan (West Java), Nagari (West Sumatra), Marga (South Sumatra and Jambi), Binua (West Kalimantan), Banjar (Bali), and Lembang (Toraja) to name but a few. However villages decide to present their views and concerns, the essential point is that village organization should be decided by them and not by top-down dictates. In the past, for instance, a *bupati* might decide he was only prepared to receive village delegations from one county at a time and with the approval of the county leader. The problem of the county administration is that currently it is not elected and owes its existence to the approval of the *bupati*. County leaders are unlikely to wholeheartedly support village efforts to do anything that will be perceived as making life difficult for the *bupati*. To date, this has been a serious constraint to village-driven accountability. This situation could conceivably change if *bupatis* were to give clear and unambiguous signals to county leaders of the importance of properly receiving, recording, and if necessary relaying to the regency concerns of village communities about government mismanagement.

Public Record

Scheduling times when regency government would meet with village delegations, though no easy matter, should not present insurmountable difficulties. Problems not resolved by the *bupati's* office in a timely manner would be automatically scheduled for submission to the regional House of Representatives.[9] Actual processes could be worked out locally. To avoid mismanagement of such processes, their development and implementation has to be transparent and timely, involving the appropriate levels of local government and including the establishment of a public registry of complaints that could be readily accessed by political parties, NGOs, the media, and others. There should be a public archive of all village community complaints to regency government, recording all relevant decrees, correspondence, and meetings as well as newspaper articles. Ideally, a more independent agency, perhaps a commission or NGO, would maintain a similar archive. Posting the archive on the Internet would be helpful, perhaps along the lines of the new <www.surabayadomain.com> website (Owen 2000).

Local government decisions should be justified in writing. *Bupatis* or even the regional House of Representatives, of course, might choose to ignore inconvenient complaints (e.g., when government officials are involved in illegal logging of traditional or state forest reserves). Following are the key points:

- Village community complaints and local government action should be properly recorded and accessible to the public.
- "Responsible" government officials or representatives should know that a well-documented archive will make them liable to future investigation by higher levels of government or the media, even after those officials or representatives have moved to other positions or professions.

Regency governments might balk at the prospect of having to deal with an avalanche of village complaints as well as managing a public archive for each. There would be fewer such complaints or petitions if regency and county administrations adopted a more participatory approach in the allocation, management, and taxation of resources; provision of services; and formulation of policies in general.

In sum, the most important relationship to the development of village democracy and village-driven accountability should be that between village (and its voluntary association with other villages) and regency government. Over time, regency government answerable to its village electorate would be more likely to involve them in the earlier stages of resource allocation and regulation decisions, choosing participation over later confrontation. Village-driven accountability, then, could be a practical and potent instrument to encourage responsible local government, especially during the critical early stages of decentralization while more conventional institutional instruments of democracy are developing. In short, village-driven accountability is in the national interest.

Village Democracy as Political Liability or Human Capital Asset

Empowering village communities within the process of decentralization might be seen by some in national government, particularly those with authoritarian inclinations, as too great a political liability whether they have their own interests or the interests of the nation in mind. Authoritarian governments typically distrust the self-reliance of villagers, especially farmers and community forest managers, above all their traditional forms of village governance (sometimes embarrassingly more democratic). The relative lack of village dependence on central government is awkward for state and private agencies that would like to exploit natural resources in village areas. The political loyalty of village communities is conveniently questioned, ostensibly as an obstacle to nationhood. In Indonesia, UU 5/1979 epitomized the response of an autocratic government to traditional village governance. UU 22/1999 could change this deeply ingrained perception.

Among those in government who are sincerely concerned with village welfare, a patronizing, if not condescending, attitude is all too common, perpetuated by perceptions of superiority as the result of higher formal education as well as misperceptions about the behavior of poor farmers and other natural resource managers. Stereotypes persist. Smallholder farmers are considered as essentially ignorant and resourceless. Village communities are seen as the source of threats to economic stability and environmental sustainability. They are seen to be involved in illegal logging and gold mining, extorting money from forest concessions, converting natural forests to agriculture, cultivating steep slopes vulnerable to erosion, setting forest fires, and fishing by bombing or poisoning coral.

In fact, smallholder farmers are consummate micro managers of their farming systems, far from ignorant and far better described as resourceful. They make the most of what they have and generally make rational choices about investing their time and energy in agricultural investments. This may include only partially adopting or even rejecting technological recommendations from the Ministry of Agriculture. For example, smallholder farmers in Semendo, South Sumatra, rejected the nitrogen component of the recommended fertilizer package for their coffee trees because they subsequently observed that not only did it increase pest damage to the coffee berries but it also stimulated leaf production over flowers; smallholder coffee farmers in North Sumatra rejected supposedly disease-resistant arabica coffee varieties introduced from the coffee research center because they were less resistant to local disease than local varieties.

Illegal timber extraction by local communities, however, can be traced to the fact that they have been formally excluded from access to forest resources within their village lands. At the same time (formally or informally), government-approved private logging businesses not only have been permitted to log in these areas but also have created more damage than traditional harvesting methods by using bulldozers and road-building machinery that destroy nontarget trees and pollute the waterways they cut across. Denied formal rights over natural forests, it has made more sense to convert forest to agricultural use to which communities perceive they have a more certain claim, especially if they plant trees or other perennials (i.e., rubber, damar, teak, fruit trees, cinnamon, rattan). In fact, unlike the parastatal Inhutani timber companies and private companies, smallholder farmers have for decades grown trees for timber without subsidies or any other form of government assistance (e.g., surian in West Sumatra, sengon in West Java, and teak in South Sulawesi). Timber trees with other uses, like rubber in West Sumatra and damar in Lampung, encourage farmers to cultivate them in degraded areas such as alang-alang grasslands. The Inhutanis and private companies, on the other hand, have preferred to establish timber plantations by replacing natural forests (logged-over but capable of recovery).

Community-Based Natural Resource Management

Village communities generally have a more complete knowledge of land use within their areas than any government officials or databases. Long-established community-based systems of natural resource management are common, although over the years they have been eroded by top-down interventions in village boundaries and administration "justified" by UU 5/1979. Other strains on traditional systems of land use have been government-approved forest concessions, timber plantations, estate crop schemes, transmigration schemes, and mines. These have reduced the land accessible to villagers and increased pressures on their remaining land; denying local people adequate rights of access and management of forest areas has further disrupted community-based resource management. Nonetheless, village communities (often unknowingly and unacknowledged by government) support a range of national development programs related to sustainable natural resource management. Following are some examples.

- **Fire Management:** A traditional system of fines and penalties is imposed for the destruction of fruit and rubber trees destroyed by fire that escapes from poorly managed burn sites being cleared for rice cultivation (e.g., Belaban Ella, Nanga Pinoh, and Sintang in West Kalimantan; Guguk and Bangko in Jambi). Fines are set according to tree variety and age, and they vary over time according to changing economic conditions.

- **Sustainable Resource Harvesting:** Cutting trees that are too small is prohibited. Among the Kanayatn Dayak (West Kalimantan), for instance, trees less than seven hand spans (*kilan*) in girth may not be cut in hill forests is prohibited. This corresponds approximately to the 50 cm dbh (diameter at breast height) limit of the Indonesian Selective Logging and Planting System. Similarly, in South Aceh, customary rules prohibit the use of nets that would catch too many fish in river estuaries or along the coast.

- **Reducing Illegal Logging:** Some village communities have chased away illegal loggers when they believe they have the legitimacy to do so because the forestland is perceived as being formally theirs. Local guardians of a traditional forest area in the village of Desa Baru Pangkalan bordering Kerinci National Park (Jambi), recognized by a *bupati* decree in 1993, for instance, have prevented illegal loggers from removing the wood they cut, in turn reducing the incidence of illegal logging.

- **Conserving Natural Forests:** Among the various land uses recognized by many village communities (discussed later in this section) are natural forest areas to be left as such for the foreseeable future, allowing minimal extraction of useful products, usually under some sort of traditional system of approval by village elders (e.g., Kampung Galao of the Iban Dayak, Putussibau [West Kalimantan] or Hutan Cadangan of the Depati [Marga] in Jambi). The possibility of some future conversion of part of these areas remains, but this allows an ecological pause during which time local communities could be persuaded to emphasize conservation. Incentives might include payments for ecological services to downstream and global stakeholders (cf. funds from rattan ecolabeling, carbon offsets, even debt for nature swaps).

- **Spatial Planning:** Villagers generally have a better understanding of land and water use types and allocation within their village areas than any current government agency. Land-use categories recognized and managed through long-established systems of village governance include (a) natural forests kept as strategic reserves, as wildlife habitats, and as safeguards against degradation of water systems (especially springs) or sacred areas; (b) shifting cultivation with its agriculture and forest cycles; (c) agroforestry and tree crop areas; and (d) irrigated rice land as well as settlement areas and house gardens.

Assisted by skilled NGOs in many provinces across Indonesia, villages have been able to produce maps that demarcate village boundaries and land use within those boundaries, gaining agreement with surrounding villages of different religious and ethnic backgrounds. Participatory village mapping has been supported by the NGO Pancur Kasih in West Kalimantan, where adjacent Muslim Melayu and Christian Dayak communities have formalized generally agreed upon boundaries between their villages (including negotiating agreement over conflict zones). Similar mutual agreements have been obtained between Dayak and Maduran settlements. County leaders have in some cases approved such village maps, arguing they show better land-use detail than previous official maps.

Village Empowerment and Adat

Through village empowerment, sectoral departments—with the best interests of their sectors and social welfare in mind—could enhance national oversight of sectoral management by regency government. For example, the MoF frets over the risk of decentralized forest resource management leading to a proliferation of small concessions ostensibly managed by cooperatives or customary (*adat*) institutions, which are in fact created by business interests. This problem argues for a participatory process (currently lacking) in the granting of forest management licenses involving village government (preferably in line with UU 22/1999).

Village communities will be the best judges of whether the candidate cooperative or customary community holder of a forest management license in their area is truly local and supportive of village development. Similarly, approvals for formal customary forest management should involve greater community participation than is suggested in *Peraturan Menteri Negara Agraria/Kepala Badan Pertanahan Nasional Nomor* 5/1999 (Ministerial Decree of State Minister of Agrarian Affairs/Head of National Land Agency 5/1999 on the Resolution of Traditional Rights Conflicts), Forest Law 41, and the draft Government Regulation on Customary Forest Management. Each policy outlines a top-down process for deciding whether local custom (*adat*) is alive or not. Given the entrenched bureaucratic mindsets (MoFEC 2000), reliance on interdepartmental teams (which purport to include local community representation) to decide whether *adat* is viable in a particular area is questionable. Villagers themselves are better placed to decide what customary institutions should be given formal authority over natural resource management. Customary institutions should then be able to develop and adapt to meet local needs. Top-down empowerment runs the risk of favoring the well-connected elite rather than majority choice. It also imposes rigidities demanded by an inevitably bureaucratic process of defining, codifying, and fixing *adat*, thereby denying its inherently adaptable nature. Such bureaucratic processes could deleteriously require that various officials be involved in deciding whether any future changes, like the adjustment of fines in line with evolving economic conditions, should be allowed. The same issue applies to formal recognition of existing traditional institutions for management of agricultural and fisheries resources at the village level.

Village community resourcefulness is not restricted to natural resource management. Where government programs have failed to deliver essential services, villages have strived to make do as best they can. For example, in a village in West Java, local people gave up requesting a bridge to their village and funded its construction themselves, thereafter levying a well-managed toll (Haeruman 2000). The list of village community ingenuity is surely endless. The point is not to create a romantic notion about village life. Villages are not entirely self-reliant or always right in their dealings with higher levels of government; nor is village life necessarily idyllic. After all, many villagers move to towns for better employment opportunities and services. The point is that village communities can and should be equal players in the development of decentralized governance, above all in exerting pressure on regency governments to behave responsibly.

Conclusion

Village communities should (a) be entrusted with their own representational governance (building from long-established forms of governance, strengthened by implementation of the intent of UU 22/1999) and (b) be key instruments of regency government accountability, discouraging misgovernment and encouraging appropriate participatory governance (to reduce the likelihood of being called to painful and public account).

Will national government have the vision to realize this and act upon it through appropriate policy development, including workable mechanisms for access of village communities to central government if their local government fails them? Are they to be considered as 65,000 allies or 65,000 threats? Both national and regional governments remain wary of empowering villagers in the spirit of UU 22/1999. Will the opportunity for village-driven accountability be seized, or will political opportunism or bureaucratic inertia or both result in a continuation of the status quo ante, whether or not it is displaced from the center to the regencies? Perhaps lip service to the principle will be as subtle as the difference between *memberdayakan* (to empower) and *memperdayakan* (to take advantage of). Time is running out.

Village-driven accountability of local government, clearly stipulated and upheld by national policy, could build trust and ultimately forge closer ties between the national government and Indonesia's villages—the rural backbone of the nation—while discouraging regency government decisionmaking that negatively affects the village community's livelihoods (especially those of the poor) and the natural resources they depend on. A sense of national unity should also result from these developments. Livelihoods, not the politics of regional separation and national disintegration, matter most to the vast majority of village communities. Strengthening of village democracy and village-driven accountability go hand in hand. They represent an opportunity for encouraging better local government, allowing a diversity of good village governance to flourish within and nurture national unity, in short, to bring Indonesia closer to the ideal of *Bhinneka Tunggal Ika*—Unity in Diversity.

Endnotes

1. In August 2000, there was significant discussion about whether, in fact, decentralization would be focused on regency government (as stipulated in UU 22/1999) or whether greater emphasis would be placed on a role for provincial government. Since then, the

regencies have appeared to be in the ascendancy. Regardless of the degree of devolution to the regency level, the core argument for greater accountability at that level to local communities and the role that village communities can play remain the same.

2. Local government might justifiably reply that such short-sighted and elitist approaches to natural resource management have been one of the principal shortcomings of overly centralized decisionmaking.

3. As pointed out by Owen (1999), there are three fundamental determinants of successful decentralization—accountability, accountability, and accountability.

4. Accountability is usually mentioned in decentralization documents but not as one of the foremost considerations. When mentioned, it is generally said to be important but then "left hanging" without clear statements of how it might work.

5. *Tanggung gugat sosial* might best convey the idea of public accountability (Siscawati 2000).

6. I am using MoF uniformly here, although it was for a time (late 1999 to late 2000) called Ministry of Forestry and Estate Crops (MoFEC).

7. *Preman* (criminals) were convenient allies when, in the wake of UU 5/1979, the government wanted to ensure that traditional forms of local governance did not survive to challenge any of the tenets of the New Order. I observed one of many such instances in 1986. The head of the village of Bumi Agung in Lahat Regency, South Sumatra, was a notorious armed highwayman who had held up convoys of trucks laden with coffee bound for Palembang until halted by an embarrassingly placed bullet, which in no way stopped him from subsequently being appointed as village headman. The *Pasirah* (respected traditional leader) was ignored, so too the traditional grouping of Marga (villages) for which the *Pasirah* had been responsible. The new county boundary was designed to cut across the *Marga*. The *Pasirah* was warned in no uncertain terms to stay out of village administration.

8. These are hunter–gatherer groups in Kalimantan and Sumatra, respectively.

9. One way to achieve this would be for the bupati's office or a regional government registration agency to simply stamp the petition with a submission date. If unresolved within a specified time period, the bearers of the petition would then have the right to bring the matter directly to their regional representative.

References

Bennett, C.P.A.. 2000b. *Decentralisation and Domestic Trade: Divisive Threats to Intra- and Inter-Regional Trade in Indonesia.* Working paper. Development Planning Assistance, Sub-Project: SP-81 Natural Resource Management Policy under Decentralisation, Bappenas—Hickling (CIDA). Draft. July 11.

———. 2000b. *Opposition to Decentralisation of Forest Resource Management in Indonesia—Sowing the Seeds of Future Conflict.* Working paper. Development Planning Assistance, Sub-Project: SP-81 Natural Resource Management Policy under Decentralisation, Bappenas—Hickling (CIDA). Draft. June 25.

Crook, R.C., and S. Sverrisson. 1999. *To What Extent Can Decentralised Forms of Government Enhance the Development of Pro-poor Policies and Improve Poverty-alleviation Outcomes?* Unpublished manuscript.

DCM (Donor Coordination Meeting). 2000. *Capacity Building Needs Assessment for Local Governments and Legislatures—Status, Interim Findings.* Jakarta, Indonesia: DCM.

DFID (Department for International Development). 2000. *Environmental Sustainability and Eliminating Poverty. Strategies for Achieving International Development Targets.* Consultation document. London: DFID.

Frerks, G., and J.M. Otto. 1996. *Decentralization and Development: A Review of Development Administration Literature.* Van Vollenhoven Institute Publication Series, Research Report 96/2. Leiden, The Netherlands: Van Vollenhoven Institute for Law and Administration in Non-Western Countries.

Haeruman, H. 2000. Personal communication with the author, May 2000.

Indonesian Observer. 2000. E. Nusa Tenggara Governors Implicated in Sandalwood Destruction. July. Cit. joyo@aol.com.

The Jakarta Post. 2000a. Experts: Regions unprepared for regional autonomy. August 2.

———. 2000b. Workshop questions Indonesia's autonomy laws. From the online archive, July 18, 2000.

MoFEC (Ministry of Forestry and Estate Crops). 2000. *Gugus Tugas Kelembagaan Kehutanan dalam Rangka Desentralisasi.* Report on work from December 1999 to February 2000. Jakarta, Indonesia: MoFEC.

Moore, M., and J. Putzel. 1999. *Politics and Poverty. Background Paper for the World Development Report 2000/1.* Unpublished manuscript.

Owen, P. 1999. Input to inter-donor discussions on decentralisation, Aryaduta Hotel, Jakarta, August.

———. 2000. From the webpage at <http://www.surabayadomain.com>. Posting on e-mail group EAPINDEC%WORLDBANK@worldbank.org. Cit. B. Hofman.

Pedoman Rakyat. 2000. *Lelang Danau, Pemda Diminta Memihak Rakyat Kecil (Lake Auction, PEMDA Asked to Side with Small-scale Producers).* Pedoman Rakyat (Sultan/pr), No. 143, Th ke-54. Ujung Pandang.

Siscawati, M. 2000. Personal communication with the author, July 2000.

Tim Tujuh. 1999. *Bahan masukan untuk pertemuan-2 informal tentang desentralisasi pengelolaan sumber daya hutan oleh masyarakat adat.* Version No. 5. November 9. Jakarta, Indonesia: DFID Forest Field Management.

Treisman, D. 2000. *Decentralisation and Corruption: Why are Federal States Perceived to be More Corrupt?* Paper for annual meeting of American Political Science. September 1999.

U.S. Embassy in Jakarta. 2000. IMI: Joint Chambers of Commerce Meeting with Minister of Regional Autonomy Rya'as Rasyid. *Recent Economic Reports,* July 21, 2000.

Annex 3–1: On the Regional Rush for Revenue

Source: Policy Note 01, The Regional Rush for Revenue, April 22, 2000.

Apart from the obvious implications for decentralization from regency government proposals to impose new taxes on the Newmont mining venture in North Sulawesi, there is also the question of the proper development role for regional government (with or without decentralization). The *bupati's* decision to directly manage a private fund for community development was pure New Order. More worrying is the ability of the local executive to influence the local courts. It brings to mind concerns that decentralization may substitute one king for 350 little kings. And this reminds us that, in the regional rush for revenue and the primary preoccupation of national decisionmakers with the problem of insufficient regional capacity, one critical element of successful decentralization is in danger of being left behind: the establishment of formal and informal mechanisms of accountability. In the early stages of decentralization, while local government institutions are still weak, informal mechanisms may be more effective (e.g., an open door policy at the *bupati's* office and the regional House of Representatives for public and transparent meetings with village communities dissatisfied with resource allocation decisions). Without accountability, there will be little but lip service to participatory processes for rural development.

Lest the New Order be replaced by a regional New Order, every step toward decentralization should be accompanied by corresponding and explicit increases in accountability. The nurturing of accountability, a long and difficult process going against the grain of prevailing and time-honored (though less honorable) systems of formal governance, could help to curb the excesses of devolution while motivating local government personnel to seek the capacity they need to avoid disappointing those they govern.

Accountability is indeed referred to in many official documents and papers, but it has often featured less prominently in the rhetoric of decentralization. Recognition of bottom-up village governance as described in Regional Governance Law (UU 22/1999) and its accountability relationship to regency government could play a vital role in laying the foundations of accountability, while gaining the trust of ordinary Indonesians in the decentralization process and in the good faith of central government. Among regional and central government circles, amongst NGOs and academics, on either side of the corridors of development agencies, too few promote the paramount importance of accountability in the decentralization of natural resource management.

Annex 3–2: Strategic Policy Recommendations

Village Democracy

Issue a national policy statement clarifying that implementation of village democracy be consistent with the spirit of UU 22/1999 by allowing village communities to (a) elect whomsoever they wish to village leadership or the village council without preconditions such as educational level, and (b) decide whether to be represented or associated according to traditional forms of village governance.

Village-Driven Accountability

• Issue a government regulation for implementation of Articles 113 and 114 of UU 22/1999, which among other things (Bennett 2000a) stipulates that national government may revoke new regional government decisions and policies if

1. the allocation, management, regulation, and taxation of natural resources within village areas does not include appropriate community participation;
2. village community complaints about new decisions and policies are not adequately resolved by local government; and
3. village community complaints to central government about new decisions and policies are subsequently revealed to be well founded.

- Guidelines should be produced to outline the kinds of consultative processes that would constitute village-driven accountability. These should include the following:
  1. Clear definitions of accountability, linking the concept of *tanggung gugat* (or more appropriate terminology) with *tanggung jawab* (the explanation of the concept of public record), and
  2. Clear explanation of the concept of public record.

CHAPTER FOUR

Devolution and Indonesia's New Forestry Law

Eva Wollenberg and Hariadi Kartodihardjo

On September 14, 1999, the Indonesian People's Consultative Assembly approved a major piece of new legislation—the new forestry law.[1] This law updated the previous Basic Forestry Law of May 1967, *Undang-Undang* (UU) 5. Although healthy debate has emerged about whether the overall spirit of the law has changed, one area where there has been notable change is in the new provisions for customary communities and in the promotion of community involvement in forest management. Taken together with the *Surat Keputusan* ([SK] ministerial decree) 677 (Forestry) of October 7, 1998, the law signals a significant shift in increased state support for the devolution of forest management and forest benefits to local communities.

In this chapter we provide an analysis of the new law. Our comments focus on the institutional requirements for devolution at the ground level and the two institutions through which devolution is to be channeled according to the law, customary communities, and the cooperatives. The aim of the analysis is to suggest that before we can rely on either of these two institutions to promote devolution, there needs to be a broader base of civil society organizational capacity and systematic support within government.

Devolution is defined here as the transfer of power to subnational entities such as local government or *adat* (customary) communities. It is distinct from decentralization, which involves a transfer in the locus of action but not of power or authority. Deconcentration is a transfer in the locus of action within the same organization (Goldman 1998). In the Indonesian context and usage, devolution, decentralization, and deconcentration have specific connotations. Devolution is not commonly used. Instead, decentralization is used to refer to transfers of power, and deconcentration is used to refer to transfers of activity without increased power or authority. The term autonomy is often associated with decentralization.

As this analysis was prepared only two weeks after the law was signed, there has been little opportunity for public discussion of the law. The analysis presented here is therefore an initial interpretation. The subsequent implementing regulations will provide more detail, as will the practice of the law.[2] The comments we present here are offered therefore in the spirit of initiating debate, rather than resolving it.

We review first the content of the law and then discuss the nature of the two institutions—customary communities and cooperatives—and their suitability as the means for implementing devolution. We conclude with several suggestions for action to further strengthen devolution consistent with the principles of empowerment and equity stated by the law.

The Law

In this section, we discuss the excerpts of the law and its accompanying interpretation that pertain to customary communities and customary forest. For a more detailed understanding of the law relevant to local communities, see Annex 4–1.

Customary Communities and Forests

According to the law, "customary forest" is defined as state forest in the area of a customary community. The creation of the concept of customary forest is the single most important innovation of the new law for devolution, as it marks the first time in Indonesian legal history that a national law supports the transfer of territorial-based rights on state forestland to a customary institution.

Beyond this innovation, the capacity of the law to achieve devolution must be understood in terms of how the law enables the state to retain strategic control over these customary forests. First, the law classifies a customary forest as a state forest. The interpretation accompanying the law explains that state forestlands are those that do not have legally preexisting private rights associated with them, as allocated in the Basic Agrarian Law of 1960. The interpretation further explains that this classification is derived from the principle of the unified state[3] that makes the state the organization with authority over its citizens. These justifications are consistent with previous forest law that has historically been at odds with the agrarian law. The agrarian law allocated private agricultural lands according to the principle that cultivated lands best serve production needs when they are under the control of those managing and using them. This principle is now widely applied in local forest management (Ostrom 1998) and has been one of the driving forces behind devolution policies in other countries (Lynch and Talbott 1995). Furthermore, many customary "forests" are in fact cyclical agricultural and horticultural systems. These lands might have qualified for registration as agricultural land in the 1960s had swidden agriculture then been better understood.

A second way in which the new forestry law ensures that the state maintains strategic control is that it gives the state the power to recognize and revoke the status of "customary community," and therefore of customary forest. This power is vested in local government through regional regulations that remain to be determined and according to criteria determined by national government. According to the new law, the following criteria are used to recognize customary communities:

- The community constitutes an association.
- There is a local institution dealing with customary law.
- There is a clear area regulated by customary law.
- Legal judiciary institutions exist, and their decisions are obeyed.

Rights to customary forest are not automatic or in perpetuity in the law. They do not address more deep-seated concerns of customary communities about their rights to a place of ancestral and cultural heritage. They do not provide secure tenure. The rights given in the new law are in this way distinct from those associated with customary communities in other countries, such as the Ancestral Domain Claims in the Philippines or the indigenous *comunidades* of Mexico.

Third, the law states that customary communities' rights will be given as long as they do not conflict with national priorities. Although the need for flexibility is important, legal provisions such as these have been invoked in the past to limit customary communities' claims.

Fourth, the current definition of customary forest could be interpreted to allow the state to claim customary forest anywhere, including on private land (Kartodihardjo 1999). The law is unclear on this point, but it does suggest that compensation would be paid to those whose lands are turned over. Depending on how the law is implemented, if all customary forests were to become state forests, the law could create perverse incentives for customary communities to deforest their land to keep it out of state forest and retain control over it.

Fifth, the new law places the burden of proof on customary communities for applying for customary rights. The law is based on the premise that state control of forestland has been legitimate. This premise has been questioned, however, by customary communities who feel they still have historical claims to their land (Florus et al. 1994). Historically, customary communities controlled much of Indonesia's forestlands through customary institutions. During the Dutch period, forestlands and labor in Dutch-controlled Java and some parts of Lampung were treated as the jurisdiction of the Forestry Department (Fay et al. 2000). Customary law in areas not controlled by the Dutch was nevertheless respected as legitimate. After Independence, Indonesia's agrarian law acknowledged customary historical claims again by respecting customary areas as private land. Yet with the onset of the New Order regime and the rise of a lucrative timber industry in the Outer Islands, the state claimed forestlands as its own and customary practices lost their legitimacy. Areas assigned to logging companies were automatically made into state forest and the directorate of forestry designated about three-quarters of the country as state forestland in the mid-1970s (Fay et al. 2000). The principles and interests of the state in that period differ substantially from those that exist now and therefore bear reexamination.

Thus, the new law can be applauded for its pioneering efforts to devolve control of customary forestlands to communities. The law also gives government several avenues to maintain its own control. Who actually makes decisions about forest management will depend largely on how the law is implemented.

Rights on Customary Forests and Lands Outside Customary Forests

We can also look at the functions and use rights permitted on different types of forestlands (Table 4–1). Each tenure and function category is associated with permitted users or managers:

- State forest for conservation or protection is managed by the state.
- State forest for production is managed by private enterprise, cooperatives, or state-owned enterprise, under the supervision of the state.
- State forest with customary forest for conservation, protection, and production is managed by customary communities.
- State forest for special purposes is managed by customary communities, research centers, educational institutions, or social and religious institutions.
- Private forest for conservation, protection, and production is managed by the owner.

Table 4–1 shows that the types of uses and users permitted are very similar on customary forest to those on forests outside customary areas. The same functions are applied to customary forest as to noncustomary forestlands: protection, conservation, and production. The same types of users can apply for permission to use production forest on customary forest and noncustomary forest: individuals, cooperatives, private companies, or the state companies such as Inhutani. Notably, cooperatives can be managed by local communities, but they can do this on customary forest as well as noncustomary forests. The interpretation document suggests that communities can be given permission directly for use rights on production forest as well; however, it is not clear if this refers to any community or specifically customary communities. The status of customary forest appears to confer few new rights. Anyone with official use rights is also subject to taxation for forest products removed. The central government is responsible for determining the level and distribution of use rights.

Table 4–1 also shows that special purpose areas can be designated on both land types for religious, cultural, educational, or research purposes, and, in support of devolution, customary communities can have rights to manage these areas. Given the precedent of the special purpose designation (*Kawasan dengan Tujuan Istimewa*) for communities managing the damar agroforests in Krui, Sumatra (SK 47/1998), it is feasible that the special purpose designation could be used to extend rights to communities ineligible for customary communities status (Chapter 6).

From Table 4–1, we can see that only two sets of rights are uniquely associated with customary communities: (a) the right to use the forest for daily consumptive needs and (b) the right to undertake forest management activities according to customary rules (as long as these rules do not conflict with state laws). The new law strengthens these rights, which had been available to customary communities through decrees rather than laws.[4] SK 251/1993, which granted use rights to nontimber forest products and timber for consumptive use, is such an example. Some rights have not been actualized because they were interpreted to be in conflict with national priorities. In other cases, local people were simply not aware of or able to claim the rights.

According to the law, the most lucrative rights—those for enterprise—are to be given to cooperatives or companies. On the one hand, the availability of enterprise rights to cooperatives is a major milestone toward devolution, especially because local communities can form cooperatives. On the other hand, by relying on cooperatives, the law creates a firm division between two kinds of institutions: those for enterprise-oriented use of the forest and those for customary use rights to local communities. Presumably customary communities must form cooperatives if they want to use the forest for cash income generation (although this is not clear in the law, as communities technically may be able to receive rights directly). Looking at how institutions for local forest management have been organized in other countries (e.g., Forest Users' Groups [Nepal], Forest Protection Committees [India], Ejidos [Mexico], and Farmers' Associations [Philippines]) where the rights to income are usually integrated with subsistence rights, one might question the necessity of such a division. The burden of forming, registering, and monitoring two institutions among

Table 4–1. Forest Function, Status, and Utilization Based on UU 41/1999 on Forestry

Forest Function	Forest status		Private forest
	State forest		
	Noncustomary forest	Customary forest	
Conservation forest	This forest is to be used for biodiversity conservation.Other uses are possible, except in nature reserves, core zones, and forest zones in national parks (Article 24).	Customary communities can use for conservation and protection purposes where these uses do not conflict with the designated functions and law (Article 37).	The owner can use the forest for conservation and protection purposes as long as these uses do not conflict with the designated functions (Article 36)
Protection forest	Protection forest is to be used for environmental services and nontimber forest products (NTFP) extraction (Article 26).		If changed to state forest, the government will compensate owners (Article 36).
Production forest	Production forest is to be used for environmental services, timber, and NTFP extraction (Article 28).	Customary communities can use the customary forest for daily subsistence purposes (Article 67). Customary communities can undertake other uses as long as these uses do not conflict with the designated function and law (Article 37). If forest products are traded, the customary community must pay forest taxes (Article 37)	Forest use is managed by the owner.
Special purpose forest	Special purpose forest is to be used for research, development, education, training, religious, or cultural functions (Article 8).	Special purpose forests are not necessarily customary forests, but customary communities can manage forest with special purpose (Article 34).	Not specified
Urban forest	This includes public urban areas designated as forest by the government (Article 9).	Not relevant	Not relevant

Table 4–1. *Continued.*

Use options	
Permitted enterprise use of the area	**Forest conversion**
None	Conservation forest cannot be converted to nonforestry use.
None	Protection forest can be converted to nonforestry use (e.g., mining).
Permitted enterprise use can be granted to— •Individuals •Cooperatives •Private companies •State companies •BUMN, BUMD (*Badan Usaha Milik Negara/Daerah*)	Production forest can be converted to nonforestry use (e.g., mining).
Not specified	Not specified
Not specified	Not specified

local communities, let alone ensuring coordination between the two, may prove to be ambitious. The administrative burden of dealing with one local institution alone has proven to be sufficiently challenging in most countries (Fox 1993).

The degree of genuine devolution will depend on the extent that cooperatives are formed primarily by local communities and the extent that they primarily benefit these communities. The current public impression of cooperatives would need to be more positive for the cooperatives to be considered credible and legitimate institutions for devolution. According to the vision of cooperatives promoted during this reform period, many different groups, including the employees of timber companies, can form local cooperatives. The implementing regulations of the new law should provide guarantees that local cooperatives represent or benefit local communities. The current law further stipulates that government and private companies should work with local cooperatives; this is with the intention of distributing forest benefits to local communities. The nature of this work, however, is not specified, other than that the companies should assist local cooperatives to become more professional. There is no provision that suggests the form of the collaboration or how it would increase material benefits to local communities. Anecdotal evidence from a number of sites in Kalimantan between 1999 and February 2001 indicates that the collaboration has been used by some concessionaires at the expense of communities.

Aside from the rights associated with customary forests, customary communities, and cooperatives, the law also includes the following progressive provisions about people in forest management that could be supportive of customary communities:

- Determination of the forest area is to take into account local culture, economy, and institutions (including customary institutions).
- Monitoring is the responsibility of government, individuals, and the community.
- Society has the right to know about forest management and to monitor it.
- If communities suffer pollution or deforestation that affects their lives, government forest agencies are responsible to act on behalf of the communities' needs.
- Nongovernmental organizations (NGOs) can support local people's efforts in reforestation or forest rehabilitation (not in forest management).
- A forestry watch forum composed of central government and local government partners is to work to formulate and manage the perceptions, aspirations, and innovations of communities as input to forest policy. Scattered throughout the law are references that suggest that forests should be managed according to principles of social equity, empowerment of customary communities, fairness, prosperity, and sustainability. Among these provisions, the creation of a forestry watch forum and the granting of permission to NGOs as support organizations are significant measures, potentially important for further strengthening devolution.

In sum, the new law potentially strengthens the rights of customary communities on forestland by creating legal entitlements for these groups on customary forests and special purpose zones. Customary communities have rights to use the forest for daily consumption needs and to manage the forest according to their customary law, as long as these laws do not conflict with national law. Through cooperatives, customary communities as well as other groups can now acquire enterprise management rights. The state retains hegemony in ways that enable little to change from the current distribution of control between the center and local managers.

Despite this strengthening and partial expansion of rights, vagueness in some parts of the law could work against the transfer of authority to customary communities. For example, who has priority rights of enterprise on customary forests? Use rights on customary forests are presently not exclusive. Without exclusive rights, there is always insecurity and the risk of competition with (and losing to) more powerful groups.

Similarly, what are the permitted uses of customary forest? If swidden farming is the major source of livelihood and means of meeting daily needs, yet forest burning is prohibited by law, how will customary communities meet their needs? Is it reasonable to assume that these groups should not practice swidden, especially when it is an integral and sustainable part of their economy and culture? To the extent that permitted functions and uses of customary forest reflect the functions and land uses required by customary communities, the more they will fulfill these communities' needs and provide incentives for good management. Yet the functions and uses in government guidelines reflect an approach to management very different in style and purpose from that of customary communities. The scale and distribution of management units in customary forests tend to be smaller and determined by more limited transport networks. Local people are more likely to shift land uses in customary forest according to changes in their needs and external conditions like markets, rather than assign permanent land uses to fixed units of land (Leach and Fairhead 1993). Customary forest is likely to have a higher mix of planted trees and modified wildlife populations and be managed for more diverse products. If customary forest is retained as state land, serious adaptation of past management regimes will be required to accommodate these very different systems.

The institutional relationships among the customary communities, cooperatives, and the government or private companies required to work with the cooperatives also need further clarification. Where all three exist, how will decisions be made equitably and fairly? Can neutral power relations and equitable distribution of benefits exist under such arrangements (Edmunds and Wollenberg 2001)? Despite the intentions of the law, will the relationship among these groups develop to be one of competition for scarce financial or natural resources? What elements of accountability exist on the part of the cooperatives and companies to the customary communities?

As with any good law, there is much room for interpretation in the new Forestry Law of 1999. The degree to which devolution occurs to customary communities will depend on how the law is implemented. In the next section, we discuss the institutional factors that will play a major role in influencing this implementation.

The Role of Local Institutions

The viability of the law's provisions for devolution to customary communities should be stronger to the extent that there are correspondingly strong local institutions to support the law. Institutional support from local civil society is necessary for implementation. Institutional support across sectors of civil society (e.g., the media, universities) and government can provide the checks and balances necessary to guard the intent of the law. Here we highlight the needs for institutional development in customary communities and cooperatives to foster more robust devolution.

Customary Communities

Just as local governments can be highly variable, customary communities similarly vary in the strength of their leadership, quality of decisionmaking, and extent of democratic practice (see Chapter 5). The criteria for selecting legally recognized customary communities should identify the stronger among these groups. The law could, however, be strengthened to address possible conflicts of interest within customary communities.

For example, customary leaders in many communities are currently struggling with how to position their identity vis-à-vis government and to ensure their legitimacy among a range of constituencies. Many customary leaders serve as village government leaders and as such are members of Golkar, the party of Soeharto's ousted New Order government. Others are appointed as customary leaders within existing government apparatuses that have little or nothing to do with traditional customary leadership. Others have developed alliances with local timber or mining companies, police, or traders and received associated demonstrations of gratitude from these groups. Community members usually begrudge these arrangements and are consequently not always sure whose interests their leader represents. Also, in many communities, there has been a shift in the factors influencing who holds power in the community. Inherited power and traditional titles are becoming less important determinants of influence compared with education and economic success.

Customary systems are not necessarily more democratic, equitable, or transparent than many local governments. There are ample instances of hierarchical decisionmaking, feudal-style tribute payments, and gender inequities in customary societies around the world (Ribot 1999). Conflict across neighboring areas with different customary laws is also common. If devolution is to be meaningful to a significant proportion of the population, not just to the elite of local communities, is there a responsibility on the part of the government to promote democratic values among these groups, even if they are not strictly consistent with traditional practice? This is a question that is not easily answered, but it does suggest the need to give more attention to the "living" and fluid nature of customary systems.

Cooperatives

Cooperatives in Indonesia have not historically been linked to forest management or customary communities' needs. This may change if the government's vision of cooperatives as the unit of economic organization at the village level is successfully implemented over the next several years. In September 1999, we predicted that problems would persist, and indeed they have. In many villages, there is no cooperative and there never has been. Few people at the village level know how to create a cooperative, let alone know what a cooperative's function is supposed to be. (Where cooperatives do exist, the official state cooperatives have had a less than positive reputation for effectiveness.) There is evidence from some communities in East Kalimantan that the ministerial decree for community forestry (SK 677/1998) is being used by concessionaires to form cooperatives to organize labor for timber harvesting, and the number of such reports has blossomed over the past two years. Unless there is better legal literacy among communities about the functions of the new cooperatives and a shared understanding about these functions among different stakeholders, their uses are liable to be misinterpreted to the detriment of local communities.

As noted earlier in this chapter, one potential for misuse of cooperatives is that they can be formed by anyone. There is no indication of how the people organized in cooperatives will relate to forest user groups, be accountable to local communities, or work collaboratively with customary institutions. Also, the cooperatives' orientation is enterprise, not forest management. Cooperatives may not be well placed to make balanced decisions about the trade-offs between profitability and sustainable management. We know that in some other countries, cooperatives have had mixed success in forest management (Campbell 1999).

Devolution: From Policy to Practice

So what do these attributes of the law and the local institutions imply for the practice of devolution? Although more precise implications will only become clear after the implementing regulations are issued, according to the new law, the territorial rights to customary forest are not exclusively tied to any use or beneficiary. Customary systems and cooperatives will be empowered to manage forests, but they will need stronger checks and balances to ensure their congruence with the interests of a broad range of local community members and accountability to them. Because of the potential for government intervention to maintain control over customary forests, the degree of devolution achieved will depend largely on the vision and values of the government officials responsible for the implementation of the law.

With the decentralization of implementing regulations about what constitutes a customary forest, implementation will vary by region and not necessarily in consistent ways. In provinces where timber values are still high, we can expect to see higher levels of red tape, more state-driven regulation, and more burdensome criteria for recognizing customary forest in efforts to reduce the claims of customary communities. We can also expect higher frequencies of permission granted for enterprise use of customary forest by noncustomary groups. Similarly, the organizational capacities and influence of customary communities themselves vary tremendously by region. A customary group in Papua is less likely to even know about the rights associated with the new law, compared with, say, farmers in Lampung. Valuable forests in Kalimantan, Sumatra, and Papua for instance are thus likely to stay in the hands of noncustomary groups, unless customary groups are well organized and probably assisted by third parties. What provisions can the implementing regulations make to protect the intent of the law?

These conditions point to critical uncertainties in the law that could be improved to achieve devolution. The approach to devolution in the new law raises general questions about the key points of legal leverage for achieving real transfers of authority in countries such as Indonesia, where local people must compete with government and private industry for valuable forest resources. Under these circumstances, it would appear that the real benefits of a devolution law are the ability to create legal possibilities for communities to manage with more certainty, to gain secure access to valuable economic benefits, and to overcome conflicts with more powerful groups. The existing law takes steps in this direction. The implementing regulations could help strengthen this aspect of the law to some extent. At present, however, rights to customary forest can be revoked by the government, economic benefits are de-linked from customary institutions, and there are no protections for communities to pursue their interests if these conflict with those of more powerful people. As it is difficult for policy to control all these things on the ground anyway, especially under frontier forest conditions (Kaimowitz et al. forthcoming), there is still the opportunity for the implementing regulations and complementary policies to strengthen both government's and civil institutions' capacity to implement the devolution aspects of the current law.

The delegitimation of customary law under the past law raises the question of how implementation of the new law will effectively recognize, strengthen, and legitimize existing customary systems of management. Whether customary institutions continue to manage forests sustainably under current pressures is an open question that can be assessed on a site-by-site basis. We know customary management is strong in some places (Michon and de Foresta 1995; Lubis 1996; Eghenter and Sellato 1999), and in others it has been displaced by state management (Padoch and Peluso 1996). In yet others, the concept of customary rights has been used to regain control over resources (Zerner 1994). Will the new forestry law allow recognition and empowerment of existing customary systems, or will it seek to bring these lands under a regime of state forest management that destroys their meaning and effectiveness? The existing law may burden the customary systems through additional registration, regulations, and reporting that weaken these systems. Checks must be put in place to ensure that opportunists do not seek to take advantage of the law to invent customary systems or take control over legitimate customary areas.

The challenge is therefore how to ensure the legitimacy of customary forest and to create the local institutional capacities, transparency, and checks and balances that increase the security of customary communities' rights and better channel benefits to them. Measures in the current law such as the forestry watch forum and the role of NGOs as support organizations make important strides in this direction. Future policymakers will have to work hard to foster an era that embraces local diversity and innovation. Devolution will work better to the extent that customary management systems are themselves treated as valuable resources and given the security to develop their own initiatives. This is not to say that local communities should be given rein to destroy forests. On the contrary, there need to be systems for coordination among stakeholders to establish management objectives and monitor progress. But such coordination requires strong local institutions and a clear and secure distribution of rights across groups.

Five actions—by a mix of actors—are therefore required to enhance the effect of the current law on devolution. All involve strengthening civil society at the ground level and upward, as well as improving the relationship between civil society and the state.

- Build local institutional capacities, especially to improve the responsiveness and accountability of cooperatives, customary institutions, and other local forest management entities to the interests of customary communities and to make them more democratic in creating a shared agenda toward sustainable forest management—requiring bottom-up efforts by communities, NGOs, and civil society at large.

- Improve the security of rights to customary communities to enable local innovation and incentives for sustainable management over the long term—a legislative and judicial issue.
- Enhance information flows and accountability regarding equity and sustainable management by relying more on civil society organizations, including the media and NGOs.
- Develop interinstitutional arrangements that protect the priority rights of customary communities to customary forest, with checks through civil society organizations for protecting customary communities' interests against those of more powerful groups.
- Work out institutional arrangements by which valuable economic benefits can go directly to customary communities.

These measures rely on a widespread concern—among communities, NGOs, the government, donors—of empowering local communities. They require cooperation among a variety of stakeholders. Each suggested action, by itself a challenge, would strengthen devolution in the new law to help it meet its own intended purpose of giving rights to customary communities to "achieve empowerment within the context of improving their prosperity" (Article 67). The new forestry law sets out an impressive vision for the role of communities, especially customary communities. The task now for civil society and government is how to ensure that the vision is achieved.

Acknowledgments

We are grateful to Martua Sirait, Chip Fay, Mark Poffenberger, Jeff Campbell, Ida Aju Pradnja Resosudarmo, Carol J. Pierce Colfer, Bambang Soekartiko, Rachel Wrangham, David Edmunds, and David Kaimowitz for lively discussions about past and current policy developments, as well as their helpful contributions to this analysis.

Endnotes

1. *Rancangan Undang-Undang* 41/1999 *Republik Indonesia Tentang Kehutanan.* The law was signed by President Habibie on September 30, 1999.

2. When this chapter was written (February 2001), no implementing regulations had been issued related to customary communities and their rights on forestland. As of January 1, 2001, the regency governments now have the right to issue their own implementing regulations.

3. Negara Kesatuan Republik Indonesia.

4. A law is a more permanent legal instrument than a decree, whereas the latter is tied to the individual making the decree.

References

Campbell, J. 1999. Personal communication with the authors, April 10, 1999.

Edmunds, D., and E. Wollenberg. 2001. Multistakeholder negotiations and disadvantaged groups of people. *International Journal of Agricultural Resources, Governance, and Ecology* 32(2):231–53.

Eghenter, C., and B. Sellato (eds.) 1999. *Kebudayaan dan Pelestarian Alam*. Jakarta, Indonesia: World Wide Fund for Nature.

Fay, C., M. Sirait, and A. Kusworo. 2000. *Getting the boundaries right: Indonesia's urgent need to redefine its forest estate*. Paper presented at the 8th Conference of the International Association for the Study of Common Property. May 2000, Bloomington, IN.

Florus, P., S. Djuweng, J. Bamba, and N. Andasputra (eds.). 1994. *Kebudayaan Dayak, Aktualisasi dan Transformasi*. Jakarta, Indonesia: LP3ES-Institute of Dayakology Research and Development and PT Gramedia Widiasarana.

Fox, J. (ed.). 1993. *Legal Frameworks for Forest Management in Asia: Case Studies of Community State Relations*. Occasional paper no. 16. Honolulu, HI: East–West Center.

Goldman, I. 1998. Decentralization and sustainable rural livelihoods. In *Sustainable Rural Livelihoods: What Contribution Can We Make?*, edited by D. Carney. London: Department of International Development, 39–51.

Kaimowitz, D., A. Faune, and R. Mendoza. Forthcoming. Your biosphere is my backyard. The story of Bosawas in Nicaragua. Manuscript submitted to the *Journal of Environmental History*.

Kartodihardjo, H.1999. *Analisa substansi UU Kehutanan*. Posted on Forum Komunikasi Kehutanan Masyarakat listserv. September 17.

Leach, M., and J. Fairhead. 1993. Whose social forestry and why? People trees and managed continuity in Guinea's forest-savanna landscape mosaic. *Zeitschrift fur Wirtschaftgeographin* 37(2): 86–101.

Lubis, Z. 1996. *Repong Damar: Kajian Tentang Proses Pengambilan Keputusan Dalam Pengelolaan Lahan Hutan di Pesisir Krui, Lampung Barat*. Master's thesis. Jakarta, Indonesia: Universitas Indonesia.

Lynch, O., and K. Talbott (eds.). 1995. *Balancing Acts: Community-based Forest Management and National Law in Asia and the Pacific*. New York: World Resources Institute.

Michon, G., and H. de Foresta. 1995. The Indonesian agro-forest model. In *Conserving Biodiversity Outside Protected Areas. The Role of Traditional Agro-ecosystems*, edited by P. Halladay and D. Gilmour. Gland, Switzerland: The World Conservation Union, 90–106.

Ostrom, E. 1998. *Self-Governance and Forest Resources*. Center for International Forestry Research (CIFOR) occasional paper no. 20. Bogor, Indonesia: CIFOR.

Padoch, C., and N. Peluso. 1996. *Borneo in Transition. People, Forests, Conservation and Development*. New York: Oxford University Press.

Ribot, J. 1999. Decentralization, participation and accountability in Sahelian Forestry: Legal instruments of political administrative control. *Africa* 69(1): 23–65.

Zerner, C. 1994. Through a green lens: The construction of customary environmental law and community in Indonesia's Maluku Islands. *Law and Society Review* 28(5): 1079–122.

Annex 4–1

Summary of Sections in the 1999 Forestry Law Pertaining to Local and Customary Communities

Translated by Diah Y. Raharjo of the Ford Foundation,
September 1999

Chapters and Articles in the 1999 Forestry Law Pertaining to Local and Customary Communities

1. Considering

(a) that forests, as the Almighty God's blessing and mandate bestowed upon the Indonesian nation, are assets that are controlled by the state and provide multifarious benefits for mankind, and for that we must give thanks to God, and manage them and make use of them in an optimal manner, and ensure that they are pre served for the greater good of the people, for both present and future generations

Elucidation:
The control of forests by the state does not constitute ownership; rather, that the state confers upon the government the authority to regulate and manage all that pertains to forests, forest zones, and forest products; to designate forest zones or to change the status of forest zones; to regulate and stipulate the legal relationship between people and forests or forest zones or forest products; and to regulate lawmaking concerning forests. The government has the authority to grant permits and rights to other parties to operate in the forestry sector.

(c) that sustainable and globally-oriented management of forests must accommodate the aspirations and the participation of communities, customs, and culture, as well as community value systems that are based on national legal norms.

Elucidation of Paragraph IV:
Forest resources play a major part in [providing for continued] availability of forest for industrial raw materials, sources of income, and job creation. Forest products are commodities that can be converted into processed goods to give added value and to open up opportunities for employment and enterprise. Such processing of forest products must not cause damage to the forests as a source of industrial raw materials. To ensure a constant balance between the capacity to supply raw materials and the processing industries, the regulation, guidance, and development of forest product primary processing industries shall be arranged by the minister of forestry. [The definition of] forest exploitation is not restricted to the production of wood and nonwood products; but it must be extended to [include] other types of exploitation such as germ plasm and environmental services, in order to optimize forest benefits.

Elucidation of Paragraph VII:
In anticipation of the development of community aspirations, in this law forests in Indonesia are classified into state forest and private forest. State forest is defined as forests on lands that are not encumbered with land titles based on UU 5/1960, including forests previously controlled by customary communities that are referred to as hutan ulayat, hutan marga, or other types of forest. The inclusion of forests controlled by customary communities in the definition of

state forest is a consequence of the state's right to control and manage as the organization of authority over the people under the principle of the Unitary State of the Republic of Indonesia. Customary communities, therefore, insofar as they actually exist and are recognized as such, can manage forests and harvest forest products. Private forest, meanwhile, is forest on land that is encumbered with land titles in accordance with the provisions of UU 5/1960 regarding Basic Agrarian Regulations, such as right of ownership, right of exploitation, and right of use.

Elucidation of Paragraph VIII:
In respect of deriving maximal benefit from forests and forest zones for the prosperity of the communities, in principle all forests and forest zones can be exploited by taking into account their nature, characteristics, and vulnerability, without allowing their primary function to be altered. The exploitation of forests and forest zones must be reconciled with their primary functions, that is, conservation, protection, and production. To ensure that primary forest functions and forest conditions are maintained, rehabilitation activities such as land and forest reclamation are also carried out, with the objective not only of restoring the quality of the forest but also to empower and improve the welfare of the community, such that community participation is the key to their success. The reconciliation of these three functions is highly dynamic, and the most important factor is to ensure that there is synergy in exploitation. The conversion of natural forest that is still productive into plantation forest must as far as possible be avoided if the quality of the environment is to be protected.

Elucidation of Paragraph X :
With respect to the development of economic justice, small- and medium-scale enterprises and cooperatives shall have the widest opportunities to exploit the forests. State-owned enterprises (BUMN), local government-owned enterprises (BUMD), and Indonesian private enterprises (BUMS Indonesia) licensed to operate in the forestry sector must work together with cooperatives in local communities and gradually empower them so that they can become strong, independent, and professional cooperative enterprises on a par with other economic agents.

2. Article 1

(4) State forest is forest on lands that are not encumbered by land titles.
(6) Customary forest is state forest that lies within the zone of a community under customary law.

3. Article 4

(1) All forests in the territory of the Republic of Indonesia including the assets therein are controlled by the state for the greater good of the people.
(2) State control of forests as intended in Paragraph (1) entitles the government to:
   a. regulate and manage all matters pertaining to forests;
   b. designate certain areas as forest zones or as nonforest zones; and
   c. regulate and determine the legal relationships between people and forests, as well as regulate legal actions concerning forestry.
(3) State control of forests will uphold the rights of customary communities if they actually exist and are recognized as such, and do not conflict with national priorities.

Elucidation:
• The definition of "controlled" does not mean "owned," rather it embodies the obligations and authority in public law as set forth in Paragraph (2) Article 4 of this law.

• *The government's authority pertaining to matters that are highly important, strategic, or have national and international repercussions shall be exercised with the approval of the House of Representatives (DPR).*

4. Article 5

(1) Forest is categorized by status into:
  a. state forest
  b. private forest

(2) State forest as intended in Paragraph (1a) can also be customary forest.

(3) The government stipulates the status of forests as intended in Paragraph (1) and Paragraph (2); and customary forest is designated if the customary community concerned still exists and is recognized as such.

(4) If the customary community no longer exists, the right to manage the customary forest reverts to the government.

Elucidation of the Article:

• *State forest may take the form of customary forest, that is state forest of which the management is delegated to customary communities. This customary law was formerly referred to as hutan ulayat, hutan marga, hutan pertuanan, or various other terms.*

• *Forests managed by customary communities are included in the definition of state forest as a consequence of the state's right of control as the organization of authority over the people at the highest level and the principles of the Unitary State of the Republic of Indonesia. The inclusion of customary forest in the definition of state forest does not invalidate the rights of customary communities to manage forests, insofar as those customary communities actually exist and are recognized as such.*

• *State forests managed by villages and exploited for the welfare of such villages are referred to as village forests.*

• *State forests whose exploitation is aimed principally at empowering communities are referred to as community forests.*

5. Article 17

(1) Forest management districts shall be formed at the following levels:
  a. province
  b. regency/town
  c. management unit

(2) The establishment of forest management districts at management unit level shall be implemented by taking into account the characteristics of the land, forest type, forest function, watershed conditions, sociocultural conditions, the economy, and local community institutions including customary communities and government administrative boundaries.

(3) The establishment of forest management units that straddle government administrative boundaries due to forest type, conditions, and characteristics shall be specifically regulated by the minister.

Elucidation:

• *"Management unit" shall refer to the smallest unit of management of a forest that can be managed in an efficient and sustainable manner in line with its main function and designation and includes protected forest management units, production forest management units, conservation forest management units, community forest management units, customary forest management units, and watershed management units.*

- *The stipulation of management districts at management unit level must also take into account the relationship between the community and the forest, and the indigenous knowledge and aspirations of the community.*

The establishment of forest management units is based on the criteria and procedures stipulated by the minister.

6. Article 18

(1) The government determines and retains a sufficient area for forest zones and forest coverage for each watershed to optimize the environmental, social, and economic benefits for the local communities.

(2) The forest zone area that must be retained as intended in Paragraph (1) is at least 30% of the area of the watershed and/or a proportional spread.

Elucidation:

- *"Forest coverage" refers to the coverage of land by vegetation with a specified composition and density, in order to create forest functions such as micro climates, water circulation, and habitat for fauna as a forest ecosystem.*

"Optimizing the benefits" is the balancing of environmental, social, and economic benefits in a sustainable manner.

- *Given that Indonesia is a tropical country that has a high volume and intensity of rainfall in most areas and an undulating, hilly, and mountainous land profile that is susceptible to imbalances in water circulation such as floods, sedimentation, and erosion, and drought, the area of forest zones for each watershed or island is stipulated at a minimum of 30% of the land area. Henceforth, the government will stipulate the forest zone area for each province and regency/city based on biophysical conditions, climate, population, and the socioeconomic conditions of the local communities.*

7. Article 21

Forest management as intended in Paragraph (2b), Article 10, covers the following:

    a. forest plans and the formulation of forest management plans,

    b. forest exploitation and the utilization of forest zones,

    c. forest rehabilitation and reclamation, and

    d. forest protection and nature conservation.

Elucidation:

- *Forests have been entrusted to us by the Almighty God, and forest management is therefore undertaken on a moral and honorable basis for the greater good of society. Thus the implementation of each component of forest management must take into account the cultural values, aspirations, and perceptions of communities and give due attention to the rights of the people; therefore the local communities must be involved.*

- *In principle, forest management comes under the authority of the government or local government. Given the varied features of each area, and the social and environmental conditions that are closely related to forest conservation and the interests of the wider community that require specific management capabilities, the implementation of forest management in certain areas may be delegated to the BUMN (state-owned enterprises) that operate in the forestry sector, whether in the form of public utilities (Perum), departmental agencies (Perjan), or public limited companies (Persero), which are under the supervision of the minister.*

- *The actualization of sustainable forest management requires supporting institutions such as financial institutions that back forestry development, as well as research and development, education and training, and extension institutions.*

8. Article 23

Forest exploitation as intended in Article 21b is aimed at deriving the maximum benefit for the prosperity of society as a whole in an equitable and sustainable manner.

Elucidation:
Forest exploitation must be distributed equitably by widening community participation, with the result that communities are increasingly empowered.

9. Article 27

(1) Permits to exploit the zones intended in Paragraph (2) of Article 26 may be granted to:
   a. individuals
   b. cooperatives
(2) Permits to take advantage of the environmental services as intended in Article 26 Paragraph (2) may be granted to:
   a. individuals,
   b. cooperatives,
   c. Indonesian private enterprises, and
   d. state-owned enterprises or regional government-owned enterprises.
(3) Permits to harvest nonwood forest products as intended in Article 26 Paragraph (2), may be granted to :
   a. individuals
   b. cooperatives

Elucidation:
In using the permits to exploit these zones, individuals, local communities, or cooperatives can collaborate with state-owned enterprises (BUMN), regional government-owned enterprises (BUMD), or Indonesian private enterprises (BUMS).

10. Article 28

(1) Exploitation of production forest may take the form of exploitation of zones, exploitation of environmental services, exploitation of wood and nonwood forest products, and the collection of wood and nonwood forest products.
(2) Exploitation of production forest is implemented through the purchase of business permits for zone exploitation, business permits for the exploitation of environmental services, business permits for the exploitation of wood and nonwood forest products, permits for the collection of wood-based forest products, and permits for the collection of nonwood forest products.

Elucidation:
* *The exploitation of zones in production forest is implemented in order to exploit the space in such a way as to maximize environmental, social, and economic benefits, for example the cultivation of crops beneath forest stands.*
* *The exploitation of environmental services in production forest refers to all forms of enterprise that exploit the potential of environmental services without damaging or prejudicing the forest's primary function.*
* *The exploitation of forest products in production forest can take the form of natural forest and plantation forest exploitation enterprises.*
* *Plantation forest exploitation enterprises may be monoculture and/or multiple crop plantation forests.*

- *Plantation forest exploitation is carried out mainly in unproductive forest in the context of maintaining natural forest.*
- *The produce from plantation forest exploitation enterprises constitutes an asset that may be used as collateral.*
- *Permits to harvest forest products in production forest are granted for the collection of both wood and nonwood forest products, with certain restrictions on duration, area, and/or volume, with due attention to the principles of conservation and equity.*
- *Collection covers harvesting, skidding, transportation, processing, and marketing, permission for which is given for specified periods.*

11. Article 29

(1) Zone exploitation as intended in Article 28 Paragraph (2) may be granted to:
   a. individuals
   b. cooperatives
(2) Business permits for the exploitation of environmental services as intended in Article 28 Paragraph (2) may be granted to:
   a. individuals,
   b. cooperatives,
   c. Indonesian private enterprises, and
   d. state-owned enterprises or regional government-owned enterprises.
(3) Business permits for the exploitation of nonwood forest products as intended in Article 28 Paragraph (2) may be granted to:
   a. individuals,
   b. cooperatives,
   c. Indonesian private enterprises, and
   d. state-owned enterprises or regional government-owned enterprises.
(4) Business permits for the exploitation of wood-based forest products as intended in Article 28 Paragraph (2) may be granted to:
   a. individuals,
   b. cooperatives,
   c. Indonesian private enterprises, and
   d. state-owned enterprises or regional government-owned enterprises.
(5) Business permits for the collection of wood or nonwood forest products as intended in Article 28 Paragraph (2) may be granted to:
   a. individuals
   b. cooperatives

Elucidation:
Self-explanatory

12. Article 30

As part of the effort to empower the people's economy, all state-owned enterprises, regional government-owned enterprises, and Indonesian private enterprises that have business permits for the exploitation of environmental services or business permits for the exploitation of wood or nonwood forest products are required to collaborate with local community cooperatives.

Elucidation:
- *Collaboration with local community cooperatives is intended to ensure that the communities in and around the forest derive and enjoy forest benefits directly, with the result that they can improve their welfare and quality of life, and at the same time be able to grow the*

trees they own. *Under such collaboration indigenous knowledge and principal values, which are rooted in community value systems, can be made into mutually agreed rules.*
• *The compulsory cooperation between BUMN, BUMD, and Indonesian BUMS is aimed at empowering local community cooperatives so that they will eventually become strong, independent, and professional.*
• *If local community cooperatives have not been established, the BUMN, BUMD, and Indonesian BUMS shall urge the immediate establishment of such.*

13. Article 34
The management of forest zones for specific purposes as intended in Article 8 may be granted to:
    a. customary communities,
    b. educational institutions,
    c. research institutions, and
    d. social and religious institutions.

Elucidation:
The management of forest zones for specific purposes is management with specified objectives such as research and development, education and training, and for sociocultural purposes and for the application of indigenous technology. The implementation thereof must take into account the developmental history of communities and indigenous institutions, and the conservation and care of the ecosystem.

14. Article 35
    (1) All holders of forest exploitation permits as intended in Article 27 and Article 29 shall be charged fees for the permits, commission and reforestation, and performance guarantee funds.
    (2) All holders of forest exploitation permits as intended in Article 27 and Article 29 must provide investment funds to finance forest conservation.
    (3) Holders of permits to collect forest products as intended in Article 27 and Article 29 shall only be charged commission.
    (4) The further provisions intended in Paragraph (1), Paragraph (2), and Paragraph (3) shall be set forth in government regulations.

Elucidation:
• *Forest exploitation permit fee is the levy imposed on forest exploitation permit holders for a specified forest zone, which is paid once upon the issue of the permit. The amount of the fee is determined by a progressive tariff according to hectarage.*
• *Resource royalty provision is the levy imposed as compensation for the intrinsic value of the forest products collected from state forests.*
• *Reforestation fund is the fund collected from holders of permits to collect forest products in the form of wood from natural forests, for reforestation and forest rehabilitation. This fund is used only to finance reforestation and rehabilitation, and activities to support such.*
• *Performance guarantee funds are funds belonging to forest exploitation permit holders, as a guarantee for the implementation of their permits, which may be liquidated by permit holders once their activities are deemed to have fulfilled the provisions concerning sustainable forest exploitation.*
• *Forest conservation investment funds are funds designated for financing all forms of activity undertaken in respect of securing forest preservation, including the costs of conservation, forest protection, and forest fire control. These funds are managed by institutions*

established jointly by the forestry sector business community and the minister. The management of these funds and the operations of these institutions are under the coordination and supervision of the minister.

15. Article 36

(1) Private forests shall be exploited by the holders of the rights to the land concerned, in line with their function.

(2) Customary forest that has protection and conservation functions may be exploited provided that this does not interfere with its functions.

Elucidation:

• *Exploitation of private forest that has protection and conservation functions shall be carried out in accordance with the provisions intended in Article 24, Article 25, and Article 26. The government shall give compensation in accordance with the prevailing legislation to forest title holders if said private forest is converted to forest zones.*

16. Article 37

(1) Customary forests shall be exploited by the customary communities concerned, in line with their function.

(2) Customary forests that have protection and conservation functions may be exploited provided that this does not interfere with their functions.

Elucidation:

Customary forests shall be subject to the same requirements as those imposed upon state forests, insofar as the products of such forests are traded.

17. Article 42

(2) Land and forest rehabilitation is implemented principally through a participatory approach in order to develop the potential of and empower communities.

Elucidation:
Self-explanatory

18. Article 43

(1) Everyone who owns, manages, or exploits forest that is critical or unproductive must rehabilitate the forest for protection and conservation purposes.

(2) In undertaking the rehabilitation as intended in Paragraph (1), any person may request assistance, service, and support from nongovernmental organizations, other parties, or the government.

Elucidation:
Government support may take the form of technical assistance, funds, extension, seedlings, and so on, according to requirements and the government's capacity.

19. Article 48

(5) To ensure proper forest protection, the community shall participate in forest protection measures.

Elucidation:
Self-explanatory

20. Article 50

(3) It is prohibited for anyone to:

a. work, use, or occupy forest zones illegally;

b. clear forest zones;

c. fell trees in forest zones within a radius or distance of up to:

1. 500 meters from the banks of a reservoir or lake,

2. 200 meters from the edge of a spring and from either side of a river in swamp areas,

3. 100 meters from either side of the banks of a river,

4. 50 meters from either side of the banks of a tributary,

5. 2 times the depth of a ravine from the edge of the ravine, and

6. 130 times the difference between the high water mark and the low water mark from the edge of a beach;

d. burn forest;

e. fell trees, harvest, or collect forest products in a forest without holding rights or permits from the competent authority;

f. accept, buy, sell, receive in exchange, be entrusted with, store, or own forest products that are known to originate or are strongly suspected of originating from forest zones and were taken or collected illegally;

g. conduct general investigations or exploration for or exploit minerals within zones without the permission of the minister;

h. transport, control, or own forest products that are not furnished with a document attesting to their legality;

i. herd livestock in forest zones that have not been specifically designated for such purpose by the competent authority;

j. bring heavy and/or other equipment that is commonly used or suspected of being used to transport forest products into a forest zone without a permit from the competent authority;

k. bring equipment commonly used for logging, cutting, or splitting timber into a forest zone without a permit from the competent authority;

l. dispose of objects that could cause fire or damage and endanger the existence or continuity of the forest function within the forest zone; and

m. remove from or bring into forest zones or transport plants and wildlife originating in forest zones and that are not protected by law without a permit from the competent authority.

Elucidation of Letter a:

• *"Working a forest zone" refers to the working of land in a forest zone without a permit from the competent authority, such as for cultivation, agriculture, or other purposes.*

• *"Using a forest zone" refers to the exploitation of a forest zone without a permit from the competent authority, such as for tourism, herding, camping, or the use of a forest zone for purposes other than that for which the permit was issued.*

• *"Occupying a forest zone" refers to the control of a forest zone without a permit from the competent authority, for example to build a settlement, building, or other construction.*

Elucidation of Letter b:

• *"Clearing" refers to the opening up of a forest zone without a permit from the competent authority.*

Elucidation of Letter c:
• In general the distances specified are sufficient to safeguard the interests of land and water conservation.
• The minister may grant exemption from this provision by taking into consideration the interests of the community.

Elucidation of Letter d:
• In principle, the burning of forests is prohibited.
• Limited forest burning is allowed only for specific purposes or when it is unavoidable, such as to control forest fires, eradicate pests and disease, or to cultivate plant and wildlife habitats.
• Such limited burning must have the permission of the competent authority.

Elucidation of Letter e:
• The "competent authority" refers to the officials in the center or area who are authorized by law to issue permits.

Elucidation of Letter f:
Self-explanatory

Elucidation of Letter g:
• "General investigation" refers to a general geological or geophysical investigation on land, water, or from the air, with the intention of producing geological maps or to detect indications of extractive minerals.
• "Exploration" refers to all extractive geological investigations to establish more thoroughly and in greater detail the presence of extractive minerals and the nature of their location.
• "Exploitation" refers to the mining and exploiting of minerals.

Elucidation of Letter h:
• "Furnished with"means that all transportation, control, or ownership of forest products must be accompanied at the same time and place by legal documents as evidence.
• If there is a discrepancy between the content of said legal documents for the forest products and their physical condition with regard to type, quantity, or volume, the forest products concerned shall be declared as lacking legal documents as evidence.

Elucidation of Letter i:
• The competent authority shall stipulate specific places for herding livestock in forest zones.

Elucidation of Letter j:
• "Heavy equipment" refers to heavy transportation equipment, such as tractors, bulldozers, trucks, logging trucks, trailers, cranes, barges, motorboats, helicopters, jeeps, tugboats, and ships.

Elucidation of Letter k:
• This provision does not cover communities that carry implements such as parang, mandau, golok (types of machetes or swords), or other similar implements, in accordance with local traditions and culture.

Elucidation of Letter l:
- *Self-explanatory*

Elucidation of Letter m:
- *Self-explanatory*

21. Article 56

(1) Forest extension is aimed at enhancing knowledge and skills and changing the attitudes and behavior of communities so that they are willing and able to support forest development on a foundation of faith in and devotion to the Almighty God, and to create awareness of the importance of forest resources for human life.

(2) Forest extension is provided by the government, the business community, and communities.

(3) The government creates and promotes conditions conducive to the provision of forest extension.

Elucidation:
Given that forest extension cannot be provided only by the government, community and business community participation is greatly needed. To realize this, the government must take the initiative and coordinate the promotion and creation of conducive conditions.

22. Article 60

(1) Central and local government must exercise supervision over forests.

(2) Communities and individuals shall play a part in the supervision of forests.

Elucidation:
Self-explanatory

23. Article 64

The government and local communities shall monitor aspects of forest management that have national and international repercussions.

Elucidation:
- *"National repercussions" refers to forest management that has an effect on the life of the nation, for example unauthorized logging, timber theft and smuggling, forest clearing, and mining in forests without permits.*
- *"International repercussions" refers to forest management that has an effect on international relations, for example forest fires, ecolabeling, research and development, forest denudation, and various breaches of international conventions.*

24. Article 67

(1) Customary communities insofar as they actually exist and are recognized as such are entitled to:

a. collect forest products to meet the daily consumptive needs of the customary communities concerned,

b. undertake forest management that is in accordance with customary law and is not against the law, and

c. empower themselves by improving their prosperity.

(2) Confirmation of the existence and disappearance of customary communities as intended in Paragraph (1) is stipulated by government regulations.

(3) The further provisions intended in Paragraph (1) and Paragraph (2) shall be set forth in government regulations.

Paragraph (1)
Customary communities are recognized if they truly embody elements such as the following:
    a. the community is still in the form of an association;
    b. there are institutions in the form of customary control apparatus;
    c. there are clear customary law regions;
    d. there are legal institutions, specifically a customary judicature, that are obeyed; and
    e. forest products are still collected from the surrounding forest regions to fulfill daily needs.

Paragraph (2)
Local regulations are drawn up taking into consideration the results of research by customary law experts, the aspirations of the local communities, prominent figures from the customary communities in the area concerned, and any other agencies or parties involved.

Paragraph (3)
The government regulations regulate matters such as:
    a. research methods,
    b. the parties to be involved,
    c. research content, and
    d. the criteria for evaluation of the existence of customary communities.

25. Article 68
    (1) The community is entitled to enjoy the environmental quality generated by the forest.
    (2) Other than as intended in Paragraph (1), the community can:
        a. exploit forests and forest products in accordance with the prevailing legislation;
        b. know about planned forest allocation, forest product exploitation, and forestry information;
        c. provide information, suggestions, and considerations in forestry development; and
        d. directly or indirectly monitor the implementation of forestry development.
    (3) Communities in and around forests are entitled to compensation for the loss of access to the surrounding forest that constitutes a working area that provides their living due to the stipulation of forest zones, in accordance with the prevailing legislation.
    (4) All persons are entitled to compensation for the loss of rights to the land they own as a consequence of the stipulation of forest zones in accordance with the provisions of the prevailing legislation.

Elucidation of Paragraph (1):
The definition of "enjoy environmental quality" includes deriving social and cultural benefits for the communities living in and around the forests.

Elucidation of Paragraph (2):
Self-explanatory

Elucidation of Paragraph (3):
• *A change in the status or function of a forest can influence the termination of the relationship between communities and the forest and potentially even cause them to lose their source of income.*
• *To ensure that such changes of forest status and function do not cause suffering, the government together with the recipients of forest exploitation permits must seek to provide appropriate compensation, such as a new source of income and involvement in the exploitation of the surrounding forest.*

Elucidation of Paragraph (4):
Self-explanatory

26. Article 69
    (1) The community is required to participate in maintaining and safeguarding the forest zone against disturbance and damage.
    (2) In undertaking forest rehabilitation, the community can seek assistance, services, and support from nongovernmental organizations, other parties, or the government.

Elucidation:
• *In implementing forest rehabilitation for protection and conservation purposes, the community can seek assistance, services, and support in the form of technical assistance, training, and financial aid.*
• *Assistance is allowed because of the social benefits such as flood and drought control, prevention of erosion, and stabilization of the condition of water circulation.*
• *Nongovernmental organizations are intended to work as partners in the establishment of a strong, independent, and dynamic social infrastructure.*

27. Article 70
    (1) The community shall participate in development in the forestry sector.
    (2) The government must encourage community participation through a range of useful and productive forestry-related activities.
    (3) In order to increase community participation, central and local government may be assisted by a forestry watch forum.
    (4) The further provisions intended in Paragraph (1) and Paragraph (2) shall be set forth in government regulations.

Elucidation:
• *The forestry watch forum is a partnership between central and local government to increase community participation in the forest industry and serves to formulate and manage community perceptions, aspirations, and innovations as input for the government in respect of policymaking.*
• *Membership of the forum is drawn from professional organizations in the forestry sector, nongovernmental organizations operating in the forestry sector, community leaders, and forestry observers.*
The government regulations regulate matters such as:
        a. institutionalization,
        b. the forms of participation, and
        c. the procedures for participation.

28. Article 71

    (1) Communities are entitled to file claims to the court and/or report to law enforcers in respect of damage to forests that causes loss to said communities.

    (2) The right to file suits as intended in Paragraph (1) is limited to claims against forest management that do not accord with the prevailing legislation.

Elucidation:
Self-explanatory

29. Article 72

If communities are found to be suffering as a result of pollution or damage to forests to the extent that it affects the life of said communities, the forestry agencies responsible at the central or local government level may take action on behalf of such communities.

Elucidation:
Self-explanatory

CHAPTER FIVE

Differing Perspectives on Community Forestry in Indonesia

Jeffrey Y. Campbell

T he ongoing debate over the future of Indonesia's vast forestlands and forest resources, and in particular the new opportunities that present themselves for increased community control and management, is characterized by a complex continuum of contending perspectives. Different actors are seeking to speak for the people through a puzzling plurality of discourses (i.e., legal, social, political, economic, ecological), and the dialogue is striking in the dichotomy between rhetoric and intent. This chapter attempts to illustrate the creative confusion of the debate by painting, in broad strokes, some of the major themes that color this unprecedented opportunity for change. Although few of these themes are new, they have taken on an interesting life within the dynamic context of post-Soeharto Indonesia, and in particular, during the transitional government of President B.J. Habibie and the tenure of his minister of forestry, Muslimin Nasution. This context provides a new arena for public discussion and contestation, opening real possibilities for restructuring fundamental principles of natural resource ownership and distribution and for

An earlier version of this chapter has been published in Indonesian as Hutan Untuk rakyat, masyarakat adat atau Koperasi? Beragam Perspektif dalam Debat Publik tentang Hutan Kemasyarakatan, in *Sumber Daya Alam dan Jaminan Sosial*, edited by F. von Benda-Beckmann, K. von Benda-Beckmann, and J. Koning. Yogyakarta, Indonesia: Pustaka Pelajar, 2001.

realigning power and influence. Finally, this chapter focuses on one of the discrete new policies—the new community forestry program based on Ministerial Decree (*Surat Keputusan* [SK]) 677/1998—and discusses efforts to build an adaptive learning process into its implementation, which might accommodate the pluralism of local variations.[1]

Context

Through a process of land appropriation and extension of state authority that began in colonial times and accelerated with Independence, the national government of Indonesia has exerted its control more than 70% of Indonesia's land, officially classifying this vast resource as state forests. Power over this area (making up 80–90% of many provinces) gradually came to rest in the state through central and provincial forest departments. More than one-third of this area was classified as production forest. With the backing of regency and provincial government and the military, a closely linked network of large private companies was given use rights to more than 90% of the production forests.

At the same time, large areas rich in biological diversity were declared as strict nature reserves, national parks, and protection forest with accompanying restrictions on access and use of natural resources within them. In a kind of "reverse land reform" project, existing land-use patterns of local communities, many of whom had long histories of prior access and rights, were completely ignored, and forestland was effectively transferred from the hands of the poor to the hands of a small, mostly urban elite. Complex land rights and local management systems were transformed into single-use, single-user timber concessions or timber estates and estate crop plantations. Transmigration programs and spontaneous migration shuffled populations of people from region to region and island to island, usually without prior consultation with existing communities, further complicating the character of land rights, natural resource use, and the overall human ecology of different areas. The administrative regularization of village boundaries cut through historical and customary social and political landscapes, ignoring complex relationships between settlements and land. Collective or community-managed resources were automatically aggregated into the national collective of the central government.

While timber fueled the remarkably rapid pace of Indonesia's "dramatic development" in the 1970s and 1980s, communities living in and around the source of this green gold were frequently plunged into conflict and remained among the poorest in the country. The thorough plundering, both legal and illegal, of the country's forests, with annual deforestation rates as high as 1.5 million ha, has led to a dramatic reduction in forest cover from 152 million ha in the 1950s to fewer than 100 million today. Informal estimates suggest that little more than 50% of the remaining forests could be considered healthy.

A recent study by experts from Great Britain's Department for International Development suggests that only 14 million of the country's 64 million ha of production forest are still untouched. Rapid clearing for ongoing conversion and alterations to the forest structure due to excessive logging contributed to the extensive fires that continue to destroy even more forests.

The reform era that has followed the fall of Soeharto has provided an opportunity for community groups, nongovernmental organizations (NGOs), university activists and scholars, "reform-oriented" national politicians, sympathetic officials in the forest department, and resentful regional governments to call for change. Depending on the point of view and the stated or implied objectives and interests of different actors, a wide variety of issues have been raised. These can be grouped into three broad categories: rights and access, distribution of resources, and management and regulation.

Rights and Access

The issue of rights and access is of course viewed in a number of different ways depending on whether the prior right of communities is considered. In other words, perspectives differ according to which of the two major overlapping legal schools of thought dominate—national law (often referred to as "positive law") versus customary law. In many cases, arguments are based on a very simplified understanding of these legal settings, although the reality in the "local law" is of course far more confusing, overlapping, and context specific (von Benda-Beckmann et al. 1998). From the official perspective that all forests are part of the state (national) forests, the issue is how can rural communities living in and around forests gain improved access and utilization rights to these important resources? From the perspective of local government officials in the field and the industrial timber sector, the issue is more a question of what kinds of compromises may be needed to resolve conflicts among the continuing concession rights of timber companies, local community needs, and customary (*adat*) rights?

For many local community leaders and the activist NGOs that support them, the question is how can the preexisting customary rights of traditional communities over forestlands and traditional forest management systems be recognized and returned? This has led to a renewed call for a reclassification of forestland rights that would recognize and carve out customary community forests (*hutan adat*) from the national forest estate.

Distribution of Resources

The second set of issues, although related to the first, focuses more on the economic and commercial implications of forest management and addresses what is viewed as the inefficient and inequitable distribution of forest assets. How should the monopoly control over timber processing, marketing, and exports be dismantled to ensure a more equitable distribution of benefits from forest resources? How can the state ensure a larger percentage of the rent from forest concessionaires? How should the distribution of rent be shared between the central and local governments? How can local, forest-dependent communities and small- and medium-scale enterprises benefit from forest resources? Here again, there are different perspectives on how, to whom, and in what quantities this redistribution should take place.

Management and Regulation

Finally, there are a number of technical issues based on the assumption that better management and more effective regulation can be used to address problems. How can the existing timber concession management systems be monitored more effectively by the department and by independent parties to reduce forest degradation, environmental damage, corruption, and collusion? How should the large-scale conversion of degraded forests to plantation crops be discouraged and reversed? How can the large-scale illegal timber harvesting and the widely distributed processing and marketing business be reduced and legalized? How can disincentives to private and small-scale forest product marketing be removed? What role should public sector state forest enterprises (the Perum Perhutani and Inhutanis) play in the future? How can the remaining primary natural forests be protected more effectively to conserve biodiversity and preserve environmental functions? How should revised forestry policy relate to the push for greater regional and local autonomy and the devolution of power?

Rights of Customary Communities Versus the "People's Economy"

Two dominant and competing arguments for reform are ironically encapsulated in the rhetoric of the populist, ex-minister of forestry and estate crops, Muslimin Nasution's slogan: forests for people (*hutan untuk rakyat*). The first is an argument based on people's rights that draws its legitimacy from customary claims, calling for the "rights of customary communities;" the second is an argument based on a people's economy. The first calls for the recognition and return to customary rights over forests, for a redress of the historic misappropriation of these rights,[2] and for a reclassification of the nation's forests as a necessary precondition to reform. The second calls for a redistribution of access to forest resources and income from forests as a means to reorient the economy away from the monopoly control of a small elite, toward a network of small- and medium-scale businesses, organized as cooperatives. An emerging network of customary leaders supported and, to some extent still represented by NGOs and intellectual advocacy groups, is behind the first argument.

A major ideological group within the reformist government of President B. J. Habibie (and others who have followed) supports the second argument.

Recognizing or Reviving Customary Communities?

The rallying cry for the assertion of local claims to forest resources focuses on the recognition of preexisting community rights and claims to land and calls for the revival of customary institutions and law. This responds to a very clear historical process of marginalization and, frequently, violent intimidation of forest-dependent communities. Interestingly, both "local law" (von Benda-Beckmann et al. 1998) and national law are used to justify customary claims. Many community leaders are arguing that their traditional rights and customary land-use patterns and management rights were ignored with the application of new national laws, particularly since Independence. They have begun to question the validity of national law in public forums such as the 1999 Congress of Indigenous People of the Archipelago, which brought together more than 250 representatives of customary communities from throughout the archipelago. This remarkable event, which would have been unthinkable only two years earlier, attracted a significant amount of press attention, and several of the sessions on land rights were attended by senior government officials. Unfortunately senior officials from the forest ministry were conspicuously absent. Frustration with national laws is being expressed by such groups in calls for devolution of natural resources through greater regional and local autonomy and, in the most desperate cases, in calls for Independence and secession from Indonesia.

Ironically, a number of customary rights advocates seek to use national or state law as the means of proving the existence of customary law. Most recent forest department definitions of customary law communities (*masyarakat hukum adat*) insist that the final indicator of this definition in any particular case is the recognition of this status by local government. In a further twist, the "formalization" of customary leaders through the creation of official Councils of Customary Leaders can in some cases mean that local governments recognize communities as "customary law communities," when in fact they may already have relegated most decisionmaking matters to the new government regime and national law. Customary rights advocates working on drafting new government policies to recognize customary forests within the formal legal framework have convincingly cited a string of national laws and administrative decisions that recognize customary rights to forests (Sirait et al. 1999).

There are a number of interesting cases where customary communities (such as Desa Temudak, Nenek Limo Hian Tinggi, and Nenek Empat Betung Kuning, which border the Kerinci Seblat National Park in Jambi, Sumatra) have in fact effectively established their preexisting claims over forest areas through a regency-level decree (SK *Bupati*) in spite of lack of higher authorization (Edison 1998). Contradictions between agrarian law (which recognizes community land rights) and forest law (which claims all forests as state property) are finessed in these arguments in favor of agrarian law by making the distinction that agrarian law must adjudicate use and ownership of the land, while forestry law should pertain only to the access and use of forest resources—not forest territory. High hopes are therefore attached to a new decree from the State Ministry of Agrarian Affairs/National Land Agency— Guidelines to Resolve Customary Communal Rights Conflicts (*peraturan menteri* [PM] or ministerial regulation 5/1999). This order calls for the registration of community land rights and transfers the responsibility for this process to provincial and regency governments (see Chapter 6).

With the intensity of the focus on rights that has been taken up by the NGO advocates and an emerging Alliance of Customary Communities, there is a danger that the argument will, perhaps inadvertently, be overly simplified. By placing *adat* at the center of the rights argument, there is a danger of loading too much expectation on customary institutions, of romanticizing customary processes, and of encouraging a static interpretation of *adat* as a fixed set of customary prescriptions. This in turn endangers the more nuanced understanding of *adat* as a dynamic and evolving process of community decisionmaking, interacting and interlocking with external legal, political, social, and religious influences. By depicting a romanticized version of *adat* as a glorious living tradition of harmony with nature that is fully operative in forest-dependent communities, it is easier for government critics to push their equally simplistic view that most customary systems (as static self-perpetuating operating systems) have already broken down. Conversely, to admit that *adat* is part of the plural legal reality of decisionmaking and understanding at the village level can make it easier for critics to say that it is impossible to define what constitutes a "functioning" customary community. If nothing else, the efforts to revive *adat* as a competing legal system have gained a much greater hearing and have stimulated vigorous debate, spawning a range of "experts" from village customary leaders to intellectuals and politicians. The de facto management of much of Indonesia's more remote forests by customary communities, practicing a sophisticated array of traditional agroforest and forest management systems, can now be given the respect it has been denied by the policymakers for so many years.

One danger with the politicization of the debate is that earlier arguments of community rights advocates, which focused on the economic and ecological sustainability of community-based forest management systems, are in danger of being submerged or ignored. Failure to maintain these additional arguments can lead to a tendency to assume that if customary communities are only given back their rights, sustainable forest management will automatically follow in all cases. This is far from guaranteed.

Because of the political power of the customary rights argument, there is also a danger that the equity concerns, which in many cases prompted NGOs and academic involvement in the movement in the first place, might also be suppressed. There is relatively little discussion of the feudal characteristics of many *adat*-based land-use and management arrangements, the role of women versus men, and the transparency of decisionmaking processes in traditional customary forums. Younger villagers in some areas (Krui, Lampung, for instance) are worried that the new "fashion" of *adat* is providing an opportunity for old and "out of touch" customary leaders to regain their power. Adding to their argument is the fact that many of these customary leaders have already managed to establish themselves within the formal political structure serving as a village head or in other government positions. In this way many customary leaders are in fact as much representatives of the Soeharto era as they are of community consensus.

Another issue is the concern that the resurgence of customary claims will rekindle ethnic tensions, a very real concern given the recent and ongoing interethnic and interreligious violence in West Kalimantan, Central Kalimantan, and Maluku. In the call for community forestry policy, much less attention is being given to the many complicated mixed-community villages where people from different customary backgrounds, and even people who no longer consider *adat* a defining characteristic of their culture, are thrown together. These groups are also dependent on forest resources, and their rights to access and participation in natural resource decisionmaking cannot be ignored. Some scholars are calling for the much more generalized application of the term *adat* to apply to the dynamic process by which any community develops common rules and understandings in order to avoid a polarization of communities (Tjitradjaja 1999).

Events in the field add a further layer of complexity as, increasingly, communities are taking matters into their own hands, directly confronting logging concession holders, and often using violent and intimidating methods (including the burning of logging camps) to demand compensation for forest degradation and damage. In some cases customary law is more or less forcefully applied, and concession holders are tried in "customary courts" and fined punitive damages. At times different groups within the same customary community "sue" the companies for damages of different amounts (Nugroho 1999). It can be argued that these direct action campaigns in the field have caused many concession holders to engage more actively in policy debates[3] and to express an interest in identifying and accommodating "customary claims" (see Chapter 6). The choice for many logging companies is whether to continue to "buy their way out" of conflicts or to "manage their way out." Those interested in the latter approach are discussing collaborative management or participatory mapping to designate customary forest areas.

The use of *adat* for extortion of rent and taxes weakens the argument that community groups would like to reclaim the forests for their own direct use and for more sustainable management. If anything it increases the argument that the commercial paradigm of forests, primarily as a source of revenue, has a certain acceptance within communities or at least certain elements of customary communities as well. If this is the case, how will customary forests be managed in the future? Will the forest resources be converted to assets that add value and appreciate over time, so that they can become a sustainable investment that can be transferred to future generations (Coward et al. 1999)? What are the economic implications of community forest management? Will many of the forests be converted into agroforestry systems dominated by estate crops, albeit more ecologically diverse and complex forest gardens than the monocultures of large plantations? Evidence shows that many such systems are quite successful in providing a steady stream of benefits and, when linked to international markets, can be quite resilient in times of local economic crisis. What incentives will there be to retain natural forests and conserve biological diversity on a large scale? Will the merciless pull of the market and the layers of corruption and collusion and armed power that currently control large-scale illegal forest products trade entice or force communities to sell off or log natural forest remnants? The experience with community-owned forests in neighboring Papua New Guinea shows that traditional (customary) chiefs and local leaders can be as easily corrupted as distant government officials.

The possibility of decentralization, increasing regional autonomy, and the devolution of authority over natural resources to more local levels further complicates the customary rights argument. The new law on decentralization (*Undang-Undang* [UU] 22/1999) calls for the eventual election of representative village councils, which will presumably function at the village level in the same way that newly elected representative assemblies will work at the regency level—currently the locus of devolved authority. Should new opportunities for village-level democratic governance be guided primarily by traditional *adat* institutions and considerations? Should these be seen as the vanguard of a new phase of local *adat* processes? Or should the focus turn to how communities can most effectively access and use the new local governance structures to effectively manage local resources, gradually replacing customary processes? How can democratic governance accompany decentralization to ensure that the concerns and needs of local people are not simply ignored by a new set of village, regency, or regional elite?

Finally, of course, there is the incredible pluralism and complexity of reality in the field, where the forces of the market, the power of corrupt local officials, and the armed might of the military still determine events around and within the forests of many customary villages. In making use of *adat* arguments to create "situations" and make use of "room to maneuver," Tsing (1999) described how village leaders have had to tread a careful balance between attracting sympathy and understanding as a "traditional" community and conveying a serious commitment to join the development bandwagon. During the reform period, the portrayal of a strong customary culture is finding greater air space in the ongoing dialogue for local land and forest rights. In the process, village leaders and NGO advocates face the danger of portraying customary rights not only as a necessary condition but also as a sufficient condition for forestry reform. These concerns do not imply that Indonesia's forests would be better managed by anyone other than local communities. Indeed, the evidence has already shown us that the timber industry with or without government supervision is not a strong contender. The track record speaks for itself. It is important, however, that these legitimate concerns not fall out of an oversimplified debate.

Forests for People or Forests for Cooperatives?

If the issue of the rights of customary communities is layered by paradoxes and plural agendas, then the rhetoric and reality of the "people's economy" as a rallying cry for change is equally complex. As has already been mentioned in this chapter, most of the changes that have so far been made in forest policy assume that economic solutions will solve the problems. This assumption stems from a continuing commercial- and timber-oriented understanding of forest resources as engines of national (as opposed to local) development and completely ignores the complex social, cultural, and institutional factors that tie local communities to forests. Building on a major push within the transitional government for a people's economy, championed by the minister for cooperatives, the forest department has also fully embraced the logic and rhetoric of cooperatives as the medium for "people" to participate more actively in the national economy via small- and medium-sized business enterprises. Cooperatives are thought to combine the legal status necessary for small-scale business enterprises with the distributive and democratic elements required by pressures for political reform. It is widely assumed—based on direct communication from villagers all over Indonesia—that people will somehow forget their grievances against many of the village-level cooperatives from the Soeharto era, which were often controlled by the local elite and the cooperatives department.

Many people both within and outside of the forest department are perplexed by this new institutional orthodoxy that insists on reviving "new" cooperatives as the only legitimate format for community natural resource management, indeed as the only alternative to large-scale industrial forest management. While firmly based in the rhetoric of asset distribution and "people-centered development" as part of the new people's economy, there is concern that the insistence on cooperatives reflects a continuing pattern of state control and social engineering. The assumption that a cooperative will automatically represent the community is widely questioned, although the term "cooperative" is often substituted for the terms *rakyat* (the people) or *masyarakat* (the community) in many rhetorical statements of top political leaders.

A more cynical view sees cooperatives as an avenue for the forest industry to get around new limits to the size of forest concessions and regulations stipulating that 20% of shares in new timber concessions must be given to cooperatives (new decree, SK 732/1998). Clarifications to the latter rule state that the preference should be for cooperatives genuinely formed by local community members, but that cooperatives formed by more distant members, including those formed by employees of private firms and even the forest department, may also be considered. This is borne out by the flood of applications from newly formed cooperatives for small forest concessions (areas less than 50,000 ha can be approved at the provincial level, and forests fewer than 10,000 ha can be approved at the regency level under SK 732/1998). A similar rush by cooperatives with dubious membership has been seeking community forest utilization rights (under a new community forestry program outlined in decree SK 677/1998). To add to the confusion, special encouragement is being given to Muslim schools to form cooperatives and apply for forest concessions. Several of these schools on Java have been given forest concessions in Kalimantan, often in partnership with the forest industry, as well as in teak forests on Java, without consultation with local communities (Cohen 2000).

Another development within the forestry ministry that sends mixed messages is the quiet but persistent push toward the extension of the Perum Perhutani (currently the Java State Forest Corporation) model to the Outer Islands. A massive concession in East Kalimantan that borders Malaysia was given to the Perum Perhutani, and a visit by provincial forestry heads to study the functioning of the Perum Perhutani in Java is an indication of the government's commitment to this process. Unlike the state forest corporations that have functioned as forest concession holders off Java (Inhutanis), and that subcontract most of their forestry activities to private timber companies, the Perum Perhutani holds a monopoly over the production forests of Java and combines the role of forest industry with that of the provincial forest department. This means that Perum Perhutani staff directly control and use forest resources, combining a regulatory role with a profit motive and an obligation to undertake community development and welfare activities. Extending the Perum Perhutani model to the Outer Islands is in some ways an extension of centralized control over forest resources and goes against the trend toward increasing privatization of state-owned enterprises that is supposedly being encouraged by the current reform government in other sectors. Handing over large forest areas to Perum Perhutani or new provincial government corporations set up along the lines of Perum Perhutani would seem to be a direct contradiction to the call for a redistribution of assets to local communities.

Policy Change toward Community Forestry

A flurry of policy revisions within the Ministry of Forestry and Estate Crops (MoFEC) in 1999 began to respond to these questions (see Chapter 6). Foremost among these is the new forestry bill (UU 41/1999, discussed in Chapter 4). Yet the initial deluge of policy responses to demands for change were in the form of government regulations (*Peraturan Pemerintah* [PP]) and ministerial decrees (SK). The first major government initiative was a ministerial decree, SK 677/1998, revising a previous "community forestry" program (SK 622/1995) that focused on involving community groups in the rehabilitation of degraded forestland on production and conservation forests and planting a mixture of timber and multipurpose tree species. Under SK 622/1995, community groups were given rights to nontimber forest products from the multipurpose tree species, but they had little say in the overall management of the forests and no rights to final timber harvests. Under the New Order, all forest areas not currently under long-term timber leases are eligible for community forest utilization rights. For the first time, forest-dependent communities will be given the right to the utilization of production forests, forests protected for environmental functions, and national parks and conservation forests.

Community Forestry

The initial process of formulating SK 677/1998 for community forestry was remarkably open and involved a number of actors from outside the forest department. Enthusiastic officials in the Directorate of Rehabilitation and Social Forestry solicited input and set up an advisory team to help them draft a very different approach to community forestry. This was based on a number of important principles, among others a recognition of traditional forest management systems and a very clear mandate to let communities take a lead role in determining their own forest management institutions and objectives. However, the order went through a number of consecutive drafts, and the final product is considerably changed. SK 677/1998 has a number of shortcomings stemming primarily from the department's reluctance to move away from a commercial orientation to forest management. Communities, like industrial forest concession holders, can be given a "utilization right" but not a "management" right. This stems from a fundamental perception within the forest bureaucracy that only the forest department, and by extension scientifically trained foresters working for the department, can "manage" the forest. This interpretation is traced back to Paragraph 33 of the national constitution, which specifies that the state "controls" all natural resources for the greatest benefit of the people. There is a widespread perception that to grant management rights is to lose control over the forests and that therefore the state can only grant commercial utilization rights or collection and usufruct rights.

To be eligible for a 35-year renewable "forest utilization right," communities must first form a cooperative.[4] This stipulation directly contradicts one of four important principles laid out in the order, which states that communities are to determine their own institutions. It stems from an assumption that rights to commercial utilization can be given only to "legally recognized bodies." Cooperatives are seen as the ideal form for an egalitarian business venture, in spite of the widely perceived failure of the village-level cooperatives of the Soeharto New Order regime. There is already considerable evidence to support the widespread concern that cooperatives are proliferating, claiming to represent communities, and applying for commercial forest utilization rights. A further difficulty is that communities applying for a community forest utilization right may be required to prepare fairly rigorous long-term, medium-term, and annual forest management plans, much along the lines of commercial logging firms.

These shortcomings in the new government decree are in contradiction with the basic premises of community forestry, which are to secure access of communities to the forests on which they depend and to place the communities in control of forest management decisionmaking as the primary actors. The latter premise also is clearly laid out in the basic principles of the decree, which stress that communities are the primary implementers and that the community will determine the forest utilization system. A further principle states that government will only facilitate and monitor community forestry.

Many NGOs and academic critics of SK 677/1998 feel that the community forestry program will be abused by small- and medium-scale businesses through fake cooperatives, that it is "the wine of privatization in community bottles" (Tadjudin 1999). This concern draws from disappointment about the process and final form of a higher-level government regulation (PP 6/1999) governing the utilization of production forests. PP 6/1999 is notable only for adding cooperatives to the list of legal institutions allowed to gain utilization rights to production forests in addition to private firms and government corporations at the national and provincial levels. PP 6/1999 consigns mere collection rights to customary law communities.

Draft Government Order on Customary Rights

Perhaps the greatest problem with both SK 677/1998 and PP 6/1999 is that they do not address the issue of conflicting land claims on forests that have already been leased to industrial logging companies. These orders do not explicitly recognize customary rights; existing traditional forest management systems, which are still practiced throughout the country; and local decisionmaking institutions. In response to an initiative by customary rights advocates, a second government order at the ministerial level is under consideration that would address those areas under current timber leases that directly overlie forests claimed by traditional forest communities, whose long struggles for recognition of their customary rights have been the source of intense conflict. In this second order a process of application would be clarified for communities seeking recognition of their *adat*-based rights to forests. Progress on this order saw the preparation of an initial draft and an informative background paper known as an "academic draft" (Sirait et al. 1999). As mentioned earlier, a major difficulty lies in the definitions of customary communities, which require local government recognition to validate their existence. In spite of laudable efforts by the drafting team to move the process forward, there does not appear to be a strong commitment from within the ministry.

The Basic Forestry Law was hastily revised, and, at the time of writing, the proposed new law was being debated by Parliament.[5] A critical debate took place about the inadequacy of the consultative process leading to this bill. In fact, critics of the draft bill insisted that the final draft sent to Parliament is totally different from the draft prepared by a reform committee established by the minister for the purpose. While environmental activist groups like *Wahana Lingkungan Hidup Indonesia* (Indonesian Forum on the Environment) and even ex-ministers of the environment and forestry requested that this draft bill be left to the discretion of the next government to establish a much more consultative preparatory process, there are indications that the current Parliament will try to push it through, along with a large number of other bills, in its last month of power.[6] The commission discussing this bill invited comments from a number of stakeholders, but many community rights advocates and NGOs avoided becoming involved. One group that has sought to actively engage in this process is the *Forum Komunikasi Kehutanan Masyarakat* ([FKKM] Communication Forum on Community Forestry).

A policy group within the FKKM is advocating a reclassification of forests into three categories: private forests, customary forests, and public forests. The idea of recognizing a new category of customary forests appears to have struck a reformist chord, and a number of the official factions have requested clarification on this concept from FKKM members. As of this writing it appears unlikely that customary forests will be accorded a status independent of the national forest. Oddly, while community groups, NGO advocates, and government officials are trading rhetoric and adopting a variety of stances on this important issue, the current Parliament may pass a new law with an entirely different interpretation of community forestry and *adat* rights within the month (see Chapter 4). FKKM members have begun to strategize on how to target their inputs on the development of the next government's long-term development plan if efforts to address customary rights in the new draft bill fail.[7]

A number of other government decrees, such as PM 5/1999 from the State Ministry of Agrarian Affairs/National Land Agency and two new laws on decentralized governance and revenue sharing between the central government and the provinces, will have a profound effect on the nature of local control over natural resources.[8]

Conclusion

As the Indonesian forestry sector faces the process of necessary change and reforms, old paradigms of custodial state control and the comfort of cronies within a small circle of power holders are undergoing a period of trauma and slow transformation. Despite the growing strength of rhetoric and opinion in favor of community rights on the one hand and the "people's economy" on the other, new policies are still rooted in conventional, centralized management approaches.

Nevertheless, the opportunity provided by the new government community forestry program for communities to gain utilization rights to forest areas where timber concessions have expired or been canceled is an important interim step in the struggle for community forestry. Through a collaboration between the Ford Foundation and the MoFEC, efforts are being made to ensure that the implementation of this new community forestry program is based on a learning process that takes into consideration variations in local context and places community forest managers at the center of the process of experimentation. Only through the messy process of experimentation in the field can forest-dependent communities and the forestry ministry reach some sort of negotiated settlement on how to manage these forests. Multistakeholder working groups are being established at the national level and in at least seven provinces to guide an adaptive process of working together on pilot community forestry sites.

There are many challenges to be faced. Communities must be given information on the various management options available to them as new laws and regulations are issued. Clear but flexible guidelines need to be sent to field-level forestry staff and community members. These guidelines must illuminate the spirit and philosophy behind the community forestry initiative and lay out participatory processes to be followed without imposing a rigid and uniform model encumbered with onerous bureaucratic steps. In particular, local forest departments will need help in wading through the sea of applications from cooperatives that have been hastily formed to gain access to forests to determine whether they represent community members or a small elite. Community-based institutions must be given the authority, time, and trust to build on traditional decisionmaking systems and management practices. NGOs and other facilitating groups must strengthen these community institutions and assist them to make use of new opportunities, to discuss sustainable and equitable management options, and to develop indicators to monitor and correct their progress.

Once rights are granted, attention will need to be given to new silvicultural practices that are specific to the multiple needs and objectives of community managers. Marketing support and value addition for forest products and forest-based enterprises will be needed if community forestry is to contribute to local development. Local government will have to play an increasingly greater role as a facilitator and regulator, which will require transparency and accountability mechanisms to resist the urge to squeeze revenue from forests and to succumb to local cronies and corruption. It is hoped that the experiences gained through a learning process connecting community-managed sites—by community groups, NGO community organizers, university researchers, and local government officers—will help guide the process of implementation, illuminate the difficulties with the current community forestry policies, and suggest modifications and changes.

It is hoped that the incremental pace of policy change will speed up and provide ever more space for a far more consultative and adaptive process of decisionmaking at the macro level. But the real contests will be in the field, where new alliances and institutional formats will create opportunities and challenges for local community members to organize among themselves and to negotiate compromises with local government officials, the forces of the market, old and emerging bases of power, and the national government. The political crisis offers new space for regional-, local-, and community-based forest management. The economic crisis can be used as an argument to redistribute assets to the small- and medium-scale business sectors while posing new pressures on forests as sources of quick capital and investment. New policies are beginning to respond to this space. Taken together, the way responses to these crises play out will have extremely long-term effects on the forest resources of Indonesia.

Endnotes

1. There have been dramatic changes in Indonesia since this chapter was originally written, including the first free elections in 32 years. Abdurrahman Wahid was elected president, and Nur Mahmudi was appointed minister of forestry. The ministry itself has been amalgamated with the Ministry of Agriculture and then separated again. Most recently (July 2001), Megawati Soekarnoputri became president, and in August 2001, Muhammad Prakosa was appointed as the minister of forestry.

2. Franz von Benda-Beckmann (1997, 30) captures this movement: "What people claim is not so much the recognition of their law as a solid going concern or a return to 'the olden ways,' but the recognition and unmaking of historical injustice and the legitimate power to regulate their own affairs."

3. The head of *Asosiasi Pengusaha Hutan Indonesia* (Association of Indonesian Forest Concession Holders) was involved in discussions for the draft government order on recognizing customary forests.

4. With the change to a democratically elected government, the rhetoric insisting on cooperatives and the call for a "people's economy" have faded. Devolution and decentralization to local-level government and greater regional autonomy have taken over the discourse. Yet the condition that local communities must form a cooperative to obtain the community forest utilization rights is still in force.

5. It was passed on September 30, 1999, although implementing regulations have taken a long time in preparation.

6. This was passed on the last day of the transition government, and Abdurrahman Wahid took the position that it must be respected.

7. Since this chapter was written, there have been many new developments that relate to the issues discussed, among them the new forestry law (UU 41/1999) has been passed. In this act, customary forest is recognized as a legal category within the national forest zone, not as a forest owned outright by communities. Regulations clarifying the process for identifying and gazetting customary forest areas have yet to be issued.

8. The new laws on decentralization have raised the intensity of the debate with local autonomy having taken force in 2001. Many customary rights groups are calling for a redrawing of village boundaries (returning to customary clusters) and a clarification of customary territorial rights as part of a decentralized reassessment of land use and natural resource management planning.

References

Cohen, M. 2000. Faith in the forest. *Far Eastern Economic Review*, 163(4):21.

Coward, E.W., M. Oliver, and M. Conroy. 1999. *Building Natural Assets—Rethinking the Centers' Natural Resources Agenda and Its Links to Poverty Alleviation*. Paper prepared for the Meeting on Assessing the Impact of Agricultural Research on Poverty Alleviation. September 1999. San Jose, Costa Rica.

Edison, A.E. 1998. *Studi Banding Jambi*. Paper presented at the Third Regular Meeting of the Indonesian Communication Forum for Community Forestry (FKKM). April 1999. Madiun, Indonesia.

Nugroho, A. 1999. Personal communication with the author, May 20, 1999.

Sirait, M., C. Fay, and A. Kusworo. 1999. *Bagaimana Pandangan Pemerintah Atas Hak-Hak Masyarakat Hukum Adat Di Dalam Kawasan Hutan?* Paper presented at the workshop on Decentralization and Natural Resources. August 1999. Pontianak, West Kalimantan, Indonesia.

Tadjudin, D. 1999. *Hutan Kemasyarakatan: Anggur Privatisasi dalam Botol Kemasyarakatan*. Paper presented at the Indonesian Tropical Institute. August 1999. Bogor, Indonesia.

Tjitradjaja, I. 1999. Personal communication with the author, April 6, 1999.

Tsing, A.L. 1999. Becoming a Tribal Elder, and Other Green Development Fantasies. In *Transforming the Indonesian Uplands: Marginality, Power and Production*, edited by T.M. Li. Singapore: Harwood Academic Publishers and Institute of Southeast Asian Studies, 159–202.

von Benda-Beckmann, F. 1997. Citizens, Strangers and Indigenous Peoples: Conceptual Politics and Legal Pluralism. In, *Law and Anthropology. International Yearbook for Legal Anthropology.* (Volume 9), edited by R. Kuppe and R. Potz. The Hague: Martinus Nijhoff Publishers, 1–42.

von Benda-Beckmann, F., K. von Benda Beckmann, and J. Spiertz. 1998. Equity and legal pluralism: taking customary law into account in natural resource policies. In *Searching for Equity, Conceptions of Justice and Equity in Peasant Irrigation*, edited by R. Boelens and G. Van Gorcum Davila. Assen, The Netherlands: Van Gorcum, 57–69.

CHAPTER SIX

Reforming the Reformists in Post-Soeharto Indonesia

Chip Fay and Martua Sirait

In the early 1980s, in what could be considered one of the largest land grabs in history, the Indonesian government implemented a forest zonation system that classified most of the Outer Islands as state forestlands. Seventy-eight percent of Indonesia, or more than 140 million ha, was placed under the responsibility of the Ministry of Forestry and Estate Crops (MoFEC). This included more than 90% of the Outer Islands. Estimates place as many as 65 million people living within these areas.[1] According to the Ministry of Forestry (MoF), the creation of the state forest zone nullified local customary (*adat*) rights, making thousands of communities invisible to the forest management planning process and squatters on their ancestral lands.[2] As a result, logging concessions, timber plantations, protected areas, and government-sponsored migration schemes have been directly overlaid on millions of hectares of community lands, causing widespread conflict. Yet, in fact for many local people, traditional or customary law still governs natural resource management practices.

Indonesian law governing the environment and natural resources is a combination of overlapping and conflicting regulations. While the constitution of 1945 recognizes the traditional land rights of local people, Article 33 clearly

Revised from a paper presented at the American Association of Rural Sociology, Chicago, Illinois, August 6, 1999.

states that all natural resources, including land, are controlled by the state. The 1960 Basic Agrarian Law also recognizes customary law and specifies other rights that can be attached to land. The Constitution, however, has the final say, making it clear that even private rights of ownership are not private in the Western sense. All rights are still controlled by the state. This allows various customary property rights regimes to continue to develop, but only as long as they do not interfere with the interests of the state. For example, when the state decides that a golf course is to be developed just near Jakarta, the rights of local farming families are not respected, regardless of whether they have tilled those lands for generations or have bought them outright and have official deeds of sale certified by local government. The appropriation of the land for the golf course is ostensibly done in the national interest and this reasoning is seen to justify the arbitrary usurpation of local property rights.[3]

In another example, an agroforestry farmer in Sumatra was told by a forestry official that the forest gardens he and his family had created and managed over the past 80 years were state forests. The farmer replied, "but even the Dutch recognized my family's rights over our area." The official responded in earnest, informing the farmer that while that may be true, he must understand that was "before we had our freedom."[4]

At the local level, it is also important to recognize that natural forests have often been replaced by a variety of agroforestry systems, which for local communities are more productive and profitable than the original ecosystems. In fact, agroforestry products such as clove, nutmeg, mace, pepper, and cinnamon placed the archipelago on the international trade maps hundreds of years before Indonesia became a nation. The forest gardens in Krui, Lampung (Sumatra), are examples of such systems. Over the past 100 years, Krui communities have created many thousands of hectares of highly productive forest gardens and agroforests. Numerous other systems are still found throughout Indonesia.[5]

Rapid withdrawal of foreign capital from Indonesia and other Asian countries during the first quarter of 1998 triggered the Asian economic crisis. Yet agroforestry communities with trading links to export markets, producing such products as resins, cacao, and coffee, enjoyed a boon while other agricultural communities suffered losses due to increases in production costs that were not offset by domestic price increases (see Chapter 11).

Civil Society Demands for Forestry Reform and the Recognition of Customary Rights

The May 1998 Soeharto resignation led to a flurry of political maneuvering by local and national opposition activists. Public forums were held where discussions focused on redefining the state. Aceh and West Papua were viewed by some activists as prepared for nationhood, while the remaining provinces were poised for federalism. The Habibie government was viewed as illegitimate. Demands emphasized the creation of a caretaker government that would oversee free and fair elections. Yet soon it became apparent that a caretaker government was unrealistic and those who had controlled political and economic decisionmaking during the Soeharto period were still making the decisions. Unlike the "People Power Revolution" in the Philippines, there had not been a transfer of power to the opposition. As a result, the nongovernmental organization (NGO) movement began a more focused period of political advocacy. Efforts focused on legal change in specific areas such as agrarian reform and forestry. Three important coalitions have emerged to address forestry issues:

- *Koalisi untuk Demokratisasi Pengelolaan Sumberdaya Alam* ([KUDETA] Coalition for the Democratization of Natural Resources),
- *Forum Komunikasi Kehutanan Masyarakat* ([FKKM] Communication Forum on Community Forestry), and
- *Jaringan Pembelaan Hak-hak Masyarakat Adat* ([JAPHAMA] Indigenous People's Rights Advocate Network).

KUDETA

KUDETA is a network of 82 Indonesian NGOs and student organizations. KUDETA came together immediately after the Soeharto resignation. The coalition demands that the transitional government ensure the return of natural resource management and benefits to local communities. The student movement set the early tone of this coalition, organizing several demonstrations at the Parliament and the first demonstration ever at the MoF. This June 1998 protest saw banners flying and microphones blaring in the lobby of the ministry. There were three main demands:

- redefine the boundaries of the state forest, identify customary communities, and fully recognize their rights;
- restructure state institutions responsible for environmental and natural resource management; and
- redirect all development efforts toward community-based resource management.

The minister and some of his senior staff met the protestors and briefly discussed these issues. He then invited them to nominate a representative to sit on the forestry reform committee that was taking shape at that time. The protesters declined the offer on the grounds that the government was illegitimate.

A second KUDETA protest took place in December 1998. Protesters hung a large banner on the 14th floor that covered the ministry sign. It called on the ministry to "stop converting forest to oil palm plantation." This action followed a research report that several corporations were given licenses to convert large areas of forests to oil palm plantations (see Chapter 10). The participants expressed their demands and left without a dialogue with the forestry officials.

KUDETA's next large demonstration took place in June 1999. The group of several hundred demanded that the ministry take back the draft forestry law submitted to the Parliament in April 1999. They also demanded that the ministry restart the process of drafting the forestry law and ensure transparent and open consultations. The group then demonstrated at the heavily guarded Parliament. They were allowed to enter and spoke with members of the Parliament's commission on natural resources.

FKKM

FKKM was established on September 23, 1997, eight months before Soeharto's resignation. Founders included several Indonesian NGOs, university professors and students, and reform-minded forestry officials. During the reform period, the FKKM become an effective voice advocating on behalf of local communities located within the state forest areas and an important counterbalance to industrial foresters.

FKKM has a broader base than KUDETA, and its work focuses more on developing detailed critiques of forestry policy and advocating a new paradigm for natural resource management. Strategies focus more on the use of the media; meetings with high-level forestry officials, including the minister; and lobbying in Parliament. FKKM received initial support from the Ford Foundation and was intended to include all groups and individuals concerned about forestry issues in Indonesia. Throughout its early days, FKKM included several high-level MoF officials and some from the private sector. By mid-1998, FKKM took the lead in defining a new vision for forestry under the new government.

FKKM has taken the position that genuine reform can only happen after the government recognizes the failure of previous forest management practices. It has called for a new paradigm that is politically, socially, economically, and environmentally sustainable. Proceedings from FKKM's first assembly after the Soeharto resignation were published as "The Right Starting Points toward the New Era of Indonesian Forestry." The document presented a vision that is democratic, just, and supportive of forest management based on existing natural resources and ecosystems. It called on government to abandon its focus on timber management and to adopt a strategy that emphasizes forest ecosystem management. FKKM said these changes would require a complete shift in approach to one that is pro-people, location specific, decentralized, and publicly accountable. Specifically, it called for a broad reorganization of the MoF and revision of the Basic Forestry Law. To accomplish these objectives, FKKM carried out collaborative research and organized workshops and cross-visits among participants. FKKM also regularly sent comments on emerging policies directly to the forestry ministry, often in the form of open letters to the minister.

FKKM is the coalition that took the lead on the development of new forestry legislation, a process that was marked by disappointment. After initial consultations on the new law were organized by the ministry's reform committee, the committee's draft was, in a process that was not transparent, superceded by a draft that emerged from within the ministry. It is this draft that was approved by Parliament and passed into law in September 1999 (see Chapter 4). In response, FKKM members organized an intensive, inclusive, and transparent effort to draft a natural resource management law that included forestry.

FKKM representatives presented this bill to the natural resource management committee in the Parliament, and a lobbying effort ensued. Emphasis was placed on stopping the MoF's version from being considered, and debate over the draft law was heated. In June 1999, Djamaludin Suryohadikusumo and Emil Salim, the recently retired ministers of forestry and environment, respectively, held a press conference and called on the Parliament not to act on the draft law submitted by the ministry. Their main criticism was that the ministry draft did not represent enough of a break with the past, because the question of customary rights was avoided and the emphasis was still on timber exploitation rather than on forest management. The former ministers joined the calls from numerous NGOs that a new forestry law wait until the new government and Parliament were formed.

Emergence of an Indigenous People's Movement

At a meeting in Tanah Toraja, Sulawesi, in 1993, indigenous leaders and supportive NGOs established JAPHAMA. An important outcome of the meeting was a consensus among participants to use and promote the term "customary community" (*masyarakat adat*). The term refers to a community that has maintained its traditional community-based property rights, customs, and institutions. The term was selected in direct response to existing government terms like "isolated communities" or "communities not yet modern," which were viewed as pejorative. It is important to note that the equivalent word for "indigenous" in Indonesian is not used by customary leaders because most Indonesians can rightfully claim to be indigenous. The primary distinction is that customary communities have maintained a level of customary law and other practices distinct from the homogeneous political structure imposed by the central government.

JAPHAMA set out to bring attention to the many human rights abuses being suffered by customary communities. Network members addressed national policies that worked against the interests of customary communities and helped link their efforts to gain recognition of customary rights to the international arena. International Labor Organization Convention 169 on Indigenous and Tribal Peoples was translated into Indonesian and the network lobbied the national government to ratify it. Overall, during its first few years, JAPHAMA was successful in consolidating the network and raising public awareness, particularly in the Indonesian media, of the problems customary communities face in Indonesia.

In early 1999, JAPHAMA and associated NGOs organized a nationwide consultation of customary communities. The National Congress of Customary Communities, held in Jakarta in March 1999, followed numerous regional meetings. The meeting was a high-profile gathering of customary leaders, men, and women, and it represented a diverse political force. More than 200 representatives from 121 ethnic groups attended, sharing their culture through formal and spontaneous performance. The national media helped give the congress a high profile prior to and during the weeklong gathering. Sessions were divided by sectoral and legal issues. Government ministers were invited to hear the concerns of the participants and to share what they, as members of the reform cabinet, were doing to address the problems presented. Representatives from several of the newly formed political parties were also invited to share their platforms and to explain how they would deal with state- and *adat*-related tensions.

The theme of the meeting was "improving the bargaining position of customary communities." In nearly all sessions, land rights was the central issue, with the government transmigration and forestry policies receiving the most attention. A full day was given to the discussion of problems related to forestry and the state-defined forest zone. Approximately 160 people, with 160 stories of how state-sanctioned forest industries had taken their lands, attended this session. Problems included logging and reforestation schemes, but the greatest encroachments were reported to be from *hutan tanaman industri* ([HTI] industrial tree plantations). Although invited, no representative from the MoF attended this session.[6]

On the final day of the congress, participants formed the Alliance of Customary Communities of the Archipelago (AMAN 1998).[7] Forty-seven people were elected to form an Assembly of the Alliance. An executive committee and a five-point, three-year program of work were created.[8]

Forestry Reform in the Post-Soeharto Era: Year One

President Soeharto's resignation marked the beginning of political change that was referred to in Indonesia as "reform." Soeharto's vice president, B.J. Habibie, became president, established a reform cabinet, and promised to hold elections within a year. Elections were held in June 1999, and Abdurrahman Wahid took office as president in November 1999.

When President Habibie appointed his reform cabinet in June 1998, he chose Muslimin Nasution to be his minister of forestry. During the later years of the Soeharto government, Minister Nasution had been a senior official in Indonesia's powerful planning agency. Prior to that, he had been a high-level administrator in the Ministry of Cooperatives.

The call "forests for the people" featured prominently in Minister Nasution's early speeches as he laid the groundwork for developing a populist image. The center of his reformist approach was a strategy of redistribution of benefits derived from forest resources. The minister challenged the close partnership between government and the forest industry that resulted in widespread corruption and mismanagement of forest resources during the Soeharto period. Allowing cooperatives to manage forestlands, reducing the area that forest concessions can manage, and requiring that a portion of all forestry companies that have government-awarded concessions be owned by a cooperative were a the initial actions taken by the minister to promote his redistribution strategy. Other actions taken were in line with requirements set forth in Indonesia's January 1998 agreement with the International Monetary Fund.

Another important initiative Minister Nasution took in June 1998 was the creation of the Forestry and Estate Crops Reform Committee (FECRC), an independent body tasked to make recommendations on the forestry reform process. Those invited to join this committee came from universities, NGOs, and the forest industry, as well as reform-minded staff from the forestry ministry. The creation of this committee generated an interesting debate within the NGO community. During the early months of the Habibie government, many NGOs and Indonesians were reluctant to recognize its legitimacy. They viewed the transition as unconstitutional and called for the creation of a caretaker government that would oversee elections. This position became problematic when some of these NGOs were formally asked to advise the new government. In the end, two out of the three NGO people asked to sit on the FECRC agreed to participate.

From July through September 1998 the main work of the committee centered on four tasks submitted directly to Minister Nasution:

- an overall vision document that detailed new directions for forest management,
- recommendations for restructuring the MoFEC,
- a draft regulation governing all production forests (focused on the management approach and beneficiaries), and
- a draft forestry law.

During the last quarter of 1998 and through the early months of 1999, the committee spent much time conducting field visits and consulting local NGOs and local government. In Jakarta, committee members monitored policy developments and struggled at times to understand the status of their recommendations. It soon became apparent that an internal ministry group was also drafting new policies, particularly the regulations on production forests and a draft forestry law.

On January 29, 1999, President Habibie signed government regulation (*Peraturan Pemerintah* [PP]) 6, the new production forests regulations. PP 6/1999 replaced PP 21/1970, the government regulation that defined who could (and implicitly who could not) harvest timber from natural forests. PP 21/1970 had enabled a few corporations with close ties to the Soeharto family to monopolize timber extraction from the 65 million ha of production forests. The only significant change in the new regulation was that cooperatives, in addition to state and private corporations, could now manage these forests.

The new regulation bore little resemblance to the draft submitted by the FECRC. Forest policy advocacy NGO groups such as FKKM, the FECRC, and even the World Bank were surprised by the content of the new regulation; only the World Bank, at the last minute, was able to comment on it. The main criticism of PP 6/1999 is that it does not address the overlapping rights problem in the state-defined forest zone, it offers little opportunity to local communities, and it still treats timber as the only product to be managed in the forest ecosystem. In short, most civil society observers believe PP 6/1999 falls far short of government rhetoric and the spirit of reform.

The lack of transparency in the process of developing the final version of PP 6/1999 led many NGOs, as well as those sitting on the reform committee, to complain. In his efforts to project a populist image, the new forestry minister promised to hold broad consultations during the development of important new policies. The reform committee, seeing this as their mandate, held many such consultations on their draft and invited written comments as well. While this was happening, a separate group from within the ministry developed the draft that was eventually signed. This caused some NGOs to view the reform committee as little more than a ruse, designed to deflect efforts to promote changes that threaten the status quo.

Overview of Efforts to Secure Community Forestry and Customary Rights in State Forest Areas

The Government Community Forestry Program

On October 7, 1998, Minister Nasution signed *Surat Keputusan* ([SK] ministerial decree) 677. It set out the framework for the second generation of the community forestry program (*hutan kemasyarakatan* [HKm]). This program is the government's most advanced effort to increase participation of communities living inside the state-defined forest zone in the management of forest resources. On balance, the new framework represents a significant improvement over the earlier regulations. There are four main areas of improvement:

- Through most stages, the process of developing the policy was open, transparent, and participatory. Several NGOs and university staff were deeply involved in the conceptualization of the new framework as well as in the actual drafting of the decree (the weaknesses and limitations of this process are discussed later in this chapter).
- The program allowed the harvesting of both natural and planted timber, unlike the original framework that allowed only for the harvesting of nontimber products.
- The time limit of the contract awarded to participants was increased from 20 to 35 years and made renewable.
- The program was defined by a set of internationally recognized community forestry principles. The two most important were that local communities are the primary actors and that the forest management system for project areas is rooted in existing community-based forest management practices.

Regrettably, the further the process evolved the further the ministry moved away from many of the basic principles. Clear contradictions appeared in the final decree. The most blatant was that all community organizations must take the form of cooperatives, ignoring a central principle stated earlier in the decree that the community must define its own organizations. Other contradictions emerged in the drafting of the implementing and technical guidelines. The tendency was that ministry staff, when tasked to draft such guidelines, reverted to familiar, prescriptive approaches that ran counter to the objectives stated in the community forestry policy framework.

Overall, the greatest weakness of the new framework was its scope. Given the prescriptive and still heavily regulated approach, it was likely that the program would be implementable only in a few very limited areas (appropriate for a small cross-section of circumstances in the state forest zone). These would be areas where communities are, as the program requires, prepared for and capable of forming a cooperative and fulfilling the program reporting requirements. There was also the important consideration of land rights. Many if not most communities inside the state forest zone believe, and can often demonstrate, that they have rights over areas that precede state delineation of their lands as national forest. It was likely that these communities would not be satisfied with being awarded conditional rights over areas they claim as their *adat* lands.

Dialogue on the Recognition of Customary Rights

In November 1998, a group of reform-minded individuals from inside and outside the MoF, recognizing that the new community forestry decree SK 677/1998 did little to recognize customary rights and traditional agroforestry systems, approached the minister of forestry to consider developing an additional community forestry policy that focused specifically on traditional agroforestry systems and customary communities. Policy specialists from the International Center for Research in Agroforestry (ICRAF) and the Center for International Forestry Research (CIFOR) joined hands with Djamaludin, a former minister of forestry. Over a period of several months, they assisted MoF staff to develop a draft policy that would secure the rights of customary communities inside the state-defined forest zone.

The draft was based largely on experience gained in the Krui agroforests when Djamaludin was minister. In January 1998, he signed a groundbreaking decree that placed 29,000 ha of state forest zone under the management of the Krui agroforestry farmers. He did this because he was convinced that procedures needed to be developed to protect and promote community-based agroforestry (the Krui indigenous agroforestry systems were threatened by a palm oil company). He was also convinced by many years of research and his own visits to the area that the Krui agroforests are a sustainable form of forest management. The minister's action came in response to several years of demands by the Krui people and local NGOs that the Krui agroforests be taken out of the state forest zone, because they were created long before the state forest was gazetted. The new classification, which the minister termed "Zone with Special Purposes," was a compromise. While the status of the forest area as state forest did not change, the minister, for the first time, created a classification of forest management that was based on an already existing community agroforestry system. Equally important, he placed the management responsibility of the area in the hands of customary institutions, in this case the clans.

The Krui classification was unprecedented in that it implemented the following actions:

- sanctioned a community-based natural resource management system as the official management regime within the state forest zone;
- allowed NGOs working with local people to be directly involved in the drafting of a forestry decree;
- allowed the harvesting of timber from within the state forest zone by local people;
- allowed the limited harvesting of timber from within a watershed, provided the watershed functions were still met;
- devolved the management responsibility of state forestlands to a traditional community governing structure; and
- provided a right without a time limit.

The minister's decision was viewed at the time as an important breakthrough in the struggle of *adat* communities to gain tenurial security over their areas that the state had classified as forestlands. While Krui community leaders were not completely satisfied, early indications were that most saw the classification as a significant improvement. Prior to the issuance of the decree, most of the area covered by the Krui agroforests was under the jurisdiction of a parastatal logging company. When the resignation of President Soeharto opened the way for broad political reform, Krui community leaders returned to their original position, demanding that their agroforests be excised from the state forests. They are currently working with NGOs to explore options to accomplish this objective. These options are discussed later in this chapter.

The Krui classification served to significantly broaden the perimeters of discussion within the ministry of what is possible. The draft regulation on recognizing customary areas inside the forest zone can be described as taking what was determined to be possible in Krui and applying it throughout the forest zone.

In December 1998, former Minister Djamaludin met Minister Nasution and shared ideas on how customary lands and agroforestry systems could be recognized. Staff from ICRAF and CIFOR joined this meeting. Djamaludin outlined a two-track approach to dealing with community forestry. The first approach focused on the existing HKm that he, during his time as minister, had helped initiate. The second and complementary approach emphasized on a Krui-type arrangement for customary communities with proven forest management capacities. Minister Muslimin accepted the two-track approach and requested that his senior staff work with Djamaludin, ICRAF, CIFOR, and interested NGOs to develop what six months later was known as the draft *adat* decree.

A first version of the draft *adat* decree was written by a small team that included government and nongovernment members. The head of the association of timber concessionaires was an active member of this team. He said his participation was prompted by the need for logging companies to know exactly who are the communities within and around their concessions that have customary rights. Following the change of government in May 1998 and Minister Muslimin's pronouncements of "forests for the people," numerous logging companies were besieged by communities demanding the removal of concessions from their lands and compensation for resources taken and destroyed. It is not uncommon for one group to demand compensation for a given area one day, and another to demand compensation for the same area the following day. This behavior has led to a situation in many concessions and tree plantations that industry people are referring to as anarchy.

The first draft of the *adat* policy, or "draft zero" as it was referred to in Indonesian to emphasize that there had yet to be any public comment on its contents, was distributed in May 1999. Its completion marked the beginning of a complicated process of having the draft concept work its way through the forestry bureaucracy, meanwhile being open for public scrutiny. Minister Muslimin himself, having been criticized for a lack of transparency in policy development, insisted that discussion on this policy be open for broad public participation. At that time, the drafting team was asked to prepare an accompanying "academic draft" that detailed the technical and legal justifications for such a new policy. This draft was completed in June 1999.

"Draft zero" attempted to deal with the most difficult questions that arise when a government makes a good faith effort to recognize the property rights of communities who have claims that predate the existence of the state. First, what is a customary community? Second, what are the procedures for the government to recognize a customary community? Third, what are the rights that such communities have that can be recognized by government, and how can these rights be delineated? And fourth, how does the government deal with conflicts that arise from overlapping rights, particularly in areas where the government has already awarded rights, such as logging concessions and timber plantations?

The drafting team carefully studied how other countries have dealt with the government recognition of indigenous rights, particularly to land. Of the countries looked at, the Philippines offered experience that most closely resembled Indonesian conditions. In 1993, the Philippine Department of Environment and Natural Resources, the agency that manages areas classified as public forestlands, developed the Certificate of Ancestral Domain Claim (CADC). The CADC is a special certificate that is issued to customary (ancestral) communities who have reasonably demonstrated their claims over classified forestlands. Although the classification did not go as far as legally recognizing community-based property rights, the CADC did provide the customary community exclusive and open-ended rights over areas they claim as ancestral. Between 1994 and 1998, 2.5 million ha (close to 20% of the Philippine forest zone) were classified as ancestral areas.

The Philippine CADC experience offered Indonesia an excellent point of reference. Similar to the CADC, the initial concept of the Indonesian *adat* policy outlined a process by which the difficult questions and problems would be answered and addressed. The draft definition of a customary community was taken from the government regulation on Krui, mainly because it is highly inclusive and had already been accepted by the MoF. It simply states that a customary community is "a traditional community still bound together in association, having customary institutions, customary law that is still adhered to, a territory defined by customary law, and whose existence is affirmed by the community itself together with government."

The draft also called for the creation of a permanent commission at the national level and a commission at the regency level (*kabupaten*, a layer of government one step below the province). Both would be made up of government and nongovernment individuals. The national commission, based at the MoF, would develop criteria for how a community would gain government recognition as a customary community. The commission at the regency level would be formed by the *bupati* (regency head) and provide a recommendation as to whether a community that requested recognition met the criteria determined by the national commission.

When a community defines itself as a customary community in the state forest zone and gains recognition from the government, the next question is how to shape and secure its property rights in the forestry context. The MoF has legal jurisdiction to determine whether such a community is managing the natural resources within its area in a way that meets ministry approval. Therefore, any right given to an officially recognized customary community would be conditional. Expecting communities to demonstrate that it is managing its resources sustainably may be unreasonable. Many of those developing the *adat* policy hope that, at least local customary communities must merely demonstrate it is not harming its environment, and the burden of proof that they are causing harm should be in the hands of government. Criteria for sustainable management are not clear, as they are not clear in most forest management situations throughout the world, making this condition one of the more difficult in the *adat* recognition process.

The weaknesses of the process outlined in the draft policy are obvious. The most important is that the initiative is still within the boundaries of the state forest zone. It therefore accepts the deeply flawed process by which the state forestlands were demarcated and determined. Following the open dissemination of the draft for comment, much debate took place over this question. Proponents of the policy say that it is essential that customary communities articulate where their territories are within the forest zone and gain security of tenure so no other rights can be awarded over their areas, and existing forest industry rights can be canceled or at minimum not extended. Critics tend to agree that developing procedures by which customary communities inside the forest zone can be formally recognized is important, but the process should explicitly include steps by which *adat* lands that should never have been classified as state forests can be declassified, and communal rights can be recognized. Such processes arguably already exist. The MoF has long had a procedure of creating enclaves inside the forest zone. In these areas, other rights clearly exist, and there is no significant ecological justification that the land in question serves only a forest function.

Redefining the Boundaries of the State Forest

Based on PP 62/1998 (Government Regulation on the Granting of Governmental Affairs in Forestry to the Region), responsibility for forest delineation is devolved to local governments. The final gazette, however, remains in the hands of the minister of forestry in Jakarta. This devolution requires a revision of the ministerial decree on Forest Delineation and the Enclave Policy (SK 634/1996).

In September 1998, the ministry invited nongovernmental participation in a working group tasked to improve ministry procedures for redrawing the boundaries of the forest zone. NGOs promoted greater participation of local people in determining the boundaries and creating community enclaves within the forest zone. Customary rights proponents joined the working group, viewing it as an important opportunity to get large areas of *adat* lands excised from the forest zone.

Community Enclaves within State Forests. The policy debate on creating enclaves focused on the types of prior rights that would be recognized by the ministry and just how far an enclave should extend. Conservative forestry legal staff took the position that only lands that have land certificates or the highest form of land title should qualify, and this should only be for immediate settlement areas and fixed agriculture in close proximity to settlements. *Adat* rights proponents on the working group argued that traditional territories, and not just lands with formal certificates, should be recognized as prior existing rights and that all customary areas, including agroforestry areas and natural forest, should be included within an enclave. Currently the definition of prior rights is more flexible, but the "enclavable" areas do not yet include agroforestry lands, arguably the most important component in many customary land-use management approaches. Yet just as the working group appeared to be making some progress, the ministry's legal bureau sent its own draft enclave policy to the minister. This draft showed little improvement in the original enclave process and, according to *adat* proponents, would do little to address conflicts on the ground. Like other forest policy development processes in the reform era, the new enclave policy was clouded in uncertainty and confusion.

Participatory State Forest Boundary Setting. The issues taken up in the working group's discussions on procedures for redrawing the boundaries of the state forest are more complicated. As of February 1999, government figures revealed that only 68% of the areas the MoF claims as being state forest zone were actually formally delineated and gazetted.[9] As a result, 32% of the forest zone is not yet under the legal jurisdiction of the MoF. Information as to which areas have completed the formal gazetting process is unavailable to local communities. In some areas, local communities claim that the process by which their areas were gazetted (part of the 68%) was illegal. Forest boundary delineation and gazettement procedures require that all local communities be informed of the creation of state forest in their areas and that community leaders sign documents saying they were informed. *Adat* rights proponents estimate that much of the ministry's 68% delineation violated this requirement. This may be accurate considering how unlikely it would be for a forestry staff member to organize a village meeting to inform the community that the government has classified its village, rice fields, and agroforests as state forests under the control of the MoF; that its occupation of the area is illegal; and that a timber plantation might soon clear the entire area to plant eucalyptus.

While the major issues were all discussed in the working group, ministry staff members were resistant to most of the suggestions that would lead to a significantly smaller area of state forest. Still, the July 1999 draft policy is an improvement on the 1996 policy, as shown by the following examples:

- The role of local government in the process of forest delineation has increased significantly; many hope this will lead to greater participation by local people.
- The methods to determine state forest are no longer based on a scoring system (e.g., considering rain, slope, and type of soil) that was heavily biased toward justifying most anywhere as state forest.
- Local communities can participate from the early stages of the delineation process.
- The procedure of delineation will no longer be determined by the length of the border but will be measured by blocks in hectares.
- Communities who live or have claims inside state forest will be treated the same as a community outside the forest by being involved in the delineation process.
- There will be a process of participation and notification that will determine if the state forest area is free from third-party (community) claims. This process will precede the placing of permanent markers, making it more difficult for forestry staff to bypass the participation of local communities in the process.

Another policy initiative that stands above and that will govern those just described is a draft government regulation on forest solidification. This regulation will be the umbrella law that allows for new policies on forest delineation and the creation of community enclaves. Consistent with the development of other new forestry policies, the ministry has not made an effort to ensure coordination between drafting groups. The draft regulation, which is being developed by an internal ministry team, does not yet reflect the progress made in the working group on forest delineation and the enclave policies, leaving those involved in this process confused as to how or even whether to proceed.

A Potentially Groundbreaking Policy Initiative from the National Land Agency

On March 25, 1999, the minister of agrarian affairs attended the Congress of Customary Communities. He listened to the numerous land conflicts that result from *adat* rights being invisible to the government development planning process. He stated at the time that he was committed to addressing this problem. Over the next two months the *Badan Pertanahan Nasional* ([BPN] National Land Agency) within his ministry, with some assistance from *adat* lands specialists, developed SK 5/1999 (Guidelines to Resolve Customary Communal Rights Conflicts).

This decree sets into motion a process that, similar to the MoF policy initiative on *adat*, will determine criteria for the recognition of customary territories. The main difference is that the BPN accepts the registration of customary lands and treats them as a communal and nontransferable right, unlike the forestry classification that would provide only a management right.[10] In addition, the policy allows customary communities to lease their lands to government, and the government can in turn transfer these rights to the private sector.

The decree turned over complete responsibility for this process to provincial and regency governments. This has led some critics to say the national government has done little more than to pass the problem onto local government. Critics also question why local government should play such a pivotal role in determining whether customary communities exist.

Although not completely satisfied with the new policy, some customary leaders and NGOs have nonetheless decided to test the BPN process and determine what form of recognition can be gained. The foremost question is, what happens in the overlapping areas? The state has already given 65 million ha to the timber industry and 15 million ha to plantations, and 48 million ha are set aside as protected forests, including national parks. Added to this list are 482 mining concessions and transmigration areas.

Conclusion

Progress has been made in Indonesia toward developing policies that will secure the rights of customary communities. Certainly the *adat* policy initiative in forestry and the communal rights policy from the BPN were only distant hopes during the Soeharto period. Yet, enormous challenges still exist for customary and other forest-dependent communities, NGOs, and government. Much effort is still needed as Indonesia attempts to develop a national policy framework that provides guidance and enables local communities and local government to sort out the many overlapping rights on the ground. A reassessment of the role of the MoF at the national level is a necessary step in this process.

The failure of the ministry policies and management practices to protect natural forest areas and improve the welfare of forest-dependent people is self-evident. There is increasing consensus among forest policy analysts in Indonesia that what drives the ministry is the desire to maintain control over as much of the Indonesian land base as possible. When opportunities to profit from the logging of natural forests end in the near future, the control of land for timber plantations and reforestation projects will become the main arena for rent-seeking activities. Only after a fundamental shift in orientation—toward protecting what remains of the natural forest and privatizing the millions of hectares of lands that justifiably cannot be classified as state forest—can the ministry hope to become a positive force in Indonesia's efforts to remake the nation.

The mechanisms for such a fundamental shift in orientation exist, even within the current legal framework. But the political will and leadership in forestry appear to be lacking. Clearly, an important first step is to redefine the state forest zone. Government must then make a firm commitment to forest protection and develop innovative management approaches that focus on a far smaller forest estate. These changes would increase the potential of government to rescue what remains of some of the world's most important reserves of biological diversity. They would also make major advances toward resolving the widespread conflict that results from the MoF's belief that it has the rights over and can manage more than 70% of the fourth largest country in the world.

Endnotes

1. There is no accurate figure for the number of people living within, or the number of people indigenous to, areas classified by the state as forest zones. This figure is based on a rough analysis of government figures done by Lynch in 1992 and may well be a low estimate today.

2. The legality of how the forest zoning process, called Forest Functions Based on Consensus (TGHK—Tata Guna Hutan Kesepakatan), was carried out is currently being questioned by legal experts. The 1992 Spatial Planning Law has also led to negotiations between local government and the MoF over which areas are to remain as permanent forest. Most provinces have developed new maps with the ministry through a *paduserasi* process (or compromise through "integration") of provincial planning and ministry maps. Following the *paduserasi* process, 108.8 million ha are listed as permanent forest and 3.7 million ha are listed as conversion forest (suitable for conversion to other uses). Eight main provinces with large areas of natural forest still use the TGHK data because the MoF has yet to reach an agreement with local government. Much confusion remains at both local and national levels as to where the compromise boundaries actually are on the ground. As a result, the ministry tends to continue to use the original TGHK classifications. The World Bank and local nongovernmental organizations are calling for a complete redrawing of the permanent forest estate to reflect current realities. A draft ministry policy on new boundary setting procedures is discussed later in this chapter.

3. Some compensation is nearly without exception paid, but levels are well below market value. Local communities in the Jakarta-Bogor area who have actively resisted losing their land have been intimidated by the military and in some cases arrested. One golf course in the Java highlands has been retaken by local farmers. It is now not uncommon to see security forces guarding the perimeters of golf courses during peak playing times.

4. Field visit to the Krui agroforests by senior MoF officials in April 1997.

5. For a detailed treatment of traditional agroforestry systems in Indonesia, see Michon et al. (2000). For an excellent analysis of a specific system in Kalimantan, see Salafsky (1993).

6. An advisor to the minister of forestry and a ministry lawyer did attend the final session of the congress.

7. *Aman* in Indonesian means peaceful.

8. For a full report on the congress, see AMAN (1998). Publication available from the Alliance Secretariat: *AMAN, komp. Bumi Indah Khatulistiwa Blok* A No. 5, Pontianak, Kalbar, Indonesia.

9. Estimates on the progress in the delineation and gazettement of the state forest zone are based on numbers of notification units signed by the minister of forestry in February 1999. From a total of 2,531 units identified during the TGHK process that began in 1984, only 1,719 units have been signed, leaving 812 units still unfinished (INTAG 1999).

10. There would be no restriction on land transfers within the community. The intention is that land under *adat* would not enter the land market.

References

AMAN (*Aliansi Masyarakat Adat Nusantara*—Alliance of Traditional Communities of the Archipelago). 1998. *Notes of Outputs from the Congress of* Adat *Communities of the Archipelago*. Pontianak, West Kalimantan, Indonesia: AMAN.

INTAG (*Biro Inventarisasi dan Tata Guna Lahan*—Bureau of Forest Inventory and Land Use). 1999. Unpublished internal document. Jakarta, Indonesia: INTAG.

Lynch, O. 1992. *Securing Community-Based Tenurial Rights in Tropical Forests of Asia*. Washington, DC: World Resources Institute.

Michon, G., H. De Foresta, A. Kusworo, and W.A. Djatmiko. 2000. *Ketika Kebun Berupa Hutan: Agroforest Indonesia, Sebuah Sumbangan Masyarakat*. Bogor, Indonesia: International Center for Research in Agroforestry.

Salafsky, N. 1993. *The Forest Garden Project: An Ecological and Economic Study of a Locally Developed Land-use System in West Kalimantan, Indonesia*. Ph.D. thesis. Durham, NC: Duke University.

CHAPTER SEVEN

Structural Problems in Implementing New Forestry Policies

Hariadi Kartodihardjo

orest management and the forest industry in Indonesia have undergone significant policy shifts that will have both present and future effects. Efforts have been made to achieve justice in the forestry business, such as promulgating a new policy on the redistribution of forest assets. Yet there is one condition that has made forest resources increasingly vulnerable: the growth of looting and timber theft, which has increased business uncertainty. Meanwhile, weaknesses in forest conservation efforts remain an important issue needing speedy resolution, through both policy improvement and implementation and through other measures. The following questions are then raised:

- What are the fundamental problems of forest management in Indonesia?
- Do the policies that have been implemented over the last two years constitute a solution to the problem of forest management as a whole?
- If they are deemed inadequate, is this because the substance of the policies has not changed in principle or because the preconditions for policy implementation are not in place?
- Are there other factors that do not support the implementation of these policies?

The answers to these questions can be a starting point in determining whether the objectives of forest management and business can be met through

This chapter is adapted from Kartodihardjo (1999a, b).

the traditional mechanisms for policy formulation and implementation. The lack of institutional support has proven to be a potent barrier to implementing new ideas on forest management and regulation (see Chapters 15 and 16). This chapter attempts to explore the structural conditions and developments in the implementation of forest management policy during 1998 and 1999.

Economic Loss and the Emergence of Structural Problems
Quantitative Estimates

Data on log production by forest concessions reported by the Ministry of Forestry and Estate Crops (MoFEC) between 1977 and 1998 show only around 51% of estimated real log production (MoFEC 1999). If the national log production reported by the MoFEC is divided by the area of productive forest calculated in each Annual Management Plan, the productivity of natural lands categorized as "production forest" is negligible, between 28 m³/ha and 11 m³/ha.

An estimate of real production from forest productivity can be made. Estimating from conservative national production figures—45 m³/ha in 1977, falling to 30 m³/ha in 1998 (FAO and GOI 1990; MoFEC 1999)—we can simulate calculation of real log production. The volume of logs not reported during the period 1977 to 1998 is estimated at 477.4 million m³, or approximately 12.8 million m³ per year. The results of the simulation of unreported log production are presented in Figure 7–1.

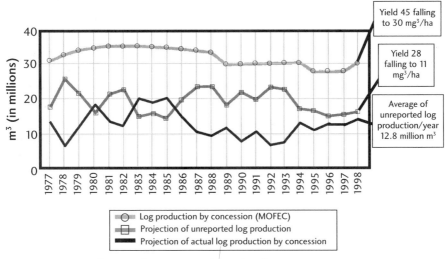

Figure 7–1. Simulation of Unreported Log Production

Note: During the ban on log exports in 1985, reported log production fell, although in fact real production remained at the same level as in the previous period (MoFEC 1999). At the beginning of the log export ban, unreported logs were actually still being exported. During the period 1987 to 1998, the government consistently recorded log production by forest concessions (HPH) at between 20 and 30 million m³ per year. Actual log production was, in fact, much greater: 28 to 36 million m³ per year.

Based on the aforementioned estimated figures, we can conclude that the state suffers huge economic losses. If the average price of logs is reckoned at US$90 per m³ at the current value, the material loss over this 22-year period is US$25.3 billion, or approximately US$1.3 billion per year. At this value, the state has also forgone the opportunity to earn income from its additional Resources Royalty Provision (*Provisi Sumberdaya Hutan*) of around US$239 million per year and Reforestation Funds amounting to some US$311 million per year.

If it were "merely" that some production went unreported, while the volume of this production remained dependent on forest capability and forest protection was implemented properly, forest destruction would not occur. Yet according to data from the MoFEC (1999), by the end of 1998, around 16.6 million ha of the natural production forest currently being worked had been destroyed. In addition to unreported production in the forestry industry, logging is also taking place in excess of production quotas and outside stipulated logging zones.

The estimated value of this loss has only been assessed for natural forests for logging carried out by concession holders. Other losses, the value of which is more difficult to estimate, are those from the coordinated theft of wood, which occurs in both production forest areas and in other forest. Scotland et al. (1999) estimated the figure for unauthorized logging for the whole of Indonesia to be 32 million m³ per year. Using this figure, the average annual theft of wood outside authorized activities amounts to an estimated 19.2 million m³ per year (i.e., 32 minus 12.8). If this is the case, using the current values for log prices, the Resources Royalty Provision and Reforestation Fund, we can estimate that the material losses from activities other than authorized timber concession (such as *Hak Pengusahaan Hutan* [HPH] or Forest Concession, Forest Exploitation Rights]) activities amount to US$900 million annually, with another US$270 million every year in losses to the state from forgone Resources Royalty Provision and Reforestation Funds (see Chapter 12 to put these losses in national perspective).

The estimated loss from these two sources results in a total material loss of some US$2.2 billion per year, as well as the loss of potential income from the Resources Royalty Provision and Reforestation Funds of an average of US$820 million per year. This US$2.2 billion per year has obviously affected both regional and national growth. It has already given rise to business links that have become institutionalized within society (see Chapter 16). Furthermore, the monies in the amount of US$820 million from the Resources Royalty Provision and Reforestation Fund not received by the state have contributed to the "drive" to form rent-seeking behavior and personal benefit within the government, business, and the wider political-economic sphere, which have grown from the destruction of forest resources.

Contreras and Hermosilla (1997) identified several sources of corruption in forest industry practices. Following are examples of the corruption that is likely occurring in Indonesia:

- **illegal logging:** logging of tree species protected by the Convention on International Trade in Endangered Species, logging outside stipulated zones, logging within protected forest and conservation areas;
- **problems in assessment:** the total reported production of logs being lower than the actual amount; manipulation of financial accounting; reduction of the amount of forestry levies by manipulating log grading; and
- **bribery:** to obtain forest utilization concessions, to get annual logging quotas, to expedite export, to avoid a bad assessment of forest management performance.

New Structural Problems of Forest Policy

Acknowledged or not, the economic effect of activities that have caused the depletion of forest resources has played a part in ensuring the stability of the people's economy, whether at the individual, household, small enterprise, or large enterprise scale or among the vast array of other economic agents involved. As a result, it is not easy to stop the theft of wood because of the profitability of the forest to people's economy in this rent-seeking situation within the government.

A boost for economic growth in the form of illegal funds, however, if left unchecked, will eventually be halted by limits on the forests' natural supportive capacity, which is by no means inexhaustible. In other words, nature will have the final say. Given these circumstances, we are left with two questions in particular.

- How do you dismantle these institutions that have arisen structurally and that continue to stimulate the destruction of forest resources?
- Who is going to consider the economic condition of the more disadvantaged segments of society (the upper and more privileged segments are able to deal more easily with the problems they face) when these "illegal institutions" collapse, particularly when such collapse is not by choice on the grounds of moral development but because the natural forest resources have been exhausted?

The Urgency of Institutional Reform and the Role of the Bureaucracy

Table 7–1 presents a recalculation of natural forest destruction from available data prepared by the Ministry of Forestry (MoF). The highest rate of forest degradation, calculated at about 89%, is in production forest managed by concessionaires, while degradation in protection and conservation forests has been calculated at 46% and 38%, respectively.

Table 7–1. Recalculation of Areas of Production Forest, Protection Forest, and Conservation Forest Condition

| Forest function | Forest condition | | | | | |
| | Primary/Virgin forest | | Secondary forest, degraded forest, nonforest | | Total | |
	Million ha	%	Million ha	%	Million ha	%
Production forest (managed by concessions)[a]	18.4	45	22.8	55	41.2	100
Production forest (state-delivered concessions)[a]	0.6	11	5.1	89	5.7	100
Protection forest[b]	6.7	54	5.8	46	12.5	100
Conservation forest[b]	10.8	62	6.6	38	17.4	100
Total	**36.5**	**47**	**40.2**	**53**	**76.7**	**100**

Source: MoF 2000.
Notes:
[a]Based on interpretation of 320 concessions using LANDSAT images dated April 1997 to January 2000.
[b]Based on interpretation of air photo and airborne radar (1996/1997). These data present evaluation of the condition of only 42% and 58% of the total existing area of protection forest and conservation forest, respectively.

In this discussion, the issue of forest destruction focuses on weaknesses in the management of production forest. Damage to natural production forest is a result of both management policy and other causes (e.g., development of plantations, mining, wood theft, use of production forest as agricultural land by the people).

Without improvements in the functioning of formal forest management institutions, the following extant situations are likely to continue in natural production forest management:

- The policy formulation processes are unable to develop viable solutions to the variable problems in the field.
- There are weaknesses in identifying common values for parties in dispute over the use of forest resources. In many cases the problem is left to the private sector (the concession holders).
- Forest management policy is unable to generate a sense of "ownership" of forest resources, with the result being that the forest concession has no genuine initiative to protect the standing stock of forest.
- Regulation of forest management is centralized and, in many cases, provides an argument for reducing the size of the government apparatus. In fact the problem is poor management in regulating the role of the bureaucracy, including spreading the risk of failure to implement policies already initiated.

- Data and information relating to forest management are seriously deficient. Decisionmaking focuses more on finding solutions to administrative rather than field-based problems.
- There are weaknesses in information and knowledge gathering on various matters related to forest management (necessarily highly location specific), with the result being that effective policy improvement is difficult.

Most of the forest in Indonesia is designated as state forest, and its management is undertaken by the government. To a great extent, the government's performance determines the success of forest management. Table 7–2 shows the government's formal role in exercising guidance and control over the management of forests by concessions. It appears to be fairly tight, and among other things, it requires certain activities and by implication at least 58 visits to each forest industry site per year (Prasetyo and Hinrichs 1999). The volume of wood not reported and the area of forest destroyed suggest that the government's control and guidance have proven ineffective. Previous research indicates that concessionaires must pay between 26% and 48% of their operational costs in dealing with the government.[1]

The weak internal controls within government organs—which result in their output actually obstructing the implementation of the policies they proclaim—result from the reality of the weakness of civil society, with a range of negative effects on forest management as a whole. In the context of efforts to save the forest, therefore, the reform of government institutions and the bureaucracy can be considered the real issue, while the other matters are only symptoms.

Without reform of government institutions and the bureaucracy, redistribution of forest benefits has become limited to the redistribution of forest commodities that are easily liquidated or the opening of opportunities to obtain shares in commercial enterprises. However, conflicts over the use of forest resources, respect for entitlements within the forests such as customary forest, and the existence of illegal economic institutions based on the theft of wood are not yet the focus of forest management policy.

Problems of Policy Improvement
Shortcomings in the Spirit of the Law

To discuss production forest management policy, we will examine nine decrees of the MoFEC issued in 1999, as shown in Annex 7–1. By identifying the components with which to evaluate these policies, we can demonstrate the following points:

- Clarifications of decisionmaking processes on the application of policies are unclear and have the potential to create further business uncertainty

Table 7–2. Guidance and Control of Forest Concessions by Government

Activities (checking/guidance)	Dinas TK I	Dinas TK II	MoFEC Kanwilhutbun	BEH-PHH	BIPHUT	Ditjen PHP	Ditjen RLPS	Ditjen PKA	IRJEN	BPKP	Depnaker	Government/ Bupati
Working block boundary	•	•	○	•	•							
Timber cruising	•		○	•	•							
Infrastructure (road construction)	•	•	○	•	•							
Cutting/harvesting	•			•	•							
Exploitation equipment	•	•		•	•							
*Tebang Pilih Tanam Indonesia*ª	•			•	•	•						
Scaling and grading	•	•			•							
Employment of forestry technician	•			•	•							
Stock checking	•				•							
Financial obligation payment				•	•				•	•		
Timber administration (production reports)		•		•	•							
Timber supply and circulation	•			•	•	•						
Local community assistance	•			•		•	•					•
Laborers and their welfare											•	
AMDAL results implementation				•				•				
Forest protection	•							•				
Biodiversity conservation								•				
Recommendation for RKL and RKPH												•
General checking				•		•						

Source: Prasetyo and Hinrichs 1999.

Note: ª *Tebang Pilih Tanam Indonesia* is the Indonesian selective cutting and planting system.
• = the guidance and checking activities are done at least once a year; ○ = involved in preparation of tasks only; AMDAL = *Analisis Mengenai Dampak Lingkungan* (Analysis for Environmental Impact Assessment); RKL = *Rencana Karya Lima Tahun* (Five-Year Work Plan); RKPH = *Rencana Karya Pengusahaan Hutan* (Forest Utilization Work Plan); Dinas TK I (Forestry Services at Provincial Level); Dinas TK II (Forestry Services at Regency Level); Kanwilhutbun (Regional Offices of MoF); BEH-PHH (Forest Exploitation and Forest Product Collection Branch Office); BIPHUT (Forest Inventory and Mapping Agency); Ditjen PHP (Directorate General of Production Forest Management); Ditjen RLPS (Directorate General Land Rehabilitation and Social Forestry); Ditjen PKA (Directorate General of Nature Protection and Conservation); IRJEN (Inspectorate General); BPKP (State Financial Accountancy and Development Agency); Depnaker (Ministry of Manpower); Government/Bupati (Head of Province/Regency)

(*Kesatuan Pemangkuan Hutan Produksi* [KPHP] or Production Forest Management Units, *Hak Pemungutan Hasil Hutan* [HPHH] or Forest Product Harvesting Rights, applications for HPH, auctions, and concessions by indigenous communities).

- Policies with varied content do not necessarily burden the people if there is good coordination between the MoFEC and the other parties involved in their implementation. But evaluation of the nine decrees actually suggests a likely increase in inefficiency, potentially pushing the high-cost economy even higher.
- Policies do not yet touch on strengthening forest management and improved definition of forest status,[2] so they cannot support efforts to preserve forest product businesses.
- Policies in general are still centralized. Delegation to governors and regents still contains weaknesses in that the regulations concerning the allocation of forest resource exploitation rights based on the regulation of products are not strictly enforced (see Chapter 15).
- In addition to the previous four points, policies are drawn up without first consulting public opinion, which is required by the Policy Reform Support Loan (PRSL) II.[3]

    —An examination of the substance of the policies contained in these nine decrees indicates that, other than potentially contributing to increased opportunity to achieve economic justice based on reallocating rights to forest asset exploitation, there are no significant signs of improvement in the prospects for the forest industry. In addition, it can be seen that the principal objective of production forest management, namely exploiting the benefits of forest resources in a sustainable manner, has not really been addressed.

    —The strong impression here is that the government is captured in an internal disagreement relating to revisions in policy on forest management. In its efforts at policy improvement, the government has not succeeded in reconciling the interests of justice with the sustainability of forest benefits. Moreover, efforts to improve bureaucratic efficiency and minimize costs and collusion seem to have received no attention whatsoever.

    —This is also evident in the government's implementation tools for *Undang-Undang* (UU) 41/1999 regarding forestry, including the substance of the draft government regulation regarding forest planning and the drafting of forest management plans, as well as the exploitation of forests and the use of forest zones (see Appendix for a timeline showing relevant laws and regulations, including SK 310/1999, SK 312/1999, SK 313/1999, SK 317/1999, SK 318/1999). As a result, it is probable that the changes made in forest enterprise policy will be insufficient to tackle the problems of forest destruction described earlier in this section.

—Leaving aside the existing weaknesses,[4] the implementation of the 1999 Forestry Law (UU 41/1999) demands a deeper understanding of forest problems if the spirit of the law is to be realized. In addition, if the preconditions and the instruments required do not contribute to the implementation of regulations, many obstacles will be encountered.

- A basic instrument needed for this appreciation of the law's substance is an institution whose function is to regulate the coordination of forest management by taking into account inherent conditions, like watersheds or areas that should be conserved because of their unique flora and fauna or because of the culture of their communities. Such areas are very likely to straddle local administrative boundaries, be they regencies or provinces. With due attention to regional autonomy, as set forth in UU 22/1999 regarding local government, there needs to be coordination between regencies or between provinces, whether touching on the planning or management of conservation areas.

- The UU 41/1999 should be publicized in such a way that all parties involved understand it. It contains clauses concerning representation and the resolution of forestry disputes, as well as several articles that explain transparency and public participation in the management of forests, which should be used as an instrument for dialog between stakeholders. The government needs to be proactive in organizing such dialogs.

- The elucidation of article 31 of the UU 41/1999 states that "in order to realize the principles of justice, equity, and conservation, as well as business certainty, rearrangement of the business permits for exploitation is required." This rearrangement should also be tied to problems that relate to regional autonomy. For example, the production forest management unit boundaries, the principal purpose of which is to support regional economic development, need to be reconciled with regional administrative boundaries. This requirement may conflict with the first bullet.

The implementation of the Forestry Law will, of course, take time. If it is to be accelerated, there are two important issues to be considered: (a) the need to make adjustments to forestry organizations and institutions so that they are in accord with the desired objectives of the Forestry Law and other laws, and (b) the need to have the content of the government regulations define the necessary preconditions, mainly the strengthening of institutional capacity and capability in the organization of regional autonomy. It seems that neither of these two issues has yet been incorporated into the draft government regulations.

Early Stage of Regional Autonomy

UU 22/1999 on regional autonomy gave authority for production forest management to the regency level. The central as well as provincial governments act more as facilitators in providing references, such as principles, criteria, indicators, procedures, and standards. The question then is, can decentralization stimulate the regional ownership toward state forests that is warranted, given the strengthening of forest management authority by the regional government? As the existing problems in production forest management become complicated, how can the central government improve its effectiveness, limited as it is to the role of facilitator by the regional autonomy law?

Before and at the time of the implementation of regional autonomy (January 1, 2001), two important issues on the status of production forest management emerged:

- The central government's policy instrument, used as a reference to implement regional autonomy, was late in its release. Although the authority of the central and regional governments was defined by January 1, 2001, the function of forest management organizations at central, provincial, and regency levels had not been established. This is due to the existence of internal disagreement in the implementation of regional autonomy, especially in the field of forestry (Communication Forum on Community Forestry 2000). A serious conflict remains between the central and regional governments over authority. Immediately prior to the implementation of regional autonomy, the central government was still releasing new, long-term concession permits. During the same period, most regional heads had also released hundreds of licenses to use forest products (Sudiono 2000). The implementation of regional autonomy has also been hindered by the activities of forestry state-owned enterprises. As centralistic forest management institutions, these enterprises (e.g., Perum Perhutani in Java and PT Inhutani in the Outer Islands) have not defined their position, even after the era of regional autonomy had begun. In this situation, the MoF came out strongly in favor of state-owned enterprises being designated to conduct forest management together with the local government. According to an Institut Pertanian Bogor ([IPB] Bogor Agricultural Institute) study, this initiative was rejected by local governments (IPB–Faculty of Forestry 2000).
- Regional autonomy is being implemented in a situation of economic and political crisis and with weak forest management practices, reflected by dramatic rates of illegal logging, forest plundering, corruption, and more. In relation to efforts to overcome the economic crisis, donor countries (Consultative Group on Indonesia) have instituted conditions requiring reform in forest management policies for debt restructuring. Based on this demand, the government—through presidential decree 80/2000—established an Inter Department Committee on Forestry (IDCF) to define and implement

forestry action programs. These action programs are related to the following requirements: taking measures against illegal logging, completing a forest resource assessment, evaluating policy on conversion forest and putting a moratorium on all natural forest conversion until the National Forest Program is agreed upon, downsizing and restructure wood-based industry and increasing its competitiveness, closing heavily indebted wood-based industries and linking proposed debt write-offs to capacity reduction, connecting the reforestation program with existing forest industries and those under construction, recalculating the real value of timber, using the decentralization process to enhance sustainable forest management, handling the tenure problem, strengthening institutions for forest management, resolving the forest fire problem, and finalizing the National Forest Program (IDCF 2000)

Ideally forest management institutions, if established and strengthened at the central as well as local levels together with other sectors, could implement the action programs defined by IDCF. Although it is too early to predict the performance of forest management institutions in the era of regional autonomy, the weak ownership of the IDCF program performed by the MoF was clear in the implementation of the letter of intent in 1998 and PRSL II in 1999.[5] The bureaucracy was more interested in reforming governmental organization than in reforming forest management policy.

Conclusion

The most important factor for better performance in forestry management is strengthening the role of forest management institutions, which can identify specific problems in certain areas. These institutions could then make decisions based on information about the limits to the supportive capacity of the forest or the growing aspirations of the communities. Forest managers at the regional level should formulate policies for forest management and forest product businesses. If the substance of this policy is formulated at the central level without relating it to actual conditions in the regions, the results will continue to be plagued by weaknesses.

The size of the government organizations involved in forest management in Indonesia gives rise to inherent deficiencies in internal controls, including delays in the reactions needed to overcome the very rapid dynamics of problems in the field. This inherent weakness therefore needs to be resolved through transparency in the policy formulation process, as well as a number of broad-based dialogs between stakeholders in operational decisionmaking in the field. Such a decisionmaking mechanism is the most direct way for the parties involved to seek the most accurate information as needed for effective bargaining at various levels. In sum, the form of the institutions will determine the degree of professionalism and not the other way around.

If all this is to be realized, it will require that decisionmakers be willing to change their ways of thinking about forestry and regional autonomy, because conditions have undergone considerable change in the last three years.

Endnotes

1. The various procedures for legalizing documents, permits, entertainment expenses, and other things results in an increase in operational costs. If the companies did not pay the officials, they could not continue with their field activities. A fuller explanation can be found in Kartodihardjo (1998).

2. Official forest management principally concerns the formation of product conservation units by taking into account regional biophysical characteristics before the allocation of small-scale forest resource exploitation rights (like HPHH and HPH of fewer than 10,000 ha) to communities. Strengthening the definition of official forest status, meanwhile, is part of the solution to the still-unresolved problem of community rights in state forest areas.

3. PRSL II is an agreement between the government and the International Monetary Fund and the World Bank to revise several forest management policies. One of the platforms of this agreement is public consultation on all policies the government issues. This transparency in forestry management is also explicitly stated in Articles 2, 11, 68, and 70 of the Forestry Law (UU 41/1999).

4. A member of the Indonesian legislative assembly explained that UU 41/1999 on forestry has been listed as one of the decrees that will be revised. Many parties that joined in the Communication Forum on Community Forestry have also agreed to revise the UU 41/1999.

5. The success of policy reform is highly dependent on the existence of genuine interest to do it. Genuine interest is shown by strong ownership and care for the success or failure of the policy. So far, this genuine interest has not been manifested. The implementation of the letter of intent (1998) and PRSL II (1999) on policy on the auction of forest concessions, the issuance of performance bonds, the reduction of natural forest conversion, and the reform of multistakeholders forestry policy were not carried out well. The facts show that pressure from the international funding agencies was not effective in promoting ownership in forestry policy reform. See Kartodihardjo (1999c) and World Resources Institute (WRI 2000) for a detailed discussion on this aspect.

References

Contreras, A., and Hermosilla. 1997. *Country Sector Planning*. Paper presented at the 11th World Forestry Congress. Antalya, Turkey.

Communication Forum on Community Forestry. 2000. *A Half Hearted Decentralization*. Proceeding of the Regular Meeting IV. February 2000. Samarinda. Yogyakarta, Indonesia: Aditya Media.

FAO (Food and Agriculture Organization) and GOI (Government of Indonesia). 1990. *Situation and Outlook of the Forestry Sector in Indonesia (Volume I: Issue, findings and opportunities)*. Jakarta, Indonesia: FAO and GOI.

IDCF (Inter Department Committee on Forestry). 2000. *Position of the 12 Forestry Commitments in the Achievement of Sustainable Forest Management and Establishment of Priority Programs*. Paper presented to Ministry of Forestry. Jakarta, Indonesia.

IPB (Institut Pertanian Bogor or Bogor Agricultural Institute) Faculty of Forestry. 2000. *Forest Management Feasibility Study of the Ex-HPHs in the North Sumatera Region*. Cooperation between Faculty of Forestry—IPB and the Planning Bureau, Ministry of Forestry, Jakarta, Indonesia.

Kartodihardjo, H. 1998. *Improving the Performance of Natural Production Forest Industry through the Policy of Institutional Reform.* Ph.D. dissertation. Bogor, Indonesia: Institut Pertanian Bogor.

———. 1999a. *Conversion and Degradation of Natural Forest: Critiques on Policy of Forest Management.* Paper presented at the Panel Discussion on Natural Conversion Forest Practices, World Wide Fund for Nature Indonesia. September 1999. Jakarta, Indonesia.

———. 1999b. *Policy Problems on Natural Forest Management.* Paper presented at the Forestry Development Platform Going into the 3rd Millennium: Anticipating Social Conflicts Caused by Miscommunication, held by the Development Communication Study Program, Class of 1999, Institut Pertanian Bogor Postgraduate Program. October 1999. Bogor, Indonesia.

———. 1999c. *The Shackle of IMF and the World Bank: Structural Barriers on the Forestry Development Policy Reform in Indonesia.* Bogor, Indonesia: Pustaka Latin.

MoF (Ministry of Forestry). 2000. MoF website, http://dephut.gov.id.

MoFEC (Ministry of Forestry and Estate Crops). 1999. *Rearrangement of Large-Scale Land Ownership and Forest Utilization in Connection with Resources Benefit Distribution* (in Indonesia). Jakarta, Indonesia: MoFEC.

Prasetyo, B., and A. Hinrichs. 1999. *The Existing Guidance and Control System for HPH. Inputs for the team on incentives for HPHs in certification process.* Unpublished report to MOFEC. Jakarta, Indonesia.

Scotland, N., A. Fraser, and N. Jewell. 1999. *Roundwood Supply and Demand in the Forest Sector in Indonesia. Indonesia–U.K.* Tropical Forest Management Programme, report no. PFM/EC/99/08 (November 23rd draft). Jakarta, Indonesia: Indonesia–U.K. Tropical Forest Management Programme.

Sudiono, E. 2000. *Sistem HPHHC (IPHH) Banjir Kap Model II. Paper on the Development of Forestry Management in East Kalimantan.* Unpublished. Samarinda. Indonesia.

WRI (World Resources Institute). 2000. *The Right Conditions: The World Bank, Structural Adjustment and Forest Policy Reform.* Washington, DC: WRI.

ANNEX 7–1. Identification of the Substance of the Decrees of the MoFEC That Relate to Forest Enterprises

Evaluation Component	SK 307/1999	SK 308/1999	SK 310/1999
Content	HPH	KPHP	HPHH (wood or non-wood)
Decisionmaker	Minister	Minister	Regent (regent reports to the directorate of production forest management [Ditj. PHP] every three months
Copied to/ acknowledged by/evaluated by	Governor, Ditj. PHP, Planning, Secretary General	Planning agency	Governor, regional office, level-I and level-II service offices
Clarification of the decision made	Relies more on administrative aspects; tends to lack transparency	Does not take into account basic problems in implementation	Upon recommendation of level-II forestry service office; tends to lack transparency
Subject/beneficiary	The HPH concerned	Forestry and Estate Crops regional office	Community gets 100 ha for 1 year
Obligations	Transfer excess hectarage; guide cooperatives	Not stated	Wood—in conversion forest, and compulsory replanting; nonwood—in conversion, production, protected forest; use of mechanical tools prohibited for wood
Necessary preconditions for the policy to work	Evaluation of performance by independent institutions	Functioning forest management institutions at regional level that have forest resource allocation plans with a clear master plan	Level-II forestry service offices must have a master plan as a basis for the considerations given
Conditions/existence of preconditions	Not put into operation	No institutions yet	Unclear authority of level-II forestry service offices with respect to forest resources
Potential problems/ high-cost economy	Problematic clarification/high-cost economy	Structural/ownership rights obstacles	Weak basis for decision-making and control/ high-cost economy
Strengthening of forest management	Not relevant	Encourage reinforcement of forest management	Not relevant

Notes: For ministerial decrees 312/1999 and 313/1999 two components are analyzed here. HPH =Renewal of Forest Utilization Concession Rights, KPHP =Production Forest Management Unit, HPHH = Forest Product Harvesting Rights.

ANNEX 7−1. *Continued.*

Evaluation Component	SK 312/1999		SK 313/1999
Content	HPH by application (area 10,000–50,000 ha)	HPH by application (area < 10,000 ha)	Auction of natural HPH (area 50,000–100,000 ha)
Decisionmaker	Minister	Governor	Minister, after accepting three prospective winners
Copied to/ acknowledged by/ evaluated by	Ditj. PHP; Planning, Regreening, and Nature Conservation (PKA); governor, regional office	Head of service office, regional office, regent	Ditj. PHP, Auction Committee
Clarification of the decision made	Evaluators lack objective arguments based on specific field facts	Regional office, using KPHP; if there is no KPHP, the planning agency provides clarification	Auction committee must have sufficient information concerning management units to be auctioned
Subject/beneficiary	Small- and medium-scale enterprises, cooperatives	Small- and medium-scale enterprises, cooperatives	Closed to foreign institutions
Obligations	Survey potential and conduct an AMDAL study; pay HPH fees; plantation HPH must be in nonproductive areas and accompanied by a feasibility study	Not stated	AMDAL study; produce a management plan
Necessary preconditions for the policy to work	Functioning forest management institutions at regional level that have forest resource allocation plans with a clear master plan	Functioning forest management institutions at regional level that have forest resource allocation plans with a clear master plan	Monopsony problem can be overcome; transparency and accountability in evaluation methods
Conditions/existence of preconditions	Administrative and coordinating leadership of Ditj. PHP and regional offices; no KPHP yet	Administrative and coordinating leadership of regional offices and planning; no KPHP yet	Auction evaluation has not been transparent up to now
Potential problems/ high-cost economy	Weak basis for decision-making and control/high-cost economy	Weak basis for decision-making and control/high-cost economy	High-cost economy
Strengthening of forest management	Reinforcement of forest management if tied to master plan/KPHP	Reinforcement of forest management if tied to master plan/KPHP	Not relevant

ANNEX 7–1. *Continued.*

Evaluation Component	SK 313/1999	SK 314/1999	SK 315/1999
Content	Auction of plantation (HPH)	Forest Utilization Master Plan (RKPH), Environmental Management Plan (RKL), Annual Management Plan (RKT), Work program	Sanctions in forest industry and forest product fees
Decisionmaker	Minister, after accepting three prospective winners	Ditj. PHP, except RKT by Regional Offices	Minister
Copied to/ acknowledged by/ evaluated by	Ditj. PHP, auction committee	Level-I service offices	Echelon-I officials
Clarification of the decision made	Proposal evaluation method not explained in decree	Legalization mechanism not stipulated	Based on official reports by forestry agency teams
Subject/beneficiary	Private foreign companies can participate	Concession holders	Specially formed forestry agency teams
Obligations	Technical proposal without AMDAL	Undertaking field activities according to plan	Not explained; transparency and its relation to other evaluations (e.g., the performance of forest certification) are not considered
Necessary preconditions for the policy to work	Industrial forest plantation auction concept is still not clear. What is the state expecting from unproductive forestland? Why is the private sector interested?	Guarantees such as performance bonds can function	The performance of forest industries should be open to the public
Conditions/existence of preconditions		Incentive policy and law enforcement are not supportive	At present, forest industry performance is kept confidential
Potential problems/ high-cost economy	It may be difficult to implement this decree to achieve the objective of economic justice	High-cost economy	High-cost economy
Strengthening of forest management	Not relevant	Centralized; this plan tends to be administrative in nature, thus not strengthening forest management	Sanctions in the form of reduction of hectarage will weaken forest management efforts

ANNEX 7–1. *Continued.*

Evaluation Component	SK 317/1999	SK 318/1999
Content	HPHH for customary communities in production forest hectarage (wood, nonwood)	Role of community in forest industries (natural, plantations)
Decisionmaker	Regent	Regional offices
Copied to/ acknowledged by/ evaluated by	Designation of hectarage determined by level-II forestry service offices and HPH holders and stipulated outside annual logging blocs. If outside HPH, there must be clearance in principal from the Governor.	Level-I forestry service offices and concession holders
Clarification of the decision made		Not explained
Subject/beneficiary	Forest utilization concession holders	Local communities
Obligations	If communities need forest products, HPH holders must permit this after following the procedures noted earlier in this table; communities must pay Reforestation Funds and Resources Royalty Provision	HPH must give communities the opportunity to take part in planning and implementation; HPH must make plans and quarterly activity reports
Necessary preconditions for the policy to work	All forms of forest resource exploitation should be stipulated and unified in RKPH, RKL, and RKT	The clarification of participatory mechanisms and processes should be stipulated in this decree
Conditions/existence of preconditions	Implementation of forest industry policy is still far from efficient	A climate of transparency through dialog still needs to be developed.
Potential problems/ high-cost economy	Very bureaucratic	Very bureaucratic
Strengthening of forest management	Strengthening of forest management will be possible if all aspects of the HPH management plan are unified to make them efficient	If this decree is put into operation it will strengthen forest management

CHAPTER EIGHT

Timber Management and Related Policies: A Review

Ida Aju Pradnja Resosudarmo

Since the early 1970s, the forestry sector in Indonesia has played a major role in national development as the largest source of non-oil foreign exchange earnings, a promoter of industrial development and employment opportunities, and a contributor to regional development. It is therefore in the country's best interests to maintain its forest resources in a way that sustains this sector's production.

Beginning in the 1980s, growing environmental awareness led to scrutiny of the way these forest resources were being managed. Since then, there has been growing concern that Indonesia's forests are not being managed sustainably. The concept of sustainable forest management, in the broadest sense, refers to managing forests in such a way that their economic, ecological, and social functions are maintained over time (FAO 1993, 11; ITTO 1992, 2). Recognizing the complexities inherent in the idea of sustainable management (i.e., the need to address and balance all three functions of forest resources), and without any intention of elevating one function over the others, this chapter focuses specifically on the forest's economic services. The other two functions are discussed, however, in a limited fashion as they relate to economic considerations included herein.

Available evidence strongly indicates that commercial forest harvests in Indonesia have been conducted in an unsustainable manner. Logs of adequate quality and size have become increasingly difficult to obtain, resulting in a decline in production in recent years. With regard to forest management practices that have led to this situation, we might ask, does unsustainable logging result from bad forest policies or from sound policies that have not been enforced or followed adequately?

The economic crisis in Indonesia has spurred the government to undertake structural reforms in many areas, including policy reforms in forestry and related sectors, in exchange for a multibillion-dollar loan pledged by the International Monetary Fund (IMF). Reforms in the forestry sector in some ways provide a means for testing the conventional policy wisdom prescribed by development agencies with regard to natural resource management. This brings us to the second question: can policy reforms lead to sustainable forest management?

The Role of the Forestry Sector in the Indonesian Economy

Commercial development of the forestry sector in Indonesia began in the late 1960s, when extensive timber harvesting was done in response to an urgent need for sources of national revenue. Two laws supporting these activities were enacted in 1967: the Foreign Investment Law (*Undang-Undang* [UU] 1/ 1967) and the Basic Forestry Law (UU 5/1967). Since then, the forest industry has undergone three phases marked by different areas of emphasis. The first phase (1967–1979) focused on the export of logs, the second phase (1980–1990) saw the development of the plywood industry, and the third phase (the 1990s) witnessed the considerable expansion of the pulp and paper industry has considerably expanded (Hardjono 1994, 211).

The forestry sector has contributed substantially to the national economy, as reflected in the export value of forest and related products. Until 1991, wood products were second only to oil and liquefied natural gas as a source of foreign exchange in Indonesia. Since then, the export value of textiles has surpassed that of wood products. In 1997, forestry products (including pulp and paper) constituted 17% of the value of non-oil exports (Bank Indonesia 2000), and earnings from this sector have expanded rapidly over time. According to figures from Bank Indonesia and the World Bank, the value of forest product exports increased from slightly more than US$1 billion in 1984[1] to more than US$7 billion in 1997 (Bank Indonesia 2000; The World Bank 1996, 141). The role of this sector in the national economy is even more evident in the period of the economic crisis, in which the export value of forestry products in 1999 could still be maintained at US$6 billion, which is about 16% of the total non-oil/liquefied natural gas export value (Bank Indonesia 2000). Although the export of plywood once made up a large part of the foreign exchange earned from the forestry sector, its influence has diminished in recent years because of the declining legal timber supply, increased competition from substitute products, pressure from the environmental movement in major export markets, and other problems (MoF 1997, 20; Nusapati and Keeling 1996, 9; Rashid Hussain Securities 1996; Fletcher 1994, 2; see also Chapter 9 in this book).[2]

Another important way in which forestry activities contribute to Indonesia's national economy is employment opportunities. Estimates of employment in the country's forestry sector range from 700,000 people, or about 1% of the total work force, to 2.5 million people (The World Bank 1995, 5; MoF 1995, 2, 5).[3] Yet these figures may underestimate this sector's full contribution because of difficulty in calculating related to indirect employment. Estimates of indirect employment range widely from a ratio as low as 1.18 additional jobs for every person working directly in the forest sector to as high as 22 jobs for each forestry-related position (Nasendi 1996, 4; MoF 1995, 2: 5; Pudjowidodo and Santoso 1990, 10).

Forestry is also important in the context of regional development in Indonesia. As an industry with resource-based and labor-intensive characteristics, it is suited especially for development of the Outer Islands, which, although endowed with abundant natural resources, have limited infrastructure and skilled labor.[4]

Forestry Practices in Indonesia

Three decades of continuous timber harvesting for commercial purposes have degraded the quantity and quality of Indonesia's natural forest resources. This is reflected in the decline of forest cover and in the figures showing a decline in the forests' (sustainable) capability to produce timber over the years. A World Bank estimate suggested that the country lost about 20 million ha during 1985–1997 (The World Bank 2001, ii). According to the MoF's documents, during the first four of the country's five-year development schemes, *Pembangunan Lima Tahun* (PELITA I–IV) Indonesia's forests were able to produce about 40 million m^3 of timber, declining to 31.4 million m^3 in PELITA V, and to 22 million m^3 in PELITA VI.[5] The decline is expected to continue to below 20 million m^3 per year by PELITA VII (Departemen Kehutanan 1997c, 14; MoF 1997, 38).

Commercial logging in Indonesian forests is supposed to follow the selective cutting and replanting system known as *Tebang Pilih Tanam Indonesia* (TPTI).[6] This system, which calls for leaving some trees of a certain size and growth capability unfelled in the forests, was intended to ensure that natural forests could regenerate for successive harvests. Provisions for replanting were part of the system.

Although the system seems straightforward on paper, in practice it has been difficult to implement. Among other problems, it offers the temptation for some concessionaires to re-log a regenerating stand prematurely, and monitoring of the program requires too high a level of forest management skills (D'Silva and Appanah 1993, 33). Even the MoF acknowledged that, although the TPTI system is ecologically sound, in reality it is difficult to put into practice (Departemen Kehutanan 1997c, 5). Other observers, however, believe the TPTI system itself is incapable of achieving sustainability (Setyarso 1990, 7).

Large numbers of concession holders are known to have violated the TPTI regulations by overharvesting, damaging residual stands, failing to replant, or logging outside their cutting blocks. A study on 60 concessions revealed that in 1995 only 52% of the TPTI provisions were implemented (Kartodihardjo 1998b, 1). As a result of unsustainable practices such as overcutting, forest industries face difficulties in obtaining sufficient raw material, thus reportedly leading them to operate well below capacity (Rashid Hussain Securities 1996). This subcapacity performance has occurred in spite of the fact that the industry has at times imported logs to make up for the supply shortfall (Roesad 1996, 253). Of the 18 log-producing provinces, only 3—East Kalimantan, Central Kalimantan, and Aceh—have not experienced a deficit in the supply of raw material for forest industries (Departemen Kehutanan 1997c, 14; see also Chapter 7 of this book). Some of the characteristics of the country's forestry sector that promote unsustainable management include the following:

- rates of timber extraction higher than the rates determined to be sustainable,[7]
- inefficient logging methods,
- logging methods that cause excessive ecological disturbances,
- logging methods that contribute to unplanned forest conversion to nonforest uses, and
- poor reforestation and forest regeneration practices.

Rates of Timber Extraction Higher than the Rates Determined to be Sustainable

To ensure sufficient and continuing production of natural forests, the rate of harvesting must not exceed the forests' capacity to regenerate. An examination of timber extraction in Indonesia shows a record of log production that exceeds the assumed sustainable rate (see Chapter 9). Although official government data show that annual production surpassed the sustainable rate only in 1994, estimates by the Food and Agriculture Organization of the United Nations indicate that log production has been higher than the sustainable rates since 1989 (Table 8–1).[8] A decline in the ability of Indonesia's forests to produce timber is an indication that more has been harvested than the official data suggest. Following are some of the contributing factors:

Table 8–1. Log Production

Year	Log production (millions of m³) [a] (MOF)	Year	Sawlog and veneer log production (millions of m³) [b] (FAO)	Production capacity of Indonesian forests (millions of m³) [c] (MOF)
1983–1984	15.2	1983	25.5	40
1984–1985	16.0	1984	27.0	40
1985–1986	14.6	1985	23.5	40
1986–1987	19.8	1986	27.4	40
1987–1988	27.6	1987	31.2	40
1988–1989	27.8	1988	34.8	40
1989–1990	22.3	1989	36.7	31.4
1990–1991	26.1	1990	32.0	31.4
1991–1992	23.8	1991	35.4	31.4
1992–1993	28.2	1992	35.3	31.4
1993–1994	26.8	1993	35.3	31.4
1994–1995	24.0	1994	31.8	22
1995–1996	24.9	1995	31.1	22

Sources:
[a]Departemen Kehutanan 1994; Departemen Kehutanan 1996; Departemen Kehutanan 1997d.
[b]FAO 1996 and 1997.
[c]Departemen Kehutanan 1997d; MOF 1997.

- Cases of illegal logging are rampant, resulting in underestimated official statistics.[9]
- The demand for logs exceeds the forests' sustainable production threshold.[10]
- The size and the amount of logs cut are not in conformity with the rules, which has led to an underreporting of the number of logs felled.[11]

One of the most clear and alarming signals of decline in the country's natural forest production is the government's acknowledgement of the need to depend on high levels of supply from planned timber plantations. The directorate general of Forest Inventory and Land Use of the MoF had planned to obtain 23 million m³ per year of logs from timber plantations during 1999 to 2004 (Departemen Kehutanan 1997b, 20). Reaching this goal will be virtually impossible, because the 1997 production capacity was reportedly 1.8 million m³ per year (Departemen Kehutanan 1997a, II–10). If timber plantations do not follow the planned schedule—which at this point appears to be very likely—incentives to overharvest natural forests will be all the greater.

Temporarily, logs obtained from the conversion of forests to nonforestland uses such as oil palm plantations could partly offset the shortage of legal supply from forest concessions, in addition to wood supply from forests that are cleared for timber plantation development. Yet it is estimated that the expansion and development of oil palm and rubber plantations will be saturated in the next 10 years (Data Consult Inc. 1997a, 70; see also Chapter 10 of this book), meaning that forest industries will have to find other sources of raw material to fill the gap. In the MoF's strategic plan draft report released during its 2000 annual national meeting, one aim of the government's forestry policies was to stop natural forest conversion to nonforest uses, until an agreed National Forest Program could be established (Dephutbun 2000, 17). Following are some of the scenarios that may develop:

- Mills will run further below capacity.
- Logs will have to be imported in significant amounts.
- Mills will maintain current production levels by further overexploitation of the natural forests—that is, by overcutting production forests, expanding felling areas to nonproduction forests, or both.

Inefficient Logging Methods

Besides evidence of harvesting in excess of the forests' capacity, data indicate concessionaires have been engaging in inefficient logging practices (Table 8–2). The inefficient use of timber resources is reflected in the portion of logs recovered, the amount of wood wasted, and the damage done through current logging practices compared with sustainable practices. Of the 85 m^3 of commercial logs per hectare, only 55 m^3 are recovered in current practices, compared with a harvestable level of 72 m^3 for sustainable practices. The logs wasted and left remaining in the forest total 30 m^3 per hectare, or more than double the projected amount if harvesting was done sustainably.

Logging Methods That Cause Excessive Ecological Disturbances

Unsound logging practices have contributed to undesirable ecological and environmental effects, such as the loss of biodiversity, siltation, erosion, and flooding. The damage incurred in current logging practices is substantial. Effects include damage to the residual trees, decreases in species composition of residual stands as a result of extraction of the best trees, and destruction of residual stand structure as the upper canopy layer is reduced (Sagala 1997, 115; Kartawinata and Vayda 1984, 117). Table 8–2 shows that forest harvesting methods in Indonesia damage more trees than necessary.

Table 8–2. Timber Recovery and Losses Under Current and Sustainable Logging Practices

	Forest harvesting practices 1990s (m^3 of commercial logs per ha)	Sustainable practices (m^3 of commercial logs per ha)
Stock of commercially harvestable logs/ha	85	85
Recovered	55	72
Waste	30	13
Damage	18	14

Source: The World Bank 1994b.

Forest harvesting through Indonesia's selective cutting and planting system has been shown to inflict damage in the range of 28% to 48% of the remaining trees (Sist et al. 1998, 255; Sist and Bertault and Sist 1997, 215; Elias 1996, 13). Improved logging methods can reduce damage to residual stands to 25–30% (Sist and Bertault 1998, 153). Most of the trees that were damaged had little chance to recover because their growth was affected by the damage (Elias 1996, 19).

Another adverse ecological effect of logging activities is related to the construction and use of logging roads and skidding tracks, which may leave large portions of forest bare. Because dry road conditions are necessary for log hauling, logging roads are often built in a wide swath to prevent shading, thereby increasing the amount of cleared forest area (Fenton 1996, 86). In East Kalimantan, the average size of opened area associated with the harvesting of one tree is 396 m^2 (Elias 1996, 16).

Research also has shown that soil compaction in Kalimantan related to logging operations reduced water infiltration 21 times, resulting in high erosion rates and flooding (Tarrant et al. 1987, 27). Stadtmuller and Hardiwinarto (1990, quoted in Riswan and Hartanti 1995, 49) showed that soil erosion in East Kalimantan was nearly four times higher in the freshly clear-cut forest compared with untouched forest, and the surface runoff in the clear-cut forest was about 2.5 times greater than that of untouched forest. Silt loads in the streams of Kalimantan have been found to increase 33-fold in some logging areas (Tarrant et al. 1987, 27).

Logging Methods That Contribute to Unplanned Forest Conversion to Nonforest Uses

Recognizing that nonforest forms of land use are necessary and legitimate, the Government of Indonesia (GOI) has designated some 35 million ha of forestlands for conversion to other uses, of which 22.7 million ha are forested. Other classifications of forestlands include 61.9 million ha designated for timber production and 47.6 million ha for protection and conservation (GOI/FAO 1996, 31). It is important to note, however, that not all forestlands are forested.[12]

These classifications, known as *Tata Guna Hutan Kesepakatan* ([TGHK] Forest Functions Based on Consensus), were developed in 1982, after the granting of concession areas. As a result, some areas of forest classified as other than production forests overlap with areas allocated to timber concessions. As many as 4.8 million ha of protection and conservation forests were found to be located within concession areas (Mulyana 1990, 6). Analysis of timber concession areas in 1989 indicated that, on average, some 25% of the total area was located in other forest categories (GOI/FAO 1990, 18). As concessionaires have faced limited obstacles to logging in conversion, protection, or conservation forests located within their concession boundaries, their activities may have led to "unplanned" conversion of forests to nonforest uses.

Another activity that can contribute significantly to unplanned deforestation is the common practice of reentering logged-over forests before they have returned to harvestable conditions. This often causes damage to the stock and permanently prevents regrowth (The World Bank 1994a, 53; Thiele 1994, 86; Yayasan Adi Sanggoro 1989, 20). The prevalence of subcontracting has been shown to aggravate this problem, because subcontractors are often not held liable for their actions (MoF 1995, 4, 12; Yayasan Adi Sanggoro 1989, 20).

Although logging practices of short-term–oriented concessionaires result in forest degradation and unplanned deforestation, the indirect consequences of logging often lead to more severe, irreversible deforestation than actual logging (RePPProT 1990, 153; Tarrant et al. 1987, 28).[13] Logging roads have been known to promote forest loss by providing access for activities other than logging, such as the opening of new settlements.[14] Although there are no comprehensive national data showing the relationship between the development of new settlements and the establishment of logging roads, several case studies have shown that migration to forested areas is greatly facilitated by these roads (Anyonge and Nugroho 1996, 110; Vayda and Sahur 1985, 594). In East Kalimantan, the removal of big trees made it easier to clear the forests for swiddens (Poffenberger and McGean 1993, 16). Furthermore, although concessionaires are responsible for safeguarding forest areas within their concession boundaries, the presence of logging roads in unattended logged-over forests make these forests easy targets for timber theft and illegal logging.[15] Networks of logging roads on Indonesia's Outer Islands are extensive and reach far into the hinterlands, to forests that otherwise would be inaccessible. Up to 1993, some 38,000 km of roads had been built across 19 provinces for the purpose of timber exploitation (Departemen Kehutanan 1995, 25). Poor logging practices have also contributed to preconditions for major uncontrolled forest fires (State Ministry for Environment, Republic of Indonesia/United Nations Development Programme 1998, 74). Such fires occurred in East Kalimantan during 1982–1983 and in Sumatra and Kalimantan from the latter half of 1997 to April 1998 (see Chapters 13 and 14 of this book).

Poor Records of Reforestation and Forest Regeneration Practices

An unsatisfactory record of reforestation and forest regeneration in Indonesia has exacerbated the effect of poor logging practices. From 1976 to 1994, fewer than 800,000 ha of areas designated as protection forests had been reforested (Kartodihardjo 1998a, 10). It is not known how much of this reforestation effort has actually succeeded, but the national success rate of reforestation is estimated to be below 40% (Kartodihardjo 1998a, 10). Meanwhile, the proportion of logged-over areas that have been replanted is minimal, as low as 4% (Pramono 1992, 168). In the Riau province, by 1991–1992 only 10% of concessionaires had done any replanting activities in their logged-over areas (Awang 1993, 77).[16]

The present rate of replanting will not keep pace with the rate of forest areas lost. If the latest estimate of 1.6 to 1.7 million ha of annual deforestation is accurate, then to compensate for annual deforestation from all causes (not only from timber sector activities but also by the expansion of agriculture and other causes) would require approximately the same area of successful reforestation each year.[17] Given the gloomy statistics just discussed, this seems unlikely.[18]

Forestry Policies and Institutional Issues[19]

The record of commercial forest utilization tends to indicate that the current policies by which these practices are governed are inadequate to encourage sustainable forest management. The policy deficiencies appear to be of two kinds: (a) policies that undermine sustainability and (b) policies that may aim for sustainability but are not adequately enforced or are in fact unenforceable.

Policies and Institutional Arrangements Leading to Practices that Undermine Sustainability

Following are several policies and economic imperatives that have influenced the way the commercial timber sector has operated in Indonesia:

- the centralization of control and jurisdiction of forestlands,
- overdependence on forest resources for national income,
- patronage and partiality in concession allocations,
- a log ban and vertical integration of the forest industry,
- low fees and royalties,
- duration of concession cycle and tenure insecurity, and
- promotion of agroexport commodities.

Centralization of Control and Jurisdiction of Forestlands. Control over the country's forest resources lies with MoF, which is charged with assigning and distributing forest exploitation rights while also controlling and protecting these resources.[20] The first task involves the granting of concession rights; the second requires setting the rules and regulations that these concessionaires must adhere to and making sure that the rules are enforced.

MoF controls 144 million ha of forestland or 75% of the total national land area. The centralized governance of the country's forestlands entails planning (forest) land uses, allocating financial and human resources, and distributing forestry-derived earnings. Among the consequences of this approach are inconsistencies in implementation at the regional and local levels: although planning has been done at the national level, there is a lack of incentives at lower levels of government to manage concessions well.

The distribution of both human and financial resources is skewed against the provinces outside Java. Half of the forestry department staff is located in

Java, which has only 2% of the country's forests (The World Bank 1990, xxii). In 1995, every forester working in concessions outside Java on average oversaw 26,700 ha of forestland, while a counterpart on Java oversaw 6,906 ha of forest (Kartodihardjo 1998c, 13).

A similar situation occurs in relation to the distribution of forestry-derived earnings. While natural forest resources are located far from the center, the central government has acquired a large proportion of the sector's earnings.[21] Between 1983 and 1995, the contribution of the forestry sector to gross regional earnings was on average 1.2% per annum (Kartodihardjo 1998c, 7). The small contribution that concessionaires and their logging activities make toward regional development has been a disincentive to maintaining the forests' existence (Mulyana 1990, 7, 22). The fact that local government has no authority over the granting of forest exploitation permits is a further disincentive. This encourages the local government, especially at the regency levels, to look for more alluring investment possibilities in other sectors. Depending on investment choices, investment in other sectors such as agriculture or mining could potentially put more pressure on forests if forest conversion is needed.

Overdependence on Forests for National Income. The GOI has depended heavily on forest resources as a source of foreign exchange, and the economic crisis is increasing this dependence. The pressure to favor foreign exchange earnings through the exportation of forestry products and to ignore conservation is great (see Chapter 11). Indonesia has the right to utilize its resources for the benefit of the country as a whole, especially at a time of crisis when foreign exchange and employment opportunities are needed more than ever. Yet excessive dependence on these forests for income can lead to even greater destruction and prevent their future utilization. It is precisely this reason—to be able to enjoy the values of the forests now and in the future—that justifies an appropriate balance between forest utilization and forest conservation.

Patronage and Partiality in Concession Allocations. As noted earlier in this chapter, commercial exploitation of forests in Indonesia began at a time of national economic collapse. In the beginning, this exploitation depended on foreign capital; nationalization followed several years later. Because the main focus was on quick generation of cash, concessions were given to large companies able to invest sufficient capital (Suryohadikusumo 1997, 3). As a result, concession rights were concentrated in the hands of a few individuals, and each concessionaire was allocated vast areas of forests. Moreover, the allocation was based on patronage, rather than occurring through a market mechanism or bidding system. Cases of "sleeping partners," in which forests are harvested by an enterprise other than the concession licensee, are common. In such situations, the companies conducting the harvest are not liable for violations of the terms stipulated in the forestry agreement, which has the effect of encouraging them to log as they please.

At the same time, the excessively large size of concession areas provides few incentives for protecting against encroachment (Thiele 1994, 187). However, for control purposes, large concessions are easier for the MoF to monitor and penalize (Nusapati and Keeling 1996, 11). In 1994–1995, 17 of 98 timber groups had control over concessions from more than 1 to 6 million ha, while 16 groups controlled from 500,000 to 1 million ha (Brown 1999, 12–13). Meanwhile, a study by Scotland (1998, 19) shows that the size needed for concessions to be profitable is on the order of 80,000 ha.

The most important implication of this policy appears to be the "overempowerment" of several large concessionaires. Some observers believe the government has been overgenerous to a few concessionaires. The consequence is that the government appears to have lost control over these timber companies and has not been capable of implementing its forestry development program (Samego 1997, 3; Mubyarto 1996, 13).

Log Ban and Vertical Integration of the Forest Industry. In the 1980s, the government issued a ban on log exports, and subsequently applied a high export tax on sawn wood. This was done in the quest for higher value-added production by promoting downstream forest-based industries, especially plywood.[22] This policy, along with financial incentives, resulted in industrial overcapacity in relation to the supply of raw materials and encouraged inefficient resource utilization (Sumitro 1995, 184).[23] The requirement to invest in downstream wood processing industries forced smaller concessionaires to transfer their concession rights to larger ones. As a consequence, Indonesia's forest resources became even more concentrated (Sumitro 1995, 184; Ramli and Ahmad 1993, 56).

Why, then, did the government adopt this policy? Subsequent vertical integration of processing industries, apart from seeking domestic added value, was meant to encourage the concessionaires to run their concessions well (Rashid Hussain Securities 1996, 11). It appears, however, that the policy backfired. The low price of timber resulting from the ban promoted inefficient and wasteful logging.[24] Production of 27 m³ of plywood and derivatives per hectare entailed 15 to 22 m³ of waste at the industrial plants and 20 to 70 m³ of log waste in the forest (Fenton 1996, 67).

Low Fees and Royalties. Analysts have tended to support the notion that the fees and royalties charged for the right to harvest timber are too low, resulting in low government rent capture (Prakosa 1996, 43).[25] Low rent capture encourages inefficient and wasteful logging and processing (Thiele 1994, 190), and excessive profits are collected by concessionaires.

Duration of Concession Cycle and Tenure Insecurity. Reports claim that the duration of a concession permit (20 years) that falls short of the stipulated 35-year harvesting cycle promotes unsustainable management because concessionaires have insecure tenure for the subsequent harvesting cycles (Kartodihardjo 1998c, 16; Thiele 1994, 186). As a result, concessionaires tend to harvest the entire area of their concessions within that 20-year period (Toha 1997, 5). Other observers believe that regardless of the duration of a lease, forestry companies will not change their behavior in managing forests (WALHI 1996, 6). An analytical study by Boscolo and Vincent (2000) using Malaysian data shows that a longer concession period alone provides little incentive for loggers to adopt reduced-impact logging practices or to comply with minimum diameter cutting limits. Many companies with natural forest concessions are short-term in outlook—that is, they do not reinvest in the forestry sector with the aim of maintaining their stream of income from this resource for the long term (Nusapati and Keeling 1996, 16; Toha 1997, 4, 7).

Promotion of Agroexport Commodities. The capability of the forests to secure foreign exchange is challenged by the competitiveness of agroexport commodities. The expansion of oil palm and rubber plantations in Indonesia over the years has been tremendous. The area of oil palm plantations increased 24-fold in 30 years, from 105,000 ha in 1967 to 2,630,000 ha in 1998 (see Chapter 10); the area of rubber plantations increased from 2 million ha in 1967 to 3.5 million ha in 1998 (Direktorat Jenderal Perkebunan 1998).

In contrast with oil palm plantations where the operations are mostly owned by large companies, rubber plantations are mostly run by smallholders. In 1998, smallholder rubber plantations consisted of about 80% or 2.83 million ha of the total rubber plantations in the country (Capricorn Indonesia Consult 1999, 3). In 1998, exports from this commodity amounted to US$1.1 million (Capricorn Indonesia Consult 1999, 16).

Consequently, forestlands in Indonesia are under increasing pressure for conversion. Until 1998, it would have been in the interests of the MoF to maintain jurisdiction of these forestlands by favoring them for conversion to timber estates (including pulp plantations) over conversion to agricultural uses. In 1998, however, with the transfer of responsibility for plantation development from the Ministry of Agriculture to the MoFEC, different sorts of challenges and issues were expected to arise. On the one hand, control by the MoFEC over the designated use of the land, whether for agricultural activities or for forestry, was intended to make planning easier in terms of consistency in policy and better oversight of the designated land use. On the other hand, pressures to develop crop plantations could have led the MoFEC to set priorities to the detriment of forest cover. The latter fears may have been important in the recent decision to revert to an MoF.

Although the need to develop tree crop plantations both for export goals and development in general is easily understood in the context of Indonesia's economic crisis, it is widely suspected that many companies clear forests with the stated intention of developing tree crops but do not do so. In West Kalimantan, companies cleared timber on large tracts of land but did not subsequently establish oil palm and rubber plantations (*The Jakarta Post* 1998a, 8). The development of tree crop plantations may not necessarily pose a threat to forest cover, insofar as they are located on unused sites or as a means to improve the quality of the sites. Tree crop plantation developments raise a concern when they are developed inappropriately through the incentives provided and along with inadequately addressed regulatory issues such as how much forest area should be converted for this purpose, where the designated sites are located, and how they are established. It is widely known that some of these plantations have been established on customary, or *adat*, lands, leading to conflicts with local communities.

Potentially Positive Policies That Are Not Adequately Enforced or Are Unenforceable

Recognizing that sustainable forestry has not been achieved and that concessionaires are responsible for some forest destruction and degradation (Departemen Kehutanan 1997c, 6), beginning in the early 1990s the MoF adopted several policies to address this issue. These policies included community development schemes, sanctions and penalties, and timber plantation development.

Community Development Schemes. One important component of sustainable management of forest resources is the fulfillment of appropriate economic and social functions of these forests with regard to communities living in these forest areas. More recent policies governing the forest sector have shifted from focusing exclusively on economic considerations to giving greater attention to conservation and social goals. The HPH *Bina Desa* program, later known as *Pembinaan Masyarakat Desa Hutan* (PMDH), was established in 1991 as a legal arrangement to involve local communities in forest management (also discussed in Chapter 1). Yet the program has had many shortcomings and failures. The needs of the communities have not been adequately assessed through their participation in planning, the rights of communities with regard to access to land have not been acknowledged, forest communities have not been granted the right to harvest timber for commercial purposes, and timber companies do not see any benefit from participating in the program (Kartodihardjo 1998d, 2). Effective implementation would entail giving relevant communities a greater share of decisionmaking in forest use and access to forest wealth. Failure to involve forest communities in forest management and to incorporate their rights and needs may encourage "illegal logging," thereby contributing to unsustainable forest management.

Sanctions and Penalties. Some observers believe that the GOI not only has been overgenerous to the commercial timber sector, but also has been too lenient in applying sanctions and penalties for infractions of government regulations and the forestry agreements. While the most severe sanction stipulated by law is a 10-year prison term (Pamulardi 1995, 351), it appears that the most serious sanctions acted upon have been the revocation of licenses, and there are no records of any action to prosecute offenders. Given the existence of other policies designed to promote the development of forest industries, the government is likely to favor concessionaires that have little regard for forest sustainability but that contribute significantly to the nation's gross national product (Samego 1997, 3). In recent years, however, and particularly under the current political atmosphere of reforms, we have seen revocation of licenses as opposed to repeated warnings and fines.[26]

Timber Plantation Development. Timber plantation development potentially supports the economic sustainability of natural forests by helping to reduce pressure on remaining natural forests. In Indonesia, the establishment of timber plantations has been seen as a way to offset timber shortages resulting from the continuing loss of natural forest cover (MoF 1995, 2, 6). Yet there are indications that the country's timber plantation development has fallen far short of expectations.

Timber plantations were to have been established only in "unproductive" areas within production forests or in areas to be designated as production forest.[27] Anecdotal evidence, however, shows that there has been a tendency to clear the most productive forests for timber. Land-clearing activities by timber and oil palm plantations have been blamed in large part for initiating many of the devastating 1997–1998 forest fires in Indonesia (Dennis 1999, 14; see Chapters 13 and 14 of this book).

In recent years, timber plantations have given priority to the production of raw material for the pulp and paper industry (MoF 1995, 5, 2). This industry grew rapidly in the 1990s and is now one of the 10 major categories of export commodities from the industrial sector (Data Consult Inc. 1997b, 8; Bank Indonesia 2000). In 1997 there were 15 pulp producers in Indonesia with a total production capacity of 3.9 million metric tons per annum (Indonesian Business Trend 1998, 5). Between 1993 and 1997, pulp production increased by 37.1% annually (Indonesian Business Trend 1998, 6). Export earnings from pulp and paper production have increased from less than US$0.5 billion in 1993 to US$2.7 billion in 1999 (Bank Indonesia 2000).

Rapid development of the pulp and paper industry is posing a threat to natural forests. One threat is the emerging disparity between the overcapacity of the pulp and paper mills and the undersupply of raw materials from timber plantations (Data Consult Inc. 1997b, 11; Mulyadi and Roesad 1996, 278).

As with plywood, this encourages overexploitation of natural forests to pay back the high capital costs of establishing such plants. Many of the pulp plants face difficulties in procuring raw material because of the slow development of timber estates (Data Consult Inc. 1997b, 8; Mulyadi and Roesad 1996, 278). By October 1998, out of the 5 million ha of land with timber plantation permits, more than 3 million ha were reserved for the development of pulp plantations (MoFEC 2000). Of these, only 1 million ha have been established (MoFEC 2000).

The negative effect of the pulp and paper industry on the forests may be even greater in the future because of the potential attractiveness of this industry compared with the plywood industry. There are two reasons for the increasing desirability of pulp and paper. First, the increasing substitutability of plywood makes it less attractive over time. Second, in contrast with nonpulp plantations, the shorter period between planting and harvest for pulp plantations is an obvious advantage for quicker returns on investment and involves less risk. This is further supported by the government's policy to promote the industry with incentives and subsidies, similar to those applied in support of the plywood industry.[28] The attractiveness of the pulp and paper industry would appear to offer incentives for stakeholders in the plywood business to invest in this industry, and it has been shown that producers of pulp are often stakeholders in plywood and oil palm enterprises (Capricorn Indonesia Consult 1995).

The government's policy of promoting timber plantation development with the goal of achieving timber sustainability and reducing pressure on natural forest cover can be questioned for two reasons. First, the existing plywood industry's requirement for timber is far larger than the requirement of the pulp and paper industry, yet the development of timber plantations has been geared toward the supply of the latter industry. Second, even given the problem of (structural) timber deficit faced by the plywood industry (i.e., the inadequate legal supply from production forests and conversion forests), the government still implements a policy that has failed to ensure sufficient raw material is produced from timber plantations for plywood mills prior to the establishment of new pulp plants. The problem is exacerbated by the revocation of many concession licenses, bringing the legal timber supply even lower (*Bisnis Indonesia* 1999c, b; *The Jakarta Post* 1999a, 1).

Although timber plantation development could potentially sustain timber supply and help maintain the remaining natural forest cover, it has actually increased pressure on the remaining natural forests because it has been done ineffectively. In addition, the development of pulp and paper industries induced the prioritization of pulp plantations, thus undermining any efforts or intentions to develop timber plantations to address the raw material problem faced by the plywood industry.

How Will Proposed Policy Reforms Affect Forests and Forest Management?

We have seen that the policies in place until early 1999 in Indonesia are inadequate to meet the goals of forest sustainability, either because they are not the right policies or because they have not been enforced properly. The need for reforms in policies that affect the forest has been recognized for some time, but in general such changes have not gained the support of decisionmakers. The current economic and political crises have forced the government to make structural policy commitments in many sectors, including in the forestry and related sectors, as specified in the agreement between the IMF, the World Bank, and the GOI.

Reforms in the forestry sector and other sectors affecting forest management are under way. Reform measures under the responsibility of the MoFEC include ones that affect the following:

- forest market structure and access;
- direct taxation of forest product enterprises;
- the management and ownership of forestlands; and
- agriculture and plantations, with indirect effects on forestry.

Because the effects of these policy reforms on forests and forest management can only be seen in the medium to long term, this section will provide only a preliminary and indicative (and to a certain degree rather speculative) analysis of the possible effects of these measures on the commercial timber sector and the forests in general, based on information gathered up to the date that this chapter was written.

Measures That Affect Forest Market Structure and Access

Among the reform measures that affect forest market structure and access is the elimination of the plywood export marketing arrangements, which were previously done through the monopoly of the Indonesian Wood Panel Association (APKINDO). APKINDO assigned plywood companies export quotas. The association played a critical role in setting prices and controlling international distribution (Barr 1998, 2). It has been blamed for the loss of Indonesia's market share abroad by setting prices too high and has been accused of collecting unnecessary fees, thereby adding to the industry's costs.

How would the elimination of this marketing arrangement affect the timber sector? In the short run, companies might face difficulties in finding buyers because they have been out of touch with the market. In the long run, however, elimination of such marketing arrangements should benefit companies with regard to prices, market preferences, and market potential. Direct access to international markets, leading to better prices and higher profits, along with other improvements such as a stronger concession tenure, may promote better management of forests. However, it could also promote the behavior of "produce as much as you can while the business is profitable," with the corresponding "log as much as you need while you can" behavior, leading to even worse destruction of the natural forests.

Reports covering the period after the abolishment of APKINDO's role in marketing arrangements and price control have noted competition among Indonesian plywood producers in the form of a price war that has contributed to the decline in world prices for Indonesian plywood (*Bisnis Indonesia* 2000d). Another reform provision in this category is the reduction of export taxes on logs to a maximum of 30% ad valorem in mid-1998 and further reductions to 10% by the end of 2000.[29] This essentially means the lifting of the log export ban.

There are two schools of opinion on the virtues and the sins of banning log exports.[30] The log export ban is said not to be good for forests because it reduces the domestic price of timber, promotes more inefficient logging and processing, leads to fewer plantations and investments in forest management, and makes agriculture a more competitive land use option compared with forestry. The following arguments are raised by proponents of log export bans:

- Reduced domestic log prices may lead to less logging and associated forest degradation in the short run.
- If agriculture and logging complement each other through the opening of logging roads, then less logging can make agriculture less competitive rather than more competitive.
- Inefficiencies must be analyzed in a dynamic context, and there should be a positive learning curve of industries involved in processing.

Although the export ban has been lifted, priority is still being given to guaranteeing an adequate log supply for domestic industry through controls on export volume, export licenses, and exportable wood species (*Bisnis Indonesia* 1998; *The Jakarta Post* 1999b, 8; U.S. Department of Agriculture 1999, 8). Nevertheless, reports have indicated that halfway to the 2000, log exports were blamed as a contributing factor to the increasing difficulties in meeting the needed supply for the plywood industry and the resulting decline in plywood exports (*Republika* 2000). The lifting of the log export ban has reportedly bolstered illegal logging activities even further and promoted illegal export of logs (*Bisnis Indonesia* 2000a, b, c). There is much discussion now (February 2001) about the possibility of reinstating a log ban.

Measures That Affect Direct Taxation of Forest Product Enterprises

A measure has been suggested (as stated in the IMF memorandum of understanding) that increases the proportion of the market value of land and buildings assessable for tax purposes to 40% of the assets' value for plantations and forest property. This tax is collected by the regional governments of the areas where the enterprises are located. One of the reasons why some concession areas are so large is because the price of acquisition and fees and royalties are low. In the past, the prices of land in concession areas are known to have been assessed at very low levels, sometimes as low as a mere 300 Rp per hectare (Prakosa 1996, 37).[31] Although concessions do not buy lands (where their concessions are located), they are obligated to pay land tax according to the assessment made on the value of the land. From a scale of 1 to 50 of land value classifications in Indonesia, with class 1 being the highest valued, the value of land assigned for concession areas is in class 47, or the 4th lowest (*Bisnis Indonesia* 1999a). If this continues to be the case, then there are few incentives to limit the size of concessions and the use of land in inefficient ways under contract.

The government has acknowledged that some concessions are too large to be manageable and that the size of concession areas should be such that they guarantee efficiency while being sufficient in size to supply processing requirements. In 1998, the government decreed new regulations on the extension of concession rights that limit the size of a concession area to 100,000 ha in one province or 400,000 ha throughout Indonesia (*Surat Keputusan* [SK] or ministerial decree 732/Kpts-II/1998).

Measures That Affect the Management and Ownership of Forestlands

This category includes the following types of reform measures:

- auctioning of concessions,
- lengthening of concession periods,
- transferability of concessions,
- review and increase of stumpage fees and creation of new resource rent taxes on timber resources,
- implementation of a system of performance bonds for forest concessions,
- de-linking of concession ownership from forest product processing industries,
- incorporation of the reforestation fund into the state budget, and
- the redirection of the fund uses other than forestry purposes.

The auctioning of concessions, the lengthening of the concession period, and the transferability of concessions are incentives intended to promote long-term management by increasing the value of the land (and the resources on it) to the concessionaire. The lengthening of the concession period aims to provide security of tenure. The transferability of concessions is expected to provide an incentive for concessionaires to maintain the "value" of their concessions, to obtain a favorable price when they decide to sell. All of these provisions will require an appropriate mechanism of forest resource allocation. In addition, because forest areas are inhabited by indigenous and local peoples, issues of property rights and equity need to be addressed as well (see Chapters 1, 2, 4, 5, and 6).

In mid-September 1998, the government announced that 149 concessions would be awarded through an auction system (*The Jakarta Post* 1998c). These concessions originally belonged to companies that had had their licenses revoked for breaching logging regulations and for failing to manage their concessions sustainably. To prevent further destruction of the forests, no new forest concessions were to be awarded—only vacant concession areas were opened for bidding (*The Jakarta Post* 1999a, 8; 1998b, 8). Some 11 million ha of forest concession areas were anticipated to be taken over by the government by 2000, 10 million ha of which would be offered to the public for auction (*The Jakarta Post* 1999c, 12). Before new concessions are granted through auction, the government should obtain sufficient information on the market potential of the forests, to assess the value of the forests realistically. One significant problem has been that the private sector has been able to secure more complete information than the government on the potential of forest resources (Kartodihardjo 1998c, 15).

An increase in stumpage fees is meant to bring the value of timber felled in line with its real value. The increase in stumpage fees may result in more illegal logging unless it is accompanied by improvements in all components of the forestry system, including appropriate policies and effective regulations. In the absence of such improvements, illegal logging is currently rampant. The gradual decrease in the imposition of a log export tax (to reach a level of 10% by 2000) must be compensated by the phasing in of a resource rent tax to prevent the excessive utilization of the resource (Pangestu 1998). The maximum resource rent tax has been set at 6% of the selling price, which is based on both the international and the domestic prices. Given the drastic depreciation of the national currency because of the economic crisis (and with the domestic price quoted in the national currency), this could mean a low resource rent in real terms and therefore may not work in favor of sustaining forest resources. Furthermore, it is important that the selling price be reviewed often to adequately reflect the prevailing market price.

The implementation of a system of performance bonds for concessionaires has the objective of improving environmental protection by internalizing the environmental and social costs of forest utilization. A performance bond is an amount of money that concessionaires have to pay up-front to the government before they carry out logging activities. This amount of money, including interest, will be returned to them only if they prove to have harvested their concessions sustainably. It is therefore crucial to have the right set of criteria and indicators in place with which to measure the performance of concessionaires. An appropriate mechanism for collecting and redistributing the funds also is needed.

The dismantling of vertical integration between concession owners and downstream processing industries, along with the lifting of the log export ban, is expected to adjust the price of logs to what they are really worth in the market. The risk of timber harvest over and above the capacity of the forest resource appears to remain; only now, assuming that there are no obstacles to the exportation of logs, it is dictated both by the price of (and hence demand for) logs on the domestic and international markets. In the short term, because inefficient industries will only be able to compete if they can obtain logs cheaply, this may prompt increased efforts to seek supply from illegal harvest.

The incorporation of the reforestation fund into the state budget is intended to increase public control over its use. The use of the fund for purposes other than forestry can be minimized, and it may provide the local governments with a new source of funds. However, the MoFEC is now more restricted in its use of the fund because the ministry no longer has control over it. Developments in early 1999, however, have seen efforts by the MoFEC to determine at which bank the reforestation funds are to be kept, where at least part of the funds would be used as a working asset for establishing an alternative funding institution to finance agribusinesses (*Bisnis Indonesia* 1999a). While the use of reforestation funds is restricted to only forestry purposes, the fact that there were intentions to direct some of the funds to support agribusinesses was clearly one consequence of moving the estate crops sector from the Ministry of Agriculture to the MoF.

Measures That Affect Agriculture and Plantations, with Indirect Effects on Forestry

This category includes the following types of reform measures:

- the removal of restrictions on foreign investment in oil palm plantations;
- the replacement of a ban on palm oil product exports with an export tax, which was down from 60% in July 1998 to 10% in early 2000; and
- the reduction of land conversion targets to environmentally sustainable levels.

The first two of the above provisions probably pose one of the greatest threats to forest resources. The pressure is large because the country is badly in need of foreign exchange, and virtually any foreign investment in such a difficult situation will be welcomed. The low exchange value of the national currency to the dollar means that larger areas of land can be obtained by foreign investors. The low "price" of forestlands works to the benefit of investors, potentially accelerating the conversion of forestlands to plantations.

The third provision is potentially in contradiction with the first. The extended role of the MoF to include estate crops/plantations could have contributed to maintaining a sufficient area of natural forest, because control of forestlands would have been made easier (Suryohadikusumo 1998). However, the conversion of forestlands to estate crops would face fewer obstacles because the decisionmaking process was designed to take place within the same ministry.

Conclusion

The natural forest wealth of Indonesia has been ruined in part by excessive timber harvesting and inappropriate silvicultural practices. We have seen that inappropriate policies and institutional arrangements along with nonenforcement of potentially good policies have contributed to the problem.

The following are the main inappropriate policies:

- centralization of forest administration and finances leading to low incentives and capabilities for appropriate forest management at the local level (see Chapter 15);
- excessive dependence on natural forests for national development, which has led to liquidation of forest resources for the benefit of other sectors and to the enrichment of the few;
- favoritism in the allocation of concessions, which leads to a perverse situation whereby many concessionaires are above the law and are "overempowered" in relation to the state;
- low fees and royalties, which are directly related to the problem of favoritism, lead to inefficiency and waste, and contribute to overempowerment;
- a log export ban and vertical integration policies, which have led to industrial overcapacity, overuse of natural forests, and inefficiency and waste; and
- inappropriate development of tree crop plantations, notably oil palm. Although oil palm development is potentially helpful as a means to address the economic crisis, it is important to recognize that it is driven partly by inappropriate land-use practices of timber concessionaires and that bad plantation siting decisions have undermined some forest communities and sustainable livelihoods, among other problems.

The following are the main potentially positive policies:

- community development schemes, which are intended to increase the share of forest communities in access to forest wealth and in decisionmaking over the use of forest resources, but which have fallen far short of these ideals;
- imposition of fees and sanctions, which through their nonimplementation have contributed to the problem of "overempowerment" of concessionaires and to destruction of forest resources; and
- timber plantation development, which if done appropriately would reduce pressure on natural forest resources, but because it has been done inappropriately has actually contributed to increased pressure on remaining natural forest resources.

The economic crisis and the presidential transition and subsequent reform movement of 1997–1998 presented a golden opportunity to implement much-needed, drastic policy reforms, but these conditions also presented daunting challenges. Large-scale reforms are already under way. Some reforms, imposed through the IMF negotiation process, address some of the inappropriate policies of the past. These new policies undermine favoritism by requiring that new concessions be auctioned; they raise fees and royalties and government rent capture; and they require a dismantling of the log ban, vertical integration, and the plywood monopoly in marketing arrangements. These adopted policies, however, do not address the problem of centralization,[32] the need to alleviate overexploitation of remaining natural forests, the need to improve decisionmaking with regard to oil palm development, the need to improve community development and timber plantation policies, and the need to increase the inadequate power of the state to impose sanctions on concessions.

But even if drastic reforms are implemented soon, one must ask to what extent they can alleviate the dire effects of bad policies and poor implementation of good policies. In closing, three "skeptical" questions are posed that are intended not to fuel despair, but rather to challenge those involved in the reform process to produce better and more meaningful policies. First, is it really possible to construct a system of incentives that motivates concessionaires to protect the natural forest resources over the long term? After all, concessionaires are in the business for the money, and money is not made while waiting for forests to grow back. Second, isn't the aim to limit pressure on natural forests in the midst of a drastic currency depreciation a bit like trying to walk north and south at the same time? The currency depreciation makes the sale of timber, palm oil, and other agricultural export commodities very lucrative, and this can only increase pressure on forests. Finally, how much can forest policy reform in and of itself do to turn the tide and create the conditions for a sustainable timber economy? Some of the strongest pressure on the remaining natural forests comes not from within but from outside the forest sector.

Endnotes

1. This refers to the fiscal year April 1 to March 31.

2. Proconservationist lobbies in many of Indonesia's major markets have gained support for their activities focusing on the alleged destruction of the tropical rain forests. As a result, some countries have committed to phasing out tropical timber imports from unsustainably managed forests (Fletcher 1994, 43).

3. The total economically active population (including people working or looking for work) in 1994 was 84 million (BPS 1996, 52–3).

4. With regard to local employment, however, several studies have shown that the benefit of employment opportunities in terms of strata of work and related earnings in logging companies are enjoyed more by nonlocal workers. Local workers, who are generally less skilled, are confined to the lowest paying jobs (Awang 1992, 250). Local labor is often also unwilling to work for the low wages paid by timber companies

5. PELITA (or *Rencana Pembangunan Lima Tahun* [REPELITA]) refers to the country's Five-Year Development Plan: PELITA I 1969/1970–1973/1974, PELITA II 1974/1975–1978/ 1979, PELITA III 1979/1980–1983/1984, PELITA IV 1984/1985–1988/1989, PELITA V 1989/1990–1993/1994, PELITA VI 1994/1995–1998/1999.

6. This silviculture system (i.e., the selective cutting and replanting system or TPTI) was developed from the previous silviculture system (i.e., the selective cutting system or TPI) in 1989. TPI was first adopted in 1972 and revised in 1980. The current version of TPTI was revised in 1993 (Soerianegara 1996, 61).

7. In 1997, the area of virgin forest remaining was estimated to be 21 million ha, with potential log production of 22 million m^3 per annum (Departemen Kehutanan 1997b, 15). By the year 2003, the sustainable rate from natural forests is estimated to decrease to 18 million m^3 per annum (MoF 1997, 20).

8. Three data sources for log production and for forestry product exports provide different figures. These sources are MoF, BPS, and FAO. For analysis on these different estimates, see Fenton (1996) and ITFMP (1997).

9. The magnitude of timber theft or illegal logging in 50 concessions in 1995 was reported to be almost equal to the concessions' officially recorded production (Marzali 1997). Approximately 30 million m^3 of roundwood extracted from Indonesia's forests are illegal or unreported (ITFMP 1999, 13). See also endnote 11, and Chapters 7 and 16.

The loss from illegal logging is estimated to be in the range of US$3.5 billion to US$4.6 billion annually (King 1996, 218). There are still many unlicensed wood processing mills that rely on logs from illegal logging; limited employment alternatives have made it difficult for the authorities to close down these mills (Sumitro 1995, 186). Kartodihardjo found that the rate of primary forest loss in 60 concessions outside the legal harvest area and outside the areas intended for conversion is on average 2.5% annually (1998b, 10).

10. Much of the problem is rooted in the imbalance between roundwood supply and demand or the imbalance between the supply that the forests of Indonesia can sustain and the industry's capacity. In 1997, the total consumption of roundwood was estimated to be 82.3 million m^3, while the total supply from official harvesting, imports, and recycling totaled 45.3 million m^3. This means a shortfall of 37 million m^3 had to have been met through unrecorded, undocumented, or unreported production and illegal logging (Scotland et al. 1999, 6).

11. In some places such as West Kalimantan, logs are cut 20% to 30% over the annual allowable cut. In addition, felling of logs less than the 50 cm dbh (diameter at breast height) threshold—the minimum allowable diameter for felling—reach as much as 25% to 40% of the logs supposedly felled under the TPTI system (Alqadrie 1994, 254). The Minister of Environment was quoted as saying that the actual volume of timber cut in 1993 was nearly 50 million m^3, although officially only 35 million m^3 was recorded (EIA 1996, 8).

12. Forest area estimates have always been a contentious issue because of the particular nature of these kinds of data. The National Forest Inventory (GOI/FAO 1996) suggested that 112 million ha of forestlands are forested. A study by Scotland and Fraser (1999) revealed that as of 1996, Indonesia had 47 million ha of production forests in commercially viable forest types (including 15 million ha classified under conversion forests) and only 19.5 million ha of unlogged forests.

13. The World Bank estimated that logging contributes to about 80,000 ha of deforestation annually (The World Bank 1994, 52). Compared with the high annual deforestation rate estimate from 1985 to 1997 (see endnote 17) and considering the intensity of logging activities during these years, this contribution appears to be rather understated.

14. In East Kalimantan, the opening of new swiddens is based on three considerations: proximity to the community, a river or water source, and a road (Poffenberger and McGean 1993, 19).

15. The responsibility of protecting forest areas under concessions from encroachment is laid upon the concessionaires, regulated by *Peraturan Pemerintah* ([PP] government regulation) 28/1985 and the Forestry Minister's Decision Letter (SK) 523/1993.

16. At least three factors undermine the obligation of replanting in logged-over areas in this province: (a) concessionaires are not inclined to replant due to the uncertainty of their exploitation rights after the expiration of their 20-year lease, (b) some concession holders find the inconsistencies of control by the forestry staff to be disappointing, and (c) the selective felling and replanting system has many weaknesses that are difficult to implement in the field.

17. Estimates of the annual rate of deforestation in Indonesia vary widely, ranging from 263,000 ha to 2.4 million ha (Sunderlin and Resosudarmo 1996: 3). More recent estimates suggested 1.6–1.7 million ha per year of deforestation between 1985 and 1997 (Toha 2000; The World Bank 2001, 7).

18. To fill in the deficit from natural forests (the 22 million m³ per annum sustainable rate), an additional supply of logs originated from hutan rakyat or community forests (11.4 million m³) and from forest clearing (3.7 million m³) (Fakultas Kehutanan IPB 1996: 12). The total, however, still amounts to 37.6 million m³, short by half of the total demand.

19. This chapter covers mostly the period up to about a year after the demise of the New Order, or 1999. Since then, many changes have occurred rapidly (see Chapter 15).

20. In 1998, the MoF's task was extended to become the Ministry of Forestry and Estate Crops (or MoFEC). This was recently reversed, and Indonesia again has an MoF.

21. For a discussion on the types of levies imposed and how much of each type is apportioned to the local government, see Prakosa (1996, 32–8) and Ramli and Ahmad (1993, 33–8).

22. Plywood, which absorbs 70% of log production, ranks fifth in value added among other wood products, after handicrafts, furniture, molding, and sawnwood (Solahuddin 1997, 4).

23. The plywood industry's overcapacity with regard to raw materials has been acknowledged by its placement on the negative investment list—that is, no new industries are permitted (Roesad 1996, 247).

24. Royalties are determined at the processing industries' logpond. This encourages wasteful logging, where only the most profitable logs are taken out of the forests without consideration of the remaining logs that have been unnecessarily felled (Subari 1990, 21).

25. Calculation of rent capture depends on the average log prices, production costs, and return on investment; therefore, it varies. Yet estimates of the rent from 1989 to 1998 were in the range of 17–31% (Gray and Hadi 1990, 118; Reid 1992 [as quoted in Prakosa 1996, 43]; Ramli and Ahmad 1993, 36; Pangestu 1998; Sutopo and Darusman 1992 [as quoted in Kartodihardjo 1998b, 4]).

26. Kartodihardjo (1998b, 19) concluded that revoking licenses prior to the expiry date does not serve as a disincentive for concessionaires but exactly the opposite. This policy frees the concessionaires from their accountability to rehabilitate and protect the degraded forests throughout their concession period.

27. The requirements for timber plantation developments are contained in PP 7/1990. The new PP 6/1999 on Forest Utilization and Forest Product Harvesting in Production Forests annulled the 1990 regulation.

28. To promote the development of timber estates, the government provides a large subsidy by extending a 32% interest-free loan, 14% government equity, and 32% market-rate loan. Both the interest-free loan and the market-rate loans were taken from the nation's reforestation funds.

29. By January 2000, the Ministry of Finance had applied a 15% export tax to logs.

30. The following discussion on the pros and cons of the log export bans draw heavily on David Kaimowitz's internal discussion circular, unpublished.

31. Throughout much of the 1990s the *rupiah* was valued at Rp 2,000 to Rp 2,500 to the U.S. dollar. In April 1998, it jumped to Rp 17,000 to the U.S. dollar; and it is now about Rp 11,000 to the U.S. dollar (June 2001).

32. Indonesia is now in the process of decentralization, including forest management (see Chapter 15).

References

Alqadrie, S.I. 1994. Dampak perusahaan pemegang HPH dan perkebunan terhadap kehidupan sosial ekonomi dan budaya penduduk setempat di daerah pedalaman Kalimantan Barat. In *Kebudayaan Dayak: Aktualisasi dan transformasi*, edited by P. Florus, S. Djuweng, J. Bamba, N. Andasputra. Jakarta, Indonesia: Grasindo, 244–60.

Anyonge, C.H., and Y. Nugroho. 1996. *Rural Populations Living within Logging Concessions in Indonesia: A Review of Social Development Programmes and a Case Study from S. Kalimantan.* Imatra, Finland: ENSO Forest Development Oy Ltd.

Awang, S.A. 1992. Kehutanan sosial untuk pengembangan perekonomian rakyat Kalimantan. In *Perekonomian Rakyat Kalimantan*, edited by Mubyarto, Sulistiyo, and S.A. Awang. Jakarta, Indonesia: Yayasan Agro Ekonomika, 247–61.

———. 1993. Hutan, industri kehutanan, dan pembangunan masyarakat. In *Riau Menatap Masa Depan*, edited by Mubyarto, I. Setiawati, E. Djatmiko, S.A. Awang, L. Soetrisno, A.S. Dewanta, A. Mawarni, P. Sudira, E. Pratiwi, N.S. Rejeki, Sulistiyo, and Santiasih. Yogyakarta, Indonesia: Aditya Media, 51–82.

Bank Indonesia. 2000. *Financial Statistics, March 2000, Non-Oil/Gas Export Value by Group of Commodities.* From the webpage http://www.bi.go.id/ datastatistik/index.htm (accessed May 31, 2000).

Barr, C. 1998. Bob Hasan, the rise of APKINDO, and the shifting dynamics of control in Indonesia's timber sector. *Indonesia* 65:1–36.

Bertault, J., and P. Sist. 1997. An experimental comparison of different harvesting intensities with reduced-impact and conventional logging in East Kalimantan, Indonesia. *Forest Ecology and Management* 94: 209–18.

Bisnis Indonesia. 1998. MPI: Umumkan daftar log untuk diekspor. September 11. From the webpage http://www.bisnis.com (accessed September 14, 1998).

———. 1999a. Dana Apkindo dan DR jadi alternatif. March 23. From the webpage http://www.bisnis.com (accessed March 23, 1999).

———. 1999b. HPH KKN resmi dicabut. July 9. From the webpage http://www.bisnis.com (accessed July 16, 1999).

———. 1999c. Sejumlah HPH kembali ditutup: Nasib industri perkayuan kian tak menentu. July 13. From the webpage http://www.bisnis.com (accessed July 16, 1999).

———. 2000a. Kayu bulat ilegal diselundupkan ke Cina. June 6. From the webpage http://www.bisnis.com (accessed June 12, 2000).

———. 2000b. Kebijakan dephutbun kurang dukung bisnis. May 29. From the webpage http://www.bisnis.com (accessed June 2, 2000).

———. 2000c. Kinerja industri kayu lapis nasional anjlok. June 7. From the webpage http://www.bisnis.com (accessed June 12, 2000).

———. 2000d. MPI: Kayu lapis terancam jadi sunset industry. April 28. From the webpage http://www.bisnis.com (accessed April 28, 2000).

Boscolo, M., and J.R. Vincent. 2000. Promoting better logging practices in tropical forests: A simulation analysis of alternative regulations. *Land Economics* 76(1): 1–14.

BPS (*Biro Pusat Statistik*). 1996. *Statistik Indonesia 1995*. Jakarta, Indonesia: Biro Pusat Statistik.

Brown, D. 1999. *Addicted to Rent: Corporate and Spatial Distribution of Forest Resources in Indonesia: Implications for Forest Sustainability and Government Policy.* Jakarta, Indonesia: ITFMP (Indonesia–U.K. Tropical Forest Management Programme).

Capricorn Indonesia Consult. 1995. Konsumsi pulp tahun 1995 diperkirakan mencapai 1.77 juta ton. *Indochemical* 177:57–61

———. 1999. *Prospects of Natural Rubber Industry and Market in Indonesia* 230:3–24

Data Consult Inc. 1997a. Log supply from land clearing will finish in 10 years. *Indonesian Commercial Newsletter XXIII*(222):70.

_____. 1997b. Pulp and paper industry faced with scarcity of basic materials. *Indonesian Commercial Newsletter XXIII*(222):8–26.

Dennis, R. 1999. *A Review of Fire Projects in Indonesia (1982–1998)*. Bogor, Indonesia: CIFOR.

Departemen Kehutanan. 1994. *Data dan informasi 1992/1993*. Jakarta, Indonesia: Departemen Kehutanan.

_____. 1995. *Konsep XVI Rencana Pembangunan Lima Tahun Keenam Kehutanan*. Rapat Kerja Nasional Departemen Kehutanan Tahun, 1995. Jakarta, Indonesia: Departemen Kehutanan.

_____. 1996. *Statistik Kehutanan Indonesia 1994/1995*. Jakarta, Indonesia: Sekretariat Jenderal Departemen Kehutanan, Biro Perencanaan.

_____. 1997a. *Arahan teknis Direktur Jenderal Pengusahaan Hutan tanggal 6*. Reboisasi dan Rehabilitasi Lahan. Rapat Kerja Nasional Kehutanan Tahun. April 1997. 3E: 9. Jakarta, Indonesia: Departemen Kehutanan.

_____. 1997b. *Pokok-pokok arahan Menteri Kehutanan tanggal*. Rapat Kerja Nasional Kehutanan Tahun, April 1997. Jakarta, Indonesia: Departemen Kehutanan.

_____. 1997c. *Sambutan Menteri Kehutanan pada acara pembukaan*. Rapat Kerja Nasional Kehutanan Tahun, April 1997. Jakarta, Indonesia: Departemen Kehutanan.

_____. 1997d. *Statistik Kehutanan Indonesia 1995/1996*. Jakarta, Indonesia: Departemen Kehutanan.

Dephutbun (Departemen Kehutanan dan Perkebunan). 2000. Draft rencana stratejik. Rakernas 2000. June 26–29. Jakarta, Indonesia: Dephutbun.

Direktorat Jenderal Perkebunan. 1998. *Statistik Perkebunan Indonesia 1997–1999: Karet*. Jakarta, Indonesia.

D'Silva, E., and S. Appanah. 1993. *Forestry Management for Sustainable Management*. An EDI policy seminar report no. 32. Washington, DC: The World Bank.

EIA (Environmental Investigation Agency). 1996. *Corporate Power, Corruption and the Destruction of the World's Forests: The Case for a New Global Forest Agreement*. Washington, DC: Environmental Investigation Agency.

Elias. 1996. A case study on forest harvesting damages, structure and composition dynamic changes in the residual stand for dipterocarp forest in East Kalimantan, Indonesia. In *Forest Operations for Sustainable Forestry in the Tropics*, edited by D. Dykstra. Proceedings of a symposium organized by IUFRO Subject Group S3.05-00 at the XX IUFRO World Congress, August 6–12. Finland.

Fakultas Kehutanan IPB (Institut Pertanian Bogor). 1996. Pembaharuan kebijakan pengelolaan hutan produksi menuju era sertifikasi ekolabel. In *Pengelolaan Hutan Produksi Lestari di Indonesia: Konsep Permasalahan dan Strategi menuju Era Ekolabel*, edited by E. Suhendang, H. Haeruman, I. Soerianegara. Proceeding simposium Penerapan Ekolabel di Hutan Produksi, 11–25. August 10–12, 1995, Jakarta, Indonesia.

FAO (Food and Agriculture Organization). 1993. *The Challenge of Sustainable Forest Management: What Future for the World's Forests?* Rome: FAO.

———. 1996. *FAO Yearbook of Forest Products 1994*. Rome: FAO.

———. 1997. *FAO Yearbook of Forest Products 1995*. Rome: FAO.

Fenton, R. 1996. *The Indonesian Plywood Industry: A Study of the Statistical Base, the Value-Added Effects and the Forest Impact*. Field report series no. 29. Singapore: Institute of Southeast Asian Studies.

Fletcher, D.G. 1994. *Assessment of Future Prospects for the Indonesian Plywood Industry*. Jakarta, Indonesia: ITFMP.

GOI/FAO (Government of Indonesia/Food and Agriculture Organization). 1990. *Situation and Outlook of the Forestry Sector in Indonesia: Issues, Findings, and Opportunities.* Vol. 1. Jakarta, Indonesia: Directorate General of Forest Utilization, MoF, GOI, and FAO.

———. 1996. *National Forest Inventory of Indonesia: Final Forest Resources Statistics Report.* Jakarta, Indonesia: Directorate General of Forest Inventory and Land Use Planning, MoF, GOI, and FAO.

Gray, J.A., and S. Hadi. 1990. *Fiscal Policies and Pricing in Indonesian Forestry.* Jakarta, Indonesia: Ministry of Forestry/Food and Agricultural Organization.

Hardjono, J. 1994. Resource utilization and the environment. In *Indonesia's New Order,* edited by H. Hill. Sydney, Australia: Allen and Unwin.

Indonesian Business Trend. 1998. Perkembangan industri pulp di Indonesia. *Indonesian Business Trend* 63: 4–12. November 15.

ITFMP (Indonesia–U.K. Tropical Forest Management Programme). 1997. Nilai Manfaat Hutan Indonesia. Jakarta, Indonesia: Indonesia-U.K. Tropical Forest Management Programme.

———. 1999. *Threats to Sustainable Forest Management in Indonesia: Roundwood Supply and Demand and Illegal Logging.* Draft position paper. Jakarta, Indonesia: ITFMP.

ITTO (International Tropical Timber Organization). 1992. *Criteria for the Measurement of Sustainable Tropical Forest Management.* ITTO policy development series no. 3. Yokohama, Japan: ITTO.

The Jakarta Post. 1998a. Minister asked to punish plantation firms. June 8, 8.

———. 1998b. No new forest concessions will be awarded. June 13, 8.

———. 1998c. Forestry Ministry to offer public 149 concessions. June 15, 8.

———. 1999a. Government revokes vast forest concessions. July 9, 1.

———. 1999b. Government reduces export taxes on wood products. March 24, 8.

———. 1999c. One million hectares of forest to be allotted to cooperatives. April 19, 2.

Kaimowitz, D. nd. Internal discussion circular. Unpublished.

Kartawinata, K., and A. Vayda. 1984. Forest Conversion in East Kalimantan, Indonesia: The Activities and Impact of Timber Companies, Shifting Cultivators, Migrant Pepper-farmers, and Others. In *Ecology in Practice, Part I: Ecosystem Management,* edited by F. Di Castri, F.W.G. Baker, and M. Hadley. Dublin: Tycooly International Publishing Limited and Paris: UNESCO, 98-126.

Kartodihardjo, H.. 1998a. Dengan sistem pengusahaan hutan saat ini tidak memungkinkan mencapai upaya pelestarian hutan. In *Analisis Kebijakan Pengelolaan Hutan Alam Produksi di Indonesia: Sebuah Kumpulan Naskah Lepas,* edited by H. Kartodihardjo. Fakultas Kehutanan IPB. Unpublished. Bogor, Indonesia.

———. 1998b. Kebijaksanaan dan Implementasi Desentralisasi Urusan Kehutanan. In *Analisis Kebijakan Pengelolaan Hutan Alam Produksi di Indonesia: Sebuah Kumpulan Naskah Lepas,* edited by H. Kartodihardjo. Fakultas Kehutanan IPB. Unpublished. Bogor, Indonesia.

———. 1998c. Masalah dan kebijaksanaan penataan institusi pengusahaan hutan alam produksi di Indonesia. In *Analisis Kebijakan Pengelolaan Hutan Alam Produksi di Indonesia: Sebuah Kumpulan Naskah Lepas,* edited by H. Kartodihardjo. Fakultas Kehutanan IPB. Unpublished. Bogor, Indonesia.

———. 1998d. Pemberdayaan ekonomi masyarakat dalam pembinaan masyarakat desa hutan (PMDH). In *Analisis Kebijakan Pengelolaan Hutan Alam Produksi di Indonesia: Sebuah Kumpulan Naskah Lepas,* edited by H. Kartodihardjo. Fakultas Kehutanan IPB. Unpublished. Bogor, Indonesia.

King, D.Y. 1996. The political economy of forest sector reform in Indonesia. *The Journal of Environment and Development* 5(2): 216–32.

Marzali, A. 1997. Dampak kegiatan HPH terhadap masyarakat desa sekitarnya. In *Proceedings Seminar Sehari Program Pembinaan Masyarakat Desa Hutan: Pengalaman di Lapangan Bersama Perusahaan Pemegang HPH*. Laboratorium Antropologi FISIP UI, Kampus Universitas Indonesia. June 12. Depok, Indonesia.

MoF (Ministry of Forestry). 1995. *Country brief. Indonesia Forestry Action Programme*. Jakarta, Indonesia: MoF.

————. 1997. Draft REPELITA VII. Jakarta, Indonesia: MoF.

MOFEC (Ministry of Forestry and Estate Crops). 2000. From the webpage http://www.dephut.go.id/ (accessed May 8, 2000).

Mubyarto. 1996. Peran ekonomi dan sosial hutan di Indonesia. In *Berbagai Aspek Pembangunan Pedesaan*, edited by Mubyarto, E. Djatmiko, and R. Winahyu. Yogyakarta, Indonesia: Aditya Media, 11–25.

Mulyadi, J., and K. Roesad. 1996. Kertas dan pulp: Harapan masa depan. In *Transformasi Industri Indonesia Dalam Era Perdagangan Bebas*, edited by M. Pangestu, R. Atje, and J. Mulyadi. Jakarta, Indonesia: Center for Strategic and International Studies, 263–85.

Mulyana, Y. 1990. Perkembangan tata guna hutan kesepakatan dan saran penyempurnaannya. Makalah Penunjang 112. Bidang Pembinaan Kawasan, Kongres Kehutanan Indonesia. October 22–25. Jakarta, Indonesia.

Nasendi, B.D. 1996. Deforestation in Indonesia: Policy, model, driving forces, scenarios, constraints, opportunities and strategies. A manuscript for the book *Forest in the South and the North in Context of Global Warming*, submitted for review at the UNU/WIDER 3rd Workshop. Finnish Forest Research Institute METLA. October 1996. Helsinki, Finland.

Nusapati, W., and W. Keeling. 1996. *Barito Pacific: Not for the Faint of Heart*. March 29. Hongkong: Kleinwort Benson Research, Kleinwort Benson Securities (Asia) Ltd.

Pamulardi, B. 1995. *Hukum Kehutanan dan Pembangunan Bidang Kehutanan*. Jakarta, Indonesia: Perseroan Terbatas, Raja Grafindo Persada.

Pangestu, M. 1998. IMF Watch: Konsistensi kebijakan pemerintah. *Bisnis Indonesia*. From the webpage http://www.bisnis.com (accessed May 18, 1998).

Poffenberger, M., and B. McGean (eds.). 1993. *Communities and Forest Management in East Kalimantan: Pathway to Environmental Stability*. Center for Southeast Asia Studies. Research network report no. 3. Berkeley: University of California.

Prakosa, M. 1996. *Renjana Kebijakan Kehutanan*. Yogyakarta, Indonesia: Aditya Media.

Pramono, A.H. 1992. Tata guna hutan dan deforestasi di Indonesia: sebuah tinjauan singkat. In *Melestarikan Hutan Tropika*, edited by M. Lubis. Jakarta, Indonesia: Yayasan Obor Indonesia, 157–81.

Pudjowidodo, P., and H. Santoso. 1990. Pembinaan kawasan hutan dalam pembangunan wilayah. Makalah Penunjang, 114. Bidang Pembinaan Hutan. Kongres Kehutanan Indonesia II. October 1990. Jakarta, Indonesia.

Ramli, R., and M. Ahmad. 1993. *Rente Ekonomi Pengusahaan Hutan Indonesia*. Jakarta, Indonesia: Wahana Lingkungan Hidup Indonesia.

Rashid Hussain Securities. 1996. Plywood: Culling the herd at sunset (I) Indonesia: market dateline. November 2. Jakarta, Indonesia.

RePPProT (Regional Physical Planning Programme for Transmigration). 1990. *The Land Resources of Indonesia: A National Overview*. London, U.K., & Jakarta, Indonesia: Overseas Development Administration and Department of Transmigration.

Republika. 2000. Pemerintah diminta hentikan ekspor log. From the webpage http://www.republika.co.id (accessed May 16, 2000).

Riswan, S., and L. Hartanti. 1995. Human impacts on tropical forest dynamics. *Vegetatio* 121: 41–52.

Roesad, K. 1996. Daya saing industri kayu lapis. In Transformasi Industri Indonesia dalam Era Perdagangan Bebas, edited by M. Pangestu, R. Atje, and J. Mulyadi. Jakarta, Indonesia: Center for Strategic and International Studies, 244–62.

Sagala, A. 1997. Field design of a sustainable production forest management unit using gap cutting in South Kalimantan Indonesia. In *A State-of-the-Art Report on Some Recent Forestry Policies, Initiatives and Achievements in Indonesia: Concepts, Strategies and Actions for Sustainable Forest Management and Forestry Development Towards 21st Century*, edited by B.D. Nasendi. Collection of Indonesian papers contributed independently to the XI World Forestry Congress. October 1997. Antalya, Turkey, 115–19.

Samego, I. 1997. Ekonomi politik hutan, untuk rakyat. In *Proceedings National Seminar Tinjauan Pembangunan Kehutanan di Indonesia: Peningkatan Nilai Tambah Dalam Perspektif Kesejahteraan Rakyat*. Jakarta, Indonesia: Center for Information and Development Studies.

Scotland, N. 1998. *The Impact of the Southeast Asian Monetary Crisis on Indonesian Forest Concessions and Implications for the Future*. Jakarta, Indonesia: Indonesia-U.K. Tropical Forest Management Programme.

Scotland, N., and A. Fraser. 1999. *Indonesian Forest Inventory Data*. Draft. Jakarta, Indonesia: ITFMP.

Scotland, N., A. Fraser, and N. Jewell. 1999. *Roundwood Supply and Demand in the Forest Sector in Indonesia*. Draft. Jakarta, Indonesia: ITFMP.

Setyarso, A. 1990. Pemantapan tebang pilih tanam Indonesia. Makalah Penunjang 213. Bidang Pembinaan Hutan. Kongres Kehutanan Indonesia II. October 1990. Jakarta, Indonesia.

Sist, P., and J.G. Bertault. 1998. Reduced impact logging experiments: Impact of harvesting intensities and logging techniques on stand damage. In *Silvicultural Research in a Lowland Mixed Dipterocarp Forest of East Kalimantan*, edited by J.G. Bertault and K. Kadir. Montpellier, France: Centre de Cooperation Internationale en Recherche Agronomique pour le Development, Forestry Research and Development Agency, and PT Inhutani I, 139–61.

Sist, P., T. Nolan, J.G. Bertault, and D. Dykstra. 1998. Harvesting intensity versus sustainability in Indonesia. *Forest Ecology and Management* 108:251–60.

Soerianegara, I. 1996. Aspek Ekologi dalam Pengelolaan Hutan Alam Produksi Lestari. In *Pengelolaan Hutan Produksi Lestari di Indonesia: Konsep Permasalahan dan Strategi Menuju Era Ekolabel*, edited by E. Suhendang, H. Haeruman, and I. Soerianegara. Proceeding simposium penerapan ekolabel di hutan produksi. August 1995. Jakarta, Indonesia, 56–65.

Solahuddin, S. 1997. Peningkatan nilai tambah dalam industri kehutanan. In *Proceedings National Seminar Tinjauan Pembangunan Kehutanan di Indonesia: Peningkatan Nilai Tambah Dalam Perspektif Kesejahteraan Rakyat*. Jakarta, Indonesia: Center for Information and Development Studies.

State Ministry for Environment, Republic of Indonesia/United Nations Development Programme. 1998. *Forest and Land Fires in Indonesia: Impacts, Factors, and Evaluation*. Vol. 1. Jakarta, Indonesia: State Ministry for Environment.

Subari, D. 1990. Pemungutan hasil hutan. Makalah Penunjang no. 312. Bidang Pengusahaan Hutan. Kongres Kehutanan Indonesia II. October 1990. Jakarta, Indonesia.

Sumitro, A. 1995. Industrial pressures for overexploitation of forest: The Indonesian experience. In *Management of Tropical Forests: Towards an Integrated Perspective*, edited by O. Sandbukt. University of Oslo. Oslo, Norway: Center for Development and the Environment.

Sunderlin, W.D., and I.A.P. Resosudarmo. 1996. *Rates and Causes of Deforestation in Indonesia: Towards a Resolution of the Ambiguities*. CIFOR occasional paper no. 9. Bogor, Indonesia: CIFOR.

Suryohadikusumo, D. 1997. Sambutan Menteri Kehutanan R.I. In *Proceedings National Seminar Tinjauan Pembangunan Kehutanan di Indonesia: Peningkatan Nilai Tambah Dalam Perspektif Kesejahteraan Rakyat*. June 1997. Jakarta, Indonesia: Center for Information and Development Studies.

————.1998. Personal communication with the author, May 1998.

Tarrant, J., E. Barbier, R.J. Greenberg, M.L. Higgins, S.F. Lintner, C. Mackie, L. Murphy, and H. van Veldhuizen. 1987. *Natural Resources and Environmental Management in Indonesia: An Overview*. Jakarta, Indonesia: U.S. Agency for International Development.

Thiele, R. 1994. How to manage tropical forests more sustainably: The case of Indonesia. *Intereconomics* July/August:184–93.

Toha, M. 1997. *Pengelolaan Hutan Yang Berorientasi Kesejahteraan Rakyat*. Paper presented at the national seminar tinjauan pembangunan kehutanan di Indonesia: Peningkatan nilai tambah dalam perspektif kesejahteraan rakyat. June 1997. Jakarta, Indonesia: Center for Information and Development Studies.

——————. 2000. *Estimated deforestation rate for Indonesia*. Seminar presented at the Consultative Group on Indonesia seminar on Indonesian forestry. January 2000. Jakarta, Indonesia.

U.S. Department of Agriculture. 1999. *Indonesian Forest Products*. GAIN report #ID9063. Washington, DC: Foreign Agricultural Service.

Vayda, A.P., and A. Sahur. 1985. *Forest Clearing and Pepper Farming by Bugis Migrants in East Kalimantan: Antecedents and Impact*. Reprint no. 83. East-West Environment and Policy Institute. Honolulu, HI: East-West Center, 588–605.

WALHI (*Wahana Lingkungan Hidup Indonesia*). 1996. *Mitos-Mitos Pengelolaan Hutan di Indonesia*. Kertas Posisi no. 02. Jakarta, Indonesia: WALHI.

The World Bank. 1990. *Indonesia: Sustainable Development of Forests, Land and Water*. Washington, DC: The World Bank.

——————. 1994a. *Indonesia: Environment and Development*. Washington, DC: The World Bank.

——————. 1994b. *Indonesian Production Forestry*. Unpublished report quoted in M. Ahmad and U. Djalins. 1997. *Sustaining Growth in Indonesia's Forest-Based Industry*. Paper presented at Sustaining Economic Growth in Indonesia: A Framework for the 21st Century, Conference on the Indonesian Medium-Term Economic Prospects. December 1997. Jakarta, Indonesia.

——————. 1995. *The Economics of Long-Term Management of Indonesia's Natural Forest*. Washington, DC: The World Bank.

——————. 1996. *Indonesia: Dimensions of Growth*. Washington, DC: The World Bank.

——————. 2001. *Indonesia: Environment and Natural Resource Management in a Time of Transition*. Washington, DC: The World Bank.

Yayasan Adi Sanggoro. 1989. *Report on Field Case Studies of Forest Concessions*. Indonesia Forestry Studies, field document no. 1–5. Jakarta, Indonesia: MoF0, Government of Indonesia, and Food and Agriculture Organization.

CHAPTER NINE

Timber Concession Reform: Questioning the "Sustainable Logging" Paradigm

Christopher Barr

Since the mid-1980s, policy discussions aimed at promoting sustainable forest management in Indonesia have focused almost exclusively on reforming the *Hak Pengusahaan Hutan* ([HPH] Forest Concession, Forest Exploitation Rights) timber concession system.[1] This emphasis on HPH reform is hardly surprising given the pressures that Indonesia's commercial logging industry has put on the nation's forests over the last three decades. Since 1967, when the New Order regime opened the rich Dipterocarp forests of the Outer Islands to large-scale timber extraction, the Government of Indonesia (GOI) has allocated a total of 585 HPHs, covering 62 million ha, to private and state-owned logging companies (Brown 1999). According to official figures, HPH holders generated 612 million m³ of roundwood between 1970 and 1999, or 20.4 million m³ annually for 30

This chapter has been extracted from C. Barr's (2001) The Political Economy of Fiber and Finance in Indonesia's Pulp and Paper Industries, Chapter 4 in *Banking on Sustainability: Structural Adjustment and Forestry Reform in Post-Suharto Indonesia*, published by the Center for International Forestry Research (CIFOR) and World Wide Fund for Nature Macroeconomics for Sustainable Development Program Office, Washington, D.C. Research described herein was conducted in Jakarta during 1999 and involved in-depth key informant interviews with representatives from government policymakers, forest sector industry associations, 15 Indonesian timber conglomerates, civil society organizations, and international donor agencies involved in the forest sector.

years. Some industry analysts have argued that actual timber removals by HPH holders during this period were, in fact, approximately twice this volume (Kartodihardjo 1999a; see Chapter 7 of this book).

Policy analysts advocating reform of the HPH system as a means to achieve sustainable forest management have generally prioritized three objectives. First, they have sought to increase the government's capacity to enforce the technical aspects of sustainable concession management (MoF 1995; The World Bank 1993; Gray and Hadi 1989). In practice, such efforts have largely been oriented toward designing more effective mechanisms for monitoring concessionaires' harvesting practices to ensure that they adhere to the selective cutting guidelines stipulated in the HPH contract.[2]

Second, forest economists have advocated a sharp increase in the government's timber royalties and fees to halt the flow of resource rents—that is, revenues above a "normal" rate of return—to concession holders (Brown 1999; Scotland and Whiteman 1997; The World Bank 1993; Ingram 1989; Gillis 1988). From a fiscal perspective, they maintain that the government's failure to fully capture timber rents implies the loss of funds that might otherwise be used by the state for formal budgetary allocations. In terms of sustainability, they argue that access to excessive profits leads concession holders to undervalue the resources under their control, which effectively undermines their incentive to manage their HPHs sustainably over the long term.

Third, policy analysts have long called on the Indonesian government to lift the prohibitive restrictions on log exports that it has maintained since the early-1980s (Manurung and Buongiorno 1997; The World Bank 1995; Vincent 1992; Lindsay 1989). They emphasize that these restrictions have led concession holders to sell virtually all of the timber they produce to Indonesia's wood-processing industries at prices that are well below international market rates. Underpricing of this sort is believed to promote inefficiency both at the point of log harvesting and during processing operations.

Taken together, these three sets of prescriptions—selective cutting, full rent capture, and market-based efficiency—represent the essential pillars of what can be called the "sustainable logging" paradigm. Although the policy prescriptions associated with this paradigm have been proposed, in some form, for practically every timber-producing country in the world, they have been advocated especially loudly in the case of Indonesia. This approach to sustainability has been articulated most recently and most comprehensively by the World Bank following the onset of the current economic crisis in late 1997. In the early months of the crisis, the World Bank took steps to ensure that conditions aimed at reforming the country's timber concession system were pointedly included in the International Monetary Fund's US$43 billion bail-out loan agreement with the Indonesian government. Key elements of the reform proposals included the following policy interventions:

- strengthening HPH contracts by extending them to 35 years and making them transferable;
- enforcing improved concession management by introducing performance bonds and independent monitoring;
- removing market-distorting practices by lifting restrictions on logs, sawnwood, and wood panels; and
- increasing the state's rent capture by raising timber royalties and introducing area-based fees for logging concessions (The World Bank 1998).

Five basic assumptions have supported efforts by the World Bank and others to achieve sustainable management of Indonesia's forests by reforming the HPH system.

1. Controlling log supply, without taking any direct steps to reduce demand for industrial timber, is an effective strategy for sustaining the nation's natural forest resource base.
2. The most effective means of reducing Indonesia's log harvests to a sustainable level is by reforming the HPH system.
3. Increased efficiency will promote the conservation of natural forests.
4. Sustainable concession management is profitable.
5. The GOI has the institutional capacity to enforce the proposed changes in the HPH system and the forest products trade.

In this chapter, I examine each of these assumption and the policy prescriptions that emerge from them. Based on this analysis, I argue that the "sustainable logging" reform agenda is quite unlikely to succeed in reducing Indonesia's timber harvests to the government's own widely cited sustainability threshold of 25 million m^3 per year.[3] I maintain that for structural reasons this may, in fact, be an unachievable goal. Reform of the HPH system alone fails to address key factors that are encouraging unsustainable rates of log removals—most notably, effective demand for timber on the part of the nation's wood-processing industries and new technologies that have made previously marginal areas and species commercially viable (see Chapter 16).

The reforms of the HPH system proposed by the World Bank and others have also failed to address significant qualitative changes that have occurred in the sources of timber supply over the past decade. These include a marked decline in the volume of logs generated by concession holders, as well as a corresponding rise in large-scale forest conversion and other unsustainable harvesting practices. Moreover, in assuming that sustainable concession management is profitable, proponents of the "sustainable logging" paradigm erroneously conclude that most private timber operators will be willing—over both the short and long term—to employ environmentally sustainable logging practices if required to do so. Finally, advocates of HPH reform as a strategy for achieving sustainability generally overestimate the GOI's political will to impose a substantial reduction in the nation's timber supply, as well as its institutional capacity to carry out such a policy.

Assumption #1: Controlling Log Supply, without Taking Any Direct Steps to Reduce Demand for Industrial Timber, Is an Effective Strategy for Sustaining the Nation's Natural Forest Resource Base

A central objective for advocates of the "sustainable logging" paradigm has been to establish tighter controls over Indonesia's timber supply to reduce log removals to the supposedly sustainable level of 25 million m³ per year. Since the late 1980s, the World Bank has sought to accomplish this by persuading the Indonesian government to enforce improved HPH management practices through the implementation of performance bonds and an independent monitoring system (The World Bank 1993, 1998). Moreover, to give logging companies an economic incentive to adhere to the government's selective cutting guidelines and to reduce damage to the forests under their control, the World Bank has called for the GOI to extend the HPH contract from 20 to 35 years and to make concessions transferable.

Collectively, these policy interventions have been intended to introduce more effective mechanisms for restricting the volumes of logs that are harvested from areas managed by timber concession holders. To the extent that the World Bank and proponents of HPH reform have addressed the issue of demand for logs on the part of wood-processing industries, they have done so only indirectly. Their attention to industrial timber demand has generally been limited to advocating policies designed to push Indonesia's wood processors to invest in efficiency, which will presumably lead these processors to reduce the overall volume of wood they consume. In seeking to remove restrictions on log exports and to raise timber royalties, for example, the bank has sought to bring Indonesia's domestic log prices up to international parity levels. Its primary aim in doing so has been to force the country's plywood factories and sawmills to use fewer logs in generating their processed wood outputs.

By focusing almost exclusively on controlling timber supply rather than reducing effective demand for logs, advocates of the "sustainable logging" paradigm have essentially failed to recognize the degree to which overcapacity exists within Indonesia's wood-based industries and the structural problems that it poses. In fact, the installed production capacities of the nation's sawnwood, plywood, and pulp industries have created a demand for logs and fiber that substantially exceeds the supply capacity of Indonesia's formal timber production apparatus. Table 9–1 shows the installed production and wood utilization capacities of these three industries in 1997.

Table 9–1: Production Capacity and Roundwood Consumption of Indonesia's Major Wood-Based Industries, 1997

Industry	Units	Production capacity	Estimated real production	Estimated roundwood consumption
Sawnwood and molding	2,345	18,975,000 m³	13,300,000 m³	24,180,000 m³
Plywood	115	12,600,000 m³	10,080,000 m³	20,160,000 m³
Pulp	15	3,900,000 t	3,400,000 t	16,660,000 m³
Total				61,000,000 m³

Sources: APKI 1997, APKINDO 1999, and ISA 1999.

Notes: t = metric tons. Production capacity figures included in this table are based on statistics provided by the respective industries' producers associations. Yet several assumptions are made to estimate real production levels and roundwood consumption. In the aggregate, sawnwood and molding producers are estimated to have operated at 70% of their installed production capacity and to have had an average recovery rate of 55% for the roundwood they consume. Plywood producers are estimated to have operated at 80% of their installed capacity and to have had an average recovery rate of 50%. Pulp producers are estimated to have operated at 87% of installed capacity, with 4.9 m³ of roundwood needed to produce each metric ton of pulp.

While aggregate roundwood consumption capacity for the three industries stood at approximately 78 million m³ during 1997, it is conservatively estimated that these three industries consumed 61 million m³ of raw materials.[4] This figure is 36 million m³ higher than the volume of timber removals that the Ministry of Forestry and Estate Crops (MoFEC) claims is sustainable as an annual harvest.

The existence of such a substantial "structural timber deficit" poses fundamental problems for the "sustainable logging" reform agenda in terms of both the policy formulation and implementation. On the one hand, the very existence of these industries promotes an expectation among policymakers that processors should have access to raw materials—that is, that they are literally machines that need to be fed. As a plywood officer at the Barito Pacific Group explained in an interview,

> The government won't let the industry collapse from lack of raw materials because plywood is too important for the economy. The Forestry Department will always find a way to make more timber available, as long as the demand exists. In fact, this is what they have done over the last several years in opening large areas of *izin pemanfaatan kayu* ([IPK] permission to use the timber in conversion forest), carrying out the *Proyek Lahan Gambut* ([PLG] Peat Lands Project) Million Hectare Sawah Project, and so forth. (Soedibyo 1999)

Policymakers are likely to feel particularly strong pressure to ensure a continuous supply of raw materials to industries, such as pulp and paper, in which processing facilities entail extremely high fixed costs or in which processors have close ties to state elites.

The structural demand for substantial volumes of timber above and beyond those generated by the official log supply is a central factor driving Indonesia's illegal timber trade. Estimates of illegal log removals in recent years have ranged from 12 to 32 million m^3 per year (ITFMP 1999). There is anecdotal evidence suggesting that illegal logging may have expanded dramatically in many parts of the country since the financial crisis began. Undocumented harvesting is often carried out by licensed concession holders who extract logs above their annual allowable cut or by logging in areas that have not been approved by the MoF[5] (Kartodihardjo 1999a). At times, this includes forests located outside their concessions. Moreover, organized syndicates of illegal loggers are known to be active in most timber-producing provinces (Telapak Indonesia and EIA 1999). While these groups are often financed by local businesspeople—in some cases HPH holders—they are said to almost always involve some degree of collusion with members of the armed forces, the local forestry bureaucracy, and other elements of the government's law enforcement apparatus (see Chapters 7 and 16). In parts of Kalimantan and Sumatra, whole units of the armed forces and national police are known to run rogue timber operations as a means of supplementing their official budgets (Asnawie 2000; WWF and DFID 1998; Sacerdoti 1979).

The pervasiveness of illegal logging and the Indonesian government's relatively weak capacity to enforce its own forest boundaries suggest that any efforts to control timber supply without reducing effective demand on the part of the nation's wood-based industries are likely to be futile. Indeed, there is widespread sentiment within the industry that the establishment of an effective log monitoring and regulatory system would take several years to implement, even under the most favorable of circumstances. Continued demand for illegal timber on the scale that currently exists in Indonesia is likely to seriously undermine this process and to keep log removals well above the government's own sustainability targets. In this way, it would appear that any serious attempt to cut harvest levels substantially must, at some point, involve proactive steps to reduce production capacity on the part of Indonesia's wood-processing industries.

Assumption #2: The Most Effective Means of Restricting Indonesia's Log Harvests to a Sustainable Level Is by Reforming the HPH System.

A majority of the forestry sector policy interventions put forth by the World Bank and other proponents of the "sustainable logging" paradigm have focused on reforming the HPH system to bring about a sharp reduction in timber production levels. Proposed interventions to the HPH system have included enforcing concession management practices better through the introduction of performance bonds and independent monitoring, extending the HPH contract and making it transferable, de-linking HPHs and processing facilities, and raising the state's rent capture by increasing timber royalties and introducing area-based fees. By contrast, proposed reforms have directed scant attention toward reducing log output levels from other (i.e., non-HPH) legal sources of timber production or toward controlling illegal log removals outside of HPH areas.

This emphasis on reforming the HPH system made a fair amount of sense in the late-1980s when Indonesia's timber concessions formally generated 26–27 million m³ of logs per year, accounting for approximately 90% of the country's official timber supply (Departemen Kehutanan 1994). Over the last decade, however, Indonesia's legal timber supply has experienced significant changes, which recent policy proposals aimed at promoting sustainable logging have largely failed to address. Specifically, there has been a steady decline in the volume of logs officially produced within the HPH system since 1990. According to MoF statistics, timber production levels realized under concessionaires' *Rencana Karya Tahunan* ([RKT] approved Annual Work Plans), in effect, the cumulative legal output for all HPH holders—dropped from just under 24 million m³ in 1990–1991 to 15 million m³ in 1996–1997 (Direktorat Bina Pengusahaan Hutan 1999a). This 37.5% drop in RKT output at the national level was, in fact, surpassed by the declines recorded for many of Indonesia's major timber-producing provinces. RKT levels during this period dropped by 48% (from 6.0 million to 3.2 million m³) in East Kalimantan and by 79% (from 2.9 million to 600,000 m³) in Riau.

This sharp decline in RKT production levels stems from the fact that large numbers of HPHs were taken out of production during the 1990s. Indeed, by the time President Soeharto was forced to step down in mid-1998, only 389 of the 652 concessions that had been distributed during the New Order period remained in operation.[6] Seventy-seven HPHs covering 5.5 million ha were either returned to the state or revoked by the MoF before the concessionaire's initial 20-year contract had ended. More significantly, the MoF chose not to renew the license for 186 HPHs covering 15.7 million ha after their initial contract period had expired. Unfortunately, detailed information on why these HPHs were revoked or not extended is not publicly available, so it is difficult even to speculate on the extent to which these areas remain at all commercially viable. Of the 263 HPHs that reverted to the state, only 33 covering 3.3 million ha were reallocated to other concession holders. A far larger number—147 HPHs covering 9.5 million ha—were assigned to the control of the state's five Inhutani forest enterprises for "rehabilitation."

Over the past several years, the MoF has adopted a number of strategies to make new supplies of timber available to Indonesia's wood-based industries to compensate for the HPH system's declining output. Within the parameters of the HPH system, the MoF has responded to the growing scarcity of accessible and commercially valuable logs in many parts of Kalimantan and Sumatra by opening the expansive forests of Irian Jaya (now referred to as Papua) to large-scale logging. It has done so by allocating 40 HPHs in Papua, covering an area of 9.7 million ha, between 1989 and 1997 (Direktorat Penyiapan Pengusahaan Hutan 1998). Papua's role as the timber industry's new frontier is made clear by the fact that the province's RKT output levels rose from 732,000 m³ in 1990–1991 to 2.3 million m³ in 1997–1998, in sharp contrast to the declines recorded in most other timber-producing provinces (Direktorat Bina Pengusahaan Hutan 1999a).

During this period, the MoF has also taken steps to broaden and deepen the nation's legal timber production system to generate significant volumes of logs from new sources. It has done so by implementing the following strategies:

- slating large areas of forest for conversion to other uses and making these available to logging companies for clear-cutting,
- allowing private timber operators to extract logs from areas under Inhutani control through ad hoc contractual arrangements, and
- weakening the HPH system's *Tebang Pilih Tanam Indonesia* ([TPTI] Indonesian Selective Planting and Cutting System) guidelines.

Although each of these strategies poses direct challenges to the sustainability of natural forests, they have thus far largely gone unaddressed by those advocating policy interventions aimed at promoting sustainable logging through HPH reform.

The Growing Reliance on Forest Conversion

The most significant strategy the MoF has used for maintaining Indonesia's formal timber supply has been to make vast tracts of conversion forest available to logging companies for clear-cutting. Since the early 1990s, this policy has been tied to the government's efforts to support the development of the nation's pulp and palm oil industries by opening up forested areas for the establishment of tree plantations (see Chapters 8 and 10). Under the MoF's forest conversion policy, a private timber operator is able to obtain an *izin pemanfaatan kayu* ([IPK] wood utilization permit) to harvest the timber from areas that have been slated for conversion. In contrast to the HPH contract, the IPK agreement allows the logging company to employ nonselective harvesting techniques and to pay minimal royalties (and no reforestation fee) on the logs that are cut. Although some of Indonesia's timber groups have made investments in oil palm plantations, it is not uncommon for IPK holders to abandon these sites once they have removed all stems of commercial value.

As Figure 9–1 shows, the aggregate volume of timber produced through IPK forest conversion rose from 4.2 million m³ in 1994–1995 to 10.1 million

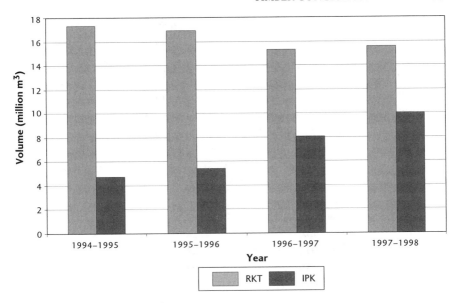

Figure 9–1. Roundwood Production from RKT versus IPK

m³ in 1997–1998, compensating substantially for the sharp decline in logs produced under the HPH system (Direktorat Bina Pengusahaan Hutan 1999b).

In its 1998 issues paper, the World Bank acknowledges the very major threat to sustainability posed by widespread conversion of natural forests, calling it "one of the most insidious forces operating in the forests at present in Indonesia" (The World Bank 1998, 16). Significantly, however, the bank fails to recognize the degree to which the GOI's conversion policy is linked to the aggregate decline in timber yields from the HPH system over the last several years. In fact, it identifies "the most significant forces for conversion of forest" as being largely exogenous to the forestry sector per se: oil palm and cocoa projects, livelihood-based agriculture, and transmigration (The World Bank 1998, 16). This leads the World Bank to offer the astonishing conclusion that "most of the conversion pressures on the forests in recent years in Indonesia have originated from decisions made by stakeholders and interest groups outside the official Ministry of Forestry."

The World Bank's failure to appreciate the central role that forest conversion currently plays in the MoF's roundwood supply strategy leads it to grossly underestimate the pressures that exist both within the private sector and within the state to keep a large-scale conversion policy in place. Given the fact that IPK forest conversion accounts for roughly 40% of the nation's legal timber and pulpwood supply, it is difficult to imagine that the MoF will not seek to maintain current conversion levels, for as long as possible, to meet the demand for timber among Indonesia's wood-based industries. While estate crops were formally under the

MoF's jurisdiction, it could even promote large-scale forest conversion without losing administrative authority over the areas allocated for agroindustrial estates.

Exploitation of Areas Under Inhutani Control

A second strategy employed by the MoFEC was to allow select logging companies to extract timber from areas under the jurisdiction of the Inhutani state forestry enterprises, which currently total just under 10 million ha.[7] This typically occurs in one of two ways: In some cases, the MoF allocates an area with remaining stands of commercially valuable timber as an HPH that is run as a joint venture between a private timber operator and one of the Inhutanis. More often, an Inhutani will engage a private logging company—at times, an area's former concession holder—to harvest timber stocks under an informal work contract known within the industry as a *Kerja Sama Operasi* ([KSO] Operational Collaboration).

Little public information exists about the terms of these contracts, the types of areas exploited, the management practices used, or the volumes of logs produced under such arrangements. Yet many industry observers claim that KSO contracts often enable logging companies to harvest timber from degraded areas, to cut in logged-over areas before their 35-year rotation has passed, and to engage in a variety of other practices that technically would not be allowed under an HPH contract. Indeed, Titus Sarijanto, former director general of forest production, acknowledged in an interview that it is not unusual for the Inhutani enterprises to permit private timber operators to log in areas classified as rehabilitation forest. As he explained,

> This occurs for two reasons: Often an area needs to be cleared before it can be rehabilitated. Sometimes, too, the Inhutanis don't have the funds to carry out the rehabilitation, so they will allow a portion of the area to be logged to finance the rehabilitation of the rest. (Sarijanto 1999)

A senior officer at Inhutani I in East Kalimantan also stated that "To ensure security of these areas, Inhutani needs to have activity there. If we don't log in these areas, it is certain that other parties will come in and take whatever wood is left" (Inhutani I 2000).

Some industry observers suggest that one of the Inhutanis' motives for exploiting the forests under their jurisdiction is that the funds generated play an important role in supporting the MoF's formal and informal budgetary needs (Ascher 1998). Moreover, it is widely believed that the individual Inhutani enterprises have a significant degree of discretion in deciding which logging companies will have access to KSO contracts, which areas will be opened to timber operations, and what types of harvesting practices will be permitted (Kartodihardjo 1999b; Ahmad 1999). Many of these decisions—which play a critical role in determining whether sustainable harvesting practices are used—are apparently made by Inhutani field officers and the contractors working with them. It is likely that the challenges to sustainability posed by such arrangements would increase if the MoF moves forward with its recently announced plan to transfer all privately held HPHs to the Inhutanis and to allow existing concessionaires to function as contractors (*Reuters* 2000).

Weakening of Selective Cutting Guidelines

Finally, the MoF has sought to bolster the output from Indonesia's remaining HPHs by modifying the principles of the TPTI system. It has done so most significantly by introducing a new silvicultural system, *Tebang Pilih Tanaman Jarak* ([TPTJ] Selective Logging and Line Planting), in November 1998. The TPTJ guidelines may be applied on areas of production forest with a slope no greater than 25% and with altitudes up to 500 m above sea level.[8] Ostensibly designed as a modification of the TPTI system to make it more appropriate for logged-over areas, the TPTJ scheme may also be applied to tracts of primary forest as well.

Under the TPTJ system, the timber operator is permitted, first, to carry out selective logging of a designated block using a 40-cm maximum diameter cutting limit. This initial harvest is followed by the use of clear-cutting to open up "planting strips," which are then to be planted with high-value local species. By reducing the cutting limit from the 50-cm diameter prescribed under the TPTI guidelines and by permitting a portion of the area to be clear-cut, TPTJ will make substantially larger volumes of logs available from a given area of forest than would be possible under TPTI. Some industry observers have also speculated that the introduction of the TPTJ system may, in fact, be a first step toward MoF's opening of logged-over areas to commercial timber extraction without regard to where those forests are in the 35-year rotation originally designated under the HPH contract.

Assumption #3: Increased Efficiency Will Promote the Conservation of Natural Forests

Proponents of the "sustainable logging" paradigm have long argued that raising efficiency levels in all segments of the timber sector is a critical component in any strategy for conserving Indonesia's natural forests. The World Bank (1995, 16), for instance, argues that "sustainability should be sought through the promotion of efficiency, rather than an attempt to simply administer a reduced flow of raw materials to the sector, while leaving cost and price conditions and incentives unchanged." The bank and others calling for increased efficiency in the timber sector have generally addressed the issue in both allocative and operational terms. Whereas allocative efficiency refers to who produces and where, operational efficiency is concerned with how efficiently each producer conducts its activities.

Proponents of the "sustainable logging" paradigm seek to raise the sector's allocative efficiency to promote the optimal distribution of the nation's timber resources in accordance with market-based calculations of cost and scarcity. To the extent that efficient producers receive a larger share of the nation's timber output, the sector's overall efficiency is expected to improve. At the same time, proponents promote an increase in operational efficiency for individual producers through a reduction of waste in timber harvesting and higher log utilization rates in processing. The rationale is that even if the same producers account for the same share of total production, any increase in efficiency will reduce pressure on forests. Most proponents of the "sustainable logging" paradigm consider the two types of efficiency to be closely linked. Policy interventions that raise allocative efficiency within the timber sector are generally deemed to be a crucial mechanism for increasing operational efficiency on the part of timber producers and wood processors.

To raise allocative efficiency in the timber sector, the World Bank has long sought to remove several of the major market-distorting policies put in place by the New Order state. Since the current economic crisis began, the bank has taken steps to lift restrictions on log and sawnwood exports, to eliminate controls over plywood marketing held by the *Asosiasi Panel Kayu Indonesia* ([APKINDO] the Indonesian Wood Panel Association), to de-link logging concessions and processing facilities, and to make HPHs transferable. The bank justifies these reforms by arguing that the government's restrictive policies have led to an uncompetitive and inefficient processing sector, "characterized by high levels of rent-seeking which has become totally dependent on highly subsidized log prices" (The World Bank 1995, 16). The World Bank maintains that the log export ban, in particular, has undermined sustainability by leading "the sector [to] substitute logs, which should be regarded as a scarce factor of production for other factors…[encouraging the forests to be] treated as a low value resource by both the private sector and government agencies" (The World Bank 1995, 16).

In calling for the removal of log export restrictions, the World Bank and others have maintained that they are seeking to enable Indonesian timber producers to obtain full market value for their logs (Manurung and Buongiorno 1997; Barbier et al. 1995; The World Bank 1995; Vincent 1992; Lindsay 1989). They claim that policies that have kept domestic timber prices below international parity levels have led processing companies to use their wood inputs carelessly. This, in turn, has kept the volume of timber being logged higher than would have been necessary if wood panel producers and sawmills were able to generate their processed wood products in a more efficient manner. These analysts argue that higher log prices will promote the sustainability of Indonesia's natural forests in two ways. First, increased profits from timber sales should lead concession holders to attach greater value to the forest resources under their control and, in doing so, to take steps to reduce the volume of waste associated with their harvesting operations. Second, substantially higher raw material costs are likely to lead Indonesia's wood-based industries to invest in more efficient processing techniques, which will presumably generate greater levels of output with a smaller volume of logs.

In their efforts to raise domestic log prices, the World Bank and other advocates of efficiency-based sustainability have largely ignored the additional pressures that the removal of log export restrictions would place on Indonesia's forests. Nonetheless, it is probable that open access to international timber markets—where roundwood prices are often considerably higher than they are domestically—would introduce a substantially greater structural demand for Indonesian logs than currently exists.[9] Such additional demand on the part of foreign buyers can be expected to create pressures for increased levels of timber removals in both Indonesia's legal and illegal logging industries, leading to large volumes of roundwood being shipped overseas. The correlation between reduced export taxes and increased logging is, in fact, predicted by most econometric studies that have analyzed the marketing restrictions imposed in Indonesia's timber sector over the last 20 years (Manurung and Buongiorno 1997; Barbier et al. 1995). Together with the World Bank, however, these analyses generally assume that pressures for additional logging will be offset by steps taken to raise efficiency on the part of wood processors. Unfortunately, none of these studies provides compelling evidence to support this assumption.

The effects of such pressures to increase log supply will be particularly acute if Indonesia's log export restrictions are removed before effective mechanisms are installed to control timber extraction and marketing. In the absence of such controls, higher log prices are likely to support a proliferation of illegal logging above the current high levels that exist in most timber-producing provinces. A similar problem arises with the World Bank's proposal to de-link HPHs from processing facilities. The bank's rationale for trying to separate the two is that it will "weaken the official monopoly over log supplies that large-scale processing complexes have hitherto benefited from" (The World Bank 1998, 20) and, in doing so, remove a major structural factor contributing to the undervaluing of Indonesian forests. The bank envisions the development of a domestic log market in which processors would be forced to purchase the bulk of their raw materials at market rates (which would presumably be on par with international prices if log export restrictions were successfully removed). As with opening log exports, however, the Bank's efforts to de-link HPHs and mills are likely to encourage an expansion of illegal logging if they are carried out before an effective chain of custody system is put in place.

Over the past several years, many Indonesian panel producers have, in fact, purchased a growing portion of their logs from outside their own concessions. The Barito Pacific Group—Indonesia's largest panel producer—has reportedly purchased 30–40% of its logs since 1994 (Soedibyo 1999). Similarly, the Korindo Group is reported to purchase more than one-half of the 1.3 million m³ that its mills consume, because of the declining productivity of its own concessions and the fact that several of its own HPHs have been involuntarily revoked (Cheol 1999).

Several industry officers interviewed in the course of this study indicated that their firms often have little information on either the source of these logs or the conditions under which they are harvested. As one plywood executive, in a confidential interview in Jakarta, on February 9, 1999, put it,

> We buy logs from a broker. Sometimes they have documentation, but often they do not. We generally do not know where the logs come from. If the Forestry Department finds out that we're using logs without documentation, we point to the broker and he's the one that gets penalized.

The World Bank and others seeking to deregulate Indonesia's timber trade have done so to encourage both concession holders and wood processors to invest in measures that will improve the efficiency of their operations. Investments in harvesting efficiency might include the use of new technologies or practices that allow logging companies to extract more timber from each hectare of forest, more wood out of each stem that is cut, or larger volumes of timber harvested in shorter time frames or at reduced cost. Similarly, measures to raise processing efficiency would include the adoption of new equipment or techniques that enable wood processors to raise the volume or value of output from each unit of wood that their mills consume.

The arguments used to promote greater operational efficiency are rooted in the assumption that improvements in efficiency at both the harvesting and processing levels will relieve pressures on Indonesia's forests. Embedded in this assumption is a belief that if firms are able to obtain greater output from each cubic meter of wood (or hectare of forest) by improving the efficiency of their operations, they will thereafter demand the same or possibly a smaller volume of timber (or exploit a smaller area). Efficiency becomes associated with conservation because it is assumed that investments in efficiency will produce greater volumes of processed output without generating increased demand for raw materials. Yet there is little evidence to indicate that either logging companies or processing firms would voluntarily place a cap on their earnings by restricting the volume of timber they harvest or process if access to this timber were not otherwise constrained. On the contrary, basic economic theory would suggest that firms able to raise profits through increased efficiency would have an incentive to expand their operations, thereby increasing their demand for logs.

Moreover, technological innovations that increase efficiency in timber extraction or processing—the widespread adoption of the chain saw, for instance—have, at times, changed the nature of demand or accelerated the pace of forest destruction quite considerably.[10] The growing adoption of small-spindle rotaries on the part of Indonesian plywood producers may be having just such an effect.[11] Introduced in the mid-1990s, the new rotaries allow panel producers to peel logs as small as 15 cm in diameter, leaving a core of 6–8 cm. The old, large-spindle rotaries, by contrast, would generally leave a 15- to 25-cm core that could not be peeled. According to several producers interviewed, the use of the new technology has had the practical effect of raising their log recovery rates—particularly when their preexisting machinery had become highly depreciated—from the 45–50% range to that of 55–60%.

The new rotaries have enabled producers both to peel logs from younger trees and to process a variety of timber species that were previously considered to be marginal. In this sense, the widespread adoption of the new rotaries is likely to increase the burden on Indonesia's forest resource base quite substantially. Indeed, several producers interviewed for this study indicated that the new rotaries had given them incentive to return to logged-over areas for a second harvest or to seek harvesting rights in areas without old-growth Dipterocarps. Most admitted that both of these processes would have been uneconomical just a few years ago, when their mills' capabilities were limited by the constraints of the large-spindle peelers that were then in place. As a timber manager with the Korindo Group explained, "The new rotaries are what has made IPK profitable, as we can cut trees with diameters of 20 cm and up and all species but *ulin* and *bengeris*. With the old technology, we would not have been able to use most of this for plywood" (Cheol 1999).

Assumption #4: Sustainable Concession Management Is Profitable

Beyond seeking to rescind Indonesia's log export restrictions, the World Bank and other proponents of the "sustainable logging" paradigm have called on the government to raise timber royalties and to introduce a system of performance bonds to ensure that logging companies manage their concessions sustainably. Implicit in these proposals is an assumption that HPH holders will be able to generate profits in spite of the additional costs that these new fees impose on their operations. That is, Indonesian-based concessionaires are assumed to be enjoying such high rents that they are able to afford the additional financial obligations that sustainability imposes. To the extent that sustainable concession management is not profitable for private timber operators, they can be expected either to withdraw from the timber sector or, more likely, to resort to increasingly unsustainable practices for as long as they are able to. Simply put, HPH holders will not play by the rules if it is not profitable for them to do so.

Through much of the New Order period, there was a general consensus that Indonesia's HPH system did, indeed, generate high rents and that a substantial portion of these accrued to private timber operators in the form of excess profits. Ruzicka (1979), for instance, estimated that in the mid-1970s, medium- and large-scale concessionaires in East Kalimantan were able to capture 67–75% of the rents associated with their logging activities, yielding average annual returns of 120–150%. Similarly, Ahmad and Ramli (1991) concluded that the government allowed private concession holders to capture no less than 83% of the rents generated in the timber sector during the period 1980–1990, or roughly US$80 in rent for every cubic meter these companies harvested.

Several concessionaires contacted in the course of this study, however, indicated that the profitability of timber extraction on at least some of their HPHs had declined markedly over the past decade. Some attributed this to the fact that the most productive parts of their concessions—particularly those areas with stocks of high-value, high-diameter *meranti* (*Shorea spp.*)—have already been logged over, and they are now harvesting stands of lesser commercial value. Several also claimed that they are having to travel greater distances than in the past to obtain commercially valuable timber and that the added transport costs have cut into their profits. Although anecdotal claims of this sort should not be interpreted to mean that rents no longer exist in Indonesia's timber sector, they do suggest that some concessionaires may no longer be enjoying the high excess profits that they did in the past.

Assessment of Current Rent Levels

To better assess whether sustainable concession management is, in fact, viable for a majority of Indonesian HPH holders, it is useful to examine the concession rent studies conducted by the Indonesia–U.K. Tropical Forest Management Programme (ITFMP). These studies offer the most detailed calculations of timber sector profitability in recent years. Based on the results of a 1995 survey of 31 concessions located in five provinces, ITFMP has developed a Forest Concession Model, which estimates the economic rent that concessionaires obtain from their operations for a given log price and production costs. Using this model, Scotland (1999) estimated that before the onset of the economic crisis in July 1997, a timber operator with a 15-year old concession of 115,000 ha—characteristics purportedly selected "to represent an average concession in Indonesia"—enjoyed an internal rate of return of 19%. Total economic rent under those conditions stood at US$42.00 per m³, corresponding to excess profits of US$3.16 per m³ for the concessionaire, assuming a 15% discount rate.

In estimating rent levels after the monetary crisis began, Scotland assumes that most concessionaires adopted a range of cost-cutting measures to compensate for the sharp devaluation of the *rupiah*: switching to exclusive use of the *rupiah* to minimize dollar expenditures; placing a moratorium on all large capital purchases; and reducing by 50% all nonessential expenditures—that is, anything not directly related to felling operations and the sale of timber. With these adjustments, it is estimated that timber operators were able to generate an internal rate of return of 27%, which was just slightly higher than the assumed post-crisis discount rate of 25%. In response to the precipitous drop in domestic log prices, rent levels are believed to have fallen to US$13.50 per m^3 during the months after the crisis began, leaving concessionaires to capture US$0.60 per m^3 in excess profits. From these figures, Scotland estimates that during the first year of the crisis, aggregate rents associated with Indonesia's logging industry were US$447 million, of which approximately US$16 million accrued to the private sector as excess profits. By comparison, total rents before the crisis began were on the order of US$1.1 billion per annum, of which US$84 million went to concession holders (Scotland 1999, ii).

What is striking about these numbers is the relatively small portion of the total rents generated by the HPH system that are actually collected by concession holders as excess profits—7.6% before the crisis and a mere 3.5% since the crisis began.[12] Under either set of conditions, it is not at all clear that a substantial majority of Indonesia's concession holders would be able to continue operating profitably if timber royalties were raised significantly and a performance bond equivalent to 30% of annual operating costs were imposed, as the World Bank has recommended. Unfortunately, the ITFMP model does not account for the considerable variation in operating costs or productivity—and, therefore, rent levels—that exists across geographic space and among firms with different processing capacities, investment strategies, and management objectives. As such, it does not reliably predict what portion of HPH holders would lose money if they did not manage their concessions sustainably.

As Scotland's study was based on figures derived from a hypothetical "representative" concession, its conclusions extrapolate from the assumption that all concessions are able to obtain 28 m^3 of commercial timber per hectare and that 70% of their species mix is made up of valuable *meranti*. While it is acknowledged that these figures are "undoubtedly higher than production in marginal and degraded concessions, the latter of which there are many," the study offered little sense of the ranges of productivity or profitability associated with such sites either before or after the crisis (Scotland 1999, 15). In fact, however, the rent survey on which the ITFMP Forest Concession Model was constructed found that no fewer than 10 of the 31 firms covered had productivity levels of 15 m^3 per hectare or less. The least productive of these sites reported yields of only 5 m^3 per hectare.

Moreover, anecdotal evidence from interviews conducted during the course of the present study suggests that meranti accounts for substantially less than 70% of the timber currently being harvested at many HPHs. Several industry sources indicated that there has been a marked decline in high-value, large-diameter *meranti* in most timber-producing regions over the past 10–15 years. As such, many concessionaires are now cutting smaller-diameter stems and a broader range of species than in the past. Former APKINDO chair, Bob Hasan, described this process as follows:

> Through the 1970s and 1980s, most of what we cut was *meranti*. The trees were enormous and we could pick which ones we wanted. Generally, we chose those 60 cm and up. Now, the big *meranti* is much more scarce and harder to get. At least half of what we harvest is other species. (Hasan 1999)

To some extent, this decline in high-value meranti logs has been obscured by the fact that since the early 1990s the *Masyarakat Perhutanan Indonesia* (Indonesian Forestry Society) has encouraged its members to market a variety of species with properties similar to Shorea as "meranti group."

Scotland used the ITFMP model to estimate forest concession profitability and levels of economic rent associated with HPHs of varying sizes. He found that under the post-crisis scenario, there was a substantial economy of scale in the timber sector and that concessions only began to register a profit when they are 80,000 ha or larger (Scotland 1999, 19–20). At the assumed post-crisis discount rate of 25%, he argued that concessions smaller than this show a negative net present value and that economic rent on each cubic meter of roundwood produced falls below the log levies collected by the government. These findings, therefore, suggest that a significant portion of Indonesia's concessionaires have not been able to maintain their economic viability if they adhered to the GOI's regulations through much of the period since the crisis began.

In addition, Scotland's analysis was prepared in early 1999 when international petroleum prices were low and when domestic fuel prices were being heavily subsidized by the GOI to keep them at roughly 30% of international rates. As a result, the potentially large effect of fuel costs on profit margins is not readily apparent in the rent levels calculated. Because it is improbable that domestic fuel prices will remain at such low, subsidized rates for very long, many concessionaires—particularly those which must haul their logs overland—are likely to face substantially higher transportation costs over the medium term than those estimated.

The point of this discussion is not to critique Scotland's study—which, indeed, offers the most serious analysis of concession-holder profits since the economic crisis began. Nor is it to imply that Indonesian concession holders are no longer making profits. It is, rather, to underscore the manner in which discussions of Indonesian timber rents have often overstated the profits available to a substantial portion of the nation's concessionaires. Timber companies with the largest, most productive, and most accessible HPHs were clearly capturing sizeable rents before the crisis, and most have apparently continued to enjoy excess profits on a more modest scale since the crisis began. Yet timber companies with smaller, less productive, or remote concessions have been operating much closer to the margins of profitability. It is likely that many have resorted to illegal—and presumably unsustainable—practices to maintain their profit levels.

This poses an important practical challenge for the World Bank and other agencies that have sought to have the GOI raise its timber royalties and to introduce performance bonds. Together, these two fees will need to be large enough that they motivate concessionaires to employ sustainable management practices, but not so high that they inhibit timber operators from generating a reasonable profit at the prevailing discount rate. As mentioned above, concession holders cannot rationally be expected to manage their HPHs sustainably if it is not sufficiently profitable for them to do so. Given the range of rent levels that appears to exist across space, companies, and time, it is difficult to imagine how the government will be able to increase its own rent capture and impose effective performance bonds without also pushing a segment of the industry's concession holders out of business. Several industry officials interviewed indicated that to the extent these fees reduced the profitability of their own logging operations, their firms would shift toward sourcing their logs from the open market. In practical terms, this would imply a growing reliance by many wood processors on illegally and unsustainably harvested timber (De Kock, 1999).

Dwindling Prospects for Rents Over the Long Term

By definition, sustainable concession management also involves the maintenance of a site's productivity at a commercially viable level for an indefinite number of harvests beyond the first logging rotation. Such systems generally take into account the fact that second harvests are almost always lower than first harvests. At least in theory, they are designed to maintain all subsequent harvests at levels that are similar to the second cut and are profitable. Indonesia's TPTI system is based on the assumption "that a residual stand after logging will contain an adequate stocking of sound, commercial species trees of 20 cm dbh or more, which will grow into economically harvestable timber in 35 years from the original logging date" (The World Bank 1993, 38). To be successful, the TPTI system is dependent on commercial species in the logged-over forest regenerating at a rate of at least 1 cm per year, so that there is an adequate number of stems with a diameter of 50 cm and up when the second rotation begins.

With a growing number of concessions in Indonesia's Outer Islands nearing the end of their first 35-year rotation, the question of whether there will be trees of adequate size and value to make sustainable management profitable during the second harvesting cycle is emerging as a critical issue. Many of the concession holders interviewed for this study indicated that they anticipate that the second rotation may, in fact, not be profitable if the concession is managed for sustained yield. Some questioned the theory behind the TPTI system, claiming that the trees at their concession sites did not grow at a rate of 1 cm per year and, therefore, would not fully regenerate in 35 years. Others reported that noncommercial or lesser-value species dominated the residual stand after the first rotation. Several industry studies have documented the fact that collateral damage during logging operations is often severe, with the effect that it sharply limits the site's future productivity. Post-logging surveys in the early 1990s estimated that damage and mortality in residual stands was frequently in the range of 35–50% (The World Bank 1993).

In interviews, several industry officials noted that logging companies frequently have little incentive to leave commercially valuable stems standing in residual forests, as there is often scant hope that these trees will remain in place—or that their firms will have continued access to them—until the second rotation begins. Although the World Bank has used this to justify extending the HPH contract from 20 to 35 years, there is growing evidence that, in fact, longer concession periods will hardly be adequate to counteract such pressures. With timber roads and skid trails providing easy access, logged-over areas are often highly susceptible to encroachment on the part of illegal loggers and settlers. Some companies also reported that after their initial harvest, portions of their concession areas have been reclassified by the MoF for other uses such as plantations and transmigration. Consequently, it is common practice for concession holders to re-log a regenerating stand prematurely, a practice known as *cuci mangkok* (literally, "washing the bowl"). In fact, some concessionaires are known to have intentionally logged in degraded and cut-over areas to encourage the Forestry Department to reclassify their HPH sites as conversion forest. Logged-over areas have also been particularly susceptible to the widespread forest fires of the last few years, which have further diminished the availability of second-rotation timber (Dennis and Hoffmann 2000; Hoffmann et al. 1999; see Chapters 13 and 14 of this book).

The combination of these factors raises serious doubts as to whether sustainable concession management practices will be at all profitable in areas entering their second rotation—a prospect facing concessions allocated in the late 1960s within the next five years and a rapidly growing number after that. In fact, there is growing evidence that in many parts of Sumatra and Kalimantan, timber concessions subject to repeated logging and other forms of disturbance will have no commercial volume remaining at the point that the second logging rotation is due to begin.

Assumption #5: The GOI Has the Institutional Capacity to Enforce the Proposed Changes in the HPH System and the Forest Products Trade

To be implemented effectively on any large scale, the reforms put forth by proponents of the "sustainable logging" paradigm would require a considerable degree of institutional capacity on the part of the Indonesian government.

According to the reform agenda proposed by the World Bank, the government's central task in the forestry sector is to reduce aggregate roundwood production by roughly 30 million m³ per year. The bank argues that the GOI will be able to achieve this by regulating concession management practices more tightly and by removing restrictions on the marketing of logs and other wood products. To be even minimally successful in accomplishing these, the government would need to have the following institutional capabilities:

- mechanisms to monitor and enforce the use of sustainable practices on the part of concessionaires within their HPHs,
- the capacity to enforce concession boundaries to restrict outside actors from encroaching on HPHs,
- the ability to keep concession holders and others from logging in areas that have not been designated for commercial timber extraction, and
- an effective system of surveillance and chain-of-custody to control both the domestic timber trade and log exports.

For several reasons, it appears highly unlikely that the Indonesian government will, at any point in the near future, have the institutional capacity needed to make systemic changes in the HPH system and the nation's forest products trade (see Chapter 7). From a purely logistical perspective, the need to enforce rigid, exclusionary boundaries around areas designated as HPHs and to monitor the harvesting practices of close to 400 concession holders poses a number of formidable challenges. Indonesia's total concession area currently extends over 49 million ha, much of which is located in remote regions or covers terrain that is difficult to access. The state forestry bureaucracy—which, since 1967, has been charged with managing 75% of the nation's landmass—is understaffed, poorly trained, and ill-equipped to administer such a large area. Moreover, the vast majority of the MoF personnel are concentrated in Jakarta, Java, and provincial capitals (see Chapter 8).

Some observers anticipate that such institutional weaknesses are likely to be exacerbated by the current decentralization process, in which authority over forest administration is shifting from Jakarta to provincial and regency (*kabupaten*) level governments (see Chapter 15). Until now *kabupaten* governments have played a minimal role in administering the forests within their jurisdictions. Most have little technical capacity to assess whether timber companies are adhering to the government's regulatory guidelines for sustainable concession management. Likewise few, if any, have the enforcement capacity needed to regulate the activities of either formal concession holders or the various actors involved in informal timber harvesting. Under the decentralized system, significant responsibilities for forest sector policymaking and planning are also likely to remain with the MoF in Jakarta, while implementation responsibilities lie with the provincial and *kabupaten* governments. This implies that implementation of a coherent policy for sustainable timber extraction will require a considerable amount of coordination across the various tiers of government, which in many cases have competing institutional interests.

Complicating matters significantly, units of the military, national police force, and other arms of the state apparatus are known to be heavily involved in illegal logging in most timber-producing provinces (McCarthy 2000; Telapak Indonesia and EIA 1999). It is likely that the involvement of such actors could become more entrenched as the state becomes weaker or more decentralized and as these agencies are less able to rely on formal budgetary allocations to support their operations.[13] While the World Bank and others have proposed the establishment of an independent monitoring system to regulate concessionaire management practices, it is difficult to imagine how such a system could function without the active support of the state's own law enforcement agencies. In any case, it would appear that reducing effective demand for logs by closing some processing mills would be an easier, and arguably more effective, strategy to implement than controlling log supply.

Conclusion

Reorienting Timber Sector Reform

Over the last 15 years, the policy dialogue in Indonesia's forestry sector has been dominated by proposals to reform the HPH timber concession system. The central aim of these reforms has been to reduce Indonesia's aggregate timber extraction rates to the supposedly sustainable level of 25 million m^3 per year. As argued in this chapter, the World Bank and others promoting environmental sustainability through improved concession management are unlikely to achieve this objective under the circumstances that currently exist in Indonesia's forestry sector. The effectiveness of the proposed policy interventions is likely to be limited in that they perform the following acts:

- seek to control timber supply without reducing effective demand on the part of Indonesia's wood-based industries;
- overlook or inadequately address roundwood extraction from large areas, including areas designated protection and conversion forest, as well as areas under Inhutani control;
- fail to provide a credible plan for reducing illegal logging;
- encourage investments in efficiency without regard for the often-damaging effects that such investments may have on natural forests;
- assume that sustainable concession management is profitable over both the short and long term, despite strong indications to the contrary; and
- assume, without evidence, that the GOI has the institutional capacity needed to make systemic changes to the HPH system and the forest products trade.

In assessing the prospects for environmental sustainability in Indonesia's forestry sector, this analysis has largely focused on policy reforms proposed by the World Bank since the mid-1980s. It is important to recognize, however, that the bank has hardly been alone in arguing that sustainability can best be achieved by modifying the HPH concession system and regulatory structures framing the nation's forest products trade. Indeed, many forest economists and policy analysts have joined the Bank in calling on the Indonesian government to better enforce its selective cutting guidelines; to increase its capture of timber resource rents; and to encourage market-based efficiency in log harvesting, processing, and trade. Moreover, proponents of the "sustainable logging" paradigm have advocated a very similar set of policies in many countries besides Indonesia. These include tropical timber-producing countries as diverse as Cameroon, Guyana, Malaysia, and Papua New Guinea.

While sustainable forest management is clearly an important goal to be pursued by the World Bank or other agencies seeking to leverage reforms on the part of the Indonesian government, it loses much of its legitimacy to the extent that it is fundamentally unachievable on any large scale. This, in turn, raises important questions about what priorities should guide the policy reform process in Indonesia's timber sector. The following sections outline three major directions in which the reform process should be reoriented.

Limiting Demand for Roundwood

The considerable logistical difficulties associated with controlling timber supply in Indonesia suggest that any serious effort to relieve pressures on the nation's remaining natural forests should involve proactive steps to limit demand for wood on the part of domestic forest-based industries. With illegal logging going virtually unchecked in most timber-producing provinces, it is probable that Indonesia's annual log harvest will greatly exceed the legal and sustainable harvesting levels as long as a substantial "structural timber deficit" remains in place. Industrial overcapacity in Indonesia's wood-processing sector was identified as a critical problem facing the forestry sector at the February 2000 meeting of the Consultative Group on Indonesia, placing the issue squarely on the forestry sector policy agenda. There, both the GOI and the international donor community agreed to take immediate steps toward "closing illegal sawmills" and the "downsizing and restructuring of [Indonesia's] wood-based industry to balance supply with demand for raw materials" (Keating 2000).

To implement these commitments, it will be necessary for the Indonesian government and international donors to define practical steps that can be taken to reduce demand for wood on the part of domestic processing industries and to identify which agencies would need to carry these out. In this regard, it is significant that the Indonesian Bank Restructuring Agency (IBRA) now controls many of Indonesia's wood processors, either in whole or in part. To the extent that

IBRA chooses to call in outstanding loans held by forest sector debtors, it can exert a great deal of leverage in carrying out reductions in processing capacity at both the firm and industry levels. In playing such a role, it would clearly be necessary for IBRA to work closely with policymakers from a range of government agencies, civil society organizations, and forest industry groups.

As a first step, these actors would need to develop criteria for determining which mills should be subject to capacity reduction measures or closure. Clearly, this should not be based simply on which mills hold the largest amounts of outstanding corporate debt. Rather, it should include detailed and transparent assessments of whether they reflect the following characteristics:

- These mills have verifiable access to legal and sustainable raw material supplies.
- Their operations have a profoundly negative effect on the surrounding environment.
- Their activities have led to social conflicts with local communities that threaten either the viability of the processing enterprise or the sociopolitical stability of the region in which they are operating.
- The processing enterprise carries an inordinate degree of financial risk.

Slowing Forest Conversion

To the extent that policymakers seek to control Indonesia's wood supply, their focus will need to extend beyond restricting log output from the HPH system. Sharp reductions in roundwood harvests can only be achieved if steps are taken to significantly reduce the pace at which Indonesia's remaining natural forests are being converted to other uses. To its credit, the World Bank secured from the GOI a temporary moratorium on the allocation of forested land for conversion to oil palm and other agroindustrial crops in late 1998 (see Chapter 10). This moratorium should be maintained at least until detailed surveys have been carried out to determine whether appropriate nonforested areas are available for such projects and until existing legal claims on such lands have been resolved. Moreover, efforts should be made to ensure that subsidies in the form of underpriced IPK wood, discounted capital and loan guarantees, and corporate debt write-off do not offer perverse incentives for agroindustrial conglomerates to clear new tracts of forested land.

In addition, Indonesian government policymakers should be encouraged to seriously consider placing restrictions on the allocation of new IPK licenses to pulp mills and other wood processors. Companies seeking access to IPK wood should be required to provide verifiable documentation that they are making adequate progress in establishing plantations to ensure that their operations will eventually be sustainable over the long term.[14] Policymakers may also wish to consider requiring IPK license holders to pay higher royalties on the wood they harvest to ensure that its costs are comparable to the costs associated with obtaining wood from industrial wood plantations.

Finally, the GOI should be encouraged to restrict the use of logging in areas allocated to the Inhutani state forestry enterprises for "rehabilitation" purposes. More generally, efforts should be made to establish a clear code of accountability for the Inhutanis and mechanisms for monitoring the forest areas under their control, although such efforts would almost certainly be hindered by many of the same factors that limit monitoring of existing HPHs. This latter point is especially critical in light of the MoF's proposal in mid-2000 to transfer all of Indonesia's existing HPHs to Inhutani management.

Shifting the Agenda toward Equity

The recognition that, at this point, sustainable concession management is fundamentally unachievable on any large scale begs the question of who should have access to and control over the nation's forest resources. Through the New Order period, both the MoF and many advocates of the "sustainable logging" paradigm routinely argued that large, privately owned logging companies connected to processing facilities are the most appropriate actors for managing areas designated as production forest in Indonesia's Outer Islands. The stated rationale was that such actors would have an incentive to manage their concessions sustainably because they have both a long-term investment in processing, which relies on continued access to timber supplies, and an economy of scale that enables them to run their harvesting operations efficiently. In this way, the principle of sustainability has often been used to legitimize the extreme inequity around which the HPH system has been structured over the past three decades. In practice, it appears that some large-scale timber operators may, indeed, have adhered to the GOI's selective harvesting and replanting regulations. Yet a far larger number have employed indiscriminate logging practices to liquidate as rapidly as possible the timber resources made available to them by the state.

Recognizing sustainability of forest management by large-scale enterprises to be untenable under the current circumstances makes it impossible to justify maintaining the New Order regime's policy of categorically excluding forest-dependent communities from areas that the state has defined to be production, protection, or conversion forest. On the contrary, the demise of sustainability as an achievable policy goal suggests that equity for local communities with clear historical or customary (adat) claims to forestland should, in fact, be a central principle guiding forestry sector reform in the present context (see Chapters 5 and 6). Clearly, the legal recognition of local tenure would not, in itself, guarantee that any given tract of forest would remain standing longer than if a timber concessionaire managed it. It would, however, provide the basis for ensuring that members of forest-based communities would have legitimate authority to determine how the forest resources on which their livelihoods depend should be managed and to share equitably in the benefits of any products harvested from the areas under their jurisdiction.

Moreover, numerous studies have shown forest-dependent communities in many parts of Indonesia to consist of highly skilled resource managers who have sustained complex forest ecosystems for generations (Fried 1995; Dove 1986).

Acknowledgments

This research was supported by CIFOR and WWF-International's Macroeconomics Program Office. I am indebted to David Kaimowitz for his conceptual guidance and input on various drafts of this chapter and to David Reed for his support for this work.

Endnotes

1. The HPH timber concession system was established with the adoption of Indonesia's Basic Forestry Law in 1967, shortly after Soeharto's New Order regime came to power. Under this system, private logging companies and state-owned enterprises have been able to obtain concession licenses to harvest timber in areas designated as production forest and limited production forest for a period of 20 years. For details on legal and institutional aspects of the HPH system, see Gray and Hadi (1989). Barr (1999) provides a political-economic history of the HPH system during the New Order period.

2. Key elements of the *Tebang Pilih Tanam Indonesia* ([TPTI] Indonesian Selective Planting and Cutting System) guidelines include the use of a 35-year harvesting cycle; restrictions on cutting commercial species that are below 50 cm dbh (diameter at breast height); rehabilitation of skid trails and enrichment planting; and thinning of noncommercial species at 10, 15, and 20 years. Djamaludin (1989) provides a detailed account of the development and implementation of the TPTI guidelines during the 1970s and 1980s.

3. For the purposes of this chapter, I do not examine how this figure was derived, nor do I analyze whether it, in fact, represents a realistic estimate of the volume of wood that can be sustainably harvested from Indonesia's natural forests. Rather, I maintain that even if this figure is assumed to be a reasonably accurate estimation of the nation's sustainability threshold, it is doubtful that the HPH reforms advocated by proponents of the "sustainable logging" paradigm will effectively reduce timber removals to this level.

4. By comparison, Scotland et al. (1999) estimated that in 1997, total consumption of roundwood in Indonesia may have been as high as 82.3 million m^3.

5. During most of the 1990s, Indonesia had an MoF. The MoF was changed to the MoFEC during the Habibie regime, but it was changed back to the MoF in 2000.

6. The figures in this paragraph are drawn from MoF data presented in Kartodihardjo and Supriono (2000).

7. There are currently five Inhutani state-owned forestry enterprises. PT Inhutani I controls 3.9 million ha in East Kalimantan; South, Central, and North Sulawesi; and Maluku. PT Inhutani II controls 3.8 million ha in South, East, and West Kalimantan and Central Sulawesi. PT Inhutani III controls 2.9 million ha in South, Central, and West Kalimantan. PT Inhutani IV controls 500,000 ha in North Sumatra, West Sumatra, Aceh, and Riau. PT Inhutani V controls 400,000 ha in South Sumatra, Jambi, Bengkulu, and Lampung (Departemen Kehutanan 1998).

8. The TPTJ system is specified in Keputusan Menteri Kehutanan 435/Kpts-II/1997 and 338/Kpts-II/1998, and in Keputusan Menteri Kehutanan dan Perkebunanan 625/Kpts-II/

1998. A critical examination of the implications of the TPTJ system is provided by Purnama et al. (1999).

9. Industry analysts have speculated that international demand for Indonesian logs and wood products could increase substantially as a result of China's recent ban on logging and entry into the World Trade Organization. Indeed, there are indications that Chinese wood processors have imported a growing volume of logs from Malaysia and Indonesia (in some cases illegally) as domestic sources have diminished.

10. Colfer (1983), for instance, describes a rapid acceleration in timber harvesting in rural East Kalimantan following the introduction of the chain saw in the late 1970s and early 1980s.

11. The new rotaries cost between US$1 million and US$2 million, and as such they are a form of technology that is accessible (though by no means inexpensive) to plywood producers of all sizes. Indeed, 12 of the 15 firms interviewed indicated that they had either already installed or initiated the purchase of new rotaries in at least one of their mills. For many producers, the installation of the new rotary has been part of a broader restructuring process, which has often involved the purchase of new driers, kilns, and hot presses, as well as other capital investments to improve efficiency. There is general belief within the industry that all of Indonesia's plywood producers will eventually buy new rotaries, although many will now have to wait until after the economic crisis is over.

12. Clearly, it is important to recognize that most of Indonesia's timber concessions are controlled by integrated timber conglomerates, through which they are linked to plywood and sawmills. A portion of the rents associated with a concession is often transferred to these industries through the sale of roundwood to an allied processing firm at artificially low prices, a process known as transfer pricing. Moreover, by adding value to the logs they consume, these industries generate additional rents for each cubic meter of roundwood processed (Scotland and Whiteman 1997, 12). As concessions and processing operations become increasingly separated, however, timber groups will have no reason to use rents generated from processing to subsidize concessions if they are not profitable in their own right.

13. In a news interview, Minister of Defense Juwono Sudarsono stated that formal budget allocations "only account for around 25 percent of the minimum budget needed for TNI [Indonesian Army] operational costs" (*The Jakarta Post* 2000). Juwono noted that "because minimum standards to enhance professionalism are not met, there are many [military officers] who are involved in unsavory activities, including 'influencing' legal processes."

14. For large-scale plantation projects, such as those associated with Indonesia's major pulp mills, this could be accomplished at relatively low cost through the use of satellite or aerial imagery, coupled with independent third-party audits by trained forestry experts. In this way, it is conceivable that effective monitoring could occur in spite of the limited institutional capabilities of the government's forest regulatory agencies, as discussed under "Assumption 5" in this chapter.

References

Ahmad, M. 1999. Personal communication with the author, May 4, 1999.

Ahmad, M., and R. Ramli. 1991. *Rente Ekonomi dalam Pengelolaan Hutan Alam*. Jakarta, Indonesia: Wahana Lingkungan Hidup Indonesia.

APKI (Asosiasi Pulpdan Kertas Indonesia). 1997. Indonesian Pulp and Paper Industry 1997 Directory. Jakarta, Indonesia: PT Gramedia.

APKINDO (Asosiasi Panel Kayle Indonesia). 1999. *Production and Export of Indonesian Wood Panels*. Unpublished data.

Ascher, W. 1998. From oil to timber: the political economy of off-budget development financing in Indonesia. *Indonesia* 65:37–61.

Asnawie, S. 2000. Penjarahan kayu diperbatasan kembali marak. *Tarakan Post*. January 15–22.

Barbier, E.B., N. Bockstael, J.C. Burgess, and I. Strand. 1995. The linkages between the timber trade and tropical deforestation—Indonesia. *World Economy* 18(3):411–42.

Barr, C. 1999. Discipline and Accumulate: *State Practice and Elite Consolidation in Indonesia's Timber Sector, 1967–1998*. Master's thesis. Ithaca, NY: Cornell University.

———. 2001. Chapter 4: The Political Economy of Fiber and Finance in Indonesia's Pulp and Paper Industries. In *Banking on Sustainability: Structural Adjustment and Forestry Reform in Post-Suharto Indonesia*. Washington, D.C.: the Center for International Forestry Research (CIFOR) and World Wide Fund for Nature Macroeconomics for Sustainable Development Program Office, 70–95.

Brown, D. 1999. *Addicted to Rent: Corporate and Spatial Distribution of Forest Resources in Indonesia; Implications for Forest Sustainability and Government Policy*. Jakarta, Indonesia: ITFMP.

Cheol, K.Y., manager of the Forestry Division, Korindo Group. 1999. Personal communication with the author, February 25, 1999.

Colfer, C.J.P. 1983. Change and indigenous agroforestry in East Kalimantan. *Borneo Research Bulletin* 15(1&2):3–20, 70–86.

De Kock, R.B. 1999. *Yield Regulation for KPHP*. Report no. PFM/SILV/99/3. Jakarta, Indonesia: ITFMP.

Dennis, R., and A. Hoffmann. 2000. *Large-scale, catastrophic fires and secondary forests in Indonesia*. Paper prepared for the workshop "Tropical secondary forests in Asia: Reality and perspectives," Center for International Forestry Research, German Agency for Development, and Expertisecentrum LNV (formerly IKC Natuurbeheer). April 2000. Samarinda, Indonesia.

Departemen Kehutanan. 1994. *Statistik Kehutanan Indonesia*. Jakarta, Indonesia: Biro Perencanaan, Sekretariat Jendral Departemen Kehutanan.

Departemen Kehutanan, Sekretariat Jenderal Pengusahaan Hutan, Direktorat Penyiapan Pengusahaan Hutan. 1998. *Laporan Hasil Monitoring dan Evaluasi Perkembangan HPH Sampai Dengan Bulan Maret* 1998. Jakarta, Indonesia: Departemen Kehutanan.

Direktorat Bina Pengusahaan Hutan. 1999a. *Realisasi produksi kayu bulat, khusus RKT-PH*. Jakarta, Indonesia: Departemen Kehutanan, Direktorat Jenderal Pengusahaan Hutan. Unpublished statistics.

——————. 1999b. *Produksi kayu bulat areal konversi*. Jakarta, Indonesia: Departemen Kehutanan, Direktorat Jenderal Pengusahaan Hutan. Unpublished statistics.

Direktorat Penyiapan Pengusahaan Hutan. 1998. *Laporan Hasil Monitoring Dan Evaluasi Perkembangan HPH Sampai Dengan Bulan Maret 1998*. Jakarta, Indonesia: Departemen Kehutanan, Direktorat Jenderal Pengusahaan Hutan.

Djamaludin. 1989. The implementation of Indonesian selective cutting and replanting (TPTI) silviculture system for timber improvement in the logged-over areas. In *Proceedings of the Fourth Round-Table Conference on Dipterocarps*, edited by I. Soerianegara et al. Special publication no. 41. December 1989. Bogor, Indonesia: Biotrop.

Dove, M. 1986. The ideology of agricultural development in Indonesia. In *Central Government and Local Development in Indonesia*, edited by C. McAndrews. Singapore: Oxford University Press, 221–47.

Fried, S. 1995. *Writing for Their Lives: Bentian Dayak Authors and Indonesian Development Discourse*. Ph.D. dissertation. Ithaca, NY: Cornell University.

Gillis, M. 1988. Indonesia: Public policies, resource management, and the tropical forest. In *Public Policies and the Misuse of Forest Resources*, edited by R. Repetto and M. Gillis. NY: Cambridge University Press, 43–114.

Gray, J., and S. Hadi. 1989. *Forest Concessions in Indonesia: Institutional Aspects.* Forestry Studies report no. UTF/INS/065. Jakarta, Indonesia: Ministry of Forestry/Food and Agriculture Organization (FAO).

Hasan, M., former chair of APKINDO 1999. Personal communication with the author, May 3, 1999.

Hoffmann, A.A., A. Hinrichs, and F. Siegert. 1999. Fire Damage in East Kalimantan in 1997/ 98 Related to Land Use and Vegetation Classes: Satellite Radar Inventory Results and Proposal for Further Actions. IFFM–SFMP report no. 1a. Jakarta, Indonesia: Ministry of Forestry and Estate Crops, German Agency for Development, and KfW.

Ingram, D. 1989. Analysis of the Revenue System for Forest Resources in Indonesia. Forestry Studies report no. UTF/INS/065, field document no. VI-2. Jakarta, Indonesia: Ministry of Forestry/FAO.

Inhutani I. 2000. Author's confidential interview with Inhutani I, Tarakan, East Kalimantan, March 25, 2000.

ISA (Indonesia Sawmillers Association). 1999. *Statitik Industri Sawnwood dan Molding Indonesia.* Unpublished data.

ITFMP (Indonesia–U.K. Tropical Forest Management Programme). 1999. Illegal Logging in Indonesia. Report no. PFM/EC/99/03. Jakarta, Indonesia: ITFMP.

The Jakarta Post. 2000. Military faces acute budget problems: Juwono. May 24, 2000.

Kartodihardjo, H. 1999a. *Economic loss of the state in managing natural forest.* Unpublished paper prepared for Telapak Indonesia and Environmental Investigation Agency. August 24.

————. 1999b. Personal communication with the author, February 10, 1999.

Kartodihardjo, H., and S. Supriono. 2000. *Dampak Pembangunan Sektoral Terhadap Degradasi Alam: Kasus Pembangunan HTI dan Perkebunan di Indonesia.* Occasional paper no. 26 (I). Bogor, Indonesia: Center for International Forestry Research.

Keating, J. 2000. New hope for Indonesia's forests. *The Jakarta Post.* February 4.

Lindsay, H. 1989. The Indonesian log export ban: An estimation of forgone export earnings. *Bulletin of Indonesian Economic Studies* 25(2).

Manurung, E.G.T., and J. Buongiorno. 1997. Effects of the ban on tropical log exports on the forestry sector of Indonesia. *Journal of World Forest Resource Management* 8:21–49.

McCarthy, J. 2000. "Wild Logging:" *The Rise and Fall of Logging Networks and Biodiversity Conservation Projects on Sumatra's Rainforest Frontier.* CIFOR occasional paper no. 31. Bogor, Indonesia: CIFOR.

MoF (Ministry of Forestry). 1995. *Country Brief—Indonesian Forestry Action Programme.* Jakarta, Indonesia: MoF.

Purnama, B., W. Rusmantoro, and P.R. van Gardingen. 1999. *The Selection of Silvicultural Systems for the Management of Primary and Logged-Over Dipterocarp Forests in Indonesia: The Case Against the Application of TPTJ.* Jakarta, Indonesia: Balai Penelitian Kehutanan Samarinda and Department for International Development, ITFMP.

Reuters. 2000. Indonesia to hand forest control to state firms. May 4.

Ruzicka, I. 1979. Rent appropriation in Indonesian logging: East Kalimantan 1972/1973– 1976/1977. *Bulletin of Indonesian Economic Studies* XV:45–74.

Sacerdoti, G. 1979. Where timber is booty. *Far Eastern Economic Review.* November 30.

Sarijanto, T. 1999. Personal communication with the author, May 3, 1999.

Scotland, N. 1999. *The Impact of the Southeast Asian Monetary Crisis on Indonesian Forest Concessions and Implications for the Future.* ITFMP, ODA–Department for International Development report no. SMAT/EC/98/02. Jakarta, Indonesia

Scotland, N., and A. Whiteman. 1997. *Economic Rent in the Indonesian Forest Sector, Volume 4: The Forest Concession Industry.* ITFMP, ODA–Department for International Development report no. SMAT/EC/97/04, Jakarta, Indonesia.

Scotland, N., A. Frazer, and N. Jewell. 1999. *Roundwood Supply and Demand in the Forest Sector in Indonesia.* Report no. PFM/EC/99/08 (November 23rd draft). Jakarta, Indonesia: ITFMP.

Soedibyo, director of the Barito Pacific Group. 1999. Personal communication with the author, February 19, 1999.

Telapak Indonesia and EIA (Environmental Investigation Agency). 1999. *The Final Cut: Illegal Logging in Indonesia's Orangutan Parks.* Bogor, Indonesia: Telapak Indonesia and EIA.

Vincent, J.R. 1992. The tropical timber trade and sustainable development. *Science* 256:1651–55.

The World Bank. 1993. *Indonesia—production forestry: Achieving sustainability and competitiveness.* Unpublished draft working paper. October.

———. 1998. *World Bank involvement in sector adjustment for forests in Indonesia: The issues.* Unpublished draft issues paper. October.

———. 1995. *The economics of long-term management of Indonesia's natural forest.* Unpublished paper. August.

WWF (World Wide Fund for Nature) and DFID (Department for International Development). 1998. *Laporan perkembangan sawmill di wilayah selatan Taman Nasional Bukit Tigapuluh & di sekitar KPHP Pasir Mayang.* Jambi, Indonesia: ITFMP.

CHAPTER TEN

The Political Economy of Indonesia's Oil Palm Subsector

Anne Casson

Oil palm has been one of the most dynamic of Indonesia's agricultural subsectors. Dating from the late 1960s, the oil palm subsector expanded from around 106,000 ha to 2.5 million ha in 1997. This prolific growth has conferred important economic benefits inasmuch as it has become an important source of foreign exchange and employment. Yet it has also become a source of concern because much of the oil palm expansion has occurred at the expense of Indonesia's humid tropical forest cover.[1] Oil palm expansion has also been held partly responsible for the 1997–1998 forest and land fires that affected more than 5 million ha in Kalimantan alone (Departemen Kehutanan dan Perkebunan 1998a; see Chapters 13 and 14 of this book).

During Indonesia's recent period of economic crisis and political change (mid-1997 to mid-1999), the boom subsided. From early 1998 through to mid-1999, oil palm area expansion slowed significantly. For 1999, the government estimated that only 177,197 ha of oil palm would be planted. Although this is still a significant increase in oil palm area, it is a 33% decline in growth compared to the 266,565 ha planted in 1997.

In 1998, crude palm oil (CPO) production declined for the first time since 1969. Total production only reached 5 million metric tons in 1998. This was a 7% decline from 1997 production, which almost reached 5.4

million metric tons. The reduction is mainly attributed to the 1997–1998 El Niño Southern Oscillation phenomenon.

The subsequent slowdown in oil palm area expansion and decline in CPO production is ironic because in the latter half of 1997, conditions seemed to be optimal not only for continued growth but also for accelerated growth due to increasing world and domestic demands and cheap production costs in Indonesia. Just prior to the crisis, the Soeharto government had reduced the export tax on CPO products from a progressive tax to 5%, promoted the development of oil palm in Eastern Indonesia through the *Kredit Koperasi Primer Anggota* ([KKPA] Prime Cooperative Credit for Members) scheme, and designated large tracts of land for oil palm development. In 1996, the Soeharto government pledged to overtake Malaysia as the world's largest oil palm producer by doubling the area for palm oil production to 5.5 million ha by 2000. Half of this was to be allocated to foreign-owned private estate companies. Most of these plantations were to be established on the Outer Islands of Indonesia, primarily Kalimantan, Sumatra, Sulawesi, and Irian Jaya. Correspondingly, Indonesian palm oil production was also expected to increase, reaching 7.2 million metric tons in 2000 and 10.6 million metric tons in 2005 (Arifin and Susila 1998a).

This chapter (a) explains factors behind the extraordinary growth of the oil palm subsector up until late 1997, (b) explains the causes of the slowdown in area expansion since the beginning of 1998, and (c) assesses the possibilities for renewed growth in the sector. It then goes on to focus on the implications of renewed growth on Indonesia's forest cover. The Center for International Forestry Research (CIFOR) commissioned this study because oil palm development is viewed as a major cause of forest conversion in Indonesia. This development has also been linked to an increase in social conflict resulting from allocation of large tracts of land to oil palm companies. This was brought to the fore by a groundbreaking study on the trends, effects, and directions of tree-planting activities, including oil palm, by Potter and Lee (1998a). A further understanding of factors underlying or impeding the growth of the oil palm subsector is therefore considered necessary to determine the extent to which such growth will pose a threat to Indonesia's existing forest cover.

The present study draws largely on a much larger study that I conducted in 1999 entitled *The Hesitant Boom: Indonesia's Oil Palm Subsector in an Era of Economic Crisis and Political Change.* That study primarily focused on economic and political change during the period of President Habibie's government. The study was researched through three approaches. First, a review of secondary literature, including scholarly articles, industry literature, and the print media. Second, the research involved semistructured interviews with industry representatives, nongovernmental organizations (NGOs), and government officials in Indonesia and Malaysia. Third, field visits were made to North Sumatra, West Kalimantan, Jambi, and Riau.

Also provided in this chapter is a summary of basic information on the growth of oil palm in Indonesia up until the end of 1997. This summary provides a context through which to understand the pace and character of oil palm growth and the conditions and policies encouraging growth. The chapter then identifies and analyzes the conditions leading to a slowdown in area growth during the recent period of economic crisis and political change. Lastly, the chapter analyzes the prospects for resumed growth and the implications for tropical forest cover in Indonesia.

The Rapid Development of Indonesia's Oil Palm Subsector

The Indonesian oil palm subsector has experienced remarkable growth since the late 1960s. The area of oil palm plantations has increased from 106,000 ha in 1967 to 2.5 million ha in 1997, implying an average growth rate of 11.2% per annum (Departemen Kehutanan dan Perkebunan 1998b). Most of this oil palm plantation area is concentrated in the six provinces of North Sumatra, Riau, South Sumatra, West Kalimantan, Jambi, and Aceh (Figure 10–1). While North Sumatra could be perceived as a traditional area,[2] the others are areas of new development that have experienced sharp growth in the last decade. For example, Riau and West Kalimantan experienced 12.1% and 25.4% average annual area growth rates, respectively, between 1991 and 1997.

As the plantation area increased in Indonesia, CPO production has correspondingly increased by around 12% per annum, from 167,669 metric tons in 1967 to 5.4 million metric tons in 1997. This remarkable growth made Indonesia the world's second largest CPO producer after Malaysia, with a 30% contribution to the 1997 global palm oil supply (Figure 10–2).

The prolific growth of the oil palm subsector has conferred important economic benefits; palm oil has become a valuable source of foreign exchange. In 1997, 2.9 million metric tons of palm oil were exported, bringing in earnings valued at US$1.4 billion (Departemen Kehutanan dan Perkebunan 1998b). This was 31% of Indonesia's agricultural exports in 1997, and 3.5% of Indonesia's total non-oil and gas exports. The main destinations of Indonesian CPO exports were the Netherlands, Germany, Italy, Spain, and Kenya (Figure 10–3).

In addition to bringing in valuable foreign exchange, CPO is considered to be a strategic commodity because it is the raw material of the main cooking oil consumed in Indonesia. Palm oil industries are also considered to be important because they are labor-intensive and are able to provide employment opportunities for Indonesia's growing population. In 1997, Indonesia's oil palm industry employed more than 2 million people (Arifin and Susila 1998a, 1).

In light of the economic importance of palm oil to the Indonesian economy, the Soeharto government facilitated the growth of the sector through various

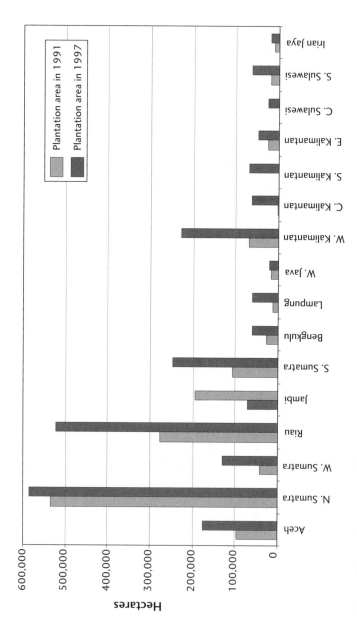

Figure 10–1. Geographical Distribution of Oil Palm Plantations, 1991–1997

Source: Departemen Kehutanan dan Perkebunan 1998b.

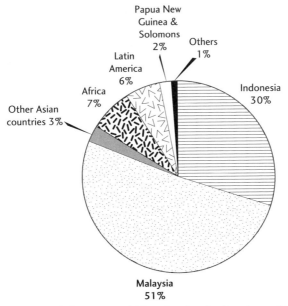

Figure 10–2. Share of CPO World Production by Producer Country, 1997

Sources: Departemen Kehutanan dan Perkebunan 1998b; Oil World 1999b.

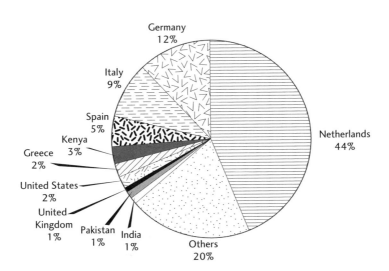

Figure 10–3. Indonesia's Palm Oil Exports by Country of Destination, 1997

Sources: Departemen Kehutanan dan Perkebunan1998b; Oil World 1999a.

schemes. These schemes have led to the emergence of three categories of oil palm estates: state-owned estates, smallholder estates, and privately owned estates. The privately owned oil palm estate subsector has experienced the most rapid growth in recent years. By 1996, 1.1 million ha of oil palm had been planted by the private sector compared to just 144,182 ha in 1986. This was a 23% average annual growth rate compared to a 7.6% average annual growth rate between 1969 and 1986. The Soeharto government encouraged greater private sector involvement in the oil palm sector between 1986 and 1996 by granting access to credit at concessionary rates for developing estates, planting new crops, and purchasing crushing facilities. Newly established companies could then draw on a loan from an "executing bank" at a rate of 11% during land preparation and tree establishment and 14% after the trees yielded. In turn, the executing bank was eligible to borrow from the Bank of Indonesia at a concessionary rate of 4%. The interest subsidies were intended to help investors overcome risks and uncertainties associated with establishing estates involving smallholders (Larson 1996).

In 1997, the Indonesian private estate oil palm subsector was dominated by 10 conglomerates:[3] the Salim Group, the Sinar Mas Group, the Texmaco Group, the Raja Garuda Mas Group, the Astra International Group, the Hashim Group, the Surya Dumai Group, the Napan Group, the Duta Palma Group, and the Bakrie Group. By 1997, these 10 conglomerates owned land banks[4] totaling approximately 2.9 million ha. This was approximately 400,000 ha more than the total planted area of oil palm plantations in Indonesia. Yet only around 812,000 ha of the total land bank acquired by these companies had been planted by the end of 1997 (Table 10–1). This is still significant, as it means that around 64% of the total planted area owned by private companies was owned by just 10 conglomerates.

Prospects for the Oil Palm Subsector Before the Crisis

Before the crisis, prospects for the Indonesian oil palm subsector looked extremely promising, and all three producer groups, particularly the private sector, were expected to rapidly expand for several reasons. First, the CPO production process in Indonesia was highly efficient because of the relatively high yield obtained from trees[5] and the potential to harvest trees throughout the year. These factors, combined with low labor costs, favorable climate and soil conditions particularly in Sumatra, and the perception that Indonesia had an abundance of undeveloped land, resulted in lower production costs than for other edible oils. Indonesia was, therefore, one of the most cost-efficient countries in the world for the establishment of oil palm plantations.

Second, from an investor's perspective, the domestic and international markets for CPO looked promising. Before the economic crisis hit Indonesia,

Table 10–1. Land Holdings Owned by Some Indonesian Oil Palm
Conglomerates, 1997

Group	Holding company	Total Land bank area (ha)	Total area planted (ha)
Salim Group	PT Salim Plantations	1,155,745	95,310
Sinar Mas Group	PT Golden Agri Resources	320,463	113,562
Texmaco Group	—	168,000	35,500
Raja Garuda Mas Group	PT Asian Agri	259,075	96,330
Astra international Group	PT Astra Agro Lestari Tbk	192,375	125,461
Hashim Group	—	244,235	105,282
Surya Dumai Group	—	154,133	23,975
Napan Group	PT PP London Sumatra Indonesia Tbk	245,629	78,944
Duta Palma Group	—	65,800	25,450
Bakrie Group	PT Bakrie Sumatra Plantations	49,283	23,392
Total		2,854,738	723,206

Source: Badan Planologi 1999.

palm oil was projected to replace soybean oil as the world's most consumed oil
by 2000 (Danareksa Sekuritas 1998, 2) Growth in global demand for palm
oil was attributed to world population growth and rising spending power.
There had been an increasing preference for CPO over other edible oils because it was cheaper than other vegetable oils such as soybean and rapeseed
oils prior to 1998.

On the international market, the compound average growth rate of palm oil
consumption was the highest among vegetable oils and all major categories of oils
and fats since 1992. Between 1992 and 1997, global demand for palm oil grew
around 7% per annum, followed by soybean oil at 5%, while other vegetable oils
grew less than 4% per annum (Goldman Sachs 1998, 5). Most of this palm oil
was consumed in Asia, primarily by Indonesia, China, India, Malaysia, and Paki-
stan (Figure 10–4). Foods consumed in this region are usually fried.

The processing of CPO by various industries in Indonesia, especially for
cooking oil, was also expanding with an average annual growth rate of 13%
since 1986. In 1986, domestic consumption was just 0.66 million metric
tons, and it jumped to 2.8 million metric tons in 1997 (Oil World 1999b).
This sharp increase is explained by several factors, mainly increasing population and income per capita. In 1990, per capita consumption was 6.9 kg, and
it rose to 10.4 kg in 1995—implying an 8.6% annual increase (Arifin and
Susila 1998a). In 1997, the Indonesian market consumed around 55% of
domestic CPO production (or 20% of global production), making Indonesia
the world's largest market for palm oil (Ing Barings 1998).

The third reason that the Indonesian oil palm subsector looked promising
was that the government had demonstrated its commitment to development

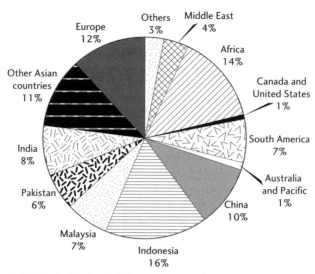

Figure 10–4. 1997 Global Palm Oil Consumption by Country

Source: Oil World 1999b.

of the palm oil subsector by offering numerous incentives to both domestic and international investors. Just prior to the crisis, the government had reduced the export tax on CPO products from a progressive tax to 5%, promoted the development of oil palm in Eastern Indonesia through the KKPA scheme, and designated large tracts of land for oil palm development. In 1997, the Soeharto government pledged to overtake Malaysia as the world's largest oil palm producer by doubling the oil palm area to 5.5 million ha by 2000. Correspondingly, Indonesian palm oil production was also expected to increase, reaching 7.2 million metric tons in 2000 and 10.6 million metric tons in 2005 (Arifin and Susila 1998b).

Most of these new plantations were to be established on the Outer Islands of Indonesia, primarily Kalimantan, Sumatra, Sulawesi, and Irian Jaya. Half of the area allocated for oil palm development was to be offered to foreign-owned private estate companies. As a result, the sector attracted considerable investment from overseas, primarily from Malaysia, Singapore, England, Hong Kong, Belgium, South Korea, and the British Virgin Islands. In fact, foreign investor interest had become so strong that the government was forced to close the oil palm subsector to foreigners in early 1997 because domestic companies had begun to complain about having to compete for land with foreign investors, those from Malaysia in particular. Malaysian investors had been especially active in the Indonesian oil palm subsector because land had recently become scarce in Malaysia and rising wages had increased the cost of CPO production in that country. With much encouragement from the Indonesian government,[6] Malaysian investors were able to acquire land banks totaling at least 1.3 million ha before the crisis hit Indonesia. Most of these land banks were in West Kalimantan, Central Kalimantan, South Sumatra, Riau, and Jambi (for details on Malaysian investors in the Indonesian oil palm subsector see Casson 2000).

The Hesitant Boom

From the beginning of the economic crisis (mid-1997) through early 1998, it appeared that the Indonesian oil palm subsector would continue to expand. Indeed, it seemed as if changes resulting from the crisis would not only allow continued growth but also encourage faster growth. Most important were windfall profits made possible through depreciation of the *rupiah* against the dollar and a low export tax of 5%. By increasing sales to the export market, companies were able to take advantage of high international CPO prices and low production costs. The government then issued a directive removing barriers to foreign investment in oil palm plantations and sped up the processing of applications, in line with International Monetary Fund (IMF) demands. With the collapse of many industries across the country, the plantation sector was hailed as the prima donna of the Indonesian economy (Tripathi 1998).

Yet by 1998 it became clear that several companies had begun to experience difficulties, and it was revealed that they had not performed so well in the midst of the economic crisis. In fact, 1997 marked the first year in which many oil palm companies recorded negative net profits.[7] For instance, LonSum achieved a net profit of Rp 76.5 billion in 1997, a 5% decline against Rp 80.6 billion in 1996 (Ing Barings 1998). In 1998, LonSum recorded a negative net profit of Rp 274.6 billion. Yet LonSum failed to recognize certain losses in its 1998 profit and loss statement. If the company had recognized these losses it would have booked a net loss of Rp 1.5 trillion in 1998.[8] Technically the company is bankrupt. Similarly PT SMART, a subsidiary of the Sinar Mas Group and one of Indonesia's largest oil palm companies, recorded a negative net profit of Rp 87.7 billion in 1997 compared to Rp 37.0 billion in 1996 (PT SMART Tbk 1997). Bakrie recorded a profit of Rp 28.2 billion in 1998 compared to Rp 50 billion in 1997, and PT Indofood Suksus Makmur recorded a negative net profit of Rp 1.2 trillion in 1997 compared to Rp 351.3 billion in 1996 (Figure 10–5).

Because of the financial difficulties many companies began to face in 1998, oil palm expansion began to slow down. According to the Indonesian government, an average of approximately 200,000 ha of oil palm was planted per annum between 1990 and 1997. Oil World (1999c, 32) estimated that from January to December 1998 only 70,000–80,000 ha were newly planted. The Indonesian government's planting figures for 1998 are much higher than this,

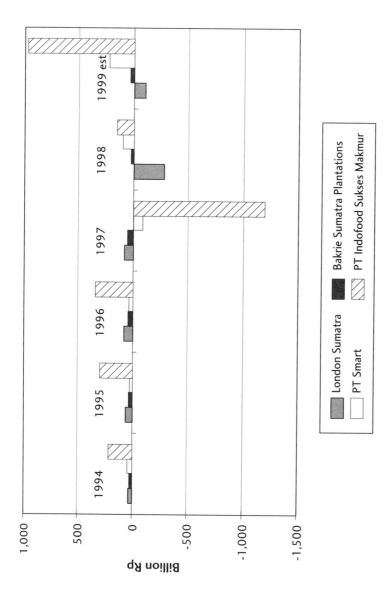

Figure 10–5. Net Profits of Some Listed Oil Palm Plantation Companies, 1994–1999 est.

Sources: Annual reports of companies involved, Danareksa 1998, 1999a, b and Ing Barings 1998, 1999.

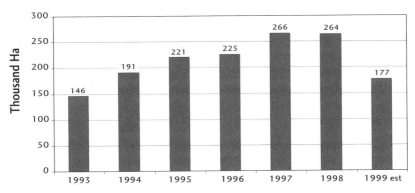

Figure 10–6. Growth in Area Planted to Oil Palm, 1993–1999 est.

Source: Departemen Kehutanan dan Perkebunan 1998b.

but they do show that area expansion started to slow down, and the government's most recent estimates were that 177,197 ha of oil palm were to be planted in 1999 (Figure 10–6). This constitutes a 33% decline in plantation establishment compared with the 266,565 ha planted in 1997.

The decline in new plantings occurred because many companies, burdened with U.S. dollar liabilities and various other factors arising from political and economic crisis,[9] reduced their plantation targets in 1998. For instance, PT Astra Agro Lestari previously planned to plant around 20,000 ha per year. Yet it was only able to plant 3,000 ha in 1998. Similarly PT Asian Agri Agro, a subsidiary of the Raja Garuda Mas Group, planned to plant 30,000 ha per year but reduced its planting target to 10,000 ha in 1998. PT SMART planned to plant 70,000 ha per year but reduced its planting target in 1998 to 20,000 ha per year. And LonSum was forced to cut its planting program altogether except on already prepared land (Lauw and Eastaugh 1999). As a consequence, the sales of Indonesia's three oil palm seed suppliers—LonSum, Socfindo, and *Pusat Penelitian Kelapa Sawit* ([PPKS] Oil Palm Research Centre)—declined. Socfindo's seed sales decreased from 17 million in 1997 to 14 million in 1998. Similarly, seed sales recorded by PPKS declined from 51 million in 1997 to 37 million in 1998. PPKS estimated that it would be able to sell only around 20 million seeds in 1999 (Lauw and Eastaugh 1999; Asmady and Rasep 1999) and PPKS (Wayono and Quritno 1997).

Palm oil production also declined in 1998. Despite a large expansion in the average area of mature oil palm in 1998 by more than 12%,[10] in that year, CPO production only reached around 5 million metric tons. This was a 7% decline in CPO production from 1997 when it reached almost 5.4 million metric tons (Figure 10–7). The decline in 1998 signaled the first time that CPO production had stagnated since 1969.

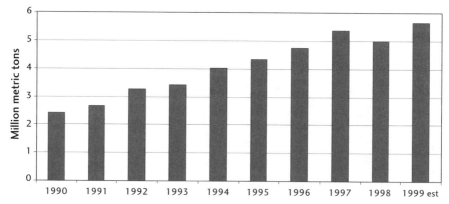

Figure 10–7. CPO Production, 1990–1999 est.

Source: Departemen Kehutanan dan Perkebunan 1998b.

Prospects for Renewed Growth and the Fate of Indonesia's Forests

It is possible to surmise that the oil palm subsector will continue to expand in the near future, in spite of the problems encountered during the recent period of economic and political change.[11] In fact, many companies have already started to boost their planting targets. PT Astra Agro Lestari has increased its planting target from 6,000 ha in 1998 to 10,000 ha in 1999.[12] PT SMART also expects to increase its planting target from 20,000 ha in 1998–1999 to 50,000 ha in 2000. These new plantings will come into production in the next four to five years.

CPO production was also expected to increase in 1999 to 5.6 million metric tons , a 12% increase over the 5 million metric tons produced in 1998. The increase in CPO production is mainly explained by increased rainfall once the El Niño drought subsided in mid-1998 and by the maturation of plantings prior to the crisis. Increased yields per unit area will make investment more attractive in terms of improved returns.

As the economic and political situation improves in Indonesia, it is important to determine where this growth will occur and what implications it will have for Indonesia's forest cover. Before the crisis, most oil palm development occurred within Sumatra. Yet from the late 1980s, the Soeharto government attempted to redirect development into Eastern Indonesia. This has resulted in some oil palm development in Kalimantan and Irian Jaya (Figure 10–1). The Habibie government was committed to former President Soeharto's policy of directing plantation development to Eastern Indonesia, primarily Kalimantan and Irian Jaya. To facilitate this growth, the Habibie government allowed companies wishing to establish plantations in Irian Jaya to double their land holdings. Companies were able to use 40,000 ha of land in Irian Jaya as opposed to 20,000 ha in other provinces.

The Habibie government also demonstrated its willingness to support further development in Irian Jaya by giving permission to 28 Indonesian private companies to open large-scale oil palm plantations in that province. If realized, the investment would make the province one of the world's main CPO producers (*The Jakarta Post* 1999). Five of the 28 investors have already opened plantations in Irian Jaya.[13]

In addition to Irian Jaya, the Habibie government also had large-scale plans for oil palm expansion in Kalimantan. In October 1998, the government announced plans to establish 1 million ha of oil palm in East Kalimantan in the Kutai, Pasir, and Bulungan regencies.[14] Moreover, according to a report published by the West Kalimantan regional plantation office, Dinas Perkebunan, the government has already allocated around 1.5 million ha of land to oil palm companies for development in the near future (Dinas Perkebunan 1999a).

Yet despite the government's grand plans for expansion of the oil palm subsector, some oil palm companies are hesitant about establishing plantations in Irian Jaya and Kalimantan for the following reasons:

- **Ethnic unrest.** This is often attributed to the government's *perkebunan inti rakyat* ([PIR] nucleus estate plantations) transmigration program, which established plantations with transmigrant labor in the Outer Islands of Indonesia and often resulted in social conflict between local people and transmigrants. These conflicts have increased during the reform era.
- **Poor infrastructure.** Oil palm trees produce fruit on a continuous basis, with seasonal variations. Once ripe, the fresh fruit bunches must be processed quickly to prevent a buildup of acid in the oil. Fruit not crushed within 48 hours of harvest has limited value. Roads in Kalimantan and Irian Jaya tend to be poor compared with roads in Sumatra, and this can greatly affect the ability of companies to process the fruit within 48 hours.

Companies are, however, interested in the timber that can be harvested from oil palm concessions in Irian Jaya and Kalimantan. This explains why the majority of companies setting up in these regions have strong links with logging companies.[15] It also may explain poor performance in realizing their plantation targets. For example, by March 1999, the government had issued location permits for the development of 871,211 ha of oil palm plantations in West Kalimantan, yet only 18,278 ha had actually been planted (Dinas Perkebunan 1999a). Admittedly some companies have been unable to plant oil palm because of the difficulties encountered during the economic crisis. But despite these difficulties, performance has been extremely poor, and this fuels the suspicion that these companies are more interested in exploiting the timber from allocated concessions than in establishing oil palm plantations.

Companies actually interested in establishing oil palm are more likely to develop estates in the provinces of Riau, Jambi, and South Sumatra in the near future. Oil palm investors prefer to establish estates in these regions because Sumatra possesses the best climate and soil conditions in the country for cultivating oil palm and has the necessary infrastructure already in place for palm oil processing. Companies also prefer to invest in Sumatra because the estate workers (primarily Javanese in origin) are used to plantation life and culture and are thought to work harder than the indigenous peoples of Kalimantan, Sulawesi, and Irian Jaya.[16]

The desire to open oil palm plantations in Sumatra is confirmed by the recent forest fires that occurred in August 1999. Using satellite imagery, these fires have already been linked to oil palm companies wishing to clear land for further oil palm development.[17] The director of Dinas Perkebunan[18] in Pekanbaru, Riau, also revealed that investors, particularly Malaysian investors, are continuing to expand and develop estates in the province, despite the problems arising from recent political and economic change. The regional forestry and plantation office is hard-pressed to find land for these new developments and has asked the Malaysians to invest in downstream processing plants rather than oil palm plantations. The Malaysians rejected the offer and stressed their desire to invest only in plantations (Dinas Perkebunan 1999b).

Because most plantation companies still wish to open estates in Sumatra, forest area allocated for conversion to plantations has been placed under considerable pressure. According to the Ministry of Forestry and Estate Crops (MoFEC), approximately 4.1 million ha of forestland has been converted to plantations since 1982.[19] Most of the land converted (3.3 million ha) was on conversion forestland—forestland actually designated for plantation development. Yet plantations were also developed on 166,532 ha of limited production forest,[20] 455,009 ha of production forest,[21] and 129,449 ha of forestland designated for other uses (Figure 10–8).[22]

According to the division of the MoFEC responsible for the release of forestland for conversion, Badan Planologi, 12 groups had been given permission to convert approximately 1.5 million ha of forestland to oil palm plantations between 1982 and 1999. The same 12 groups had also received *izin prinsip*[23] permits to convert approximately 2.8 million ha of forestland to oil palm plantations between 1982 and 1999. This constitutes almost 70% of the total forestland converted to plantations since 1982 (Figure 10–9). Almost 1.2 million ha, or 43%, of this forestland had been allocated to just one conglomerate—the Salim Group. The Salim Group was able to obtain these permits through its connection to the Soeharto family. The founder of the Salim Group, Liem Sioe Liong, is a close friend of former President Soeharto (Robison 1986).

The conversion of forestland to plantations has resulted in significant conversion forest deficits[24] in the provinces of Aceh, Riau, Jambi, Bengkulu, West Sumatra, and South Sulawesi. This is confirmed by statistics (Badan Planologi 1999) released by the government in 1999, which show conversion forest

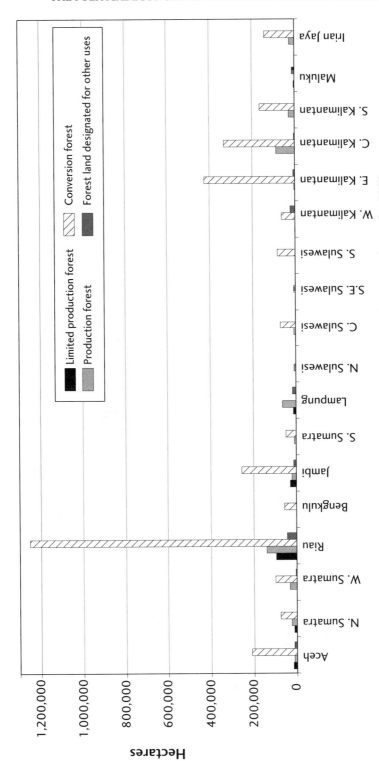

Figure 10–8. Forestland Converted to Plantations According to Forest Type and Province Since the 1982 Forest Land Use Consensus (TGHK)

Source: Badan Planologi 1999.

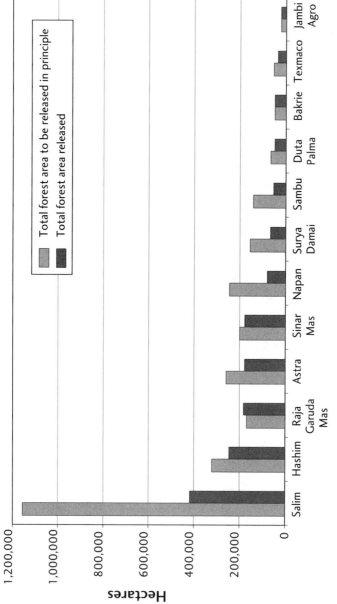

Figure 10–9. Forestland Released to Conglomerates between 1982 and 1999

Source: Badan Planologi 1999.

deficits in a number of Sumatra's provinces (Figure 10–10). The existence of conversion forest deficits in much of Sumatra partly explains why large areas of production forest and limited production forest are now being allocated to plantation companies in Aceh, North Sumatra, Riau, Bengkulu, Jambi, South Sumatra, and Lampung. Yet it does not explain why production forest is also being allocated to companies in the provinces of Central Kalimantan, East Kalimantan, and Irian Jaya. Large areas of conversion forest are still available in these three provinces, but a significant area of production forest has already been allocated to plantation companies there (Figure 10–8). This suggests that oil palm plantations are going directly onto former *Hak Pengusahaan Hutan* ([HPH] Forest Concession, Forest Exploitation Rights)[25] sites. This has far-reaching implications, as it means that logging companies are clear-cutting their concessions to make way for oil palm plantations.

In recent years, the Indonesian government has faced mounting criticism from international donors and NGOs about its policy to develop oil palm plantations on forestland. The Habibie government did take progressive steps to address the conversion of forestland to plantations by (a) revoking the licenses of companies that failed to realize their plantations, (b) placing a temporary moratorium on any new applications for forest conversion in October 1998, and (c) reassessing existing forestland in Indonesia through the 1999 *Rencana Tata Ruang Wilayah Propinsi* ([RTRWP] Provincial Spatial Plan). The RTRWP acknowledges that there is little conversion forest remaining in Sumatra's provinces, especially Aceh, Jambi, North Sumatra, and Bengkulu. Yet the RTRWP also states that 334,521 ha of conversion forest remain in Riau despite the significant conversion forest deficit revealed in Figure 10–10. Clearly there are discrepancies in these numbers, and they cannot be considered accurate. They do, however, reveal the fact that serious problems exist in terms of forestland allocation and the way in which forestland is classified in Indonesia.

Questions surround the remaining outstanding applications for the release of 4.5 million ha of forestland to plantations. The government decided that any outstanding applications for the release of forestland agreed to in principle and received before February 1999 would be processed. Preliminary data indicate that the outstanding applications already agreed to in principle wil' consume around 843, 058 ha of forestland. Around 70% of this land will ' converted to oil palm (the director of planning, MoFEC, 1999). Most of forestland is in Riau (417,503 ha), Lampung (74,779 ha), Central Kalim (100,100 ha), and East Kalimantan (168,848 ha). Once these outs applications are processed, there will be conversion forest deficits Riau, Jambi, East Kalimantan, and Central Kalimantan in accor the 1999 RTRWP. Although we can expect to see real oil palm in Aceh, Riau, South Sumatra, and Lampung, many devel'

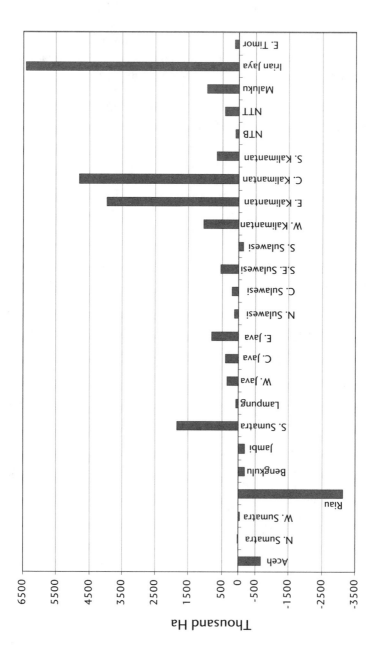

Figure 10–10. Remaining Conversion Forest According to the 1982 TGHK as of March 1999

Notes: NTB = Nusa Tenggara Barat (West Nusa Tenggara); NTT = Nusa Tenggara Timur (East Nusa Tenggara)

Source: Badan Planologi 1999.

extract the timber they can fell in Central and East Kalimantan in the near term. This may, however, change once the environment for oil palm development in Indonesia becomes more favorable.

The fate of the remaining 3.6 million ha already agreed to in principle is uncertain. The moratorium on further forest conversion for plantation development is only temporary and can be lifted at any time. If the government allows the remaining applications to be processed on conversion forestlands in accordance with the 1999 RTRWP, there would still be conversion forest deficits in Aceh, North Sumatra, Riau, and Jambi, and significant conversion forest deficits would arise in East Kalimantan and Central Kalimantan (Figure 10–11). This would inevitably mean that some of the outstanding applications will be located on remaining production forestland and increasingly on limited production forestland, particularly in East and Central Kalimantan. This has now been legitimized by the new Mixed Forest Plantings regulation and the decision to allow Inhutani to convert 30% of their logging concessions to oil palm. Mounting anecdotal evidence also suggests that estate developments are moving into national parks and other forest areas of high conservation value (Potter and Lee 1998b; Sunderlin 1998; EIA/Telapak 1999; Basyar 1999).

Alternatively, there is potential for outstanding applications and any future applications to be directed onto degraded lands.[26] Large areas of degraded land exist in many of the provinces earmarked for plantation development (Figure 10–12). This is particularly the case for Central and East Kalimantan. Redirecting plantation development to degraded lands would allow the government to continue to facilitate the development of the oil palm subsector while minimizing the effect of further development on Indonesia's existing forest cover. Yet great care will be needed to ensure that further plantation development does not displace local people who have already occupied these lands. Care will also need to be taken to ensure that such a policy does not encourage plantation companies to purposely light fires to reclassify forestland as degraded land.

Conclusion

The Indonesian oil palm subsector expanded rapidly after 1967. Much of this growth has occurred in the last decade and posed a significant threat to Indonesia's existing forest cover. It has also displaced local communities and increased social conflict. At the beginning of the economic crisis in 1997, there was every expectation that the oil palm boom would not only continue but also be propelled by the currency depreciation and lifting of foreign investment constraints. But a slowdown in area expansion and CPO production took hold instead. From early 1998 to mid-1999, oil palm area expansion slowed significantly, and CPO production declined for the first time since

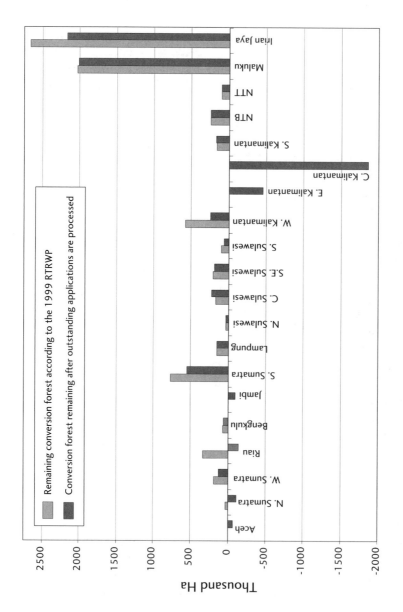

Figure 10–11. Remaining Conversion Forest According to the 1999 RTRWP and Conversion Forest Remaining after Outstanding Applications Are Processed

Source: Badan Planologi 1999.

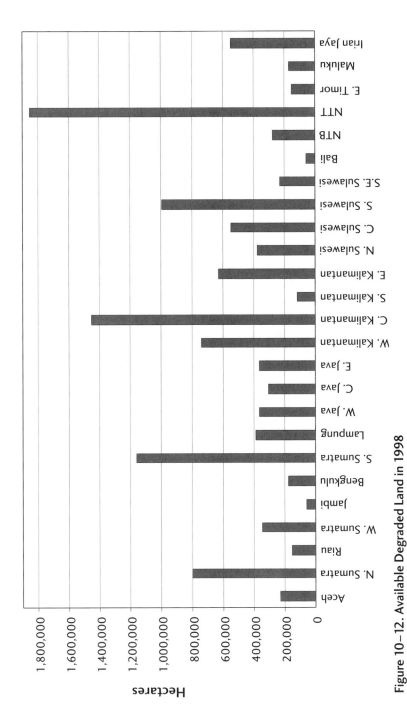

Figure 10–12. Available Degraded Land in 1998

Notes: NTB = Nusa Tenggara Barat (West Nusa Tenggara); NTT = Nusa Tenggara Timor (East Nusa Tenggara)

Source: Departemen Kehutanan dan Perkebunan 1998a.

1969. It now looks like the sector is poised for further growth because many companies increased their planting targets for 1999, and share prices of oil palm companies have stabilized.

As the oil palm subsector is poised for further growth, this chapter has attempted to determine where growth has already occurred, what effect this growth has had on Indonesia's forest cover, and the implications of further growth on Indonesia's forests. Over the last decade, oil palm development has primarily occurred within Sumatra and increasingly in Kalimantan. The Habibie government was committed to the Soeharto government's policy of directing plantation development to Eastern Indonesia, primarily Kalimantan and Irian Jaya, but the industry was more interested in developing oil palm plantations in Sumatra. This is because Sumatra has the necessary infrastructure required to process palm oil and an established plantation labor force. The rapid development of oil palm in much of Sumatra has already resulted in significant conversion forest deficits. This has increased the potential for further expansion to be located within production forest, limited production forest, and, increasingly, protected forest areas.

While there has been less interest in developing oil palm plantations in Kalimantan and Irian Jaya, companies continue to apply for concessions so that they can gain access to timber readily available in these two Outer Island provinces. Although some of these companies actually intend to plant oil palm, many are primarily interested in the timber they can extract. This explains why many oil palm developments are occurring on production forestland in Kalimantan and Irian Jaya, despite the availability of large areas of degraded land in much of Kalimantan. The allocation of production forestland to oil palm developers has accelerated conversion and environmental degradation.

Given Indonesia's ongoing financial crisis, the administration of Abdurrahman Wahid was under considerable pressure to boost the gross national product and particularly to raise the country's export revenues. Under his regime, considerable emphasis was placed on renewed development of Indonesia's oil palm subsector. Yet further oil palm development will undoubtedly have an adverse effect on Indonesia's forest cover unless fundamental changes are made in the way such development is implemented in the near future.

Endnotes

1. For further information on this see EIA (1998); Potter and Lee (1998a, 1998b); Wakker (1998a, 1998b); Basyar (1999).

2. North Sumatra is viewed as a traditional area for oil palm development because the Dutch initially established estates in this region. Early oil palm plantations were established there because the province has some of the most suitable soil conditions for this crop.

3. Four of these conglomerates had their plantation holding companies listed on the Jakarta and Surabaya Stock Exchanges: PT Astra Agro Lestari Tbk (Astra International Group), PT PP London Sumatra Indonesia Tbk (Napan Group), PT SMART (Sinar Mas Group), and PT

Bakrie Sumatra Plantations (Bakrie & Brothers). The Salim Group has a listed company called PT Indofood, which has some investments in oil palm plantations and commands a 60% share of the cooking oil industry.

4. Area of land agreed to be developed in principle by the governor of a given province.

5. In 1997, Indonesia's oil palm trees produced an average of 3.37 metric tons per ha. This is slightly below the Malaysian average of 3.68 metric tons per ha but higher than the world average of 3.21 metric tons per ha (Oil World 1997, 251).

6. The Indonesian government had pledged to allocate 1.5 million ha of land to Malaysian developers for oil palm development.

7. It is important to draw a distinction between net profit and operating profit. Net profit refers to the net excess of all the revenues over all the expenses. Operating profit refers to revenues generated from sales minus operational expenses. The operating profit referred to in the *Far Eastern Economic Review* did not, therefore, take into account expenses incurred from U.S. dollar liabilities.

8. These losses mainly arose from unfulfilled off and on balance sheet contractual obligations, including U.S. dollar sell forward contracts to Credit Agricole Indosuez, Union Bank of Switzerland, and Citicorp Financial Services Limited; an interest swap extension contract between the company and Citicorp Financial Services Limited; a commodity par-forward contract with Citibank; losses on advances to smallholder projects; and doubtful affiliates receivable. These losses totaled around Rp 1.2 trillion.

9. For further information on the various factors that have contributed to a decline in new oil palm plantings, see Casson 2000.

10. This is a consequence of record new plantings in 1994 and 1995, primarily in Kalimantan.

11. For further information on factors that have the potential to contribute to renewed expansion in the Indonesian oil palm sector, see Casson 2000.

12. PT Astra Agro Lestari has in fact performed very well during the economic crisis, recording a net profit of Rp 223.4 billion in 1998 compared to Rp 90.6 billion in 1997. The company is expected to record a net profit of Rp 187.3 billion for 1999.

13. These five investors are state plantation company PT Perkebunan Nusantara II, PT Varita Majutama, PT Sinar Mas Group, PT Texmaco, and PT Korindo. PT Perkebunan Nusantara II is a *Badan Usaha Milik Negara* (state-owned plantation company), which in 1982 opened oil palm plantations on 10,000 ha in the Arso district, Jayapura regency, and on 4,000 ha in the Prafi district, Manokwari regency. The state company has also developed a CPO processing plant and is currently harvesting. Varita Majutama has opened a 2,500-ha oil palm plantation in Babo district, Manokwari regency. Sinar Mas, one of the country's biggest CPO producers, opened oil palm plantations on 4,000 ha in Lereh, Manokwari regency. Texmaco and Korindo opened plantations in the Merauke regency, each on 3,000 ha.

14. The project is estimated to need Rp 7 trillion in investment.

15. A number of conglomerates are involved in the pulp and paper as well as the plywood sector. Some of these include Raja Garuda Mas, Sinar Mas, Korindo, Benua Indah, Astra International, Barito Pacific, and the Salim Group.

16. This view was expressed by a number of plantation companies interviewed during the period in which this research took place.

17. See for instance, the Centre for Remote Imaging, Sensing and Processing (CRISP), National University of Singapore website at http://www.crisp.nus.edu.sg/. This has also been confirmed by field visits conducted by U.S. Agency for International Development.

18. This is the provincial office for plantations. Dinas Perkebunan is answerable to the governor of a given province.

19. This figure includes rubber, coffee, tea, and other estate crop plantations, as well as oil palm.

20. According to the government, limited production forest can only be selectively logged.

Only logs more than 50 cm dbh can be extracted from limited production forest.

21. Production forest is designated for timber extraction.

22. In accordance with the original *Tata Guna Hutan Kesepakatan* ([TGHK] Forest Land Use Consensus], this category does not exist. It seems to have been created to accommodate conversion and timber extraction.

23. Permits for the release of forestlands that have been agreed to in principle by the MoFEC.

24. This implies that land already converted to plantations and used for transmigration exceeds forestland designated as conversion forestland in the 1982 TGHK.

25. Areas of land where a company has been granted a license for the selective harvest of natural forests over a 20-year period. This license is renewable for another 15 years. In 1998, Indonesia had 464 HPHs spread across 51.5 million ha, with 30% licensed to just five conglomerates (Brown 1999, vi).

26. This alternative is supported by a number of international institutions including the IMF and World Bank.

References

Arifin, S., and W. Susila. 1998a. *Indonesia as a Major Oil Palm Producer: Prospects and Challenges*. Bogor, Indonesia: Center for Economic Studies, Research and Development, Department of Agriculture.

_____. 1998b. Development and prospects of the palm oil industry in Indonesia. IARD Journal 20(2): 25–32.

Asmady, A.S., and A. Rasep Socfindo. 1999. Personal communication with the author, April 1999.

Badan Planologi. 1999. *Laporan Perkembangan Permohonan Pelepasan/Pencadangan Kawasan Hutan untuk Budidaya Pertanian dan Pemukiman Transmigrasi S/D 30 November 1999*. Jakarta, Indonesia: Departemen Kehutanan dan Perkebunan.

Basyar, H. 1999. *Perkebunan Besar Kelapa Sawit: Blunder Ketiga Kebijakan Sektor Kehutanan*. Jakarta, Indonesia: ELaw Indonesia and CePas.

Brown, D. 1999. *Addicted to Rent: Corporate and Spatial Distribution of Forest Resources in Indonesia; Implications for Forest Sustainability and Government Policy*. Report no. PFM/EC/99/06, U.K. Department for International Development (DFID)/ Indonesia–U.K. Tropical Forest Management Programme (ITFMP). Jakarta, Indonesia: ITFMP.

Casson, A. 2000. *The Hesitant Boom: Indonesia's Oil Palm Subsector in an Era of Economic Crisis and Political Change*. Occasional paper no. 29. Bogor, Indonesia: CIFOR.

Danareksa Sekuritas. 1998. *Plantation Sector Review*. Jakarta, Indonesia: Danareksa Sekuritas.

Departemen Kehutanan dan Perkebunan. 1998a. *Eksekutif Data dan Informasi Kehutanan dan Perkebunan*. Jakarta, Indonesia: Biro Perencanaan, Sekretariat Jenderal, Departemen Kehutanan dan Perkebunan.

———. 1998b. *Statistik Perkebunan Indonesia, 1997–1999, Kelapa Sawit*. Jakarta, Indonesia: Departemen Kehutanan dan Perkebunan.

Dinas Perkebunan. 1999a. *Informasi pembangunan perkebunan di Kalimantan Barat*. Pontianak, Indonesia: Dinas Perkebunanan.

———. 1999b. Personal communication with the author, with the director of Dinas Perkebunan, Pekanbaru, Riau, October 1999.

EIA (Environmental Investigation Agency). 1998. *The Politics of Extinction: The Orangutan Crisis, the Destruction of Indonesia's Forests*. London: EIA.

EIA/Telapak. 1999. *The Final Cut: Illegal Logging in Indonesia's Orangutan Parks*. London: EIA; Bogor, Indonesia: Telapak Indonesia.

Goldman Sachs. 1998. *Plantation Industry Indonesian Research*. Singapore: Goldman Sachs.

Ing Barings. 1998. *Plantation Sector Review*. October. Singapore: Ing Barings.

_____. 1999. *Plantation Sector Review*. January 29. Singapore: Ing Barings.

The Jakarta Post. 1999. Irian Jaya attracts 29 local oil palm investors. November 9, 11.

Larson, D.F. 1996. *Indonesia's Palm Oil Subsector*. Policy research working paper no. 1654. Washington, DC: International Economics Department, Commodity Policy and Analysis Unit, The World Bank.

Lauw, C., and G.C.Eastaugh of LonSum. 1999. Personal communication with the author, April 1999.

Oil World. 1997. *Oil World*. Hamburg, Germany: Oil World.

_____. 1999a. *Oil World 2020: Supply, Demand, and Prices from 1976 through 2020*. Hamburg, Germany: Oil World.

_____. 1999b. *Oil World Annual 1999*. Hamburg, Germany: Oil World.

_____. 1999c. *Oil World* No. 4, Vol. 42, January 29. Hamburg, Germany: Oil World, 32.

Potter, L., and J. Lee. 1998a. *Tree Planting in Indonesia: Trends, Impacts and Directions*. CIFOR occasional paper no. 18. Bogor, Indonesia: CIFOR.

_____. 1998b. Oil Palm in Indonesia: Its Role in Forest Conversion and the Fires of 1997/98. A report for World Wide Fund for Nature (WWF), Indonesia Programme. Jakarta, Indonesia.

Robison, R. 1986. *Indonesia: The Rise of Capital*. Canberra, Australia: Asian Studies Association of Australia.

PT SMART Tbk (Sinar Mas Agro Resources and Technology). 1997. *Annual Report*. Jakarta, Indonesia: PT SMART Corporation Tbk.

Sunderlin, W.D. 1998. *Between danger and opportunity: Indonesia's forests in an era of economic crisis and political change*. From the webpage http://www.cgiar.org/cifor/ (accessed September 11).

Tripathi, S. 1998. Natural advantage: An Indonesian plantation company sticks to what it does best, making it a rare winner in the region's worsening downturn. *Far Eastern Economic Review*. January 29.

Wakker, E. 1998a. *Introducing Zero-Burning Techniques in Indonesia's Oil Palm Plantations*. Report prepared for WWF, Indonesia Programme. The Netherlands: AIDEnvironment

_____. 1998b. *Lipsticks from the rainforest: Palm oil, crisis and forest loss in Indonesia: the role of Germany*. WWF, A Forest Campaign Project of WWF–Germany in collaboration with WWF-Indonesia.

Wayono, T. and P. Quritno of PPKS. 1999. Personal communication with the author, April 1999.

CHAPTER ELEVEN

Effects of Crisis and Political Change, 1997–1999

William D. Sunderlin

Beginning in mid-1997, Asian currencies lost value against the U.S. dollar, leading to an unprecedented regionwide economic crisis. Among all the Asian countries affected, none fared worse than Indonesia. As explained by the World Bank (1998, 1), "No country in recent history, let alone one the size of Indonesia, has ever suffered such a dramatic reversal of fortune."[1] In the period 1967–1997, Indonesia had experienced average annual economic growth of 6.5%; in 1998, the economy contracted 13.6%. This was by far the biggest setback among Southeast Asian countries, and Indonesia was the only country in the region to experience serious inflation in 1998 (Hill 1999, 23–4). A study for the World Bank (Poppele et al. 1999, 14)

This chapter, written on November 15, 1999, is the latest in a series of papers by the Center for International Forestry Research (CIFOR) that provides an overview of how recent changes in Indonesia have affected the country's forests and the people who rely on them. It summarizes the preliminary findings of several streams of research on the crisis and policy changes under way. It is not a comprehensive report on the subject; because much of the research is still in midcourse, some of the findings should be considered preliminary and tentative. Like past versions, this chapter draws liberally on media sources to fill in the information gaps. These sources often provide timely insights on issues that are not yet adequately understood. For the best explanation of the information summarized in the following pages, the reader is urged to consult the primary research documents referred to in this chapter once they have been published.

showed the aggregate poverty rate in Indonesia increased from 11% in 1996 to 14–20% in 1998.[2] Assessments of why the crisis was so bad in Indonesia focus on the fact that a high degree of corruption during Soeharto's administration had allowed dollar-denominated private sector debts to proliferate with little monitoring and control (Sadli 1999, 16; Cole and Slade 1998; see Chapter 12 in this book).

Although it is still too early to say that Indonesia is emerging from the economic crisis, the rate of economic growth expected in 1999 was about 0%, a considerable improvement over 1998. Other signs of possible improvement included a trend toward strengthening of the *rupiah* against the U.S. dollar, positive gross domestic product growth in the first half of 1999, negative inflation from March to June 1999, and a decline in benchmark interest rates (Pardede 1999, 5–8). Political and economic events in 2000 have not proven particularly hospitable to economic recovery.

Economic observers and policymakers stated early on during the crisis that agriculture (and natural resources in general) would play a key role in moderating the effects of economic decline and in leading the way to recovery. This has proven to be the case. An analysis of the first three-quarters of each year in the period 1994–1998 shows that all sectors declined in absolute terms in 1997–1998 except the joint agriculture, livestock, forestry, and fisheries sector. When this sector is disaggregated, the forestry subsector demonstrated by far the fastest growth in the period 1997–1998 (NRMP 1999, 7, 12). The output of the agriculture sector, including the forestry and fisheries sectors, has been constant during the crisis, whereas the construction sector collapsed dramatically, and all other sectors fell between these two extremes (Hill 1999, 25–6).[3] During the crisis, the agriculture sector has shown the largest year-on-year improvement of all sectors, but it is still down overall since September 1998. The main reasons for the slowdown are increased competition from exports from other countries, the collapse of demand in other Asian countries, and a general decline in commodity prices (Pardede 1999, 12–3).[4]

Although the relative share of agriculture in the economy has declined substantially over the years, agriculture remains extremely important because at the beginning of the crisis it employed an estimated 41% of the total national workforce (Johnson 1998, 16–7). From 1997 to 1998, agriculture's share of the total workforce expanded from 40.7–45.0%—the only sector in which the workforce expanded (Hill 1999, 39). Because of the crucial role of agriculture during the crisis, the Department of Agriculture plans to make the case for recognizing agriculture as the leading sector of the country in the government's forthcoming five-year planning period (*Bisnis Indonesia* 1999h).

The following are the main reasons the agriculture sector has been crucially important during the crisis:

- It has been relatively independent of the debt-laden dollar economy and has therefore suffered less than other sectors.
- It provides basic needs commodities that are a strategic priority of the government for preserving the conditions for stable and legitimate rule.
- It can help absorb unemployed people forced out of the manufacturing and industrial sectors, as well as new entrants to the labor force who are unable to find work in urban areas.
- It can help reduce costly imports of agricultural commodities.
- It provides the opportunity for lucrative export income, because the depreciation of the *rupiah* makes Indonesian commodities cheap on the international market and because earnings are in U.S. dollars whereas most costs are in the local currency (Sunderlin 1998).

This last point is true not only of agriculture in the narrow sense but also of natural resources in general, including forests, fisheries, and minerals.

An assessment of how the economic crisis and policy changes have affected forests and the people who live in and around them must be grounded in an analysis of changes in the agriculture sector. People living in forests depend largely on agriculture for their livelihood; thus, crisis-induced changes in the sector are likely to have a direct effect on their economic status and their use of the forest. In addition, the growth of agricultural and commercial timber activities in recent years has greatly influenced forest conversion and degradation, so understanding how the crisis and policy changes have affected these economic activities is important (see Chapters 8 and 9).

At the level of theory, the economic crisis could have either positive or negative effects on the livelihood of forest-dwelling people and the existence of remaining natural forests. Inflation and the increased costs of living and agricultural inputs, for example, would pose a setback for many households. However, livelihood may be improved by developments such as increased profitability of export crops. A breakdown of law and order during the crisis, as has occurred in Indonesia, is a contributing factor that also cuts both ways. It allows greater access to resources that may have been off limits in the past. Yet some farmers may decide to curtail production because they cannot be sure that they, and not others, will derive the benefits of their labor.

At the same time, natural forest cover can either benefit from or be harmed by the effects of economic crisis. When the profitability of export crops increases, more forestland is likely to be converted for agriculture; similarly, higher profitability of exported forest products can be expected to promote greater exploitation of the forest and its resources. In a different scenario, however, forests may benefit if national or regional demand for agricultural and forest products is depressed or when concessionaires and plantation owners are unable to realize their development targets because of debt burden or other economic problems.

Sorting out these interrelated and often contradictory effects of the economic crisis to better understand the extent of their effect on forests and forest people is a considerable challenge of this research. This chapter reviews preliminary research findings in five areas:

- the effects on small farmers;
- the effects on the commercial timber sector (in particular the plywood and pulp and paper subsectors);
- the effects on the oil palm subsector, considered to be one of the leading causes of forest conversion;
- the effects of miscellaneous extrasectoral factors such as export crops, roads, and mining; and
- the effects of policy change.

This chapter closes with a summary of the findings and their implications.

Effects on Small Farmers in Forested Areas

This section is based on research by Sunderlin et al. (2000). The two main objectives of the research project were to determine (1) how the crisis has affected the economic well-being of people in forested areas and (2) how changes in farming practices have affected forest clearing. It was assumed that both of these effects were strongly determined by how much access farmers had to export commodity markets and income during the crisis. Agricultural export production was an attractive option because of the higher prices such commodities command in *rupiah* terms, as a result of depreciation of the *rupiah* against the dollar.

The research was conducted through a sample survey of 1,050 households in five provinces: Riau/Jambi,[5] Lampung, West Kalimantan, East Kalimantan, and Central Sulawesi. Thirty-five households were selected randomly in each of six villages in each of the five provinces. The household survey focused mainly on family members' recollection of household status, farming practices, and forest-clearing practices in three periods: (a) the year before the onset of the economic crisis (mid-1996 to mid-1997); (b) the first year of the crisis (mid-1997 to mid-1998), which included the period of severe drought and fires related to the El Niño-Southern Oscillation (ENSO) phenomenon;[6] and (c) the second year of the crisis, after the drought had ended (mid-1998 to mid-1999).

A key preliminary finding related to the first objective was that two-thirds of the respondent households viewed themselves as worse off, and one-fifth as better off, during the second year of the crisis compared with the year before the crisis (Figure 11–1). This confirms a preliminary assessment of the researchers that "the crisis had a larger negative impact than initially hypothesized" (Angelsen and Resosudarmo 1999, 1). This finding contradicts the conventional wisdom about the effects of the crisis in rural Indonesia. It was

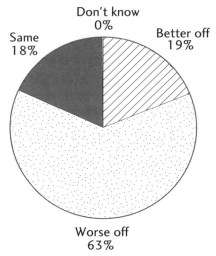

Figure 11–1. View of Respondents on Their Status in 1998–1999 Compared with 1996–1997

Source: Sunderlin et al. 2000.

generally assumed that most rural Indonesians, notably those outside of Java, would suffer relatively little from the crisis, and some would in fact prosper. For example, Evans (1998, 34) said that people outside Java "have been doing somewhat better (than people in Java), with their tradable commodities securing higher prices (at least in *rupiah* terms)." From May 1997 to May 1998, farmers' terms of trade were lower in Java but higher in Bali, Sulawesi, and Sumatra (Evans 1998, 28). Hill (1999, 27–8, 45) concurred with other researchers in assuming that, generally speaking, people in rural areas have either not been badly affected by the crisis or have actually benefited from the depreciation of the *rupiah*.[7] Jellinek and Rustanto (1999) said the Javanese poor have not suffered greatly because of resilience in the agriculture and informal sectors. Booth (1999, 137) said, "the devaluation [sic] will increase the *rupiah* price of agricultural products and boost producer incomes."

Why do our findings differ from the conventional wisdom? Specifically, why is it that two-thirds of the respondents find themselves worse off, in spite of the fact that the majority (77%) have had at least some income from export commodities? It is because the costs of living and agricultural inputs[8] have, in some cases, increased faster than the rise of income from certain export commodities. Moreover, the export prices of many commodities peaked in mid-1998 and then tended to decline. Two case studies corroborate this phenomenon. The high increase of input costs for rice producers in Java, in connection with a low increase in the price of rice, meant a net drop in income for producers (Ratnawati et al. 1998, 23–4). A study by Elmhirst et al. (1998, 106–11) in Lampung showed that food growers were not always shielded from the effects of the crisis, as commonly assumed. Through the combined effects of the crisis and the drought, most respondents were worse off than they were before the crisis.

With regard to the second objective of the study, the respondents were asked to indicate whether they had cleared forestland in each of the three survey years and, if so, for which of the following three purposes: (a) shifting cultivation only, (b) shifting cultivation and cultivation of permanent crops, or (c) cultivation of permanent crops only. The results are shown in Figure 11–2.

It can be seen that there was a substantial increase in the frequency of forest clearing in the second year of the crisis (1998–1999) compared with the prior two periods (1996–1997 and 1997–1998). Among the factors that explain the increased forest clearing are that 36% of the households that were worse off during the crisis decided to expand their area of cultivated land, and 17% of those who were better off decided to buy land or to otherwise increase their area of cultivated land. Declining government capacity to control entry into the forest played a role in increased forest clearing in some areas.

It should be noted that there was a pronounced change in emphasis between 1996–1997 and 1998–1999 from shifting cultivation (mainly production of food crops) toward cultivation of permanent crops (especially production of tree crops). Farmers were motivated to plant rubber (in spite of its relatively low price during the crisis) because of the "safety net" characteristics of this crop.[9] Farmers who could afford the expense were motivated to plant pepper, cocoa, and coffee because of the relatively high price of these crops during the

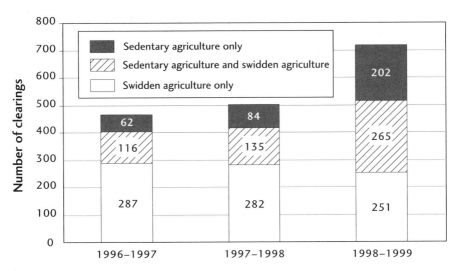

Figure 11–2. Clearings of Land for Agriculture in 1996–1999 According to Intended Purpose

Source: Sunderlin et al. 2000.

crisis. It is not clear whether this significant increase in attention to sedentary agriculture is transitory and linked to price instability or is instead a more long-lasting effect.

Effects on the Plywood and Pulp and Paper Subsectors

This section draws largely on research done by Barr (1999a). The plywood and pulp and paper subsectors account for approximately 90% of total annual export revenues in Indonesia's forestry sector. Indonesia has been the world's leading exporter of tropical plywood since 1987. In recent years it has aspired to become one of the world's leading pulp and paper producers, and it has made strides in that direction. Figure 11–3 shows annual export revenues from plywood and pulp and paper from 1993 to 1999. Figure 11–4 shows the production of plywood in millions of cubic meters from 1990 to 1999. And Figure 11–5 shows changes in installed capacity of pulp and paper production from 1982 to 1999 (The numbers for 1999 are estimated.)

Together these figures demonstrate that in 1998 and 1999, the pulp and paper subsector overtook the plywood subsector as the leading contributor to Indonesia's forestry export earnings. If this is indeed a lasting change—and it gives every indication of being one—it has major implications for the nature of timber-based industries in Indonesia and their effect on forests. As Barr explains,

> From the mid-1980s through the mid-1990s, the timber industry was structured to channel the bulk of the forestry sector's rents to plywood producers, particularly those that controlled the export of Indonesian wood panels through APKINDO's (Indonesian Wood Panel Association's) marketing cartel. Over the last several years, however, large sums of investment capital have been channeled into the nation's rapidly growing pulp and paper industry. Although the investment costs in pulp and paper are exponentially higher than they are in plywood, so too is the value added per unit of wood and, therefore, the potential profits. In this way, the primary locus of rent capture in Indonesia's forestry sector is shifting markedly in the direction of pulp and paper. (Barr 1999b)

The Decline of Plywood

The fact that pulp and paper have overtaken plywood during the crisis suggests that the crisis itself had a role in bringing about this change. Some commentators have argued that the crisis has had a key role in the downturn of the fortunes of the plywood subsector. For example, Kristiyono Fajari, director of APKINDO, said that the downturn in plywood exports in the period 1997–1999 was attributable largely to the decline in demand of some of the leading importers of Indonesian plywood (notably Japan, South Korea, and Taiwan)[10] and to competition from low-cost producers such as China and

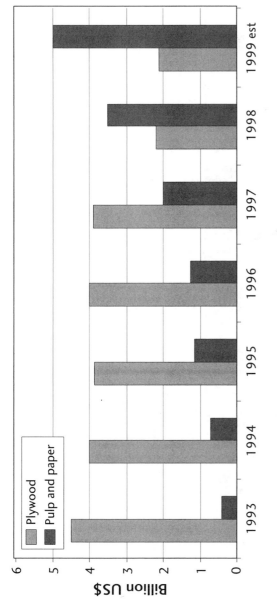

Figure 11–3. Value of Plywood and Pulp and Paper Exports, 1993–1999 est.

Sources: NRMP 1999; Adli 1999.

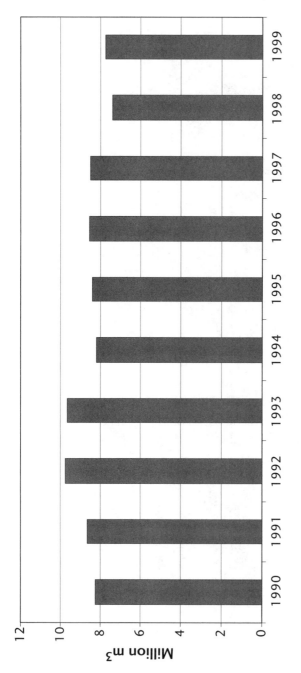

Figure 11–4. Volume of Plywood Exports, 1990–1999

Source: FAO 2001.

Brazil. He added that the government's decision to reduce the export tax to 10% and the revocation of various timber concession licenses obtained through corruption, collusion, and nepotism was likely to further damage the plywood industry (Adli 1999; Nirang 1999).

Although there is much to be said for this explanation, a look at Figures 11–3 and 11–4 shows that it is only part of the story. The decline of plywood production began long before the onset of the crisis, and Barr (see Chapter 9) explained increasing constraints on plywood production over time in this way:

> Over the years, a structural timber deficit has emerged in the timber sector. As a result, annual log consumption (55 million m³ in 1997) now greatly exceeds legal log production from officially sanctioned sources (26 million m³ in 1997). This means that 29 million m³ annually are coming from illegal sources. The amount of timber coming from production forests has declined from 24 million m³ in 1990 to 16 million m³ in 1998. This decline in supply from production forests is the result of past exploitation at rates that exceeded those of renewal. The decline is concurrent with an abrupt reduction in concessions, from a high of 652 in the early 1990s to 389 in 1998. The reason for this decline is that the licenses were either revoked (because of poor management) or not renewed (because of lack of interest in continuing). The shortfall of timber from concessions in production forests has been made up by increasing the extraction of timber from conversion forests. This trend is clearly unsustainable not only because of the progressive drain on legal sources of timber but also because dependence on conversion forests is increasing at the same time that the amount of such forests is shrinking.[11]

The Rise of Pulp and Paper

The rapid growth of the pulp and paper industry in Indonesia long predates the economic crisis, as can be seen in Figures 11–3 and 11–5. Indonesia has been well suited for this kind of economic activity because of its ample raw materials, the abundant seed capital available to industrialists through loans, and existing marketing channels to meet growing demand in other Asian countries. It is possible, but by no means clear, that there is a relationship between the decline of the plywood industry and the rise of the pulp and paper industry. It stands to reason that the degraded forest resources left behind from plywood and sawn timber production are now more optimally suited to conversion to pulp and paper, but there is no clear causal link at the aggregate level. Research is needed to determine to what extent such a causal link might exist.

It is noteworthy that international pulp and paper prices were extremely favorable in 1999 and that this spurred a hopeful outlook in the industry. International prices of pulp and paper had been declining since 1995 before showing an increase in 1999. The price of pulp rose from US$410 per metric ton] in 1998 to US$550 per metric ton in 1999 (Lazuardi and Ardi 1999), and the price of

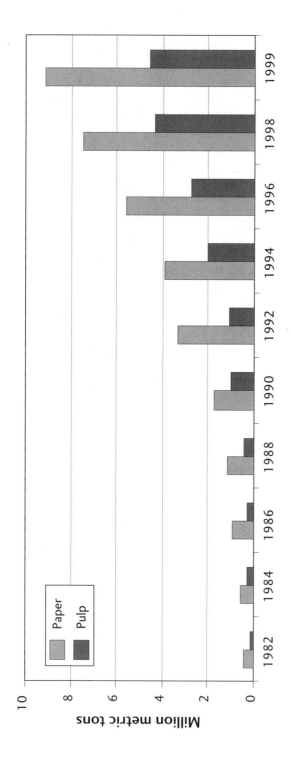

Figure 11–5. Pulp and Paper Capacity, 1982–1999

Source: APKI 2001.

medium-grade paper rose from about US$190 to US$235 per metric ton (Winarto 1999). These prices continued to rise through 2000, with international pulp prices reaching US$615 per metric ton in May of that year. The Indonesian Pulp and Paper Association estimated that the value of Indonesian pulp and paper exports would have increased from US$3.5 billion in 1998 to US$5 billion in 1999 (Lazuardi and Ardi 1999).

Illegal Logging and Effects on Protected Areas

It has been widely assumed during the crisis that illegal logging has increased significantly. There is ample evidence to support this assertion. A report by the Indonesia–U.K. Tropical Forest Management Programme (ITFMP) finds that the illegal supply of logs from the natural forest is now about equal to the legal supply (ITFMP 1999, 13; see Chapter 7 of this book). The international auditing firm Ernst & Young stated in November 1999 that 52% of Indonesia's log consumption comes from illegal sources (*Bisnis Indonesia* 1999l). According to Hartadi, the director of production for the State Forestry Corporation, the value of teak timber lost to theft in Java increased 700% in 1998 as compared with 1997 (*Bisnis Indonesia* 1999c). A case study by Elmhirst et al. (1998, 113) at a site in Lampung province showed that illegal logging existed before the crisis but was greatly aggravated by the crisis to the point where local supplies of timber were exhausted.

It has been widely assumed that the increase in illegal logging can be wholly explained by crisis-related factors such as increased poverty and greater difficulty in guarding forests because of a decline in law and order. But as Barr's research indicates, the tendency toward increased illegal logging predates the crisis.[12] It is clear that both noncrisis and crisis factors explain the situation (see Chapter 16).

The research literature as well as media reports indicate that illegal logging is taking a noticeable—and in some cases alarming—toll on conservation areas and protection forests. Researchers from the U.S. Agency for International Development's Natural Resource Management Project have noted increased illegal logging at Kutai National Park in Kalimantan and Lore Lindu National Park in Sulawesi (Merrill and Effendi 1999, 15).[13] Their research showed that one-third to one-half of national park managers in Indonesia believed there had been increased encroachment by local people during the crisis. At the same time, the budget for protected area management was inadequate. Although it has risen in current *rupiah* value, it has declined year by year since 1996 in real terms (NRMP 1999, 48).

Other accounts provide additional evidence of increased illegal logging in protected areas. According to an exposé by the Environmental Investigation Agency (EIA)/Telapak (1999, 14), illegal logging in Tanjung Puting National Park in Central Kalimantan—one of the major reserves in the world for orangutans—has increased dramatically in the last year. Such activity reportedly has been done in full view of the authorities. In another major conservation area for orangutans, Gunung Leuser National Park in the Aceh province, illegal logging has also grown considerably during the crisis. This theft is said to involve timber barons, the military, and the police—and even conservation authorities—acting to take advantage of a power vacuum (EIA/Telapak 1999, 14, 31–4; *Kompas* 1999g). Meanwhile, thousands of hectares of reforestation trees in the Gunung Balak conservation forest in the province of Lampung have been cut down for charcoal production (*Kompas* 1999d), illegal logging recently became rampant in conservation forests in Sumatra's Jambi province (*Kompas* 1999h, *Media Indonesia* 1999b), and the situation of illegal logging in the conservation forests of Kalimantan has in general become dire (*Kompas* 1999f). Three converging factors—declining log supply from production forests, collapse of government forest access controls, and crisis-related search for alternative incomes—propel current illegal logging and give it strong momentum.

Effects on the Oil Palm Subsector

This section summarizes research by Casson (2000). Oil palm development has received much attention in recent years because it is viewed as an important cause of the conversion of Indonesia's natural forests to nonforest uses. Indeed, from 1967–1997 the oil palm subsector increased 20-fold in amount of planted area (from 106,000 ha to 2,516,000 ha), and crude palm oil (CPO) production increased 12% annually (Casson 2000).

At the beginning of the crisis in late 1997, it seemed that conditions would propel even faster growth in oil palm development. The depreciation of the *rupiah* against the U.S. dollar made the export of palm oil products even more profitable than before, and conditions imposed by the International Monetary Fund (IMF) removed constraints on foreign direct investment in palm oil. But as it turned out, the growth of the oil palm subsector slowed during the crisis. The total area of planted oil palm continued to grow but at an increasingly slower rate since its peak in 1997 (Figure 11–6). In 1998, production of CPO declined for the first time since 1990 (Figure 11–7).

These changes can be explained by nine factors:

- a 40–60% export tax on oil palm products imposed by the government from April 1998 to January 1999 to ensure adequate domestic supplies of cooking oil,
- higher-than-expected production costs,
- political instability and a subsequent decline in foreign investment,
- changes to the government-regulated system for marketing and distributing oil palm products,

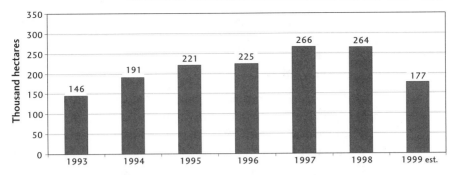

Figure 11–6. Palm Oil Area Growth in Indonesia, 1993–1999 est.

Source: Departemen Kehutanan dan Perkebunan 1998.

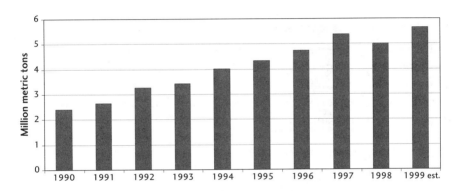

Figure 11–7. CPO Production Growth, 1990–1999 est.

Source: Departemen Kehutanan dan Perkebunan1998.

- credit access difficulties,
- changes in the state-owned plantation sector,
- reformist policies that targeted the oil palm sector (for example, revocation of license if cleared land was not planted),
- damage to crops resulting from the 1997–1998 drought and fires, and
- a steep decline in the world price of oil palm products.

This slowdown is only temporary, and growth of the oil palm sector can be expected to resume. Following are some of the factors that will stimulate growth:
- a drastic reduction of the export tax imposed earlier,
- lower interest rates,
- various regulations that remove obstacles to oil palm development,
- collusion between Indonesia and Malaysia in setting the world price of oil palm products,

- the availability of additional land cleared during the drought and forest fires in 1997–1998,[14]
- debt restructuring opportunities, and
- growing global demand for CPO.

Although the Indonesian government is committed to oil palm development in eastern Indonesia over the long term, particularly in Kalimantan and Irian Jaya, most expansion in the near term can be expected to occur in Sumatra. Oil palm companies, however, will continue to apply for concession areas in Kalimantan, Irian Jaya, and Sulawesi to gain access to timber (see Chapter 9). Unless there are fundamental changes in the way forestland is allocated in Indonesia, further oil palm expansion will continue to pose a significant threat to the country's natural forests.

Effects of Miscellaneous Extrasectoral Factors

Other factors outside the forest sector also affect the amount of natural forest in Indonesia. This section briefly examines the effect of the crisis on several export commodities other than palm oil on mining, the construction and maintenance of major roads in forested areas, and the Indonesian government's transmigration program.

Other Export Commodities

Cocoa and coffee are two smallholder crops that have important implications for natural forest cover. Figure 11–8 shows that in 1997 there was a decrease in the volume of cocoa and coffee exports. The decrease in cocoa production is largely the result of the ENSO drought phenomenon (*The Indonesian Observer* 1998). The decrease in coffee production is linked in part with the drought, but it also occurred because of the high cost of inputs and weak international demand related to excessive world supply (CIC 1998a, 60). Both crops showed a strong recovery in 1998 in both the volume and value of exports.

In the recent cocoa production marketing year (October 1998 to September 1999), 336,000 metric tons were produced, representing an increase of 6% over the previous year. The reason is that many cocoa trees planted four to five years ago in Sulawesi—the center of cocoa production in Indonesia—have begun to bear fruit. Production for the marketing year 1999–2000 is expected to reach 350,000 metric tons because of favorable weather and price conditions. Price increases have been a strong incentive for production. The price rose dramatically from 3,300 Rp/kg prior to the crisis to 17,500 Rp/kg in July 1998; it then declined to 6,000 Rp/kg in August 1999. Traders contend that the crop will remain profitable as long as the farmgate price (or the price to farmers at the

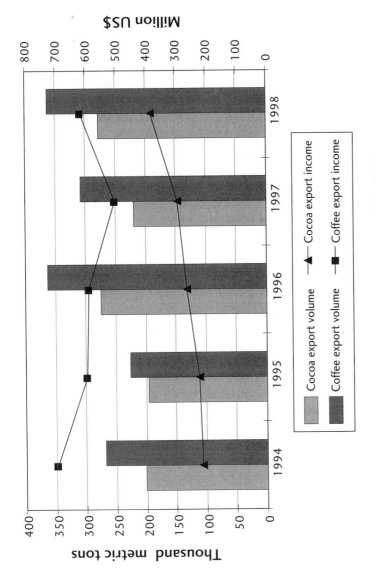

Figure 11–8. Volume and Value of Cocoa and Coffee Exports, 1994–1998

Sources: CIC 1998a; USDA 1999a, b.

place of production) remains above 5,000 Rp/kg (USDA 1999a, 1–2). The Indonesian Cocoa Association projects that 500,000 metric tons of cocoa will be produced in the year 2005 (*The Jakarta Post* 1999d, 10; *Media Indonesia* 1999g).

Coffee experienced a gradual recovery from the effects of the 1997 drought. Production levels increased because of strong blooms after heavy rains in early 1999. Domestic consumption of coffee has been decreasing during the crisis, so producers have relied more heavily on a growing export market motivated by strong *rupiah* returns (USDA 1999b, 1–2). The head of the Association of Indonesian Coffee Exporters, Oesman Soedargo, predicted that coffee production would increase to 450,000 metric tons from October 1999 to September 2000—an increase of 18.5% over the previous period (*Bisnis Indonesia* 1999j).

Other farm commodities that have important implications for natural forest area are rubber, pepper, and aquaculture shrimp. The depreciation of the *rupiah* against the U.S. dollar did not stimulate higher rubber latex production for several reasons: weak demand at the world level, high cost of inputs, and importers of Indonesian rubber (such as Japan and South Korea) who were also suffering from the crisis (CIC 1998a, 61–2). In mid-1999 the price of rubber fell to its lowest level in the last 25 years (*Bisnis Indonesia* 1999e), dimming prospects for increased production. With regard to pepper, Indonesia is the world's leading producer of white pepper and the second highest producer of black pepper after India. From 1994 to 1997, Indonesian pepper production ranged from 50,000 to 59,000 metric tons (CIC 1998a, 63). Yet, production was expected to plunge from 47,000 metric tons in 1998 to 26,000 metric tons in 1999 because of heavy rains in the key growing areas of Bangka Island and Lampung (*The Jakarta Post* 1999c). Finally, high export prices for shrimp during the crisis—a trend that appears likely to continue—appear to be the reason behind increased reports of uncontrolled clearing of coastal mangrove forests in Indonesia for conversion to shrimp aquaculture.[15] This is an underresearched issue that should receive urgent attention. Of special note is the fact that the gestation period for shrimp can be relatively short (less than a year), which means investors may have a high incentive to clear land immediately to take advantage of existing high prices. This situation differs from that of tree crops (such as palm oil, cocoa, and rubber) in which the gestation period is measured in years, thus lowering the degree of producers' confidence that they can take advantage of peaks in prices.

Mining

Mining (including for coal, gold, iron, and nickel) has potentially important effects on forest cover in Indonesia in relation to the crisis because the *rupiah* depreciation has boosted export incentives and because some mineral reserves are in forested areas,[16] including protection forests. Of particular concern, although predating the crisis, are reported intentions to mine coal in Kutai

National Park and Bukit Soeharto Recreation Park in East Kalimantan[17] and Lorenz National Park in Irian Jaya (Sunderlin 1998).

Sources differ on whether the crisis has affected the mining sector positively or negatively. A report by NRMP (1999, 7) said that, measured in terms of constant 1993 *rupiah* returns between 1996–1997 and 1997–1998, there has been a decline in the growth of the mining and quarrying sector. A report by CIC (1998b, 94), however, indicated that, as in the case of agriculture, the crisis has either helped the mining sector or not affected it and has created opportunities for large profits in *rupiah* terms. Kuntoro Mangkusubroto, the former minister of mining and energy, said in May 1999 that even though Indonesia tends to charge higher royalties from mining than other countries, foreign investors remain interested in the opportunities offered in Indonesia (*Bisnis Indonesia* 1999b).

In coal exports, a strong year-to-year increase from 1994 to 1997 was followed by a downturn in 1998 (CIC 1999, 16). Growth is expected to resume because of high world demand along with government attempts to diversify local energy sources. With the exception of the slump in 1998, coal production has generally benefited from increased growth during the crisis related to the industry's low content of imported materials, the *rupiah* depreciation, and increased world demand (CIC 1999, 3).

The experience of other mineral commodities has been mixed. Bauxite production underwent a steep decline from 1994 through 1997, followed by an increase in 1998 driven by higher export sales. The production and export of nickel (with the exception of nickel mate) declined in 1998 compared with 1997. For tin, there was a steady increase in exports from 1991 through 1998, but the value of exports declined in 1997 and 1998 because of a weaker international market (CIC 1998b, 101–4). In spite of the sluggish market for tin, the net profits of Tambang Timah, one of the leading tin mining companies in Indonesia, soared 190% from 1997 to 1998 because of the *rupiah* depreciation (*The Jakarta Post* 1999a). The company's mining activities on Bangka Island reportedly have caused serious environmental problems (*Bisnis Indonesia* 1999f, *Kompas* 1999b). The production of iron grew steadily from 1990 through 1998 (CIC 1998b, 101–4).

Gold exports during the crisis have increased 10% (*Bisnis Indonesia* 1999a), and gold mining has become an important alternative source of income for thousands of people, notably in Kalimantan.[18] A negative effect is that small-scale mining activities have extended into sensitive conservation areas, such as Tanjung Puting National Park in South Kalimantan, where it is reportedly causing serious environmental problems (*Banjarmasin Post* 1999a). The then-minister of mining and energy (Mangkusubroto) has decried the environmental and health effects of small-scale mining (*The Jakarta Post* 1999k). But large-scale mining is also a source of concern. For example, the mining company PT Aneka Tambang has been accused of causing environmental destruction from its gold mining operations in Gunung Halimun National Park in West Java (*Media Indonesia* 1999d).

Roads

The construction of roads is recognized as one of the main indirect causes leading to conversion of natural forests to other uses. Road (and bridge) construction facilitates tropical deforestation by enabling logging and the establishment of plantations in areas that were formerly inaccessible and by facilitating spontaneous and directed settlement. There has been a considerable decline in government funding for the construction and maintenance of major highways in Indonesia during the crisis, meaning that certain negative effects on forests may have been (inadvertently) avoided. Of special concern are plans to link the major urban areas in Kalimantan, although as of late 1998 the situation apparently remained largely unchanged. For example, the completion of a 190-km road between Palangka Raya and Buntok in Kalimantan will be delayed until 2005 because of a lack of funds (*Banjarmasin Post* 1999c). Severely limited government funds will also make it difficult to put an asphalt surface on the southern leg of the Trans-Kalimantan highway (between Central and South Kalimantan) (*Media Indonesia* 1999e), although Japan is set to provide some foreign assistance for maintenance of the road (*Banjarmasin Post* 1999b).

Transmigration

Indonesia's long-established transmigration program has been an important institutional source of pressure on natural forests.[19] Since 1905, more than 6 million people have been moved under the program from land-scarce Java and Bali, mainly to once-forested areas of Sumatra, Kalimantan, and Sulawesi. A key aim of the program since the early 1980s has been to supply labor to plantations producing timber and tree crops such as rubber and palm oil. On the eve of the economic crisis in mid-1997, the transmigration program focused heavily on supplying labor to then-President Soeharto's controversial 1-million ha peat land project (*Proyek Lahan Gambut* [PLG]; also discussed in Chapter 13) in Central Kalimantan. The plan entailed resettling 316,000 families at the PLG site over six years; 20,000 families were to be moved to the site in 1997–1998, about three-quarters of all transmigrants for that period.

Since mid-1997, the PLG project has collapsed. It was terminated because of budget constraints and because it was deemed an inappropriate use of the designated lands. (President Soeharto had insisted on clearing the area in spite of strong objections from the scientific and nongovernmental organization [NGO] communities.) Meanwhile, the transmigration program has been reoriented and no longer poses the institutional threat to forests that it once did. Whereas it previously supplied labor to plantations, now it is used mainly to accommodate the many people in Indonesia who seek to relocate to other areas for a variety of reasons. These refugees are being settled mostly in urban or already-settled areas rather than on forestlands cleared for agriculture.[20] During the crisis, the transmigration budget decreased by 22% in nominal terms (and even more in real terms).

Despite the transmigration program's change in focus, it should not be assumed that migration and settlement are no longer a threat to natural forests. Tree crop and timber plantations continue to be established, and they require large labor forces. Yet recruitment is now done largely through the private sector and government institutions other than the transmigration program.

Effects of Forest Policy Change

In the 17-month regime of President B.J. Habibie and the tenure of Muslimin Nasution as Minister of Forestry and Estate Crops (May 1998 to October 1999), there has been tremendous ferment in forest policy reform. These reforms can be classified into two categories. The first, here called "exogenous reforms," are those that were imposed on Indonesia through the provisions of the IMF's US$40 billion debt relief agreement with the government (see Chapters 9, 10, and 12). Among the provisions of the agreement, the Government of Indonesia was required to implement the following changes:

- remove restrictions on oil palm investment;
- make changes in the forest concession system that included implementing a performance bond, introducing new resource rent taxes, increasing stumpage fees, allocating concessions through auctions, and delinking the ownership of concessions and processing facilities;
- eliminate APKINDO's monopoly over plywood exports;
- transfer control over all government-owned commercial forestry companies from the Ministry of Forestry to the Ministry of Finance; and
- incorporate the reforestation fund into the national budget and use the money in the fund only for reforestation purposes.[21]

A second group of reforms, here called "endogenous reforms," have been introduced by various groups with a stake in Indonesia's forests rather than being imposed from the outside. One example is former Forestry Minister Nasution's initiatives to allocate concessions to cooperatives and to ratify a new forestry law (see Chapter 4). Another is a campaign by NGOs to raise the status of community-based forest management and to ensure the rights of traditional forest communities (see Chapters 5 and 6).

In spite of the exuberance many people felt during the 17-month period in anticipation of reforms, the outcome has fallen far short of the vision. On one hand, there has been notable achievement in the elimination of some of the excesses of corruption, collusion, and nepotism that prevailed during the Soeharto years. APKINDO's influence has been reduced, many of the concession contracts of Soeharto family members and associates have not been renewed,[22] and some of the money allocated through the Reforestation Fund that had been misused has been returned. On the other hand, there has been little progress in reducing the huge industrial overcapacity (especially for plywood and pulp and paper) that threatens remaining natural forests. In relation to this, there has also been little progress in reorienting forestry priorities from production to protection and conservation. Moreover, there has been little meaningful progress in ensuring the rights of forest dwellers and increasing their access to forest resources.

Because a new government was recently installed and many policy and program changes are likely, little attention will be given here to reviewing policies that were enacted during President Habibie's term in office or that are pending. Nonetheless, it is useful to briefly examine some of the recent policy changes and debates inasmuch as they might be carried over into the subsequent era of policy reform. The remainder of this section examines the following topics: area limits on forest concessions and resource rents, allocation of concessions to cooperatives through auctions, community forestry, and *adat* (traditional) rights and the new forestry law.

Area Limits and Resource Rents

In 1998, Minister Nasution created a regulation that limited forest concessions to 50,000 ha.[23] When he took office, individual concession areas ranged from 22,000 to 560,000 ha (Kartodihardjo 1998), and nine holding companies had total concession areas of 1.3 million to 3.5 million ha (*Bisnis Indonesia* 1998). The stated intention of the new regulation was to curb collusion, corruption, and nepotism in the forestry sector and to lay the groundwork for the transfer of smaller units to cooperatives (see the next section on "Cooperatives").

Researchers, NGO activists, and industry representatives alike disapproved of the limitation on concession size. Scotland (1998, x–xi) said that concessions smaller than 50,000 ha are not commercially viable and do not capture sufficient rents for the government.[24] He argued that 80,000 ha is the threshold for profitability, and the optimum area is 100,000 to 150,000 ha. Indro Tjahjono, the coordinator of *Sekretariat Kerjasama Pelestarian Hutan Indonesia* ([SKEPHI] the Secretariat for Cooperation in Indonesian Forest Conservation—the NGO Network for Forest Conservation in Indonesia) opposes small concessions on the grounds that they are unprofitable and encourage deviations from regulations and thus may hasten the process of deforestation (*Media Indonesia* 1999g). The head of Masyarakat Perhutanan Indonesia (Indonesian Forestry Society) contends that area limits would make it difficult to attain sustainable management of Indonesia's forests (*Bisnis Indonesia* 1999i).

In mid-September 1999, the Ministry of Forestry and Estate Crops (MoFEC) announced an intention to revoke the regulation limiting the size of concession areas. Waskito Seojodibroto, director general of production forest utilization, acknowledged that the change was made in response to a request by industry (*Bisnis Indonesia* 1999i). As of November 1999, timber firms were pressing for definitive revocation of the regulation (*The Jakarta Post* 1999l).

Auction System and Cooperatives

The allocation of concessions through an auction system was implemented to introduce efficiency and fairness into the award of timber access rights. Likewise, Minister Nasution (who has since been replaced) championed the idea of awarding concessions to cooperatives to ensure that forest wealth was not monopolized by the rich and powerful. The auction system began in May 1999 with an offer of 170,000 ha in Irian Jaya and Central Kalimantan that had belonged to concessions whose licenses were suspended (*The Jakarta Post* 1999e). By April 1999, five cooperatives had been awarded concessions of 10,000 ha each in Irian Jaya (*Kompas* 1999a).

In spite of the good intentions, both the auction system and the practice of awarding concessions to cooperatives have been criticized. The IMF has criticized the auction system developed by the MoFEC because it imposes stipulations on the suitability of awardees and is therefore not fully free-market oriented (*Bisnis Indonesia* 1999d). Minister Nasution introduced restrictions on who could participate in the bidding, which were based on the size of a company and its past silvicultural practices (*The Jakarta Post* 1998).

The award of concessions to cooperatives has also been subject to criticism for a variety of reasons. Tjahjono of SKEPHI said that only 15% of concessions whose licenses should have been revoked because of corruption, collusion, and nepotism have been acted on. Furthermore, he rejected the idea of distributing concessions to cooperatives on the basis that they will not be accepted at the local level, in part because the term "cooperative" has acquired a bad reputation as a result of past failures of government-established cooperatives (*Media Indonesia* 1999f). Brown (1999, ii) said cooperatives constitute a "new system of patronage" because they can be used to favor politically connected recipients and will be inefficient. He said that experience in Sabah, Malaysia, suggested that small, short-tenure concessions are unsustainable. Zain Masyhur, the head of the reform wing of Masyarakat Perhutanan Indonesia, said the new system is not transparent (*Media Indonesia* 1999c) and has requested a government investigation into whether new incidents of corruption, collusion, and nepotism have occurred in the award of concessions. Similar charges have been made in the national media (*Media Indonesia* 1999h).

Community Forestry and Adat *Rights*

Fay and Sirait (see Chapter 6), researchers at the International Center for Research on Agroforestry, said that significant progress is being made in the reform era to improve systems of community forestry and to secure the rights of *adat* communities. Two tracks of formal policy reform are being pursued: the government's community forestry program (called *hutan kemasyarakatan* [HKm]) and a draft *adat* decree. As discussed in Chapter 6, the Hkm program has improved compared with the situation during the Soeharto years. Yet the MoFEC has moved away from some of the guiding principles. Among the main deviations is that only conditional rights will be awarded on *adat* lands. The Bureau of Lands has issued potentially groundbreaking "Guidelines to Resolve *Adat* Communal Rights Conflicts," which will spell out criteria for the recognition of customary common property rights (see Chapter 6). Campbell (see Chapter 5) says the Hkm program is an important first step forward, but new policies related to community forestry unfortunately remain rooted in the assumption that the government has the sole right to control forestlands.

New Forestry Law

An Indonesian forestry law enacted in 1967 had long been regarded as out of date when deliberations on a new forestry law were begun in 1989. Subsequently, more than 10 draft laws were produced over a decade. During the Habibie presidency, Minister Nasution pressed hard for passage of a new forestry law, and one was finally ratified on September 30, 1999 (see Chapter 4).

Before ratification, the new forestry law came under heavy criticism for a variety of reasons. Two former ministers (former Minister of Forestry, Djamaludin Suryohadikusumo and former Minister of Environment Emil Salim) said the law should be substantially revised prior to approval. Suryohadikusumo criticized the proposed law on the grounds that it did not recognize the rights of forest-dwelling people; did not encourage giving sufficient value to forest biodiversity; and was not in accordance with international conventions on forests, biodiversity, and climate change. Salim said the proposed law would allow the timber industry to increase its production capacity by 30% (*The Jakarta Post* 1999h).

The NGO community has reacted strongly against the proposed law. *Wahana Lingkungan Hidup Indonesia* ([WALHI] or Indonesian Forum on the Environment) believes the new forestry law is quite similar to the 1967 Basic Forestry Law, which treated natural forests as resources to be exploited, and thus has asked the House of Representatives to drop it. Emmy Hafild (of WALHI) urged that a more overarching natural resources bill be considered to reduce competition among economic sectors in the governance of resource use (*The Jakarta Post* 1999j). According to Hasanu Simon, then-head of *Forum Komunikasi Kehutanan Masyarakat* ([FKKM] Communication Forum on Community Forestry), the process by which the forestry law was written was not open and the issue of *adat* rights was neglected (*Media Indonesia* 1999a). Abdon Nababan of Forest Watch Indonesia says customary forest should be treated separately from state forest, but this is not reflected in the proposed legislation. Without such a provision, state rights would continue to prevail over local rights (*Bisnis Indonesia* 1999i).

Conclusion

Although some people living in forested areas have benefited from certain income-enhancing effects of the crisis, the majority of households were worse off two years into the crisis than they were in the year before the crisis. The differential effects of the crisis on levels of living are largely explained by the degree of household access to export commodity income, as balanced against increased costs of living and of agricultural inputs.

The effects of the crisis on the forests themselves are not as easy to ascertain because no time-series satellite imagery data are available yet to compare the precrisis and crisis situations. Nonetheless, as this chapter has indicated, there clearly have been both positive and negative consequences. In spite of the lack of precise knowledge at the aggregate level about the effects of the crisis on forest cover, some tentative conclusions can be made at the subaggregate level.

- Small farmers (with considerable regional variation) have tended to clear more forestland in response to the crisis, and they have mainly been interested in planting tree export crops, although whether this pattern is a lasting one is not clear.
- The commercial forest sector appears to be placing ever-growing demands on forest resources that are reaching increasingly unsustainable levels, but this trend predates the crisis and it is not known precisely how it is affected by the crisis.
- Oil palm development, both in terms of area growth and production of CPO, slowed during the crisis; but there are signs that growth will resume.
- The higher export value of certain commodities (such as cocoa, shrimp, and coal) has clearly increased pressure on forests, including protected areas.
- The government has found it difficult to meet budget requirements for building and maintaining major roads in forested areas, which presumably has alleviated additional pressure on natural forests from roads.

Although it is important to understand the effects of the crisis on the forest sector, it is critical to keep this point in mind: The country's natural forests are under serious threat, and the threat predates the economic crisis. Excess processing capacity by the industrial timber industry, an overcommitment to production at the expense of conservation, and insufficient forest access rights at the local level are the key policy issues, as they were long before the crisis. The Habibie administration made only tentative progress in addressing these critical issues, and it remains to be seen if the current administration, with its stated commitment to reform, will be able to make meaningful progress in securing the rights of forest-dwelling people, enforcing greater guarantees of biodiversity protection, stemming the rampant illegal felling of trees, and implementing other measures that are needed to protect Indonesia's remaining natural forests.

Acknowledgments

Valuable comments on this chapter were made by Chris Barr, David Brown, Anne Casson, Carol J. Pierce Colfer, Ida Aju Pradnja Resosudarmo, and Michael Spilsbury. Diana Parsell did the copyediting. Any errors in the finished product are entirely the responsibility of the author.

Endnotes

1. Evans (1998, 5) offers another assessment, saying that "Indonesia's economic collapse is the most profound to affect any significant market-oriented economy in decades."

2. Early studies by Indonesia's Central Bureau of Statistics and the International Labor Organization put the poverty rate at 30–40%, an assessment that has been criticized as methodologically flawed and overly pessimistic (Cameron 1999, 13–4). Hill (1999, 41–2) stated that the Poppele et al. (1999) estimate of poverty at 14–20% is the most reliable.

3. In recent years the rates of annual agricultural growth have been 4.2% (1995), 1.9% (1996), 0.7% (1997), and 0.2% (1998) (Hill 1999, 25–6).

4. The decline in exports during the crisis is unexpected, given the depreciation of the *rupiah* against the U.S. dollar. The main reason for this decline, according to Hill (1999, 30–1), is the low price of oil and gas. (Exports other than oil and gas declined in dollar terms but rose in *rupiah* terms.) Other important reasons for the export decline include cancelled orders, problems getting credit, shipping bottlenecks, the weak Japanese economy, disruption of law and order, and the reduced presence of export-oriented multinational corporations (Hill 1999, 30–1). According to Rahardi Ramelan, then minister of industry and commerce, the drop in exports to Asian countries affected by the crisis has been compensated for by increased exports to countries not badly affected, such as Australia, Singapore, Belgium, China, India, Canada, Malaysia, and Thailand (*Bisnis Indonesia* 1999g).

5. Riau and Jambi were considered a joint province for purposes of the research. Three villages were surveyed in each of the two provinces.

6. We judged it important to differentiate, to the degree possible, the effects of the drought and fires from the economic effects of the crisis because the effects of ENSO were so severe in Indonesia. As explained by the World Bank (1998, 1.11), "What the financial crisis has done

to wreck Indonesia's urban firms, nature seems to be doing to ruin its rural farms." Hill (1999, 37) said that through 1998, the rural poor were affected much more by the drought than by the crisis. The Food and Agriculture Organization of the United Nations views this as one of the severest droughts this century (Johnson 1998, 37).

7. Hill (1999, 27–28, 45) said that the welfare of those in the agricultural sector has not been adversely affected directly, that "export growth rose, to the benefit of those deriving income from the sector," and that "many in the agricultural and informal sectors have experienced no great hardships, and possibly even an increase in incomes." He stated further, "the deterioration of living standards is serious but not catastrophic."

8. Various kinds of agricultural inputs, such as pesticides, and various kinds of fertilizers have to be imported and have become very expensive (CIC 1998a, 53).

9. Among the characteristics of rubber that make it appealing to farmers facing economic crisis and seeking to increase their long-term security are that it (a) requires relatively low cost in time and expenditure for establishment and maintenance; (b) is limited, in terms of latex production, more meaningfully by labor expenditure than by the number of trees; (c) can be harvested throughout most of the year; and (d) is nonperishable, meaning that it can be stored and sold at a time when the price is advantageous.

10. Tjipto Wignjoprajitno, executive director of APKINDO, said on March 2, 1999, that the 35% fall in the value of plywood exports from 1997 to 1998 (to $2.5 billion) was because of "weak demand and depressed prices rising from economic crises affecting several main importing countries, particularly Japan and South Korea" (*The Jakarta Post* 1999b, 8).

11. Christopher Barr prepared this paragraph especially for this chapter (Barr 1999b).

12. See also Brown (1999, ii), who indicated that the minimum annual illegal log supply was 20 million m^3, and the legal production forest supply had declined from 18 million to 16 million m^3 in the period 1994–1998. In the same period, Brown claimed that the conversion forest supply had increased from 5 million to 10 million m^3.

13. Lore Lindu is also experiencing increased land clearing for cocoa and coffee, as well as increased mining (Merrill and Effendi 1999, 15).

14. Colfer (1999) argued, based on July 1999 field observations in East Kalimantan, that "the land will have to be recleared because much of it has been covered again by vines and alang alang (*Imperata cylindrica*)."

15. For example, according to the Environmental Impact Control Agency in southeast Sulawesi, thousands of hectares of mangroves have disappeared in that region of the country (see *The Jakarta Post* 1999f). Clearing of mangroves for shrimp aquaculture can damage the productivity of coastal fisheries (Usher 1999, 18).

16. Among the 668 mining contracts in Indonesia as of April 1999, 372 (56%) were in Sumatra and Kalimantan, two of the most important forest resource regions.

17. Kuntoro Mangkusubroto, then minister of mining and energy, announced on June 15, 1999, that coal mining would not be allowed in Bukit Soeharto. It had been assumed initially that removing the coal would help relieve the problem of forest fires. The government changed its position when it was shown a low-cost method of putting out coal fires by the U.S. Office of Surface Mining Reclamation and Enforcement (see *The Jakarta Post* 1999g). Regardless of this positive step for the interests of conservation, thousands of hectares of Bukit Soeharto are threatened with conversion to nonforestland uses, in spite of the desire of the local government to maintain the area as a conservation forest (see *Kompas* 1999e).

18. See for example the story of the Kahayan River (*Kompas* 1999c).

19. This section is based on an interview conducted on November 5, 1999, with Patrice Levang. Levang is a researcher who worked from 1980 to 1987 and from 1996 to 1999 in the Transmigration Ministry.

20. The transmigration program's current activities involve resettling 10,000 Madurese families from West Kalimantan, 23,000 mainly Bugis and Buton families from Ambon, about 2,000 transmigrant families from Aceh, and 32,000 East Timorese families.

21. Kartodihardjo (1999a, 49) said the IMF forestry provisions can be helpful to improve forest management, but they will be ineffective unless accompanied by institutional and political/economic reform. Obstacles to implementing these reforms include a weak domestic Indonesian constituency and an international constituency strong enough to push through the reforms but focused merely on administrative reform without a sense of ownership of the process. What is needed, according to Kartodihardjo (1999b, 44–6), is a link between domestic and international constituents, with full transparency on the part of the international institutions, to build legitimacy and support within Indonesia.

22. By July 1999, eight forest concessions with a total area of 1.17 million ha owned by Soeharto's children and their business associates were revoked because it was assumed they were obtained through corruption, collusion, and nepotism. Thirteen additional concessions with a total area of 1.36 million ha were expected not to be renewed when they expired in March 2000 (see *The Jakarta Post* 1999i).

23. For each industry group, the limits on timber concessions were 100,000 ha per province, with a nationwide limit of 400,000 ha. A ceiling was also placed on the area of plantations: 20,000 ha at the provincial level and 100,000 ha at the national level.

24. Scotland (1998, x–xi) argued, moreover, that the current resource rent tax, based on a percentage of log prices, means an ever decreasing rent share to the government as log prices increase in the process of economic recovery. He said the current resource rent tax should be replaced with an area-based charge.

References

Adlin, S.E. 1999. Ekspor menciut, industri plywood susut. *Bisnis Indonesia*. September 14. From the webpage http://www.bisnis.com (accessed September 20, 1999).

Angelsen, A., and I.A.P. Resosudarmo. 1999. *Krismon, Farmers, and Forests: The Effects of the Economic Crisis on Farmers' Livelihoods and Forest Use in the Outer Islands of Indonesia.* May 14. Unpublished report from the Center for International Forestry Research (CIFOR).

APKI (Asosiasi Pulp dan Kertas Indonesia/Indonesian Pulp and Paper Association). 2001. *Kapasitas Industri Pulp dan Kertas 1960–2001.* Jakarta, Indonesia: APKI. Unpublished.

Banjarmasin Post. 1999a. *Petugas PHPA tak Berdaya.* June 16.

_____. 1999b. *Trans Kalimantan Poros Selatan Makin Parah.* May 12.

_____. 1999c. *Jalan Palangka Raya-Buntok Selesai Tahun 2005.* May 14.

Barr, C. 2001. Chapter 4: The Political Economy of Fiber and Finance in Indonesia's Pulp and Paper Industries. In *Banking on Sustainability: Structural Adjustment and Forestry Reform in Post-Suharto Indonesia.* Washington, D.C.: CIFOR and World Wide Fund for Nature Macroeconomics for Sustainable Development Program Office, 70–95.

_____.1999b. Personal communication with the author, November 4, 1999.

Bisnis Indonesia. 1998. *Konsesi HPH cukup sejuta hektar saja?* From the webpage http://www.bisnis.com (accessed August 20, 1998).

_____. 1999a. *Penjualan emas menurun.* From the webpage http://www.bisnis.com (accessed March 15).

_____. 1999b *Iklim investasi pertambangan tetap menarik bagi PMA.* June 1.

_____. 1999c. *Penjarahan hutan semakin brutal.* From the webpage http://www.bisnis.com (accessed June 14).

————. 1999d. *IMF ragukan sistem lelang HPH*. From the webpage http://www.bisnis.com (accessed June 25).

————. 1999e. *Harga karet capai titik terendah*. From the webpage http://www.bisnis.com (accessed July 21).

————. 1999f. "*Kehadiran PT Timah di Bangka Diusik*. From the webpage http://www.bisnis.com (accessed July 26).

————. 1999g. *RI masih mampu tingkatkan ekspor*. From the webpage http://www.bisnis.com (accessed August 16).

————. 1999h. *Pertanian akan jadi andalan*. From the webpage http://www.bisnis.com (accessed August 30).

————. 1999i. *Sejumlah kritikan atas RUUK*. From the webpage http://www.bisnis.com (accessed August 31).

————. 1999j. *Produksi kopi diduga naik 18.5%*. From the webpage http://www.bisnis.com (accessed September 6).

————. 1999k. *Pembatasan HPH dicabut*. From the webpage http://www.bisnis.com (accessed September 17).

————. 1999l. *Industri kayu pakai 52% log ilegal*. From the webpage http://www.bisnis.com (accessed November 9).

Booth, A. 1999. The impact of the crisis on poverty and equity. In *Southeast Asia's Economic Crisis: Origins, Lessons, and the Way Forward*, edited by H.W. Arndt and H. Hill. Australia: Allen & Unwin, 128–41.

Brown, D. 1999. *Addicted to Rent: Corporate and Spatial Distribution of Forest Resources in Indonesia: Implications for Forest Sustainability and Government Policy*. Report no. PFM/EC/99/06. Jakarta, Indonesia: ITFMP

Cameron, L. 1999. Survey of recent developments. *Bulletin of Indonesian Economic Studies* 35(1):3–40.

Casson, A. 2000. The Hesitant Boom: Indonesia's Oil Palm Subsector in an Era of Economic Crisis and Political Change. Occasional paper no. 29. Bogor, Indonesia: Center for International Forestry Research.

CIC (Capricorn Indonesia Consult Inc.). 1998a. *Perkembangan Sektor Pertanian*. No. 216. December 26. Jakarta, Indonesia: CIC.

—————. 1998b. *Perkembangan Sektor Pertambangan dan Energi*. No. 216. December 26. Jakarta, Indonesia: CIC.

—————. 1999. *Prospects of the Industry and Marketing of Coal in Indonesia*. No. 221. March 19. Jakarta, Indonesia: CIC.

Cole, D.C., and B.F. Slade. 1998. Why has Indonesia's financial crisis been so bad? *Bulletin of Indonesian Economic Studies* 34(2): 61–6.

Colfer, C.J.P. 1999. Personal communication with the author, July 7, 1999.

Departemen Kehutanan dan Perkebunan. 1998. Statistik Perkebunan Indonesia, 1997–1999, Kelapa Sawit. Jakarta, Indonesia: Departemen Kehutanan dan Perkebunan.

EIA (Environmental Investigation Agency)/Telapak. 1999. *The Final Cut: Illegal Logging in Indonesia's Orangutan Parks*. London: EIA; Bogor, Indonesia: Telapak Indonesia.

Elmhirst, B., Hermalia, and Yuliyanti. 1998. "Krismon" and "Kemarau": A downward sustainability spiral in a North Lampung translok settlement. Preliminary report of research findings. In *Agroforestry in Landscapes Under Pressure: Lampung Research Planning Trip, June 17–21*, edited by M. van Noordwijk and H. de Foresta. Bogor, Indonesia: International Center for Research in Agroforestry.

Evans, K. 1998. Survey of recent developments. *Bulletin of Indonesian Economic Studies* 34(3): 5–36.

FAO (Food and Agriculture Organization). 2001. Indonesia: Plywood Exports Volume (m³). In *FAOSTAT Database*. Rome: FAO. http://apps.fao.org/ page/collections?subset=forestry (accessed June 18, 2001).

Hill, H. 1999. *The Indonesian Economy in Crisis: Causes, Consequences, and Lessons.* Singapore: Institute of Southeast Asian Studies.

The Indonesian Observer. 1998. Cocoa harvest this year 310,000 tons: Association. November 6, 9.

ITFMP (Indonesia–U.K. Tropical Forest Management Programme). 1999. *Threats to Sustainable Forest Management in Indonesia: Roundwood Supply and Demand and Illegal Logging.* Draft position paper. Report number: PFM/EC/99/01. Jakarta, Indonesia: ITFMP.

The Jakarta Post. 1998. Scoring system for bids in logging auction. August 25, 12.

———. 1999a. Timah's profits up 190% due to the rupiah plunge." February 20, 8.

———. 1999b. RI plywood exports fall 35% due to tardy market. March 5, 8.

———. 1999c. Pepper production to plunge this year. April 15, 8.

———. 1999d. RI set to produce 500,000 tons of cocoa in 2005. May 3, 10.

———. 1999e. Auction opens for forestry concessions. May 26, 12.

———. 1999f. Shrimp ponds sweep away SE Sulawesi Mangrove Forests. June 8, 7.

———. 1999g. Minister bans coal mining at Bukit Soeharto. June 16, 8.

———. 1999h. Revise forestry bill, say former ministers. June 16, 8.

———. 1999i. Govt revokes vast forest concessions. July 9, 1.

———. 1999j. House urged to drop new forestry bill. July 31, 2.

———. 1999k. Government having difficulty with illegal miners. August 28.

———. 1999l. Timber firms in drive to keep power. November 15, 10.

Jellinek, L., and B. Rustanto. 1999. *Survival Strategies of the Javanese during the Economic Crisis.* Jakarta, Indonesia: The World Bank.

Johnson, C. 1998. Survey of recent development. *Bulletin of Indonesian Economic Studies* 34(2):3–60.

Kartodihardjo, H. 1998. Personal communication with the author, September 9, 1998.

———.1999a. Redistribusi dan Pelestarian Manfaat Sumber Daya Hutan: Hambatan Struktural dan Masalah Implementasi Paket IMF. (Redistribution and protection of forest resources: Structural impediments and the problem of implementation of the IMF Package.) *Analisis CSIS* 28(1):49–61.

———.1999b. *Belenggu IMF and World Bank: Hambatan Struktural Pembaharuan Kebijakan Pembangunan Kehutanan di Indonesia. (IMF and World Bank shackles: Structural impediments to forest development policy reform in Indonesia).* Bogor, Indonesia: Pustaka Latin.

Kompas. 1999a. Lima Koperasi Diberi HPH. April 26, 15.

———. 1999b. Bangka: Mumpung Terumbu Belum Musnah. July 13, 15.

———. 1999c. Emas Ditambang Elmautpun pun Datang. July 19, 23.

———. 1999d. Hutan Gunung Balak Dibabat Gerombolan Penjarah. August 13, 24.

———. 1999e Dikapling, Ribuan Hektar Bukit Soeharto. August 25, 17.

———. 1999f. Hutan Lindung Kalimantan Mulai Gundul. August 28, 20.

———. 1999g Paru-paru Dunia Terluka. August 28, 19.

———. 1999h. Penjarahan Hutan di Jambi Makin Dahsyat dan Mengerikan. September 3, 19.

Lazuardi, H., and Y. Ardi. 1999. Pulp-Kertas Selamatkan Sektor Industri (Pulp and paper rescues the industrial sector.) *Bisnis Indonesia.* September 20. From the webpage http://www.bisnis.com (accessed September 20, 1999).

Levang, P. 1999. Personal communication with the author, November 5,1999.

Media Indonesia. 1999a. Penyusunan RUU Kehutanan Tertutup dan Abaikan Hak *Adat.* From the webpage http://mediaindo.co.id (May 14, 1999).

———. 1999b. Penjarahan Taman Berbak makin Ganas. Patroli Rutin Jagawana tak Berdaya. From the webpage http://mediaindo.co.id (August 2, 1999).

———. 1999c. Cabut HPH Kroni Cendana. From the webpage http://mediaindo.co.id (August 4, 1999).

———. 1999d. PT Aneka Tambang Dituding Merusak Taman National. From the webpage http://mediaindo.co.id (September 2, 1999)

———. 1999e. Proyek Jalan di Kalimantan Sulit akibat Tanah Berair. From the webpage http://mediaindo.co.id (September 7, 1999).

———. 1999f. Indro Tjahjono (Koordinator SKEPHI): Saya Memang Curiga. From the webpage http://mediaindo.co.id (September 9, 1999).

———. 1999g. Kecil iturugi. September 9, 1999.

———. 1999h. Reformasi Hutan Menggandeng Kroni Baru. From the webpage http://mediaindo.co.id (September 9, 1999).

Merrill, R., and E. Effendi. 1999. Impact of Indonesia's crisis: IV. Protected areas management. *NRM News* 1(1):15. Jakarta, Indonesia: Natural Resources Management Project.

Nirang, S.G.M. 1999. Indonesia's plywood exports face challenges. *The Jakarta Post.* September 27. From the webpage http://www.thejakartapost.com (accessed September 28).

NRMP (Natural Resources Management Project). 1999. *Analysis of Natural Resource Impacts of Indonesia's Financial Crisis.* (Briefing on a Study Commissioned by Deputy V of Bappenas, with updates through the third quarter of 1998) January 28. Jakarta, Indonesia: NRMP.

Pardede, R. 1999. Survey of recent development. *Bulletin of Indonesian Economic Studies* 35(2):3–39.

Poppele, J., S. Sumarto, and L. Pritchett. 1999. *Social Impacts of the Indonesian Economic Crisis: New Data and Policy Implications.* Jakarta, Indonesia: Social Monitoring and Early Response Unit.

Ratnawati, A., R.N. Suryana, and D. Rachmina. 1998. *Dampak Krisis Ekonomi Terhadap Industri Kecil Menengah Pangan dan Komoditas Pertanian Serta Alternatif Kebijakan (The impact of the economic crisis on small- and medium-scale food industries and agricultural commodities and alternative policies).* Jakarta, Indonesia: The Asia Foundation.

Sadli, M. 1999. The Indonesian crisis. In *Southeast Asia's Economic Crisis: Origins, Lessons, and the Way Forward,* edited by H.W. Arndt, and H. Hill. Australia: Allen & Unwin, 16–27.

Scotland, N. 1998. *The Impact of the Southeast Asian Monetary Crisis on Indonesian Forest Concessions and Implications for the Future.* Report no. SMAT/EC/98/02. Jakarta, Indonesia: Indonesia–U.K. Tropical Forest Management Programme.

Sunderlin, W.D. 1998. *Between danger and opportunity: Indonesia's forests in an era of economic crisis and political change.* From the webpage http://www.cgiar.org/cifor/ (accessed September 23).

Sunderlin, W.D., I.A.P. Resosudarmo, E. Rianto, and A. Angelsen. 2000. *The Effect of Indonesia's Economic Crisis on Small Farmers and Natural Forest Cover in the Outer Islands.* CIFOR Occasional paper no. 28 (E). Bogor, Indonesia: CIFOR.

USDA (U.S. Department of Agriculture). 1999a. *Indonesia cocoa annual 1999.* Global Agriculture Information Network report no. ID9068. Jakarta, Indonesia: USDA.

———. 1999b. *Indonesia coffee annual 1999.* Global Agriculture Information Network report no. ID9044. Jakarta, Indonesia: USDA.

Usher, G. 1999. Impact of Indonesia's crisis: V. Coastal and marine resources. *NRM News* 1(1): 118–9. Jakarta, Indonesia: Natural Resources Management Project.

Winarto, W. 1999. Kinerja Emiten Pulp dan Kertas Bakal Membaik. *Bisnis Indonesia.* From the webpage http://www.bisnis.com (accessed August 9).

The World Bank. 1998. Indonesia in crisis: A macroeconomic update. Pre-publication draft. Jakarta, Indonesia: The World Bank.

CHAPTER TWELVE

Corporate Debt and the Indonesian Forestry Sector

Christopher Barr, David Brown, Anne Casson, and David Kaimowitz

L arge outstanding debts owed by private conglomerates currently constitute a major obstacle to the rapid recovery of the Indonesian economy. Companies that depend heavily on forest products and palm oil for their revenues account for a significant portion of that debt. Weak government regulation of the banking sector allowed banks to engage in risky business practices that proved unsustainable once the Indonesian *rupiah* depreciated in 1997.[1] Unless the government stringently regulates such risky practices in the future, the current crisis will be prolonged and financial crises will inevitably recur. The forest and estate crops sector presents particular risks because the long-term availability of raw materials is uncertain, high potential exists for social conflict, and the industry relies heavily on inherently unstable political connections to obtain access to raw materials and subsidies (see Chapters 9, 10, and 16).

How the government handles the financial crisis will directly affect the forest and estate crops sector in three major ways:

- Loan write-offs and debt restructuring will, in effect, subsidize the sector and encourage it to expand its activities. Because many of these activities have adverse social and environmental effects, this may lead to greater political unrest and forest degradation.

- The Indonesian Bank Restructuring Agency (IBRA) now controls two very large conglomerates closely tied to the forest and estate crops sector and has the legal authority to influence the management of most other corporations in the sector because the great majority have large nonperforming loans. Nevertheless, IBRA has taken no significant steps to improve the management of most of these firms.
- If the government fails to put in place adequate due diligence procedures to ensure that banks do not lend money to support illegal or excessively risky practices, banks will continue to lend money for questionable forest-related activities. Until now Indonesian banks have assumed that even if they lose large sums, the government will cover part of those losses.

The general public in Indonesia and taxpayers in Europe, the United States, and Japan have a special interest in these issues because they will pick up much of the bill for bank and business mismanagement. Foreign donations and loan subsidies reduced spending for public goods and services, and higher taxes will have to cover a great share of the enormous fiscal cost of the financial crisis. Taxpayers also may be concerned to know their money could be used to subsidize illegal logging and other practices with negative environmental and social effects.

The following pages document each of these claims. Many of our findings are preliminary, but they clearly point to the need for the Government of Indonesia (GOI) and the international community to give greater attention to these issues. In the first section, we discuss the importance of forest-related debt within Indonesia's overall financial picture. In the second section, we analyze how financial policies may affect the forest and estate crops sector. In the third section, we look at who will pay costs related to the financial crisis. We end with some central questions that policymakers and their advisors will need to address over the coming months.

The Magnitude of the Forest and Estate Crops Debt and the Issue of Risk

The Magnitude of the Debt

We estimate that private corporations owe IBRA a total of Rp 345 trillion (US$51.5 billion at the current exchange rate of Rp 6,700 = US$1.00).[2] Of this figure, nonperforming debt—which includes all loans that are more than three months past due plus all restructured debt—accounts for Rp 230 trillion (US$34.3 billion) (Muhammad 1999). To put this in perspective, this represents approximately 32% of Indonesia's 1998 gross domestic product (S&P 1999). (See Annex 12–1 for the sources and assumptions we used to derive our debt figures).

Forest and estate crops activities make up 8% of the amount that companies owe IBRA. This is currently on the order of Rp 28 trillion or US$4.1

billion, of which Rp 18 trillion (US$2.7 billion) is nonperforming. As of January 1999, conglomerates with substantial forest sector holdings had US$3.4 billion in nonperforming loans. Of this, US$1.8 billion was directly tied to forest and estate crops activities, while the remaining US$1.6 billion involved investments in other sectors. Since the data on these conglomerates were collected, the value of nonperforming loans in IBRA's portfolio has grown by 50%, suggesting that the forest-related and non-forest–related bad debt held by forest-linked conglomerates may now be on the order of US$2.7 billion and US$2.4 billion, respectively. According to the January 1999 data, 10 large groups (Andatu, Astra, Bakrie, Barito Pacific, Bob Hasan, Djajanti, Gemala, Raja Garuda Mas, Salim, and Sinar Mas) accounted for more than 70% of the bad debt in the forest and estate crops sector and virtually all of the nonperforming loans in other sectors that were held by forest-linked conglomerates (See Table 12–1). (See Chapter 10 for an account of many overlapping companies.)

In addition to their domestic obligations, these groups have substantial dollar-denominated debts to foreign creditors. The Sinar Mas group, which controls 50% of the nation's pulp production, has more than US$9 billion in international debts, mostly via Asia Pulp & Paper, a Singapore-based subsidiary (Hill 1998).[3] The Raja Garuda Mas group has borrowed US$1.6 billion from offshore debt markets through its own Singapore-incorporated holding company, Asia Pacific Resources International, Ltd. (APRIL) (*PR Newswire*

Table 12–1. Bad Debts (in billions Rp) Owed to Distressed Indonesian Banks by Indonesia's Top 10 Forest-Linked Conglomerates (excluding the Soeharto family) as of January 1999

Conglomerate group name	Plywood subsidiary debt	Pulp and paper subsidiary debt	Oil palm subsidiary debt	Other subsidiary debt	Total debt (Rp)
Andatu	314	—	—	—	314
Astra	—	—	—	411	411
Bakrie	—	—	—	2,353	2,353
Barito Pacific	146	—	—	6,249	6,395
Bob Hasan	1,973	2,480	—	24	4,477
Djajanti	2,418	—	—	98	2,516
Gemala	15	—	—	401	416
RGM	404	485	28	—	917
Salim	—	—	18	834	852
Sinar Mas	80	—	—	343	423
Total	5,350	2,965	46	10,713	19,074

Source: Compiled from raw, company-level debt figures posted on IBRA's web site (http://www.bppn.go.id) in June 1999.

1999). The Astra and Bakrie Groups, both of which have made large investments in oil palm, each have more than US$1.1 billion in outstanding obligations with foreign lenders (Solomon 1999). The Salim Group has well in excess of US$1 billion in foreign debt, much of this attached to its PT Indofood holding company that is heavily involved in oil palm processing and plantations (Indofood 1998). Barito Pacific, Indonesia's largest plywood producer and owner of the Tanjung Enim Lestari pulp mill, owes more than US$1 billion in loans to a consortium of foreign banks (Fung 1998).

The Indonesian treasury is preparing to inject US$3.9 billion into nine banks being recapitalized by IBRA, three of which are closely linked to the forest and estate crops sector (*The Jakarta Post* 1999a): Bank International Indonesia (BII) of the Sinar Mas conglomerate; Bank Universal of the Astra conglomerate; and Bank Bukopin, the largest shareholder of which is the Indonesia Wood Panel Association (APKINDO).

Incentives for Risky Behavior

The failure by banks to exercise due diligence (i.e., seriously assess the potential for loan default) when Indonesia's forest-linked conglomerates sought to borrow funds, greatly contributed to the current high level of nonperforming loans. Before the current crisis, the nation's state-owned banks, in particular, frequently based their loans on political instructions rather than prudent risk calculations (*Kompas* 1999b). They often set interest rates and repayment terms on a discretionary basis to favor politically connected borrowers (Winters 1992). They routinely approved loans for projects backed by senior state officials regardless of whether these ventures were likely to be profitable (Wangkar and Rohadian 1994; England 1986). In effect, many state bank loans were nonperforming from the moment they hit the books.

By the same token, several of Indonesia's largest private banks were actually owned or controlled by the forest-related conglomerates that borrowed money from them (Table 12–2). Given this situation, the banks could not be expected to critically assess their loans to these companies. Although the government formally placed a 10% limit on related-party lending, weak enforcement of banking regulations allowed many groups to obtain loans with no real collateral (Hasjim 1999). Analysts also have reported that Indonesia's forestry conglomerates used their banks to help convince other lenders to provide funds for projects with high financial markups—that is, projects where the company claimed to invest much more than it actually spent. In some cases, the additional finance was injected into the forestry project as working capital, creating what is known in the industry as "profit before operating" (Box 12–1). In other cases, the conglomerates redirected the money to other sectors.

Although not related to financial sector policies per se, direct government subsidies for forest and estate crops activities also encouraged corporate risk

Table 12–2. Banks Owned or Controlled by Conglomerates with Substantial Investments in the Forest and Estate Crops Sector before the Crisis and Current Status

Group	Bank	Status of bank
Astra	Bank Universal	Recapitalized
Bakrie	Bakrie Bank (Bank Nusa)	Taken over
Barito Pacific	Bank Andromeda	Closed
Bob Hasan	Bank Umum Nasional	Closed
Bob Hasan	Bank Duta	Taken over
Bob Hasan/APKINDO	Bank Bukopin	Recapitalized
Raja Garuda Mas	UniBank	Not under IBRA program
Sinar Mas	Bank Internasional Indonesia	Recapitalized
Salim	Bank Central Asia	Taken over
Salim	Bank Risjad Salim Internasional	Taken over

taking. As long as companies were investing someone else's money, they had less incentive to ensure that their investments would prove viable in the long run. Since the late 1960s, the government has made timber available to forestry companies under the forest concession system for less than its true stumpage value (Gillis 1988). It has also used money in the state's Reforestation Fund to give companies cash grants of up to 42.5% of their initial investment in forest plantations. Over the last five years, the government has allowed plywood and pulp producers, as well as investors with permits to establish oil palm estates, to use the wood clear-cut from areas designated as conversion forest—or even production forest—at nominal cost (Brown 1999; Chapter 9 of this book). Moreover, forestry conglomerates with close ties to senior officials have often had access to informal grants—at times totaling hundreds of millions of dollars—from the Reforestation Fund or from institutional fees collected by the APKINDO plywood marketing cartel (Barr 1998). Box 12–1 illustrates some of these issues.

Forest and Estate Crops Investment as a High-Risk Endeavor

Weak government regulation of the financial sector and poor due diligence were clearly not unique to the forestry sector. Nor do we claim that the particular political, environmental, and social risks associated with the sector explain the failure of most forest-related conglomerates to bring their loan payments up to date. Nevertheless, strong evidence suggests the future risks specifically associated with forest and estate crops sector activities will be greater than the risks involved in most other sectors. This implies banks and the government need specific measures to ensure those risks are adequately assessed and avoided.

The lack of due diligence to keep banks from lending money for illegal forest and estate crops activities is a separate but related issue. Throughout the world,

---

Box 12–1. Government Subsidy and Financial Markup: The Case of Kiani Kertas

In 1997, PT Kiani Kertas built a 500,000–metric-ton-per-year greenfield pulp mill in East Kalimantan. To finance the project, Kiani owner, Bob Hasan, drew on his close ties to former President Soeharto. The firm received at least US$300 million in loans from four state-owned banks, as well as at least US$100 million from the Reforestation Fund (*Kompas* 1999a; Borsuk 1997). The government further subsidized the mill by providing Kiani a 10-year tax holiday and access to low-cost wood from more than 2.7 million ha in timber concessions and plantation licenses then controlled by Hasan's timber group (Brown 1999; Departemen Kehutanan 1998). When the crisis hit, Mr. Hasan also reportedly channeled part of the US$868 million in liquidity credits that Bank Indonesia injected into his Bank Umum Nasional to the Kiani Kertas project (*Asian Wall Street Journal* 1998).

Kiani has reported that it spent US$1.3 billion to develop the mill (Pranasidhi 1998). Yet industry analysts claim that the figure most likely represents a significant markup over the mill's real cost, which they believe to be closer to US$600 million. That the investment costs per unit of annual processing capacity among similar mills in the region have generally ranged between US$1,000 and US$1,500 per metric ton, or 40–60% lower than what Kiani claims to have spent, supports that allegation (Spencer and Choi 1999). In fact, Mr. Hasan may have sought to profit twice from the markup of the mill. When IBRA moved to close Bank Umum Nasional for failing to repay the Bank Indonesia liquidity credits, he offered to surrender Kiani Kertas if the agency would cancel US$1.3 billion of the bank's debt (Pranasidhi 1998).

---

governments prohibit banks from lending funds for illegal practices. A 1999 audit of the government's Reforestation Fund, carried out by the international accounting firm Ernst & Young, estimates that 52% of the total log consumption of Indonesia's wood-based industries originates from illegal sources (Bisnis Indonesia 1999; see Chapters 7, 8, 9, and 16 of this book). Analysts widely acknowledge that most of Indonesia's forest and estate crops sector companies regularly pay illegal bribes to government officials (Telapak Indonesia and EIA 1999). Nevertheless, to our knowledge the government has never restricted any bank from lending to companies engaged in these practices.

During the 1990s, many forestry companies assumed an inordinate degree of risk by investing large sums of capital in wood-processing industries without first securing a legal supply of raw materials that can be sustained over the long term. This problem particularly characterizes the rapid growth in Indonesia's pulp and paper industries. Since the late 1980s, conglomerates have invested approximately US$12 billion in the pulp and paper subsector to raise the pulp industry's processing capacity from 605,000 to 4.9 million metric tons per year and the paper industry's capacity from 1.2 to 8.3 million metric tons per year (Barr 2000). Yet, they failed to develop plantations at this same pace, and in only one instance did a company actually wait for its plantation to come on line before operating its pulp mill. Instead, most producers have chosen to obtain a large portion of their fiber by clear-cutting natural forests. This strategy is unsustainable and, in some cases, leads pulp mills to rely on illegally harvested wood for a substantial portion of their raw materials.

By 2000, Indonesia's pulp industry consumed the equivalent of 20 million m³ of roundwood per year (Barr 2000). Yet according to industry figures, only one-quarter of that comes from plantations. Moreover, a recent assessment of the plantation programs associated with the country's two largest pulp mills found that if companies continue to plant trees at the present rate, plantations will continue to provide no more than one-half of the mills' raw materials until at least 2007 (Barr 2000; Cossalter 1998). Ministry of Forestry statistics suggest that since 1994 approximately 50–60% of the pulp industry's aggregate raw material supplies have come from legal clear-cutting of mixed tropical hardwoods under the *izin pemanfaatan kayu* (wood utilization permit) licensing system. The *izin pemanfaatan kayu* system is designed to allow companies to remove timber from land designated for conversion to other uses, though in many cases such conversion is never carried out once the wood is removed (Barr 2000; Chapter 10 of this book). Much of the remaining fiber that Indonesian pulp mills have consumed has come from undocumented and presumably illegal sources (ITFMP1999). From a financial perspective, investing billions of dollars in pulp mills without any assurance that they will have a sustainable and legal source of raw materials is inordinately risky behavior.

More generally, Indonesia's forest industries will probably face greater difficulties in the coming years in obtaining access to sufficient raw materials from legal sources. Both the quantity and the quality of the country's forest resources have declined markedly over the last two decades. Scotland and colleagues (1999) estimated that between 1984 and 1996, Indonesia lost 14 million ha of forest or 1.2 million ha per year. The entire country now has only 17 million ha of production forest estate—which includes areas designated as production forest, limited production forest, and conversion forest—that has still not been logged, and the government has already slated 5 million ha of that for conversion (Scotland et al. 1999).

Forest-related projects that have generated active conflicts with local communities are another major source of financial risk. Private timber operators and plantation companies frequently encounter opposition from local peoples when they seek to log or clear forests on land traditionally controlled by those communities (Fried 1995; Casson 2000). Often this takes the form of arson and similar acts of destruction that have high financial costs (see Chapter 14). Some pulp and paper companies have also faced violent community protests in response to their release of toxic emissions into the air and watersheds near their mills (Box 12–2). Under the previous government, forestry conglomerates were largely able to ignore local communities' grievances because the government was willing to take harsh measures to guarantee social control (Fried 1995). Under the current administration, however, the central government is substantially weaker and considerably less willing to use force to resolve conflicts between local communities and large business interests in favor of the latter (Chapter 5). The ongoing case of the Indorayon pulp mill in North Sumatra, presented in Box 12–2, illustrates the financial risks inherent in projects employing problematic social and environmental practices.

The Effect of Bank Recapitalization and Debt Restructuring on Forests and Estate Crops

Debt Write-Off as Subsidy

Policy analysts interested in Indonesia's forestry sector have had a long-standing concern about the government's failure to capture a substantial portion of the potential timber revenues from the logging concessions it allocates to private companies (Ruzicka 1979; Repetto 1988; Scotland 1998). In part, this concern has been motivated by a desire to increase government revenues to reduce inequality. Another important consideration, however, has been that the conglomerates might use the additional revenues to expand their activities beyond environmentally sustainable levels (see Box 12–3). This latter aspect has particular significance at present because many large companies

---

Box 12–2. Indorayon and the Financial Costs of Social Conflict

PT Inti Indorayon Utama is a US$600 million pulp and rayon mill in North Sumatra owned by Indonesia's Raja Garuda Mas group. For several years, *Batak* communities living near the mill have voiced concerns over environmental problems associated with its operations, including forest degradation, the release of noxious fumes, and a drop in the water level of nearby Lake Toba. In July 1998, local residents blocked trucks entering the mill to keep them from bringing in raw materials, forcing Indorayon to halt production for four months (Thoenes 1998). Then in January 1999, violent clashes between community members and security forces led President Habibie to close the mill, pending an independent audit (*The Jakarta Post* 1999c). The Jakarta Stock Exchange, in turn, suspended trading of Indorayon shares.

Indorayon has paid a considerable financial cost for its conflicts with the communities. The company posted net losses of US$40 million in 1998 (Fung 1999a). In March 1999, it failed to pay US$15 million in bond coupon obligations as well as US$144 million owed to bond holders who wished to cash in their guaranteed notes. At that point, S&P downgraded its ratings on US$110 million unsecured Indorayon notes due in 2000 and US$150 million guaranteed notes due in 2001 to D from double-C (Dow Jones News Service 1999). The company has since entered into discussions with creditors to restructure its overall debt of US$360 million (Fung 1999b). Financial analysts generally agree that the success of Indorayon's restructuring proposal will depend on the outcome of the mill's still-pending environmental audit and the company's ability to negotiate an effective settlement with the surrounding communities.

Box 12–3. Debt Restructuring and the Expansion of Forest Industries

To date, only a handful of Indonesian-based companies have reached debt-rescheduling agreements with their creditors. In some cases, these agreements have led directly to an expansion in the companies' forest-related activities. In September 1999, for instance, the APRIL pulp and paper conglomerate signed an agreement to restructure US$800 million in short- and long-term debts (*The Jakarta Post* 1999b). Under the plan, creditors will roll over the debt's maturity until 2005 and waive interest payments on the principal to allow APRIL to expand processing capacity at its PT Riaupulp facility from 850,000 to 1.3 million metric tons of bleached hardwood kraft pulp per year. In April 2000, the group's parent conglomerate reached a similar agreement with IBRA and other large domestic creditors, again linking debt rescheduling to the installation of a second processing line at PT Riaupulp (Barr 2000). This expansion in processing capacity will raise the volume of wood that the mill annually consumes from 4.2 million to 6.5 million m³. Since reaching these agreements, APRIL also has reportedly sought to identify additional sources of finance to support further expansion at Riaupulp and to install a second paper machine at the group's PT Riau paper mill (*The Jakarta Post* 1999b).

have curtailed their plans to expand their pulp and paper, oil palm, and plywood operations because of lack of available funds (*Pulp & Paper Week* 1997; Sunderlin 1998; Casson 2000). Writing off or restructuring these companies' debts would probably contribute to a spurt of investment that is likely to have negative environmental consequences and to promote social unrest.

Depending on how the government handles the financial crisis, debt write-offs and loan restructuring may well provide Indonesia's forest-related industries with another substantial subsidy. Many analysts expect that the government will eventually write off or discount the majority of the companies' nonperforming loans (Linnan 1999; Ismawan 1999). In late 1999, then-chair of IBRA, Glenn M. Yusuf, stated that he expects the government to recover only 3–4% of the nonperforming loans owed to state banks and recently nationalized private banks, respectively (*The Jakarta Post* 1999d). S&P has suggested that in general Indonesian banks will require a 70% loan loss provisioning level for their nonperforming loans, which is another way of saying that the banks should expect to recover only 30% of those debts (S&P 1999). Recent claims by domestic financial analysts that the real value of the total assets held by IBRA amounts to only 30% of their book value further support the idea that IBRA may have great difficulty in recovering more than that (Ismawan 1999).

Based on this information, we believe that if current trends continue, IBRA will eventually write off 50–70% of forest-linked conglomerates' bad debts (Table 12–2). As noted earlier, we estimate that IBRA holds some Rp 18 trillion (US$2.7 billion) in nonperforming loans related to timber, wood processing, pulp and paper, and oil palm investments. This implies that IBRA would write off between Rp 9 trillion (US$1.3 billion) and Rp 12.6 trillion (US$1.9 billion) of these debts. If one also includes the anticipated write-offs on non-forest–sector loans incurred by the large forest and estate crops conglomerates mentioned earlier, these figures could rise to between Rp 17.3 trillion (US$2.6 billion) and Rp 24.2 trillion (US$3.6 billion).

To put these figures in perspective, the total write-off of bad debt in the forestry sector is likely to be two to three times higher than the US$1.2 billion that the APKINDO plywood cartel extracted from Indonesian panel producers between 1985 and 1998 (Brown 1999). Analysts estimate that during the 1990s the government failed to capture approximately US$1 billion per year in potential royalties and stumpage fees from vertically integrated concession-plymill companies (Brown forthcoming). The debt write-off figures could grow substantially if foreign banks and companies write off or discount the forest and estate crops corporations' offshore debts to any significant degree.

Forest and Estate Crops Companies in Effective or Potential Receivership

Through the banking sector recapitalization process, IBRA has emerged in its own right as the most important holder or potential holder of forest and estate crops assets in the country. IBRA's total forest- and non-forest–related assets have an aggregate book value of Rp 573 trillion (US$86 billion) (Ismawan 1999). Two of the country's largest forest-related conglomerates, the Bob Hasan and Salim groups, have pledged a mixture of cash, property, and assets to IBRA to pay for liquidity injections made by the government to their banks amid bank runs during the early weeks of the crisis. Although IBRA could directly manage those assets if it chose to do so, it has instead allowed the previous owners to continue running their companies with virtually no supervision (McCarthy 1998; *Pulp & Paper International* 1999).

In fact, IBRA has far-reaching legal authority to call in nonperforming loans and to seize corporate assets of any companies that do not pay their debts to banks under IBRA's management, which includes nearly all of Indonesia's forest-linked conglomerates. Once again, however, it has allowed the prior management to continue to operate most of these companies, in spite of the fact that many are technically bankrupt. Given that its total staff is limited to 600 people, IBRA has minimal ability to supervise such firms (Jusuf 1999). Although IBRA has recently begun to sell some companies under its control, the agency has moved slowly to liquidate the assets that it holds. One explanation for this behavior is that IBRA anticipates being able to obtain more money for these assets if it waits to sell them when market conditions improve.

IBRA's current lack of supervision over the forest-related companies that owe it large sums of money likely will serve as an impetus for debtor firms to continue to engage in practices involving an inordinate degree of financial risk. This includes practices that have negative social and environmental effects as well as those that are unsound in other ways. At the same time, the fact that IBRA owns or potentially controls a substantial share of Indonesia's forest-related industries provides a unique opportunity to improve the management of the nation's remaining forest resources. By bringing in forestry management experts to audit these companies' practices, IBRA could play a vital role in reducing Indonesia's unsustainable rate of forest degradation, minimizing the social instability that often accompanies these activities, and ensuring a higher likelihood of eventual loan repayment.

Who Will Pay for Debt Write-Off and Rescheduling?

Preliminary estimates suggest that the GOI will have to spend US$87 billion—equivalent to 82% of the nation's 1998 gross domestic product—to cover the up-front fiscal costs of revitalizing the country's commercial banking sector (S&P 1999). This figure includes funds the government provided to initially recapitalize distressed banks and pay out their creditors, as well as the first three years of interest on bonds issued by the government to fund the recapitalization program. To the extent that the government fails to recover these costs by collecting on bank loans and selling the assets of bankrupt companies, it will have to cover them itself. Ultimately, the people of Indonesia and the taxpayers of the industrialized G-7 countries (France, the United States, the United Kingdom, Germany, Italy, Japan, and Canada) will bear most of the costs of these write-offs.

During the 1999–2000 fiscal year alone, the major bilateral donors contributed US$5.9 billion dollars to Indonesia. Although some of these funds are earmarked for specific purposes, economists have realized for some time that foreign assistance funds are fungible. Hence, most grants and subsidized loans will directly or indirectly contribute to helping the GOI cover the costs of any debt write-offs. We speculate that many taxpayers in the G-7 countries would feel concerned if they realized that part of their support for Indonesia might be used to subsidize the expansion of forest and estate crops activities, many of which are currently illegal and have deleterious environmental or social consequences.

The Export Credit Agencies (ECAs) of the G-7 and other northern country governments may also end up paying substantial sums to indirectly subsidize the write-off of private conglomerates' foreign loans. A recent study of Indonesia's largest ECA-supported projects during the period 1994–1997 indicated that the pulp and paper sector was the second largest recipient of ECA-linked finance, just behind the power sector (Fried and Soentoro 1999). Four of the ten largest projects receiving ECA-backed financing were pulp and paper companies, with a combined US$4 billion. Typically, ECAs provide guarantees for commercially syndicated loans and help to leverage further finance for projects involving the export of capital goods to ensure that exporting-country vendors will receive payment for goods sold. In many cases, the ECAs' loan guarantees require no collateral, suggesting that lenders bear little direct risk and that the costs to the ECAs are likely to be quite substantial in the event that these projects fail or the purchasing company is unwilling to pay (Stephens 1998). Because ECAs are government entities, whatever costs they incur will eventually be assumed by the exporting-country taxpayers.

Conclusion

Given the magnitude of the problems currently facing Indonesia's financial and forest and estate crops sectors and the paucity of reliable data on each, we are not prepared to offer definitive solutions at this time. We recognize that Indonesia's economic recovery is likely to necessitate some degree of corporate debt forgiveness. Yet we are concerned that the very real pressures for rapid recovery in the short term will fail to address the underlying causes of the crisis and could, in turn, either prevent economic recovery or intensify the conditions for yet another collapse in the years ahead. We feel that over the coming months government officials, donors, and members of civil society organizations must address the following three questions if they wish to avoid future financial and political crises and seriously improve the management of Indonesia's remaining forest resources.

- How can we keep IBRA and the bank recapitalization process from providing additional large subsidies to Indonesia's forest-related industries?
- How can we ensure that stronger practices of due diligence are followed by banks and investors to discourage investments in inordinately risky and illegal activities, many of which also have adverse environmental and social effects?
- How can IBRA manage the assets currently or potentially under its control in a manner that promotes social and environmental sustainability, as well as financial viability?

Endnotes

1. This chapter was written in December 1999. Figures cited in the text were based on available data at that time.

2. Currency values have fluctuated regularly and sometimes dramatically over the past three years. In February 2001, the rate had gone down to Rp 9,650 to the U.S. dollar. In June 2001, it was Rp 11,500 to the U.S. dollar; in August 2001, it was Rp 8,000 to the U.S. dollar.

3. By early 2001, aggregate dollar-denominated debt held by the Sinar Mas group was estimated to have reached US$11 billion (*Reuters* 2001).

References

Asian Wall Street Journal. 1998. Associate of Soeharto says his firm used central bank funds. September 4.

Barr, C.1998. Bob Hasan, The Rise of APKINDO and The Shifting Dynamics of Control in Indonesia's Timber Sector. *Indonesia* 65:1–36.

———. 2001. Chapter 4: The Political Economy of Fiber and Finance in Indonesia's Pulp and Paper Industries. In *Banking on Sustainability: Structural Adjustment and Forestry Reform in Post-Suharto Indonesia.* Washington, D.C.: Center for International Forestry Research (CIFOR) and World Wide Fund for Nature Macroeconomics for Sustainable Development Program Office, 70–95.

Bisnis Indonesia. 1999. Industri kayu pakai 52% log illegal. November 9.

Borsuk, R. 1997. Costly Borneo mill opens as Hasan makes pulp move. *Asian Wall Street Journal.* August 7.

Brown, D.W. 1999. *Addicted to Rent: Corporate and Spatial Distribution of Forest Resources in Indonesia; Implications for Forest Sustainability and Government Policy.* Report no. PFM/EC/99/06. Jakarta, Indonesia: Department for International Development/Indonesia–U.K. Tropical Forest Management Programme.

———. Forthcoming. *The political economy of timber reform in Indonesia, Sarawak, and Sabah (1970–1999).* Seattle: University of Washington.

Casson, A. 2000. *The Hesitant Boom: Indonesia's Oil Palm Sub-Sector in an Era of Economic Crisis and Political Change.* Occasional paper no. 29. Bogor, Indonesia: Center for International Forestry Research.

Cossalter, C. 1998. *Pulpwood Production and Deforestation in Indone*sia. Unpublished manuscript. Bogor, Indonesia: Center for International Forestry Research.

Departemen Kehutanan, Sekretariat Jenderal Pengusahaan Hutan, Direktorat Penyiapan Pengusahaan Hutan. 1998. *Laporan Hasil Monitoring dan Evaluasi Perkembangan HPH Sampai Dengan Bulan Maret 1998.* Jakarta, Indonesia: Departemen Kehutanan.

Dow Jones News Service. 1999. S&P cuts Indorayon's bond ratings to D; off watch. April 1.

England, V. 1986. Two steps, forward…. *Far Eastern Economic Review.* December 4.

Fried, S. 1995. *Writing for Their Lives: Bentian Dayak Authors and Indonesian Development Discourse.* Ph.D. dissertation. Ithaca, NY: Cornell University.

Fried, S., and T. Soentoro. 1999. *Export Credit Agency Finance in Indonesia.* Unpublished manuscript.

Fung, N. 1998. Barito Pacific: 1st quarter performance. *Dow Jones Newswire.* August 20.

———. 1999a. Indonesia's Indorayon presents debt proposal to creditors. *Dow Jones News Service.* June 29.

———. 1999b. Indonesia's Indorayon '98 losses IDR 323.78 billion vs. IDR 444.01B. *Dow Jones Business News.* May 2.

Gillis, M. 1988. Indonesia: Public policies, resource management, and the tropical forest. In *Public Policies and the Misuse of Forest Resources,* edited by R. Repetto and M. Gillis. New York: Cambridge University Press, 43–114.

Hasjim, S. 1999. Personal communication with the authors, December 2, 1999.

Hill, C. 1998. Asia pulp & paper's fall from grace. *Global Finance* 1:41.

Indofood. 1998. *Annual Report.* Jakarta, Indonesia: Indofood.

Indonesian Pulp and Paper Association. 1997. *Indonesian Pulp and Paper Industry 1997 Directory.* Jakarta, Indonesia: PT Gramedia.

Ismawan, I. 1999. Soal penyusutan aset BPPN. *Bisnis Indonesia.* November 15.

ITFMP (Indonesia–U.K. Tropical Forestry Management Programme). 1999. *Threats to Sustainable Forest Management in Indonesia: Roundwood Supply and Demand and Illegal Logging. Draft position paper.* Report no. PFM/EC/99/01. Jakarta, Indonesia: ITFMP.

The Jakarta Post. 1999a. Analysts question market capacity to absorb government bonds. November 26.

————. 1999b. APRIL gets relief to expand Riau pulp. September 20.

————. 1999c. Government suspends Indorayon operation. March 20.

————. 1999d. Only 4 percent of state banks' problem loans can be recovered. November 27.

Jusuf, G.M.S. 1999. Dampaknya sangat kritis. *Panji Masyarakat.* December 1.

Kompas. 1999a. *Aset konglomerat dialihkan ke pemerintah.* July 8.

————. 1999b. *Rincian kucuran kredit dari BI ke Texmaco.* December 1.

Linnan, D.K. 1999. Insolvency reform and the Indonesian financial crisis. *Bulletin of Indonesian Economic Studies* 35(2):107–38.

McCarthy, G. 1998. Jakarta sees full recovery of debt from 2 big groups. *Asian Wall Street Journal.* October 2.

Muhammad, M. 1999. Prospects for RI's recovery. *The Jakarta Post.* October 23.

PR Newswire. 1999. APRIL reports first quarter 1999 results. May 11.

Pulp & Paper International. 1999. Kiani Kertas' management will remain in place. January 1999.

Pulp & Paper Week. 1997. Southeast Asian turmoil prompts some expansion delays. December 8.

Pranasidhi, E. 1998. Indonesia's "Bob" Hasan offers paper company to government for funds used. *Dow Jones Newswires.* September 7.

Repetto, R. 1988. *The Forest for the Trees: Government Policies and the Misuse of Forest Resources.* Washington, DC: World Resources Institute.

Reuters. 2001. Jakarta tries to edge out APP creditors. From the webpage <www.paperloop.com> (accessed February 16, 2001).

Ruzicka, I. 1979. Rent appropriation in Indonesian logging: East Kalimantan 1972/73–1976/77. *Bulletin of Indonesian Economic Studies* XV:45–74

S&P (Standard & Poor's). 1999. Indonesian banking: World's worst banking crisis since the 1970s. *Standard & Poor's Credit Week.* June 23.

Scotland, N. 1998. *The Impact of the Southeast Asian Monetary Crisis on Indonesian Forest Concessions: Implications for the Future.* Report no. PFM/EC/98/02. Jakarta, Indonesia: ITFMP.

Scotland, N., A. Fraser, and N. Jewell. 1999. *Roundwood Supply and Demand in the Forest Sector in Indonesia.* Report no. PFM/EC/99/08. Draft dated December 6. Jakarta, Indonesia: Department for International Development/Indonesia-U.K. Tropical Forest Management Programme

Solomon, J. 1999. Indonesian firms begin to resolve debt, but full workout is still years away. *Wall Street Journal.* May 7.

Spencer, C., and A. Choi. 1999. *Positioning for Asia's Recovery.* Singapore: Morgan Stanley Dean Witter.

Stephens, M. 1998. *Export Credit Agencies, Trade Finance, and South East Asia.* International Monetary Fund working paper. December. Washington, DC: International Monetary Fund.

Sunderlin, W.D. 1998. *Between danger and opportunity: Indonesia's forests in an era of economic crisis and political change.* From the webpage <http://www.cgiar.org/cifor/> (accessed September 11).

Telapak and EIA (Environmental Investigation Agency). 1999. *The Final Cut: Illegal Logging in Indonesia's Orangutan Parks.* Bogor, Indonesia: Telapak and Environmental Investigation Agency.

Thoenes, S. 1998. A nation let loose to protest, but to what end? In Indonesia a mill accused of ecocide is closed but reopened after protesters waver. *Christian Science Monitor.* November 2.

Wangkar, M., and A.R. Rohadian. 1994. Eddy Mencencang, Bapindo memikul. *Tempo.* April 16.

Winters, J. 1992. *The Political Economy of Banking Reform in Indonesia.* Paper prepared for the annual conference of the Association of Asian Studies, April 2–5. Washington, DC.

Annex 12–1:
Explanation of Assumptions and Sources of Figures Used

Unless otherwise specified, the exchange rate used in this paper is Rp 6,700 = US$1.00, which was the current rate in December 1999 when the policy memo was initially written. The figure of Rp 345 trillion for the total amount of corporate debt held by IBRA has been derived through an extrapolation from the Rp 230 trillion in nonperforming loans that the agency was known to hold in October 1999 (Muhammad 1999). This extrapolation is based on the conservative assumption that 67% of Indonesia's total corporate debt is nonperforming, defined on a three-month, past-due basis and including all restructured loans.

Our estimate that forest and estate crops industries account for 8% of total nonperforming loans in IBRA's portfolio is derived from the list of the 1,689 largest debtors that the agency published on its website in June 1999 (http://www.bppn.go.id). This list contains all nonperforming loans that IBRA had assumed from state banks through January 1999, from closed banks by December 1998, and from private banks taken over by IBRA through December 1998. By totaling the debts of all companies and individuals on the list that had investments in forest-related industries, we determined that these industries accounted for at least Rp 12 trillion in bad debt, broken down as follows: timber/plywood (Rp 7.8 trillion), pulp/paper (Rp 3.6 trillion), and oil palm (Rp 0.6 trillion). To calculate the percentage of total nonperforming loans represented by forest-related industries, we divided Rp 12 trillion by Rp 155 trillion—the aggregate value of bad debt held by all 1,689 debtors.

In estimating the current value of performing and nonperforming corporate debt linked to the forest and estate crops sector, we multiplied Rp 345 trillion (our estimate of total corporate debt currently in IBRA's portfolio) by 0.08 (the percentage of forest-related debt on IBRA's list of 1,689 debtors) to arrive at the figure of Rp 28 trillion (US$4.1 billion). We estimated the current value of nonperforming loans linked to the forest and estate crops sector by multiplying Rp 230 trillion (the known value of all nonperforming loans currently held by IBRA) by 0.08 and thus arrived at the figure of Rp 18 trillion (US$2.7 billion).

We calculated the value of nonperforming loans held by forest-linked conglomerates by totaling the value of debts held by each group's subsidiaries identifiable on IBRA's list of 1,689 debtors. The total value of nonperforming loans held by each group was disaggregated according to four categories: plywood, pulp and paper, oil palm, and other subsidiary debt. The totals for each of the top 10 forest-linked conglomerates appear in Table 12–1.

In estimating the total anticipated write-offs of nonperforming debt held by forest and estate crops conglomerates, we added the estimated values of forest-related (US$2.7 billion) and non-forest–related ($2.4 billion) bad debt incurred by these groups. We then multiplied this sum (US$5.1 billion) by 0.5 and 0.7 (the estimated range at which IBRA will write off nonperforming loans). This produced the range of US$2.6 billion to US$3.6 billion.

CHAPTER THIRTEEN

Forest Fires in Indonesia: Impacts and Solutions

Grahame Applegate, Ross Smith, James J. Fox, Andrew Mitchell, David Packham, Nigel Tapper, and Graham Baines

Indonesia experienced extensive fires during 1997–1998 that burned vast tracts of forest and forestland, especially on the islands of Borneo and Sumatra. These forest and land fires and the accompanying smoke caused (a) serious damage to the forest areas, (b) air pollution, (c) damage to public health, (d) loss of life, (e) destruction of property and livelihood options, and (f) other substantial economic losses in much of southern Southeast Asia. There are various opinions among institutions and others about the area of land burned in forest fires and other land fires during that period. Estimates range from a low of several hundred thousand hectares to a high of many millions of hectares (ADB 1999; Barber and Schweithelm 2000).

Some figures quoted include only those land and forest fires that were not planned (i.e., legal fires that were regarded as wildfires). It is important to recognize that land conversion fires, while illegal, were planned and contributed enormously to smoke and haze production. The inputs from this source of atmospheric particulates may be far more significant than previously expected, especially when the fires occurred in areas dominated by peat soils.

The existence of comparatively large areas of burning for conversion of natural forest to other uses in Sumatra and Kalimantan needs to be factored into the overall consideration of the 1997–1998 fire event and the resultant haze. It is also important to accept that accidental wildfires, some as a result of careless or misguided land conversion and agricultural burning, obviously did occur, as did deliberate ignition of wildfires by people who were aggrieved, generally as a result of disputes over changes to traditional land-use rights (see Chapter 14).

A further important contribution in terms of area burned, but less important in terms of haze production, was agricultural burning. There is an unquantified area of agricultural land burned annually to dispose of unwanted agricultural by-products that have no apparent use or value, such as straw and husks. This material is burned when it is biologically cured and is fired after harvest.

It is also important to understand that areas burned in 1997–1998 did not always equate to areas damaged or destroyed. For example, many of the open woodlands and forests in the drier parts of eastern Indonesia burn annually. Fire in these environments is a regeneration tool for many species and prepares the site for the regeneration of seedling or assists with the reduction of competitors.

Much of the fire and associated haze resulted from illegal burning by large and small land holders, inadequate fire management planning and practices to protect resources, as well as inappropriate land-use policies and the inadequate implementation of existing policies designed to minimize fire in the landscape. Another El Niño event is expected within two years, and unless policies and practices are altered, a similar disaster will again strike many parts of Indonesia and its neighbors.

Effect of Fire

Area Burned

Estimates prepared by Asian Development Bank (ADB) and Bappenas (the Indonesian National Planning Agency) in 1999 (ADB 1999) indicated the following areas burned in the 1997–1998 fires in Indonesia (in hectares): Sumatra—1.7 million, Kalimantan—6.5 million, Java—0.1 million, Sulawesi—0.4 million, and Irian Jaya (now called Papua)—1 million. Area estimates (in hectares) for forest types and land-use categories are as follows: Montane forest—0.1 million, lowland forest—3.3 million, peat and swamp forest—1.5 million, agricultural and open grassland—4.6 million, and timber plantation and estate crops—0.5 million. The area burned in 1997–1998 was 9.7 million ha as detailed in Table 13–1. The estimates were based on information from a number of sources.

Peat Fires and Conversion Forests

Fires in areas of peat soils and in cleared areas categorized by the Indonesian Ministry of Forestry and Estate Crops (MoFEC) as conversion and production forests are identified as major contributors to smoke and haze production. Conservative estimates suggest that 60% of particulates and carbon dioxide in smoke and haze arose from peat fires and 20% from

Table 13–1. Estimated Extent of Spatial Damage by Fire in 1997–1998 (hectares)

Island	Montane forest[a]	Lowland forest[b]	Peat and swamp forest[c]	Dry scrub and grass[b]	Timber plantation[d]	Agriculture[b]	Estate crops[e]	Total
Kalimantan	—	2,375,000	750,000	375,000	116,000	2,830,000	55,000	6,501,000[f]
Sumatra	—	380,000	300,000	260,000	70,000	670,000	60,000	1,740,000[f]
Java	—	25,000	—	25,000	—	50,000	—	100,000
Sulawesi	—	200,000	—	—	—	200,000	1,000	401,000
Papua	100,000	300,000	400,000	100,000	—	100,000	3,000	1,003,000
Total	100,000	3,280,000	1,450,000	760,000	186,000	3,850,000	119,000	9,745,000

Notes:

[a]Estimate from aerial survey technical assistance member, in United Nations Disaster Assistance Commission Disaster Assessment Report, Field Visit, Papua, October 3–8, 1997 (NSWRFS 1997).

[b]Total area estimate extrapolated into land cover categories of lowland forest, scrub and grass, and agriculture, based on estimates of Liew et al. (1998) and Burnt Scar Maps from the 1999 Centre for Remote Sensing and Processing; division of areas on other islands based on land cover data from the National Forest Inventory of Indonesia (1996), the National Development Planning Agency (1993, 62–9), and ADB (1999).

[c]Papua and other islands based on estimated 20% peat areas and peat distribution in Biodiversity Action Plan (Liew et al. 1998).

[d]Estimate based on Soedarmo (1998), and plantation loss estimates provided by the East Kalimantan Provincial Office of the Ministry of Agriculture—Food Crops Subsector (*Dinas Pertanian Tanaman Pangan Propinsi Kalimantan Timur* 1998) of 13,769 ha 1997, 101,922 ha 1998.

[e]Soedarmo (1998) estimated 112,000 ha burned in 1997 and the Government of Indonesia, State Ministry of Environment, and United Nations Development Programme (1998) estimated the area at 119,070.32 ha.

[f]Liew et al. (1998) estimated 3.06 million ha in Kalimantan (similar estimate for 1998—1.5 million ha in Sumatra [E. Nabet, SPOT ASIA Pte Ltd.]). Makarim et al. (1998) reported that the European Union estimate for Sumatra may be 2,798,000 ha, including 700,000 ha of forest.

forest conversion burning (ADB 1999). In 1997–1998, the fires in Indonesia contributed 22% of the world's carbon dioxide production. These fires produced more than 700 million metric tons of carbon dioxide (ADB 1999; Reily 1999) that were released into the atmosphere from the burning of the peat (fossil fuel), thus elevating Indonesia to one of the largest polluters of carbon dioxide in the world. If this situation is allowed to continue in future years, Indonesia will be classified as one of the largest contributors to global warming in years of severe drought and fire. A reduction in burning on these land classes would lead to a large reduction in haze and carbon emissions, which would significantly reduce the problems related to health, international criticism, reduced travel and tourism, and interrupted transportation systems.

Economic Costs of the 1997–1998 Drought and Fires

To date there have been two major attempts to value the effects of the 1997–1998 fires and haze: one by the World Wide Fund for Nature (WWF) and the other by the Environmental Emergency Project (EEP) of the Ministry of the Environment. These estimates valued the losses at US$4.1 billion and US$2.4 billion respectively. The valuation of the costs of the fires was based on surveys using case studies in a number of fire-prone regencies in Sumatra and East Kalimantan, national statistics, private company information, and a review of two previous estimates on the 1997 fires (ADB 1999). The valuation also included the extra damage from the fires that occurred in 1998.

A modeling approach was used in the ADB analysis so that the estimates can be updated as more data become available. The approach to valuing the losses was to sum the value of the individual components, which were valued using the most appropriate technique. The value of the timber destroyed was based on surveys designed to estimate the true economic rent of the forest by island group. Two estimates of the economic rent are given, one based on current forest practices and the other assuming reform of the log market. The total estimated timber destroyed had a minimum value of US$1.4 billion and maximum value of US$2.1 billion. Estimates of the reduced volumes growing into the exploitable size classes were also estimated. These volumes were discounted into net present volumes and given a value based on the economic rent models. The lost growth from production forest is estimated at a minimum of US$287 million and a maximum of US$423 million. Based on the assumptions derived for the degree of burned and lost trees and the assumption that nontimber forest products (NTFP) production would gradually be reestablished over a 20-year period, the loss of NTFP production was estimated at US$631 million.

Forests also have indirect benefits, which are often more valuable than the direct benefit derived from production. Forests can protect areas from flooding and can prevent erosion and siltation. Using the assumption just discussed about loss of tree cover, an estimated lost flood protection value of

US$413 million was estimated. The protective function for erosion and siltation was given a total value of US$6,040 per hectare assuming that when forest is converted it is lost forever. By calculating the discounted cash flow that would yield a net present value of US$6,040, it is possible to estimate the protective function for the first few years. When this figure is multiplied by the area affected by the fires, an estimated loss due to erosion and siltation of US$1.3 billion is computed.

A total of 757 million metric tons of carbon dioxide was estimated to have been produced during the 1997–1998 fires (more than 75% of this was a result of the combustion of peat). The total cost of the carbon dioxide released into the atmosphere (based on US$7 per metric ton) was calculated to be US$1.446 million. This figure is conservative; other estimates have put the amount of carbon dioxide produced at 3.7 billion metric tons, or nearly five times the previous estimate.

The estimated losses from timber plantations were calculated by assuming that the areas burned were evenly distributed over the different age classes. Based on field observations, plantations fewer than three years old were completely destroyed but plantations older than three years were only 30% destroyed. Estimates of profit forgone have also been included. The estimated lost timber plantation value is US$91 million.

Official area estimates of the estate crops destroyed are similar to the area estimates made in the study. The economic losses for estate crops calculated by EEP came to US$319 million. Agricultural losses incurred during 1997–1998 were due to drought, as well as the haze and fires. By analyzing the past trends of agricultural production, it was possible to predict the level of production for 1997–1998 had there been no drought and haze. The total economic cost of lost rice production is estimated at US$1.9 billion. In addition to the lost production, there is an economic cost in importing rice as a substitute. The economic cost of importing the rice is the difference in price between the local rice and imported rice for the equivalent of the production lost. This additional cost was estimated at US$496 million, giving a total estimated agricultural loss of US$2.4 billion. The impact on health was estimated at US$148 million and was based on official estimates, care costs, and estimates for lost productivity.

Tourism, an important sector in the Indonesian economy, was also significantly reduced over the period of the fires. Yet, not all the reduction in tourism can be attributed to the fires; other factors such as the Asian economic crisis and the political unrest in 1998 have also contributed to the decline. Assuming standard profit margins and overheads, it was then possible to estimate the economic loss in tourism due to the fires. The tourism loss was estimated at US$111 million (The WWF study estimated a loss worth US$70 million from just the 1997 fires [Barber and Schweithelm 2000]).

The officially reported loss for transmigration areas, transport, and fire fighting was US$46 million. The total losses resulting from the 1997–1998 drought and fires were estimated at between US$8.7 and US$9.6 billion, with an average of US$9.1 billion. A summary of these costs by component is presented in Table 13–2.

Fire Management

Institutional Capacity for Fire Prevention and Suppression

In the case of fires that were accidental or those that escaped (intentionally or unintentionally) from areas where fire was used as a site preparation tool, the capacity of Indonesia to deal with these fire events in terms of early warning systems (EWSs), detection, fire control, and coordination at local (regency or village) and institutional (agency) levels was severely tested in 1997–1998.[1] A number of agencies stated that there is a need to strengthen fire management capacity at regency and subregency levels through education programs, equipment supply, training, enhanced fire intelligence, and communications and coordination systems. This solution is only likely to succeed when dealing with fires that are not a direct result of fire being used to resolve land-use conflicts or to seek revenge.

Table 13–2. Summary of the Economic Cost of the 1997–1998 Drought and Fires

Sector	Estimated economic losses (US$ in millions)		
	Minimum	Maximum	Mean
Agriculture			
Farm crops	2,431	2,431	2,431
Plantation crops	319	319	319
Forestry			
Timber from natural forest (logged and unlogged)	1,461	2,165	1,813
Lost growth in natural forest	287	423	355
Timber from plantations	91	91	91
Nontimber forest products	631	631	631
Flood protection	413	413	413
Erosion and siltation	1,354	1,354	1,354
Carbon sink	1,446	1,446	1,446
Health	148	148	148
Buildings and property	1	1	1
Transportation	18	49	33
Tourism	111	111	111
Fire fighting costs	11	12	12
Total	**8,723**	**9,593**	**9,158**

Interagency coordination at the national level is minimal, with several co-ordinating groups operating, sometimes independently of each other, at the individual agency level, monitoring fire activity, hotspots, and resource needs and allocation. Benefits will emerge by rationalizing these bodies to create a peak body with representation from appropriate agencies to determine policy. There has been very little attention in the past to strengthening the capacity of various groups in coordinating input to manage fire.

Transfer of policy and implementation guidelines to provincial, regency, and subregency levels is necessary. There is a need to facilitate timely fire ground intelligence flow upward from field centers through provinces to the national level. Local area representatives must have the opportunity to develop their own fire management plans, under a national policy framework, to ensure relevance of plans for their areas. Areas that require strengthening were identified and form the basis of recommendations to build a stronger fire management capacity:

- rationalization of national, provincial, and local fire management coordination;
- strengthening of the capacity to develop local fire management plans to facilitate ownership;
- decentralized fire training for local residents;
- education and publicity programs to enhance prevention programs;
- development of EWSs;
- enhanced detection capability;
- upgraded mapping;
- improved communications between fire locations, local, provincial and national centers; and
- enhanced fire research capabilities.

There is little evidence in the provinces or at the central level of a substantial institutional prevention and preparedness program to control fires that are accidental or have escaped accidentally. Following are reasons for this lack of readiness:

- inadequate structure to respond to early warnings and provide information and guidance to field operators;
- no clear ownership of communal lands, so no protection or preparedness compared with owned lands;[2]
- no formal procedures in place to eliminate or minimize the use of fire during dangerous fire periods;
- no system of permits to regulate the use of fire in dangerous periods;
- no systematic appropriate education and information process to minimize fire during dangerous periods; and
- clear need for a systematic approach to prevention commencing with a dedicated public education campaign and distribution system to ensure the message is received at the level where fire is used.

These conclusions suggest that solutions will not be found with the high-technology solutions on the ground, where the fires occur. There is a need for well-equipped, trained, and coordinated firefighters and the development of a fire management system by Indonesian agencies to fight those fires that are "socially" possible to extinguish or have accidentally escaped into areas that need to be protected.

Climate and EWS

Indonesia lies at the heart of a region that exhibits intense tropical cloudiness and plays a major role in the general circulation of the global atmosphere. Other distinguishing features of Indonesia's climate are the seasonal reversal of wind flow associated with the monsoon, the generally light winds year round, and the strong seasonality of rainfall over much of the country (Ramage 1968; Sturman and Tapper 1996; McBride 1992).

El Niño–Southern Oscillation. The greatest source of year-to-year variability in Indonesian rainfall is associated with fluctuations in the Walker circulation across the Pacific (Allan et al. 1996). These fluctuations have important implications for drought and fire in the region. In its normal mode, rainfall is relatively high and vertical motion is enhanced over Indonesia, forest fire activity is suppressed, and the modest products of burning are relatively efficiently dispersed away from the source both horizontally and vertically. During an El Niño–Southern Oscillation (ENSO) event, the intense cloud convection normally over Indonesia moves eastward into the Pacific Ocean, fire activity increases because of drought, and haze dispersion is reduced as wind and vertical dispersion drop. Twenty-six of 28 drought years in Indonesia since 1877 have been associated with an ENSO, along with all of the major fire events (ADB 1999).

ENSO events are associated with global-scale variations in sea surface temperature and pressure. Because there is a good degree of persistence and predictability in some of these parameters, this offers possibilities for statistical forecasting of seasonal rainfall at least three months in advance. Many different studies on Indonesian rainfall have confirmed this. Predictability is best for dry season rainfall and wet season onset and for the south and east of Indonesia (Hastenrath 1987).

Currently the only operational seasonal prediction scheme in Indonesia provides for 102 rainfall districts by the *Badan Meteorologi dan Geofisika* ([BMG] Meteorological and Geophysical Agency). The information derived from the data suggests that the forecasts can reasonably predict wet season rainfall and wet season onset but are less reliable at predicting dry season onset. They are relatively poor at predicting dry season rainfall, especially during ENSO years. The 1997–1998 drought was one of the strongest this century, but it showed many characteristics typical of ENSO-induced droughts in Indonesia. The March to May 1997 rainfall was close to or above normal across much of the north of the country, but dry conditions in the south were associated with an early monsoon retreat. By June to August, the dry conditions had expanded to the western part of the country, with the exception of northern Sumatra. The drought peaked during September to November, with rainfall returning to close-to-normal from December 1997 to February 1998, except for pockets of East Kalimantan, Sulawesi, and Nusa Tenggara.

Horizontal Air Motion and Haze Transport. The most significant large-scale influence on horizontal air motion and haze transport in the region is the position of the intertropical convergence zone (ITCZ). When the ITCZ is well north of Indonesia, the haze transport in the trade winds has a strong north–south component in it. This was the case during September and early October 1997, when haze from fires in West and South Kalimantan and east-central Sumatra was transported north over Singapore and Peninsular Malaysia. As the ITCZ moved south in October, the transport had more of a zonal component, and most haze was moved out into the Indian Ocean. When fires and haze reappeared, particularly in East Kalimantan between March and April 1998, the ITCZ was located across Borneo. The light and variable winds associated with the ITCZ resulted in relatively localized haze impacts (ADB 1999).

Climate Monitoring and Modeling. The ability of Indonesia to monitor its climate in a timely and efficient manner is at least as important as the development of a climate modeling capability. Development of current drought indices and fire hazard ratings require up-to-date information. Haze monitoring and prediction (transport and dispersion modeling) also require good knowledge of the current state of the atmosphere. Indeed, a high-quality database is essential to any further development of climate prediction models. The best advances in climate modeling are likely to occur with collaboration between interested parties, in particular between BMG, the Agency for the Assessment and Application of Technology, and the National Space Agency. It is important that BMG be involved in these activities.

EWS. The aim of an EWS is to provide a measure of the risk of fires and to communicate that information in a timely manner to central, provincial, and regency authorities and the community as a whole. Simplicity is the primary criterion for any EWS. The ENSO Index (ENSOI) would constitute a wide-area, but long-range, warning system. Rainfall deficit, however, would constitute a local, short-range warning system. Fire behavior models such as Keetch and Byram's (1968) Drought Index may be useful in the future, when ENSOI and rainfall deficit information are known. Haze warning should be based on a simple model that will complement the regional haze forecasting. Ground truthing for both fire and haze is necessary for this process to be credible and useful.

Fire in Peat Soils

Calculations on the available data confirm that peat and conversion forest fires are the major haze generators. About 80% of the haze problem is caused by burning on peat soils. This problem can be avoided by implementing appropriate land-use policies. Control of peat fires should take the form of prevention and, in particular, the permanent draining and rendering flammable of the extensive peat areas should cease (Pearce 1998; Liew et al. 1998). Clearing on peat soils, followed by draining to enable the top layer to irreversibly dry out, should be prohibited and replaced by partial drainage and utilization of forest residue as practiced by some forest plantation companies when managing their plantation operations on peat soils.

Biodiversity

Large biodiversity losses in forest ecosystems resulted from the 1997–1998 fires and, with the added impacts of previous fires, this resulted in an acceleration of degradation of globally important protected areas such as Kutai National Park in East Kalimantan. Severe damage was not only limited to natural biodiversity but also included agricultural ecosystems. Although a great deal of the vegetation burned was secondary, with depleted biodiversity, this biodiversity loss is nevertheless important. For example, a drop in the recorded numbers of rare and endangered animal species caused directly by fire has been compounded by the hunting for food, for sale, and from fear of animals whose habitats have been destroyed or who are forced into areas where people live. Some of the animals are dangerous and people fear them, so they kill them. Extensive fire damage to the peat soils of swamp forest ecosystems is also expected to accelerate the changes brought about by drainage works and to drastically alter the role of this ecosystem in water storage to sustain regional forest, agricultural, and aquatic ecosystems.

In Kalimantan, Sumatra, and Papua, a particularly dangerous ecological trend is the degradation of large areas of peat soils through fire. Fire adversely affected the marine environment and its biological resources by means of increased sediment from burned water catchments following a period of heavy rain. This effect resulted in a reduction of primary aquatic productivity through light suppression and imposed stress on filter feeding organisms. This primary productivity decline led to reduced growth in aquatic organisms dependent on solar energy. The slower growth was caused by a reduction of solar energy from smoke haze during the fires. The haze also reduced solar radiation and so reduced the productivity of all species with food chain links to the mangrove ecosystem.

A substantial area of Indonesia's secondary forest has been damaged by fire on more than one occasion, thus leading to widespread forest fragmentation. This fact needs to be encompassed in approaches to forest biodiversity management and should also affect considerations for ecosystem rehabilitation or restoration where appropriate. Fire has been added to the list of development-associated factors that are subverting indigenous cultures. National interests are better served by supporting traditional communities to maintain their long-established resource management practices, where they are consistent with the objective of sustainable management of biodiversity.

Policy Initiatives for Drought and Fire Management

Policy Reform

Indonesia is in a period of substantial transformation. Many of the basic foundations of the New Order continue to come under scrutiny during the process of reform. The directions of this reform process are embodied in the 12 Acts of Parliament passed in the Indonesian Parliament session held November 10–13, 1998. Out of this process, two fundamental directions are discernible and were supported by enabling legislation in the government presided over by ex-President Abdurrahman Wahid. Policies have thus been in place at the highest level and have been pursued to accomplish the following objectives:

- provide greater opportunities to small- and medium-sized enterprises, to local communities, and to cooperatives (see Chapter 4); and
- transfer far greater functional and budgetary authority to the provinces and regencies in the use of natural resources (see Chapter 15).

The policy interventions discussed below focus on those technical and institutional aspects related to improved land use, fire prevention, and management. The issues that are addressed are major problems, which, if they were dealt with effectively, would significantly reduce the occurrence and spread of fires in Indonesia along with a majority of the smoke and haze. These policies are discussed under four headings:

- Land-use zoning and management for effective fire prevention;
- Land clearance for conversion to cultivation;
- Drought and fire information systems; and
- Institutional strengthening: development of local capacities.

Land-Use Zoning and Management for Effective Fire Prevention

Spatial planning and land-use zoning are critical issues, especially at the provincial and regency levels. By law, all provinces are required to have well-developed and fully agreed upon *Rencana Tata Ruang Wilayah Propinsi* ([RTRWPs] provincial spatial plans). On the basis of these plans, land-use identification and land-use zoning are supposed to be established. The evidence is overwhelming that these plans have not yet been completed and agreed on. Neither their quality, reliability, nor transparency can be assured. They often differ in their classification of land from the older functional forest plans, which are still relied on by the MoF. Many of these RTRWPs are also subject to local political manipulation or are simply ignored in the allocation of access to provincial land. Efforts should be made to provide the capacity and facilities to complete RTRWPs as a matter of high priority so that these plans can be used for reliable local land zoning, use, and management.

All peat soils should be identified and delineated within each province and incorporated into the land-use plans because of (a) the considerable risk of fire posed by these soils, which are predisposed to clearing and draining, and (b) the capacity to generate harmful haze and smoke. Peat soils should be subject to special regulations on land clearing. Burning of any kind, including managed burning, should be strictly prohibited.

Efforts should be made immediately to rehabilitate the hundreds of thousands of hectares of land on peat soils that were cleared at former President Soeharto's insistence for irrigated rice planting in Kalimantan, commonly referred to as the "Million Hectare Grand Scheme." Careful attention needs to be given to the location and production capacities of all pulp mills in order to (a) develop appropriate and realistic capacities in relation to future resource supply and (b) to locate the mills in areas that are both environmentally and economically sound with respect to their locations, as well as their fiber resource requirements.

Land Clearance for Conversion to Cultivation

All licensing processes should be simplified and set out in a consistent set of standard procedures for timber and agricultural plantations and transmigration schemes. All *izin pemanfaatan kayu* ([IPKs] wood utilization permits), licenses for clearing timber on governmentally identified lands for conversion, should be presented for auction at the provincial level. These local auctions would need to occur before the "transfer" of the forestland is carried out for other uses, such as oil palm production. The proceeds from these auctions should be placed in a Provincial Fire Prevention Fund. Thus, land clearance would contribute to fire prevention. All those who are awarded IPKs or those awarded land for plantation or other clearance should be required to post a substantial "Responsible Land Clearance Bond," with the provincial government guaranteeing their compliance with correct methods of land clearance.

Given Indonesia's unique position with enormous possibilities to sequester carbon dioxide by strategic timber plantations on areas covered in *Imperata cylindrica* grassland, it is critically important that Indonesia undertake a high-level assessment of all possibilities for emissions trading. The rehabilitation of the grasslands with a productive plantation crop and a positive market outlook would reduce the pressure on the clearing and burning of peat soil areas for conversion to agriculture and forest plantations.

Drought and Fire Information Systems

BMG is a national resource whose information management capacities need to be maintained and extended to provide weather forecasts as an essential part of a national EWS. BMG should have reliable electronic communication with its weather stations and with all Provincial Fire Management Centers in all provinces. BMG should maintain a continually updated website for national and regional forecasting. Indonesia should have a network of Provincial Fire Management Centers with computer facilities able to access and analyze weather and fire information derived from both national and international sources.

Each province should maintain a "Provincial Fire Danger Index" and regularly inform the general public of fire danger conditions. These Provincial Fire Management Centers, as strategic headquarters during periods of fire, should have the communication capacities to pinpoint local fires and to communicate effectively with its local fire brigades.

Institutional Strengthening: Development of Local Capacities

In conjunction with each province's RTRWP, a "Provincial Fire Prevention and Suppression Plan" should be designed to suit the distinctive characteristics of the province. Issues of coordination among national agencies (e.g., who, when, how) should be clearly defined in this plan. A National Fire Research and Development Center should be established and research should be conducted into the nature of fire and haze in different parts of Indonesia. This research should be used to assist provinces in preparing their fire prevention and suppression plans.

Strengthening of the enforcement of forestry rules at the provincial and regency levels to enhance forest fire prevention and to provide the key coordinators for fire suppression would be of value. There is a need to increase the number of trained forest protection personnel and to upgrade systematically in each province the capacities of the entire service including the forest authority at the regency level and Forestry State-Owned Enterprises (see Chapter 9).

A training program is needed at the national level to train the trainers in fire preparedness and fire prevention. These trainers should then be sent to the provinces to train local populations in the necessary techniques and to carry out simulated fire-fighting operations as training exercises in different provincial localities. Because community awareness and willingness to participate in fire prevention, mitigation, and suppression is essential to an effective management program, a nationwide community awareness program should be initiated immediately. Some support funds to initiate this program could come from a regency based grant provided by the Government of Indonesia (GOI).

For effective fire prevention and suppression, clear and well-developed provincial-level planning, training, and strategic operations are required. There are considerable differences between Indonesia's provinces in their natural and human environments. Some have more forests than others, some have larger areas of peat soils, others have more savannah and grasslands, and yet others have large deposits of coal. Some provinces have a higher proportion of timber concessions or timber estates, while others have a greater proportion of smallholder agriculture or plantations. There can be no one fire prevention and suppression plan to fit all the needs of Indonesia's diverse provinces.

The first need is for more directed research into the nature of fires in different forest types and different parts of the country. For example, a fire in an Acacia plantation poses different problems to a Dipterocarp forest fire; coal fires require different methods of suppression from those used in *Imperata cylindrica* or on peat soils. A wild bush fire in West Timor or in Papua can be very different from a plantation fire in Jambi. It is only on the basis of this research that one can begin to design provincial plans with different local emphases. The design of provincial fire prevention plans is a high priority. This has even more significance now that decentralization and local autonomy are under way in Indonesia.

The second need is for a training program in fire prevention and suppression. Such a training program would require several stages. At the national level, there would need to be a high-quality, intensive training program to train the trainers in fire preparedness and in fire-fighting techniques. Once trained, these trainers would need to be sent to different provinces to conduct local-level training schools and to carry out, in coordination with provincial-level agencies, simulated fire-fighting operations in different localities. In large provinces with diverse ecosystems, the training would require a substantial commitment. One model for this kind of training, developed through Bappenas, is that of the "field schools for integrated pest management." Such schools were able to transfer knowledge rapidly from the national to the village level.

Conclusion

The implementation of the proposed policy reforms for fire management in Indonesia will require a phased approach involving three major stages. The first stage is to prepare an investment accepted at both the central and provincial levels and incorporated into an Integrated Action Plan for Fire Management in Indonesia. The second stage is dependent on the GOI's ensuring that the necessary policy changes and improvements are in place with appropriate regulations universally adopted at the provincial and regency levels. There were provincial issues associated with the 1997–1998 fires that will need careful management under the decentralization policy to ensure comparability across the major fire-prone areas in the affected provinces in Sumatra and Kalimantan. The third stage is to have the components of any strategy implemented by promoting its value and effectiveness to donor agencies and the GOI so that feasibility studies can be prepared for a number of projects that need to be undertaken as part of ensuring that any strategy is implemented.

We proposed that the GOI further develop an integrated action plan for forest fire management to accomplish the following tasks:

- establish the necessary policies, legislation standards, and guidelines at the national and provincial levels;
- strengthen the coordinated response to fire prevention at the central, provincial, and regency levels;
- develop strong coordinated national and provincial EWSs;
- strengthen the coordinated response to fire suppression at the central, provincial, and regency levels;
- develop a coordinated and integrated approach to the maintenance of biodiversity, including the economic rehabilitation and restoration of degraded lands caused by fire in selected high-priority or protected areas; and
- enhance the institutional capacity and capability of the fire management organizations at the provincial and central levels.

Although the difficulty in implementing such a plan for Indonesia is clear, so is the magnitude of the losses that can be expected to result from fire during the next El Niño event without such action.

Acknowledgments

This chapter is based on work undertaken as part of the Planning for Fire Prevention and Drought Management Project for the Asian Development Bank and GOI during 1998–1999.

Endnotes

1. Many fires were set as a tool in land-use and tenure disputes. Many of these fires were reset after being extinguished (ADB 1999).

2. Colfer has found that in several parts of Kalimantan fire danger increased significantly in areas where there were unclear boundaries between and disagreements over community territories. See, for instance, Dennis et al. (2001).

References

ADB (Asian Development Bank). 1999. *Planning for Fire Prevention and Drought Management Project*. Final report. Jakarta, Indonesia: Asian Development Bank.

Allan, R., G. Beard, A. Close, A. Herczeg, P. Jones, and H. Simpson. 1996. *Mean Sea Level Pressure Indices of the El-Niño-Southern Oscillation: Relevance to Stream Discharge in Southeastern Australia.* CSIRO Division of Water Resources report 96/1. Canberra, Australia: CSIRO.

Barber, C.V., and J. Schweithelm. 2000. *Trial by Fire. Forest Fires and Forestry Policy in Indonesia's Era of Crises and Reform.* Washington, DC: World Resources Institute Forest Frontiers Initiative in collaboration with WWF-Indonesia and Telapak Indonesia Foundation.

Dennis, R., C.J.P. Colfer, and A. Puntodewo. 2001. Forest cover change analysis as a proxy: Sustainability assessment using remote sensing and GIS in West Kalimantan, Indonesia. In *People Managing Forests: The Links Between Human Well-Being and Sustainability,* edited by C.J.P. Colfer and Y. Byron. Washington, DC: Resources for the Future.

Dinas Pertanian Tanaman Pangan Propinsi Kalimantan Timur. 1998. *Laporan Keadaan Tanaman Pangan Th. 1997 dan Perkiraan Th. 1998 serta Upaya Antisipasi Kemarau.* Samarinda, East Kalimantan Timur, Indonesia: Dinas Pertanian Tanaman Pangan Propinsi Kalimantan Timur.

Hastenrath, S. 1987. Predictability of Java monsoon anomalies: A case study. *Journal of Climate and Applied Meteorology* 26:133–41.

Keetch, J.J., and G.M. Byram. 1968. *A Drought Index for Forest Fire Control. U.S. Department of Agriculture (USDA), Forest Service research paper SE-38, Southeastern Forest Experiment Station.* Asheville, NC: USDA Forest Service.

Liew, S.C., O.K. Lim, L.K. Kwoh, and H. Lim. 1998. A Study of the 1997 Forest Fires in Southeast Asia Using SPOT Quicklook Mosaics. Paper presented at the International Geoscience and Remote Sensing Symposium. July 6–10. Seattle, WA.

Makarim, N., Y.A. Arbai, A. Deddy, and M. Brady. 1998. Assessment of the 1997 land and forest fires in Indonesia: National Coordination. *International Forest Fire News* January (18):4–12.

McBride, J. 1992. *The Meteorology of Indonesia and the Maritime Continent, Extended Abstracts.* Fourth International Symposium on Equatorial Observations over Indonesia, November 10–11, 1992. Jakarta, Indonesia.

Nabet, E., SPOT ASIA Ptc Ltd. 1998. Personal communication with the authors, June 1998.

National Development Planning Agency. 1993. *Biodiversity Action Plan for Indonesia.* Jakarta, Indonesia: National Development Planning Agency.

National Forest Inventory of Indonesia. 1996. *Final Forest Resources Statistics Report.* Jakarta, Indonesia: Directorate General of Forest Inventory and Land Use Planning, Ministry of Forestry, Government of Indonesia.

NSWRFS (New South Wales Rural Fire Service). 1997. *Indonesian Fire Emergency.* Report to AusAID and NSWRFS. October. Jakarta, Indonesia.

Pearce, F. 1998. Playing with fire. *New Scientist* 157(2126):36–8.

Ramage, C. 1968. Role of a tropical "maritime continent" in the atmospheric circulation. *Monthly Weather Review* 96:365–9.

Reily, J. 1999. Personal communication with the authors, July 1999.

Soedarmo. 1998. *Forest Fire in Indonesia, Condition, Causes, Impacts, and Future Programs.* Unpublished report. October. Jakarta, Indonesia: State Ministry of Environment, Republic of Indonesia, and United Nations Development Programme.

State Ministry of Environment, Republic of Indonesia, and United Nations Development Programme. 1998. *Forest and land Fires in Indonesia: Impacts, Factors, and Evaluation* (Volume 1). Jakarta, Indonesia: State Ministry of Environment.

Sturman, A., and N. Tapper. 1996. *The Weather and Climate of Australia and New Zealand,* First edition. Melbourne: Oxford University Press.

CHAPTER FOURTEEN

Ten Propositions to Explain Kalimantan's Fires

Carol J. Pierce Colfer

I n 1997–1998, an estimated 5.2 million ha of East Kalimantan went up
in smoke (Hoffman et al. 1999).[1] This area was 2 million ha more than
the area that burned in the 1982–1983 fires (Mayer 1996; Sakuntaladewi
and Amblani 1989). Both burns were related to the El Niño–Southern Oscillation (ENSO) events. There is also evidence that disastrous burns like those
in 1982–1983 and in 1997–1998 degrade the landscape in such a way that
future fires are liable to occur again and are likely to be more severe (King
1996; Mori 2000; Nepstad et al. 1999; Nicolas and Beebe 1999).

Because of this likelihood that Kalimantan (and perhaps increasingly other
areas)[2] will again be vulnerable to widespread fire, a better understanding of
both proximate and underlying causes of the 1997–1998 fires is critical. This
research is based on the assumptions that effective solutions to the fire problem cannot be devised unless they are appropriate to both the proximate and
underlying causes and that fire causes vary by location. The Center for International Forestry Research (CIFOR) has been examining this issue at the
macro level (see Chapter 13), but the development of appropriate solutions

This research is part of a multiyear, multiparty project to document the underlying causes of
fires in Indonesia. The fieldwork on which this chapter is based was supported by CIFOR and
the U.S. Forest Service. Comparable research is being conducted in three sites in West Kalimantan
and in four sites in Sumatra.

and preventive measures also depends on an understanding of the specific or particular causes behind the fires (Vayda 1999; Vayda and Broad 1999).

In search of such micro level understanding, I conducted a month's field research in East Kalimantan in July and August 1999. This area was selected because of my long-term research experience there and the probability that I might get more honest responses to sensitive questions about fire from people who trusted me. I interviewed people in Kenyah (an indigenous Dayak group) communities where I have worked periodically since 1979, and I interviewed newcomers to the area, including community members and government and company officials. Surveys on the changes that have occurred and the impacts of the fires on people's lives were also conducted (Colfer Forthcoming; Colfer et al. 2000). I visited four major areas in Kalimantan's interior and two more near Samarinda—all in areas seriously affected by the fires (see Annex 14–1).

In the past, fires have been consistently blamed on the activities of the small farmers who normally burn in August or September before planting their upland rice fields—regardless of the month of fire occurrence. This time, satellite imagery made it clear at the time of the burning that the fires tended to occur in and around plantation areas (Suyanto 2000; Suyanto and Ruchiat 2000; Dennis 1999; Stolle and Tomich 1999). The official explanation from government (and sometimes industry) evolved to one that emphasizes the role of extreme drought in causing the fires. I heard the same government refrain, as Harwell (2000) did, that fires require (a) dry fuel, (b) oxygen, and (c) a spark. The technical accuracy of this explanation was confirmed by forest fire experts (Oliver and Larson 1990; White 1999). Like Harwell, I heard the same addendum, less widely held outside Kalimantan, that tree limbs rubbing together sometimes provide the required spark. The fires are also sometimes blamed on the coal seams that occur in certain parts of East Kalimantan and burn underground normally. There is disagreement among experts on the relative importance in tropical forests of the two factors most subject to direct manipulation: the availability of fuel and the spark (Sayer et al. 2001).

I am more inclined to share Harwell's (2000, 11) view that this disaster is more humanmade than natural (Byron and Shepherd 1998; Stolle and Tomich 1999). Harwell said,

> "Disaster"…in the sense of social impact, is not "natural" but distinctly humanmade. Hewitt (1995) suggests we read this increasing vulnerability of populations to climatic extremes….as a consequence of development initiatives which have radically restructured patterns of resource access and social relations.

Striking, human-induced changes have definitely occurred in Kalimantan over the past 20 to 30 years that have made the environment more sensitive to fire (Mackie 1984, Leighton and Wirawan 1986). One fundamental change is simply in the overall humidity. Whereas even 20 years ago the island was primarily humid tropical rain forest, now only small areas of that habitat remain (Brookfield et al. 1995). There has been a continual process of conversion, which is particularly notable in the areas that burned, from humid tropical rain forest to logged (and degraded) tropical rain forest to industrial timber plantations, oil palm, and other cash crop plantations or transmigration locations (see Potter and Lee 1998a,b). Each change has decreased the humidity—not the rainfall, but the humidity—in comparison with the previous ground cover.[3]

Accompanying these biophysical changes has been the introduction of major new actors in Kalimantan's forests. Whereas in the past the forests were inhabited only by local ethnic groups (various groups of Dayaks and Malays), a whole raft of new stakeholders has emerged such as logging companies, industrial timber plantation companies, various kinds of cash crop plantations (e.g., oil palm, coconut, cacao, rubber), and conservation agencies—each supported by governmental officials of various stripes. These new activities are, by and large, supported by explicit governmental policy initiatives.

There have also been dramatic demographic changes. The influx of official and spontaneous transmigrants has resulted in a clear shift in the island's ethnic composition and in its population density. Whereas East Kalimantan (indeed all of Borneo) has always been marked by ethnic diversity, centuries of cohabitation produced some complementarity among local ethnic groups in resource use. Informal agreements evolved into customs that reduced conflict between neighboring groups.[4] In interactions with newcomers from other islands, such informal agreements and customs have yet to be worked out. Resource use patterns, values, and use of fire differ among the ethnic groups and have led to conflict.

From a purely local perspective, there has been a clear increase in insecurity about land tenure and in perceptions of inequity (for the importance of these issues for human well-being, see Wollenberg and Colfer 1996; CIFOR 1999). Whereas in the past local people were blissfully unaware (or at least unconcerned) about their lack of formal, legal rights to the resources they traditionally considered their own, they are now painfully aware that they can be booted out of the places they have called home without recourse. They are also increasingly aware of the benefits that outsiders have reaped from the forest they considered their own. This is partially a function of increasing educational levels and improved communication with the outside world and partially a function of increasing competition from outsiders for Kalimantan's resources.

Some have wondered if governmental repression tended to increase or decrease the prevalence of forest fires. In Kalimantan, there has rarely been direct repression, in the sense of harsh penalties or governmental retribution for acts like disobeying laws, engaging in conflicts, or starting fires. Instead repression has taken the form of gradual, usually sugar-coated, usurpation of traditional rights (through granting of timber concessions, transmigration programs, plantations, and so forth). In this sense, governmental "repression" has contributed to alienation and levels of conflict that can lead to purposeful forest destruction. Severe law enforcement and governmental retribution have been rare in Kalimantan, and I know of no cases where such repression has had a direct influence in reducing forest fires.

Finally, local people's traditional mechanisms for dealing with fire (a normal agricultural tool) evolved in a very humid context. It may be that the mechanisms for fire control that worked very well in humid tropical rain forest (Aspiannur and Abberger 1999; Colfer et al. 2001; Colfer et al. 2000) are inadequate for dealing with this much drier environment. Indeed, newcomers to Kalimantan may have less experience dealing with fire as an agricultural tool, and thus less knowledge about how to control it.

Ten Propositions

In this chapter, I suggest 10 (sometimes related) propositions about fire causes in Kalimantan. For each proposition I provide evidence, including examples of the kinds of accusations heard in the field that lend credence to the proposition. I stress that the accusations are in no way substantiated, though they are all possible causes of fire. Several actual burning cases from other areas, where the facts are known, are also described. The propositions have been further categorized to correspond to the framework suggested by CIFOR's fire team: fire as a weapon, fire as a tool, and fire caused by carelessness. Because the propositions have emerged in an inductive manner, they may subsequently be further whittled as we compare these findings with those from other areas where fire has been a problem (Suyanto 2000; Suyanto and Ruchiat 2000; Vayda and Broad 1999). Although several propositions follow from new interactions among people (numbers 4–9), I have separated them because their importance differs in certain locations, thus affecting the fireproneness of respective sites. These six propositions also represent different motivations, even though they are ultimately attributable, in many cases, to the same phenomenon (the addition of new stakeholders). The first three propositions pertain to underlying conditions that prevailed at the time of the fires in Kalimantan and affect fire danger—one biophysical, one social, and one political.

1. As the prevailing ground cover becomes drier, fire danger increases.

Much of Kalimantan has been converted from humid tropical rain forest to an environment that is significantly drier than it was previously. The governmental refrain explaining fires (i.e., dry fuel, oxygen, a spark) is pertinent to this proposition. There is more dry fuel for fires now than there was when

Kalimantan was covered in primary forest. This condition contributes to but does not explain the fires (dry conditions are necessary but not sufficient for fires to occur).

2. Insofar as actors are not used to combating large-scale wildfire, the danger of fire damage increases.

When people's traditional systems evolved in very humid contexts, their concern about wildfire is likely to be less than among people used to dealing with very dry (or windy) conditions. The many accusations relating to cooking fires left unattended and cigarettes thrown out the window in conditions of high fire danger support this, as do similar observations about fire causes in West Kalimantan in 1992–1993. To examine these cases in detail, see Luttrell (1994) and Vayda and Broad (1999),

The "readiness" of most parties to combat fire was also minimal in East Kalimantan, with the government apparently playing no local role at all.[5] In two Dayak communities the people, used to a situation where they only expected to control the fires they set, had little recourse when walls of fire approached them from afar.[6] They battled the fires with pesticide sprayers (access to water was dependent on rivers that were nearly dry), hoes, sticks, and soil. They made fire breaks around their village and sometimes around tree crops with bush knives and hoes. The logging companies helped where they could[7] with water tankers and heavy equipment near roads, but their capacity was also limited. They had a reduced workforce due to the financial crisis and a 200,000-ha concession to try (unsuccessfully) to protect.

One functioning 15-year-old industrial timber plantation with a comparatively good reputation (probably more interested in combating fire than a newly clearing plantation) reported having had the following fire equipment for its more than 50,000-ha concession: 3 water tankers, 12 portable water tanks, 6 high-pressure pumps, 4 bulldozers, 1 grader, 1 pickup truck, 10 motorcycles, 8 fire towers, 15 radio communication units, and 11 water storage areas. They also said they had a fire protection committee of 30 people, aided by both the company's employees and a steady supply of workers from the four transmigration areas within the plantation. Yet, an estimated 90% of the plantation burned to the ground. Fire was reported as coming from every direction during the height of the crisis.

Some of this lack of readiness was due to the history of a more humid environment. In the United States, where fire danger has been recognized as a problem in forested areas for decades, effective responses have evolved with governmental support. Firefighters can be quickly organized, including hiring of short-term labor (often students) and the mobilization of the National Guard (a U.S.-based arm of the military).

3. Insofar as the government acts in an uncoordinated and corrupt fashion about issues relating to land use, fire danger increases.

In East Kalimantan, there is uncertainty about the appropriate uses of the land. Different ministries are reportedly maneuvering to divide East Kalimantan. Certain parties are interested in converting large areas to oil palm plantations. In the past there has been serious pressure from Jakarta to convert to industrial timber plantations as well. However, timber concessions still function, implying and requiring a very different kind of ground cover, and National Parks officially dot the East Kalimantan landscape. Meanwhile, local people have continued to practice swidden agriculture, gradually adapting it to include tree crops. Although in the past there has been competition among governmental agencies about land use, now there appears to be something of a policy vacuum relating to land use in East Kalimantan. One timber official said in 1999 that they were living under "the law of the jungle." The same phrase continues to be used in describing field conditions in East Kalimantan in 2001, with the addendum that decentralization, as practiced, seems to be exacerbating the problems.

My view is that converting East Kalimantan's lowland Dipterocarp forests to plantations is a travesty. But this is a decision for the Indonesian people. The level of corruption that has characterized the Indonesian bureaucracy (and field observations suggest that it continues, perhaps even more rampantly than before *Reformasi*, the current reform movement) has adverse effects on rational decisionmaking about land use in the province (see Dudley [2000] for a system dynamics view of such corruption). When officials of various ranks can be bought, they are likely to become proponents of the views of the parties with the most money. This is highly unlikely to be the local communities whose livelihoods depend on these resources—despite the ministry's recent decision that the forests are now for the people.

In a 1999 meeting of an oil palm plantation company, several local communities, and the local government, the local government came out strongly in support of the proposed oil palm expansion. Local people's concerns about their rights to their land and resources were met with the loaded question, "Do you want rights to land or modernity?" Participants in the meeting reported it as reminiscent of a Golkar political campaign from the New Order, in favor of oil palm expansion. Foreign experts in Samarinda and in Pontianak have also reported strong support for oil palm expansion from higher-level local officials. Informal discussions with officials and others suggest that this support is, in some cases, bought by the companies.

The same issue of corruption affects the value of potential sanctions against burning. When everyone believes that officials can be bought, and officials themselves accept this as a normal supplement to their low salaries, the possibility of getting a fair hearing in court cases (including those related to fire) is also considered minimal. I heard of only one example, involving an oil palm plantation in conflict with the local timber concession, in which sanctions were brought against those who were believed to have set fires. Sanctions, in the current climate, are likely to be less effective than efforts to enhance social capital, resolve the conflicts deriving from land disputes, and mount fire danger awareness campaigns. Effective sanctions can be another important deterrent, especially in areas where there are many different kinds of actors.

The next two propositions (numbers 4 and 5) pertain to issues of social conflict (fire as weapon).[8]

4. As the number of new, external actors increases, so does the likelihood that fire will be used as a weapon.

The areas visited in this study fell into four categories (with the last coming from Gonner's 1999 study) along this continuum, each considered more likely to involve the use of fire as a weapon:

- a small cluster of villages with two ethnic groups who had lived in close proximity within a timber concession for decades, with only occasional mention of fire as a weapon;
- an area with four ethnic groups living in a transmigration site within an established industrial timber plantation, adjacent to an established timber company, with an intermediate level of suspicion about purposeful fire;
- an area where there were at least four major ethnic groups living in a transmigration area, a number of indigenous communities of various ethnicity nearby, a new oil palm plantation, and an established industrial timber plantation and logging company with a great deal of suspicion about purposeful fires; and
- in Gonner's (1999) description, significant conflicts between communities[9] and industrial tree and oil palm plantations had occurred for several years when the drought came. Additionally two new transmigration settlements were recently opened. There was a series of comparatively well-documented fires purposely set (see Harwell [2000] for a similar account).

In some ways, this proposition subsumes important elements in the next four propositions. I have kept them separate because the importance of the respective motivations varies from site to site.

5. As the diversity of value systems and natural resource use patterns increases, so does the likelihood that fire will be used as a weapon.

In one transmigration area, the Javanese and Kenyah live side by side with people from Nusa Tenggara Timur. Each ethnic group has negative stereotypes about the others, and there were many interethnic accusations about starting the fires. The Kenyah, for instance, argued that the other ethnic groups set fires all the time, burning grasses (*Imperata cylindrica*) throughout the year. The Javanese considered the other ethnic groups to be poor farmers because they were unwilling to burn and then hoe such invasive grasses. The people from Nusa Tenggara Timur regularly burned the grass to encourage the growth of young shoots for their cattle. The Kenyah themselves burned Imperata growing under their coconut and cacao orchards, to protect them from wildfire. The traditional fire-control mechanisms of each group tend to be more difficult to implement when others sharing the knowledge of those systems are interspersed with ethnic groups characterized by different systems and knowledge of fire control and use.

The next two propositions (numbers 6 and 7) pertain to psychological issues that may increase the chances of fire used as a weapon.

6. As perceptions of inequity or injustice increase (and a consequent interest in revenge emerges), so does the use of fire as a weapon.

In a Kenyah village with comparatively little interethnic conflict or outsider involvement, the residents maintained that the Kutai (both indigenous groups) had purposely burned a rubber garden that the Kenyah had managed to protect until May 1998. They suspected the Kutai of jealousy because all the Kutai gardens had already burned; they argued that Kutai hunters had made a cooking fire while looking for turtles and purposely let it burn Imperata adjacent to the Kenyah rubber gardens.

A Kenyah man in the transmigration area reported his coconut and cacao orchard purposely burned, with a group of people from Nusa Tenggara Timur as the suspects. The Kenyah man had repeatedly caught people stealing from his orchard during the monetary crisis and brought them to the village headman or the police who required an apology of eight and put four in jail. The perceived motivation is explained as jealousy that the Kenyah's orchard remained when theirs had already burned, tinged with revenge.

Revenge was also considered the motivation when a timber company was accused of having set fire to a new oil palm plantation. The plantation was clearing land on the timber company's concession without permission. Gonner (1999, 16) reported similar stories from his sites:

> ...those villagers who had not yet been compensated [by another oil palm plantation] became more and more envious about their neighbours' newly bought TVs and motor cycles.... Enhanced by the drought and the beginning of the economic crisis the social situation became increasingly tense and unstable, while financial problems were also getting worse. When the first fires (maybe even unintentionally caused by the company) destroyed people's gardens the trigger was pulled, and a vicious circle started. Although the biggest fires were either directly or indirectly related to the company's land clearing activities, the social conflicts (often induced by the compensation system) caused many smaller forest fires....it remains speculative, whether these "social fires" would have happened without the presence of the oil palm company.

In several locations, disgruntled workers, unhappy with their treatment by a logging or plantation company, were thought to have started fires in the timber concession or plantation.

7. As perceptions of insecurity of access to resources increases, so does the use of fire as a weapon.

People from an indigenous village with whom an oil palm plantation had clashed over land were accused of setting the plantation ablaze in retribution. Four hundred villagers from nine villages burned down four buildings belonging to an oil palm plantation that had taken over considerable amounts of local land in an unspecified location in East Kalimantan in December 1998 (Gonner 1999). In West Kalimantan, in April 1996, a whole village burned down the base camp of a timber concessionaire that had cut the timber from an area the community had been saving for its children (Colfer et al. 2001).

The next proposition (number 8) relates to fires caused by carelessness.

8. As social capital decreases, the danger of fires caused by carelessness increases.

People who are not closely bound by feelings of respect, affection, and trust to their neighbors are likely to take less care with fire than are those who are enmeshed in such systems. In one Kenyah village, the ties that bind people with neighboring fields are typically strong enough to withstand the losses occasionally incurred from wildfire due to carelessness.[10] In the transmigration area, neighbors, having little respect for each other, have little motivation to take extra precautions to prevent fires from spreading (particularly in the absence of more formal sanctions).

The last two propositions (numbers 9 and 10) relate to the undesirable use of fire as a tool when there are no effective sanctions against burning that adversely affects others.

9. As unfulfilled subsistence needs increase, potentially uncontrollable uses of fire as a tool may increase.

In one Kutai village, people are believed to use fire to encourage the regrowth of young shoots of Imperata to draw deer that are then caught in snares for sale (as in the area Gonner [1999] studied). During the drought when the rice harvest had failed, people may have burned in conditions they would otherwise have eschewed because of the need for a source of income and food. Some have accused the Kenyah of burning fields, either to plant their rice fields in August 1997 or subsequent crops in early 1998 (though the Kenyah vehemently deny this).[11]

10. As possibilities for financial gain from potentially uncontrollable uses of fire increase, fire danger increases.

Many accused the oil palm plantation of intentionally burning its own fields as an inexpensive land-clearing method (either directly or via their subcontractors; this interpretation is widely reported in the literature as well; see Chapters 10 and 13 of this book). This accusation was supported to some extent by a criminal court case brought against the oil palm plantation, which reportedly had to pay the court costs and reimburse farmers who had replanted trees supplied by the timber company near roads. That they did not have to reimburse the timber company for burned forest (reportedly because of insufficient evidence of culpability) was widely viewed as a result of illegal payments made by the company to government officials involved in the decision.

Harwell (2000) found a similar suspicion among the indigenous people living near the Mahakam lakes, who believed the oil palm plantation owners had purposely burned their lands as a means of acquiring lands (newly cleared by fire and thus without the previous value) the people had refused to sell to the company. If these interpretations are correct, the desire to burn will decrease as forest conversion progresses, and the same parties then need to protect their mature plantations from fire. If mass conversion of Kalimantan's forests to oil palm is ultimately the government's and the people's decision, it will imply very different levels of fire danger and a consequent improved level of fire-fighting readiness than have been the case in the past.

Conclusion

These 10 propositions are offered as a modest starting point to contribute to the development of a typology of causes of fires in Kalimantan and to complement the national-level data more typically collected. Table 14–1 provides scores for each study site along the continua stipulated by the propositions. The higher the number, the more accurate and intense the relevance of the proposition in that context (from 1 = not too important to 3 = very important).

Although all of the areas visited in this study were affected by the fires of 1997–1998, in disastrous ways, the likelihood of fires starting in a given village varies. The average scores listed in the table serve as an index, showing the likelihood of fires starting in a given village.[12] It seems probable that this likelihood will increase as we move from left to right in the table. Fires, then, would be most likely to start in Long Tutung (LT) and least likely to start in Long Umit (LU) and Lepo' Mading (LM), with Long Apui (LA) nearly as unlikely a source of fire. More refined attention to specific causes in specific locations should allow the development of focused fire management strategies—if these propositions prove relevant to other fireprone regions.

Table 14–1. Scores on Factors Affecting Fire Danger in Research Sites

Propositions	Villages					
	LU	LM	LA	LB	BB	LT
1. Environment becoming drier (as a result of human activity)	3	3	3	3	3	3
2. Actors not used to combating large-scale wildfire	2	2	2	2	3	3
3. Government acting in an uncoordinated and corrupt fashion	3	3	3	3	3	3
4. Number of new, external actors	1	1	1	2	2	3
5. Diversity of value systems and natural resource use patterns	1	1	1	2	2	3
6. Perceptions of inequity and injustice (revenge)	2	1	2	2	2	3
7. Perceptions of insecurity of access to resources (no stake)	2	2	2	2	2	3
8. Internal suspicion and lack of respect among people (low social capital)	1	1	2	1	2	3
9. Unfulfilled subsistence needs linked to uncontrollable uses of fire	1	2	1	2	2	3
10. Possibilities for financial gain from potentially uncontrollable uses of fire	1	1	1	1	1	3
Average score	**1.7**	**1.7**	**1.8**	**2.0**	**2.2**	**3.0**

Notes: 1 = low, 2 = medium, 3 = high; LU = Long Umit; LM = Lepo' Mading; LA = Long Apui; LB = Lalut Bala; BB = Batu Bulan; LT = Long Tutung. Pseudonyms are used to protect privacy. See Annex 14–1 for brief descriptions of the villages.

To clarify some of the internal links among these propositions, a few possible causal chains are postulated. Historically in East Kalimantan, there has been strong political pressure to convert lands from forest to agriculture (offset by other parts of government). These pressures (particularly from transmigration and plantation agriculture) have resulted in increasing numbers of new, external actors. The increase in new actors has resulted in insecurity related to continuing access to resources (reinforced in the Kalimantan case by the political will to convert). Such pressures can easily evolve into unfulfilled subsistence needs. The increase in new actors also means a greater diversity of value systems, which can lead to perceptions of inequity and injustice.

The causal chain can go a different way as well. The introduction of new actors can occur spontaneously, with resulting insecurity of access to resources and feelings of injustice or inequity for original inhabitants and eventual unfulfilled subsistence needs. These can result at any step along the way in degradation of the environment (e.g., more fires), prompting a greater political will to convert than existed earlier.

Possibilities for financial gain from uncontrollable uses of fire are closely related to the political will to convert, each reinforcing the other. The political will to convert encourages alternative uses; alternative uses tend to degrade forestlands, encouraging policies that recognize that and attempt to "rehabilitate" such lands to make productive use of them.

A low level of social capital can occur with or without the introduction of new actors, but the introduction of new actors is likely to result in at least a short-term lowering of the level of social capital due to disagreements and misunderstandings among people not used to each other.

In sum, these issues are interrelated, all potentially contributing to the fire sensitivity that we now see in the Kalimantan context. This analysis is intended as a preliminary step in a long-term process of identifying the proximate and underlying causes of fires in Indonesia, in pursuit of the most effective steps to minimize their negative effects, both on the people and on the forests. The likelihood of another El Niño event is not disputed. Indeed, early signs of a new El Niño were reported on *CNN News* in February 2001. So there is considerable urgency for developing practical solutions to Kalimantan's fire problem.

Endnotes

1. This represents the largest part of the estimated 9.5 million ha that were burned in Indonesia that year (Suyanto 2000).

2. Anderson (1999, xix) reported that virtually no fire research has been undertaken in the Amazon. Yet by April 1998, 3.3 million ha in Roraima, Brazil's northernmost state, had burned related to the same El Niño phenomenon we are examining in Borneo, including 1.3 million ha of rain forest.

3. There is of course also the issue of global climate change (e.g., global warming) that may be influencing Kalimantan's forests in as yet uncertain ways.

4. In Long Segar, East Kalimantan, in the 1980s for instance, the Kenyah consciously left commercial rattan collection and shingle making to the Kutai from neighboring Kernyanyan. In the Danau Sentarum Wildlife Reserve in West Kalimantan, the Iban and the Melayu have long divided the resources by exploiting the forest and the lakes, respectively.

5. Byron and Shepherd (1998) pointed out that the Ministers of the Environment and of Forests strongly supported measures to control fires and rein in the perpetrators but faced such powerful opposition that their success was limited. Harwell (2000) has a more skeptical perspective on this ministerial support.

6. Local people in East Kalimantan are used to setting, controlling, and combating the small-scale fires they set. Fire has been part of their subsistence setting for millennia, and we have records documenting its periodic importance over the past century (Brookfield et al. 1995). What local people are not used to is large-scale wildfire blanketing the countryside, as happened in 1982–83 and again in 1997–98.

7. These communities were in Bob Hasan's PT Kiani Lestari concession. Its employees are human beings who could not be unaffected by the disaster unfolding around them. They did what they could to help.

8. The proposal for this research identified three fire types: fire as a tool, fire as a weapon, and accidental fire (CIFOR et al. 1998).

9. The number of ethnic groups is unspecified, but it is highly probable that there were several new ethnic groups included in the transmigration development area.

10. Although there are customary fines for setting fires that escape (without the proper

preventive measures, like making a fire break and notifying the other land owner beforehand), they are rarely either sought or levied. Technically such fires are considered purposeful. An assessment of motivation also enters into the decision by the "customary committee" to fine or not to fine.

11. My focus has been on the Kenyah, so I tend to have heard more thorough and convincing rebuttals from the Kenyah about the actions of which they have been accused—in contrast to my lesser experience with the other ethnic groups and parties involved.

12. Using an average score, as is done here, may not be justified because there has not yet been any attempt to weigh these respective factors. But this kind of analysis does provide a rough and ready means of assessing possible susceptibility to fire.

References

Anderson, A. 1999. Preface. *In Flames in the Rain Forest: Origins, Impacts and Alternatives to Amazonian Fire*, edited by D. Nepstad, A. Moreira, and A. Alencar. Brasilia, Brazil: Pilot Program to Conserve the Brazilian Rain Forest.

Aspiannur, B.U., and H.M. Abberger. 1999. *Metode Tradisional Pembersihan Lahan Pada Salah Satu Suku Dayak di Kalimantan Timur: pembukaan ladang di desa Long Sungai Barang*. Samarinda, Indonesia: Ministry of Forestry, Deutsche Gesellschaft für Technische Zusammenarbeit, and KfW (integrated Forest Fire Management Project).

Brookfield, H., L. Potter, and Y. Byron. 1995. In *In Place of the Forest: Environmental and Socio-Economic Transformation in Borneo and the Eastern Malay Peninsula*. Tokyo, Japan: United Nations University Press.

Byron, N., and G. Shepherd. 1998. Indonesia and the 1997–98 El Niño: Fire problems and long-term solutions. *Overseas Development Institute Natural Resource Perspectives* 28: 1–7.

CIFOR (Center for International Forestry Research). 1999. *CIFOR C&I Toolbox*. Bogor, Indonesia: CIFOR.

CIFOR, ICRAF, and UNESCO (Center for International Forestry Research; International Center for Research in Agroforestry; and United Nations Educational, Scientific and Cultural Organization). 1998. *Fire: The underlying causes and impacts of fires in Southeast Asia*. Draft proposal. Bogor, Indonesia: CIFOR, ICRAF, and UNESCO.

Colfer, C.J.P. Forthcoming. Fire in East Kalimantan: A panoply of practices, views and [discouraging] effects. *Borneo Research Bulletin*.

Colfer, C.J.P., R.L. Wadley, E. Harwell, and R. Prabhu. 2001. Assessing intergenerational access to resources: Using criteria and indicators. In *People Managing Forests: The Links Between Human Well-Being and Sustainability*, edited by C.J.P. Colfer and Y. Byron. Washington, DC: Resources for the Future.

Colfer, C.J.P., R. Dennis, and G. Applegate. 2000. *The Underlying Causes and Impacts of Fires in Southeast Asia. Site 8. Long Segar, East Kalimantan Province, Indonesia. Site report*. Bogor, Indonesia: CIFOR and ICRAF.

Dennis, R. 1999. *A Review of Fire Projects in Indonesia (1982–1998)*. Bogor, Indonesia: Center for International Forestry Research.

Dudley, R.G. 2000. *The Rotten Mango: The Effect of Corruption on International Development Projects. Part 1: Building a System Dynamics Basis for Examining Corruption*. Presented at the Eighteenth International Conference of the System Dynamics Society "Sustainability in the Third Millennium." August 6–10. Bergen, Norway.

Gonner, C. 1999. *Causes and Effects of Forest Fires: A Case Study from a Sub-District in East Kalimantan, Indonesia*. Paper presented at the ICRAF's methodology workshop, Environmental Services and Land Use Change: Bridging the Gap between Policy and Research in Southeast Asia. May 31–June 2. Chiang Mai, Thailand.

Harwell, E. 2000. Remote sensibilities: discourses of technology and the making of Indonesia's natural disaster, 1997–98. *Development and Change* 31:307–40.

Hewitt, K. 1995. Sustainable disasters? Perspectives and powers in the discourse of calamity. In *Power of Development*, edited by J. Crush. New York: Routledge, 115–28.

Hoffman, A.A., Hinrichs, A., and Siegert, F. 1999. *Fire Damage in East Kalimantan in 1997–98 Related to Land Use and Vegetation Classes: Satellite Radar Inventory Results and Proposal for Further Action.* Integrated Forest Fire Management–Sustainable Forest Management Project Report No. 1a. Samarinda, East Kalimantan, Indonesia: Ministry of Forestry and Estate Crops, Deutsche Gesellschaft für Technische Zusammenarbeit, and Kreditanstalt für Wiederaufbau.

King, V. 1996. Environmental change in Malaysian Borneo. In *Environmental Change in South-East Asia: People, Politics and Sustainable Development*, edited by M.J.G. Parnwell and R.L. Bryant. New York: Routledge, 165–89.

Leighton, M., and N. Wirawan. 1986. Catastrophic drought and fire in Borneo associated with the 1982–83 El Niño-Southern Oscillations event. In *Tropical Rainforests and the World Atmosphere*, edited by G. Prance. Washington, DC: American Association for the Advancement of Science, 75–102.

Luttrell, C. 1994. *Forest Burning in Danau Sentarum.* Asian Wetlands Bureau (AWB)/ Perlindungan Hutan dan Pelestarian Alam (PHPA—Forest Protection and Nature Conservation) report. Bogor, Indonesia: AWB/PHPA.

Mackie, C. 1984. The lessons behind East Kalimantan's forest fires. *Borneo Research Bulletin* 16:63–74.

Mayer, J. 1996. Impacts of the East Kalimantan forest fires of 1982–83 on village life, forest use, and land use. In *Borneo in Transition: People, Forests, Conservation and Development*, edited by C. Padoch and N. Peluso. Kuala Lumpur, Malaysia: Oxford University Press, 187–218.

Mori, T. 2000. Effects of droughts and forest fires on Dipterocarp forest in East Kalimantan. In *Rainforest Ecosystems of East Kalimantan*, edited by E. Guhardja, M. Fatawi, M. Sutisna, T. Mori, and S. Ohta. Tokyo: Springer, 29–45.

Nepstad, D.C., A.G. Moreira, and A.A. Alencar.1999. *Flames in the rain forest: Origins, impacts and alternatives to Amazonian fires.* Brasilia, Brazil: Pilot Program to Conserve the Brazilian Rain Forest.

Nicolas, M.V.J., and G.S. Beebe. 1999. *Fire Management in the Logging Concessions and Plantation Forests of Indonesia.* Samarinda, Indonesia: Government of Indonesia—Ministry of Forestry and Estate Crops, European Union, and Deutsche Gesellschaft für Technische Zusammenarbeit.

Oliver, C.D., and B.C. Larson. 1990. *Forest Stand Dynamics.* New York: McGraw-Hill.

Potter, L., and J. Lee. 1998a. *Tree Planting in Indonesia: Trends, Impacts and Directions.* CIFOR occasional paper no. 18. Bogor, Indonesia: CIFOR.

_____. 1998b. *Oil Palm in Indonesia: Its Role in Forest Conversion and the Fires of 1997/98.* A report for the World Wide Fund for Nature (WWF), Indonesia Program. Jakarta, Indonesia: WWF.

Sakuntaladewi, N., and M. Amblani. 1989. *Investigation of the Steps Needed to Rehabilitate the Areas of East Kalimantan Seriously Affected by Fire: Socioeconomic Aspects of the Forest Fire 1982–83 and the Relation of Transmigrants Toward Forestry and Forest Management in East Kalimantan.* Deutsche Forstscervice GmbH FR-Report No. 11. Samarinda, East Kalimantan, Indonesia: Deutsche Forstscervice GmbH FR.

Sayer, J., G. Applegate, and A.P. Vayda. 2001. Personal communication with the author, January 28–June 1, 2001.

Stolle, F., and T. Tomich. 1999. The 1997–98 fire event in Indonesia. *Nature and Resources* 35(3): 22–30.

Suyanto, S. 2000. *Fire, Deforestation and Land Tenure in the North-Eastern Fringes of Bukit Barisan Selatan National Park, Lampung.* Socioeconomic report: Site 1, Sekincau. Bogor, Indonesia: ICRAF and CIFOR.

Suyanto, S., and Y. Ruchiat. 2000. *Impacts of Human Activities and Land Tenure Conflict on Fires and Land Use Change: Case Study of Menggala-Lampung-Sumatra. Socioeconomic report: Site 2, Menggala.* Bogor, Indonesia: ICRAF and CIFOR.

Vayda, A.P. 1999. *Findings and Causes of the 1997–98 Indonesian Forest Fires: Problems/Possibilities.* Jakarta, Indonesia: WWF.

Vayda, A.P., and K. Broad. 1999. *Studying Indonesian forest-fire situations for identifying potential uses of seasonal-to-interannual (s–i) climate forecasts.* Draft proposal prepared for submission to National Oceanographic and Aeronautic Administration's Economics and Human Dimensions Program.

White, R. 1999. Personal communication with the author, August 5, 1999.

Wollenberg, E., and C.J.P. Colfer. 1996. Social sustainability in the forest: A progress report of a project aiming to test criteria and indicators for the social dimensions of sustainable forest management. *Tropical Forest Update* 6(2):9–11.

Annex 14–1
Snapshot descriptions of the communities visited
(Pseudonyms are used.)

BB: Batu Bulan is a base camp for a major timber concession, which now has industrial timber plantations (HTI) nearby and associated HTI transmigration communities of four ethnic groups. The population of Batu Bulan itself was originally the indigenous Kutai, but it is now very mixed. The conflict levels are less obvious than in Long Tutung.

LA: Long Apui is a Kenyah village, originally settled in 1962 by people who moved from the remote interior of Borneo. It is adjacent to a Kutai village in the center of East Kalimantan within a timber concession not far from industrial timber estates, transmigration, and oil palm plantations.

LB: Lalut Bala is an offshoot of Long Apui, located about three hours up a river that is about one hour out of Samarinda. A road was built but has not been maintained. The community is surrounded by other ethnic groups, and it is located on the previous base camp of a timber concession that is no longer operating. There is industrial timber estate development nearby, with which the community has had both positive and negative interactions.

LM: Lepo' Mading is another offshoot of Long Apui, located about a one-half hour walk from a paved road that is less than one hour from Samarinda. There is talk of developing oil palm. So far there seems to be minimal conflict with the other ethnic groups, with the most obvious disagreements relating to land and to the political contacts and savvy of Bugis settlers (from the neighboring island of Sulawesi) who live along the paved road.

LT: Long Tutung is a large transmigration area with oil palm, logging, and industrial timber concessions immediately adjacent. It is composed of at least four ethnic groups, including Kenyah who moved from Long Apui in the late 1980s, all in routine conflict, among themselves and with indigenous communities not far away.

LU: Long Umit is an offshoot of Long Apui, originally settled in the 1980s by Kenyah. It is located on a logging road, within a timber concession and, like Long Apui, not far from other developments.

CHAPTER FIFTEEN

Forests and Regional Autonomy: The Challenge of Sharing the Profits and Pains

**Ahmad Dermawan and
Ida Aju Pradnja Resosudarmo**

In the preceding chapters of this book we have examined three decades of the centralized nature of forest management in Indonesia. This characteristic of forest management mirrored the operational style of the Indonesian government during the same period. That is, decisionmaking authority over most aspects of policy was largely in the hands of the central government. The first day of 2001, however, marked a momentous change in Indonesian history—the authority or power over a significant chunk of decisionmaking for a number of responsibilities was formally transferred to local governments.

We begin this chapter by discussing briefly what we mean by decentralization, because frequently there is confusion over the use of the term. Readers will be shown snapshots of the history of attempts to decentralize governance, particularly focusing on the development of laws and regulations pertinent to decentralization in forestry. We then examine two recent laws on regional autonomy—the regional governance law and the fiscal balance law—as they relate to forestry. Next we discuss progress in the regions during the transition period toward effective decentralization based on the

The earlier version of this paper was presented at the Indonesian Regional Science Association International Conference held in Jakarta, Indonesia, March 20–21, 2001, and will appear in its proceedings.

preliminary findings of research by the Center for International Forestry Research (CIFOR) and the most current debate on the issue. This discussion will highlight some of the new regulatory regimes in the study regions. In the next section, we attempt to illustrate the tug of war between levels of government over the decisionmaking authority in forestry. In the chapter's final section we discuss the possible implications and challenges of decentralization for forests and forest communities and reflect on possible avenues for Indonesia to move forward.

The Long (and Winding) Road to Decentralization

"Decentralization" is a term that has been used by different people to mean different things. Recognizing that this could be problematic in any discussion of the issue, we need to begin with a common understanding of the term.

What Is Decentralization?

Decentralization, according to Cheema and Rondinelli as cited in Cohen and Peterson (1996, 10–11), can be classified into forms and types. Forms are grouped on the basis of objectives: political, spatial, market, and administrative. Each form is divided into types. For our purposes, we are concerned with political and administrative forms of decentralization. Political forms of decentralization are typically used by those interested in democratization and civil society to identify the transfer of decisionmaking power to lower-level governmental units or to citizens or their elected representatives. Administrative decentralization is the focus of those seeking to describe or reform hierarchical and functional distribution of powers and roles between central and noncentral governmental units (Cohen and Peterson 1996).

Parker (1995) uses another approach, by categorizing decentralization into three interlinked elements: political, fiscal, and institutional decentralization. Fiscal decentralization involves the access to an appropriate level of financial resources to cover the costs of public goods and services. These can be secured in basically three ways: self-generated or locally generated revenue, transfers from higher-level institutions, and resources from borrowing (Parker 1995, 27). Institutional decentralization includes identifying formal government institutions to be involved in a decentralization program and developing an appropriate legal framework to define the relationships between different institutions (Parker 1995, 32). All these elements are pertinent to our discussion.

It will also be helpful for us to be aware of the common categories of administrative decentralization: deconcentration, devolution, and delegation. As Cohen and Peterson (1996, 10–11) described it,

Deconcentration is the least extensive type of decentralization, and it is defined as the transfer of authority over specified decisionmaking, financial, and management functions by administrative means to different levels under the jurisdictional authority of the central government. Devolution occurs when authority is transferred by central governments to local-level governmental units holding corporate status granted under state legislation.[1] Delegation refers to the transfer of government decisionmaking and administrative authority or responsibility for carefully defined tasks to institutions and organizations that are either under its indirect control or independent.

As we see later, Indonesia has attempted to legally embark on the road to decentralization, but the process has mostly been in the form of deconcentration of tasks.

The Development of Decentralization Laws and Regulations Related to Forestry

In a broad and legal sense, efforts toward some degree of decentralization (which in the Indonesian case is more commonly referred to as regional autonomy) in its various forms and perhaps contrary to common knowledge, is not entirely new to Indonesia. Laws and regulations containing some elements of decentralization go as far back as the year of Independence.[2]

From a forestry perspective, at least legally, the authority for decisionmaking about forest management appears to have followed a cyclical pattern. From the second half of the 1950s until the 1960s, the authority to manage forest resources was in the hands of the then–first-level governments or *daerah swatantra tingkat I.*[3] Following the enactment of the 1967 Basic Forestry Law (BFL), however, the formal management of the country's forest resources reverted to the central government. From that time until the period leading up to 2000, the central government had almost absolute control over how these forests were to be managed, including authority over planning, administration, exploitation, and protection of the resource.[4] On January 1, 2001, however, the tables turned, with the authority over decisionmaking in most fields, including forestry, reverting again to the regions. This time decisionmaking power has been devolved, not to the provincial level (which has hitherto been the first level of government in the hierarchy), but down to the regency level, which was previously the second level of government. Three pertinent regulatory regimes describe this cycle: [5]

1. *Undang-Undang* ([UU] law) 1/1957 on Principles of Regional Governance and *Peraturan Pemerintah* ([PP] government regulation) 64/1957 on the Granting of Some of Central Government's Authority over Matters Concerning Coastal Fisheries, Forestry, and Community Rubber Sectors to First-Level Regional Governments;[6]
2. the 1967 BFL; and
3. the regional autonomy laws of 1999.

UU 1/1957 and Forestry Authority Based on PP 64/1957

UU 1/1957 on the Principles of Regional Governance and PP 64/1957 on Forest Authority provided for a relatively broad control by the then–first-level regional government. These legislations gave regional governments the authority to administer both forests with protection functions and forests for production. They included the following rights:

- issue forest exploitation permits and timber and nontimber forest products extraction permits,
- levy a tax or taxes on the holders of forest exploitation permits and timber and nontimber forest products extraction permits,
- regulate and implement forest protection, and
- regulate the transport of forest products.

The authority of the central government (in this case the then–Ministry of Agriculture) was restricted to the formulation of work plans to guide the regional governments in implementing their duties. This regulation did not state the authority of second-level regional governments (regencies) except for regions that fell under the category of the ex-State of Eastern Indonesia (see endnote 4).

BFL 5/1967

Implementation and other aspects of this law have been discussed in greater depth in the previous chapters, so here we will only mention some of the issues relevant to decentralization. The promulgation of this law returned the authority for managing the forest resource to the central government. It included control over planning, administration, exploitation, and protection of forests.

The authority for planning, for example, resulted in the establishment by the Ministry of Forestry (MoF) of the *Tata Guna Hutan Kesepakatan* ([TGHK] Forest Functions Based on Consensus). Much of the classification was made on an ad hoc basis, not only without due consideration to ecological functions of the forests but also with little regard to social, cultural, and economic functions of the forests for the communities who have been living in them for centuries (Blomkvist and Djuwadi 2000, 19; Kartasubrata 1993, 419).

On the exploitation side, this law provided the legal basis for the central government to grant permits and allocations for concessions. As explained in the previous chapters, together with the enactment of UU 1/1967 on Foreign Investment, this marked the beginning of massive exploitation of the forests to satisfy both political and economic motives. Problems began to emerge, including (a) conflicts between communities and concessionaires and those working for concessionaires, (b) inefficient logging practices, and (c) forest degradation (see Chapter 8).

Following the enactment of UU 5/1967, a government regulation was issued later in the year governing the royalty and license fees from forest exploitation.[7] This regulation stipulated that these royalties and fees would be distributed by the central government back to the regions and to other areas across Indonesia. It specified that the balance between the amount to be distributed to the regions and the amount to be retained by the central government would be determined by the central government. The justification for the structure and process of this distribution was made on grounds that these fees would be needed for both rehabilitation and development of forests in the revenue-producing regions, as well as in other regions across Indonesia.

Thus, this law conveniently provided the central government with the power to determine how the forest resources of Indonesia were going to be managed, how the proceeds from exploiting these forests were going to be used, and for what purposes. These forests immediately began to be used as a cash cow for development, particularly in the 1970s and 1980s, and provided the means for those in power to gain political patronage (see Chapters 8 and 12). Previous chapters have described the systematic destruction of the forests. This degradation not only occurred at the expense of those people living in these forest areas but also failed to bring about many benefits or compensation to those who had to bear the consequences.

The 1967 BFL allowed the central government to transfer some of its authority to regional governments. Indeed, some control over forests was devolved to the provincial-level governments—albeit only very little over the span of 30 years. Yet these rights were trivial and only the least comprehensive forms of decentralization (i.e., deconcentration, coadministration).

One of the powers given to the provincial governments was the granting of *Hak Pemungutan Hasil Hutan* ([HPHH] Forest Product Harvesting Rights), which entitled the holder to extract timber and nontimber forest products within an area of 100 ha of forest.[8] In January 1999, however, this authority was transferred to the then–second-level of regional governments (i.e., the regency level, and the permits were to be valid for a maximum of one year).[9] The issue of these small timber concessions will be discussed in more detail in subsequent sections of this chapter.

The central government also handed the authority to carry out forest protection to the provincial level through PP 28/1985. In reality, most of the policies on forest protection were made at the central level, while provincial officials only dealt with the technical functions of forest protection (Rahmadi 2000, 14). The latest formal attempt at decentralizing some powers with regard to forests prior to the enactment of the 1999 regional autonomy laws—albeit on only very trivial matters—was a 1998 government regulation granting some areas of governance in the forestry sector to the regions.[10] The desire of the central government to retain control over the most lucrative aspects of the forestry sector was very obvious in this regulation, as reflected in the powers that were transferred to the following levels:

- provincial level—including only the management of *taman hutan raya* (forest parks) and administering forest boundary arrangements; and
- regency level—including reforestation and soil and water conservation, natural silk production, honey production, management of private forests and community forests, day-to-day management of protected forests, extension in forestry, management of nontimber forest products, traditional hunting of nonprotected species of fauna in areas designated for hunting, forest protection, and training of the community in forestry skills.

Not much happened after the release of this regulation, however. Government officials of one regency studied by CIFOR maintained that the granting of control over forestry matters governed under this regulation was felt to be more of a transfer of burden from the center to the region (Soetarto et al. 2001, 43).

Based on this discussion, we can see that there have been, to a certain degree, some attempts to formalize transfer of authority in forestry to the regions. The earlier attempts with the governors having authority in forest management did not result in widespread commercialization of the nation's forest resources, and the authors have not found systematic documentation of significant environmental problems.

Following the collapse of the Soeharto government in May 1998, Indonesia experienced social unrest in a number of places. Several regions are demanding a larger share of resource revenues and even Independence. The Habibie transitional government realized that revitalizing the earlier plans for regional autonomy was perhaps necessary to avoid disintegration.[11] In May 1999, in what seemed to be a hurried action, the government passed two laws designed to decentralize both political and economic power away from the central government. The new Forestry Law (UU 41/1999) was passed in September 1999, about four months after the enactment of the regional autonomy laws. Yet in the context of devolving authority in forest administration to regions, several passages of this law appear to be inconsistent with passages of the regional autonomy law. For example, Article 4(2) of the law stipulates that the central government continues to retain its authority over forest administration.[12]

Next we will discuss the two autonomy laws that are setting the stage for what is currently happening in the country in the context of the decentralization process.

Legislation Devolving Political and Economic Power from the Center

Two laws passed in 1999 marked a new era of governance and financial relations between the central government and the regions. We will discuss the major changes that have occurred in these laws that are relevant to forestry.

UU 22/1999 on Regional Governance. This law replaces UU 5/1974 on the Principles of Regional Governance and devolves a significant set of authorities to the regency and town levels, which are now autonomous regions.[13] Provinces, however, both are autonomous regions and carry out the function of central government representatives (and will therefore perform deconcentration functions). There are no longer any hierarchical relationships among the three regions.[14] The regency heads and mayors will be elected by and accountable to the appropriate regional legislative bodies. Meanwhile, a governor, as the head of the province, will be accountable to the provincial legislative body and to the president as a representative of the central government. In effect, this represents a significant boost of power for the regional House of Representatives.

Greater authority has been given to regional governments, but the law is unclear about control over management of natural resources, including forests. At least two sections are contradictory. Article 7 states that utilization of natural resources remains with the central government, while Article 10 states that regions are authorized to manage national resources within their territories and are responsible for maintaining the sustainability of the environment according to law.

The province has authority over affairs that are interregional in nature, such as public works, communications, forestry, and plantations. In addition, this level of government exercises control over planning and regional development at the macro level, and it is responsible for conducting provincial spatial planning. Some points are ambiguous and contradictory, and they require further government regulations for effective implementation.

In May 2000, or about a year after the enactment of the law, the government passed the implementing regulation of this law.[15] It specified the breakdown of responsibilities between the central government and the provincial government on a sector-by-sector basis. This regulation tends to indicate, however, that the central government still retains as much as possible the power it previously held. For instance, PP 25/2000 specified the authority of the central and provincial governments, rather than the authority of the regency governments. Some observers (Van Zorge Report 2000, 22) viewed this as rather strange, because UU 22/1999 devolved authority and responsibilities to the regency governments. Therefore, to resolve the inconsistencies between the two laws with regard to the mandates, there would have to be an implementing regulation clearly setting out the authority of the regency governments. In fact, this implementing regulation implies that the authority of the regency governments is to be whatever remains or is excluded from the control of the central and provincial governments as defined. Therefore it perpetuates the ambiguities in the division of responsibilities in certain areas. The inclusion of a stipulation in Section 4 of the regulation—which defines the mechanism by which the central government could resume power or authority over areas where regions (province, regency, and town) are deemed not capable of carrying out the tasks—suggests that the central government is taking precautions to be able to recover some controls when needed.[16]

The substance of this government regulation indicates that the decisionmaking power related to the management of forest resources remains to a significant degree with the central government, more specifically the MoF. Indeed, discussions with various people within the MoF and other ministries it was revealed that forestry was one of the last ministries to agree to the points contained in the forestry section of the regulation (see also *Bisnis Indonesia* 2000a; *Kompas* 2000a; *Media Indonesia* 2000a).

In general, the center's responsibility with regard to forestry was to set criteria and standards for various aspects of forest administration, with the provinces and presumably regencies carrying out the day-to-day functions of forest management. Following are several important authorities and responsibilities of the central government (in this case the MoF) that reaffirm its policymaking role in forest management:

- to set forest areas and the change of their status and functions;
- to set the criteria and standards for the tariffs on forest utilization license fees, royalties, reforestation funds, and investment funds for the costs of forest conservation;
- to set the criteria and standards for licensing utilization of forest areas, environmental services, and nature recreational areas; utilization and extraction of forest products; and management of hunting parks;
- to manage nature conservation and hunting parks, including rivers flowing through these areas;
- to set criteria and standards for the management of forest products, including planning of management, use, maintenance, rehabilitation, and control of forest areas; and
- to set the criteria and standards for natural resource and ecosystem conservation in the fields of forestry and plantations.

The authority of the provinces is limited to setting guidelines for forest inventory and mapping, setting guidelines for forest boundaries, and in addressing forestry matters that affect more than one regency or town within the province.

In November 2000, or about two months before regional autonomy was to be effectively implemented, the MoF passed a decree on the Criteria and Standards of Licensing of the Utilization of Forest Products and the Licensing of Harvesting Forest Products in Natural Production Forests. The decree set the maximum areas for the utilization of forest products in a province, the maximum number of licenses a company can have in a province, and the maximum area available to one company for the utilization of forest products across Indonesia. The decree also specified the powers of regency, provincial, and central governments with regard to licensing of forest utilization.

UU 25/1999 on the Fiscal Balance between the Central Government and the Regions. This law on fiscal decentralization complements the law on regional governance by providing the legal instrument for the regions to receive a specified share of revenues from various sectors and to raise money to meet financial needs for implementing the responsibilities stipulated in the governance law. This situation is in marked contrast to the 1995 District Autonomy Pilot Programme, which did not have a legal and clear instrument to address the funding needs of the regencies.[17]

The execution of regional duties in the implementation of decentralization is financed by the regional budget, which consists of (a) self-generated income—composed of regional taxes, charges, regionally owned companies, and other legal sources such as grants; (b) funds from the central government, including revenue sharing, the general allocation funds, and the specific allocation funds; (c) regional debts and loans; and (d) other legal income.[18] The execution of central government duties by provincial apparatus in the implementation of deconcentration tasks is financed through the central government budget.

Under this law, there is an increase in the share of revenue generated by the forestry sector allocated to the regions. Thirty percent of the revenue from the forest utilization rights levy (*iuran hak pengusahaan hutan*) was previously retained by the central government, while the remainder was distributed to the provincial governments. UU 25/1999 and its implementing regulation stipulate that only 20% is to be retained by the center, and 80% is to be distributed to the regional governments—16% to the provincial governments and 64% to the producing regency or town.[19]

Similarly, 20% of the forest resource provision (royalty) will now be retained by the central government, and 80% will be distributed to the regions. Yet in the regional allocation, while the province receives 16%, the producing regency or town will get 32%, and the remaining 32% will be distributed equally among the other regencies or towns within the province. Previously, revenue from these royalties was divided as follows: 30% to the provincial government, 15% to the regency or town, 40% to national forestry development, and 15% to regional forestry development (Presidential Decree 67/1998).

Another source of revenue from the forestry sector for which the distribution and use are governed by this law is the Reforestation Fund. These payments are required to be submitted by concessionaires to the government for the sole purpose of forest rehabilitation.[20] In contrast to previous arrangements, this law and its implementing regulation stipulate distinctly what share of the Reforestation Fund can be retained by the central government and what is to be redistributed to regions.[21]

Forests, People, and Regional Autonomy in Sumatra and Kalimantan

To build an understanding of the possible implications of decentralization or regional autonomy on forests and people's livelihoods, CIFOR initiated a study at field sites in four provinces—Riau (a province in Sumatra), West Kalimantan, Central Kalimantan, and East Kalimantan. The study was an attempt to capture the perceptions of the regions about decentralization and to document what is happening in these forest areas with regard to decentralization.

The research was focused on the regency (*kabupaten*) level, although information was also gathered at the provincial, village, and central levels. The regencies studied were Kabupaten Kampar[22] and Kabupaten Indragiri Hulu[23] (Riau); Kabupaten Ketapang (West Kalimantan); Kabupaten Kotawaringin Timur, Kabupaten Kapuas, and Kabupaten Barito Selatan (Central Kalimantan); and Kabupaten Kutai Barat, Kabupaten Berau, and Kabupaten Malinau (East Kalimantan).

The methodology involved interviews with key informants and various stakeholders—from the national level down to the village level—including central and regional government officials, forestry company representatives, community representatives, legislative officials, nongovernmental organizations, and government representatives of other sectors at the provincial and regency levels. It should be noted that officials interviewed were not limited to forestry officials but included officials from other sectors such as the State Ministry of Regional Autonomy,[24] the regional treasury office, and the land agency. In addition to interviews at all levels of government and community, we also collected secondary information, statistical records of basic demographic and geographical data, forestry data, financial data, and maps and land-use or spatial planning documents related to the study areas.

It should be emphasized that this research was undertaken in 2000, while regional autonomy only became effective beginning on January 1, 2001. Therefore, this study was an attempt to document the decentralization trend that has occurred in the preparatory period leading up to formal, and effectively legal, decentralization.

This section begins with a discussion of the general attitudes of the regions toward decentralization. It is followed by presentation of the main issues relevant to forests and local communities. Information from media and other sources is also be used to enrich the fieldwork findings.[25]

General Perceptions, Attitudes, and Concerns

Until the third quarter of 2000, the general attitudes of the regions toward decentralization were a combination of enthusiasm, pessimism, confusion, and uncertainty. In Riau in April 2000, there were mixed feelings about decentralization. There was some level of pessimism and a tendency to see it as false promises, which would delay the achievement of prosperity by the people (Potter and Badcock 2000, 12). There were voices of concern that some bureaucrats in the regions were not ready to implement regional autonomy. This was primarily associated with the newly developed regency such as the regency of Kuantan Singingi. Almost all regions studied demonstrated some degree of inadequate capacity, ranging from human resources, facilities, and infrastructure to a lack of access to information.

After the enactment of PP 25/2000, there was a feeling of confusion and, to a certain degree, some suspicion that the central government had taken back regional authority over several sectors including forestry—describing it as "half-hearted autonomy" (Potter and Badcock 2000, 12; Soetarto et al. 2001, 49). These perceptions resulted in growing frustration with the central government. There were some who perceived that certain groups existed within the central government who were opposed to regional autonomy.

There was much emphasis on the fact that decisions will be made at the local level. Government officials see regional autonomy as being aimed at ensuring that the government is better able to serve local people. Forestry officials at the regency level indicated that decentralization would make it easier to regulate the companies operating within their jurisdiction, as decisions will not need to go through the bureaucratic chain.

Perceptions of local communities, at least in certain areas, were that regional autonomy would be good for the villages because the regency could concentrate on what happens at the local level, and the administration could be held responsible for its actions and programs because monitoring by local people is possible. Yet there were voices of cynicism that questioned the benefits of regional autonomy until presented with concrete evidence. As one villager put it, "So far the evidence is not the increase in benefits, but the increased exploitation of the forests around our village" (Potter and Badcock 2000, 42). The level of regional enthusiasm in some instances went as far as "all-or-nothing"—insistence that every single aspect of forest administration, including conservation, should go to the regencies (Potter and Badcock 2000, 17).

One positive development arising from the decentralization process has been the increasing interaction between the regency head and the governor, with a much greater level of independence for the regency leaders. This has enabled them to consult with central and provincial government officials, the private sector, and other leaders about decentralization. Executives in both the regency and provincial governments work closely with their counterparts to strengthen their positions in regional autonomy. The formation of an association consisting of regency governments throughout Indonesia provides a venue for improving communication among regency leaders and for strengthening their bargaining power with other levels of government. Similarly, the provincial governors are using *Asosiasi Pemerintah Propinsi Seluruh Indonesia* ([APPSI] Association of Provincial Governments across Indonesia) to enhance communication among provincial leaders and to develop a strategy to address issues on decentralization that may work against their interests.

A not-so-positive aspect of decentralization, depending on one's perspective, is the growing sentiment for *putera daerah* to hold government posts in the regions (Potter and Badcock 2000, 18; McCarthy 2000a, 25).[26] For instance, regency leaders are almost always expected to be a *putera daerah*— someone seen to be more in tune with the needs and aspirations of the local population than would be someone from outside. Although it is necessary that local interests are protected and enhanced in the process, there is a risk of disintegration and of conflicts between indigenous locals and migrants. The ethnic conflict that has plagued and continues to plague Indonesia in the past few years is a manifestation of the tension between indigenous and migrant groups generated by such feelings.

Regional government officials and local people see regional autonomy as *putera daerah* and local people finally getting to retain the benefits from resources extracted from the regions. People were aware that their areas were major sources of natural resource revenues to the central government, and they talked about the Jakarta-based officials and conglomerates getting rich in the past 30 years while very little was being returned to the regions (Barr et al. 2001, 25).

Forest concession holders were nervous about decentralization. They generally appreciate the improved revenue generation for the regions, but they indicated concerns about the security of the business environment. There was a perception that the rules of the game were no longer clear. There were claims, particularly from local investors, local brokers, and community elites working with them, that concession holders did not have legitimacy within their concession areas. Some said that local governments are now more responsive to local needs. Yet there were indications of individuals potentially manipulating local communities. Local communities, however, generally felt that regional autonomy would restore their rights to participate directly in logging activities.

What has been most striking in the findings, although not unexpected, is that the regions studied equate decentralization with revenues. This is not unexpected because all of our study areas are quite resource rich, at least in terms of forest resources. Regions have begun to calculate their share of revenue from the central government. During the interviews, the most significant concerns revolved around the issue of how the regions will support themselves financially. For some areas, this amount would presumably be a significant part of money that has to be raised, above and beyond the amount they would receive from the revenue-sharing, general allocation, and specific allocation funds from the central government.

Next we describe some of the issues and responses that have emerged with regard to decentralization. In many cases, they are not associated exclusively with the decentralization process or regional autonomy but are possibly linked to the reform process (*Reformasi*) or even with the economic crisis that has ravaged Indonesia since 1997.

Some Issues Identified in the Period of Transition toward Effective Decentralization

Preliminary research findings show similarities as well as differences among the nine research areas in the issues relating to forests and decentralization. Following are the major areas of concern, albeit far from all those identified:

- forest resources as an important source of regional income,
- spatial planning and land uses,
- large forest concessions, and
- conservation and protected areas.

Forest Resources as an Important Source of Regional Income

While there was still much uncertainty even toward the end of 2000, regions were preparing themselves for the implementation of autonomy in January 2001 with legal instruments allowing for administrative reforms and increased revenue generation. This resulted in the creation of a new regency regulatory regime, in which the regency issued regional regulations. Forestry is an attractive source of revenue for the regional governments because of the ready availability of the resource and because forests can provide immediate income (i.e., forests are comparatively ready-to-cash assets). These regional governments see it in their best interests to generate as much income as possible as quickly as possible. For precisely these reasons, many regencies are issuing regulations allowing revenue generation from forests within their jurisdictions.

One important regulation allows regency leaders to issue small concessions or HPHH licenses in various forms to cooperatives or individuals.[27] The most common reason given by the regency for the issuance of this regulation was that it would kill two birds with one stone—both the regency and the local people would benefit by generating local income for the regency and by providing forest harvesting licenses to local cooperatives or individuals.

PP 6/1999 governed these small-scale permits and was enacted in early 1999. In September 1999, the MoF issued a decree to delay the implementation of the regulation that allowed regency leaders to grant these licenses. Despite the delay—probably because the central government realized the consequences both environmentally and politically—many of the regency governments continued to grant the permits (Casson 2000a, 19; McCarthy 2000a,

10; *Kompas* 2000d). The argument for continuing to issue these permits was that the regulation has not been cancelled, only delayed. It is important to note, however, that not all of the regencies such as the one in Riau went ahead with this initiative, for fear that these regulations would conflict with national legislations. For those who did, the regency legislative bodies supported the action, thus removing any obstacles to the issuance and implementation of the permits.

For example, in one of the regencies in Central Kalimantan, by July 2000 as many as 150 small-scale utilization permit applications had been submitted to the leader; 60 of these had been granted (McCarthy 2000a, 10). In one regency in East Kalimantan, by August 2000, 223 permits had been issued (Casson 2000a, 19). On the surface, these permits may seem small and insignificant. Yet there are aspects that give reason for concern, including (a) the total area allocated for this purpose, (b) the locations of the permits, and (c) who actually benefits from these activities.

Total Area Allocated for Small-Scale HPHH and *Izin Pemungutan dan Pemanfaatan Kayu* Permits. Even though an individual area of 100 ha is relatively small, 200 permits will translate into 20,000 ha being exploited—not a small area for a regency. In addition, one must remember that these are only those permits issued during the transition period. By the time decentralization is fully implemented, the opportunity and incentives to grant these permits may increase exponentially. A more serious concern is that although it is true on paper that permits are granted over 100-ha areas, in practice this may not be the case. In at least one regency, permits are granted for areas between 100 and 3,000 ha (Barr et al. 2001, 16). With limited capacity and staff, it is difficult for the regency governments to monitor the HPHH permit-related activities. Operations can thus easily extend or spill over into adjacent and larger areas, thus effectively placing more areas (than assigned by the permits) at risk of being felled or cleared.

Areas for Small-Scale Permits Overlapping with Large Timber Concessions. Inaccurate specification of the area of concessions given in the permits has both social and environmental repercussions. Regency leaders often assign permits that overlap with existing large-scale timber concessions *Hak Pengusahaan Hutan* ([HPH] Forest Concession, Forest Exploitation Rights) assigned by the central government (Barr et al. 2001, 23; *Kompas*, 2001g). This is a potential source of conflict and is a clear disincentive for concessionaires to carry out any form of sustainable forest management. The small HPHH permits are often given to cooperatives without the fulfillment of the necessary requirement for an environmental impact assessment (*Kompas* 2000c).

Who Actually Benefits from the Permits? The argument that local people benefit from the HPHH permits may only be partially true. First, local people simply may not have the capital to obtain these permits because the costs are high—as much as 25 million Rp for one permit (McCarthy 2000a, 13; Soetarto et al. 2001, 44). Second, local communities may not have adequate technical capacity to carry out logging operations (McCarthy 2000a, 13). For these reasons, in most instances, there are large-scale concessionaires or other capital providers playing a role as "partners" behind these permits (Soetarto et al. 2001, 44; Casson 2000a, 18; McCarthy 2000a, 13; Barr et al. 2001, 35). These capital providers are using cooperatives and local communities to gain access to forest resources.

One argument for extending access to forest resources to local communities through a legal instrument was to control "informal" logging in cases where local communities are involved. On the one hand, assigning small-scale local permits to cooperatives may be an initial step to control illegal logging. On the other hand, careless and inappropriate assignment of these permits may spark conflicts between those who are involved in illegal activities but for various reasons do not apply for these permits and those who actually receive the permits. An interesting observation in one area was that before the existence of HPHH permits, there were no reports of illegal logging. After the permits were instituted, people reported illegal activities, indicating that the (future) permit holders would be disadvantaged if these illegal activities continue (McCarthy 2000a, 12).

Why did the regency governments, with the support of the regional House of Representatives, create these regulatory instruments and courageously issue permits despite a conflict with national regulations? First, it would be a source of legal income for the regency and therefore present a good report card for the regency head. Second, through this regulation the regency is seen to accommodate local demands for access to timber resources.[28] Third, the regulation opens up an opportunity for local elites to take part in the timber business by offering protection or privileges for those with permits. Fourth, those with the capital and technical capacity (who are not infrequently HPH holders) would now have to satisfy the local constituents by making new arrangements with these communities instead of with the central government.

Initially, these small-scale, local permits were not directly opposed by the central government or its line agencies in the regions (McCarthy 2000a, 16); there are a number of possible reasons for this. The central government and MoF were probably as confused as the regions in terms of the kinds of authority should be decentralized and the kinds of authority they could retain. There is most likely some sense of widespread resentment at the district level of the center's power, encouraging the MoF to accommodate local demands (McCarthy 2000a, 15). The central government and timber interests at the center are in a less powerful position to oppose local desires because of the regional autonomy laws and because the center now has considerably less power to enforce its demands. The central government will be more lenient about innovations, such as this regulation to issue local forest utilization permits, as long as the interests of the concessions with licenses from the center are not put at risk.

In some areas toward the end of 2000, strong warnings from the MoF resulted in the temporary moratorium on the issue of small-scale HPHH and *izin pemungutan dan pemanfaatan kayu* ([IPPK] wood utilization and harvesting permits) permits. At the end of February 2001, it was revealed that many small-scale local permits issued by regency leaders to cooperatives in Kalimantan had been sold to timber businesses (*Kompas* 2001g).

Another important initiative to collect locally generated income from forest resources was the creation of regulations that would levy charges on confiscated illegal timber. There are variations among regencies about how this confiscated timber is handled. Several avoided conflict with national legislation by continuing to auction captured illegal timber, as they had done before. Yet other regencies found innovative ways to make use of the confiscated timber to accumulate income for their own use and created formal regulations to impose charges on confiscated timber. After the charges are paid, these logs can be transported out of the jurisdiction of the regency. In other words, the regional governments do not care about the origins of the timber and how it was harvested; they are more concerned with whether the timber has been paid for (through charges). This effectively legalizes illegal timber. To the extent that these charges are lower than the total formal fees associated with legal timber activities, such as royalties and Reforestation Funds, the imposition of these charges create a disincentive for legal timber activities and sustainable forest management practices.

Extralegal activities in the forestry sector appeared to increase and became more open at the onset of *Reformasi*. This bonanza continued in the period of transition leading up to decentralization. In all of the regencies studied, not one escaped extralegal activities in one form or another. Activities include illegal sawmills procuring illegal timber, timber traders distributing illegal timber, pulp and paper mills fed by illegal timber, and timber felling hiding behind cooperatives.[29]

Other regulations issued or being formulated to generate earnings in the regencies under study involve imposing charges on logs or processed timber that are transported out of the regency, licensing small wood industries (i.e., sawmills), and establishing regency-owned, forestry-related enterprises. The enthusiasm of regional governments to gain as much as possible from forest resources in the quest for local income generation, unfortunately, has not been accompanied by the same level of enthusiasm to return a share of the benefits to the forests. The fact that this issue did not arise in the interviews indicates that the local governments do not consider it an important or immediate concern.

Spatial Planning and Land Uses

In general, spatial planning in Indonesia has faced severe challenges:

- lack of good on-the-ground data;
- the tendency of different sectors to produce different maps and have different interests;
- the commissioning of planning to consultants who have limited accountability to the stakeholders or the agency mission;
- planning documents produced to meet deadlines or contractual obligations rather than reflecting ground-level realities;
- consultants working with a reduced level of funding because a portion of the funds tends to be siphoned off somewhere along the way; and
- greater influence of stronger sector groups in making land-use decisions.

Spatial planning, therefore, has often been a paper exercise rather than a tool to effectively coordinate land use (Barr et al. 2001, 41).

During the period of research most of the regions were still in the process of reconciling provincial spatial planning with defining forestland use by TGHK. In general, the process of spatial planning, as well as its reconciliation with the consensus land-use definitions, has not changed from the previous situation. The decisionmaking has continued to be a top-down process, and the key players remain the provincial government, sector agencies at the provincial level, and the MoF. The involvement of the regency governments has been very limited—they were usually consulted in the process but never really involved in a meaningful way.[30]

In forestry, several issues arose with regard to spatial planning and land use in the past. First, the large-scale forest concession and small, local utilization permits often overlapped other uses or functions. This situation generated conflicts between the holders of these permits and the original users or stewards of the land. Second, the forests were assigned to various uses, in some cases without due regard to the physical and ecological conditions of the land. Consequently, vast areas of protection and conservation areas were located within concession areas (see Chapter 8).

Whenever problems developed from these conflicting land uses, however, the consequences had to be borne at the local levels. In almost every regency, there were various forms of disputes over land, commonly between local communities and logging companies or oil palm companies. Regency officials were concerned about these ongoing disputes, which they directly attributed to the licensing policies and priorities at the national level.

Decentralization provides an opportunity for spatial planning with a meaningful involvement of various stakeholders at the local level to better reflect local interests and conditions. Regency officials argue that spatial plans need to reflect more accurately local priorities and field realities. For this to happen, the regional government should have a primary role in creating the plan, including the right to turn down any development plan suggested by higher levels of government that is perceived to be inappropriate by the regency (McCarthy 2000b, 17–18). Yet it would be perhaps even more crucial for the process to include a number of perspectives and involve various stakeholders, including communities or their representative bodies.

Regencies could improve their capacity to deal with spatial planning. For example, regencies tend to hire outside consultants to assist them with spatial planning. The use of outside consultants who carry out work largely for a fee will not necessarily provide the motivation to plan land uses that reflect local conditions and local interests. The evaluation of the process of spatial planning during the transition period in a newly formed regency (Malinau) in East Kalimantan suggested that the main interest of the exercise appeared to be in assessing the economic potential of the area (Barr et al. 2001, 43). This again is consistent with the locally perceived objective of decentralization (i.e., revenue generation).

In addition to the regency's view on the process of spatial planning or its reconciliation with real land use being a top-down process, there are also concerns revolving around the process of spatial planning at the provincial level itself. As an example, one spatial planning process was being contracted out to a Jakarta-based firm. This may be an admission by the provincial planning office (Bappeda [*Badan Perencanaan Pembangunan Daerah* or Regional Development Planning Body]) that it does not have the technical capacity to undertake the exercise, but it may also be a reflection of some difficulties in the relationship between Bappeda and the *Kanwilhutbun* (*Kantor Wilayah Kehutanan dan Perkabunan* or Regional Office for Forestry and Plantations)(Potter and Badcock 2000, 8). In another province, the provincial Bappeda was not actively engaged in the planning of land uses, but it acted more as a funnel for information and for compiling decisions made by other agencies (Barr et al. 2001, 41).

There were cases showing that actual land-use policies at the regency level did not always conform to the plans reflected in the regency spatial plan. This demonstrates the lack of usefulness of the spatial plan in the past, even if it reflected actual conditions on the ground. At the time of the research, at least one regency was preparing a regulation that would require the spatial plan to be followed in all development strategies (McCarthy 2000b, 18).

One requirement for the allocation of forest utilization permits is the completion of an environmental impact assessment.[31] The study suggested that there are concerns by the local environmental agency that the capacity of the local government to fulfill the above requirement is lagging behind the rate of applications for forest utilization permits. For example, at the time of the study, one regency was still struggling with the establishment of a commission to handle the environmental impact assessment of projects, while there were already 25 applications for permits waiting to be processed (McCarthy 2000b, 19).

Large Forest Concessions

In general, the operations of timber concessions remain unwelcome among local governments and local people. Various stakeholders perceive that such concessions deliver the greatest share of the benefits from forests to outsiders. By contrast, locals are the ones who have to shoulder the consequences resulting from the operations of these activities (McCarthy 2000b, 26).

In many places, concession holders, both private and state owned (Inhutani), have lost access to the forest resources within their concession areas, except where the felling plans are very active. Extralegal harvesting, which was common, has been proliferating since the onset of *Reformasi*. In some areas, communities have taken control of heavy equipment associated with logging operations and burned logging camps, demanding compensation. In fact, small-scale forest utilization (IPPK and HPHH) licenses have been issued for areas legally assigned to Inhutani or other concession holders (*Bisnis Indonesia* 2000f). The issuance of these small licenses not only lowers the potential revenues of the concessions but also is a disincentive for the concessionaires to follow sustainable practices. As a result, holders of timber concessions were forced to change their procedures to become more responsive to local governments and local communities.

Factors determining access to forest resources have changed with decentralization. Previously, personal relationships with elements of the central government were key to access to forest resources. Now it appears that a relationship with local elites is not only an advantage but also a necessity to obtaining such access. In addition, economic considerations apply more directly, as a permit for forest utilization would be too costly for local entrepreneurs. The solution for these local entrepreneurs with limited capital is to work in partnership with capital providers (*cukong*) who can afford the costs to run a legal operation.

Clearly, the position of local communities with regard to their share of forest benefits has not changed. They generally occupy a weak position in the network, in financial as well as in political terms. In practice, cooperatives are used by those with capital and connections—now at the local level instead of at the national level—as a means to gain access to timber. Local people who are involved in felling activities in small-scale permit areas—and even worse in illegal felling—still only work as laborers for low pay (McCarthy 2000b, 31; Soetarto et al. 2001, 45).[32]

An example in East Kalimantan demonstrates how the pressures on forests are increasing with decentralization. In the regency on the border with Malaysia, local entrepreneurs function as middlepersons for Malaysian investors. These capital injections have been accompanied by a flood of heavy equipment from Malaysia, which some claim is larger than what is needed to log areas allocated for small-scale use (Barr et al. 2001, 20). This build-up of heavy equipment indicates that the holders of the utilization permits, or those benefiting from the use of the permits, are planning to log forest areas larger than those assigned for felling.

Another endeavor to generate revenues was the establishment of regional government enterprises, which perform forestry-related business activities, among other functions. Yet in many cases, these enterprises have limited technical capacity and capital to pursue logging activities on a commercial scale. To overcome this obstacle, there have been initiatives to establish partnerships with timber concession holders, including Inhutani. Such partnerships are a strategic response by Inhutani to the changing political and administrative conditions at the national and regional levels. The partnership arrangement will involve provincial governments, regency-level governments, and local cooperatives. At the time of the research, however, the details of how such partnerships would function had not been fully worked out (Barr et al. 2001, 28–29).

This kind of partnership appears to be welcomed by the regencies, as it means that they will not only enjoy a fair share of forest royalties and fees but also gain revenue directly from logging activities in their areas. To be truly beneficial for all stakeholders involved, however, the share of revenues that has been agreed upon must reach the appropriate stakeholders. In this respect, it is important that a proper mechanism is established to effectively implement the partnerships, particularly if the communities are to receive maximum benefits rather than continuing the old approach of centrally defined village programs such as the *Bina Desa* or *Pembinaan Masyarakat Desa Hutan* (Forest Village Community Development) schemes.

Conservation and Protected Areas

It can be stated with some degree of certainty that many protected areas, including national parks, are at great risk and are currently undergoing savage destruction. Although the surge in this devastation may have begun with the euphoria of *Reformasi* and been compounded by the economic crisis, in general, decentralization has yet to demonstrate any tendencies toward positive benefits for protected areas.

Illegal timber-felling activities in these areas involve virtually all elements of the industry: capital providers, entrepreneurs, communities, government officials, military, and the police (Soetarto et al. 2001, 45-48; McCarthy 2000a, 12). In addition to revenue from timber, these invasions are designed to increase the size of land holdings (Potter and Badcock 2000, 34)

To date, regional authorities have concentrated on identifying, monitoring, and prosecuting illegal activities by such means as seizure of heavy machinery and illegal timber (Potter and Badcock 2000, 33). In Riau, regency leaders more recently seem to be focused on reducing the threats to a national park by requesting the suspension of all concession licenses in the areas. Some regencies have begun to show an interest in developing parks, in addition to undertaking a conservation role (Potter and Badcock 2000, 37; Soetarto et al. 2001, 67).

Officials in one regency with a national park specifically suggested that its role in the management of national parks be extended to include the development of the tourism potential. This interest was directly linked to the opportunity to raise revenue. Stakeholders report the perception that maintenance of national parks will be difficult if benefits do not directly accrue to local communities within the boundaries of the park (Soetarto et al. 2001, 66). A member of the regional House of Representatives in Riau also reiterated the importance of providing economic alternatives for communities living around conservation areas (*Kompas* 2001b).

National parks have probably been a lower priority for regional governments because legislation defines that the responsibility for conservation areas remains with the central government. To the extent that these areas at present are a lost opportunity for revenue generation in comparison with production forests, the existence of protected areas in a region could be perceived by the relevant regional governments as a burden rather than a blessing (Soetarto et al. 2001, 26).

The best interests of protected and conservation areas may not be served by managing them according to administrative boundaries. The natural extents of these areas do not follow human-defined boundaries, but they are determined by watersheds or other geographical and ecological characteristics. Therefore, if parks were to be administered by regencies, there would have to be good coordination and working relationships between those in control.

Emil Salim, a prominent Indonesian economist and environmentalist (see Afterword), suggested that regional autonomy puts pressure on conservation areas such as national parks and protected forests. He went on to say that there is a tendency to convert conservation areas into businesses to collect revenues for the region. He cites an example of a conservation area turned into a business on the island of Kakaktua in East Kalimantan (*Kompas* 2001a).

In at least one study area in Riau, people had some residual fears about encroaching on a wildlife reserve. They remembered that others had been jailed for such offenses in the past. In this sense "fences and fines" or strict enforcement of the law may have some conservation advantages.

Having examined developments in the forestry sector in the regions in the context of decentralization, it is worthwhile to explore the situation at the national level and the responses of provinces and regencies. One key element in this scenario is the struggle for power between, at the very least, certain constituents of these governments. A review of these struggles and what has been actually happening in the regions provides us with a comprehensive picture of decentralization trends and helps us determine the anticipated possible implications for forest and local communities. The following section is based on media sources and discussions with individuals from the relevant ministries.

The Tug-of-War between the Center and the Regions

Although it is anticipated that the present move toward regional autonomy is real in comparison to previous actions, there still appears to be a tendency for a tug-of-war between levels of governments. This is particularly the case for the central government, and to some degree the provincial governments, who give the impression that they want to hold onto and even regain key responsibilities in general. The case of the management of oil resources is a clear example of a battle for power between the central government and the regions.[33] To a lesser degree, this also holds true for forest resources.

The resistance of the central government is demonstrated by its limited commitment in many aspects of the decentralization process. On the one hand, it may reflect the process by which the laws were formulated, which was hurried and without sufficient, meaningful consultation and without serious consideration of the mechanisms for implementation. On the other hand, it may also imply that there are groups within the central government who are reluctant to go ahead with decentralization in its present form and would like to retain as much power as possible.

The tendency for certain groups at the center to resist the current process of decentralization can be traced back to the earlier attempts at regional autonomy and by following the progress of the recent process. First, the reluctance to relinquish authority seems to be rooted in the history of the long process toward real regional autonomy. As discussed earlier, at least on paper, there were legal efforts to implement a certain degree of decentralization. In reality, most elements of the decentralization process were deconcentration functions, and earlier initiatives for devolving regional autonomy to the regency level did not eventuate. Failure of the District Autonomy Pilot Programme is a clear example of the not-so-serious intentions of the central government to transfer its authority.

Second, the replacement of Ryaas Rasyid (who formerly led the State Ministry of Regional Autonomy and who was known to be the architect behind the current decentralization push) by another figure (who is thought to have a different vision of decentralization) can be interpreted as resistance at the center. This was followed by Ryaas Rasyid's resignation from his new post as the minister of administrative reform in January 2001.

Third, the fact that it has taken the central government some time to prepare the necessary implementing regulations (at the time of this writing, many had not been completed) demonstrates either the difficulties in formulating these regulations or the wish to delay implementation of decentralization. At the start of the eighth week of regional autonomy, Rasyid estimated that there were still 197 presidential decrees that needed to be formulated to implement regional autonomy effectively (*Kompas* 2001f).

Finally, at the time of writing, international organizations (e.g., International Monetary Fund, the World Bank, Asian Development Bank) and donor countries such as Japan have been putting pressure on the national government to forbid foreign borrowing by the regions for the first two years of regional autonomy. In effect, they are pushing to delay the implementation of this authority to raise foreign loans as set out in the 1999 law on fiscal balancing (*The Jakarta Post* 2001a, 2001b; *Kompas* 2001d). These donors also demanded amendments to the implementing regulation of the Fiscal Balancing Law on Regional Government Borrowing (PP 107/2000) *(Bisnis Indonesia* 2001c).

There have indeed been discussions on plans to amend the two regional autonomy laws. In a hearing with the House of Representatives in mid-February 2001, the minister of home affairs and regional autonomy, Surjadi Soedirdja, revealed the government's plan to revise UU 22/1999. Earlier in that week, then–Vice President Megawati Soekarnoputri stated that many provinces were not ready to implement regional autonomy (The Jakarta Post 2001c).

There is also resistance to regional autonomy from the provinces. In a national meeting of APPSI, which was attended by governors from all over Indonesia, one topic of discussion was the request for the House of Representatives and the central government to amend the two 1999 regional autonomy laws (Kompas 2001c). One section proposed for amendment was that dealing with the structural relationship between provincial, regency, and town governments (which states that there is no hierarchical relationship between them). Resistance from the provinces is not without reason. Many government positions at the provincial level will be abolished because of decentralization. In South Kalimantan, for example, more than 3,000 officials within the provincial government will lose their seats (*Kompas* 2001e). Several regencies and towns are now disobeying provincial instructions and are indifferent about the continuing existence of the provincial governments (*Kompas* 2001c).

Some resistance to decentralization is also apparent in the forestry sector. UU 22/1999 contains ambiguous sections relating to the authority for managing forest resources. The implementing regulation of this law was not very supportive either, because it contained stipulations stating that control over important forestry matters was retained by the central government. By far the most positive direction in this regard appeared to be the release of the decree (05.1/Kpts-II/2000) by the MoF on the Criteria and Standards of Licensing of the Utilization of Forest Products and the Harvesting of Forest Products in Natural Production Forests in early November 2000.

The decree sets the maximum areas available for the utilization of forest products in a province, the maximum number of licenses a company can have in a province, and the maximum area for the utilization of forest products across Indonesia. The maximum forest area granted to a particular forest company, with the exception of Irian Jaya (Papua), is 50,000 ha. A company can hold no more than two licenses in each province. The maximum area granted to a particular licensee across Indonesia is 400,000 ha. The decree also specifies the authority of the regency, province, and central governments with respect to licensing forest utilization. The regency leader is authorized to grant forest utilization licenses over areas within his jurisdiction, a governor is able to grant licenses over areas that crosscut more than one regency (interregency), and the MoF can grant licenses over areas that crosscut more than one province (interprovince).

On the surface it appears that the level of control given to regions is quite substantial. Yet on closer examination, there are potential loopholes that allow the ministry to retain some of its authority. An important element specified in this decree that tends to provide the MoF with power is that all the licenses can only be granted over areas that have no other current legal rights over them. This will in essence exclude areas that still hold a valid concession permit, which at the time of writing was still a significant number. In June 2000, there were still 293 valid concession permits that were granted by the central government (i.e., before the issuance of the November 2000 regulation). These covered an area of 34 million ha out of an official total of 69.4 million ha of production forest.[34] Although we cannot accurately know the validity of the figures with regard to exactly how much of these areas are still actually forested, it gives some indication of the proportion of forest areas that the central government retains authority over—50%.

Another element in the decree that may appear to be insignificant is the fact that all applications submitted by December 31, 2000, will still be processed by the MoF. Interestingly, at around the same time as the release of the decree, the ministry revealed plans to issue 70 forest concession permits, of which 21 were new and 49 were extensions covering a total area of 3.5 million ha (Bisnis Indonesia 2000d). There were, however, some concerns in timber business circles that regencies may no longer honor concession permits issued by the central government (Bisnis Indonesia 2000f). This decree is also potentially a source of dispute between regency and provincial governments if there are no clear guidelines on its implementation. One possible source of disagreement is the lack of clarity about boundaries of forest areas between regencies.

One move that appears to be in the direction of resistance to decentralizing authority over the management of forest resources was the plan to manage production forests under the concept of *perumisasi*, which was to have become under the control of the Agency of Forest Management.[35] Under *perumisasi*, all production forests not under valid permits or concessions would be managed by state-owned companies. The plan is for the establishment of five agencies, one each in Sumatra, Kalimantan, Sulawesi, Irian Jaya, and the Maluku islands (*Bisnis Indonesia* 2000b). The agency will plan and issue logging permits, as well as rehabilitate degraded forests (*Bisnis Indonesia* 2000g;

Media Indonesia 2000c). These companies will be financed, at least partly, by the Reforestation Funds.

Various stakeholders have shown opposition toward this plan, because it is seen as a way for the MoF to retain its power over forest resources. Concession holders argue that placing production forests under the management of state-owned companies violates the spirit of the new Forestry Law (UU 41/1999), which clearly states that production forests are to be managed by state-owned companies, private companies, cooperatives, and individuals. Regions believe this means that decisionmaking authority over forest management is retained by the central government, even if governors and regency heads are given seats in these agencies. Forest-rich regions, such as Central Kalimantan, East Kalimantan, and Irian Jaya have been strongly opposed to this plan (*Media Indonesia* 2001).

The MoF, however, claims that this would not be the case. In fact, then-minister Nur Mahmudi Ismail insisted that this is all in the spirit of decentralization because it will involve stakeholders from the province and regency, and regions will be given an appropriate share of the revenues. It was suggested that 70% of the profit would be enjoyed by the regions—30% by the province, 30% by the regency, and 10% by forest communities (*Bisnis Indonesia* 2000b; *Media Indonesia* 2001). This last argument was also forcefully rejected by the regions, citing that they had never enjoyed much of the profits that Inhutani (the present state-owned companies who have been given the rights to manage some production forests) had accrued, and largely failed to manage production forests sustainably (*Bisnis Indonesia* 2000c, 2000e).

These examples show how, on the one hand, the MoF would very much like to retain some of its power, yet, on the other hand, it is facing fierce opposition from regions. It appears, however, that the ministry has a limited understanding of what has actually occurred in the regions since the transition period. Regional officials tend to openly act in a way that they perceive to be most beneficial to them, such as the issuance of regulations supporting the granting of small-scale forest utilization permits (HPHHs) by regency heads. As a result the center is busy making regulations and plans that may not necessarily be honored by the regions. This is reflected in one statement by ex-minister Nur Mahmudi Ismail that not everybody rejects the agency concept and that those who reject it do so because of their lack of understanding (*Media Indonesia* 2001). The ministry appears to understand that decentralization inevitably puts it in a weak position vis-à-vis the regions, demonstrated by the minister's constant effort to promote the government's plan within the regions (*Media Indonesia* 2001).[36] Now that we have looked at the trends shaping regional autonomy both on the ground and from the macro level, we examine the possible implications for forests and local communities.

Anticipating the Implications and Challenges for Forests and Local Communities

Our research was conducted during the transition period leading up to the formal implementation of decentralization; therefore, there were still many uncertainties with regard to which forest-related powers would be transferred to local governments. For example, at the time, the assignment of forest areas remained the responsibility of the central government, and it is not clear to what extent the regency has authority to issue permits for forest utilization.[37] Yet generally regencies have embarked on initiatives in forestry. Faced with financial needs, they began to follow a strategy to use forest resources in such a way as to achieve the greatest return from the opportunities that forests presented in their areas. This strategy was achieved by issuing small-scale utilization licenses, issuing sawmill licenses, and imposing charges on timber being transported outside the regency, without considering where or how the timber was harvested.

In a sense, legally imposing charges on illegal timber effectively formalizes activities that were previously largely illegal. In the short run, or while the resource lasts, as long as the charges are lower than the formal fees that have to be paid by concession holders, this creates a disincentive to continue to engage in legal timber operations. If charges were levied by every regency that the timber passed through, however, the overall charges paid could ultimately reach a level where it would not be profitable to continue illegal logging.

Nevertheless, decentralization poses another problem if regencies continue with the old way of handling confiscated timber (i.e., through auction). With decentralization, revenues from timber originating from a particular regency are shared with the center, the province, and other regencies within the province. Timber confiscated in a certain area may not originate from the area or may come from a number of different areas. As a result, disagreements may arise between regions about the origins of the confiscated timber and the distribution of the revenue from the proceeds of the auction. Either way of handling confiscated timber could potentially create conflicts among regencies.

Timber without legal letters authorizing transport may not be accepted willingly in the receiving regions, such as in the case of timber confiscated in the ports of Central and East Java (*Media Indonesia* 2000d; *Bisnis Indonesia* 2001a). But as long as illegal timber represents relatively cheap raw material, and thus increased competitiveness, there will be little reason for downstream industries not to accept it (*Media Indonesia* 2000b). Hence, it is important to cut the chain of demand for illegal logs downstream (i.e., the market). For instance, although all forest industries are strictly forbidden to use timber from Tanjung Puting National Park, industries in Java will accept it (*Media Indonesia* 2000b). CIFOR's research revealed that one of the regencies making regulations on utilization permits realized the importance of the timber being accepted in the receiving regions. It made a conscious effort to promote the acceptance of timber in receiving regions (Casson 2000b, 16).

It appears that even in the transition period regencies have attempted to address local people's concerns about accessibility to forest resources. In general the same actors continue to be involved in the utilization of forests. The difference lies with the relationship between these elements. At present, there is a closer two-way relationship between the local elites (as the group that provides protection and access to permits) and the forest entrepreneurs with capital (who use the opportunities opened up by regional autonomy). At the local (village) level, thus far, those who could enjoy the benefits of forest resources were limited to those who were quite powerful in the network of forest utilization. A large proportion of communities became laborers in logging activities, whether legal or illegal, or only enjoyed a minimum amount of the benefits brought by these activities.

The role of the regency in spatial planning and land use up to the period of research has been very minor. Decentralization may provide an opportunity to increase the role of regencies in a real sense, with the aim of lessening land conflicts or disputes and avoiding land uses that are not appropriate to the condition of the land. The role of sectors and agencies outside forestry may not be unimportant, including the National Land Agency, the industrial sector, and the plantation sector. In a case relating to the plantation sector, several regencies such as Kabupaten Ketapang in West Kalimatan and Kabupaten Kotawaringin Timur in Central Kalimantan were determined to develop plantations (notably oil palm) as a main contributor to the regency revenue. Their development would inevitably convert forestland. The overlapping of land uses and the lack of clarity and recognition about who has the rights over a piece of land—represented in this chapter by the examples of small-scale (HPHH and IPPK) permits on active timber concessions (HPH)—does not provide an incentive for those who hold the rights to follow a sustainable forest management path.

Some Reflections: How to Move Forward?

With the anticipated consequences of decentralization, how shall we move forward? Several countries around the world have implemented decentralization. We could use their forest-related experiences to anticipate the possible negative consequences in search of the best ways to manage our forests.

The Bolivian experience with decentralization, for example, suggests that strengthening the role of local governments in forest management may lead to both greater equity and more sustainable resource use. Local governments would need to have support and supervision from outside agencies to manage resources appropriately (Kaimowitz et al. 1998, 57). In addition, decentralization to a certain degree has created new opportunities for communities and small-scale timber producers in gaining direct control over a portion of timber royalties. It has also demonstrated that local governments are influenced by other forest-related stakeholders whose production systems tend to degrade the forests. Nonetheless, there were instances where these governments have been willing to promote forest management, nature conservation, and land-use planning that contribute to forests being managed more sustainably if they receive the appropriate training, resources, and incentives (Kaimowitz et al. 1998, 58).

The general tone surrounding the process of decentralization in Indonesia is one of overwhelming interest in the economic profits that can be gained from control over the utilization of forest resources in the regions. The cost in terms of capital that would have to be reinvested to maintain the sustainability of these resources is being conveniently ignored. It is important to recognize that to gain optimal benefits from forest resources, there needs to be a balance between appropriate management of the resources in the short term and the long term.

So far, the findings with regard to decentralization in Indonesia have suggested that protected and conservation areas potentially face a greater risk in this period of regional autonomy. It would be wise for all stakeholders involved to view regional autonomy as not only about power over resources, but also about responsibilities. It is all about sharing the profits and pains among all constituents of the nation.

All stakeholders, including all levels of government and communities, should recognize the different functions of forests, including their economic, environmental, ecological, and social functions. It would be desirable for all levels of governments to work together and put the nation's interests above their own. After all, it is easier to share the costs of maintaining the well-being of forests before they are destroyed, rather than wait for them to disappear, when the pains may be much worse and harder to bear.

Endnotes

1. Rondinelli et al. (1984 19–20) described devolution as

> …the creation or strengthening—financially or legally—of subnational units of government, the activities of which are substantially outside the direct control of the central government. Under devolution, local units of government are autonomous and independent, and their legal status makes them separate or distinct from the central government. Central authorities frequently exercise only indirect, supervisory control over such units. Normally, local governments have clear and legally recognized geographical boundaries within which they exercise an exclusive authority to perform explicitly granted or reserved functions. They have corporate or statutory authority to raise revenues and make expenditures.

2. For instance, sections in UU 1/1945 on the Stipulations of the Position of Regional National Committees demonstrated an early effort to set up a regional parliamentary body.

3. Based on UU 1/1957 on Principles of Regional Governance and PP 64/1957 on the Granting of Some of Central Government's Authority over Matters Concerning Coastal Fisheries, Forestry, and Community Rubber Sectors to First-level Regional Governments. In regions that were previously State of Eastern Indonesia (Negara Indonesia Timur), forestry matters were already controlled by second-level governments (regencies) (Regulation 64/1957, Article 8).

4. UU 5/1974, on the Principles of Regional Governance, did have elements of regional autonomy. In fact, Article 11 of this law specified that the focus of regional autonomy was at the regency (*kabupaten*) level. In general, however, the outcomes were as follows: (a) deconcentration has been favored as opposed to devolution by sectors; (b) most of the transfer of authority occurred from the central government to the provincial government as opposed to regency governments; (c) tasks that included important sources of revenues were seldom transferred to the regions; (d) tasks that were transferred were limited to implementation functions while policy, strategy, and decisionmaking related to funds allocation were kept at the central level; and (e) there was confusion about which tasks were devolution, deconcentration, or coadministration (Yusuf 1997, 2).

5. There are several relevant legislations in between the periods when these three legislations were enacted (e.g., UU 18/1965 on Principles of Regional Governance and UU 5/1979 on Village Governance). However, because the objective of this section is to give an overview of the process of decentralization attempts since Independence, we present only the ones most pertinent to our discussion.

6. All English version titles of the laws and regulations in this chapter are nonofficial translations.

7. PP 22/1967 on the Concession License Fees and Royalties. The explanation of this regulation explicitly specified how the implementation of the BFL benefited from the Foreign Investment Law: "With the enactment of UU 1/1967 on Foreign Investment, there opens an opportunity to massively exploit and manage the forests with overall planning by the central government."

8. PP 21/1970 on Forest Exploitation Rights and Forest Product Harvesting Rights.

9. PP 6/1999 on Forest Exploitation and Forest Product Harvesting in Production Forests.

10. PP 62/1998 on the Granting of Some Governmental Affairs in Forestry to Regions.

11. Lambang Trijono, a sociologist from Gadjahmada University, however, suggested that regional autonomy from the very outset was not meant to curb political turbulence and turmoil in the regions but specifically aimed to strengthen the central government in dealing with the economic crisis. Trijono (2001) quoted Ryaas Rasyid (who was known to be the architect of regional autonomy) as saying, "Regional autonomy was not set as a response to community or regional demands, but as a pure initiative of the central government." Rasyid went on to say that if the central government does not go ahead with decentralization, it will suffer from negative public opinion based on the idea that centralization is already outdated.

12. For a discussion on this new forest law, see Awang (1999).

13. Regions consist of provinces, regencies, and towns.

14. Under the previous law of regional governance (UU 5/1974), regency and town governments were second-level governments that reported to the provincial governments.

15. PP 25/2000 on Government Authority and Provincial Authority as an Autonomous Region.

16. This mechanism includes the following steps: first, if the regency cannot fulfill a specified responsibility, it must be given to the province; second, if the province is not capable of implementing this responsibility, it must be handed on to the central government.

17. The District Autonomy Pilot Programme was the first serious and concentrated effort to realize local autonomy at the regency level, according to UU 5/1974 (Beier 1997, 4). This program was governed by PP 8/1995 and applied to 26 regencies. The initiative is considered to have failed to address fundamental issues critical in carrying out a more comprehensive decentralization concept. The necessary condition to implement ongoing efforts in fiscal decentralization was not met (Beier 1997, 4).

18. "General allocation fund" refers to the funds allocated from the national budget for the purpose of equalizing the financial capacity between regions, to finance spending for the implementation of decentralization. "Specific allocation fund" is disbursed from the national budget to the regions to assist in financing specified needs (PP 104/2000).

19. PP 104/2000 on Distribution of Revenues.

20. As noted in several of the preceding chapters (e.g., Chapters 8 and 12), in the past this fund has been tapped and used for diverse purposes other than forest rehabilitation.

21. The regional share of the Reforestation Funds is to be treated as specific allocation funds. Specific allocation funds can be drawn from the national budget for a particular region to assist in financing specific needs. According to UU 25/1999, moneys from the Reforestation Fund are distributed as follows: 40% to the generating region to be used for rehabilitation efforts in the generating regions and 60% to the central government to be used for financing national reforestation efforts.

22. *Kabupaten Kampar* has now been formally divided into three new regencies: *Kabupaten Kampar*, *Kabupaten Rokan Hulu*, and *Kabupaten Pelalawa*n.

23. Kabupaten Indragiri Hulu has now been formally divided into two regencies: *Kabupaten Indragiri Hulu* and *Kabupaten Kuantan Singingi*.

24. The State Ministry of Regional Autonomy has now merged with the Ministry of Home Affairs.

25. The preliminary findings of the research as described in the following sections, particularly those based on fieldwork in the regions, were mostly extracted from early versions of the manuscripts synthesizing our case study findings by regencies.

26. *Putera daerah* literally means "local sons" or people who are ethnically the indigenous population of a particular area.

27. Although the differences between HPHH and IPPK permits can create some confusion, they in fact refer to small-scale timber licenses or small-scale forest conversion licenses assigned by regency leaders. In practice they are very similar (i.e., permits to harvest timber).

28. Compare this with timber concession (HPH) permits, which were mostly given to outsiders.

29. For a discussion of illegal logging, see Scotland et al. 2000 and Chapter 16 of this book.

30. In at least one of the East Kalimantan regencies studied, however, the regency government initiated its own spatial planning (Barr et al. 2001, 42).

31. Environmental Law (UU 23/1997), PP 27/1999 on Environmental Impact Analysis, and Ministerial Decree 05.1/Kpts-II/2000 on the Criteria and Standards of Licensing of the Utilization of Forest Products and the Harvesting of Forest Products in Natural Production Forests. Utilization of Forest Products is associated with timber and nontimber harvests by large-scale concessions, while the harvesting of forest products is associated with small-scale concessions.

32. In some instances, investors promise to develop agricultural plantations after the land is cleared, but there is no guarantee that this promise will be kept after the timber is removed (Barr et al. 2001, 36).

33. According to the regional autonomy laws and their implementing regulations, responsibility for the oil sector remains in the hands of the central government, and only 15% of the revenue generated is returned to the regions.

34. At the time of writing (February 2001), these data were the most recent information that could be obtained on valid concessions (Departemen Kehutanan 2001).

35. For a discussion on *perumisasi*, see CIFOR 2000.

36. By March 2001, Nur Mahmudi Ismail was replaced by Marzuki Usman. After this appointment, the concept of *perumisasi* seems to have faded from the news media. In August 2001, M. Prakosa was named Minister of Forestry under the new president, Megawati Soekarnoputri.

37. It was not until November 2000 that a Ministerial Decree (05.1/Kpts-II/2000) was issued setting out the criteria and standards for the issuance of permits of forest utilization on production forests.

References

Awang, S.A. (ed.) 1999. *Inkonsistensi Undang-Undang Kehutanan.* Yogyakarta, Indonesia: BIGRAF publishing.

Barr, C., E. Wollenberg, G. Limberg, N. Anau, R. Iwan, M. Sudana, M. Moeliono, and T. Djogo. 2001. *Decentralization of Policy Making and Administration of Policies Affecting Forests in Malinau District.* Draft paper. Bogor, Indonesia: CIFOR.

Beier, C. 1997. *Decentralization in Indonesia. Part 2: Preliminary Assessment of the Design and the Strategy of the District Autonomy Pilot Programme.* From the webpage http://www.fao.org/waicent/faoinfo/sustdev/rodirect/ Rofo0007.htm (accessed January 22, 2001). Rome, Italy: Food and Agriculture Organization.

Bisnis Indonesia. 2000a. Otonomi daerah dipercepat. From the webpage http://www.bisnis.com/ (accessed February 10, 2000).

_____. 2000b. BUMN baru kehutanan dijamin tak mengusik HPH. From the webpage http://www.bisnis.com/ (accessed November 13, 2000).

_____. 2000c. Inhutani-pemegang HPH gagal wujudkan hutan lestari. From the webpage http://www.bisnis.com/ (accessed November 17, 2000).

_____. 2000d. Dephut terbitkan 70 SK HPH seluas 3,5 juta ha. From the webpage http://www.bisnis.com/ (accessed November 22, 2000).

_____. 2000e. MPI: selesaikan "konflik" kehutanan. From the webpage http://www.bisnis.com/ (accessed November 30, 2000).

_____. 2000f. MPI: khawatir PEMDA tolak 70 HPH. From the webpage http://www.bisnis.com/ (accessed December 4, 2000).

_____. 2000g. Dephut tak lagi perpanjang HPH terhitung mulai 2001. From the webpage http://www.bisnis.com/ (accessed December 12, 2000).

_____. 2001a. Cegah masuknya kayu illegal dari Kalimantan ke Jatim. From the webpage http://www.bisnis.com/ (accessed January 6, 2001).

_____. 2001b. Lembaga donor minta PP utang daerah direvisi. From the webpage http://www.bisnis.com/ (accessed February 5, 2001).

Blomkvist, L. A., and Djuwadi. 2000. *Forest/Non-Forest Land Issues in Indonesia. Land Administration Project–C. Topic Cycle 5.* Jakarta, Indonesia: National Development Planning Agency and National Land Agency.

Casson, A. 2000a. *Decentralization of Policy Making and Administration of Policies Affecting Forests in Kutai Barat.* Draft paper. Bogor, Indonesia: CIFOR.

_____. 2000b. *Decentralization of Policy Making and Administration of Policies Affecting Forests in Kotawaringin Timur.* Draft paper. Bogor, Indonesia: CIFOR.

Cheema, G.S., and D.A. Rondinelli (eds.). 1983. *Decentralization and Development: Policy Implementation in Developing Countries.* Beverly Hills: Sage Publications. Quoted in J.M. Cohen and S.B. Peterson, *Methodological Issues in the Analysis of Decentralization.* Mimeo. (Cambridge, MA: Harvard Institute for International Development, 1996).

CIFOR (Center for International Forestry Research). 2000. Perumisasi *of Forest Management: Issues and Questions. Issues note prepared for Discussion on Models of Tropical Forest Management at Gadjahmada University.* Bogor, Indonesia: CIFOR.

Departemen Kehutanan. 2001. *Penataan Pengelolaan Hutan Produksi di Luar Pulau Jawa Melalui Restrukturisasi Kelembagaan Usaha Bidang Kehutanan.* Jakarta: Departemen Kehutanan. From the webpage http://www.dephut.go.id/informasi/umum/restrukturisasi.htm. (Accessed February 22, 2001).

The Jakarta Post. 2001a. Provinces told to resist foreign loans. January 29, 2.

_____. 2001b. Government will not let provinces go on borrowing spree. February 5, 12.

_____. 2001c. Government to revise law on regional autonomy. February 14, 2.

Kaimowitz, D., C. Vallejos, P. Pacheco, and R. Lopez. 1998. Municipal Governments and Forest Management in Lowland Bolivia. *Journal of Environment and Development* 7(1):45–59.

Kartasubrata, J. 1993. Indonesia. In *Sustainable Agriculture and the Environment in the Humid Tropics.* Committee on Sustainable Agriculture and the Environment in the Humid Tropics. Board on Agriculture and Board on Science and Technology for Sustainable Development. National Research Council. Washington DC: National Academy Press.

Kompas. 2000a. Pemerintah segera terbitkan pp otonomi daerah. February 10, 6.

_____. 2000b. Pengelolaan hutan melawan otonomi daerah. July 17, 26.

_____. 2000c. HPH skala kecil beroperasi tanpa AMDAL. November 15, 19.

_____. 2000d. Kebijakan HPH kecil sarat potensi konflik. November 24, 10.

_____. 2001a. Degradasi sumber daya hutan 1,6 juta hektar per tahun. January 30, 10.

_____. 2001b. Selaraskan relokasi gajah dengan ekonomi masyarakat. February 13, 10.

_____. 2001c. UU Otonomi diminta diamandemen. February 13, 20.

_____. 2001d. IMF masih menunggu kemajuan. February 17, 14.

_____. 2001e. 3.348 pejabat kehilangan jabatan. February 14, 19.

_____. 2001f. Ryaas Rasjid: Pelaksanaan otonomi amat merisaukan. February 20, 20.

_____. 2001g. HPH skala kecil dijual 20 juta. February 26, 13.

McCarthy, J. 2000a. *Decentralization of Policy Making and Administration of Policies Affecting Forests in Kapuas District.* Draft paper. Bogor, Indonesia: CIFOR.

_____. 2000b. *Decentralization of Policy Making and Administration of Policies Affecting Forests in Barito Selatan.* Draft paper. Bogor, Indonesia: CIFOR.

Media Indonesia. 2000a. Menhutbun tak hambat otonomi daerah. PP Kewenangan disahkan 7 Mei 2000. From the webpage http://www.mediaindo.co.id/ (accessed May 4, 2000).

_____. 2000b. Ribuan m³ kayu ramin diangkut ke Jawa. From the webpage http://www.mediaindo.co.id/ (accessed December 2, 2000).

_____. 2000c. Masyarakat Kutai tolak perumisasi HPH, Menhut dituding tidak dukung Otoda. From the webpage http://www.mediaindo.co.id/ (accessed November 18, 2000).

_____. 2000d. Kanwil Kehutanan Jateng amankan 200 m³ kayu illegal. From the webpage http://www.mediaindo.co.id/ (accessed October 27, 2000).

_____. 2001. Perumisasi HPH bersifat sentralistik. Daerah paling berwenang kelola hutan. From the webpage http://www.mediaindo.co.id/ (accessed January 5, 2000).

Parker, A. 1995. *Decentralization: The Way Forward for Rural Development?* Policy research working paper no. 1475. Washington, DC: The World Bank.

Potter, L., and S. Badcock. 2000. *The Effect of Indonesia's Decentralization on Forests and Estate Crops: Case Study of Riau Province, the Original Districts of Kampar and Indragiri Hulu.* Internal draft. Bogor, Indonesia: CIFOR.

Rahmadi, T. 2000. *Pengelolaan sumber daya hutan: Pembagian kewenangan antara pemerintah pusat dan pemerintah daerah.* Paper presented at the 2nd Insela Seminar, May 31–June 3.

Rondinelli, D.A., J.R. Nellis, and G.S. Cheema. 1984. *Decentralization in Developing Countries: A Review of Recent Experience.* World Bank Staff working paper no. 581. Washington, DC: The World Bank.

Scotland, N., J. Smith, H. Lisa, M. Hiller, B. Jarvis, C. Kaiser, M. Leighton, L. Paulson, E. Pollard, D. Ratnasari, R. Ravanell, S. Stanley, Erwidodo, D. Currey, and A. Setyarso. 2000. *Indonesia Country Paper on Illegal Logging.* Paper prepared for the World Bank-World Wide Fund for Nature Workshop on Control of Illegal Logging in East Asia. August 28. Jakarta, Indonesia.

Soetarto, E., F. Sitorus, and Y. N. Maguantara. 2001. *Desentralisasi kebijakan dan administrasi yang mempengaruhi hutan di Kabupaten Ketapang.* Draft paper. Bogor, Indonesia: CIFOR.

Trijono, L. 2001. Otonomi daerah, solusi atau pemicu disintegrasi. *Kompas.* January 29, 4–5.

Van Zorge Report. 2000. *More Questions than Answers.* September 19–23, 2000. Jakarta, Indonesia.

Yusuf, W. 1997. *Decentralization in Indonesia. Part 1: The Indonesian Decentralization Policy and the District Autonomy Pilot Programme.* December 16–18, 1997. From the webpage http://www.fao.org/waicent/faoinfo/sustdev/rodirect/ Rofo0007.htm (accessed January 22, 2001). Rome, Italy: Food and Agriculture Organization.

CHAPTER SIXTEEN

Dynamics of Illegal Logging in Indonesia

Richard G. Dudley

T ropical forests have been one of Indonesia's most important natural resources, contributing substantially to export earnings, employment, and the livelihood of local people. Roughly 300,000 people are employed in the wood-processing sector and at least 14 million are in some way directly dependent on the forest for their living. Forest products accounted for more than 11% of export earnings during 1994–1999. Although it is clear that forests have contributed substantially to the economic and social well-being of Indonesia's people, these benefits have been produced without due regard for forest sustainability. Also, a small political and economic elite have manipulated policy for their own benefit. As forest cover declines, the underappreciated local, national, and international ecological benefits of these forests are also lost (Scotland et al. 2000).

The rate of forest loss in Indonesia is alarming by any standard. During 1985–1997, almost 30% of the existing forested land on Sumatra disappeared. In Kalimantan (the Indonesian part of Borneo), 21% of the existing forest was lost over the same period. Essentially 100% of these areas was originally forested. In 1997, only about 35% of Sumatra and 60% of Kalimantan remained forested with 16.6 and 35.1 million ha of forest, respectively (Scotland et al. 2000).

Conversion of Indonesian forestland to other uses has occurred for several reasons. In many cases conversion has been a direct result of official policy. Such policies include creation of large oil palm, pulp, and (to a lesser degree) rubber plantations. Politics and corruption have played a major role in awarding plantation sites. An additional economic attraction of such conversions is the ability to sell timber from the sites as they are cleared for other uses. In the case of pulp plantations (to supply newly built paper mills), the original intent was to provide sufficient plantation area to supply the mills with fast-growing tree species. Yet mill owners found it more profitable to manipulate policy to continue to clear forest (with no fees paid) to get needed pulp logs from natural forest, while land cleared remained unplanted. (For a discussion of these issues, see Barr 2001).

Overharvest within forest concessions has also led to forest loss. Since the late 1960s, large forest concessions were awarded to entrepreneurs closely associated with President Soeharto (Barr 1998). Over time, manipulations of policy led to an overcapacity of sawmills and plywood production facilities. This overcapacity led to overharvest, which further degraded the ability of the forest to produce logs. In addition, the awarding of concessions was made with little regard for local peoples' rights to forest and land. People whose traditional rights were mostly ignored carried out "unofficial" logging within forest concessions. This "illegal logging" remained a minor problem because police and military were willing to enforce some of the laws and regulations. This willingness was related to their strong loyalty to the central government, which resulted, in part, from income they or their bosses received from their own forest concessions. Nevertheless, other factors also led to unsustainable harvest rates even within the concessions (Chapter 9).

In late 1997, serious economic difficulties and a growing resentment of increasingly obvious corruption led to the downfall of Soeharto in mid-1998. The resulting evaporation of central government control led to interethnic unrest in parts of the country. Democratic elections in early 1999 stabilized the situation, and much of the country has remained calm. Under the enigmatic President Abdurrahman Wahid, however, the central government remained weak. Decentralization, which has also been promoted by international agencies, is currently being carried out (see Chapter 15).

Will decentralization provide relief to the forestry sector? Some expect that more local control will bring less corruption and more sustainable forest management. Given recent indicators, this seems unlikely. Prior to official decentralization, de facto local control resulted from a decrease in central authority created by the political and economic uncertainty. Also, in 2000 a special law was created permitting local officials to grant small-scale forest concessions. These changes have both led respectively to illegal logging and to legal overharvest on a massive scale (McCarthy 2000; Casson 2000; Obidzinski and Suramenggala 2000). In some parts of Kalimantan, local people are now resigned to the fact that their forest will be completely converted to nonforest use in a matter of years (Wadley 2001).

The current situation is somewhat depressing. A 35-year domination of the forest resource industry by a small, powerful, and corrupt political elite has left a legacy of acceptance of feudalistic, corrupt, and illegal behavior. The current weakening of central authority has left a power vacuum in provinces rich in forest resources. The disappearance of the central elite may merely be replaced by corrupt networks at the provincial and local levels, which may include significant national and international components. This chapter represents an initial attempt to investigate these issues using a system dynamics approach to discover policies that might protect and sustainably manage remaining forest resources. The focus herein is illegal logging.

Approach Used

The work reported here was carried out during a short-term consultancy at the Center for International Forestry Research (CIFOR). It represents one attempt to formulate methods to work with various stakeholders on the growing problem of illegal logging. Numerous governmental and nongovernmental organizations are reporting incidents of illegal logging, but they are largely powerless to take action. Both donor and governmental agencies have held workshops to discuss the issue and to propose various action plans and policy proposals. But these forums have only limited means of analyzing short- and long-term implications of proposed policies. For example, new laws will have little effect if the legal system cannot enforce them, and additional taxes might merely stimulate illegal logging activity as people strive to avoid them.

A system dynamics approach provided a framework for analysis of illegal logging. It is believed that this framework could guide meaningful discussion of realistic policy options. System dynamics can portray mental models of illegal logging, which various groups reported in the literature or in person.

System dynamics is an approach to modeling that emphasizes causal relationships between variables, as well as feedback from consequences of actions back to the causes of those actions. While the use of quantitative system dynamics is an ultimate goal, activities to date have focused on a qualitative system dynamics approach known as causal loop diagramming. Causal loop diagrams provide a convenient and powerful way to clarify and display various mental models of a system. Analysis of policy options using causal loop diagrams is difficult even if the system is only moderately complex (Richardson 1986). Nevertheless, the approach certainly provides a useful starting point for examining factors that make illegal logging difficult to control. For a complete discussion of causal loop diagrams, see Sterman (2000).

The first step in building the models was to review recent reports about illegal logging that accurately detailed information from the field (McCarthy 2000; Casson 2000; Obidzinski and Suramenggala 2000; Curry and

Ruwindrijarto 2000; Newman et al. 2000; Wadley 2001). Recently completed comprehensive reviews of the Indonesian pulp (Barr 2001) and timber industry (Chapter 9) were also examined. Initial causal loop diagrams from different perspectives were created, and these were discussed with knowledgeable colleagues.[1] As appropriate, models were then discussed with stakeholders from whom the original information was obtained. These stakeholders included nongovernmental organizations, government agencies, and those involved in the timber industry. In some cases, there was a desire to return to a more general model if the details became too complicated. This was particularly true if models contained stock and flow components typical of quantitative models. All diagrams examine the question of why illegal logging in Indonesia is hard to control. Here this question is examined from just three perspectives: the evolution of the current situation, the local area perception of illegal logging, and a perception from the logging industry.

System Views of Illegal logging
The Soeharto Era and Its Legacy
In this section, I have presented a progression of four qualitative models to describe how the problem of illegal logging evolved in Indonesia. These models are based on preliminary ideas as to how factors affecting illegal logging evolved to the point that created the situation we find today. They do not describe the detail of today's situation, but rather factors leading to it.

The first model represents a somewhat idealized view of a well-managed timber industry working in cooperation with government. Sustainability of the resource is an important issue. The second model represents the role industry had in subverting sustainability for the sake of additional and more immediate profits. The third model attempts to explore how, during the Soeharto years, a timber industry largely controlled by Soeharto's family and friends and supported by the military managed to exaggerate this control by industry. The fourth model examines lingering effects of the Soeharto legacy that tend to exaggerate other factors leading to illegal logging at the local level.

Idealized View. An idealized view of the wood-processing industry might look like the representation in Figure 16–1.[2] In this view, demand for logs is driven directly by demand for and profitability of wood products. Demand for logs is also created by wood-processing mills. As demand for logs increases, the purchase price increases, stimulating increased harvest of logs using existing harvest capacity. An increase in profitability also stimulates creation of more harvest capacity (e.g., purchasing of more chain saws, hiring of more forest laborers). As the amount of timber cut increases, the supply of logs also increases, causing the price for logs to drop, which lowers potential profits

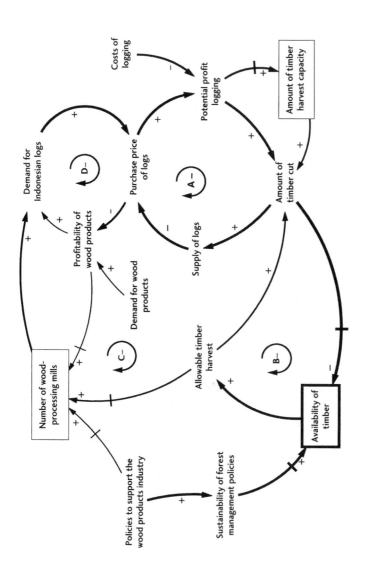

Figure 16–1. A Simplified View of an Idealized Wood Products and Timber Industry System
In this view several negative feedback loops stabilize the system and prevent both overharvest and the construction of too many processing mills.

from the log harvest. Eventually the price for logs stabilizes (stabilizing loop A). An increase in demand for logs will cause an increase in the price, which will ultimately tend to lower demand (stabilizing loop D). Taken together, these two loops also form a positive feedback loop (not labeled) whereby the increasing supply of logs lowers the price, thus increasing the demand.

Under this idealized view, the amount of timber cut is linked to an allowable timber harvest, which in turn is based on the availability of timber for harvest. As the amount of timber cut increases, the availability of timber for allowable harvest will eventually decrease (stabilizing loop B) with a delay. This negative feedback, which limits allowable timber harvest, will also limit construction of new wood-processing capacity as timber supplies and allowable harvest start to drop (stabilizing loop C). Importantly, availability of timber is influenced by the sustainability of forest management practices. In this idealized view, forest industry supports long-term management of forest for sustainable harvests over many years. Clearly this view does not present the current or past situation in the Indonesian timber industry.

Excess Influence of Industry. In Figure 16–2, I have presented a simplified view of what has happened in the Indonesian industry. This illustrates the situation that has evolved over the past several decades, the results of which still strongly influence the Indonesian forest sector. The stabilizing negative feedback loops prominent in Figure 16–1 have been overpowered by several positive feedback (growth) loops linked directly to the forest industry. Powerful interests within the forest industry were able to manipulate forest policy to directly benefit themselves. As their strength in the industry and wealth grew, their influence on policy also grew (reinforcing loop Q). Some of this policy was directed at the opening of new forest areas, which increased the availability of timber, at least in the short to medium term (reinforcing loop R). Other policy manipulations sought to bypass limits on harvest set by sustainable management practices (reinforcing loop S). Both of these actions essentially negated the effects of balancing loop B in Figure 16–1.

At the same time, greatly increasing demand and special government policies led to increased milling capacity. At first, Indonesian logs were exported. Subsequently, log exports were gradually discouraged via taxation and finally banned in 1985. This ban stimulated the growth of the domestic wood products industry. By 1992, when the log export ban was replaced with export taxes, increased milling capacity had created a strong domestic demand for logs. Continuing demand for wood from the processing sector allowed local log prices to remain high enough to stimulate continued high harvests. The relative profitability of timber harvesting has increased during the last few years as local labor costs have dropped in relation to international timber product prices. This situation benefited the large-scale timber processing industries as long as the central government could enforce the export tax.

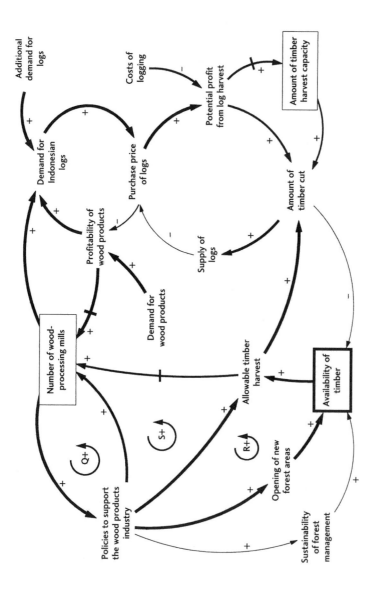

Figure 16-2. Excess Influence of Industry

In Indonesia, over the past decades, the timber industry had close ties to government. Consequently, the industry was able to directly influence and support policies that led to a larger allowable timber harvest and more wood-processing mills. At the same time, rapidly expanding demand for wood products continued to create an unfulfilled demand. These changes created positive feedback loops (Q, R, and S) that overpowered the balancing loops illustrated in Figure 16–1.

How Did Excess Influence Develop? Figure 16–2 does not fully explain why these changes came about. Figure 16–3 examines some additional information that helps explain how the Soeharto situation evolved and what potentially destructive system components remained in place when the Soeharto government collapsed in 1998.

In Figure 16–3, the relationship between Soeharto's power and timber interests is more clearly illustrated. A portion of Soeharto's power resulted from the strong support he received from the military, and a portion of that support was due to Soeharto's providing timber concessions to the military (reinforcing loop T). A spin-off from this loop is the support the military provided to the lobbying power of the timber industry, further reinforcing loop Q.

Also, as the involvement of the Soeharto family and associates grew, their influence on forest policy became dominant, providing for policies that further enhanced their own wealth and thus further strengthened their role in the industry (reinforcing loop U). These relationships weakened the role of the balancing loops illustrated in Figure 16–1, particularly those policies related to sustainability of forest resources.[3]

Importantly, as these factors further strengthened the role of the centrally controlled wood products industry, resentment began to build in the rural forested areas. The amount of dissatisfaction with central forest policy grew, but people were largely unable to do anything about it. To a certain extent, illegal logging was also a part of the centrally controlled system. Selective enforcement and insufficient monitoring allowed timber harvest outside formally agreed upon terms for forest concessions, leading to the degradation of the forest resource base. In a sense, this type of illegal logging can also be viewed as a manipulation of policy by industry. Other than this, the amount of locally based, illegal logging was kept in check by the military and police, whose bosses had timber interests themselves, and also because of the strength of the Soeharto regime in general.

Disappearance of the Soeharto Regime. With the fall of Soeharto, some of the model components disappear, some become less important, and yet others become more important. These changes are illustrated in Figure 16–4. Here model components representing the strength of Soeharto and his associates and support of Soeharto by military and police have been removed. With this change, positive feedback loops T and U disappear, and the strength of loops Q, R, and S is greatly reduced (i.e., the influence of the central timber interests on policy formulation greatly diminished).

Although the lobbying power of central timber interests decreased, the wealth of these interests and the resentment against them did not disappear. Consequently, a significant local area dissatisfaction remained and continued to grow. At the same time, the major constraint on illegal logging—support

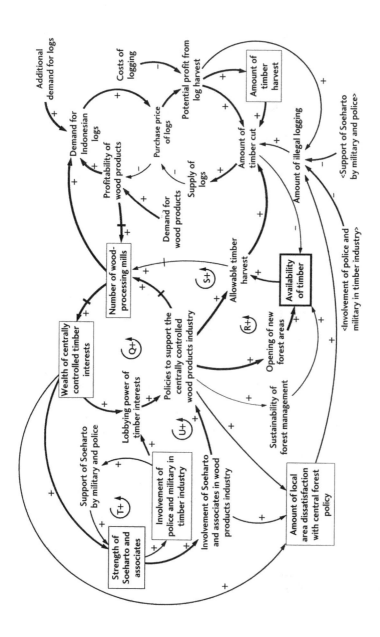

Figure 16–3. Power of Soeharto strengthens control by timber interests.

This expansion of Figure 16–1 examines some of the causal relationships that conspired to strengthen the power of centrally controlled timber interests. Of primary importance is the power of Soeharto and his own links to timber interests and military people who also had timber interests. Although dissatisfaction within communities in forested areas grew, efforts at locally controlled illegal logging during that period were kept in check by the relatively powerful police and military.

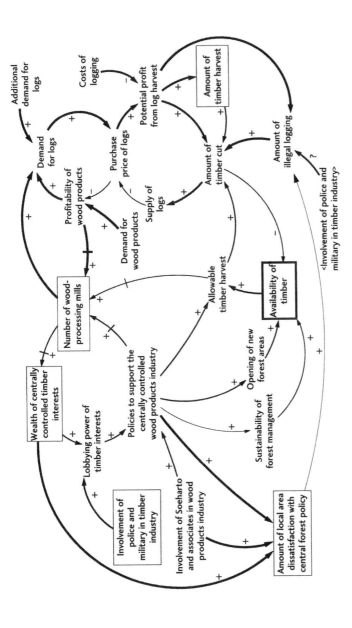

Figure 16-4. Removal of Central Controlling Interests

The timber industry shortly after the fall of Soeharto might be presented as in this figure. Soeharto lost his power as well as police and military loyalty. His family and associates retained their forestry holdings, but their influence on policy greatly diminished. Factors leading illegal logging became intensified because support of Soeharto by military and police had been removed. A major factor initiating the wave of illegal logging was the lingering resentment caused by the amount of local area dissatisfaction with central forest policies. The remaining constraint on illegal logging—involvement of police and military in timber industry—may have changed to support illegal logging.

of Soeharto by military and police—disappeared. It seems likely that residual timber involvement by military and police may tend to support, rather than limit, illegal logging. In any case, the police and military retained only limited power and thus were largely unable to enforce the law. These factors all conspired to set the framework for large amounts of illegal logging.

The aforementioned qualitative models help explain why illegal logging became such a big problem in Indonesia. These models do not explain why it persists at such a high level. The next step is to explain the factors reinforcing illegal logging with the ultimate goal of examining policies that could lead to its control.

The View of Illegal Logging at the Local Level

The previous section illustrates the situation created by the weakening of Indonesia's central government. A lingering result of the years under Soeharto, at least in the forest-rich rural areas of Indonesia, was a feeling of resentment that little of the wealth gained from forestry had been returned to the local areas. As central government power diminished, there was an initial hope that decentralization would permit some form of sustainable forest management with benefits remaining in the local area. This hope turned to concern as reports of rampant illegal logging started to come in from all parts of Indonesia. This section examines factors that caused illegal logging to flourish at the local level and that allowed illegal logging to expand so rapidly. There are three groups of factors that could each be subdivided further:

1. factors related to community values and the human situation in rural villages near forests (Figure 16–5);
2. economic factors of normal supply and demand related to the logging industry (Figure 16–6); and
3. factors related to entrepreneurs and their influence on, and collusion with, local politicians and leaders (Figure 16–7).

At the community level, as illustrated in Figure 16–5, what matters most is the provision of jobs and income. The willingness to work illegally is strongly influenced by the fact that one's neighbors and friends are also working illegally. As more people work illegally in forests and sawmills, that source of income becomes acceptable.

Community ideas concerning the long-term value of forests may limit the participation of community members in illegal logging, but several factors may weaken community resolve in these matters. Chief among these factors are the lingering dissatisfaction with central forest policy and the perception that the communities' long-term access to its surrounding forest resources is threatened. Interestingly, the perception of long-term access being lost is made more severe by increasing illegal logging. In

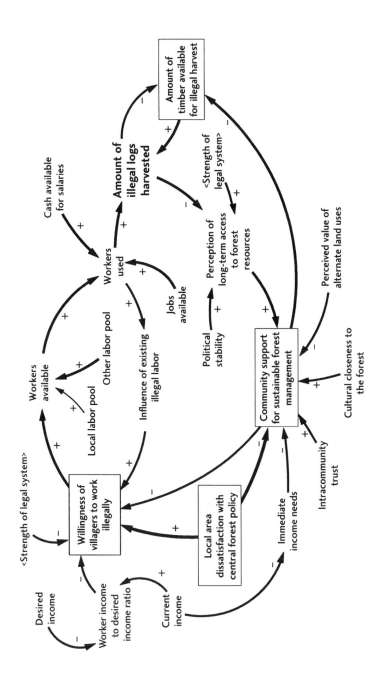

Figure 16–5. A Villager and Community Perspective
From this perspective, the other factors shown in Figure 16–8 may appear irrelevant. This is a close-up view of factors directly related to forest communities and people living in them.

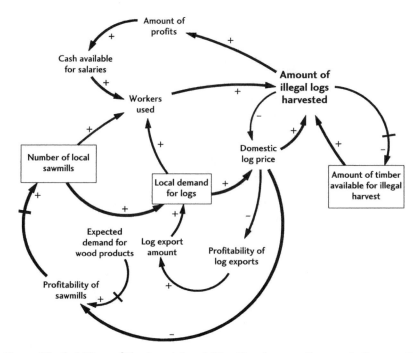

Figure 16–6. A View of the Local-Level Situation from an Economic Perspective
Opportunity for profits coupled with availability of raw materials and labor is sufficient incentive if markets are available. Business is of course possible without illegal activity.

some cases, alternates to forested land may arise and the value of these alternate uses may also change community perceptions regarding forest management.

As more and more community members participate in illegal activities, the activities become acceptable. The additional income is certainly welcome. But this logging increases forest loss, which weakens community values related to the long-term view of forest benefits. The weakening of this collective, positive, view of the forest encourages additional participation in illegal logging and milling. This whole process will be reinforced if resentment of central forest policy is strong, the legal system is weak, and the economy is poor.

A hypothesized view of how economic factors operate at the local level appears in Figure 16–6. Here the likelihood of profits generates a direct demand for logs and causes an increase in milling capacity, which creates additional demand for logs. This demand for logs creates a demand for labor and jobs for the local community.

Legal businesses provide jobs for the local communities, but because of time lags in building mills, the creation of overcapacity is possible. Overcapacity can lead to excessive demand for logs and excessive harvests even if

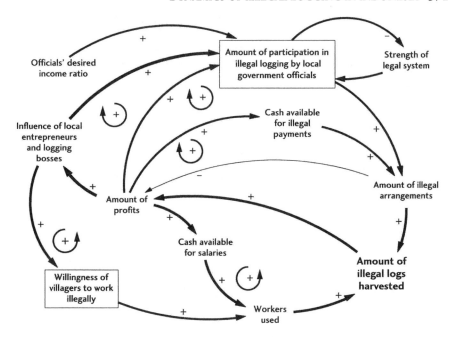

Figure 16–7. A View of Illegal Logging Activities at the Entrepreneur–Local Government Level
This view is dominated by positive feedback loops, which tend to push the system in one direction or the other, depending on the strength of other factors.

profits drop. In striving to maintain profits, mills may resort to the purchase of illegal logs if they are cheaper and the risks associated with buying them are low. For simplicity, in Figure 16–6, risks (of prosecution, for example) are included in the domestic log price.

At the political–entrepreneurial level, the likelihood of collusion appears (Figure 16–7). This happens because politicians have power to grant contracts for access to forestlands and ensure that various laws and regulations are enforced or ignored. Entrepreneurs, however, have money gained from profits in the logging business. As indicated in Figure 16–7, this subsystem contains a number of positive feedback loops that tend to reinforce and exaggerate existing conditions. As profits grow, the influence of the entrepreneurs grows, allowing more illegal arrangements to be made with local officials. Importantly, however, the loops could act with the opposite effect. If, for example, the legal system were suddenly strengthened, causing a decrease in the participation in illegal activities by local officials, then the amount of illegal arrangements and illegal profits would decrease, causing a reduction in the influence of illegal entrepreneurs. In this particular subview, the strength of the legal system is important; but as indicated in the overall view (Figure 16–8), other factors could also set such change in motion.

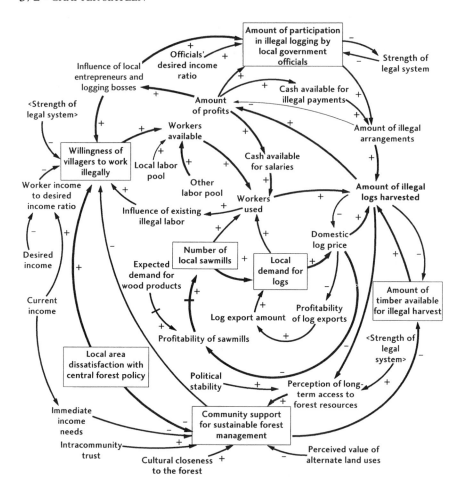

Figure 16–8. An Overall Local-Level View of Illegal Logging
In this view there are 18 feedback loops directly affecting the amount of illegal logs harvested. This view combines information found in Figures 16–5, 16–6, and 16–7.

The causal loop diagram in Figure 16–8 combines these views and represents, with many simplifications, the major forces contributing to illegal logging at the local level. Entrepreneurs tempt local officials to allow them to cut illegally to increase their profits. In some cases collusion may be necessary to gain access to forest currently allocated to other uses, especially if much of the forest is already allocated. To carry out their operations, entrepreneurs hire local people or, if the locals are not available or willing, people from distant cities or towns who are drawn by the chance for work. As illegal logging activities increase and the potential income becomes obvious, the acceptance of illegal activities by communities increases. People become dependent on this new activity and see its inevitability whether or not they participate.

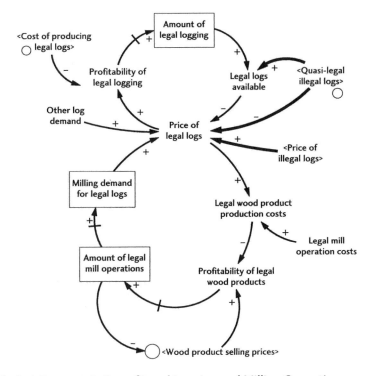

Figure 16–9. A Representation of Legal Logging and Milling Operations

One problem for legal logging operators is that illegal logs depress the log price and increase the apparent number of legal logs on the market, causing the log price to drop well below what would support legal logging. This is especially true because high taxes on legal logging operations push up the legal logging costs (Figure 16–11).

Note: Small circles indicate links to other figures in this section. Components in brackets < > indicate a component that originates from another figure.

A Business View

Obviously, large business interests see illegal logging from a different perspective. The primary issue for business is possible profits associated with the production of wood products. In simple terms this means businesses must consider the costs, potential sales, and risks associated with producing such products. Illegal producers will have a rather different view of the same issues. For simplicity we might consider two components of a timber-related businesses: (a) logging and selling logs and (b) processing logs into wood products and selling those products.[4]

A simplified view of legal logging and milling operations is presented in Figure 16–9. If profitability increases, mill operations will also increase, thus creating a higher demand for logs. Higher demand will drive up log prices, thus stimulating logging operations if logging costs are not too high.

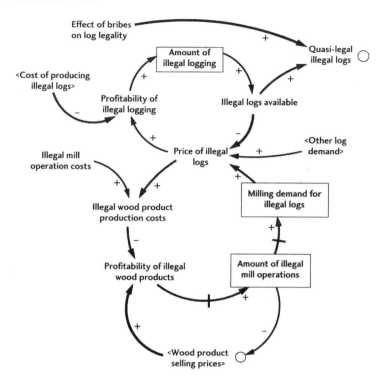

Figure 16–10. A Representation of Illegal Logging and Milling Operations
Illegal logging and milling operations have a structure similar to the corresponding legal activities. Yet the costs of the illegal activities are different. Illegal costs include bribes paid to avoid taxes and restrictions on logging location and methods. Because bribe payments are lower than taxes, illegal logs can be sold at a lower price than legal logs. Mills buying legal logs thus also have a profit advantage.

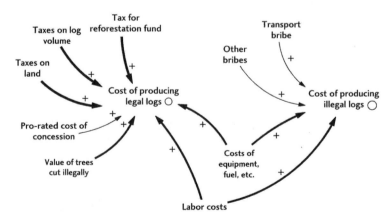

Figure 16–11. Partial List of Costs Incurred by Legal and Illegal Logging Operations

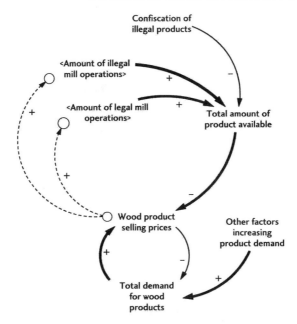

Figure 16–12. Model Components Related to Wood Product Pricing and Demand
To a large extent the legality of products produced is unknown. Thus both legal and illegal products enter the same market and their abundance helps determine the price. Other factors affecting the demand for Indonesian products might include pricing of competing products and possible substitutes.

As logging increases, log prices will drop and eventually stabilize at a price sufficiently high for the logging business and sufficiently low for the purchase of logs by the mills.

From the perspective of businesses wishing to operate legally, illegal logs on the market create problems. Illegal logs can be profitably sold at lower prices, and this will depress the overall price of logs in general. Also, illegally harvested logs may be sold as if they were legal if false documentation is purchased. Although these cheaper logs are potentially profitable for milling operations, the depressed prices discourage legal logging, creating a difficulty for mills wishing to buy only legal logs. In other words, the log market becomes flooded with low-priced but illegal logs that may give processors little choice but to buy illegal logs or none.

The perspective of illegal logging operations is different (Figure 16–10). The primary difference between this and the legal perspective is the source of the costs and resultant profitability of each type of operation. Some of the costs are illustrated in Figure 16–11. Whereas legal operations have several taxes imposed, illegal operations do not pay taxes but instead pay bribes and payoffs to officials, the police, or military. The final outcome for the manufacturing portion of the business is dependent on the pricing of the final product (Figure 16–12). If the costs for producing an illegal product are lower than the

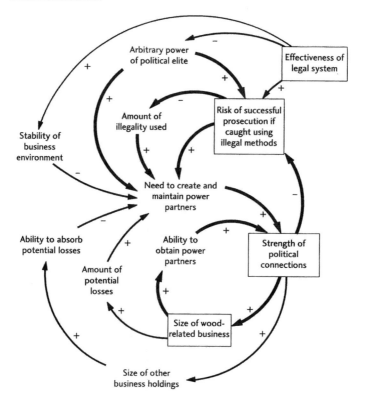

Figure 16–13. A Business View of Risks Associated with Doing Business in the Logging and Wood-Processing Sectors

Risks are increased by the effectiveness of the legal system if one is involved in illegal activities, and by possible arbitrary power of political elites in both legal and illegal cases. In order to counteract these risks, businesses tend to create and maintain power partners who can minimize these risks via political influence.

Not shown in this diagram are the arrangements made to maintain these power partners. If civil society is strong, such links would be maintained by a clean reputation, support for good causes, and appropriate political parties. If civil society is weaker, then links are more likely to be maintained by bribery, questionable business partnerships, and perhaps violence.

price of a legal product, then the legal product cannot be competitive. This is because the market price for the two is the same, unless there is a risk or premium paid on illegal products (e.g., a risk of fine or confiscation of the products). In this model, we assume that there is no way to determine if a product is produced from legal or illegal wood.

In spite of the similarity between Figures 16–9 and 16–10, the differences between them produce a very important outcome. If the illegal activities are more profitable than the legal activities, then illegal activities will become dominant, other things being equal. Legal logging and milling will disappear. Field reports indicate that illegal logging and milling is significantly cheaper, and illegal logging has become dominant in many areas. From the perspective of legal business, a major component of this problem is the level of government tax on logs. Because taxes of various sorts account for almost 50% of the cost of legal logs, a drastic reduction in this tax would make the costs of legal and illegal logging more comparable.

In addition to the operating costs of illegal and legal approaches to business, there is another related component that we can call "risk." Risk occurs in both legal and illegal operations. Here we can limit the discussion of risk to "risk of legal action, illegal action, or political action" against a business. Such action might result in jail terms or fines for illegal activity or severe limitation of business activity through confiscation of property and facilities. Risks are also faced in areas where local communities may be free to take revenge for perceived injustices by logging firms. We might imagine that these risks are only faced by illegal operators, but if other businesses and politicians are involved in illegal activities then legal operators may also face risks. These risks might involve grossly unfair business practices and biased (or lack of) enforcement of existing laws or threats, for example.

Figure 16–13 represents a model of the risks faced by logging and milling businesses as well as the actions businesses might take to minimize these risks. The major risks in the current situation might be viewed as the risk of prosecution if caught violating laws. Yet if arbitrary power of the political elite (local or national) is high, then risks might be created by actions that oppose these elites, legal or illegal. Thus, a stronger legal system may increase risk from one source (prosecution) but at the same time may lower the risk from another source (arbitrary power).

In general, all businesses will attempt to have some connection to political power to protect themselves from these risks. As the "strength of political connections" increases, the "size of wood-related business" will also tend to increase because political connections will help in the acquisition of new contracts. This will further increase the ability to obtain powerful partners but, because of the increased business, will also increase potential losses if something goes wrong. These two loops work together, increasing both the need for political partners and the ability to obtain and keep such partners.

In summary, there are both legal and illegal options for business. Legal operations require the payment of relatively high taxes on logging operations and milling operations. Illegal operators, in addition to cutting trees illegally, avoid tax costs partly by paying bribes to appropriate officials. For that reason, illegal logs are currently considerably cheaper than legally produced logs. If a mill chooses to use legally produced logs (produced at a higher price than the illegal logs), then it will produce a more expensive final product. This product will not be able to compete with the products produced by mills using illegal logs. To protect themselves from risk, both legal and illegal business interests will try to align themselves with powerful political interests who can help to minimize those risks. The reinforcing nature (or positive feedback) within this relationship means that the system will tend to move toward more legality or toward more illegality, depending on which becomes well established first. Once established, either of these modes will become more difficult to change. Because mutual benefits of this sort are possible via a number of business opportunities, none of these relationships are tied directly to healthy forest resources, and business–political partnerships could be transferred to oil palm, mining, road contract, or other endeavors. It seems possible, however, that mutually beneficial systems, for which forest wealth formed the basis, could be established.

Evolving "Illegal" Logging Systems

Obidzinski and Suramenggala (2000) and Obidzinski (2001) reported on the changing circumstances in areas where illegal logging has been common. As a part of its decentralization plans, the central government, hoping also to prevent further damage from illegal logging, passed several laws in 1998 and 1999 giving legal authority for local government to issue forest harvest permits.[5] According to Obidzinski (2001) this change immediately created a situation where buyers sought rights to cut timber via arrangements with local communities, with permits supplied by local government. This increased the role of local communities via two channels: the value of their forested lands became more obvious to them, and their legal authority over the land became clearer. Following these changes, communities were interested in protecting their lands from illegal logging, forcing logging interests to make legal deals with communities instead (Obidzinski 2001).

How do these changes affect the transparency of forest operations? The fact that log buyers are now dealing with communities and local government officials within some legal guidelines means that, technically speaking, less illegality is involved. But the arrangements whereby permits are issued by local government offices are uncontrolled. Legal and illegal fees for these permits now make up a very large portion of cash flow at this governmental level. The very high number of permits issued leads one to conclude that sustainable forest management is not the primary motivating force and that short-term profits, both legal and illegal, are still of primary interest. Only the mode of gaining access to timber resources has changed.

Under the new systems, more of the profits remain within forest communities compared with the past when profits went to Jakarta business and political interests. But the structure of the system is still similar to that presented in Figure 16–8 whereby forest entrepreneurs have captured the decisionmaking apparatus with cash payments (legal and illegal) to both officials and villagers. At this level there are few—or no— forestry advisers, and even if such advice were offered it would have little effect.

Sadly, the effect on the forest of this new logging system may be worse than the old system. Immediate economic need, rather than a long-term view of forest profitability, is likely to be the major component of community thinking given current political and economic uncertainties.

Conclusion

This chapter has demonstrated the use of system dynamics to investigate the causes of illegal logging in Indonesia. Clearly the use of even qualitative causal loop diagrams is helpful in elucidating the many factors contributing to illegal logging. The approach has been helpful in explaining how Indonesia got to its present state during the many years of the Soeharto regime, which inadvertently created a situation in which sustainability of forest management was largely ignored and dissatisfaction at the local level was increased.

This local-level dissatisfaction was an important cause, along with poor economic conditions, triggering the current illegal logging disaster. But many interlinked factors have reinforced the illegal logging system at the local level. To gain access to forestlands and avoid taxes, entrepreneurs conspire with local officials to carry out illegal logging. Members of local communities who may normally have an aversion to becoming involved with illegal logging are more willing to do so in light of their long-standing dissatisfaction with central government policy. As more and more timber is cut illegally, traditional views of the forest are eroded so people no longer see any sense in trying to protect what was once their traditional, and primary, source of livelihood.

The remaining large timber interests feel that they are significantly limited by illegal logging unless they want to become direct participants. Illegal logs on the market are significantly cheaper than legal logs from forest concessions. High taxes are claimed to be a major component of this problem. These timber interests find it difficult to compete in a market dominated by wood products based on illegal timber. Business interests at both the national and local levels attempt to minimize their risks by forming alliances with powerful politicians or community leaders. Given a weak central government, it seems likely that the large timber interests will also be compelled to reinforce such alliances at the local, rather than the national, level, and this trend will be reinforced by decentralization.

The qualitative causal loop diagrams are helpful in elucidating these situations, and they help us better understand the factors contributing to illegal logging. This understanding can help in formulating corrective policies. Yet a full analysis of such policies is best done with quantitative system dynamics models, based on the understanding provided by causal loop diagrams.

Acknowledgments

A number of people provided helpful advice and discussion during the preparation of this chapter. Among these are Joyotee Smith, Krystof Obidzinski,

Anne Casson, John McCarthy, Chris Barr, Graham Applegate, Carol Colfer, Herry Purnomo, and Lini Wollenberg of CIFOR; Erwidodo, Doddy S. Sukadri, and Subarudi of the Indonesian Center for Forestry Economic and Social Research, Ministry of Forestry; Benny Luhur, Riza Suarga, and Herman Prayudi of the Association of Indonesian Forest Concession Holders; Agus Purnomo and Agus Setyarso of the World Wide Fund for Nature, Indonesia; A. Ruwindrijarto of Telapak Indonesia; Dave Curry of the Environmental Investigation Agency (U.K.); and Elias of the Faculty of Forestry, Bogor Agricultural University.

Although I am thankful for their help, I in no way hold these colleagues accountable for what I have done with their suggestions. I hope that after reading this chapter they will have many additional comments.

Endnotes

1. See Annex 16–1 for an explanation of the conventions used to prepare these diagrams.

2. Herein we focus on the sawn timber industry. Issues related to illegal logging are somewhat different for the plywood industry and entirely different for the pulp and paper industry.

3. A similar loop structure could be applied to the role that Soeharto and his associates had in most other industries (e.g., mining, petrochemicals).

4. The relevant laws are still changing, but typically individual permits involved areas of only 100 ha, although other laws implemented at the provincial level allowed larger areas. Buyers typically have many such agreements to fulfill their log supply needs.

5. Note that land ownership in Indonesia is seldom clearly known, and even temporary resolution of land disputes may require many years of negotiation.

References

Barr, C. 1998. Bob Hasan, the Rise of APKINDO, and the Shifting Dynamics of Control in Indonesia's Timber Sector. *Indonesia* 65:1–36.

———. 2001. Chapter 4: The Political Economy of Fiber and Finance in Indonesia's Pulp and Paper Industries. In *Banking on Sustainability: Structural Adjustment and Forestry Reform in Post-Suharto Indonesia*. Washington, D.C.: Center for International Forestry Research (CIFOR) and World Wide Fund for Nature Macroeconomics for Sustainable Development Program Office, 70–95.

Casson, A. 2000. *Illegal Tropical Timber Trade in Central Kalimantan*, Indonesia. Draft report.

Curry, D., and A. Ruwindrijarto. 2000. *Illegal Logging in Tanjung Puting National Park, An Update to the Final Cut Report*. Jakarta, Indonesia: Environmental Investigation Agency and Telapak Indonesia.

McCarthy, J.F. 2000. *"Wild Logging:" The Rise and Fall of Logging Networks and Biodiversity Conservation Projects on Sumatra's Rainforest Frontier*. Occasional paper no. 31. Bogor, Indonesia: Center for International Forestry Research.

Newman, J., A. Ruwindrijarto, and D. Curry. 2000. *The Final Cut: Illegal Logging in Indonesia's Orangutan Parks*. Jakarta, Indonesia: Environmental Investigation Agency and Telapak Indonesia.

Obidzinski, K. 2001. Operational nature of illegal logging in Indonesia and its intensification in recent times. From the *Indonesian Nature Conservation Newsletter*, issue 4–10, March 11, 2001. A nonprofit Internet e-mail list for announcements and news about topics related to nature conservation in Indonesia. Contact: Ed Colijn, Indonesian Nature Conservation Database, edcolijn@bart.nl, http://www.bart.nl/~edcolijn/.

Obidzinski, K., and I. Suramenggala. 2000. *Illegal Logging in Indonesia—A Contextual Approach to the Problem*. Draft paper.

Richardson, G.P. 1986. Problems with causal-loop diagrams. *System Dynamics Review* 2(2):158–70.

Scotland, N., J. Smith, H. Lisa, M. Hiller, B. Jarvis, C. Kaiser, M. Leighton, L. Paulson, E. Pollard, D. Ratnasari, R. Ravanell, S. Stanley, Erwidodo, D. Curey, and A. Setyarso. 2000. *Indonesia Country Paper on Illegal Logging*, edited by W. Finlayson and N. Scotland. Unpublished report prepared for the World Bank-World Wide Fund for Nature Workshop on Control of Illegal Logging in East Asia. Jakarta, Indonesia.

Sterman, J.D. 2000. *Business Dynamics: Systems Thinking and Modeling for a Complex World*. Boston: McGraw-Hill.

Wadley, R.L. 2001. *Histories of Natural Resource Use and Control in West Kalimantan, Indonesia: Danau Sentarum National Park and Its Vicinity (1800–2000)*. A report for the Center for International Forestry Research Program "Local People, Devolution, and Adaptive Collaborative Management." Bogor, Indonesia: CIFOR.

Annex 16–1. Notes about Causal Loop Diagrams

The purpose of these modeling efforts is to create causal loop diagrams (which might later lead to a quantitative model) of the illegal logging problem. A modeling specialist is necessary, but ideally stakeholders should have meaningful input to improve model validity.

The primary purpose of a system dynamics model of this type is to describe the dynamics that are causing a particular problem. For example, in this case the question is, "What are the dynamics that make the illegal logging problem so difficult to solve?"

In building the diagram, the approach is to examine explicitly the causal relationships between model components, one pair of cause and effect at a time. It is often helpful to determine units of measurement to be used such as *rupiah*/m^3 or m^3/hectare. Dimensionless components might also be used, for example a ratio of "salary" to "desired salary" ($/$). Some model components have no dimension such as "influence of income on willingness to work."

For qualitative modeling it is sufficient to label the relationship between two variables as positive or negative, other things being equal. Thus, in the diagram we would label both solid arrows with a plus sign (+). In doing so we would not worry about any possible effect of oversupply on price; that would be examined in an additional connection shown by the dashed line. This connection might be given a minus sign (–) depending on how we believed logs harvested might affect price per m^3. In a qualitative model, we would not consider the shape of the relationship even though it may be very nonlinear,

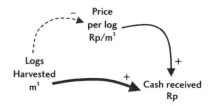

Figure 16–14. A simple example of diagram-labeling conventions.

with price remaining roughly constant until supply got very large (for example). In creating the causal loop diagrams, the following conventions have been used (Figure 16–14):

- If a relationship is marked with a plus sign (+), then the relationship is "read" as "if variable x changes, then variable y changes in the same direction (positive or negative), all other things being equal."
- If a relationship is marked with a minus sign (–), then the relationship is "read" as "if variable x changes, then variable y changes in the opposite direction (positive or negative), all other things being equal."
- Note that in a complex model it is often the case that all other things are not equal. So a particular pair-wise relationship, within the context of a model, may not produce the result we expect.
- Model components placed in boxes are "stocks" or "accumulations" that build up and dissipate over an extended period. Model components such as "number of sawmills" or "wealth of centrally controlled timber interests" are stocks.
- Stocks cause delays in a system. A line drawn across an arrow serves to emphasize this delay. A delay means, for example, that once sawmills are built, they do not disappear immediately when the price of logs becomes too high.
- In the diagrams, the thickness of lines gives a general guide as to the importance the modeler believes should be assigned to the relationship between two variables. Yet, this importance can vary.
- Feedback loops can be identified in diagrams by following arrows along any path that leads back to the original model component.
- If the arrows used along the path are all positive, or if the path includes an even number of negative arrows, then the loop is a positive feedback loop. A positive feedback loop tends to cause reinforcing behavior in the system.
- If the path contains an odd number of negative arrows then the loop is a negative feedback loop. Negative feedback loops tend to cause stability in a system.

Conclusion

So what can we conclude from this set of articles, written in the center of a maelstrom? They do not represent any sort of final "steady state." Rather they represent the kinds of problems that Indonesian policymakers have been coping with, in some cases for months, in others for decades. They also represent problems that are not so terribly unusual in the world's tropical forests and among the peoples who live in them. These articles sound alarm bells, while in most cases suggesting some practical entry points for solutions. Here we briefly summarize the main policy issues, discuss Indonesia's role on the world stage, and conclude with a policy narrative that has colored much of the policy linking people and forests in Indonesia.

Critical Policy Issues

The following significant issues still remain to be addressed:

- Kolusi, korupsi, dan nepotisme *([KKN] collusion, corruption, and nepotism) have created complex and harmful circumstances in this country.* Improvements in this realm are probably necessary if forests and forest communities are to be sustained. In late 1999, the prospects for seriously addressing these three issues seemed real and exciting. The intervening two years have tempered our optimism somewhat. No major corruption trials have resulted in suitable punishments, and incumbents are rumored to continue to practice these arts. Scientific articles abound on this subject, with suggestions ranging from "Fry the Big Fish First" (Klitgaard 1988) to salary increases for civil servants to improvements in the legal system. In the Indonesian case, the other issues discussed in this section are in fact intimately connected with KKN (Chapter 16).

• *The laws and their implementation have not been conducive to either human well-being or sustainable forest management.* There has been a lack of transparent coordination among ministries and between private industry and the government, resulting in problems like the overcapacity for processing that holds the potential for causing so much forest degradation (Barr 2000; Chapter 9 of this book) or the recent upsurge in illegal logging (Curry and Ruwindrijarto 2000; McCarthy 2000; Obidzinski and Suramenggala 2000; Wadley 2001; Chapter 16 of this book). This is linked to the previous issue. Overcapacity for processing, for instance, can be directly linked to the collusive and nepotistic mechanisms used during the Soeharto era to allocate rights to natural and other national resources (Barr 1998, 1999, 2000). That these problems have not yet been solved is unfortunately clear from the continuing surge in illegal logging and the increasing lack of clarity about rights and responsibilities of the central as opposed to regional governments (Chapter 15). Whereas the legislatures appear to have gained in power (e.g., through the Autonomy Law), efforts to reform the judicial branch seem to have fizzled out. Improvements in both branches are important for the much-needed improvements in both the laws and their implementation.

• *There has been little or no balance of power between the people and the government or even between business and government.* Particular individuals with excellent connections hold exclusive and relatively nonnegotiable rights to a variety of privileges and resources (Chapters 7 and 12). Again the strengthening of the legislative and judicial branches could be an important mechanism for addressing this problem. The obvious recent strengthening of the press, civil society, and even local communities is an encouraging sign—although some consider the press to be excessively free and irresponsible at this stage. It is certainly true that there is little experience in Indonesia with a responsible and free press, and this can carry dangers of its own.

• *Local people's traditional rights have not been respected, nor have mechanisms for resolving disputes among parties been effective.* This has resulted in a waste of rural human capital and potential contributions to sustainable management and improved livelihoods (Chapters 1, 5, and 6). Although the jury is still out, there have been increasing networks and links between nongovernmental organizations (NGOs), academics, and urban civil society, on the one hand, and forest communities on the other, with the intent of supporting local rights and developing mechanisms for conflict resolution. Attitudes within the forestry bureaucracy have shifted markedly from a complete lack of willingness to address such issues to one where a significant minority considers them important. Attempts to make policymaking more transparent have, again in fits and starts, been apparent.

Given the centrality of corruption—either directly or indirectly—in many of the problems identified, we consider it worth making some proactive suggestions. Literally thousands of analyses of corruption have been produced (see Transparency International's website at http://www.transparency.org/). But Elliott (1997, 211) summarized analyses by Klitgaard (1988) and Rose-Ackerman (1978) with these concrete suggestions for controlling corruption.

- *Improve information gathering and analysis to detect and deter corruption.*
  —Assess the organization's vulnerability to corruption and identify particular areas of concern.
  —Look for evidence of corruption (red flags, including lifestyles more lavish than honesty would allow, random inspections, and statistical analysis).
  —Increase access to information by opening channels to third parties (media and banks), clients, and the public.
  —Strengthen internal "information agents" (auditors and investigators) and protect whistle blowers.
  —Create specialized units or agencies (ombudsmen and anticorruption commissions).
- *Change incentives to discourage corruption.*
  — Increase the rewards for honesty
    o Raise low-end salaries to reduce the need for illicit supplements.
    o Introduce merit pay and incentive schemes that reward honest and efficient service, including nonmonetary rewards (for example, desirable transfers, training, travel, publicity, and praise).
    o Use contingent contracts (for example, nonvested pensions for public employees and performance contracts for private contractors).
  — Increase the penalties for corrupt behavior.
    o Raise the level of formal penalties. Where that is not possible (for political or other reasons), use nonformal penalties (e.g., undesirable transfers, negative publicity, loss of professional standing, and blackballing).
    o Increase authority to impose punishment.
    o Link the penalty to the expected gain from corruption (the size of the bribe for the public employee and the size of the expected illicit profit for the briber).

Elliott (1997, 225) also suggested a series of micro reforms that may be needed to support broad systemic reforms, for example, judicial reform, civil society and other institutional reforms, simplification of the tax and regulatory systems, use of auctions and other market-based regulatory mechanisms where possible, stronger rules relating to campaign finance and conflicts of interest, and a stronger civil society.

Dudley (2000) developed four simple prototype system dynamics models of corruption focused respectively on the amount of bureaucratic red tape, the employee–boss relationship, the likelihood that people will give or take bribes, and power. The purpose is ultimately to identify the aspects that are most amenable to change, in efforts to reduce levels of corruption (see Chapter 16 for a similar approach to illegal logging). Although the corruption models are still in development, one discouraging feature, seen when the models are run, is the stability of corruption. Changes in various parts (such as a governmental program to strengthen the judiciary) seem to typically yield only short-term gains. There is a strong tendency in the current versions for the system to revert to its previous corruption levels unless a very large commitment to change is made on several fronts. Such models may help identify the most likely entry points for making the difficult changes needed.

Indonesia's Place in the World

Indonesia has significant roles beyond its borders, of course; some of these will have become clear in the preceding chapters. Indonesia has supplied vast quantities of the world's timber and plywood (Chapters 8 and 9), palm oil (Chapter 10), and other commodities (Chapter 11). It is presently dependent on outside aid for government and businesses to function (Chapter 12). It is strategically located on important shipping lanes. And the huge population represents potentially growing markets for other countries' products. Indeed, Indonesia's low international profile is rather surprising, given its economic significance as a supplier of raw materials and its strategic location.

From a human perspective, Indonesia represents one of the most diverse regions of the world. Cultural diversity, considered on a par with biodiversity by some of us (e.g., Colfer 2000), is one of the nation's cornerstones, with "Unity in Diversity" being the national motto. Used to dealing with this diversity—of culture, of language, of ethnicity—parts of Indonesia have been models of interethnic coexistence in comparative harmony. A very high percentage of the cultures that make up this diversity are forest based. Without the forests, these cultures can no longer exist; the world's repertoire of knowledge, values, organization, and natural resource management and use strategies will be diminished.

These statements are not intended to gloss over the terrible interethnic conflicts that have exploded and festered over the last three years (in Aceh, Timor, Irian Jaya, Ambon, West Kalimantan, and most recently Central Kalimantan). But unlike citizens of many western countries, Indonesians are used to cultural and linguistic differences. They have a palpable and underrecognized advantage in terms of experience dealing with such internal differences (Colfer et al. 1989). If this fundamental understanding could be strengthened and supported by equitable and transparent policies, Indonesia could be a leader in global efforts to make full use of the diverse talents and interests of a multiethnic citizenry.

From a natural resource perspective, Indonesia's forests cover the largest area in Asia, and they represent veritable treasure troves of biodiversity—an issue of global concern. In recent years, Indonesia has been on the radar screen of conservation agencies, both national and international. The World Wide Fund for Nature (WWF), Birdlife International, Wetlands International, The Nature Conservancy, and Conservation International have all had extensive programs in Indonesia; and Indonesia has spawned its own homegrown conservation groups (including national ones like WALHI, Kehati, Telapak, and regional ones like Warsi in Jambi, Padi or Bioma in East Kalimantan). There seems to have been a stronger connection within Indonesia between conservation groups and groups concerned about community forest management and other human rights issues, than in the West. NGOs have been among the most vocal in their criticisms of formal, governmental forest management, including consistent cries for clearer community rights to land and forest (see especially Chapters 5 and 6), as well as expression of ecological concerns. And they have been active in attempts to resolve forest management conflicts at the local level (BSP/Kemala 1999, 2000a, 2000b).

Indonesia has also been a leader in global efforts to develop criteria and indicators (C&I) for sustainable forest management. When the Center for International Forestry Research (CIFOR) began research on this topic in 1994, Indonesia had already established a group called *Lembaga Ekolabel Indonesia* ([LEI] Indonesian Ecolabelling Institute), led by the well-respected Emil Salim (previous minister of population and the environment). LEI was actively involved at that time in developing C&I for the country, and its prototype set was far ahead of any other available set on social C&I. The Indonesian government also implemented a regulation in the late 1990s requiring that every timber concession be certified by 2000. Although this did not happen, significant progress has been made on developing an appropriate evaluation process and on actually evaluating a number of concessions (by LEI and by Rainforest Alliance, which uses the Forest Stewardship Council [FSC] label).

Early prototypes of LEI's C&I set were included in one of CIFOR's first tests of C&I (Burgess et al. 1995), and an active group of bright young Indonesians continued improving their efforts over the years. By 1998, LEI had a well-tested set, as did *Asosiasi Pengusaha Hutan Indonesia* (Association of Indonesian Forest Concession Holders). The process of "harmonizing" the two sets began, and an agreed upon set was created in the spring of 1998. At the same time, negotiations were ongoing between LEI and FSC in an attempt to ensure that Indonesian ecolabeling would be accepted on the world stage while not compromising Indonesian sovereignty. An agreement has now been reached that allows FSC and LEI to recognize each other's labels and to conduct joint ecolabeling activities in Indonesia. With such a promising start, it is discouraging to witness the further deterioration in management that is best exemplified by the dramatic increases in illegal logging (Chapter 16) and some of the more disturbing aspects of decentralization (Chapter 15).

Policy Narratives in Transition

In 1994, Emory Roe wrote a book called *Narrative Policy Analysis*, in which he argued that one of the driving forces behind policies is simplified "stories" about how the world works. Because reality is too complex for policymakers (or anyone else) to understand in its entirety, human beings make do with simpler stories that can help guide them in decisionmaking. This concept seems to fit with the way the Indonesian forestry establishment has dealt with the people who inhabit its "permanent forest estate." Following is one relevant narrative.[1]

> Indonesia has a vast and underutilized forest resource,[2] the primary function of which is to contribute to national development. Logging these abundant forests will provide needed foreign exchange, jobs for Indonesia's people, and wood for the nation and the world. These forests are virtually empty of people. Those few people who do inhabit the forests are ignorant and primitive, and they are an embarrassment to the nation. This behavior is shown by their animistic beliefs,[3] communal ownership patterns, and most fundamentally by their practice of the destructive slash and burn agriculture. Civilizing these people—converting them to Islam or Christianity and persuading them to practice permanent, settled agriculture, like hardworking Javanese farmers—is essential both to improving forest people's lot and integrating them into the modern Indonesian state. Such changes will contribute to modernizing the entire country.

This policy narrative goes back at least to the Dutch era. Indeed, one can find comparable, if not precisely identical, policy narratives throughout most countries that were colonized. The sad fact is that the new governments, including Indonesia, took on the views of their previous "masters" when dealing with forest peoples. In an effort to join the community of nations, to demonstrate their modernity, new nations often reject important components of their own ways of life. Barber (1997) refers to this view as the "delegitimization of local resource management practices," citing as evidence that "the Indonesian Forestry Action Programme identified shifting cultivation as the source of nearly one-fourth of all deforestation in the country, while logging concessions [were]...not even counted as a cause" (see Barber 1997; Colfer and Dudley 1993; Dove 1988; Warner 1991; and Weinstock 1989 for critiques of this one-sided view of shifting cultivation).

Similar ideas have been expressed about peoples living in forests all over Asia. Poffenberger (1990, 20) said of Thailand, Indonesia, and the Philippines: Swidden cultivators, hunters and gatherers, and migrant farmers "were generally stigmatized...as destroyers of the forest and branded practitioners of 'slash and burn' agriculture, 'encroachers,' and 'backward tribals' (see Komkris 1978 or Ratanakhon 1978 for Thai examples of such derogatory stereotypes). Indeed, forest people all over the world have tended to be seen as primitive and responsible for various kinds of environmental degradation and national embarrassment. Fairhead and Leach (1996), for instance, described a policy narrative in the West African nation of Guinea that holds local people accountable for a process of deforestation that the authors argue is not even occurring. They provide convincing historical evidence that the presence of forest patches in the local forest-savannah mosaic is the result of longstanding, purposive, local human intervention (see Leach and Mearns' 1996 compilation for other similar African examples).

Encouraging signs that this narrative might be changing began to emerge in Indonesia in the 1990s when the government allowed several explicitly phrased "experiments." In Danau Sentarum Wildlife Reserve (West Kalimantan), where the laws prescribed removing the people, Colfer participated in an attempt at comanagement, under the auspices of a British–Indonesian project (Giesen 2000). In the Sanggau area of West Kalimantan, a German-Indonesian project was permitted to experiment with community-managed timber concessions (Nolan 2001 documents the strengths and weaknesses of this experience). The last minister of forestry under Soeharto, Djamaludin Suryohadikusumo, signed approval for a *Kawasan dengan Tujuan Istimewa* (Zone with Special Purpose) in which local communities in Krui, South Sumatra, were granted legal rights to their indigenous management system (Chapter 6). The concessionaires' mandated *Bina Desa*[4] programs represented another encouraging sign that the government was beginning to recognize that local communities existed and had legitimate interests and rights that were being ignored (see also the Indonesia Forestry Action Programme [1995] for some comparatively early and encouraging governmental rhetoric). But these examples were a drop in the bucket compared with the numbers of communities actively involved in completely unrecognized, day-to-day forest management activities.

During the past decade, the complexity as well as the economic and environmental logic of swidden and other Indonesian forest agricultural systems has been widely documented (Brookfield and Padoch 1994; Chin 1984; Colfer and Dudley 1993; Colfer et al. 1997; Dove 1985; Padoch 1982; Peluso 1994). This evidence has been taken up by environmental and other researchers and activists in the country and used to construct a new policy narrative (one that Roe's theory would be the first to predict is also inevitably imprecise and subject to change). The narrative may be summarized as follows:

> Forest people have practiced an integrated and sustainable form of natural re-
> source management for centuries. They have a wealth of useful indigenous knowl-
> edge based on their long history in their area. They also have spiritual links to the
> land and traditional rules about its use that ensure a balance between people and
> local resources. If local resources are simply returned to local people, the environ-
> ment will be managed in a sustainable and equitable way.

This narrative is growing in strength and represents an improvement over the previous one. Yet in recognizing and respecting the genuine strengths and potential contribution of indigenous systems, it also carries potential threats if the policy implications of this view are directly implemented (see examples of the shenanigans of local headmen in Chapter 4 or the fire causes cited in Chapter 14). There is no evidence, for instance, that people who live in and around forests are inherently more ethical and wise than people in other contexts— although in some cases they are less able to cause serious damage because of capital and labor constraints. Effective management of Indonesia's forests will probably require some sort of balance between the potential contributions and the needs of local people on the one hand and national priorities on the other.[5] The appropriate balance was the subject of intense debate within Indonesia, as reflected particularly in Chapters 4, 5, and 6, during 1999. Although the intensity has faded somewhat, the issues remain and the decentralization process is likely to bring them to the fore again in the near future.

This rather anthropological example of a policy narrative and the way in which it is evolving is a fitting conclusion to this book. Similar policy narratives—with "before and after" renditions—could be produced for each of the policy issues that have been discussed (from how financial institutions do and should work, through the role of corruption, to the functions of oil palm or logging concessions). We remain in the midst of rapid change. In this text we have tried to document and convey some sense of the exciting, frightening, and at times incredibly hopeful and enthusiastic process under way in Indonesia. While reporting the difficult problems, we have tried to suggest entry points for constructive improvements. Finally, we remind the reader of the incredible potential for radical and positive change that remains. "Which way forward?" Indeed!

Endnotes

1. This narrative is not intended to convey the views of any particular individual but rather to summarize widely held views about the management of Indonesia's forests. It is a sort of caricature, or for some a parody, of the important elements of the most common perspective. In broad terms, it has not been unique to Indonesia.

2. This national forest estate covers around 70% of the nation's land area.

3. Within Indonesia there is an explicit and widely held view that adherence to one of the major religions—Islam, Christianity, Hinduism—indicates a more advanced level of civilization, such that animists are "behind" or *belum beragama* (not yet having religion).

4. This term means "village guidance"; it was later changed to *Pembangunan Masyarakat Desa Hutan* (Forest Village Community Development).

5. CIFOR has a program (Local People, Devolution and Adaptive Collaborative Management) that is looking at this balance in a number of field sites, both within Indonesia and in other countries (Philippines, Nepal, India, China, Brazil, Bolivia, Cameroon, Ghana, Malawi, Zimbabwe, and Kyrgyzstan) in collaboration with host-country research partners.

References

Barber, C.V. 1997. *Environmental Scarcities, State Capacity, Civil Violence: The Case of Indonesia.* Washington, DC: American Academy of Sciences and University College, University of Toronto.

Barr, C.M. 1998. Bob Hasan, the rise of APKINDO, and the shifting dynamics of control in Indonesia's timber sector. *Indonesia* 65:1–36.

_____. 1999. *Discipline and Accumulate: State Practice and Elite Consolidation in Indonesia's Timber Sector, 1967–1998.* Master's thesis. Ithaca, NY: Cornell University.

———. 2001. Chapter 4: The Political Economy of Fiber and Finance in Indonesia's Pulp and Paper Industries. In *Banking on Sustainability: Structural Adjustment and Forestry Reform in Post-Suharto Indonesia.* Washington, D.C.: Center for International Forestry Research (CIFOR) and World Wide Fund for Nature Macroeconomics for Sustainable Development Program Office, 70–95.

BSP (Biodiversity Support Program)/Kemala. 1999. *Implementation Report 7. April to September.* Jakarta, Indonesia: World Wide Fund for Nature, The Nature Conservancy, and World Resources Institute.

_____. 2000a. *Implementation Report 8. October 1999 to March 2000. Jakarta,* Indonesia: WWF, The Nature Conservancy, and World Resources Institute.

_____. 2000b. *Implementation Report 9. April to September.* Jakarta, Indonesia: WWF, The Nature Conservancy, and World Resources Institute.

Brookfield, H., and C. Padoch. 1994. Appreciating agrodiversity: A look at the dynamism and diversity of indigenous farming practices. *Environment* 36(5): 6–11 and 37–43.

Burgess, P., Elias, P.M. Laksono, R.J. Watling, and W. Razali Wan Mohd. 1995. *Final Report: Test Indonesia March 5–April 2, 1995* (with annexes). Bogor, Indonesia: CIFOR.

Chin, S.C. 1984. *Agriculture and Subsistence in a Lowland Rainforest Kenyah Community* (Volumes 1 and II). New Haven, CT: Yale University.

Colfer, C.J.P. 2000. *Cultural Diversity in Forest Management.* Keynote Address, Twenty-first International Union of Forestry Research Organizations Congress, Kuala Lumpur, Malaysia. August 7–12.

Colfer, C.J.P., and R. Dudley. 1993. *Shifting Agriculture in Indonesia: Managers or Marauders of the Forest?* Food and Agriculture Organization (FAO) Community Forestry Case Study Series No. 6. Rome: FAO.

Colfer, C.J.P., N. Peluso, and C.S. Chung. 1997. *Beyond Slash and Burn: Building on Indigenous Management of Borneo's Tropical Rain Forests.* New York: New York Botanical Gardens Press.

Colfer, C.J.P., B. Newton, and Herman. 1989. Ethnicity: An important consideration in Indonesian agriculture. *Agriculture and Human Values* VI (3):52–67. Earlier version published in Proceedings Centre for Soils Research Technical Meetings, Bogor, Indonesia.

Curry, D., and A. Ruwindrijarto. 2000. Illegal Logging in Tanjung Puting National Park, an Update to the Final Cut Report. Jakarta, Indonesia: Environmental Investigation Agency and Telapak Indonesia.

Dove, M. 1985. *Swidden Agriculture in Indonesia: The Subsistence Strategies of the Kalimantan Kantu'*. Berlin, Germany: Mouton Publishers.

_____. 1988. The agroecological mythology of the Javanese and the political economy of Indonesia. *Indonesia* 39:1–36.

Dudley, R.G. 2000. *The Rotten Mango: The Effect of Corruption on International Development Projects (Part I: Building a System Dynamics Basis for Examining Corruption)*. Paper presented at the International System Dynamics meeting. August 2000. Bergen, Norway.

Elliott, K.A. 1997. Corruption as an international policy problem: Overview and recommendations. In *Corruption and the Global Economy*, edited by K.A. Elliott. Washington, DC: Institute for International Economics, 175–233.

Fairhead, J., and M. Leach. 1996. Rethinking the forest-savanna mosaic: Colonial science and its relics in West Africa. In *The Lie of the Land*, edited by M. Leach and R. Mearns. London: The International African Institute, 105–21.

Giesen, W. (ed.). 2000. Special Issue on Danau Sentarum National Park. *Borneo Research Bulletin* 31.

Indonesian Forestry Action Programme. 1995. Jakarta, Indonesia: Ministry of Forestry, Republic of Indonesia.

Klitgaard, R. 1988. *Controlling Corruption*. Berkeley: University of California Press.

Komkris, T. 1978. Forestry aspects of land use in areas of swidden cultivation. In *Farmers in the Forest: Economic Development and Marginal Agriculture in Northern Thailand*, edited by P. Kunstadter, E.C. Chapman, and S. Sabhasri. Honolulu: East–West Population Institute, University of Hawaii, 61–9.

Leach, M., and R. Mearns. 1996. *The Lie of the Land*. London: The International African Institute.

McCarthy, J.F. 2000. "Wild Logging": *The Rise and Fall of Logging Networks and Biodiversity Conservation Projects on Sumatra's Rainforest Frontier*. CIFOR occasional paper no. 31. Bogor, Indonesia: CIFOR.

Nolan, T. 2001. *Community-Based Forest Management: Commercial Harvesting of the Rainforest in Indonesia*. Draft paper. Jakarta, Indonesia.

Obidzinski, K., and I. Suramenggala. 2000. *Illegal Logging in Indonesia—A Contextual Approach to the Problem*. Draft paper. Bogor, Indonesia: CIFOR.

Padoch, C. 1982. *Migration and Its Alternatives among the Iban of Sarawak*. The Hague, Netherlands: Martinus Nijhoff.

Peluso, N. 1994. *The Impact of Social and Environmental Change on Forest Management: A Case Study from West Kalimantan, Indonesia*. FAO Community Forestry case study series no. 8. Rome, Italy: FAO.

Poffenberger, M. 1990. The evolution of forest management systems in Southeast Asia. *In Keepers of the Forest: Land Management Alternatives in Southeast Asia*, edited by M. Poffenberger. West Hartford, CT: Kumarian Press, 7–26.

Ratanakhon, S. 1978. Legal aspects of land occupation and development. In *Farmers in the Forest: Economic Development and Marginal Agriculture in Northern Thailand*, edited by P. Kunstadter, E.C. Chapman, and S. Sabhasri. Honolulu: East–West Population Institute, University of Hawaii, 45–53.

Roe, E. 1994. *Narrative Policy Analysis: Theory and Practice*. Durham, NC: Duke University.

Rose-Ackerman, S. 1978. *Corruption: A Study in Political Economy*. New York: Academic Press.

Wadley, R.L. 2001. *Community Co-operatives, Illegal Logging, and Regional Autonomy: Empowerment and Impoverishment in the Borderlands of West Kalimantan, Indonesia*. Paper presented at Resource Tenure, Forest Management, and Conflict Resolution: Perspectives from Borneo and New Guinea. April 9–11. Australian National University, Canberra.

Warner, K. 1991. *Shifting Cultivators: Local Technical Knowledge and Natural Resource Management in the Humid Tropics*. FAO Community Forestry note 8. Rome, Italy: FAO.

Weinstock, J. 1989. *Study of shifting cultivation in Indonesia. Phase I report (draft)*. Jakarta, Indonesia: Government of Indonesia/FAO project UTF/INS/065/INS.

AFTERWORD

Indonesian Forests and People in Change

Emil Salim

This book is aptly named "Which Way Forward?" It stresses the reality that Indonesia is currently changing. But changing from where and going to where? And why these deep structural changes? What has happened to Indonesia, which in television and newspapers all over the world is projected as a turbulent and violence-filled state? What is the prospect of a future Indonesia?

All these are relevant questions for those concerned about Indonesia today. Yes, Indonesia is changing. What began in mid-1997 as a severe monetary crisis—the result of an economic contagion that spread from Thailand to Indonesia and other Southeast Asian countries—has become a series of crises that have affected almost every dimension of economic, political, and civil life in the country. Thus simple monetary measures to cope with the 1997 financial crisis were not sufficient. With the sharp decline of Indonesia's gross domestic product by 14% (1998), the structural weaknesses of the nation, long hidden by the veil of the high growth of gross domestic product, were nakedly exposed.

One of these fundamental defects was in the imbalance prevailing in the "triangle of power" at the center of Indonesian politics. The components of

---

This "Afterword" is an invited essay, designed to provide readers with a perspective from a respected Indonesian policymaker who has witnessed the changes in the country during recent history.

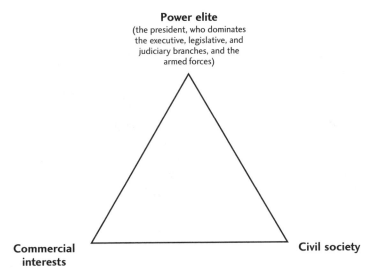

Figure A–1. Indonesian power triangle.

the triangle of power in Indonesia follow that of a normal triangle of power in any country (Figure A–1). At the top of the triangle stands the power elite, consisting of the president, who dominates the executive, legislative, and judiciary branches, and the armed forces. At the left corner of the triangle stands commercial interests, or, in the case of Indonesia, the business conglomerates that dominate the economy. At the right corner of the triangle stands civil society. What is distinctive in the Indonesian case is the dominating role that the president plays in leading the nation as head of state and of government.

The Soeharto Legacy

Indonesia at the end of President Soekarno's era (1966) was in economic shambles, with an annual rate of inflation of 650%, high unpaid official foreign debts, infrastructural breakdown among its islands, low per-capita income, and a negative rate of economic growth. The People's Consultative Assembly that rejected Soekarno and elected Soeharto as Indonesia's second president followed a student uprising against the government. If Soekarno's task was to build the nation state, President Soeharto's task was to build the nation's economy.

For a nation that has a large rural population and fertile land, agriculture was the priority of the first plans of development under Soeharto (1968 to 1983), with a special focus on rice production. This emphasis made it possible for Indonesia to allocate scarce funds and forces and to achieve food self-sufficiency by 1984. However, a strongly centralized economy dominated by the president was a by-product.

In the second era of development, from 1984 to 1998, the focus shifted from rural agriculture to industry. Motivated by a competitive desire to speed growth and catch up with the neighboring countries of the Association of South East Asian Nations, there was an unfortunate emphasis on high technology and big projects. If Malaysia could make its own national car, the Proton, why was Indonesia's capability limited to producing only spare parts? Such was the frustration among top officials: Indonesia needed to bypass stage-by-stage industrial development and leapfrog into high-technology industry. Under these plans, industrial development needed to start from the final product downstream and work its way back upstream. Because Indonesia is an archipelago, stretching a distance equal to that between London to Egypt, the transportation sector was given the highest priority. It was in this context that airplane, ship, and motorcar industries led Indonesia's strategy of industrial development. Human resource development was channeled along the high-technology path into the direction of these transportation industries, with special emphasis on building "short-take-off-and-landing" (STOL) aircraft.

In the forestry sector, emphasis was given to log-processing industries. Raw log exports were banned to increase the value added. Improved technology in forest product processing could have resulted in various benefits, such as the use of bark as an input for medicinal and cosmetics industries. Unfortunately, high technology in natural resources development was not as eagerly pursued as aviation technology. Indonesia has the human capacity to produce STOL aircrafts. The crucial question for any developing economy is "can these high-technology products be sold economically?" The answer, usually, is "no."

Another important feature of the pattern of industrial development in the late 1980s was the requirement for large amounts of capital. Only conglomerates raising foreign loans can mobilize such funds. The loans create vulnerabilities in the broader economy if projects or companies fail.

In the 1970s and early 1980s, Indonesian economic development was characterized by rural and agricultural development that not only produced self-sufficiency in food but also boosted millions of people from below the poverty line. In the late 1980s and in the 1990s, Indonesian economic development shifted to urban and mostly large-scale industrial development that produced high-cost products protected behind a high tariff wall. This transition further aided the emergence of conglomerates that were close to the ruling elite. The central government and its heavily top-down process controlled development. Both legs of the triangle of power were coopted by the power elite. Only those business conglomerates that were willing to be coopted could flourish and grow, which in turn allowed big business conglomerates close to the power elite to dominate the economy (see also Figure 16–3 in Chapter 16 to see the mutually reinforcing nature of these relationships and interactions). And only those organizations of civil society that were coopted by the power elite could function openly. All other nongovernmental organizations (NGOs), especially those critical of the government, had difficulty functioning properly.

At the top of the "triangle of power," the mechanism of *trias politica* (separation of power between executive, legislative, and judiciary branches) was not working. The president as head of the executive branch was also coopting the People's Consultative Assembly, including Parliament and the Supreme Court. Even the armed forces and political parties were being coopted. In civil society, only organizations that were considered acceptable by the government were allowed to flourish, whether chambers of commerce, women's groups, youth organizations, or other institutions. The government determined the chair and constitution of organizations.

If power is vested for too long a period in the hands of a single person and the principle of checks and balances does not operate, the system is bound to swing into authoritarianism. Power can corrupt, changing the personality of the power holder. Soeharto's overconfidence and reliance on only his own judgement grew over time. Those close to the president were saddened, observing the growing confidence gap that grew between the leader and his people.

Transition, Turmoil, and Reform

The crisis of 1997 provided the opportunity for the growing frustration of the people to burst into the open. The crisis that was initially dominated by monetary issues soon grew into a more general economic crisis that then spilled over into political and social crises. In politics it is often said "there are no permanent friends or permanent allies, but only permanent interests." Likewise, practically all important political leaders jumped off the sinking presidential ship and positioned themselves to oppose President Soeharto. By May 21, 1998, Soeharto resigned as president and was replaced by his vice president, B. J. Habibie.

Although Habibie was only briefly in power (May 1998–October 1999), he was able to float on the wave of reform that swept over the nation. President Habibie is credited with making possible the genuinely free election of 1999 that was praised all over the world. He was, however, also accused of grossly mishandling the situation in East Timor by making a spur-of-the-moment political decision, offering the region an "in-or-out of Indonesia now" referendum, and bypassing the road painstakingly walked by diplomats. And Habibie was blamed for forcing too many important legislative actions through Parliament in too short a period of time. Some of these (for example, the Law on Autonomy) raised controversial issues with huge implications for the integration of the nation.

In October 1999, the People's Consultative Assembly elected Kyai Abdurrahman Wahid as Indonesia's fourth president. Although Wahid came from a small party with 7% of the seats in the Parliament, he was supported by a broader range of political parties that rejected Megawati Soekarnoputeri, the candidate of the Nationalist-Democratic Party that had won the election. Megawati was accepted only as Indonesia's vice president.

If, initially, the leadership of President Wahid was enthusiastically received, his frequent dismissal of cabinet ministers, especially from major political parties, put him in conflict with those parties controlling Parliament. Not long after his election, the nation was soon plunged into a tug-of-war between the president and Parliament. President Wahid faced a charge of alleged misbehavior that led to his impeachment by the People's Consultative Assembly, which convened in the August 2001 session. He was, in the end, replaced by Megawati.

All these developments indicate that Indonesia is in the process of fundamental changes. Behind all this turmoil are important trends that depict five directions of constructive change:

- **Indonesia is changing from an authoritarian to a democratic regime.** Decisionmaking in the country has moved from a "top-down" to a more "bottom-up" process. The separation of power is currently more vivid. If formerly the Parliament was subordinated to the government, it is currently on a par with the president. It is precisely because of this change that the current tug-of-war between the president and parliament has become so intense.

- **Authority is becoming decentralized.** The central government is now mainly responsible for five major sectors, including foreign affairs, defense and security, finance and budget, religion, and planning.[1] All other governmental functions are in principle decentralized to the regencies and provinces. Each province and regency has its respective parliamentary bodies, which elect the local governor and district head.

- **Policy of uniformity is giving way to diversity.** The notion that was inherent in establishing unity of the nation is now yielding to a policy of diversity that allows each province to grow in a manner consistent with its own cultural and social identity. The overly strong emphasis on uniformity had almost wiped out the uniqueness of diverse village institutions in the regions. The rights of indigenous people and their title to land, forests, minerals, river, sea and natural resources, in accordance to their customary laws, were not recognized by the government because such laws are unwritten, and the government only upholds written laws. Additionally, the government actively sponsored the large migration of people from densely populated regions, predominantly Java, to outside Java where populations with different ethnic backgrounds reside. This created a serious backlash in the form of social conflicts between migrants and indigenous populations.

- **Cooptation of government by the power elite is being replaced by competition.** At the top of the triangle of power, the separation of power, *trias politica*, has taken place effectively. The legislative and judiciary branches have taken positions independent from the executive branch. Additionally, abiding by the rule of the constitution, the armed forces have now formally taken the position of supporting not the individual in an official position but rather the holder of the official position. At the business leg of the triangle of power, monopoly power and special treatments from the government, previously enjoyed by the conglomerates, have been removed and been replaced by competition on the open market. This involved opening up the market to free entry and eliminating the monopoly position of the privileged conglomerates. A Competition Watch Commission has been established to ensure that the rule of competition is properly conducted.
- **Genuine civil society is emerging.** In the past, civil society was contained; its growth was seriously clipped while the state sector played a dominant role in the economy. The economy was dominated by state rather than commercial banks and state instead of private enterprises. Labor unions were state controlled, and state-promoted community organizations predominated over NGOs. The obvious result of this arrangement was that civil society was weak. The leaders as well as the constitutions of civil society organizations had to be approved by the government. A civil society is starting to emerge, as indicated by the increased number of NGOs and the various "watch" organizations, such as the Parliamentary Watch, the Cabinet Watch, the Election Watch, the Corruption Watch, and so forth. The empowered civil society is now growing into a significant countervailing force to the government.

These five features of development are part of the reform process better known as *Reformasi*. This process reveals the urge in the society for a complete overhaul of Indonesian social, economic, and political structure. This is the way forward currently chosen by Indonesia.

Because of the radical change and the weaknesses in civil institutions that developed during the administrations of Soekarno and Soeharto, the process of implementation is not smooth. One foot of Indonesia moves forward, while the other stays behind in the past. The transition in Indonesia is full of inconsistencies and confusion. This process of *Reformasi* has taken place with many negative excesses—violent uprisings at the grass-roots level, riots, mass demonstrations, destruction of government buildings, and what appear as incomprehensible massacres.

Although democracy has allowed the accumulated, pent-up frustrations of the populace to burst into the open, it is wrong to blame democracy for the excesses that have accompanied the process of *Reformasi*. However, it is also wrong to hide behind "being on a learning curve of democracy" to justify the inaction that has taken place against these excesses. These excesses are wrong, and firm corrections must be taken (specifically in the field of eliminating money politics, eliminating bribes involved in the election of officials or members of Parliament, and ending bribing people to elect officials or members of Parliament, the discriminatory application of the law).

Reformasi and Indonesian Forests

It is against the background of *Reformasi* that one can understand the process of change in Indonesia's forest sector. Indonesian forests are valuable resources, not only for the environment but also, from the developing country point of view, for economic and political development.

After the introduction of the *"Hak Pengusahaan Hutan"* or Forest Concession, Forest Exploitation Rights, licenses were issued to exploit the resources for development. Given the dominance of the power elite in the triangle of power, these licenses were issued to "friends of the power elite," including military officers, big conglomerates, and well-connected families (see Chapters 10 and 12, for some specifics). While on the one hand forest exploitation raises the government's revenue dramatically in terms of foreign exchange, on the other hand it creates influential conglomerates that dominate forest sector development.

During the Soeharto administration, the forest sector grew into a close-knit community of conglomerates around the president. Compulsory levies were raised for the Reforestation Fund. This fund was controlled by the president, but there was no transparency and hence no control in the use of this fund. The Indonesian consortium for the environmental NGOs, known as *Wahana Lingkungan Hidup Indonesia,* in the mid-1990s accused the president of using the fund to finance aircraft development. It was also an open secret that funds from forestry were channeled to favor a particular party in the election. Forest management was then closely linked with money politics to strengthen the grip of the power elite on the conglomerates and political parties. It is therefore understandable that attempted in-roads by the World Bank or foreign governments were strongly resisted. The forestry sector became a closed sector full of secrecy. While official statistics are available on the formal forest area, it is not necessarily true that forests exist on that land.

Under these circumstances, environmental application in forest development suffered three major classic failures: market failure, institutional failure, and policy failure.

- **Market failure:** The markets did not capture environmentally related costs. Licenses for forest exploitation were not issued at the proper price level, which internalizes the environmental costs, under the pretext that it is impossible to value the environmental costs. Forests were hence exploited with no consideration of the costs in terms of ecosystem destruction, biodiversity, or soil erosion. Their value as a carbon sink was conveniently assumed to be zero because of the failure of the market to register these costs.

- **Institutional failure:** Government agencies did not take into account environmental considerations necessary for sustainable forest management. The forests were managed centrally by the Forestry Ministry. Even today, when decentralization demands a dispersion of resource management to the regions, the Forestry Ministry keeps its firm hand on the central control of forests. Meanwhile, the ministry lacks sufficient managerial and human resources to manage vast areas of protected forests and national parks, with the consequence that these lands are infiltrated by massive amounts of illegal logging. Revenues obtained by the national parks are not allowed to be used for park rehabilitation or management. They must be given to the central government. On the one hand, lack of financial resources allocated to the parks make these parks undermanaged, undermaintained, and underdeveloped. On the other hand, the private holders of forest concessions intensively exploit the production forests, raising huge revenues but paying official taxes less than any rational amount, paying low official taxes, and obtaining huge revenues, but in combination with contributions to officials responsible for forest concessions.

  Up to now, the forestry sector has been the object of various experiments by different policymakers in the Forestry Ministry. But these experiments always dealt with how to split forests into concessions for various groups rather than how to develop viable forest institutions that would make sustainable forest development possible. Since late 1998 (with the issuance of SK 677/1998 on Community Forestry), forest concessions could be given to people's cooperatives as part of the policy to create a populist economy. Forest concessions could also be given to universities as part of a process designed to implement autonomy for these institutions of higher learning. In the face of the decentralization of resource management to the regions, in 2001, the government was considering creating a single state enterprise to manage all Indonesian forests under central control. In all these cases, however, environmental issues have not been considered.

- **Policy failure:** The policy of issuing licenses for wood processing industrial development was launched without taking into account forests' carrying capacity. The total supply of Indonesian forest material in sustainably managed forests is a maximum of 17 million m^3 per annum. Total demand for wood from the licensed forest industries is 46 million m^3 per annum. This does not include demand for wood from the nonlicensed, informal forest industries or demand from households. Cheap credits are issued for those able to develop forest plantations. But this has been accomplished by transforming natural forests (which provide revenues freely) to plantation forests. The same cheap credits have been given for opening up "conversion forests" to develop oil palm plantations. The cheapest way to open forests is by burning trees. Because credits are difficult to obtain, these cheap credits are stretched by spending on burning trees to open up land for oil palm plantations, while the proportion of credit saved is used for financing other ventures.

Market, institution, and policy failures are still evident in Indonesia's forest sector. Because forestry is a billion-dollar business with powerful interest groups involved, it becomes extremely difficult to introduce environmentally sound reform in the forest sector. But the winds of change must also blow in the forestry sector. Indonesia is one of the mega diversity countries of the world, along with Brazil in Latin America and the Democratic Republic of Congo in Africa. Its forests are the main habitat for rich and diverse biological resources.

The lost opportunities from these failures multiply: the trend of the world in consumption is that buyers prefer products that are natural instead of chemical. Natural products are in fashion in the world at large—now and in the future. In this context, forests consist not only of trees but also of habitats for fauna and flora with food, medicine, and cosmetic content. Forests represent a living laboratory for science in which otherwise unavailable genetic material and species can be modified in an environmentally sound manner for humanity's survival.

Taking this trend of development into account, Indonesia's mega diversity in the tropical rain forests opens the way for building our unique competitive position in the global economy. Competition is getting fierce in the global market. Indonesia may well reach a strong competitive position by following natural resource–based development, which by applying environmentally sound biotechnology methods may raise value added on food, fruits, flowers, medicine, and cosmetics that are unique in this global economy.

"Which way forward?" is the question raised in this book. The trend of change and *Reformasi* in Indonesia indicates that even amid the turmoil seen in the news headlines, the Indonesian people are moving toward democracy in their politics, development with equity and reduced poverty in their economy, and a humane civil society in their social development.

Forest development is put within this framework. It is currently still encountering inertia in the process of *Reformasi*. But the winds of change are blowing in the right direction. Transparency as well as better insights and knowledge of forestry are required to allow these winds of change to continue along their rightful course. This book may well contribute to stimulating the necessary discussion not only on "which way forward," but also "how to move forward."

Jakarta

Endnote

1. Technically the five sectors include foreign affairs, national security and defense, judicature, monetary and fiscal, and religion. The other authorities under national control include national planning and control of macro level national development, fiscal balancing, the national administration system and national economic institutions, utilization of strategic and conservative natural resources and high technology, and national standardization.

Timeline of Significant Indonesian Legislation

ccording to the People's Consultative Assembly of Indonesia (MPR—Majelis Perwakilan Rakyat), Ketetapan (TAP) MPR TAP III/MPR/2000, there is a new hierarchy of regulations within the nation (listed below in order of highest to lowest value):

1. Indonesian Constitution (UUD—*Undang-Undang Dasar*)
2. Acts of Parliament/Decree of People's Consultative Assembly (TAP MPR—*Ketetapan MPR*)
3. Laws (UU—*Undang-Undang*)
4. Government regulations (PP—*Peraturan Pemerintah*)
5. Presidential decrees/decisions (Keppres—*Keputusan President*)
6. Regional Regulations (*Peraturan Daerah*)

Any regulation cannot conflict with those at a higher level. The important category of ministerial decrees or decision letters (SK—*Surat Keputusan*) is not listed in this official hierarchy of authority. The major difference from the previous hierarchy is the inclusion of regional regulations. The previous hierarchy (TAP MPRS XX/MPRS/1966) included two kinds of decisions by the president and ministerial decrees (with a minister's decree as the lowest listed type). The following sections divide the regulations in this book by type and present them in chronological order.

Compiled by Ahmad Dermawan. These translations are not official translations of the original version in Bahasa Indonesia.

Acts of Parliament

1. TAP MPR XV/MPR/1998: *tentang Penyelenggaraan Otonomi Daerah, Pengaturan; Pembagian, dan Pemanfaatan Sumber Daya Nasional, yang Berkeadilan; serta Perimbangan Keuangan Pusat dan Daerah dalam Kerangka Negara Kesatuan Republik Indonesia* (Decree of People's Consultative Assembly of the Republic of Indonesia concerning the Implementation of Regional Autonomy; the Arrangement, Distribution, and Equitable Utilization of National Resources; and the Fiscal Balance of Central and Regional Government in the Frame of the State Unity of the Republic of Indonesia)

2. TAP MPR XVII/MPR/1998: *tentang Hak Asasi Manusia* (Decree of People's Consultative Assembly of the Republic of Indonesia concerning Human Rights)

3. TAP MPR III/MPR/2000: *tentang Sumber Hukum dan Tata Urutan Peraturan Perundangan* (Decision of People's Consultative Assembly of the Republic of Indonesia concerning the Legal Sources and Legislative Regulations Order)

Laws

1. UU 1/1945: *tentang Peraturan Mengenai Kedudukan Komite Nasional Daerah* (Law on the Stipulations of the Position of Regional National Committee)

2. UU 1/1957: *tentang Pokok-pokok Pemerintahan Daerah* (Law on Principles of Regional Governance)

3. UU 5/1960: *tentang Pokok-pokok Pertanahan* (Basic Agrarian Law)

4. UU 18/1965: *tentang Pokok-pokok Pemerintahan Daerah* (Law on Principles of Regional Governance)

5. UU 1/1967: *tentang Penanaman Modal Asing* (Law on Foreign Investment)

6. UU 5/1967: *tentang Pokok-pokok Kehutanan* (Basic Forestry Law)

7. UU 11/1967: *tentang Pokok-pokok Pertambangan* (Basic Mining Law)

8. UU 6/1968: *tentang Penanaman Modal Dalam Negeri* (Law on Domestic Investment)

9. UU 5/1974: *tentang Pokok-pokok Pemerintahan di Daerah* (Law on Principles of Regional Governance), replaced by UU 22/1999

10. UU 5/1979: *tentang Pemerintahan Desa* (Law on Village Governance), also replaced by UU 22/1999

11. UU 10/1992: *tentang Perkembangan Kependudukan Pembangunan Keluarga Sejahtera* (Law on Population Development and Family Welfare Law)

12. UU 24/1992: *tentang Penataan Ruang* (Law on Spatial Planning, which is translated literally as *perencanaan tata ruang* and is popularly and generally understood as *penataan ruang*, which is translated as "spatial arrangement" [Zwahlen and Soewardi 2000])

13. UU 23/1997: *tentang Lingkungan Hidup* (Environmental Law)

14. UU 22/1999: *tentang Pemerintahan Daerah* (Law on Regional Governance), replaces UU 5/1974 and UU 5/1979

15. UU 25/1999: *tentang Perimbangan Keuangan antara Pemerintah Pusat dan Daerah* (Law on Fiscal Balance between the Central Government and the Regions)

16. UU 39/1999: *tentang Hak Asasi Manusia* (Law on Human Rights)

17. UU 41/1999: *tentang Kehutanan* (Law on Forestry)

Government Regulations

1. PP 64/1957: *tentang Penyerahan Sebagian dari Urusan Pemerintah Pusat Dilapangan Perikanan Laut, Kehutanan dan Karet Rakyat kepada Daerah-daerah Swatantra Tingkat I* (Government Regulation on the Granting of Some of Central Government's Authority over Matters Concerning Coastal Fisheries, Forestry, and Community Rubber Sectors to First-level Regional Governments)

2. PP 22/1967: *tentang Iuran Hak Pengusahaan Hutan dan Iuran Hasil Hutan* (Government Regulation on Concession License Fees and Royalties)

3. PP 6/1968: *tentang Penarikan Urusan Kehutanan dari Daerah Kehutanan Kabupaten ke Propinsi Di Wilayah Indonesia Bagian Timur* (Government Regulation on Withdrawing Control Over Matters on Forestry from Regency Forestry to Provincial Forestry in Eastern Indonesia)

4. PP 21/1970: *tentang Hak Pengusahaan Hutan dan Hak Pemungutan Hasil Hutan* (Government Regulation on Forest Exploitation Rights and Forest Product Harvesting Rights)

5. PP 33/1970: *tentang Perencanaan Hutan* (Government Regulation on Forest Planning)

6. PP 18/1975: *tentang Perubahan Pasal 9 Peraturan Pemerintah 21/1970 tentang Hak Pengusahaan Hutan dan Hak Pemungutan Hasil Hutan* (Government Regulation on Revision of Article 9 of PP 21/1970 on Forest Exploitation Rights and Forest Product Harvesting Rights)

7. PP 28/1985: *tentang Perlindungan Hutan* (Government Regulation on Forest Protection)

8. PP 7/1990: *tentang Hak Pengusahaan Hutan Tanaman Industri* (Government Regulation on Industrial Timber Plantations)

9. PP 8/1995: *tentang Penyerahan Sebagian Urusan Pemerintahan kepada 26 (dua puluh enam) Daerah Tingkat II* (Government Regulation on Granting of Some Governmental Affairs to 26 Sample Regions)

10. PP 62/1998: *tentang Penyerahan Sebagian Urusan Pemerintahan di Bidang Kehutanan kepada Daerah* (Government Regulation of the Granting of Some Governmental Affairs in Forestry to Regions)

11. PP 6/1999: *tentang Pengusahaan Hutan dan Pemungutan Hasil Hutan pada Hutan Produksi* (Government Regulation on Forest Utilization and Forest Product Collection/Harvesting in Production Forest)

12. PP 27/1999: *tentang Analisis Mengenai Dampak Lingkungan Hidup* (Government Regulation on Environmental Impact Analysis)

13. PP 25/2000: *tentang Kewenangan Pemerintah dan Kewenangan Propinsi sebagai Daerah Otonom* (Government Regulation on Government Authority and Provincial Authority as an Autonomous Region)

14. PP 104/2000: *tentang Dana Perimbangan* (Government Regulation on Distribution of Revenues)

15. PP 107/2000: *tentang Pinjaman Daerah* (Government Regulation on Regional Government Borowing)

Presidential Decrees

1. Keppres 67/1998: *tentang Perubahan atas Keppres 30/1990 Pengenaan Pemungutan dan Pembagian Iuran Hasil Hutan Sebagaimana telah Beberapa Kali Diubah Terakhir dengan Keppres 41/1993* (Presidential Decree on Changes on the Presidential Decree 30/1990 on the Imposition, Collection, and Distribution of Forest Royalties)

2. Keppres 80/2000: *tentang Komite Antar Departemen Bidang Kehutanan* (Presidential Decree on Inter Departmental Forestry Committee)

Ministerial Decrees from the Ministry of Forestry/Ministry of Forestry and Estate Crops

1. SK Menhut 691/Kpts-II/1991, SK Menhut 610/Kpts-II/1993, SK Menhut 69/Kpts-II/1995, SK Menhut 210/Kpts/IV-BPH/1995, SK Menhut 523/Kpts-II/1997: *tentang HPH Bina Desa dan Pembinaan Masyarakat Desa Hutan* (on Village Guidance and Forest Village Community Development)

2. SK Menhut 251/Kpts-II/1993: *tentang Ketentuan Pemungutan Hasil Hutan oleh Masyarakat Hukum Adat atau Anggotanya di dalam Areal Hak Pengusahaan Hutan* (on Stipulation of Forest Products Harvesting by Customary Communities in the Area of Forest Utilization Rights)

3. *Keputusan Bersama Menteri Kehutanan, Menteri Dalam Negeri dan Menteri Transmigrasi dan Pemukiman Perambah Hutan Nomor 480/Kpts-II/1993— Nomor 74 Tahun 1993—Nomor Surat Keputusan Bersama 69/MEN/1993 tentang Penanganan Perambah Hutan dan Perladangan Berpindah* (Joint

Decree of Minister of Forestry, Minister of Internal Affairs and Minister of Transmigration and Settlement of Forest Dwellers 480/Kpts-II/1993— 74/1993—Joint Decree 69/MEN/1993 on the Handling of Forest Dwellers and Shifting Cultivation)

4. SK Menhut 86/Kpts-II/1994: *tentang Penyerahan Sebagian Urusan Pemerintah Pusat Di Bidang Kehutanan Kepada Pemerintah Daerah Tingkat II* (on Granting of Central Government's Forestry Affairs to the second-level Government)

5. SK Menhut 622/Kpts-II/1995: *tentang Pedoman Hutan Kemasyarakatan* (on Guidelines for Community Forestry)

6. SK Menhut 101/Kpts-V/1996: *tentang Ketentuan Dan Tata Cara Penyaluran Dana Reboisasi Dalam Rangka Pinjaman Untuk Usaha Perhutanan Rakyat Kepada Mitra Usaha* (on Stipulations and Procedures on Distribution of Reforestation Fund as Loans for Social Forestry)

7. SK Menhut 634/Kpts-II/1996: *tentang Perubahan Keputusan Menteri Kehutanan Nomor 399/Kpts-II/1993 tentang Pedoman Pengukuhan Hutan* (on Changes of Minister of Forestry Decision Letter 399/Kpts-II/1993 on Guidelines of Forest Affirmation)

8. SK Menhut 47/Kpts-II/1998: *tentang Kawasan dengan Tujuan Istimewa* (on Zones with Special Purpose)

9. SK Menhutbun 677/Kpts-II/1998: *tentang Hutan Kemasyarakatan* (on Community Forestry)

10. SK Menhutbun 732/Kpts-II/1998: *tentang Persyaratan dan Tata Cara Pembaharuan Hak Pengusahaan Hutan* (on Conditions and Procedures on the Renewal of Forest Exploitation Rights)

11. SK Menhutbun 307/Kpts-II/1999: *tentang Persyaratan dan Tata Cara Pembaharuan Hak Pengusahaan Hutan* (on Conditions and Procedures of Renewing Forest Concession Exploitation Rights)

12. SK Menhutbun 308/Kpts-II/1999: *tentang Kesatuan Pemangkuan Hutan Produksi* (on Production Forest Management Unit)

13. SK Menhutbun 310/Kpts-II/1999: *tentang Pedoman Pemberian Hak Pemungutan Hasil Hutan* (on Guidelines for Granting Forest Product Harvesting Rights)

14. SK Menhutbun 312/Kpts-II/1999: *tentang Tata Cara Pemberian Hak Pengusahaan Hutan Melalui Permohonan* (on Procedures of Granting Forest Exploitation Rights by Request)

15. SK Menhutbun 313/Kpts-II/1999: *tentang Tata Cara Penawaran dalam Pelelangan Hak Pengusahaan Hutan* (on Procedures for Bargaining in the Auction of Forest Exploitation Rights)

16. SK Menhutbun 314/Kpts-II/1999: *tentang Rencana Karya Pengusahaan Hutan, Rencana Karya Lima Tahun dan Rencana Karya Tahunan atau Bagan Kerja Pengusahaan Hutan* (on Forest Exploitation Work Plan,

Five-Year Work Plan and Annual Work Plan or the Forest Exploitation Work Chart)

17. SK Menhutbun 315/Kpts-II/1999: *tentang Tata Cara Pengenaan, Penetapan dan Pelaksanaan Sanksi atas Pelanggaran di Bidang Pengusahaan Hutan dan Pemungutan Hasil Hutan* (on Procedures of Imposition, Decision and Execution of Sanctions on Violations Relating to Forest Exploitation and Forest Products Harvesting/Collection)

18. SK Menhutbun 317/Kpts-II/1999: *tentang Hak Pemungutan Hasil Hutan Masyarakat Hukum Adat Pada Areal Hutan Produksi* (on Forest Product Harvesting Rights of Customary Law Communities in Production Forest)

19. SK Menhutbun 318/Kpts-II/1999: *tentang Peran Serta Masyarakat dalam Pengusahaan Hutan* (Participation of Community in Forest Utilization)

20. SK Menhut 05.1/Kpts-II/2000: *tentang Kriteria dan Standar Perijinan Usaha Pemanfaatan Hasil Hutan dan Perijinan Pemungutan Hasil Hutan pada Hutan Produksi Alam* (Criteria and Standards of Licensing of the Utilization of Forest Products and the Harvesting of Forest Products in Natural Production Forest)

Ministerial Decrees from the State Ministry of Agarian Affairs/National Land Agency

1. *Peraturan Menteri Negara Agraria/Kepala Badan Pertanahan Nasional Nomor 5/1999: tentang Pedoman Penyelseaian Masalah Hak Ulayat Masyarakat Adat* (Ministerial Decree of State Minister of Agraria Affairs/National Land Agency Guidelines for Resolution of Traditional Rights Conflicts)

2. SK 26/1982: the Consensus Land Use Planning Decree from the Ministry of the Interior

References

Zwahlen, R., and B. Soewardi. 2000. Sustainable Development, Environmental Impacts, and the Land Development Process—Indonesian Context. Jakarta, Indonesia: National Development Planning Agency and National Land Agency, 44.

Abbreviations and Acronyms

ADB	Asian Development Bank
AEKI	*Asosiasi Eksportir Kopi Indonesia* (Association of Indonesian Coffee Exporters)
AMAN	*Aliansi Masyarakat Adat Nusantara* (Alliance of Traditional Communities of the Archipelego)
AMDAL	*Analisis Mengenai Dampak Lingkungan* (Environmental Impact Assessment)
APHI	*Asosiasi Pengusaha Hutan Indonesia* (Association of Indonesian Forest Concession Holders)
APKI	*Asosiasi Pulp dan Kertas Indonesia* (Indonesian Pulp and Paper Association)
APKINDO	*Asosiasi Panel Kayu Indonesia* (Indonesian Wood Panel Association)
APPSI	*Asosiasi Pemerintah Propinsi Seluruh Indonesia* (Association of Provincial Governments across Indonesia)
APRIL	Asia Pacific Resources International, Ltd.
ASEAN	Association of South East Asian Nations

Compiled by Ahmad Dermawan.

410

AusAID	Australian Agency for International Development
Bappeda	*Badan Perencanaan Pembanguan Daerah* (Regional Development Planning Body)
Bappenas	*Badan Perencanaan Pembangunan Nasional* (National Development Planning Agency)
BATB	*Berita Acara Tata Batas* (Register of Boundaries)
BEH-PHH	*Balai Eksploitasi Hutan dan Pemungutan Hasil Hutan* (Forest Exploitation and Forest Product Collection Branch Office)
BFL	Basic Forestry Law (UU 5/1967)
BII	Bank Internasional Indonesia
BIPHUT	*Balai Inventarisasi dan Pemetaan Hutan* (Forest Inventory and Mapping Agency)
BMG	*Badan Meteorologi dan Geofisika* (Meteorological and Geophysical Agency)
BPD	*Badan Perwakilan Desa* (Village Representatives Council)
BPDLH	*Bantuan Pengendalian Dampak Lingkungan Hidup* (Environmental Protection Aid)
BPKP	*Badan Pemeriksa Keuangan dan Pembangunan* (State Financial Accountancy and Development Agency)
BPN	*Badan Pertanahan Nasional* (National Land Agency)
BPPT	*Badan Pengkajian dan Penerapan Tekn*ologi (Agency for the Assessment and Application of Technology)
BPS	*Badan Pusat Statistik* (Central Bureau of Statistics)
Bulog	*Badan Urusan Logistik* (National Food Logistics Agency)
BUMD	*Badan Usaha Milik Daerah* (Regional Government Enterprise)
BUMN	*Badan Usaha Milik Negara* (State-Owned Enterprise)
CADC	Certificate of Ancestral Domain Claim
CGI	Consultative Group on Indonesia
CGIF	Consultative Group on Indonesian Forestry
CIC	Capricorn Indonesia Consult
CIDA	Canadian International Development Agency
CIDES	Center for Information and Development Studies
CIFOR	Center for International Forestry Research, Bogor, Indonesia
CIRAD	*Centre de Coopération Internationale en Recherche Agronomique pour le Développement* (Center for International Cooperation in Agronomic Research for Development), France

CITES	Convention on International Trade in Endangered Species
CPO	crude palm oil
CRISP	Centre for Remote Imaging, Sensing, and Processing, The National University of Singapore
CSIS	Center for Strategic and International Studies, Jakarta
dbh	diameter at breast height
DCM	Donor Coordination Meeting
Dephutbun	*Departemen Kehutanan dan Perkebunan* (Ministry of Forestry and Estate Crops)
Depnaker	*Departemen Tenaga Kerja* (Ministry of Manpower)
DFID	U.K. Department for International Development
Dinas TK I	forestry services at provincial level
Dinas TK II	forestry services at regency level
Ditjen PHP	*Direktorat Jenderal Pengusahaan Hutan Produksi* (Directorate General for Production Forest Management)
Ditjen PKA	*Direktorat Jenderal Perlindungan dan Konservasi Alam* (Directorate General for Nature Conservation and Protection)
Ditjen RLPS	*Direktorat Jenderal Rehabilitasi Lahan dan Perhutanan Sosial* (Directorate General for Land Rehabilitation and Social Forestry)
DPR	*Dewan Perwakilan Rakyat* (House of Representatives)
DPRD	*Dewan Perwakilan Rakyat Daerah* (Regional House of Representatives)
DR	*Dana Reboisasi* (Reforestation Fund)
ECA	Export Credit Agency
EEP	Environmental Emergency Project
EIA	Environmental Investigation Agency (a British nongovernmental organization)
ELSAM	*Lembaga Studi dan Avokasi Masyarakat* (The Institute for Policy Research and Advocacy)
ENSO	El Niño–Southern Oscillation
ENSOI	El Niño–Southern Oscillation index
EWS	early warning system
FAO	Food and Agriculture Organization of the United Nations
FECRC	*Komite Reformasi Kehutanan dan Perkebunan* (Forestry and Estate Crops Reform Committee)

FKKM	*Forum Komunikasi Kehutanan Masyarakat* (Communication Forum on Community Forestry)
FORDA	Forestry Research and Development Agency
GBHN	*Garis-garis Besar Haluan Negara* (State Guidelines)
GOI	Government of Indonesia
GTZ	*Deutsche Gesellschaft fuer Technische Zusammenarbeit* (German Aid Agency)
HKm	*hutan kemasyarakatan* (community forestry)
HP	*hutan produksi* (production forest)
HPH	*Hak Pengusahaan Hutan* (Forest Concession, Forest Exploitation Rights)
HPHH	*Hak Pemungutan Hasil Hutan* (Forest Product Harvesting Rights)
HPHKm	*hak pengusahaan hutan kemasyarakatan* (community forest concession)
HPHTI	*Hak Pengusahaan Hutan Tanaman Industri* (Industrial Timber Plantation Concession)
HPK	*hutan produksi konversi* (conversion forest)
HPT	*hutan produksi terbatas* (limited production forest)
HTC	*hutan tanaman campuran* (mixed forest plantation)
HTI	*hutan tanaman industri* (industrial timber plantation)
IBRA	Indonesian Bank Restructuring Agency
ICEL	Indonesian Center for Environmental Law
ICRAF	International Center for Research on Agroforestry
IDCF	Inter Department Committee on Forestry
IMF	International Monetary Fund
INTAG	*Biro Inventarisasi dan Tata Guna Lahan* (Bureau of Forest Inventory and Land Use)
IPB	*Institut Pertanian Bogor* (Bogor Agricultural Institute)
IPK	*izin pemanfaatan kayu* (wood utilization permit)
IPPK	*izin pemungutan dan pemanfaatan kayu* (wood utilization harvesting permit)
IRJEN	*Inspektorat Jenderal* (Inspectorate General)
ISA	Indonesian Sawmills Association
ITCZ	Intertropical Convergence Zone
ITFMP	Indonesia–U.K. Tropical Forest Management Programme

ITTO	International Tropical Timber Organization
IUCN	International Union for the Conservation of Nature/World Conservation Union
IUFRO	International Union for Forestry Research Organizations
JAPHAMA	*Jaringan Pembelaan Hak-hak Masyarakat Adat* (Indigenous People Rights Advocates Network)
Kanwilhutbun	*Kantor Wilayah Kehutanan dan Perkebunan* (Regional Office of the Ministry of Forestry and Plantations)
KBDI	*Keetch-Byram* Drought Index
KdTI	*Kawasan dengan Tujuan Istimewa* (Zone with Special Purpose)
KKN	*korupsi, kolusi, dan nepotisme* (corruption, collusion, and nepotism)
KKPA	*Kredit Koperasi Primer untuk Anggota* (Primary Cooperatives Credit for Members)
KPHP	*Kesatuan Pemangkuan Hutan Produksi* (Production Forest Management Unit)
KSO	*Kerja Sama Operasi* (Operational Collaboration)
KUD	*Koperasi Unit De*sa (Village Unit Cooperative)
KUDETA	*Koalisi untuk Demokratisasi Pengelolaan Sumberdaya Alam* (Coalition for the Democratization of Natural Resource Management [a nongovernmental organization])
LAPAN	*Lembaga Penerbangan Antariksa Nasional* National Institute of Aeronautics and Space of Indonesia
LEI	*Lembaga Ekolabel Indonesia* (The Indonesian Ecolabeling Institute*)*
LIPI	*Lembaga Ilmu Pengetahuan Indonesia* (Indonesian Institute of Sciences)
LKMD	*Lembaga Ketahanan Masyarakat Desa* (Village Community Resilience Council)
LMD	*Lembaga Musyawarah Desa* (Village Consensus-Reaching Organization)
MoF	Ministry of Forestry
MoFEC	Ministry of Forestry and Estate Crops
MPI	*Masyarakat Perhutanan Indonesia* (Indonesian Forestry Society)

MPR	*Majelis Permusyawaratan Rakyat* (People's Consultative Assembly)
NGO	nongovernmental organization
NRI	Natural Resources Institute
NRMP	Natural Resource Management Program [of the U.S. Agency for International Development]
NSWRFS	New South Wales Rural Fire Service
NTFPs	nontimber forest products
NTT	Nusa Tenggara Timur (East Nusa Tenggara [an Indonesian province])
PAPL	*Penyediaan Area untuk Penggunaan Lain* (Areas Designated for Other Uses)
PELITA	*Pembangunan Lima Tahun* (Five-Year Development Plan)
PEMDA	*pemerintah daerah* (regional government)
PIR	*perkebunan inti rakyat* (nucleus estate plantations)
PKA	*Perlindungan dan Konservasi Alam* (Planning, Regreening, and Nature Conservation)
PLG	*Proyek Lahan Gambut* (Peat Land Project)
PM	*Peraturan Menteri* (Ministerial Regulation)
PMA	*Penanaman Modal Asing* (Foreign Investment)
PMDH	*Pembinaan Masyarakat Desa Hutan* (Forest Village Community Development)
PNG	Papua New Guinea
PP	*Peraturan Pemerintah* (Government Regulation)
PPKS	*Pusat Penelitian Kelapa Sawit* (Oil Palm Research Centre)
PRSL	Policy Reform Support Loan
PSDH	*Provisi Sumber Daya Hutan* (Resource Royalty Provision)
Rakernas	*Rapat Kerja Nasional* (Annual National Meeting)
REPELITA	*Rencana Pembangunan Lima Tahun* (Five-Year Development Plan)
RePPProT	Regional Physical Planning Program for Transmigration
RGM	*Raja Garuda Mas* (A business group with business in the pulp and palm oil subsector)
RKL	*Rencana Karya Lima Tahun* (Five-Year Work Plan)
RKPH	*Rencana Karya Pengusahaan Hutan* (Forest Utilization Work Plan)

RKT	*Rencana Karya Tahunan* (Annual Work Plan)
RTRWP	*Rencana Tata Ruang Wilayah Propinsi* (Provincial Spatial Plan)
RUU	*Rancangan Undang-undang* (Draft of Laws)
RUUK	*Rancangan Undang-undang Kehutanan* (Forestry Law Draft)
SFDP	Social Forestry Development Project, a GTZ project in Sanggau, West Kalimantan
SFMP	Sustainable Forest Management Project
SHK	*Sistem Hutan Kerakyatan* (Community-Based Forest System Management)
SK	*Surat Keputusan* (Decree/Decision Letter)
SKEPHI	*Sekretariat Kerjasama Pelestarian Hutan Indonesia* (The Secretariat for Cooperation in Indonesian Forest Conservation [a nongovernmental network for forest conservation in Indonesia])
S&P	Standard & Poor's
STOL	"short-take-off-and-landing" aircraft
TGHK	*Tata Guna Hutan Kesepakatan* (Forest Function Based on Consensus [a widely used but controversial series of Indonesian maps supposedly based on consensus among the various parties, relating to land use classes])
TNI	*Tentara Nasional Indonesia* (Indonesian military forces)
TPI	*Tebang Pilih Indonesia* (Indonesian Selective Cutting System)
TPTI	*Tebang Pilih Tanam Indonesia* (Indonesian Selective Cutting and Planting System)
TPTJ	*Tebang Pilih Tanam Jarak* (Selective Logging and Line Planting System)
UNDAC	United Nations Disaster Assessment Committee
UNDP	United Nations Development Program
UNESCO	United Nations Educational, Scientific and Cultural Organization
USAID	United States Agency for International Development
USDA	United States Department of Agriculture
UU	*Undang-Undang* (Law)
UUPA	*Undang-Undang Pokok Agraria* (Basic Agrarian Law)
UUPK	*Undang-Undang tentang Ketenhuan-Ketenhuan Pokok Kehutanan* (Basic Forestry Law) (See BFL.)

WALHI	*Wahana Lingkungan Hidup Indonesia* (Indonesian Forum on the Environment)
WFC	World Forestry Congress
WWF	World Wide Fund for Nature, previously World Wildlife Fund

Glossary

adat: traditional and customary[1]

alang-alang: Imperata cylindrica; an invasive grass

Badan Planologi: Land Use Planning Agency

Bhinneka Tunggal Ika: Unity in Diversity; the national motto of Indonesia

Bina Desa: Village Guidance; a program required of timber companies, relating to forest communities, based on SK 691/1991

bupati: head of a regency; the administrative layer between province and county

cukong: capital provider

damar: a resin from Shorea sp.; used for lighting and caulking

Departemen Kehutanan: Ministry of Forestry

Departemen Pertanian: Ministry of Agriculture

Dinas Perkebunan: Regional Plantation Office

Direktorat Bina Pengusahaan Hutan: Directorate of Forest Utilization

Direktorat Jenderal Perkebunan: Directorate General of Plantations

---

Compiled by Ahmad Dermawan.

418

Direktorat Penyiapan Pengusahaan Hutan: Directorate of Forest Utilization Preparation

Forum Pemerhati Kehutanan: Forest Watch Forum

hak asal-usul: historical rights

hak guna bangunan: right to build and own buildings on land owned by another

hak guna usaha: right to cultivate state land, which may be granted for up to 35 years and extended for an additional 35 years

hak milik: right to own

Hak Pengusahaan Hutan: Forest Exploitation Rights

hak pakai: Right to use or collect products from state or private land for a certain period

hak ulayat: rights to a traditional territory

hukum positif: positive law

hutan adat: adat forest; traditional forest area

hutan cadangan: a kind of conservation forest held by some ethnic groups, including Depati (Marga) in Jambi

hutan kemasyarakatan: community forestry

hutan negara: state forest

hutan untuk rakyat: forests for people

Inhutani: one of the state forest companies operating in forest management (beside Perhutani)

iuran hak pengusahaan hutan: the forest utilization rights levy

izin pemungutan hasil hutan: forest products harvesting permits

izin prinsip: letter of approval

Iuran hasil hutan: royalty on forest products

jagawana: forest ranger

kabupaten: regency or district; the administrative layer between province and county

Kampung Galao: a kind of conservation forest held by the Iban Dayak, Putussibau (West Kalimantan)

Kawasan dengan Tujuan Istimewa: areas with special purpose; established on SK 47/Kpts-II/1998

kebun: garden or orchard

kecamatan: subdistrict; similar to a U.S. county

kepala desa: village head

ketua adat: adat leader

kilan: seven hand spans among the Kanayatn Dayak (West Kalimantan)

Kongres Masyarakat Adat Nusantara: Congress of Indigenous Peoples of the Archipelago

koperasi unit desa: village unit cooperatives

Marga: traditional area for which the Pasirah was responsible (Lahat, South Sumatra)

masyarakat hukum adat: customary communities

meranti: a timber tree normally translated as "Philippine Mahogany" and a member of Shorea sp.

Negara Kesatuan Republik Indonesia: State Unity of Indonesia

Orang rimba: a hunter-gatherer group in Sumatra

Orde Baru: the New Order; Soeharto's regime from 1966 to 1998

Outer Islands: Indonesian islands other than Java and Bali

paduserasi: process of reconciling the spatial plan between MoF and other parties

pancasila: the official state philosophy , which includes five components: belief in one God, humanitarianism, national unity, people's sovereignty, and social justice

partisipasi: participation

Pasirah: traditional leader in Lahat, South Sumatra

Pekan Penghijauan Nasional: National Regreening Week

pekarangan: home gardens

pengelolaan: management

pengusahaan: exploitation

peraturan daerah: regional law

peraturan menteri: ministerial regulation

perekonomian rakyat: people's economy

Perhutani: forest state company in Java

perumisasi: process of nationalizing forest companies

preman: criminal

Punan: A hunter-gatherer group in Kalimantan

putera daerah: "local son," people who were born in one region or have been living in the region for a long time

rakyat: the people

Rapat Kerja Nasional Kehutanan: Annual National Forestry Meeting

Reformasi: reform

rupiah, **Rp**: Indonesian currency

sago: traditional staple food, like rice, especially in eastern Indonesia

sawah: irrigated rice land

sengon: a fast growing plantation tree species used in "regreening" programs in Indonesia; a member of Paraserianthes falcataria.

sertifikat: certificate

surian: a well-knowm, highly valuable cabinetwood species; a member of the Meliacaca family.

talun: a garden consisting of mixed tree crops

tanggung gugat sosial: public accountability

tanggung jawab: responsibility

trias politica: separation of power between executive, legislative and judiciary branches

wilayah masyarakat hukum adat: traditional community area

Endnotes

1. *Adat* is a rich and complex concept, touching on law, tenure, religion, symbolism, practice, and ethnicity (see Introduction and Chapters 1, 4, 5, and 6 for further discussion).

Index

Chrysa Cullather copyedited and typeset the book in Adobe Garamond and Charlotte Sans. The cover illustration is a drawing by Eko Priyanto, based on a panel of traditional beadwork from Tanah Merah, Kalimantan. The beadwork is typically used by the Kenyah Dayak on a backpack for carrying a baby.